Down
the

Orval E. Faubus
1-21-81

DOWN FROM THE HILLS

by

ORVAL EUGENE FAUBUS

Printed in the United States of America

Democrat Printing & Lithographing Company
Second & Scott, Little Rock, Arkansas

Orval Eugene Faubus

TABLE OF CONTENTS

Page   Page

LIST OF ILLUSTRATIONS

Page   Page

viii

SOURCES

Sources used in the writing of this book include newspaper files, clippings, scrapbooks, correspondence and documents collected in the Governor's Office and various departments of the State Government.

DEDICATION

With gratitude for their devotion and efficiency, this book is dedicated to the people who served in state government, and to the thousands of others, who made possible the longest administration in the history of Arkansas, January 11, 1955 to January, 1967.

The rust will find the sword of fame,
The dust will hide the crown.
Ay, none shall nail so high his name
Time will not tear it down.

—unknown

George Washington on Federal Usurpation

"Let there be no usurpation, for though in one instance it may be the instrument of good, it is the customary weapon by which free governments are destroyed."

Thomas Jefferson on Centralized Power

"When all government, domestic and foreign, in little as in great things, shall be drawn to Washington as the center of all power, it will render powerless the checks provided . . . and will become as venal and as oppressive as the government from which we separated."

Abraham Lincoln on the Supreme Court

"The people of these United States are the rightful masters of both Congresses and Courts, not to overthrow the Constitution, but to overthrow the men who pervert the Constitution . . .

"At the same time, the candid citizen must confess that if the policy of the government, upon vital questions affecting the whole people, is to be irrevocably fixed by decisions of the Supreme Court, the instant they are made, in ordinary litigation between parties in personal actions, the people will have ceased to be their own rulers, having to that extent practically resigned their government into the hands of that eminent tribunal."

. . . and on Slavery

"As I would not be a slave, neither would I be a master."

Woodrow Wilson on Limited Government

"Liberty has never come from the government. The history of liberty is the history of resistance. The history of liberty is the history of limitations of government power, not the increase of it."

John Foster Dulles on Limited Government
(Secretary of State under Dwight D. Eisenhower)

"Our pride is not in what government does, but in what government does not do.

"Our system of education is local and free from Federal government influence."

The Original McMath Highway Commission

Governor McMath's choices for the 12-member State Highway Commission — one from each of the ten highway districts plus a chairman and vice-chairman at large — were announced in March in time for confirmation by the State Senate at the regular session of the General Assembly. The above picture was made at the time the appointees were administered the oath of office on March 26, 1949 in the old Highway Department building on the Capitol grounds. The commission held its first meeting the same day. Left to right, Chief Justice Griffin Smith, Sr., who administered the oath; J.B. (Jerdy) Lambert, chairman, Helena; Olen Fullerton, Morrilton; A.D. Mason, Camden; Orval E. Faubus, Huntsville; Dick Barnett, Altheimer; Truman Baker, Searcy; Jim Crain, vice-chairman, Wilson; Fred Carter, Sr., Lake City; William H. (Bill) Humphries, Little Rock; Lawrence Hunnicutt, Nashville; Roy Martin, Ft. Smith; Charley Adams, Hughes; and Governor Sid McMath. Seven of the original members were still on the commission at the end of McMath's second term. I resigned to become Administrative Assistant to the Governor and then Highway Director.

CHAPTER 1
Background of the 1954 Campaign

I returned home in 1946 after almost five years of military training camps and war.

When I arrived in Madison County I found that the Democrats had nominated me for the office of county judge. Worn out and generally fatigued, I did not wish to make the race and contacted the top county Democratic leaders to tell them I wished to withdraw, and for them to select another nominee.

A few days later the leaders told me that if I withdrew at least three other nominees, young veterans who had returned home, would quit as nominees for other offices. The leaders insisted that I continue in the campaign for county judge or the Democratic Party, for the first time in memory, might not be able to field a full slate of candidates.

I acceded to the wishes of the leaders and waged a hard campaign. The Republicans were heavily entrenched, having had for some time control of the most important offices including the one I sought. As a result the Democrats lost six of the races for the seven county offices. In my race the margin was small yet decisive. I lost by 2235 to 2340 - 105 votes, to Republican Howard Hankins, one of the most successful office holders the county has ever known.

Following my defeat Congressman J.W. (Jim) Trimble called and asked if I wanted to be Huntsville postmaster. I accepted and was appointed, going on the job November 15, 1946.

In March 1947 following the death of the venerable Alfred Hawn, owner and editor of the local newspaper, I bought the Madison County Record. I thus had two jobs and found myself as busy as we had often been in combat during the war.

The same year that I suffered defeat another returned GI was making a successful bid in the political field. Sid McMath, a handsome, energetic former Marine, won the post of prosecuting attorney of Garland and Montgomery counties, leading a Hot Springs GI team to victory.

The next election year, 1948, McMath ran for governor. He offered what I considered to be the best program for building improved roads of which Madison County had only about 12 miles at the time and no link with the outside world. I enlisted under McMath's banner. The county went for him in both primaries. McMath won the race defeating a strong political leader, Jack Holt, by a narrow margin in the runoff primary.

Without doubt the greatest desire of the people of Arkansas at the time, and one of the state's greatest needs, was improved highways. The people had alternately eaten the dust and plowed through the mud of rough, unimproved roads and, in many places, forded unbridged streams for so long, that any political leader who brought about the desired improvements was hailed as a savior by the residents of the affected area.

As a result of my efforts for McMath in the campaign and with the almost unanimous support of the people of my county, I was appointed a member of McMath's 12-member highway commission. Although Governor McMath had recommended and the people had approved a bond issue to obtain funds for road building, the commission soon discovered that the money was far inadequate to meet the demand for new roads and bridges which came from every county in the state.

As a result, McMath was in some difficulty by the time he came up for re-election. Administration critics persuaded former Governor Ben Laney, whom McMath had succeeded, to oppose him for re-election. With a full team effort and the tradition favoring a second term, McMath won handily.

However, McMath's troubles multiplied. They came to a head during the regular 1951 session of the General Assembly following his second term inauguration. Anti-administration and anti-tax sentiment prevented the Governor from securing new funds desperately needed for schools, welfare and other state services.

However the serious trouble for the McMath administration developed when the Legislature created an investigative agency to check on alleged mismanagement and wrong doing in the State Highway Department.

BRING ON THE HIGHWAY COMMISSION
By Kennedy, Ark. Democrat   *1/13/52*

The investigative body, the Highway Audit Committee, selected Attorney General Ike Murry to direct the inquiry into highway affairs. By the time the Audit Committee had finished its investigation, many people had become convinced that many of the allegations of wrong doing and mal-administration were true. The final report was strongly condemnatory of the McMath Administration's handling of highway affairs. Although many of the charges against the administration were politically motivated, and some actions of the Audit Committee personnel politically inspired, enough wrong-doing was uncovered to lend credence to a general feeling of misconduct in the minds of the people. Consequently, McMath suffered a loss

THE WITCHES COME HOME TO ROOST
By Kennedy, Ark. Democrat   1/20/52

The initial disclosures of the Highway Audit Committee were extremely unfavorable to the McMath administration in its handling of highway affairs. The cartoonist portrayed the alleged misdeeds as witches coming home to roost in the governor's office. "Clear it with Henry" referred to Henry Woods, the governor's executive secretary.

BUT HE IS - - - -
By Graham, Ark. Gazette   1/13/52

As early as January, each with campaign material already ordered, McMath and Murry each accused the other of running for governor.

OVERLOADING TROUBLE
By Graham, Ark. Gazette   1/21/52

The Gazette, supposedly friendly to McMath, viewed the Highway Audit findings with disfavor. The highway trucks overloaded with "politics" damaged the roads severely.

of faith, some of it perhaps unjustified on the part of the public, and his powerful enemies jumped on the opportunity to oppose him.

In the face of these difficulties, and the strong anti-third term tradition, McMath decided to seek re-election.

In addition to the difficulties mentioned there were others. Although all chief executives make some mistakes in appointments, it appeared McMath made a disproportionate number of such errors. Many of his appointees and political lieutenants instead of gaining adherents for McMath, did more to add to the list of his political enemies.

Another difficulty was caused by the fact that delegations constantly besieged the Governor for committments for road improvements. Almost invariably McMath would give them an affirmative answer. I believe that McMath wanted to make every highway improvement he promised. But the committments were far more than the means to fulfill, and thus the unfulfilled promises came home to haunt him in the campaign.

No amount of facts, logic or persuasion could change the anti-McMath sentiment of many of those who were disappointed by the unfulfilled promises.

As to my personal role, I entered the administration as a minor minion, and in the beginning was almost certainly the least influential member of the Highway Commission. I soon found that my greatest difficulty was with the top flight administrators of the Highway Department. Constantly I had to fight to make them fulfill even the most elementary committments of the Department itself.

In my own area with many more miles of unimproved roads than any of the ten highway districts save one, the demand for road improvements was overwhelming, but I was very careful not to promise more than could be done. I disappointed many groups and delegations seeking improvements by telling them the truth, and by showing them the extent of the overall needs and the inadequate means of accomplishment. It was a bitterly disappointing situation made even worse by those with whom I had to deal in the Department.

On one occasion a group in Washington County insisted that I accompany them to the Department to intercede for a project on Highway 16 west of Fayetteville. I told Attorney and former Chancery Judge Lee Seamster and Representative Clifton "Deacon" Wade, that from the information given me by the Department, the project could not then be accomplished, but that I would go with them. Arriving at the Department offices in Little Rock I expected to hear the top flight personnel repeat the same "facts" to the delegation as had been given to me previously. To my complete and utter astonishment, they readily promised not only that the project could be done but would be done right away. To make the case even stronger the Commission Chairman J.B. (Jerdy) Lambert of Helena, was present and concurred in the commitment. I could only reiterate to my friends on the return journey that I had been told the contrary previously but that I was glad they would get the new road. It made me look, to my friends, like a prevaricator or a weak excuse for their representative on the Commission.

Then at the very next meeting of the Commission in the same offices, with none of the delegation present — they were all at home happy in the thought that their project was assured — I was told by the same Department personnel that the project could not be done. I was dumfounded by such duplicity and bad faith, but not so dumfounded that I didn't take action.

That night I told my story to my fellow commissioners, one by one, and got enough commitments to approve the project regardless of the Department personnel. Then I appealed to Chairman Lambert in private before the Commission meeting began. He remembered the delegation and the commitment and, to his everlasting credit, he helped make the Department officials fulfill the commitment they themselves had made.

At another time I had to threaten publicly to resign in order to make the Department, and this time the Administration also, fulfill a promise to build an officially approved project on Highway 12 in Benton County.

John Fletcher, then a star reporter and feature writer for the *Gazette,* was present and heard my statement at the close of a commission meeting. He later wrote of the incident in his column The Arkansas Angle.

Another example of the double dealing of the upper echelon personnel can be cited.

At the beginning of each year the Commission had a road programming session. Each commissioner listed the projects in his district which he had selected, after which the estimated cost was given by the Department engineers. We stopped when we reached the limit of projected funds for the year. Needless to say for every project programmed, at least ten were omitted and each commissioner had to face the heat from the disappointed road seekers.

Then the Department personnel had each commissioner assign a priority to the projects in his district. On one occasion I recall that eleven projects were programmed in my large district and I dutifully listed them one to eleven, giving priority to connecting links, areas of heavy traffic or structures over unbridged streams.

"Now", said the department officers, "We may not be able to keep the projects in exact order. We need some flexibility in order to make the most efficient use of personnel. We might get number three ahead of number two or number six ahead of four and five. But we'll stick close to your assigned priorities."

Back home in meetings with interested citizens I would name the projects and reveal the priority given. Naturally those low on the list were disappointed, but they understood as well as I that not everyone could be first.

Days or weeks later I would pick up the daily newspaper and find number ten advertised for bids ahead of all other projects. To say that such news was disconcerting is an understatement hard to measure.

Thus, I found myself in constant combat with my own Department, and, in the eyes of many people, with my own administration. With roads being the greatest need, and thus of greatest interest to the people, it was almost impossible to make new friends for the governor whom I served. It was a constant battle to retard the erosion of good will which the McMath administration at first enjoyed — erosion which was inevitable under such circumstances.

Never in the wildest stretch of imagination could I ever have envisaged a situation wherein it was necessary to fight so constantly and so diligently, the forces within my own organization in an effort to compel them to live up to the most elementary precepts of truthfulness and fair dealing. If I hadn't been toughened by my war experience I would probably have been overcome.

After about 18 months as Highway Commissioner, I moved into the Governor's office as McMath's Administrative Assistant. One main responsibility was to serve as liason between the Governor's office and the Highway Commission and the Department. In such capacity I attended all commission meetings as an observer and representative of the Governor. Thus, I remained at all times completely conversant with progress in highway improvements and kept the Governor advised. Until the Governor was ready to make drastic changes to remedy the defects described, which he never did, I had to accept the situation and make the best of it.

Gradually, in spite of all the difficulties, as the months went by I was able to build a solid reputation for fairness, and truthfulness in dealing with the public and with other officials. Even the Time-Life publishers who were later numbered among my severest critics, wrote of me after my service as governor had ended in 1967 as follows:

"Young Orval [Faubus] . . . entered politics as a spokesman for the downtrodden people of the Arkansas hills, attracted the attention of Arkansas' liberal Governor Sidney S. McMath, who appointed him State Highway Commissioner. In that capacity Faubus swept away impeding departmental debris, refused to make the traditional Arkansas kickback deals with local bosses, shunned bribes from contractors and generally ran an efficient department.

"As governor, Faubus continued to try to modernize and streamline the operation of the state." . . . — From Time-Life Library of American South Central States (1967)

When Governor McMath entered the battle for a third term I had become known as one of his most staunch and dependable lieutenants. I took the stump in his behalf speaking wherever I was requested by his supporters or was sent by the campaign staff.

Once in the mid-day sun, with Bill and Clarence "Toby" Baker of St. Paul and "Fiddlin" Lou Gabbard of Ft. Smith drawing the crowd with their lively music, I spoke to a good audience on the streets of Booneville. When I had finished a countryman who had listened attentively from the edge of the crowd across the street, walked over to me. He stuck out his hand for a hand shake and said,

"Young feller, if you wuz a-runnin' I'd be for ye. But I can't be for your man."

I tried to persuade him but his mind was made up. Thus it was, I found, with too many as I spoke across the state. The tide of public sentiment was running strongly against McMath.

Four strong candidates challenged McMath's bid for a third term.

Perhaps the most prominent was former Attorney General Jack Holt who was noted as a political orator. Holt was regarded by many as the hard luck personality of Arkansas politics. Once before he had narrowly missed a victory for the U.S. Senate, and had narrowly lost to McMath four years previously in his first bid for the governor's office.

Congressman Boyd Tackett, a whirlwind campaigner, had been thrown in the same district with Congressman Oren Harris by redistricting. He chose to run for governor rather than reelection.

Attorney General Ike Murry was an early entrant in the race. Well liked by those who knew him personally, he had gained statewide name identification by heading up the Highway Audit proceedings (I had been one of his supporters in his two races for Attorney General).

Chancellor Francis Cherry of Jonesboro was perhaps the least known at the time, although he had been mentioned periodically as a possible candidate in previous political years. A very distinguished looking man, he was strong in his area and had strength in Washington County.

HOW GOOD THE AIM?
By Kennedy, Ark. Democrat   6/28/52

EARLY BOYD
By Kennedy, Ark. Democrat   4/13/52

Tackett opened up with a strong anti-McMath speech in April and Kennedy dubbed him the early bird (Boyd) of the campaign.

McMath launched his bid for a third term on June 28 at Pine Bluff with a giant rally to which the "faithful" were brought from all across the state by autos, buses and four special trains. I attended and, although I kept my council, was discouraged. The rally was a mustering of the McMath "regulars." There were few spectators along the parade route and no uncommitted in the grandstand to convert. The special trains — a Joe Martin idea — were wonderful for publicity but I wondered if they were worth the cost.

As the campaign progressed it became clear that Holt and Tackett were the main challengers for a runoff spot with McMath.

4

Then some promoters came up from Florida with a campaign gimmick known as a talkathon which had received national publicity when it was used successfully in that state. The method was to purchase 24 solid hours of time on radio during which the candidate talked or answered questions telephoned to the station by listeners. The novelty of 24 hours on radio without a break going through both night and day, attracted listeners. The sponsors helped the candidate by manning the telephones and feeding questions to him whenever the calls slacked off. The questions to which the candidate's answers found favor with the public were used over and over.

It is said the novel campaign method was first offered in turn to Tackett, Holt and Murry all of whom rejected it. It was not offered to McMath. The last offer was made to Cherry who accepted. From the outset the talkathon proved a natural for the Jonesboro chancellor. After that he couldn't be stopped. He won the run off position with McMath. The three losers combined forces with Cherry and he defeated McMath with the landslide margin of almost 100,000 votes.

When McMath was succeeded by the victorious Cherry in January 1952, I went home to Huntsville to become postmaster and editor and publisher of the local newspaper.

HIS DAY
By Graham, Ark. Gazette   5/25/52

H'M-M-M, THIS OUGHT TO BE AS GOOD A PLACE TO START AS ANY.
By Graham, Ark. Gazette   4/23/52

The Highway Audit investigation revealed that funds contributed by citizens for the improvement of the Indian Bay road in Monroe County had somehow wound up in McMath's 1950 campaign fund. Upon the revelation Highway Commissioner Charlie Adams, to whom the $2,961 check was made, voluntarily paid the amount to the Highway Department. Ike Murry, included the Indian Bay fund disclosure in the audit report and the cartoonist concluded it was a good starting point in his campaign.

McMATH UNDER ATTACK

By late May McMath was under attack from five other candidates, four Democrats and Republican Jefferson Speck. He began studying how to play the role of an underdog while chained to his record in office. Could he turn the situation to his advantage, or did the day belong to his attackers?

McMath had won the 1st place awards in 1948 and 1950. He was now being prepared for the 3rd term contest by Henry Woods and Joe Martin, an administration stalwart and advisor from Jonesboro. Martin's experience dated back to the time Huey Long came to the state to assist Hattie Caraway in a race for the U.S. Senate. He was her Northeast Arkansas campaign manager.

STAND BY FOR CONTESTANT #4
By Kennedy, Ark. Democrat   6/25/52

5

WELL, WELL, IF IT AIN'T OL' "GIVE-EM-HELL" SIDNEY!
By Graham, Ark. Gazette   7/1/52

President Harry Truman, most unpopular at the time and not a candidate for re-election, came to Arkansas to dedicate Bull Shoals Dam. McMath met the President at the Little Rock airport and they went by train to the dedication site. The last thing we told the Governor as he left the office "Don't let him endorse you!" They must have got carried away by the crowds and the acclaim as they reaped a great harvest of publicity. Harry openly endorsed Sid and his opponents proclaimed it the kiss of death. It probably made no difference in the outcome but it certainly didn't help at the time.

CARICATURES OF ARKANSAS' NEXT GOVERNOR, By Kennedy, Ark. Democrat, 7/13/52

Here is your next governor — all five of them. Jon Kennedy, the Arkansas Democrat's staff artist, gives you this preview. Of course, only one can occupy the governor's chair and the voters will decide this in the approaching primaries.

FIVE RING CIRCUS
By Kennedy, Ark. Democrat   7/6/52

The candidates settled into their campaign patterns. McMath spoke across the state after the love fest with President Truman; Jimmy Davis sang for Jack Holt's crowds; the Grand Ole Opry entertained Murry's listeners; Tackett stormed the state in a helicopter; and Francis Cherry adopted a new campaign gimmick conducted from a studio, the radio talkathon.

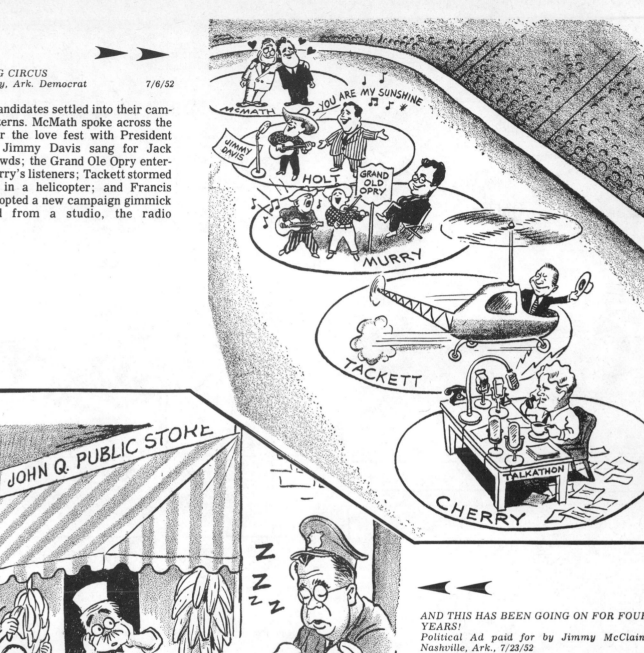

Murry had a political organization of big names that looked like the who's who of Arkansas politics with J. L. "Jim" Bland of Walnut Ridge as campaign manager. Ike was pictured as a winner with McMath frantically building roads to gain political favor. Then Tackett ran this ad against Murry who had directed the Highway Audit Committee investigation of alleged scandals in the Highway Department. Tackett said the misdeeds had been going on during the four years of Murry's tenure as attorney general. Some political observers said this was the most devastating political cartoon of all time in Arkansas. It was a good idea, humorous and attention-getting, but I never considered it that effective in changing votes. Murry was a good guy with a good organization, but somehow a poor candidate.

This was the forboding prospect faced by McMath in the runoff primary; 223,000 votes against, only 98,000 for.

... *And SO they were wed!*

AND SO THEY WERE WED
Political Ad paid for by Henry Woods, Campaign Manager, 7/52

During the runoff the long smouldering feud between McMath and U.S. Senator John L. McClellan erupted into the open. The senator came to Little Rock from Washington and openly assisted Cherry in the campaign. There were some newspaper reports that Mrs. McClellan had obtained a mink coat through improper use of her husband's influence. The senator denied the inferences and maintained he bought the coat in a proper transaction. The McMath forces ran this ad against the Cherry-McClellan combine.

◄◄

DIVORCE MILL IN CRITTENDEN COUNTY
Political Ad paid for by Henry Woods, Campaign Manager, 7/52

The McMath forces said a divorce mill had operated in Crittenden County Chancery Court over which Cherry had presided as chancery judge for five years prior to January 1951. The ad said that more than four divorces were granted each day during 1949 alone.

SHOULD AULD ACQUAINTENCE BE FORGOT
By Graham, Ark. Gazette   8/13/52

In the runoff Cherry blanketed the state with hours of his radio talkathon, while McMath feverishly campaigned from corner to corner with handshakes and speeches. Not many votes were changed. The result was determined the day the Jonesboro chancellor took second place in the first primary. McMath carried only six counties, his three best, Madison, Newton and Carroll, under my leadership. Cherry "snowed us under" by nearly 100,000 votes, a record at that time.

PRE-CAMPAIGN DEVELOPMENTS
Gains and Losses of the
Cherry Administration

As the 1954 filing deadline approached Governor Cherry had been in office more than a year. He was expected to seek and to win the traditional second term.

In the other offices, Lieutenant Governor Nathan Gordon of Morrilton, already proving to be one of the most popular state figures of his time, was expected to seek re-election without serious opposition if any at all.

Tom Gentry was in line for the traditional second term as Attorney General. Vance Clayton from a powerful political family, held a firm grip on the State Treasurer's office. The physically handicapped J. Oscar Humphrey (he had no arms), the long time State Auditor, was expected to continue his tenure without challenge. The venerable and respected Claude Rankin was solidly lodged in the office of State Land Commissioner. The well known and politically astute C. G. "Crip" Hall had been firmly seated in the office of Secretary of State for years and was expected to continue as long as he liked in that position. There were no races for the State Supreme Court judgeships.

Truly, it did not at all appear to be a good year for challengers of any incumbents for state office, especially for relatively unknown newcomers to the statewide political scene.

The only major race expected was for the U.S. Senate seat between the incumbent John L. McClellan and challenger Sid McMath.

Governor Cherry had suffered no appreciable erosion of his support among political leaders. The most obvious probable loss was the popular Jim Snoddy of Alma who had quit the job as executive secretary to Cherry only a few months after the beginning of the administration. There was some speculation that Snoddy might oppose Cherry for re-election.

On the other hand the Governor had made some gains. The budding financial mogul, W.R. "Witt" Stephens, then moving into a dominant role in Arkansas politics had, like myself, gone

AND NOW WE KNOW!
By Graham, Ark. Gazette   8/11/52

During July "State Highway 29" signs mysteriously sprouted on an unimproved county road in south Franklin County which the residents were trying to get added to the state highway system. Everyone in authority over the matter denied any knowledge or responsibility for erection of the state road signs, and the mystery deepened. Then Graham discovered that the Martians had landed.

down with McMath in the 1952 race. However, soon after Cherry's victory Stephens moved to strengthen his position with the incoming administration by employing Leffel Gentry as his attorney. Gentry was a long time personal friend of Cherry and his campaign manager in the victory over McMath. Now Stephens and many of his influential friends were solidly in Cherry's corner.

Cherry's standing with rank and file voters was a different matter. He had made a number of mistakes from which he was suffering a popularity loss.

In Cherry's use of the talkathon in the 1952 campaign he stated over and over in response to questions, that the sales tax on seed, feed and fertilizer was an unfair and unjust tax and that it should be repealed. In such statements he had implied, if not directly stated, that he favored repeal. In the regular session of the General Assembly a bill was passed effecting repeal of the tax. After the legislature adjourned the Governor vetoed the bill, thus bitterly disappointing the hard pressed poultry producers of the state. At that time there were many small poultry growers who felt directly the effects of the tax.

Governor Cherry pushed through the Legislature a constitutional amendment requiring the assessment of all property at 100 per cent of true market value. The measure was to be voted on at the general election of 1954. The Governor strongly favored the measure, stating at one time that he had rather have the reform law enacted as to be governor. Therefore many people, concerned about the effects of the law on their tax bills, were reluctant to support Cherry for re-election. They feared his re-election would be looked upon as an endorsement of the feared property tax increase.

Economic conditions were not the best at the time in the state. Two droughts in a row had worsened the economic plight of the farmers and there was considerable unemployment. In such times aid to the needy takes on greater importance and a welfare program properly handled can be a genuine asset politically. However, the administration's welfare program coupled with a harsh relative responsibility law enacted at the recommendation of the Governor, was highly unpopular. The welfare recipients could almost be counted as a bloc in opposition to Governor Cherry. He made matters even worse by referring to numbers of the aged recipients of welfare grants as "old dead heads".

A fourth irritant to the rank and file citizens was the new independent highway commission. While no one could point to any wrong doing during the brief existence of the new commission, its tenure had been sufficient to establish it as an aloof agency. No longer did members of the commission regularly attend highway improvement meetings in various communities. They were seldom seen in outlying areas inspecting the roads to determine highway improvement needs.

From these and other matters of lesser importance the administration was vulnerable, not among the business and political leaders of the state, but among the rank and file.

However, it would take a whirlwind campaign by some one who could voice the discontent of the people and offer hope of better things. In addition the candidate must some how put together sufficient political leadership in the face of the second term tradition, to create an effective organization and secure sufficient funds to reach the people through use of the media.

Would such a candidate come along? One who, to use a slang expression prevalent at the time, "could put it together?"

It didn't appear so as the deadline neared. Consequently there was an air of over confidence and complacency on the part of administration forces. An administration, they reasoned, doesn't lose a 100,000 vote margin in a small state in so short a time. They were not following Congressman Jim Trimble's political rule to "always run scared", and they appeared to have forgotten that McMath's support had shrunk from approximately 100,000 majority in 1950 to a 100,000 vote deficit in

1952. Consequently, the administration's attitude of over confidence constituted another deficit which would prove of value to any challengers.

SPEAKING OF PHENOMENA
By Graham, Ark. Gazette   4/2/53

The legislature of 1953 passed a bill exempting feed from the sales tax. Governor Cherry vetoed the bill. The poultry growers considered the veto a betrayal of a campaign pledge, and it was not forgotten.

PRELUDE TO THE CAMPAIGN OF 1954

New Year's Day, 1954, dawned with no apparent prospect of the boiling statewide races that were to come. A political headline on that date read: "Nathan Gordon To Run Again!" The Morrilton lieutenant governor was seeking his fifth term.

(On January 1 a headline on international events was a harbinger of the first disastrous military and political defeat for America: "Dien Bien Phu under Attack". The French fortress in Indo-China (Viet Nam) was besieged by the Vietnamese rebels. Its fall ultimately resulted in the division of the country into North and South Viet Nam thus setting the stage for the long drawnout war in which America became involved and was defeated.)

On January 3 Senator McClellan filed for re-election.

STATE DEMOCRATIC CONVENTION OF 1950

Party Rules Changed to Admit All Citizens

As a delegate from Madison County I attended the State Democratic party convention of 1950 in Little Rock on September 22 and 23. McMath had won renomination by an overwhelming vote in the Democratic Primary over his principal opponent, former Governor Ben Laney, and as a result held firm control of the convention. One of the main issues at the convention was a proposal to change the party rules to officially admit blacks to participation in party affairs. Blacks for some time had been voting in the Democratic Primaries but the voting had been without official sanction of the party.

Since Reconstruction days the rules of the party had restricted membership in the party to qualified white electors, the rules reading:

"The Democratic Party in Arkansas shall consist of only legally qualified White electors . . ."

The resolution for the rule change was introduced in the convention by J. Fred Parish, a delegate from Jackson County.

Leading Convention Officials

Willis Smith of Texarkana, chairman of the State Democratic Committee, called the convention to order at 12:20 p.m. on the 22nd.

Marvin Bird of Earle was named temporary convention chairman and Mayor Harold Falls of Wynne took over as temporary secretary.

Bird named Attorney George Steele of Nashville as chairman of the Credentials Committee, and D.L. Ford of Fort Smith to head the Rules and Order of Business Committee.

After a brief recess both chairmen reported back in routine fashion, and the delegates accepted their reports.

Ford informed the convention that, in keeping with the rules of past conventions, all resolutions would be channeled through the Resolutions Committee.

Then the delegates elected Floyd Barham of Fort Smith as permanent chairman and Ed Pace of Camden as secretary of the convention.

Barham then read the name of Judge Roy S. Dunn of Booneville as chairman of the Resolutions Committee and the names of the 11 members. I was named a member of this committee which was called upon to handle the hottest issues before the convention.

The chairman then followed with the name of Attorney Tom Harper of Fort Smith as chairman of the Platform Committee and the names of the 20 members.

Meeting of the Resolutions Committee

Judge Dunn called a meeting of the Resolutions Committee to convene following recess of the convention's first day activities. The Committee was packed with stalwart McMath backers who were in accord with the resolutions submitted, the main one being the stripping of the qualifying adjective "white" from the party rules of membership. No one appeared before the committee to protest or endorse the proposed resolutions and they were adopted without argument. As I recall the motion for approval of the controversial rule change was made by me.

Following the committee meeting I encountered an Eastern Arkansas planter, an official member of McMath's administration, in the lobby of the Marion Hotel, and was chastized severely by him for the committee action on the rule change.

The next day Judge Dunn made the committee report to the convention and asked for adoption of the resolutions. Attorney Jim McDaniel of Jonesboro moved for adoption with the second coming from C.E. Yingling of Searcy.

Attorney and Little Rock businessman Amis Guthridge, heading a Pulaski County group of delegates in opposition to the rule change, was recognized to speak against the resolution. Among the pro-McMath delegates Guthridge was described in a news report "as lonesome as a trapper in the Yukon."

The delegates, some protesting, let the speaker have his say, then by overwhelming voice vote adopted the resolutions.

The convention closed its sessions with the acceptance speech of McMath for his second term. The Governor spoke again that night to a fund raising banquet sponsored by the Young Democrats headed by President Doug Bradley of Jonesboro and Secretary Frank Newell of Little Rock.

The Third Term

After McMath's defeat for a third term the Gazette ran an editorial headed:

NOW LET'S END THE THIRD TERM BY LAW

It said in part —

When the voters rejected Sid McMath's bid for re-election, they were voting against . . . a third term.

This should help strengthen the anti-third term tradition that has held since Jeff Davis's day. And it is probably true that, as a practical matter, it is impossible for any governor to succeed himself a second time under the dual-primary system.

But it is time, nevertheless, to translate tradition into law. So long as it is legally possible to try for a third term there will always be governors who will believe, as Sid McMath did, that they can set a new precedent. And the act of running — even though election is impossible — can be destructive in itself.

What Arkansas badly needs is . . . a four year term for governor, (and) a simple constitutional amendment providing that no governor can succeed himself.

Karr Shannon wrote in the *Arkansas Democrat* on August 14, 1952:

STILL NO THIRD TERM

Another gubernatorial contest has been settled in Arkansas. And the third-term jinx, surmounted only by the inimitable Jeff Davis nearly a half-century ago, once more stopped an ambitious governor.

Governor Sid McMath went down fighting, and the rampart to political perpetuation still holds.

This is the third time A.D. (After Davis) that the jinx has been a barrier to the seeker of a third consecutive term. The first race was in 1912, when Joe T. Robinson stood in the way of Gov. George W. Donaghey. The second was 28 years later when Homer Adkins stopped the third-term bid of Gov. Carl Bailey.

In 1950 Ben Laney, who had served two terms as governor but did not run for a third consecutive term, unsuccessfully opposed Governor McMath for a second term.

CHERRY BESTS 'EM ALL

Judge Francis Cherry did quite a bit better than either Robinson or Adkins. He defeated McMath by over 97,000 votes.

DAVIS COULDN'T WIN — NOW

This year's primary elections prove conclusively that the people of Arkansas do not favor a third term. During a period of 46 years they have spoken out against it three times. If a constitutional amendment to limit a governor to four years is not passed, then the electorate will likely continue to vote down the third-term aspirants anyway. It is highly doubtful that even Jeff Davis could win a third term in this day and time.

POLITICAL SPECULATION BY SAM HARRIS

Sam Harris, political writer and star reporter for the *Arkansas Gazette,* had written a column of political speculation on a possible Cherry-Faubus race for Governor as early as June 1953. The column was run in J. E. Dunlap's weekly *Boone County Headlight* of Harrison on July 2, 1953.

Evidently the politicos of the state, and especially those in the Cherry organization, had either failed to take the column seriously or forgotten its prophecies.

CHERRY-FAUBUS FOR GOVERNOR NEXT SUMMER?

By Sam G. Harris in Arkansas Gazette

One of the most interesting political reports we've heard in months is stirring around the capitol these days. . . .

This report is that Orval Faubus, the Huntsville publisher and postmaster, may get his feet wet on his own account come next summer.

Faubus, being somewhat restricted by the Hatch Act, isn't talking but his friends are. It may be wishful thinking on his part because Faubus isn't going to do anything that isn't orthodox politically. He's too good a politician to make foolish moves on purpose.

However, if Faubus resigns his postmastership and enters the political arena as a candidate it'll be to win and not as somebody's stalking horse or sword carrier.

What office will he seek, if he runs in 1954? Why he'd run for governor — opposing Francis Cherry for a second term.

Faubus wouldn't oppose anybody for a second term in the face of tradition unless he figured that an upset was in the making in a big way. He's willing to take a calculated risk at reasonable odds. He'd be unwilling to run just for the sake of providing token opposition to a second term candidate.

————

Faubus is a friend of Sid McMath first, last and always. He probably wouldn't run if Sid asked him not to do so but Faubus would have a powerful big call on the same strength that Sid could muster (in a race for the U.S. Senate). They have the same set of political friends and Faubus helped make a lot of those friends while he was Highway Commissioner, Secretary, and Highway Director under McMath.

However, Faubus is a smart enough politician not to depend on a used political organization or one which someone else was depending on. He'd build his own organization and we'd be willing to bet when he got through building it, it would be highly effective.

The match-chewing pride of Madison County would keep plumb clear of the senator's race. He has about as much natural political savy as we've ever seen at the state house. He is the kind you don't just laugh off.

If Faubus chooses to run against Francis Cherry — or anybody else — it'll be a right lively race. Don't underestimate the hill-billy publisher-postmaster. He would be dangerous.

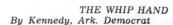

THE WHIP HAND
By Kennedy, Ark. Democrat   7/15/51

As far back as 1951 Kennedy accurately portrayed "the Industrial East" opposing, and often successfully hindering the movement of industry to the South.

CHAPTER 2
THE 1954 CAMPAIGN

ASSOCIATED POLITICAL NEWS

On January 4 the Social Security tax was one and one-half per cent, and the average weekly wage in Arkansas was $50.00.

Arkansas Democrat cartoonist Jon Kennedy showed 100 miles per hour cars on Arkansas 50 miles per hour highways, indicating the continued need for highway improvements.

Little Rock School Superintendent Virgil Blossom announced on January 8 that the school district's teachers would go without a pay raise.

The state's newest millionaire resident, Winthrop Rockefeller, was involved in divorce proceedings with his estranged wife. Other news said he would make the DAV Awards to Arkansas veterans.

SANDY McMATH AND "OLE RED" LOST

On January 9 bold headlines announced that McMath's son, Sandy, age 12, was lost in a wooded area near his Sheridan farm while on a night hunting trip with Old Red, the family owned coon dog. The police joined the ex-governor in the search.

The next day Sandy was found but Old Red was still lost.

Old Red, found a short time later, was a pure bred red bone coon dog presented to Governor McMath by a group of coon hunters of Madison County in appreciation for highway improvements in the area during his administration.

A delegation of coon hunters accompanied others from Madison County to Ione in Logan County to present the coon dog to the Governor during a dedication ceremony of a newly hard-surfaced section of Highway 23 between Booneville and Waldron on May 30, 1952.

After a fried chicken dinner prepared and served by the local residents, Lloyd Fulmer, Booneville, acted as master of ceremonies. He presented Judge R.S. (Roy) Dunn, also of Booneville, who made a speech and presented the various leaders of the Highway 23 Association. Then Bill and Clarence (Toby) Baker of St. Paul and "Fiddlin Lou" Gabbard of near Ft. Smith rendered some musical numbers. Mayor Bill Smee of Booneville introduced Governor McMath.

Among those present were Highway Commissioners Roy Martin of Ft. Smith and A.C. Mowery, Jr. of Huntsville; Ben Geren, Ft. Smith district highway engineer; Charles L. (Lee) McElhaney of Aurora, president of the Highway 23 Association; Mayor Harold Whitson of Huntsville; Perry County Judge Carl

PRESENTATION OF 'OLE RED' AT IONE
By Percy Mitchell of Huntsville. Behind Mitchell is Judge Roy Dunn holding notes.

SID McMATH AND 'OLE RED'

Adams; Perry County Representative Paul Van Dalsem; Sheriff Earl Ladd of Danville; Dave Ford and Arnold Sikes, the latter a former Logan County official, both McMath administration members of Little Rock; and me.

McMath, already an announced candidate for a third term, reviewed his highway construction program and announced he would formally open his campaign at a rally at Pine Bluff on June 28.

Old Red soon became the most famous political dog in the history of Arkansas. During the gubernatorial campaign of 1952, the red coon hound became the symbol of the administration's alleged misdeeds for McMath's critics. Years later his ghost was resurrected by my campaign staff and used in cartoons in the 1962 Democratic primary when McMath was one of my opponents.

ALLIED POLITICAL EVENTS

The February draft quota for Arkansas was 201; W. R. "Bill" Whitehead of Fordyce was named president of the Arkansas Press Association.

————

On February 25 a 12 to 2 vote of a Senate Committee approved the nomination of Earl Warren for Chief Justice of the U.S. Supreme Court.

DEMOCRAT WINS LIBEL SUIT

On February 28, the *Arkansas Democrat* was cleared of libel in a civil suit in Pulaski Circuit Court.

The suit was filed during McMath's third term bid in 1952 by Highway Commissioner A.C. Mowery, Jr., of Huntsville by his attorney, Karl Greenhaw of Fayetteville. The grounds for the suit was a story in the *Democrat* alleging that the only reason a seven-mile section of Highway 23 was improved was because it passed by Mowery's home. The improvement project, north from Huntsville to Forum, went by Withrow Spring, now a state park. The highway had been in the same location ever since the road was created many years before and was the most direct route from Huntsville to Forum and Eureka Springs. Furthermore, the project was officially scheduled before Mowery was appointed to the Commission.

I was a witness for Mowery in the trial. Since the litigation displeased the owner and publisher of the *Democrat,* August Engel, I felt the lawsuit deprived me of any possible political support from the *Democrat* for several years.

————

WARREN CONFIRMED

On March 1 the nomination of Earl Warren was confirmed in the Senate by voice vote to be Chief Justice of the U.S. Supreme Court.

FIRST FILING FOR GOVERNOR;
OTHERS INTERESTED; SNODDY WITHDRAWS

On March 5 Gus McMillan of Sheridan paid the $1,500 filing fee and filed with Secretary of State C. G. "Crip" Hall to become a surprise entry and the first candidate for governor in the Democratic primaries.

On March 7 the Army decided to forego the closing of the Army-Navy Hospital at Hot Springs. Senator McClellan relayed the news to Arkansas which gained him valuable points in his battle with McMath for the U.S. Senate seat.

Long time State Senator Lee Reaves of Warren announced his retirement.

SNODDY NOT TO RUN FOR GOVERNOR

Jim Snoddy of Alma, former state senator, former Secretary to the Senate and former executive secretary to Governor Cherry in the early months of his administration, seriously considered running for governor in 1954. He announced he would not on March 17. I had conferred with Snoddy and assured him that I would not run if he did and would back him in the race.

Our last conference was at an isolated side road off Highway 71 south of Fayetteville shortly before this announcement. I felt strongly that Snoddy was going to run and his negative decision surprised me.

In later years State Treasurer Vance Clayton and I became good friends, and he told me that he was one of those who dissuaded Snoddy from the race. It was not mentioned at the time but I knew that Clayton was very close to W. R. "Witt" Stephens.

My name was mentioned in the Snoddy withdrawal story, probably the first time it was in the news in connection with the governor's race.

The next day Boyd Tackett of Texarkana hinted he might enter the governor's race. News reports said I was silent on my plans.

Among the four challengers of McMath in 1952, Tackett, with the possible exception of Jack Holt, was the best campaigner and worked harder than any other contender. It was said that Cherry was about to drop out of the race at the time he was offered and accepted the talkathon. The method enabled him to win second place. I have always felt that Tackett, by reason of his experience in government and his diligent campaign, deserved the run-off spot with McMath which would have made him governor.

On March 19 the Hot Springs gambling casinos closed on a sudden order by a mysterious source. The Governor's office denied issuing the order. On the same day Tackett said he would not run for governor, and Jerry Campbell quit his post as publicity director in the Cherry Administration.

On March 28, McMillan, the only announced candidate for governor, was defending his plan to raise campaign funds.

McMillan had hit upon the plan of engaging campaign solicitors to raise funds on which they would be paid a ten per cent commission. An enterprising reporter soon ruined the plan by publicizing it. McMillan admitted he had agreed to pay a commission to fund raisers but denied he had proposed the selling of state jobs to supporters.

In the same story I was mentioned as a possible candidate as well as John R. Thompson of Ward in Lonoke County who was being encouraged to enter the race. Thompson had played prominent roles in both the Carl Bailey and McMath administrations.

CONGRESSMEN SEEK RE-ELECTION

The entire Arkansas Congressional delegation of the House, then numbering six, got together in Washington, as had been their custom every two years for some time, and announced for re-election. They were Trimble, Hays, Mills, Gathings, Norrell and Harris.

JONES MAY RUN, CHERRY FILES

Then State Senator Guy Jones of Conway hinted that he might be a candidate for governor.

On April 18 an attorney general's opinion ruled that Jones could legally seek the governor's office while holding his seat in the State Senate, thus removing a legal barrier to his candidacy.

On April 24 Governor Cherry filed for re-election.

NO LAW AGAINST TRYING
By Kennedy, Ark. Democrat
3/19/54

The second term wall had stood intact for all the years since Arkansas became a state and, with only one exception, had thwarted all challengers. Thus there was little interest among politicians and governor makers in supporting any candidate against Governor Cherry.

TEMPORARY WITHDRAWAL FROM GOVERNOR'S RACE

I was in Little Rock on April 2 checking my prospects as a candidate. I already had several hundred dollars which had been contributed in small amounts for my campaign fund, including $600 from a group of ordinary people from Marion County headed by former Legislator Jim Evans. Later in the day some Little Rock people who had been encouraging me began telling me that they were being subjected to tremendous pressure and inferring that it came from administration sources. Two, whom I recall, were J.C. Mitchell, a road machinery salesman, and W.L. "Doc" Hinton, a small wholesale liquor dealer who had intense competition from the larger firms. They and others were now discouraging my candidacy with some telling me flatly they couldn't support me.

Later in the day Witt Stephens walked abruptly into my hotel room and asked me, "Who is putting you up to this?"

I replied, "Did it ever occur to you that it is my own idea?" I assured him that no one was encouraging me to run for governor against the incumbent except the sentiment I gathered from ordinary people.

"You wait two years and we'll be for you," he urged. He then bluntly told me, "You run this time and we'll beat your ass." Our conference ended on that note.

Rolla Fitch, who was with me in Little Rock, told me later that when I came from the room I "looked like my whole family had died."

Some time later that day I got word that if I ran "they" would get opposition for Congressman Jim Trimble. My strong friendship for Trimble was well known to my close associates and the implied threat caused me to pause and consider.

I made a decision. I prepared a statement on the afternoon of April 3 taking myself out of the race and issued it at a press conference.

I learned later that Stephens reported the results of his conference with me to Henry Woods and Leffel Gentry jointly, the right arms respectively of McMath and Cherry, the foes of two years before. This was strange because Senator McClellan had come to Arkansas from Washington to actively assist Cherry in his victory over McMath in the Democratic run-off primary of 1952. Since I already knew that Woods had been urging our former associates and friends to discourage me from running for governor, I concluded that something very foreign to my way of thinking was happening in Arkansas politics.

After my press conference I packed my bag and went to Huntsville. However, my interest was not diminished. I continued to listen for all political news and evaluate all information. I had deliberately put in my statement the sentence, "I will not be a candidate *at this time.*"

One of those with whom I conferred was Ray Glover who traveled the north half of the state as sales agent for Little Rock Road Machinery Company. He voiced the thought that the incumbent governor could be upset, and said he would pay my filing fee if I decided to run. Some time after the campaign was underway he came to the headquarters and handed me his personal check for $750.00.

WILL ANYONE MAKE THE GRADE
By Kennedy, Ark. Democrat
4/7/54

In view of my announcement of withdrawal four days earlier, I was numbered among the fallen figures.

It portrayed the situation accurately. The moneyed men were not interested in contributing to any opponent of an incumbent governor seeking the traditional second term.

THOMPSON NOT TO RUN

John R. Thompson of Ward was urged to oppose Cherry after I withdrew. Known as the boy wonder of the Carl Bailey administration, Thompson had also been a key figure in the state government during McMath's four years as governor and consequently knew many political leaders. He was especially close to the leaders of the Rural Electric Administration cooperatives.

Thompson toured the state, sounding out sentiment and raising campaign funds. On April 26 after informing me of his decision, he announced he would not run. I had told John personally that if he decided to run I would not become a candidate and would support him.

THE 1954 CAMPAIGN
FAUBUS FILES FOR GOVERNOR

On Monday, April 26, my decision made, I quietly went down from the hills from Huntsville to Little Rock. I was accompanied by former legislator Rolla Fitch of Hindsville and O.J. Hobson, an independent telephone owner and operator of Huntsville. Since Hobson was completely unknown to the state's politicos, we traveled in his car and rented rooms in his name at the Sam Peck Hotel which was seldom frequented by politicians. I slipped unnoticed into the hotel and remained completely secluded, communicating with no one. My meals were ordered to the room and I hid during their delivery.

Rolla went out to scout the situation and returned with the information that Guy Jones was strongly rumored as a candidate but no others were in prospect.

The next morning Fitch reported on the location of the officials to receive late candidate filings, which was on the mezzanine floor of the Marion Hotel, the long-time center of state political activity. He said that Guy Jones and friends were on hand and that he appeared to be a certain candidate.

Weatherwise, the filing deadline day, April 27, was gloomy with low hanging clouds, rain and heavy mist. Shortly after 11:00 I slipped out of my room and rode with Fitch and Hobson in the latter's car to the side entrance of the Marion Hotel. While everyone was concentrating on the activity inside I stepped unseen through the rain and caught the freight elevator to a room above the mezzanine. The room was obtained by Arch Tipton who was present along with Ted Christy. Tipton and Christy were former legislators from Van Buren and Searcy Counties respectively who were ready to support me.

I thought the party officials might not accept a check for the filing fee. Not having a dime of campaign funds — previous contributions had been returned — I wrote a check for $1,500 on my personal account and Mr. Tipton went to get it cashed. I was so unknown in Little Rock at the time that Tipton had to endorse the check to cash it. He returned hurriedly in time and we went down to the filing area.

I shouldered my way through the dense crowd of on-lookers to the desk surrounded by officials, asked for and signed the proper papers and paid the filing fee.

Less than 20 minutes before the noon deadline the deed was done, and there was no time to get a candidate to Little Rock from the Third Congressional District to file against Jim Trimble. The congressman was home free in the Democratic primary.

In the meantime the news media representatives crowded around me, the reporters scribbling, the TV cameras grinding and tape recorders turning. When all the hubbub subsided and the crowd had dispersed, I felt somewhat like I thought Columbus must have felt when he launched on his voyage into the unknown with an untried crew captained by little known leaders. I, like Columbus, was going mostly on faith. But Columbus had been financed by powerful backers and I wasn't.

Shortly thereafter I went to a hotel room at the request of two friends with whom I had often conferred prior to my earlier withdrawal. Instead of a friendly meeting as I had expected, I encountered two of the maddest men I have ever seen. Anger glinted from their eyes and vibrated in their voices. They demanded to know why I had not informed them of my plans.

Taken aback, I recalled that before my earlier withdrawal they had complained of the pressure they had undergone because of their association with my possible candidacy. I explained that I filed quietly both to protect them by keeping them free from the pressure and for strategic reasons.

After some conversation they became less vehement vocally but were only slightly mollified. When I shortly departed their extreme displeasure was still readily apparent.

Months later I learned the real reason for my friends' unhappiness that day. They were to receive $30,000 for keeping me out of the race. Whether the money was advanced or was to be paid after the ticket closed, I never learned.

Were it not for one circumstance, I would conclude that the agreed sum was advanced, since one of the generally accepted means of accomplishment is to make available at least a part of the funds to the principal. Both parties knew of my errant journey and brief stay at Commonwealth College near Mena, an institution which had been placed on the Federal Justice Department's subversive list after my connection with it. They could have led their co-conspirators in the scheme to believe that I could be kept out of the race by leading me to the conclusion that the matter would be used against me and would be fatal to my candidacy.

I have no way of knowing whether Governor Cherry knew anything of the arrangement to keep me out of the race. I did not learn about it until after the 1954 campaign was over.

If I had not filed as a candidate, I would probably never have learned of the deal, and, naturally, would never have seen a dime of the money.

As the months and years went by I learned that some of the problems and burdens of any prominent public official stems from the fact that his name is often used in various schemes without his knowledge, and in ways which he would instantly veto if he only knew.

Guy "Mutt" Jones also filed for governor that day and J. M. Meyers of Springdale filed by letter.

Sam Jones of Little Rock filed against incumbent State Treasurer Vance Clayton. The respected veteran Land Commissioner Claude Rankin was faced with a young, vocal, diligent challenger, Doyle Yopp of Paragould.

The U.S. Senate candidates were McClellan, McMath, Leonard Ellis of Little Rock, and Paul Chambers of Helena.

James D. "Jim" Johnson, a young state senator from Crossett, filed for attorney general against incumbent Tom Gentry. The third candidate was Phil McNemer.

Congressman Oren Harris of the Fourth District wound up with three opponents which included G.W. Lookadoo of Arkadelphia.

What at first appeared to be a quiet political summer, except for the McMath-McClellan battle, now had contests in five state-wide races and in the Fourth Congressional District. The five statewide races became turbulent, boiling battles marked by hot words and hard fighting.

Two days later Governor Cherry, returning from a trip to Washington, said he saw only one issue in the campaign: — "Would the people turn state government back to the professional politicians."

McMILLAN FIRES OPENING CAMPAIGN GUN;
I BECOME ACTIVE

Gus McMillan, a 52-year-old former postmaster and school teacher, opened his campaign May 1 on the courthouse square at Sheridan in his home county of Grant.

At 4:20 p.m. he gave a blast on his "Jeff Davis original" fox horn and then blasted Cherry in a speech on welfare and the hiring of out-of-state people.

The Democrat on May 2 quoted the following from his speech:

"As a man who is aware of the contributions made by those who are now growing old, I strongly resent their (old folks) being called 'dead heads'. To me they are the bridge builders, lantern carriers and trail blazers, who are alone responsible for any progress this state has made."

Guy "Mutt" Jones was on hand for the McMillan opener.

On May 2 Marcus George wrote "Political observers feel either Jones or Faubus will withdraw from the race for Governor." Cherry labeled his opposition as "McMath opponents," meaning the opposition came from McMath and his political allies.

Cherry was wrong but his vocal prediction and statements on the matter helped to bring about the situation which he at first suspected.

On May 5 my resignation as Huntsville postmaster had been received in Washington.

FIRST SPLASH
By Kennedy, Arkansas Democrat   5/2/54

This cartoon, the day after McMillan's opener, portrayed the attitude of politicians toward the challenge of his candidacy. Little more credence was given to the efforts of Jones and me, and Myers was discounted completely. The politicians counted Cherry a sure winner. But three challengers knew more of rank and file sentiment than did the politicians and governor-makers who were, as usual, counseling among themselves. That dozing public figure was thoroughly aroused before the campaign was over.

MADISON COUNTY ORGANIZES CLUB
FOR GOVERNOR CANDIDATE

My home folks began organizing in my behalf. In a meeting at the courthouse on May 5 with Clay McBroom acting as temporary chairman, a Faubus-for-Governor Club was formed with plans to expand county wide. McBroom was elected permanent chairman of the group and former county official Albert King was named secretary. King later came to the Little Rock headquarters as campaign accountant.

Among those reported speaking at the meeting were a widely known northwest Arkansas attorney, Ed Fowler, E.B. Jones, a World War II veteran active in veterans affairs, and Mrs. Howard Cain, who had recently returned with her husband and family from residence in California.

At a second meeting a short time later, Joel Bunch of Fayetteville, a former Madison County World War II Air Force officer shot down by the German forces and imprisoned in the Nazi PW camps, was the main speaker.

———

REMMEL CONSIDERS RACE FOR CONGRESS

On May 11 the news again reported that Mayor Pratt Remmel of Little Rock was eyeing Congressman Brooks Hays' seat in the National Congress. National GOP backing was expected, Remmel reported, and added that he was giving the race serious consideration.

SET FOR THE SUMMER
By Kennedy, Ark. Democrat   5/16/54

McClellan had helped Fulbright in a previous political race and he felt that now Fulbright should return the favor. The junior Senator's neutral stance displeased McClellan, according to many verbal reports.

17

SPRINGDALE SUPPORT

News reports of May 18 revealed an organizational meeting in my support at Springdale. Roy Ritter, well known regionally and with a statewide acquaintance with poultry producers and feed dealers, was elected chairman of the group. Ritter announced that Springdalians who had agreed to serve on the steering committee of the Faubus for Governor Club included Harvey Jones, Luther George, John Tyson, publisher Marty Stafford, Joe McKim, Joe M. Steele, Fred Watson and Sonny Henson, all prominent business and civic leaders.

Another strong supporter at the time, although not publicly, was Gus Eidson, an old McMath ally, who was then openly connected with the McMath campaign for the Senate. Perhaps my most dedicated and loyal friend was Paul Condra, a Springdale businessman and World War II Air Force hero. Another was Bob Sanders a fellow newsman with the *Springdale News*.

o⬤⊐⬤⊐⬤⊐⬤⊐⬤⊐o

NOTHING SACRED
By Kennedy, Ark. Democrat   6/6/54

Guy Jones opened his campaign on June 5 with a speech to a gathering of supporters in Jonesboro, the hometown of Gov. Cherry.

CANDIDATES FOR GOVERNOR IN CARICATURE, By Kennedy, Ark. Democrat, 5/27/54

18

DECISION OF BROWN VS. BOARD OF EDUCATION

The U.S. Supreme Court headed by Chief Justice Earl Warren handed down a decision on May 17 in a case styled Brown vs. Board of Education, which came as a complete surprise to many people. With later clarifying rulings the decision outlawed segregation of the races in the public schools.

Banner headlines heralded the court's ruling. One such headline stated that 228 school districts would be affected in Arkansas. News stories related that the South and Border States would face vast problems of great complexity in dealing with the unexpected and unprecedented decision.

Reaction from a few sources came quickly in Arkansas. Veteran legislator Carroll Hollensworth of Bradley County, then Speaker of the House of Representatives, voiced the thought that a special session of the Legislature would be necessary to deal with the problems created in Arkansas by the ruling. The idea behind his statement was to find legal means to avoid compliance.

Governor Francis Cherry's initial reaction on the same day was that Arkansas would "meet the requirements of the decision."

On that same day an unrelated incident in Little Rock made the news. Assistant Police Chief Gene Smith was "busted" to patrolman by Chief Marvin Potts for getting drunk and creating a distrubance in a west side apartment house. The policeman's union asked for Smith to be dismissed from the force. The "busting" of Smith and the court ruling coming on the same day were coincidental, but within a little more than three years Smith's fame and fate were inextricably interwoven into the controversy resulting from the court ruling and his role as Little Rock Police Chief during the so-called 1957 crisis.

NO JOB FOR A RACE HORSE
By Kennedy, Ark. Democrat   5/19/54

Kennedy caught the attitude of the people toward integration. Everyone in Arkansas knew a race horse was not good for plowing. Making a crop was a gradual process. Likewise, radical changes in social attitudes should come gradually.

In some school districts where segregation problems were considered minor, the boards, unaware of the deep feeling of the people about the matter, made hasty decisions to integrate. Two of those were Fayetteville and Sheridan, the announcements coming on May 22.

The reaction at Sheridan, 20 miles south of Little Rock in Grant County, was swift and strong. The board rescinded its decision the next day acceding to the demands of aroused patrons of the district.

Fayetteville in the far corner of Northwest Arkansas with the only blacks in any district for at least 70 miles in any direction, did not have such a strong reaction. However the board modified its plans to provide for integration of the high schools only and continued to operate the grade schools on a segregated basis. A modifying influence there was the fact that black students were already enrolled in the University of Arkansas and many black teachers attended summer sessions along with white teachers on the Fayetteville campus.

On May 27 the Pine Bluff school board announced that integration of the city schools would be deferred indefinitely.

The turmoil continued at Sheridan. On May 30 it was disclosed that a group of patrons was seeking the ouster of the entire school board and the superintendent of the school system, notwithstanding the fact that the board had backed off from its integration plan almost as soon as it was announced. A mass meeting on June 1 demanded that segregation continue.

The developments at Sheridan were a forerunner of the turmoil and difficulty which were to ensue in many areas of Arkansas and across the nation.

On May 21 Georgia Governor Herman Talmadge announced that his state would defy the Supreme Court's integration ruling. Shortly thereafter in Louisiana strong segregation bills won final approval in the General Assembly. The state invoked its police power in defense of its schools against the federal courts.

Marcus George headlined his column Backstage at the Capitol in the Sunday, May 23, Arkansas Democrat, "Week's Biggest Question: Ruling of Supreme Court."

On May 25, the media reported that the Washington, D.C. school authority voted 6 to 2 to integrate the District schools. The decision was followed by protests, mass meetings and efforts to boycott the schools by opponents of the plan. Proponents said the Washington plan would become the great example of how well integration would work.

By June 9 Governor Cherry had begun to change his initial reaction. He picked a committee of three to attend a conference in Virginia on means of opposing the Supreme Court Decision. The members were Commissioner of Education Arch Ford; State Board of Education member Frank Bailey, son of former Governor Carl Bailey and Commander of the Arkansas Air National Guard; and Ken Francis, the Governor's executive secretary.

On June 14 the news reported that "separate but equal" school policy had been set by Governor Cherry and the Arkansas State Board of Education. In other words, segregation in the public schools was to continue under the Cherry administration. The next day the Governor urged the schools to wait, to postpone integration as "premature." He also postponed until after the Democratic primaries the naming of a committee to study and deal with the problem.

I studied the matter carefully for several days and then stated my position in a paid newspaper ad on June 5 and 6. My position was described as "local gradualism" under complete local control.

The *Arkansas Gazette* reacted to the ad in an editorial on June 8. It quoted a part of my ad as follows:

As Governor, I pledge you, the people, that the right of all will be protected but that the problem of desegregation will be solved on the LOCAL

LEVEL, with state authorities standing ready to assist in every way possible. . . .

The Gazette then commented:

The only place the problem can be solved is on the local level — not only because, as Mr. Faubus correctly states, no court ruling can force upon an unwilling people a practice the great majority disapproved, but because administrative control of the public schools is vested in the local school districts.

I dealt with the matter of integration again in my official campaign opening at Fayetteville on June 25 which was carried state wide by radio. I don't recall that the matter was mentioned again during the campaign. After Governor Cherry had made clear his policy of continued segregation, and I had taken my stand for local school determination, the matter was largely considered to be settled.

Why was the matter not discussed at length by the various candidates for the various offices in Arkansas during the campaign of 1954?

There were two basic reasons.

First the Supreme Court decision was new and its full impact had not yet been realized by the people. In fact it was handed down more than two weeks after the filing deadline for the Arkansas Democratic primaries. No candidate who filed for any office had even the faintest idea that such an issue would arise.

Certainly it was considered a problem for the long range future, months or even years in the offing. Human beings have never considered long range problems of immediate concern. History is replete with examples of how people fail to be stirred to action until the wolves are in the sheep fold or the invaders are at the gates.

Second, the school districts in Arkansas were political entities in which the locally elected school board members had sole jurisdiction and authority over the employment of faculty members, the setting of salaries and other school expenses and the assignment of student attendance. This was in accordance with the philosophy and plans of Thomas Jefferson and the Founding Fathers when the nation was established and the Constitution written and adopted. The people were firm in their belief that no legal or constitutional means existed by which either the state or federal authority could tell them what to do about their local school affairs.

Therefore the people waited with the thought, "We'll have the final say" about integration, segregation or any other school matter, supremely confident that they would prevail. Therefore why discuss the matter. They, the people, would make the decisions on any such school problems whenever they arose.

Even the *Gazette,* which later became one of the leading proponents of integration in Arkansas and the South, stated in its editorial of June 8, 1954:

The only place the problem can be solved is on the local level . . . because administrative control of the public schools is vested in the local school districts.

The general attitude of the people to the Supreme Court Decision in 1954 was a firm belief that it would never be implemented in any area where it was opposed because the court had no jurisdiction over local school affairs.

The people were firmly convinced the decision would never be enforced, at any point where the people stood in determined opposition.

FAUBUS-FOR-GOVERNOR DINNER AT HUNTSVILLE

On the evening of May 20 the Madison County Faubus-for-Governor organization held a fund-raising dinner in the Huntsville Grade School gymnasium. Clay McBroom, Chairman of the Faubus-for-Governor Club, was master of ceremonies for the $5.00 per plate affair.

The noted lecturer and writer, Harold Sherman of Mountain View, was the main speaker, and came at his own expense. My only role was to introduce Mr. Sherman and make brief remarks.

The meal was served by the senior class of the Huntsville High School under the direction of Miss Gayle Johnson.

Among the leaders were N.D. (Doc) Heathman, the Republican member of the legislature from Madison County; P.V. Blankenship, Supervisor of Schools and Vice-President of the Chamber of Commerce; and Roy "Bus" Hawkins, Huntsville mayor. The invocation was given by my pastor, Reverend R.W. "Bob" Jones of the First Baptist Church, and the benediction by Thomas R. Whiddon, the Methodist pastor.

Entertainment was by Miss Carol Ann Holland and Phillip Hawkins of Huntsville, and Bill and Clarence Baker of St. Paul.

I was presented with a check for $1,100 for the campaign at the close of the meeting.

AP&L INCREASES RATES

On May 27 came the news that a $3.9 million increase in the electric rates of the Arkansas Power and Light Company would go into effect on July 1. The higher bills would affect 263,000 electric power users.

This rate increase, along with one by Arkansas Louisiana Gas Company, (not then owned by W.R. "Witt" Stephens) was to have a significant effect on the campaign.

Telephone rates had also been increased during Governor Cherry's administration, and a water rate increase went into effect in Little Rock. A severe drought was beginning statewide, the third in a row, and business conditions were poor. The rate increases were viewed with disfavor.

CHERRY PLANS NO CAMPAIGN

A new capital drive east of the capitol building was formally dedicated on June 8.

A picture showed Governor Cherry, Secretary of State C.G. "Crip" Hall, Highway Director Herbert Eldridge, Old Line Insurance Company President W.E. (Bill) Darby and a number of legislators participating in the ceremony. The drive is beside the Old Line Insurance Company building next to the Capitol. On this occasion Governor Cherry told Hall that he really didn't have any race; that he did not intend to make a campaign except for the civic club circuit and public engagements.

————

FITCH WITHDRAWS FROM STATE SENATE RACE

On June 10 Rolla Fitch withdrew from the race for the State Senate in our district and announced he would assist me in the race for governor. He joined my campaign staff as a full time worker.

MISCELLANEOUS DEVELOPMENTS; MEYERS WITHDRAWS

On June 15 Senator J. William Fulbright of Arkansas announced that he was ready to remove Joe McCarthy from the Senate.

On the 16th Governor Cherry told the press that state employees were not expected to aid in his campaign for reelection.

On the 17th the press carried the news that Bobo Sears Rockefeller, estranged wife of Winthrop Rockefeller, had departed for Reno, Nevada, and a $6 million divorce settlement. On the 18th Mr. Rockefeller and his Arkansas attorney, Edwin Dunaway, flew from Little Rock to Reno to consumate the agreement which was completed on the 20th.

Up to that time many people in Arkansas had the thought that Rockefeller had moved to the state for the purpose of obtaining a divorce. When the filing by Bobo was made in Reno and the divorce granted there, the thought was dissipated. In the years which followed when Rockefeller remained in Arkansas the idea vanished completely.

On June 22 a $10 per plate breakfast was held in West Memphis to raise funds for the Cherry campaign. In spite of the Governor's previous announcement that no help was expected from state employees, many of them with members of their families were in attendance. Crittenden County had the strongest Cherry organization in the state.

On the same date balloons with the wording, "Jones for Governor", went up in four of the state's major cities including Little Rock. It was a novel way of advertising the candidacy of Guy "Mutt" Jones.

At about the same time I announced my scheduled campaign opening at Fayetteville. The news was carried on page 2 of one newspaper under a Cherry story headline, a strong indication that the editors did not consider my candidacy of sufficient importance to warrant a separate story.

On June 24, J.M. Meyers of Springdale, who had filed for governor by letter apparently without ever being seen by anyone including members of the press, announced his withdrawal from the race.

MANAGER APPOINTED BY FAUBUS;
12-MEMBER ADVISORY COMMITTEE NAMED

Under this headline carried on page 2 of the *Democrat*, still further indicating that my efforts were not taken seriously at the time, was the story of my appointment of R.M. "Bob" Faust of Little Rock as my campaign manager.

I had tried to get a number of people for the post, but to no avail. They expressed sympathy but made excuses, or gave reasons why they must decline. I am sure Faust was aware of this for little went on that he did not know about, but he agreed to accept the position.

I knew that Faust and Leffel Gentry — Bob always called him Lethel — Cherry's campaign manager and close confidant, were very close friends and associates. But I had to have a campaign manager, for appearances sake if nothing else, or see my campaign ship capsize early in the voyage.

Bob and I had become well acquainted when we were both sub-alterns of McMath during his administration. I came to respect his analytical ability and his propensity to tell the truth even when it was unpleasant. He was once described as a "Damon Runyon character," not of New York, but of Little Rock. He knew every political figure of the city and the state from the very top figures on down to the lowest ward-heelers, and even the jail birds in the city jail, and was intimate with many of them. His spoken pledge on any financial transaction, including the many wagers he handled, was considered as good as a government bond. To seek information from him which he did not wish to disclose was like questioning the Sphinx. So far as I could tell he was fearless. His friends were many and their trust in him was great, although a few realized he was not above the role of a con artist at times when it served his strategy.

Bob is almost certainly the only campaign manager in the history of Arkansas politics who spent no more than a half hour in the campaign headquarters in any one day and never collected a dollar for the campaign fund. However, his analysis of situations was sound, his public relations good and his advice

excellent whenever offered. Most of the conferences with him were by telephone while on the road or at night when things quieted down.

Whatever may be said by observers of, or participants in the campaign, whether true or untrue, Faust played his role and served my purpose in the political battle of 1954. I always remained grateful and our friendship continued unimpaired.

After he died at his request two of the pallbearers at his funeral were Sid McMath and Orval Faubus, then known as political enemies, which Bob knew before his death.

ADVISORY COMMITTEE

The 12-member advisory committee was made up of Rolla Fitch, a farmer and former legislator of Hindsville; Joe Hearn, Little Rock, former State Veterans Service Officer and former State Commander of the American Legion; Dwight Nichols, hotel operator and tourist advocate of Eureka Springs; Craig Holt, county political figure of Bentonville; Newt Hailey, automobile dealer of Rogers; Earl Harris, baking company executive of Rogers; J.E. Dunlap, newspaper publisher and editor and veterans leader of Harrison; Whitfield Shaver, planter and banker of Cherry Valley; Harry D. Miller, El Dorado, American Legion leader of statewide prominence; J.M. Malone, Sr., Lonoke, former county judge, a candidate for Governor in 1946 and former road machinery salesman; Roy Ritter, poultry products dealer and a restaurant operator of Springdale; and Olen Hendrix, Antoine, former highway commissioner and businessman.

I never met with these men as a group but advised with each individually as often as possible. They were most valuable as area contacts for the state headquarters staff, and for organizational efforts in their respective regions. The principal value of the advisory committee was the public use of their names for the campaign effort.

HEADQUARTERS WORKERS
Rolla Fitch

Headquarters workers until the time of the first primary were:

Rolla Fitch, who worked at headquarters until we finally obtained clerical help to handle the mail and letter writing. Then he was designated to go on the road on fact-finding trips, and finally as advance man for my speaking engagements. He proved to be excellent for this work. He was good at making contacts and arrangements for my appearances. He was probably the best member of the campaign staff for determining the attitude of political leaders toward my candidacy. He often could obtain detailed information where others failed.

Albert King

Albert King, Huntsville, former Madison County official, came to Little Rock as the campaign accountant. He meticulously recorded each contribution and expenditure of the campaign. He could tell me or the staff our financial situation, which was nearly always broke, at any time he was asked. Since I constantly urged that no indebtedness was to be incurred it was next to impossible to get Albert to write or authorize a check for any purpose unless the funds were on hand to cover it. No one could have done a better job at the task to which he was assigned.

Dr. Joe Shuffield

Many times when the campaign fund was exhausted and an expenditure had to be made, as for an ad in the Little Rock papers, those on duty in the headquarters went into their own pockets to make up the necessary amount. A few in Little Rock not connected with the headquarters would help at times. One of them was Dr. Joe Shuffield. A number of times when the campaign fund was exhausted, Fitch would go to him and "Dr. Joe", as we came to affectionately call him, would dig down and come up with $50 to $200.

Truman Baker

Truman Baker, Searcy, former highway commissioner and automobile dealer, came to headquarters one day with a $1,000 contribution and told me he would help any way he could. Soon he was almost a permanent fixture at the headquarters. He was most helpful in raising funds. Truman was also effective in calling and bringing into the campaign friends and acquaintances we had made during our four years together in state government — people I had been unable to contact because of the limitations of time. He was one of those who almost invariably contributed in time of need. A trait of his everyone liked — he didn't run away when the going got rough.

Roy Ritter

Roy Ritter, a relatively late comer, joined the staff after my supporters at Springdale got together and designated him to come to Little Rock to help. Big, bold and imposing, Roy was immediately an asset. He began to round up poultry and livestock producers throughout the state and got many of them to become active. His thinking was sound on advertising and publicity.

Carl Adams

Carl Adams of Perryville, county judge of Perry County and former president of the County Judges Association, would come to headquarters and work two or three days. When the pressure got too heavy he would go home to relax and look after official duties. Then in two or three days he would be back in the headquarters at work again.

Loid Sadler

Loid Sadler, former highway commissioner and a cotton gin operator and farmer at Morrilton, joined the headquarters staff. I don't recall just when Loid first joined but he was there when the storm broke and was one of those who did not flee. For a brief time during the Commonwealth College crisis in the runoff he was one of the few on hand. Nearly always a man of good humor, Loid later told funny stories about campaign occurrences.

Tipton, Christy, Hearn and Thompson

Christy and Tipton, along with Joe Hearn and Carl Thompson, a former employee of the Veterans Department and well known Legionnaire, helped at headquarters and worked in the field as well. Once when we were hard pressed for funds Tipton said to me as he and I were crossing Markham Street by the Marion Hotel, "I've got $5,000 saved. I'll go get it and let you have it. You can pay me back later."

I was in a great hurry at the time but stopped long enough to say, "Arch, there's no assurance we're going to win this battle. If we lose I don't know when I could pay you. I might never be able to repay you. So you keep your money," I advised him, "and don't let anyone in this campaign have it."

I had already exhausted all my meager savings and was then over $5,000 in debt at the First National Bank in Huntsville. My good friends, bank president, Tom Hargis, the well-liked Clay McBroom and Omer Basham, had permitted me to incur that indebtedness early in the campaign before I could raise sufficient funds to pay bills.

J. M. Malone, Senior and Junior

J. M. Malone, Sr., and his son Jim Malone, both of Lonoke, were at the headquarters periodically. They also volunteered as campaign speakers to represent me at affairs to which I was invited but could not attend.

John R. Thompson

Another loyal volunteer for speaking engagements was John R. Thompson of Cabot.

Jim Crain

Jim Crain of Wilson, Mississippi County, a former member of the highway commission and the Highway Audit Commission, a political leader of statewide renown, was not often in the headquarters but he was a regional organizer and, aside from Truman Baker, my only heavy contributor of the campaign. For a time he permitted the headquarters staff to draw a draft on him for $1,000 each week. His total contributions to the state campaign fund amounted to about $5,000 or $6,000.

J. Orville Cheney

J. Orville Cheney, former state senator and businessman of Calico Rock, was one of my early volunteers. He had a wide acquaintance as a result of his service in the Senate, and he knew practically every voter in his former senatorial district. He did not spend much time at headquarters at first and was assisting Guy Jones, but came in to help whenever he could. In the later stages of the campaign he was spending almost full time as a member of the staff. An excellent campaign speaker, he filled a number of engagements in my behalf and was selected to head the speakers bureau. In this role he kept a list of volunteer speakers and assigned them to fill engagements throughout the state where we had requests that I could not meet. As an experienced campaigner, his counsel on strategy was valuable and he was helpful in writing speeches, press releases and ads. Cheney wrote the first ad used by the staff in reply to Gov. Cherry's Commonwealth College charges during the runoff. Its lead line was, "For Shame, Governor Cherry."

Roy "Bus" Hawkins

Roy "Bus" Hawkins of Huntsville started with me early in the campaign as my principal driver. He was diligent, faithful, and dependable. I soon discovered he had other talents. I began the practice of turning "Bus" loose in a town while I was contacting certain acquaintances. He visited drug stores, cafes, and sometimes a pool parlor or place that dispensed beer, and picked up a wealth of information which included the names of the various political factions and political leaders of the area. Sometimes we contacted some of the leaders before leaving the area.

Clay Anderson And Tom Pearson

T. C. "Clay" Anderson of Crosses had organized a group of supporters in Fayetteville. Among them was a young attorney and Naval reserve officer, Tom Pearson. When the campaign became hectic he joined our headquarters staff in Little Rock. When the race was all over Pearson went back on active duty with the Navy before I was inaugurated.

Farrell Faubus

Farrell, my son, by that time age 15, joined the campaign as a member of the road crew with the sound trucks when my intensive speaking itinerary got under way. He was quiet, unobtrusive and observant, well-liked by the other members and made a good hand. Unknown to the general public, he observed and heard many comments that would have remained unknown to me had he not related them later.

Once in Arkansas City while I was campaigning the Desha county seat town, visiting the courthouse and the few business establishments, Farrell was seated among a few idlers near the parked sound truck. A middle-aged countryman came stalking by, stopping when he saw the brightly lettered vehicle. Aloud he spelled out the name, "F A U B U S", "Foobus" he pronounced, then commented, "He'll never make it. The name'll beat him."

The sound crew had to leave Little Rock one morning before the headquarters opened. They were all broke. On reaching Mississippi County, with Farrell acting as spokesman they obtained credit at a service station for gas for the vehicles. They did not get to eat until we caught up with them that afternoon. That night when the day's work had ended we provided them with sufficient funds to continue.

I recall that Farrell was with us on the day the Commonwealth College storm began to break at Tuckerman and Newport. The day was inordinately hot and the crew sought drinks and a brief respite from the heat in the coolness of a drug store at Newport. I remember cautioning them to always scout the speaking site to see that all was in order before taking too much rest.

Tim Canada

Then there was the giant black man, Tim Canada of North Little Rock. I seemed to acquire him along with the barren-looking garage building across Markham Street from the Marion Hotel which was our first headquarters. Tim was employed to keep the building cleaned up and soon was a fixture of the Faubus headquarters. He was diligent and faithful in his duties, friendly and outgoing in attitude and soon known to many headquarters visitors.

Mr. Canada was a strong believer in prayer. Often without hesitation he would drop to his knees on the concrete floor and there in the stifling heat offer up a fervent prayer for the success of our efforts.

Well before the end of the campaign he assured me that I would win. He had a vision, he related to me, in which he saw himself working for me while I was governor.

Besides his strong faith and firm belief in prayer, Tim's physical strength was phenomenal. In later years I saw him lift Farrell, then weighing 300 pounds, from the floor and hold him at arms length in his hands.

Tim Canada's vision was fulfilled. He was one of the first to be employed when I became Governor. He held a job in the Revenue Department under Commissioner Cheney until his death.

— o — o —

These were some of the main headquarters workers up through the first primary. All were volunteers and none received any pay whatsoever, except Mr. Canada, who got only a nominal sum. Many were loyal friends who would have supported me regardless. However, all were, in poker parlance, "betting on the come" hoping to draw a winning political hand.

— o — o —

A SIGNIFICANT MEETING

Some time early in the campaign while I was still traveling alone in a used car — provided by Truman Baker, I attended a meeting at the home of Maurice Smith, Sr. at Birdeye.

I went by Searcy and Truman accompanied me to the meeting traveling with me in the second hand auto.

Mr. Smith at the time was the patriarch of a large clan of relatives and employees on his extensive land holdings in Cross County. He was, and had been for some 40 years, the chairman of the County Democratic Central Committee and had served a comparable time as a member and chairman of an important levee board in the area.

In the campaign of 1952 he had remained a loyal part of the McMath organization. As a result of his efforts Cross County was one of the six counties carried by McMath in the runoff primary against Francis Cherry. After Cherry's victory and subsequent inauguration he refused to forgive the elderly and influential Cross County political leader for his support of McMath.

At one time Governor Cherry bluntly refused to consider a request from a Cross County delegation because of their friendship with Smith even though most members of the delegation had been his supporters. The incident occurred in the governor's office in the Capitol with Cherry dismissing the delegation with the words, "I'm not going to do anything for any friends of Maurice Smith."

The results of the conference were related to Mr. Smith and, quite naturally, he was looking for an opportunity to retaliate for the affront to him and his friends. I was selected from among the candidates opposing Cherry as the one most likely to provide formidable opposition to the incumbent governor, and invited to the meeting.

Among those attending the conference were Mr. Smith's two sons, J.H. and Maurice, Jr., various foremen and employees of Mr. Smith's operations, some businessmen of the area including Whit Shaver from a nearby town. I recall that I immediately liked the craggy-faced, outspoken Mr. Shaver. We became friends from that moment and he remained a friend and adviser throughout my administration and in the years which followed.

We had the noon meal in the rambling old plantation style home of the elder Smith. He led much of the discussion and made plain to his youthful friends and lieutenants his desires in the campaign. All were in accord. When Truman and I departed the Smith residence I was assured of strong, solid support in a county which was a part of former Chancellor Cherry's judicial district. This was most encouraging because it meant I was cutting into what would normally be considered my opponent's home area.

It must be recalled that Mr. Smith was ill at the time and confined generally to his home. That was one of the reasons for the conference there, and the fact that the aging Cross County patriarch had to depend on his relatives and friends to direct the campaign efforts in my behalf.

Later when our efforts were successful, the old gentleman's spirits were so buoyed by the victory that he was able to attend the State Democratic Convention in Little Rock where I officially accepted the nomination. A tall man wearing a dark western style hat, the elderly Smith was easily one of the most distinctive figures at the convention. I further pleased him by visiting his room where he introduced me to the Cross County delegates.

At the time of the meeting at Mr. Smith's home the state highway from the county seat of Wynne to Birdeye was unimproved. Traveling over the gravel road we had two flat tires which Truman and I had to change in the dust and heat. Said Truman with decision and finality in his voice, "We've got to get some new rubber on this car."

Safely back at Searcy Truman had his employees put four new tires on my used vehicle. They served without failure for the remainder of the campaign.

Sometime during my administration Mr. Smith's health worsened and he passed away. But I never for one moment forgot his help. The memory of the meeting at his home and of his distinctive appearance at the convention still lingers vividly in my mind.

Soon after my administration began I was pleased to see the dirt and gravel highway hardsurfaced, which was a great satisfaction to my supporters in the area. Also during my administration I had the privilege and pleasure to honor Mr. Smith's two sons with prestigeous appointments. J.H. was appointed to the Board of Trustees of Arkansas State College (now a university) at Jonesboro, and Maurice, Jr. to the much sought after membership on the Arkansas Highway Commission.

But alas, the younger inheritors of the elder Mr. Smith's powerful political organization did not prove to have his constancy. They remained loyal and helpful during my time in office, but in my last comeback political effort in 1974, the younger Smiths and their lieutenants, followed Witt Stephens, John Cooper and Bill Darby into the camp of my major opponent when their help to me could have proven decisive.

I do not think the tall, distinctive, decisive Maurice Smith, Sr. would have approved.

———

JUNE 26 —

FAUBUS OPENS AT FAYETTEVILLE; HITS UTILITY RATE INCREASE; BLAMES CHERRY ADMINISTRATION FOR BOOSTS; FAUBUS VOWS NEGRO JOBS, NOT INTEGRATION

These headlined the news of my formal campaign opening at an outdoor rally in Fayetteville on June 25 at 7:00. My speech was carried over a 34 station radio network. The following quotation from my speech was used by one newspaper.

"No ruling can force on an unwilling people a practice which a majority of the people of the affected area do not approve. True democracy is a grass roots thing. Real progress in the social and political fields wells up from the people. It is not handed down from above.

"The Negroes are entitled to state jobs, the function of which concerns their people, and to see the Governor at any time there is a need. These things I now publicly pledge."

(In the first paragraph of the quote I should have said, "can force willing acceptance of a practice which the majority opposes." The Supreme Court, acting as a virtual judicial dictatorship, and the federal government have, by military power and police state methods, forced upon the American people a number of practices not willingly accepted by the majority.)

I spoke from a flatbed truck in front of the business of Clint Walden one of my early supporters. The newsmen gave good coverage and estimated the crowd at 1,500 to 2,500. Many in the audience were from my nearby county of Madison. My principal organizer in Fayetteville was Paul Davis, former legislator, then a Washington County official. Rev. Fred Huckleberry introduced me. Two other supporters at Fayetteville were Clark and Charles McClinton who furnished me a credit card for gas and oil for my car. I used it to the amount of about $1,500. After the campaign I offered to repay them but they declined payment and said it would be their contribution.

Former Chancellor Lee Seamster was a strong supporter in Fayetteville. Another was Bryan Walker from a politically prominent family of the area.

I was disappointed with some aspects of the opener. The sound system was set in such a way that I could not hear the amplified sound of my voice. Consequently my voice was pitched too high. However, many of those who heard the speech, there and by radio, were impressed by the content.

There was a second disappointment. Jerry Campbell, former publicity director in the Cherry Administration, had been engaged to handle publicity and advertising for my campaign. He had a drinking problem of which I was unaware at the time, and before the program began had gotten hold of a bottle. When I got to the program site I found he had changed the order of the entertainment which I had previously arranged. I was angered, and as nearly as possible rearranged the program to its original order. I wanted the entertainment to close with the Tulsa (Oklahoma) Police Department Barber-Shop Quartet, former national champions, whom I had obtained for the occasion. They were Bob Howard, Sam Martinez, Les Applegate and W.C. "Choc" Roberts.

However, overall it was a good opening with a good crowd. When it was over we drove south and Jerry, still high on his booze, was a pain in the neck the entire time. Instead of getting some rest while traveling, as was my custom, I suffered all the way.

COAL HILL, ALTUS AND DANVILLE

We took lodging some time after midnight in some town now forgotten, and the next day I spoke in small towns along the Arkansas Valley, one of them Danville, on the way to Perryville. This was probably the day that I spole in Coal Hill and Altus, two small towns in Johnson and Franklin Counties. My appearance marked the last time that any candidate set up his microphones in those then declining settlements which were former boom towns of the coal mining era.

As to Campbell, after that we tried to keep him and the liquor apart. When not bothered with that problem he was knowledgeable and able in his field of responsibility, exercising both initiative and ingenuity. He was not at all hesitant about calling the television and radio media and demanding comparable coverage of my campaign under the "equal time" or "fairness" doctrine. His efforts secured much publicity which was important to a relatively unknown candidate challenging a widely known incumbent. Campbell did a very good job in his role often under difficult circumstances.

On June 26 the news reported that Cherry did not plan to make a formal campaign. Evidently this announcement was meant to display supreme confidence in the election outcome.

However the next day Leffel Gentry resigned as state chairman of the Democratic Central Committee to manage the Governor's campaign. They were treating the opposition with disdain but preparing for action. In my opinion the first announcement, even if true, was a mistake.

PERRYVILLE; CHERRY LASHES BACK AT BITTER VERBAL ATTACKS

This was the headline for the news story which related how all the candidates met at the Perry County seat of Perryville and spoke from the same platform at the back of the courthouse. Representative Paul Van Dalsem had long before arranged the event, invited all the candidates for governor and all had accepted.

Van Dalsem acted as master of ceremonies introducing the candidates. I thought he showed more enthusiasm in presenting Governor Cherry than was apparent for any of the others.

McMillan blew his fox horn and spoke with apparent confidence. Jones made an impassioned speech with a strong attack on Cherry which was received with cheers from much of the audience.

I followed with a speech which I attempted to pitch in calm, low key at the suggestion of Marcus George, *Democrat* reporter, who thought the first speeches were too high key. I agreed with George but I thought my efforts were largely a failure.

Loid Sadler was there and recorded my remarks for broadcast on Morrilton radio. We both agreed later that the speech was probably my worst effort of the campaign, but he paid for its broadcast anyway.

Cherry remained secluded in the courthouse during our speeches, making his appearance at the time of his introduction. He spoke well but responded angrily to severe heckling from the audience over his welfare policies.

The story of the veteran reporter, Sam Harris, in the *Gazette* the next day said Cherry got the most applause. For once he was in error. Guy Jones received the most applause with Cherry second best. McMillan and I got very little response. However, I judged the efforts of the challengers on that occasion as worthwhile. We mingled with the audience shaking hands and making acquaintances. Cherry remained secluded before his speech and departed as soon as it was finished, which is generally considered a poor way to campaign. Also his angry responses to his welfare policy critics still further alienated them and perhaps others.

————

GOVERNOR CHERRY DENIES RATE INFLUENCE

Governor Cherry on June 29 said he had nothing to do one way or the other with the AP&L and gas rate increases — that the matter was entirely in the hands of the Public Service Commission on which he had exercised no influence. The people did not see it that way since the Governor had appointed the members of the Commission, and since the people always look to their elected officials, who make the appointments, for redress of wrong or satisfaction of grievances. Besides, as the people knew, an elected official is often quick to claim credit when things go right, even when the decisions are made by an agency whose members are appointed. So, when things go wrong, they must bear the blame.

ARKANSAS INTEGRATION MUST WAIT, ARCH FORD SAYS

Arch Ford, director of the Arkansas Department of Education, said on July 1 that integration must wait. His stance still further confirmed the Governor's stand on the segregation-integration question.

NEWSPAPERS SAY NO HEAT IN CAMPAIGN

July 4, always considered a turning point in the primary campaigns (before the time for the primaries was changed), found the newspapers reporting that no heat had been generated. Even the political speaking at the Portia picnic in Lawrence County where many verbal duels had been fought, was reported on the "mild side". Cherry announced he would have no formal opening but planned an active campaign. The

CALLING FOR THE CATCH
By Kennedy, Ark. Democrat   6/30/54

So far as I know, this was my first depiction in a political cartoon. The rate increase developed into a crucial issue in the Governor's race. I am uncertain about its effect on the McClellan-McMath Senate contest.

writers described the McClellan-McMath battle as disappointing and said the strongest verbal attacks were directed at Governor Cherry by his three opponents.

On July 7 John Truemper, a member of Cherry's administration, joined the Governor's campaign staff.

EAST END CIVIC LEAGUE ENDORSEMENT

The East End Civic League, a Greater Little Rock organization of black voters, on July 7 announced its endorsement of my candidacy. The announcement was made by League President J.L. (Jeffrey) Hawkins, a black political leader of integrity whose word was always good.

EDITORIAL SUPPORT

Batesville News Review, July 8, 1954
By Jared E. "Jerry" Trevathan

Along the way my candidacy picked up some editorial support. One of the first and most important endorsements came from Jerry Trevathan, editor of a small weekly paper in Batesville.

This editorial was reprinted and widely distributed, giving other papers, as my own at Huntsville, time to republish it.

Jerry and I became warm personal friends during my time in office and remained so until his death.

His editorial said in part:

You don't see it happen very often, but every once in a while the people have an opportunity to look into the face of a new aspirant for office and see the fresh honesty, new promises made that have a true ring to them, and a platform that is really worthwhile and down to earth so that the average voter may know what the man is talking about.

Such a man we think is now campaigning for Governor of Arkansas and his name is Orval Faubus of Huntsville, up in Madison County.

Mr. Faubus spoke in Batesville on Saturday, July 3 and received a fine reception. . . .

. . . In addition to being a clear thinker and a good talker, he is a hand-shaker of the old school. He moves through the crowd with ease that is born of friendliness and a genuine like for people. He possesses a modesty that is becoming to his nature and as he goes from one to another shaking hands you have the feeling that you are meeting a man who has your interest at heart. . . .

. . . This man Faubus is not a politician in the sense that we usually regard those who ply the trade, but we are convinced that his experience in life has taught him that it is better to deal fairly with all people in order to operate a government today. He is the type of man who will listen to reason and be guided by the policies that will bring the greatest benefits to the largest number of people.

From his early boyhood he was brought up the hard way and he learned to appreciate how the poor man lives.

TALKATHON AGAIN

Governor Cherry, realizing that he might be in difficulty, reverted on July 15 to the talkathon for his campaign. Guy Jones asked for an invitation to participate. In 1952 Cherry kept an empty chair waiting by his side and continually renewed his invitation to McMath to join him, which McMath did for a short time on one occasion. Jones did not wait for an invitation but asked to be included saying the talkathon and his appearance would be fatal to the Cherry candidacy. Jones did not receive an invitation.

The next day the State Capitol building was picketed by union members and employees of the State Hospital led by Bitsy Simmons. The labor leader, who later became one of my most loyal and devoted supporters, had brought another state problem to the attention of the voters.

ROY RITTER JOINS CAMPAIGN STAFF

On July 18 Roy Ritter of Springdale resigned as President of the Arkansas Poultry Federation to become co-manager of my campaign. He was generally thought to represent the poultry growers of the state who were unhappy with Governor Cherry's veto of the measure to exempt feed from the sales tax. However, they were not sufficiently unhappy to contribute any substantial sums to my political expense. Pat Teague, poultry dealer and legislator of Berryville, made contributions to my campaign fund and was a substantial contributor also to Jones. Those in the poultry business, both producers and processors, were hard hit by low market prices and the drought, which was probably one reason that overall their campaign donations were negligible.

CHERRY FORSAKES HIS PROPERTY TAX

On July 18, Governor Cherry forsook his property tax equalization proposal in a paid advertisement headed "Personal Statement of Governor Cherry." The concluding part of the ad read:

"I will not use the power and influence of the Governor's office to force anyone to vote for this amendment, nor do I intend to campaign for its adoption." — Signed, Francis Cherry, Governor.

CONFEDERATE HOME INMATES

On July 18 in a telecast I hit Governor Cherry on the situation of the old Confederate ladies in the hot barracks at Camp Robinson. News reports stated that he was "mad" — very angry — with my charges.

For years the State had maintained a Home for the survivors of Confederate Veterans. It was located southeast of Little Rock near Highway 65 on a tract of land owned by the state.

It was discovered that the land was rich in bauxite ore used in the manufacture of aluminum and the property was sold to a mining company. The proceeds from the sale were to be used to build a new home for the Confederate survivors, all of whom now were women.

This was well and good, but unfortunately the sale was made and the ore mined before construction of the new home. In the mining operations the original Confederate home was destroyed and it was necessary to move the old ladies beforehand. They were placed in a military barracks at Camp Robinson, where they were still housed during the campaign of 1954 in the hottest summer on record in Arkansas.

A minister who had been ministering to their needs informed me of the situation of the old ladies in conditions which he described as intolerable. He asked me to go with him to verify his story. I found the minister to be a man of his word and with the courage of his convictions. Not only did he accompany me to the barracks on a Sunday afternoon but was willing to issue statements in connection with the suffering of the aged women.

The lady in charge that afternoon was quite hostile to our appearance. However, she could hardly refuse admittance to the minister who had been visiting the facility regularly. Without being bidden I entered the building with him.

The aged ladies reclined on crude beds or cots situated close together along the walls of the long structure. There was no form of separation, curtains or otherwise, between the beds. There was no privacy for any individual regardless of condition. The crazed babbling of those already incoherent, and others becoming so, was borne by all. The wash room and latrine was in one end of the long building as in all military barracks. The flat roofed building was exposed to the full glare of the boiling sun from early morning until sunset. The heat inside was intense.

The minister informed me that four of the old ladies had just recently died, their deaths due principally to the unusual heat. Two lay unconscious in their beds while we were there and another was becoming incoherent. How any of them endured the unbearable heat was difficult to understand. The situation was even worse than I had envisaged from the minister's description. I was amazed and shocked by the intolerable conditions and the fact that nothing was being done to alleviate the situation.

It is quite possible that Gov. Cherry did not personally know of the situation of the aged, helpless Confederate survivors. However, some aide, staff member or personnel in charge of the old ladies should have informed him of the situation. The head man must be responsible for anything that goes wrong under his jurisdiction and the only way to escape the blame is to take corrective action, including, at times, the firing of subordinates whenever wrong-doing or failure is discovered.

In the first place, the aged women should have been kept in the original home until the new one was ready for occupancy instead of placing them in a crude, rough barracks building which was comfortless enough for tough, young soldiers.

Secondly, if for some reason the inmates had to be placed in the barracks then air conditioners should have been obtained to protect them from the inordinate heat of the 1954 summer.

And thirdly, when any of the aged women became ill they should have been transferred immediately to a hospital instead of permitting them to lie on their crude beds in the heat with death as the only relief from their suffering.

Later I found that other facilities were offered for the care of the old ladies. Dr. S.J. Junkin of the Little Rock area in a sworn affidavit made available to me, revealed that he offered more adequate facilities for their care, but his offer was rejected.

THE WEATHER A CAMPAIGN FACTOR

Regardless of the heat I stayed on the road day after day, never using an air-conditioned car — there weren't many in those days — visiting as many towns and seeing as many voters as possible. I worked from early morn to late at night, sometimes past midnight.

One other challenger, Senator Jones, did much the same. Governor Cherry was no softie but he had grown accustomed to the relative coolness of the Governor's office. In his campaigning he stuck mostly to the meeting halls and the air-conditioned studios of the radio and television stations. On only a few occasions did he hit the streets to greet voters and then it was mainly for publicity purposes.

It is possible the weather was a factor in the campaign. I recall distinctly driving into Nashville, Howard County, the date now forgotten, when the thermometers reached 115 degrees. As I looked down the long stretch of the basically one-street town after parking my car, not an individual could be seen anywhere on the streets, sidewalks, storefronts or dooryards of the county seat. I found the people congregated in half-dozens, dozens and greater numbers in the cooler atmosphere of the barber shops, furniture stores and other businesses.

There was virtually no activity as people were neither buying or selling. Therefore I had a good opportunity to shake hands, visit briefly and answer questions about the campaign. Many people that day said, "Yes, I know you. I met you last night — on television." (From Texarkana where I had a 30-minute political telecast.)

Although my feet burned from the heat of the sidewalks and the blistering streets and I could feel the heat waves swirl round my tanned face and arms, I campaigned the town and, without pause, took off for the next on the schedule.

— — —

THE WEATHER IN 1954 —
      90 degrees or above on 115 days
      100 degrees or above on 46 days
        — From *Gazette* editorial, July 19, 1966

AS IF THE HEAT ISN'T ENOUGH
By Kennedy, Ark. Democrat   7/1/54

The water shortage on the farms became serious as ponds, streams and springs became dry in the continuing drought. A news report said "Bayou Meto Runs Dry". The water supply for Little Rock and other cities was threatened. Nashville was forced to obtain water through a gas line from a point near Murfreesboro. The temperature reached 107 in Little Rock and 115 in Conway.

JONES HITS AT CHERRY "EVASION"

Jones on July 22 attacked Governor Cherry for attempting to evade the responsibility for misdeeds and mistakes in his administration. In addition to the plight of the Confederate survivors, the death of a hospital patient from beating had occurred at the State Hospital and the grand jury had returned indictments against hospital employees in the case; a guard had been shot in an attempted prison break at the State Prison; telephone, gas and electric companies had been permitted stiff rate increases; and many people were unhappy with the State Highway Department whose governing body was the Highway Commission to which the Governor had appointed all five members.

BOONE COUNTY HEADLIGHT Editorial written by J.E. Dunlap, Jr., Editor — Harrison, Arkansas. The editorial endorsement said in part:

> *Why I will vote for Orval Faubus Thursday, July 22, 1954 —*
>
> *... next Tuesday, July 27, I will go to the polls and vote for Orval E. Faubus for Governor of Arkansas. ...*
>
> *Not often does a man of Mr. Faubus' character and integrity offer himself for such a high public office. With a wide experience in many fields of endeavor plus his early childhood training and background, Mr. Faubus is not only able and capable of serving Arkansas as Governor, but would be a credit to our great state.*
>
> *Mr. Faubus is a common man in the very sense of the word. He possesses a sense of modesty which is a trait not found in so many who offer their services as a public official. ...*
>
> *His entire background is one of hard work, devotion to duty in whatever field of endeavor he might be engaged, and honesty of purpose. I have never known him to betray a trust.*
>
> *... Orval Faubus has the character, the integrity and the ability to lead. I am sure the people of Arkansas want that kind of a man as Governor. That is why I will vote for Orval E. Faubus.*

Dunlap had previously given me my first opportunity for a public speech after my return home from World War II. He invited me to address the Harrison Post of the American Legion of which he was then Commander. I was then Huntsville postmaster and, like Dunlap, owner and publisher of a struggling weekly newspaper and had been separated from the Armed Forces only about a year.

After I became chief executive I gave J.E., as he is known to his friends, an opportunity for service in government on the state level by appointing him a member of the State Police Commission.

No succeeding governor has dispensed with his services since that first appointment.

HOT RACES DEVELOP

By this time we in the field knew some hotly contested races had developed. In Little Rock this was not realized by many people, even among the reporters and cartoonists.

The McMath-McClellan race was reaching fever pitch. Occasionally I saw McMath as he criss-crossed the state, working hard and making progress. Once I crossed paths with McClellan, his helicopter set down on the streets of DeQueen while he made a speech to a large audience. As soon as he finished I mounted a flatbed truck across the square from his location and began my pitch. Shortly after I began, McClellan, always mindful of courtesy, sent one of his aides to inform me he must take off in order to maintain his schedule. I halted my remarks, the helicopter roared into life, scattering the many youngsters who were clustered close by and sending a cloud of leaves and dust blowing across the area. It seemed to me the takeoff in the narrow area between trees and buildings was both precarious and dangerous.

McClellan had a battle, of which he was well aware, and he fought hard in the intense heat. Chambers I saw more often as he wearily pushed on in his hand shaking campaign, his clothes becoming more loose fitting each day as the heat and the exertion took their toll.

In the governor's race the activity of the challengers was having its effect. My campaign was finally off the ground and I was increasing my momentum each day. My speeches gained adherents each time I spoke, as increasing numbers recognized in me —as they expressed it — "governor material". I didn't see as much of McMillan as early in the campaign, but continued to hear of his activity. Guy Jones was attracting increasing notice as he carried his attack daily across the state.

All the challengers were at the long established Fourth of July picnic at Portia, and the other large gatherings at Piggott, Pollard and Corning in the Northeast where we spoke to thousands. All of us were at Paragould, the date unremembered, for a large celebration of which a huge carnival was a part. I spoke that night in the carnival area after the others had been heard during the day and had departed.

As I spoke from a prepared platform the power failed. The lights went out leaving the entire area in total darkness. The sounds of the ferris wheel, merry-go-round and other rides ceased; the voices of the concessionaires hawking their wares, and of the merry makers, died away. Silence and darkness gripped the vast throng.

My sound trucks were equipped for both electric and battery power and my crews by then were experienced. Within a minute the switch had been made and I continued my speech. In the darkness and silence my delivery was most effective. Everyone, including the out-of-state carnival personnel, listened. It was probably the most favorable conditions for a speech that I encountered during the road campaign. If some one disrupted the power to inconvenience me it had just the opposite effect. Power was not restored until my speech was concluded. Following that day I saw what I thought was the prize-winning cutline of the campaign.

The Paragould Big Picture, a tabloid newspaper of the city, ran prominent pictures and stories of all the candidates who appeared in the city that day. Under a conspicuous picture of Guy Jones in oratorical stance were these words — "The Little Lion That Roared Mightily in the Streets."

It was about that time that I became aware of the person and unusual personality of Stewart K. "Stew" Prosser, the chief aide of candidate Jones. "Stew" and I were to be close in political terms in the years to come.

Three other races had become hard fought contests.

First, Sam Jones with a political name almost the equal of Jeff Davis, was challenging incumbent State Treasurer Vance Clayton. Sam and his inseparable campaign companion, "Jelly" Street, daily pounded the streets and sidewalks, going in and out of business houses seeking votes. Sam diligently shook hands, passed out cards, and used my microphones to make his public announcements to the growing crowds at my speaking engagements. Often we found lodging at night in the same facilities and occasionally I visited Sam and "Jelly" in their room. We conversed and exchanged information while they bathed their blistered and aching feet. "Jelly" was already so thin he could hardly cast a shadow and Sam, who began the campaign with a very well-fed look, daily grew more streamlined as the lines deepened in his face.

Since the Claytons were solidly aligned with the Cherry forces neither Sam nor "Jelly" was hesitant about being for me for governor. As is always the case, as observers they gained much information about my race that I could not learn, and imparted it to me. Still, I voiced no opinion about the treasurer's race because, as they well knew, I had all I could say grace over in challenging an incumbent governor running for a second term. My aides, out of appreciation, passed on information to them that would be helpful in their effort.

Doyle Yopp, challenging the politically strong and respected Claude Rankin for the office of Land Commissioner, was making that race look like a contest. He grew so hot on the trail of the veteran Rankin that he came out to the hustings in a surprise appearance to use my microphones to answer Yopp's campaign charges. Such heated exchanges face to face by opposing candidates added zest to the campaign as a whole.

In the third race, other than for the Senate and Governor, the young State Senator from Crossett, Jim Johnson, was making a determined effort to thwart Tom Gentry's quest for a second term as Attorney General. While Gentry followed his own itinerary he sent two most diligent young lieutenants along my pathway to work the crowds in his behalf. They were Claude Carpenter and Kay Matthews. Seldom were my microphones set up that one of these determined young campaigners did not use them to make an appeal for Mr. Gentry's candidacy. Strangely enough, I don't recall seeing Jim Johnson during the campaign. I learned later that he and many of his chief supporters were aligned with Cherry which accounted for the non-appearance of Johnson or any of his representatives at any of my rallies.

And so it was that in the campaign year of 1954 many people in the hinterlands realized that some hot political races were underway before that fact ever dawned on the backroom and hotel lobby experts of Little Rock. Perhaps it can be explained by the fact that all the incumbents, including Governor Cherry, were so strong in Little Rock that their supporters were lulled into a false sense of security from which they did not awaken until late in the game.

One reporter who reached the conclusion early that a strong race for governor was developing was Mr. Alfred C. Andersson, reporter for the *Press Scimitar* of Memphis. Beginning rather early he covered most of my appearances in Eastern and Northeastern Arkansas. We visited occasionally while I was on the road, and after the campaign discussed how he realized the possibility of an upset in the governor's race before other reporters recognized it.

Two other newsmen recognized that a contest for Governor was on by the end of the first primary. They were George Douthit of the *Arkansas Democrat* and Sam Harris, then the political writer for the *Arkansas Gazette*.

X-FACTOR IN THE CAMPAIGN
By Kennedy, Ark. Democrat   7/23/54

CHERRY RAPS OPPONENTS IN ADDRESS

The Governor attacked his opponents at a $10 breakfast attended by a reported 1,700, including many state employees, at Robinson Auditorium in Little Rock on July 19. Former Mayor Dan T. Sprick was chairman of the breakfast committee and State Senator Ellis Fagan was master of ceremonies. (Sprick later served in the State Senate and became one of my strongest supporters.)

On July 21 news reports said McMath attracted 5,000 at a rally at Malvern, and that politics had turned to McCarthy on the national level and to Governor Cherry's talkathon on the state level.

TELEVISION IN THE '54 CAMPAIGN

Prior to 1954, television had never been used extensively by any candidate in an Arkansas political race. The principal means of advertising had been the radio and newspaper media and printed material. Reliance was still mainly on the stumping ability of a candidate at live political rallies. Cherry's radio talkathon in 1952 was an exception.

Some political writers and observers credited me with being the first candidate for a political office to make extensive use of television in a campaign. I did use the medium as much as finances permitted.

Use was made of one station at a time rather than a network hookup as is now customary. Payment for time was usually made by local supporters for the stations at Pine Bluff, Texarkana, Ft. Smith and Memphis, with the headquarters paying for time on the two Little Rock stations. These were the only stations with extensive coverage in Arkansas at the time. To reach all sections of the state it was necessary to use the radio network.

I went from station to station for most of my TV broadcasts. At that time no station in Arkansas was equipped to produce a telescreen or tape containing both a visual and audio recording. It was necessary to go to Memphis for such a production — which I did on two or three occasions — which could then be broadcast by any television station.

A prominent figure at that time had no way of knowing how he would look — or how he would project on the TV screen, until he obtained sufficient exposure. Fortunately for me the medium was favorable, a circumstance of which I was unaware when I began the race.

Fortunately, I was never flustered in the least by the unfamiliar surroundings of the TV studio. I pushed from my mind the studio atmosphere with all the gadgets, machinery and personnel, and envisaged myself seated in a room talking to interested people. Consequently, according to studio personnel and others, my television appearances were excellent.

HEADLINES AND A CHERRY AD

On July 25, with the election two days hence, these headlines and ads appeared.

Two Major Races Expected to Bring Out 300,-000 Votes

Candidates for Governor Speed Pace in Last Minute Appeals to Voters

Governor Cherry Does Not See Runoff; Candidates for Senate Confident

Senate Aspirants Fire Away as They Close in for the Finish

Little Rock attorney Bill Bowen, Secretary of State Democratic Central Committee, was shown in a newsphoto making preparations for the election.

A newspaper ad for Cherry read:

> *"A Personal Message from Governor Cherry"*
> *"Utility Rate Increases Have NOT Been Approved. Every effort will be made to Disprove the Need for the Increases."*
> Signed, *"Francis Cherry, Governor"*

At first the administration disavowed any authority to disapprove the telephone, gas and electric rate increases. Now that the matter was a hot campaign issue, the administration was attempting to gain credit for an effort to disprove the need for the increases and roll them back.

However, the increases had gone into effect and the harm was done.

SOUTHWEST-TIMES RECORD, JULY 25, 1954

Political ad paid for by Citizens for Cherry, Faulkner and Madison Counties, Francis Donovan, Chairman.

This two-part paid political ad had a great deal of erroneous information. The first scene depicts a situation in January, 1953 at the time Governor Cherry took office.

At the request of the new administration of Francis Cherry, I remained in Little Rock as Highway Director until January 17, 1953. We were waiting for the new highway commissioners appointed by Governor Cherry, to become qualified and select my successor. I had tendered my resignation some time before, giving it personally to Leffel Gentry. Also, I had already been installed as postmaster at Huntsville on January 1, 1953, and was waiting to assume those duties as soon as released from the position of highway director.

After the convening of the General Assembly in 1953 and while I was still in Little Rock, Senator John Cloer of Springdale, without my knowledge, circulated a petition among the state senators recommending me for some position with the new administration. The petition was signed by 17 members of the Senate.

So far as I know, Senator Guy (Mutt) Jones had nothing to do with the matter except perhaps to sign the petition. Perhaps as a result of Senator Cloer's petition, I was interviewed by the new highway commission about road matters including the position of director. I did not make application for the position.

Because he and I were both candidates against Cherry in 1954, Senator Jones was the only character identified in the ad. Others identifiable are Jim Crain of Wilson, Truman Baker of Searcy, both former highway commissioners, and Henry Woods, former executive secretary to Governor Sid McMath.

The *Cartoon* said they tried to get me installed as highway director (see application in my hand) in the new Cherry administration in 1953, a completely false insinuation.

In the second part of the political cartoon, the scene eighteen months later in 1954, the assault was being made on the Governor's office in the Capitol building. Backing me and Mutt were the same characters with the same three identifiable, Baker with the cigar, glasses and white hat with speckled band; Crain with cigarette and bareheaded; and Woods with dark hair and in a dark suit in the background. Not shown but underneath the cartoons was the opposition's version of my secret diary from 1949 to 1954.

There was a play on the name Orval Faubus—"Awful Faubus".

CHERRY RUNS SECOND UTILITY AD

On the day before the election, indicating how important the issue had become, the Cherry Organization ran still another ad on the utility rate increases which read:

> *NO utility rate increase has been approved. Every legal means at my command, or at the command of the Public Service Commission will be used to prevent any rate increase.*
> Signed, Francis Cherry

AND THEN THE PEOPLE VOTED
ON JULY 27

On July 28, these headlines appeared.

Cherry and Faubus Runoff Certain in Governor's Race

McClellan Apparently Wins

Jones, McMillan Concede; Latter to Back Faubus

Faubus Camp Shows Joy as Counting Indicates Runoff

Faubus, Cherry Square Off for Runoff; McClellan Wins; Governor's Race Looms as Hot One

Faubus Showed What Many Observers Termed "Surprising Strength"

THE RETURNS

Governor — Cherry, 154,879; Faubus, 109,614; Jones, 41,249; McMillan, 18,857

U.S. Senate — McClellan, 164,905; McMath, 127,941; Chambers, 29,733; Ellis, 3,335

Attorney General — Gentry, 175,123; Johnson, 124,327; McNemer, 14,399

State Land Commissioner — Rankin, 194,114; Yopp, 81,276; Younts, 29,615

SENATOR McCLELLAN'S ROLE IN THE RUNOFF

On either the first or second day after the preferential primary, I called Senator McClellan. "Senator," I said, "you have won your race. I know that you are now being beseeched to aid Governor Cherry in the runoff in the race for Governor. I also know that if you choose to actively take part in the race, that your influence would almost certainly be decisive. I'm not going to ask that you help me. I want to ask you to remain neutral and let us (Cherry and me) fight it out to a conclusion."

The Senator shot back, "Well, I sure didn't like the way your county came in!" (Madison County went for McMath 1,577 to 422.)

"Senator McClellan," I replied, "I told you beforehand the county would go that way. It was a McMath county and no one could do anything about it. I do want to point out that you got more votes against McMath there than any other opponent in the last three elections. You know I couldn't get involved in the Senate race anymore than you could get involved in the Governor's race in the preferential primary."

The Senator then admitted that he had been informed of the situation in Madison County regarding his race. "Well, I'll let you know," he said.

A number of my leaders had supported McClellan in the senate race. Knowing of the Cherry organization's efforts to persuade McClellan to assist the governor in the runoff many of my leaders contacted the Senator to urge him not to do so and to remain neutral. Without doubt the bulk of my supporters had voted for McMath. We were allied in the public mind because of past association. Likewise, Cherry and McClellan were similarly identified because of the latter's assistance to Cherry in the runoff in the Governor's race two years before. However, the situation did not apply to the political leadership in the state, or to some particular areas.

Perhaps, also, McClellan was aware of the behind-the-scenes maneuvering before the 1954 campaign got under way, when McMath leaders were working with Cherry aides to keep me from entering the governor's race. If these efforts had succeeded and the alliance of Cherry and McMath forces had continued through the campaign, it certainly would have been detrimental to McClellan's interests.

The Senator called me the next day and said, "I'm going back to Washington and look after my own business. I won't actively assist anyone in the campaign".

I thanked the Senator and that was the end of our contacts until the time for the Democratic State Convention in September.

During my tenure as governor I never knew of Senator McClellan doing anything detrimental to my interests. In our official capacities we worked together many times on many projects for the state. Politically he assisted me when, as the Democratic nominee, I had strong Republican opposition in 1954 and 1964. There were two or three occasions when he could have assisted me in Democratic primary politics but didn't, but that is any politician's prerogative.

Some of my friends, especially in organized labor, wondered about my continued loyalty and friendship for Senator McClellan. This hitherto undisclosed realtionship should help them to understand, for I have never yet shown the cold hand of ingratitude when gratitude was due.

J. L. "JIM" BLAND, SR.
ENTERS THE CAMPAIGN

Jim Bland, newspaper publisher and editor of Walnut Ridge, joined the headquarters staff soon after the first primary. I had tried to get him to manage my campaign in the beginning but he declined to do so.

Bland had been a casual acquaintance for some three years. I recall that during the time I was working for McMath he attended a meeting near Jonesboro to promote the continued improvement of Highway 63, and afterward wrote a very complimentary comment about my ability and efforts in seeking road improvements. Later when I was back at Huntsville after the change of administrations in 1953, our contact was renewed as I continued my efforts to secure an improved east-west highway across North Arkansas.

At first it was supposed that Bland was persuaded to enter the campaign by some of my publisher-printer friends. Frank Robbins of Conway and Bob Roach of Little Rock were supporting me openly and others quietly. My biggest booster in that field was Ira Roberts, a salesman for the Roach Paper Company.

However, Bland had written a personal letter to me as far back as July 9, explaining the situation and how he was laying the ground-work to enter the campaign if I made the runoff, and put Lawrence County in my column.

There were some objections to Mr. Bland's entry into the campaign management, the strongest from my original campaign manager, Bob Faust. I persuaded the objectors that Bland was needed and that his coming would in no way infringe on the prerogatives and authority of those already on the staff. Bland was named co-ordinator for the campaign work while Faust and Roy Ritter continued as co-managers.

In Mr. Bland I acquired a man of experience in things political and with much knowledge of campaign affairs. He had helped in the management of other campaigns for governor and had worked in the successful runoff race for the U.S. Senate of J.W. Fulbright against Governor Homer Adkins. He had served on the staff of Governor Carl Bailey, part of the time as executive secretary.

Aside from his experience and knowledge, Bland had that rare ability as an executive that is so hard to find. He had the knack of identifying and dismissing the trivial. He could recognize the importance of marginal problems, make a decision or assign them to the proper person, and then get on to the basic, bedrock questions of genuine importance. If it were not expedient or proper for him to make a decision alone on the important issues, he had the knack of gaining a consensus for a decision in a conference with others. Some matters had to be decided by the candidate himself and these Bland could determine with ease.

By some, Bland was considered impatient, and he sometimes was. Often it was due to his ability to see the minor importance of some matter which to the other person seemed major. He also had the ability to sit down with a critic or potential adversary and arrive at a working relationship. An example was the day Rolla Fitch became so unhappy that he packed his suitcase to go home. I, of course, was out on the road. Mr. Bland went to his room and inquired, "Rolla, what's wrong?" "I don't know what's going on," Fitch replied. "Have you been in one of these campaigns before?" asked Bland. Rolla admitted that he had not. "Well, I don't know what's going on either," stated Bland. "I've been in these campaigns before and that's always the case. No one ever knows fully everything that is occurring. That's the way things are in a campaign headquarters. It's up to each one to do the best he can for the campaign and the candidate. That's the only reason any of us are here. No person here can know everything or direct everything."

Then he concluded, "You've done a lot for Faubus and he has a lot of confidence in you. You've been a big help and you can do more. Rolla, I don't want you to go home and I know Faubus doesn't either."

Fitch unpacked his suitcase and stayed. More than 12 years later he and Bland were both still with me.

There were many good men in the headquarters, but there often existed too much confusion and too much work at cross purposes. Bland materially reduced that confusion — and brought more cohesion and purpose to the campaign effort. His rare executive ability was an ingredient that was needed for the campaign staff in the hectic days which followed.

CHERRY BIDS FOR VOTE OF WOMEN; MRS. FRANK DODGE NAMED TO HEAD WOMEN'S DIVISION (JULY 30)

Mrs. Frank Dodge of Little Rock, a hard worker, organized caravans of Cherry supporters to visit towns around Little Rock, going as far as Searcy, Batesville and Heber Springs. Those joining the caravan, evidently well-to-do people mostly from the capital, traveled in Cadillacs and other expensive cars. My supporters derisively dubbed the caravan "The Cadillac Brigade".

My headquarters ran a political ad on this date which said:

Which One Should You Vote For?
Their Neighbors Know Them Best!

Madison County: McMillan — 5, 0%; Jones — 27, 1%; Cherry — 25, 1%; Faubus — 2,104, 98%

Craighead County: Cherry — 51%; Faubus and Others 49%

RURAL SUPPORT

My candidacy was in great favor in some of the rural areas of the state. For example, in the first primary I got 918 votes in Newton to Cherry's 74; Montgomery, 872 to 431; Scott, 881 to 307; Izard, 637 to 345; Johnson, 1933 to 738; and Franklin, 2598 to 498.

I carried rural Nevada County in the flat lands of Southwest Arkansas 1,280 to Cherry's 1,052, while Jones and McMillan were garnering 219 and 153 respectively. That was due to the support of Olen Hendrix, and two of the best and truest friends I had in my political career, C.O. (Clyde) Wahlquist, editor of the weekly Nevada County Picayune of Prescott, and Ed Cottingham, who lived some distance out in the country. I kept hearing of Cottingham as I sought additional leadership in that area. I finally met him, a grand old countryman so honest that he was often blunt in his approach. I found him to be very effective with the rank and file voters.

I had a good rapport with Wahlquist. We were both struggling country publishers and editors, and his father, William H.V. Wahlquist, a former representative and senator from Fulton County, had worked for me in my newspaper office at Huntsville until he was well past 80 years of age.

ANOTHER SUITOR
By Kennedy, Ark. Democrat   6/30/54

32

I OPENED MY RUNOFF CAMPAIGN; COMMONWEALTH COLLEGE BECOMES AN ISSUE

These headlines appeared as I opened my runoff campaign effort:

Cherry, Faubus, Plunge into Runoff Campaign
Roads at Stake, Governor Says;
Rival Criticizes "Holier" Attitude;
Tackett, Others Join With Cherry

I plunged into the runoff effort on Saturday, the fourth day after the first primary.

Cherry named an advisory committee which contained the names of two from Northwest Arkansas, Herbert L. Thomas of Fayetteville and Joe Robinson of Springdale. Robinson had been appointed by the Governor to the Game and Fish Commission and owed Cherry his loyalty. (Both men later became friends of my administration and Robinson an active and loyal supporter.)

FAUBUS HITS AT ALLEGED WHISPERING CAMPAIGN; CITIES AFFILIATION TO PROVE LOYALTY

I opened my runoff campaign with four speeches on July 31 beginning at Tuckerman followed by Newport, Bald Knob and Searcy. Speaking from a flat bed truck in the morning heat to a large audience, I noticed Cherry workers busily distributing literature among my listeners.

The "literature" was a newspaper published and edited by John F. Wells of Little Rock in which he raised the Commonwealth College issue. Wells so strongly inferred by questions and the reproduction of alleged documents that I was subversive that the inferences and allegations raised a direct challenge to my loyalty as an American citizen. If the issue was to be met, I thought it should be done as early as possible in the brief runoff period. Nothing had yet been said publicly on the matter by any speaker. It was being handled by the Cherry forces by word-of-mouth and the widespread circulation of the Wells newspaper and photostats of alleged documents showing my presence at the college some 20 years before.

So, wisely or not, I opened the door in the Tuckerman speech for open discussion of the issue by mentioning the allegations of the whispering campaign and citing some of my affiliations as proof of my loyalty to my country. Those affiliations and service included four years as a county official; service as a private to major in the Armed Forces of World War II including ten months of combat with the Infantry; postmaster at Huntsville; membership in civic clubs, Lone Scouts of America, the Baptist Church, the Masonic Order and the American Legion.

When I got to Newport I went into a cafe for a cool drink before speaking. There the members of the press were waiting and sat at the table to question me. One of them speaking for all who were gathered said: "We've known about this for some time (the Commonwealth College matter), but we had agreed among ourselves that we would not mention it in our reports until it was raised publicly as an issue. Now that you have mentioned it as an issue in your Tuckerman speech we must mention it and must ask you about it. What do you have to say?"

I took a piece of paper and wrote on it, "I was never a student or faculty member at Commonwealth College."

When they had read the brief statement one of them asked in amazement: "Is that all?"

"Orval", said George Douthit, "if you deny it, they'll beat you to death with it!"

"I know," I replied, addressing the others as well. "I do not intend to deny my contact with Commonwealth College nor my presence there. That is well known to many of my friends and associates for many years. This," indicating the brief written statement, "is simply all I want to say on the matter at the present time."

The reporters must have wondered at my attitude as they took the statement without further discussion. I finished my drink and went to the speaking site. There was little time for me to wonder at the outcome in the hectic activity of the day.

It must be borne in mind that the Commonwealth College matter was not yet a boiling issue as it quickly became. This was the day it began to break into the open and Cherry's public use of the issue was to come the following week on Monday evening, August 2. The general public, as were my campaign workers including many of my campaign staff, were unaware of my mistaken contact with the college. Yet there was a tremendous crowd at Newport assembled in the mid-day sun by the railroad tracks in the Missouri-Pacific Railroad Park on Front Street on the west side of town.

An almost unknown mountaineer challenging an incumbent governor for a second term, had forced him into a runoff. My campaign was rapidly assuming the acceleration of a bandwagon drive. My supporters were enthusiastic while Governor Cherry's adherents were concerned, even frightened.

It is my judgment, an opinion arrived at following the campaign, and in the perspective of time since those hectic events, that my speaking ability was never greater nor more effective than on that occasion and the eventful days which were to follow.

Fred Pickens, a prominent lawyer of Newport and my leader in that area from the time of my announcement, gave me an enthusiastic introduction. It was a speech at a critical point, and I feel Pickens' support was important and crucial at the time.

In the audience that day was Curtis Swaim, then superintendent of schools at nearby Grubbs, formerly a teacher and superintendent at St. Paul and a former legislator of Madison County. Curtis and I had known each other since our early manhood. He was born and reared near St. Paul and began his teaching career at the one-room Riverside school near there. Then his school activities led him to St. Paul where he was eminently successful for many years before moving to Grubbs. I was born and reared near Combs and began my education at the one-room Greenwood school before transferring to Combs. The two towns, St Paul and Combs, only five miles apart, were then connected by the Fayetteville to Pettigrew branch line of the Frisco railroad. Later an improved Highway 16 connected the two towns.

Curtis and I became warm friends and associates when I was attending high school at St. Paul, walking the five miles through the mountains, and he was a teacher in the adjoining grade school. Regarded as bookish by many of our friends we spent hours together in long discussions of many subjects, one of which was politics. In those days he was a Republican, conservative in his views; I a Democrat, much more liberal.

Occasionally, we were teammates in basketball, but more often competitors on the rough dirt courts of that day. Occasionally we were colleagues in literary debates; at other times on opposing sides of issues. Sometimes I stayed overnight with Curtis — thus I slept in his bed and broke bread at his table, consuming much fine food prepared by his wife, Lennie, also a native of the region. Once I spent a night with them at Grubbs as I drove alone early in the campaign of 1954.

Curtis had long known of my association with Commonwealth College. We had discussed it in the spring of 1935 shortly after my return home from the institution. I remember telling him that I had learned there were "no dumb Communists" even if they were wrong about many things.

I pointed Curtis out in the audience that day at Newport and told my hearers to ask him about me - that he had known me since before I was of voting age. To a great extent I placed my political fate in his hands on that occasion. Although we had been political competitors in Madison County, he as a Republican, I as a Democrat, both of us losing as well as winning county offices, neither of us had any doubts of the other as a loyal, patriotic American.

Curtis Swaim was true to the trust. I cannot say enough for him as an industrious, hard-working citizen, churchman and public servant as well as his role as a loyal, honorable friend.

THE LETTER FROM COMMONWEALTH COLLEGE

Perhaps it is well to mention here two other circumstances, both unknown to the state at large, in connection with Commonwealth College.

In 1936, the year after my errant journey to the institution near Mena, I became a candidate for the Democratic nomination for Representative of Madison County. The Democratic township committeeman of my home township of Mill Creek, Grover Brashears, curious about my connection with the college, wrote a letter of inquiry to the institution. His reply from the college secretary stated that I "had come to the college, and left without taking any courses or paying any tuition." The information satisfied Mr. Brashears who, incidentally, had also announced his interest in seeking the same office, and he and his friends supported my candidacy.

I had a copy of the letter in my possession during the county campaigns but never found it necessary to use it. Evidently Mr. Brashears laid the issue to rest by use of the original with anyone who manifested an interest in the matter in 1936.

I lost that race by the narrow margin of four votes but two years later won the nomination and the race in the general election for the office of Circuit Clerk. After re-nomination and re-election to the same office I went to war on May 17, 1942.

The years continued to roll by. After my return home from the war I went through old papers collected over the years. I came across the letter in the jumbled collection. I recall reading it while I sat quietly reflecting over past events. Then I threw it into the pile of discarded papers. I thought the matter had long since been laid to rest but I never contemplated then that I would be a candidate for a state-wide office at a time when Senator Joe McCarthy had raised the issue of subversion to fever pitch.

At the time of the 1954 campaign Mr. Brashears was dead. I asked his relatives including Kelly Cornett, later State Comptroller in my administration, to make a search of any papers left by Mr. Brashears to see if the original letter might be found.

The search was to no avail. I mentioned the letter only once in the turbulent days of the runoff campaign. I considered it to be so self-serving to my interests as to be ineffective since there was no corroborating evidence remaining.

MEETING WITH HAROLD SHERMAN

During the McMath administration I had become acquainted with the noted writer and lecturer, Harold Sherman of Mountain View. We had become warm friends when, as a member of the Highway Commission, I had helped the people of Stone County to obtain an improved road into the county seat. Stone and Madison were two counties of six in the state which at that time had no improved highways leading to the outside world. Sherman was one of the Stone County leaders seeking to secure the improved highway for his county. Although the county was in the district served by Commissioner Truman Baker, I fought with them every step of the way in their efforts to obtain the improvement. The road was built from Mountain View east to the vicinity of Batesville before McMath left office.

In gratitude for the building of the road Mr. Sherman had acted as an adviser for the campaign staff of McMath during his ill-starred bid for a third term. I worked with him part of the time and learned that he had certain ability in evaluation of public sentiment and the public's reaction to certain types of events.

Much earlier before getting into the campaign I anticipated that the Commonwealth matter might become an issue if I became a candidate. Some time in the winter of 1953-54 I set up an appointment with Mr. Sherman and Truman Baker at Mountain View to discuss the matter.

I left Huntsville after work hours to make the drive of some 150 miles accompanied by my son, Farrell, then only 14 years of age. Except for ten miles the stretch of Highway 68 from Huntsville to Alpena was unimproved and very rough and the some 40 miles of Highway 66 from Leslie to Mountain View was unimproved and so rough it would shake a cat off a bale of cotton.

We arrived well after dark and found Sherman and Baker waiting at the appointed place. I told Mr. Sherman the full story — Mr. Baker already knew — and we discussed the matter until about midnight.

Mr. Sherman evaluated the various possibilities but there was no way to know in advance how or when the issue might be raised. The one thing I remembered from the discussion was Mr. Sherman's firm opinion that the issue need not necessarily prove fatal to my candidacy if it were raised. There again the outcome might depend entirely on how the matter was handled.

During all that time, Farrell, still too young to participate in such discussions, sat quietly listening.

The discussion over we started on the return journey and ran into one of the most torrential rainstorms I have ever encountered. Our progress was at a snail's pace as the storm continued without abatement. Twice it grew so intense we had to stop and wait for the rain and wind to slacken.

Finally, with the night waning, we reached the home stretch of Highway 68 and were out of the storm. I grew so sleepy that I turned the wheel over to Farrell. Soon I noted that he had grown drowsy and was about to lose control. I reclaimed the wheel and proceeded cautiously but in spite of my most determined efforts I could not remain awake. Finally, with the car leaving the road, I awakened with a jerk too late. I reached an arm in front of Farrell for protection while jamming on the brakes as we plowed through brambles and bushes to a halt with the car lodged against a fence. Because I was driving slowly and the car had left the road in the safest place possible neither of us was injured.

We got out and walked some two or three miles to the home of Preston Piper, a substitute mail carrier for the Huntsville office. I awakened him just at dawn and he drove us home. Farrell either went to bed or to school and I went to work at the office. Later in the day I got someone to help me retrieve the car.

WHO IS THIS MAN FAUBUS?

On July 31st appeared the first of a series of ads evidently drawn up by John F. Wells. The lead for each ad was the question, "Who Is This Man Faubus?"
August 1 headlines read:

*Faubus Charges "Whispers" Accuse Him of
Red Leaning;
Cherry Denies Starting Them.* (Faubus) *Denies
Being Student at School;
Governor* (Cherry) *Will Look Into Charges.*

CHAPTER 3
COMMONWEALTH COLLEGE AND
THE 1954 RUNOFF CAMPAIGN

August 1, Sunday—
Faubus Asserts Whispering Campaign Aimed at Him. Enters Denial; Cherry Says: Didn't Do It, Will Take Up Issue

———

Story by Sam G. Harris
"The Whispering Campaign of smears" to label him "subversive" are futile, the Huntsville publisher said, "because I am just as American as the cornbread and black-eyed peas on which I was reared. I am just as free of subversion as the spring that flows from a mountain to form the White River."

Faubus spoke to a crowd of 4,000 at Searcy, which repeatedly interrupted him with applause in his radio talk.

The aggressive challenger, serious and seemingly tireless during a long day of campaigning, also warned the Highway Department to get back out of politics.

Faubus, who often refers to himself as a working man, appeared to be well received by crowds in which khaki and denim clothing predominated. Sympathetic grins appeared on several tanned, weathered faces when Faubus recalled times "when a pair of shoes had to last all winter."

Elderly persons listened intently when Faubus tore into the "relative responsibility law" and other operating features of the Welfare Department. Many of the old-timers stepped forward to shake hands after the address.

Cherry Political ad:
Who Is This Man Faubus????? (Second in a series)
The ad discussed the Forum road, a stretch of Highway 23 north of Huntsville built during the McMath administration, inferring it was political, not needed and a waste of highway funds.

Faubus political ad:
Shame! It's your Shame! Candidate Cherry
It discussed the allegations of subversion directed toward me by the Cherry forces. The ad was prepared by J. Orville Cheney.

August 2 — *Gazette* Headlines

SENATOR JONES PUTS SUPPORT BEHIND FAUBUS
———
CANDIDATE (FAUBUS) ADDRESSED CIO, AFL MEETINGS, DERIDES PSC HEARINGS
———
GOVERNOR VOWS HE WON'T PRESS REASSESSMENT; SLATES TALK TONIGHT
———
RATE COMPLAINTS MAY SPEED AP&L HEARING
———

August 2, Monday — *Democrat* Headlines

FAUBUS HEADED GROUP AT COMMONWEALTH COLLEGE, BUT NEVER ENROLLED
———
CHERRY HINTS AT PROOF ON "COLLEGE"
———
GUY JONES JOINS FORCES WITH FAUBUS
———
PSC OPENS AP&L RATE HIKE PROBE
———

August 2, Monday — Political ads

WHO IS THIS MAN FAUBUS? I was pictured with Jim Crain. The theme of the ad was "The Same Old Gang" (Third in a series)

———

August 3, Tuesday — *Gazette* Headlines

CHERRY FLAYS HIS OPPONENT WITH COMMONWEALTH ISSUE
———
ONLY THERE A FEW DAYS, FAUBUS SAYS
———
GOVERNOR CHERRY SAYS PAPER SHOWS FOE A LEADER

CALLING OUT THE VOLUNTEERS
By Kennedy, Ark. Democrat   8/1/54

To the surprise of many Governor Cherry was in a runoff. The Cherry forces, now thoroughly alarmed, began feverishly to organize and work to win the runoff election. The Cherry volunteers rushed to the aid of the "Cherry Fire Department" as it sought to put out the fire "Faubus Runoff Drive."

One paragraph in the main *Gazette* story read: "Gov. Cherry bludgeoned his runoff opponent, Orval Faubus of Huntsville, for three-quarters of an hour last night with Faubus' identification 19 years ago with the now-defunct Commonwealth College."

———

Political ad for Faubus

THIS IS THE MAN FAUBUS
It gave facts of my life, war record and decorations, and was paid for by Joe Hearn, a prominent Legionnaire and former state commander of the American Legion.

———

August 3, Tuesday — *Democrat* Headlines

Truth is the Real Issue, Says Cherry;
Opponent's Gamble Lost, Cherry Holds

———

McLEAN FOR CHERRY
Arthur E. McLean, the banker who was critical of the Arkansas Power and Light Company and its rate increase, ran an ad in support of Gov. Cherry as a personal message saying the choice was good government or corruption.

Political Ads
There also ran the fourth of the series "WHO IS THIS MAN FAUBUS?" "IS HE REALLY A DEMOCRAT? WHY? WHY?" The ad linked me to Commonwealth College, Truman Baker, Charlie Adams and Jim Crain.

Another Cherry political ad said—

To-Night: See and Hear Boyd Tacket! The Man who Prosecuted and Closed Commonwealth College.

———

Faubus political ad —
These Are The Issues
100% Assessment, Welfare, Utility Rates

———

JONES JOINS FORCES
Perhaps it was Sunday night, August 1st, I met with Guy Jones, who had run third in the preferential primary. Others present, who had arranged the conference, were Truman Baker and Paul Van Dalsem. Jones agreed to endorse my candidacy and actively campaign for me. Stewart K. Prosser, a Jones assistant, had already joined me as an aide on the road. On Aug. 2nd Jones gave his open endorsement in a press conference.

PSC INVESTIGATES ELECTRIC RATE HIKE
The Cherry campaign was hurting severely from the electric rate increase. In an effort to mitigate the harm the Public Service Commission opened an investigation of the rate hike. Since there was no way to complete such a probe before the next primary most people thought the PSC effort was merely window dressing to assist Gov. Cherry.

COMMONWEALTH COLLEGE CHARGES
On Monday evening, August 2nd, Gov. Cherry, in a television speech over a Little Rock station, laid the Commonwealth College charges against me before the people of the area. Cherry was a lawyer and an effective speaker. His speech was like presenting one side of a lawsuit in a courtroom. He did his job well using photostats of news stories and headlines dating back to 1935.

I was on the road with an engagement at Hughes, arranged by Charlie Adams, and speeches at Bauxite and Benton, and did not get to see the telecast. Hurrying back to Little Rock, I was late for a television speech of my own. Guy Jones was filling in for me, and he was courageous in the face of Cherry's presentation. He boldly and firmly accused Cherry of "McCarthyism" of the most blatant kind. He further accused him of avoiding the issues of the campaign — the utility rate hikes, the welfare program, and the 100% assessment plan — and reverting to "smear tactics" in an effort to win the race.

I came on the program with some closing remarks about patriotism, my war service in strange lands and a lifetime of service as a citizen and an official in Arkansas. I could make no reply to the charges for I, as yet, did not know what they were. Besides, it was not yet time.

(Cherry delivered the same speech on television at Memphis on Aug. 3, Fort Smith on August 4, and Texarkana on Aug. 5.)

As I entered the lobby of the Marion Hotel that night I could sense that the Cherry charges had been effective. Those present averted their eyes or turned away. I hurried on to the headquarters rooms for information and a conference with advisers.

It was evident the next day that the Cherry speech had scattered my forces like quail from a shotgun blast. But there were some who did not waver. Two of the staunchest aides around headquarters the next two days were Orville Cheney and Loid Sadler. Truman Baker, Jim Bland, and Roy Ritter stood firm, as did Guy Jones, but the role of Jones was in the field and with the media.

Contrary to running away, as did some of my personnel temporarily, R. A. (Bob) Young, president of Arkansas Best Freight line, and Tom Harper, a prominent attorney, came to the headquarters from Ft. Smith to be of any assistance possible. Their calm counsel and advice was of much help to me and a greatly steadying influence on other aides and workers.

COMMONWEALTH COLLEGE INFORMATION
Some additional facts here about Commonwealth College might be interesting and informative. None of this information was known to the general public at the time. If my own personal experience with the school had been generally known the situation would have been in my favor and not to my detriment. Unfortunately, that was not the case.

Commonwealth College, as I recall, conducted four semesters of courses a year for students, each of twelve weeks' duration. To the best of my recollection, I arrived at the college late one month, before the beginning of the three-month semester which started the following month. Present at the time were the college officials, faculty members and those few students staying over from the previous semester to continue their studies.

Soon after the arrival of the new students an organizational meeting of all the students was held. Much to my surprise I was unanimously chosen as president of the student body.

In reflecting later on my selection it was not difficult to discover the reason. The college at that very time had come under investigation by the Arkansas House of Representatives. The resultant publicity was damaging to the institution and it very badly needed some Arkansas connections. At the time of the student body meeting the students had not had time to become acquainted, so it was an easy matter for the college officials to guide them in their decisions.

At the end of the meeting for the entire student body the students were broken into three groups to choose group leaders. At that time I got my first real eye opener. The three groups were Communists, Socialists and Unaffiliated. I, of course, went with the Unaffiliated group.

I soon gained other knowledge of the institution. Most of the students were from the East and North, the preponderant number intellectuals from New York City. I do not recall any from the South but there was one student from Cuba.

The college had a so-called museum with a few objects of interest. I concluded later that the "museum" was for the purpose of publicity. The leader of the college had been engaged in efforts in Eastern Arkansas to organize the share croppers into a union known as the Tenant Farmers Union. Reportedly, he had run into great danger from opponents of the Union and barely escaped with his life. In the museum, prominently displayed, was the rope which was to be used to lynch him, a lynching from which he had reportedly escaped. It was never explained how the rope, apparently brand new, had been obtained.

The college had a well-stocked library. Newspapers included some of the Arkansas dailies and the New York Times. There were many good books but the library contents were definitely slanted toward the left.

The college had a number of prominent supporters across the nation. William E. Zeuch, a former head of the college, was then a high official in the Franklin D. Roosevelt administration. As I recall, he was then reputed to be a member of the well-known Roosevelt brain trust. Two other supporters of Commonwealth who, it was said, also contributed financially to the institution, were the noted writer, H. L. Mencken, and Justice Brandeis of the U.S. Supreme Court.

In selecting my courses in preparation for enrollment and study, I found the institution was not recognized by other institutions of higher learning. Therefore, no credit could be obtained from the college which would help toward a continuation of study for a degree from any other college or university.

The semester study began with lectures by certain faculty members, college officials or visiting speakers.

Among the early selected speakers was a German, a refugee from Hitler's tyranny, who was a laborer on the college campus. One has but to recall, even yet, that at that time a refugee from Hitler's Germany was received with open arms anywhere in America. This refugee was a dogmatic, hard-boiled Communist labor leader who had fled from his own country. In his lecture he laid down the inflexible, dogmatic Communist line without variation. All the capitalist system was bad, including religion, and nothing good could be found in it.

One of his remarks, made with conviction and fervor, was "Marriage under capitalism is nothing but legalized prostitution!"

I immediately thought of my mother who had loved only one man, married him and been true to him all her life. I said nothing during or following the lecture but I had heard enough. Soon afterward I departed the college without paying any tuition or taking any courses.

THE CAMPAIGN

One day during the critical period of the campaign, I forged up the Arkansas River Valley. My first engagement was a breakfast at Dardanelle arranged by one of my most loyal and diligent supporters, Mack Sturgis of Dover. Mack had told me in the beginning, "You can't win, but if you run I'll support you." Mack did support me, not only then but throughout my career in state politics.

The breakfast was arranged for approximately 30 people whom Mack had invited. If my recollection of numbers is correct, 9 showed up, which together with myself, Mr. Sturgis and my driver, Horace Tarkington of Searcy, made a total of twelve.

Mack was very disappointed and clearly downcast with the turnout. I never let the situation bother me. I knew I was fighting a desperate holding battle so far as active supporters were concerned who were willing to be identified with me. My hope was to turn the tide of public sentiment through speeches, ads and publicity.

I recall sometime following the Commonwealth blast of consciously projecting myself into the role of a voter-observer of the situation. As such a voter-observer, I would possibly remain quiet, not jumping to a conclusion but waiting to hear from the other side — from the man charged. Gov. Cherry had done a powerful job in presenting one side of the case. I could understand the consternation of some of my friends, as well as the hesitancy of those not directly involved to make an immediate decision. Somehow I had faith that if I could gain a hearing and make sufficiently clear to the people the circumstances of that ill-advised journey to Commonwealth

College and its subsequent results, that they, the people, would understand.

I also sensed that by waiting while the curiosity built to a higher pitch, I would have a greater and a more attentive audience for any full-dress defense of my record as a loyal citizen, a public servant and a soldier of America. If I were successful, then those who had withdrawn in concern from any direct contact with my candidacy would come flooding back, along with thousands of others who were waiting for a resolution of the big question which had been raised in their minds. Then I would have a chance to win the election.

Therefore, I vaguely sensed, the sparse numbers at my organizational meetings during that critical period — there were good crowds for the stump speeches — along with the almost empty rooms of my headquarters would not prove decisive. The situation was building to a climax, or a series of climaxes, which would determine the fate of my candidacy.

When the breakfast meeting at Dardanelle was over, I went downtown to speak. Very few gathered close, but the sound from the mike set on the street in the open carried throughout the town where many listened from the sidewalks and the fronts of business buildings.

My speech finished and already behind schedule, I literally ran to my car and the driver took off. Tarkington was one of the best drivers with whom I have ever ridden. It was good that I had his services much of the time during those hectic days. Sturgis later reported that my determined haste that day made a favorable impression on those who observed.

From Dardanelle we were possibly bound for Ft. Smith where I had one of the best local organizations in the state. It began with Roy Martin, a personal friend, one of my most loyal supporters and a former fellow highway commissioner. Other leaders were R. A. "Bob" Young, Tom Harper, Joe Smrcker, who also worked in Little Rock, Riley Donaho and Rudd Ross, an automobile dealer. In the ranks of Labor was Dewey LeMaster, member of the Glass Workers Union, brother of my aunt, Mrs. Will (Julia) Joslin, and a boyhood school mate. Another friend was Merritt B. Wentz, a roommate when we attended high school at Huntsville. Another Ft. Smith supporter was a high official with a statewide acquaintance who shall remain unnamed, who, in the hectic days of the runoff, in numerous telephone calls to my leaders urged them not to panic, to remain calm, to remain firm and continue the fight.

The Sebastian County organization paid all expenses in that area, including a full-time headquarters in Ft. Smith, all newspaper ads and radio and television time.

On Tuesday, August 3, the day following the Commonwealth College charges, I had an early morning meeting in Pine Bluff. Only a relative few were in the room. I looked out at mostly empty seats. I recall the Freemans, the elderly owners and editors of the **Pine Bluff Commercial**, were present. One of them was a supporter throughout my career. I do not recall who arranged the meeting but G. D. Long was one of my early leaders in that area. Ed Williams, Jr., a comparatively young school teacher, took charge of my Pine Bluff headquarters about this time.

That meeting over, I went to another room where a considerable number of black leaders and their followers were gathered. I spoke to them and then took off westward along Highway 270 for Malvern. George Douthit, then traveling with me, wrote that I fell asleep and rested most of the journey.

At Malvern at 10 A.M. a fairly good crowd was waiting in the shade of the trees on the attractive courthouse lawn. Some labor leaders mounted the platform with me to show their support.

I must say that a number of Union Labor leaders and members worked even harder in my behalf following the Commonwealth charges than they had before. Many of them realized more clearly than others the meaning and implication of the smear. Still fresh in their minds was the recollection of such tactics used against them. In the long struggle upward of the Union Labor movement many honest labor leaders had been coated unjustly with the brush of subversion and ofttimes falsely painted as criminals.

I had a good reception at Malvern, due mostly, I am sure, to my Labor support in the area. After speaking I took off for Arkadelphia.

My schedule for Tuesday, August 3: Pine Bluff 8 A.M.; Malvern 10 A.M.; Arkadelphia 2 P.M.; Hope 4 P.M.; Texarkana 7:30 P.M. for a TV broadcast.

On the night of Aug. 2 I had a long conference with Attorney Kenneth Coffelt at his home in Little Rock. Coffelt had served twice in the Arkansas Legislature, the first time as a member of the House representing Benton County, the second time representing Saline County. I had seen him on the floor of the House while attending the inauguration of Governor Carl E. Bailey in 1937 — the only inauguration I had ever attended — and admired his oratory.

During the years that followed Coffelt had become controversial, but no one ever doubted his ability in a rough and tumble battle in either the courtroom or the political arena. I asked him to evaluate the situation and give me any suggestions or ideas that occurred to him as how best to combat the Commonwealth situation.

The next day as I drove into Arkadelphia for the 2 P.M. speech, to say that the situation was then hectic, turbulent, uncertain and boiling would be no over-statement. A good crowd was waiting and also someone with an urgent message to call my Little Rock headquarters.

I made the call from a county office in the courthouse and found Truman Baker waiting at the other end of the line. Truman briefly explained that Coffelt had called them, dictated a telegram and urged them to get it to me at the earliest possible moment.

Recalling my request to Mr. Coffelt, I said, "Read the telegram."

Truman read and I copied it as hurriedly as possible. When he had finished I knew as clearly as I could see the sun on that sultry day, that it was good, that it was what I needed and that I would use it. I directed Truman to send the telegram immediately to the parties indicated and to release the text of the message to the press.

I then strode to a waiting microphone to speak to the waiting crowd. There was never a more attentive audience. They stood somber and silent, hanging on every word. All passers-by stopped and became a part of the gathering. It was like throwing popcorn on a molasses ball. Even the critics and the spies for the opposition stood transfixed until I had finished.

At the close of the speech I read the telegram, which was as follows:

"While in Little Rock last evening, I consulted an attorney in whose opinion and ability I have the utmost confidence.

I am advised that to call a man a subversive, or to make this statement, either oral or written, that he ever engaged in subversive activities or an un-American act, is libel per se (in fact).

I have no objection to your condemnation of Commonwealth College, and you can talk all you want to about that institution, if the public wants to hear you. The issue is now based on the insinuation of your record that I am a subversive and have engaged in subversive activities.

Now I charge you to make this statement, that I am a subversive, or that I ever participated in any subversive activities, and if you do, knowing you do not have any proof of such charge, I will sue you immediately in the courts of my native state. Now you men get down to the

point and get on the line, and either stand or fall on this proposition."

The telegram was sent to Gov. Cherry, John F. Wells, and Boyd Tackett.

Supporters, much encouraged by the telegram, joined me in a motor caravan to Hope, some going all the way with me to Texarkana.

———

August 4 — *Arkansas Gazette* Headlines

FAUBUS DARES FOE TO SAY SUBVERSIVE; CHERRY RENEWS FIRE
GOVERNOR SLAPS AWAY OVER AIR FROM MEMPHIS
SUIT THREATENED AS CHALLENGER DENIES CHARGES
TACKETT JUMPS FAUBUS ABOUT COLLEGE ISSUE
I. S. McCLINTON BACKS GOVERNOR CHERRY.

McClinton headed an organization of black voters and was a prominent black leader in the state at the time. Later he was my supporter and adviser in the general election.

CHERRY CAMPAIGNS

The newspapers reported that Gov. Cherry, accompanied by Glen A. "Bud" Green, State Publicity Commission Chairman and Chairman of Publicity and Advertising Committee of the Cherry campaign, and his campaign driver, David Pryor of Camden, saw voters in Lonoke, Carlisle, Brinkley and Wheatley, on his way to Memphis for his second speech using the Commonwealth College charges.

COMMONWEALTH MAIN ISSUE

The news reports said that I dared Cherry to come right out and call me a Communist. I continued to hit at Cherry's first term record, including the 100% assessment program, the welfare policies and the fiscal code of state finances.

"But," I was quoted, "we are no longer debating on the issues of Arkansas government. They (Cherry forces) have made Commonwealth College the big issue of the campaign. I predict the next 48 hours will bring the crisis. I already see it turning in my favor sooner than I expected."

ENTRANCE EXAM
By Graham, Ark. Gazette   8/4/54

Before a curtained "voting booth" a sign read:
Do you believe the Commonwealth College Issue —
Is True ☐ or False ☐ (check one)

38

Faubus political ad:
A telegram of support from Paul L. Anderson of Rogers, a
war veteran and Army Reserve officer

———

Cherry political ad:
The last of a series, "Who Is This Man Faubus," All important issue — Personal integrity

READY FOR THE LAST SIX DAYS
By Kennedy, Ark. Democrat   4/4/54

In the runoff campaign with six days to go, the smoke of
"bitter charges and counter-charges (in the governor's race)"
had grown so intense that the voters were donning gas masks.

〇━〇━〇━

THE PINE BLUFF SPEECH
WHICH ASHMORE HELPED TO WRITE

It was on Wednesday night, August 4, a full two days after
Governor Cherry had laid down his devastating artillery-like
salvo of charges against me on the Commonwealth College
matter, that I gave my full dress reply. It was scheduled on the
entire radio network originating from an open air meeting in a
ball park in Pine Bluff.

I came in off the road in the afternoon to make preparation.
Robert Tipton, an attorney of Ashdown and Texarkana, filled
my afternoon speaking engagement at El Dorado.

Harry S. Ashmore, executive editor of the *Arkansas
Gazette,* aroused by the so-called McCarthy tactics of my antagonists, had started writing a speech for me. A small part of
it was handed me as I was secluded in a room to begin work.
Truman Baker was with me as I read the first part and concluded that it was good.

Thereafter a runner went back and forth between my room
and the site where Ashmore worked. As portions of the speech
were finished, I made revisions and handed them to Baker who
relayed them to a typist for conversion to final form. The
documents of the Legislature's investigation of Commonwealth
College on file in the Secretary of State's Office (C.G. "Crip"

Hall gave us full cooperation) were obtained and numbered for
use in the speech. One of the documents, which had been obtained under oath by the Legislature during the 1935 investigation, was a list of all students there and covered the period when
Cherry said I was in attendance. My name was not on the list.
Another was the sworn testimony of L. Koch, the college president, naming the Arkansas students. I was not named as one of
them.

We worked hurriedly against a deadline and barely finished
in time. The entire speech was perhaps an hour in length and we
had only 30 minutes on the radio. There was no time for major
revision. I must handle that problem as I spoke, choosing which
portions to treat briefly and which to omit entirely.

Loid Sadler was waiting with his car to rush me to Pine
Bluff. He was not the best driver in the world, as I'm sure he
would admit, and the minutes seemed to flee away as we
traversed that interminable narrow winding road from Little
Rock, at that time perhaps the worst road in the nation connecting two such cities.

We finally arrived and found a ball park. It was as empty as
the Tomb on the Third Day, but there were no watchers about.

Evidently there was another park. In search of it we plunged downtown, if the speed of the vehicle could be so described
with Loid driving. The city was empty; the work day had ended
and night was fast gathering.

Suddenly I noted we were passing the publishing plant of the
Pine Bluff Commercial. I saw an open door near the back.

"Stop here!" I directed Mr. Sadler.

Loid brought the car to a quick halt, I jumped out and dashed through the entrance into the building. I found one ink-
stained youth busily cleaning up.

I put the proper questions. "Yes," he said, "there is
another ball park," and he began to give directions to it. The
directions appeared to be complicated and I stopped him.

"Can you leave here for a few moments?" I asked.

"Yes," he replied.

"Then come with us and show us the way," I requested,
"and we'll bring you back immediately."

I ran to the car with the young man following. We piled in
and took off with him directing.

Arriving at the park I thanked our benefactor and alighted,
Loid remaining at the wheel to return him to his place of work.

Standing alone I checked my watch. It was eight minutes to
air time.

Briefly I looked around. Several spectators could be seen. I
observed men standing in the darkness behind the stands, some
singly, others in groups of twos or more conversing in subdued
tones. Those who observed me looked my way but few approached. In the half-empty stands old and middle-aged ladies
of apparently very modest means, as noted by their dress,
appeared to be dominant among those seated there.

I found a narrow side gate and entered the ball park. A lone,
bare microphone, almost spectral in appearance, stood some
twenty feet from the high fence separating the park area from
the bleachers. There was no lectern, no table or desk for papers,
no individual with instructions, assistance or guidance. Except
for the microphone I stood alone in the empty field.

With a breeze blowing just holding the loose leaves of my
speech would be some problem. I saw it would be impossible to
hold at the same time the documents from which I would read.

Putting them in order I looked around for a stone or other
object to hold them in place on the ground. The most suitable
object I found was an empty soft drink bottle, which was certainly not the best for the purpose because of its tendency to
roll.

It was not a desirable arrangement. As I would reach the
point in my speech for the use of a document, it would be
necessary to stoop to the ground to secure the paper while being

careful not to dislodge the bottle lest the remaining papers become disarranged or blown away in the wind.

As I was weighting down the documents I was, all at once, conscious of a presence by my side. "Here, Orval," a voice said, "let me hold those for you."

The presence was Jimmy Karam of Little Rock. I don't know why he was there. Whether he came as a helper, a spy, out of curiosity or whether the Lord sent him, I never knew. I did not inquire then or in the years to come. His help was sufficient for the moment.

It was air time. I handed Jimmy the papers and said, "When I reach, just hand me the one on top." And I began my speech.

It must be remembered that the brief runoff period was a series of incredibly fast-breaking developments. In fact, it was almost impossible to keep abreast of events. The political strategy and maneuver was on a daily, sometimes an hourly, basis.

In looking back it may be that Governor Cherry stuck with the Commonwealth charges too long. On the night I was delivering the radio speech at Pine Bluff, Cherry was making the same Commonwealth charges on television at Ft. Smith that he had first made the previous Monday in Little Rock, and was to make the same speech the following night at Texarkana.

It also must be borne in mind that after my use of the Coffelt-prepared telegram from Arkadelphia, about 30 hours before my Pine Bluff appearance, my opponents had backed off completely from labeling me subversive. In their fear of being sued, which was no idle threat on my part, they stated, "We do not say he's a Communist," — "We do not say he is subversive," — and "We do not question his loyalty."

In view of my life-time record as a good citizen in the hills of my native region, my war time writings, which were numerous, and my war record, such charges, had they been made, would have been impossible to prove.

Now, since my opponents had backed off completely from calling me subversive, which was clearly insinuated in the original Commonwealth charges else there was no reason to use them, the main thrust of my speech at the particular moment when I spoke at Pine Bluff, was to explain my presence at the college, a presence long known to many of my friends and which I had never denied.

Perhaps Ashmore, from his detached view as an observer, sensed this more clearly as he wrote that afternoon than did either I or the directors of my headquarters. We were caught up in the hectic, hurly-burly, rough-and-tumble of the campaign where decisions had to be made in rapid-fire order.

My headquarters made some mistakes. Once, in the early stages of the College charges while I was on the way to headquarters from a speaking engagement, some member of the staff issued a statement saying I had spent only three days at the institution. Arriving only minutes after the press release I immediately recalled it. Unfortunately, one copy could not be repossessed and was used. That statement conflicted with later statements I made which gave rise to the allegation that I was lying about the time I spent there.

The fact was that I had no way of establishing exactly how many days I spent on the campus of the far-left facility. I knew only that the stay was brief.

However, when I looked into the faces of the people in my audiences, either in person or by television, and asked each person to recall where he was twenty years ago, why he was there, what he was doing and the circumstances of his presence, each could understand the hazy recollection of such a long past event.

I began my speech that night with the knowledge that it was crucial. Not only was it crucial to the campaign but to my life thereafter and the heritage of my son. I explained my presence at the college and why I went — a naive youth of the hills seeking further education. I explained what I found and why I left.

Much of the speech was in Ashmore's rhetoric which I thought was excellent. One phrase, "When I went out from the green valley of my youth", has rung in my mind ever since.

I laid it heavily on my opponents, condemning unequivocally and harshly the smear tactics that were used. The chips were down. It was no time for pussy-footing or mealy-mouthed statements.

As I spoke, I noted the spectators were drawn, unconsciously it seemed on their part, from the darkness and the crowd grew more dense in the light along the fence. I could see many of the women in the seats crying and wiping tears from their faces. Karam, standing beside me handing over the papers as I indicated, was caught up in the emotion of the moment. He was shouting repeatedly, "Pour it on 'em, Orval! Pour it on 'em, Orval!"

When I reminded him later of his shouted encouragement he did not remember it but his voice was heard state-wide on the radio network. I do not recall a sound coming from the audience. They hung on every word as my voice rang out through the stillness of the night and died away into the darkness of the trees.

When I finished I knew I had done well. If only enough people had heard.

If there was a turning point in the campaign I think the Pine Bluff speech was it. The telegram was important, greatly important, but was perhaps not sufficient. Now the last of those who had fled at the first charges on Monday night came flocking back. Great numbers, who had waited silently with reservations, now put them aside and joined openly in the campaign. The bandwagon was beginning to roll again as more and more people urged me to get back to the original issues.

However, the opposition forces were also thoroughly aroused and working like beavers. The outcome, as I realized, was still in doubt.

In the years that followed, many of my long-time friends in the hills related to me their reaction to the speech. One, Robert W. Crabtree, a highway worker of Aurora, Madison County, related how he sprang from his chair and ran around the room.

"Yes," added his wife, "and he shouted out 'My God! Old Stonewall Jackson wasn't in it!'" (meaning I was an even greater fighter.)

POLITICAL BATTLE GROWS MORE HEATED

Headlines, political ads and editorials continued to reflect the heat of a campaign that had become the most bitter battle in the state's history. The subject of the Commonwealth College charges was the most prominent.

REMMEL HINTS HE MAY RUN AGAINST HAYS

Mayor Remmel in a speech to a civic club at Jonesboro on August 5 again indicated that he would seek the Congressional seat held by Brooks Hays. This was the third time GOP Remmel's interest in opposing Hays had surfaced in the news.

AN EDITORIAL: THE CHARGE OF BIAS

A political ad for Cherry by Bayard Taylor in the *Arkansas Democrat* accused the *Gazette* of "trying to prove" the Orval Faubus statements in regard to his "presence at Commonwealth College". Said the *Gazette* in reply: "This is a calculated and deliberate untruth."

PALMER PAPERS URGE FAUBUS TO WITHDRAW

The four newspapers at Texarkana, El Dorado, Magnolia and Hot Springs, owned and controlled by C.E. Palmer of Texarkana, in editorials urged me to withdraw from the race "or face humiliating defeat."

A Cherry political ad accused the McMath administration (and me by implication) of increasing taxes. There were "no tax increases" in the Cherry administration, the ad said. The ad then stated:

"About the 100% Amendment"
"It will not pass, that much is apparent;
public sentiment has crystalized against it."

SPEECH AT BLYTHEVILLE

On August 5 I spoke at Blytheville at 7:30 p.m. to a large and attentive audience. The speech was well covered by both Memphis daily newspapers and was carried on the Blytheville radio.

A banner headline in the *Democrat* of August 6 read:

AP&L Told to Prove Rate Boost Need
Or to Refund Increase

GUS MCMILLAN QUITS FAUBUS, JOINS CHERRY

McMillan who had endorsed me the night of the first primary, now in a press release endorsed the candidacy of Governor Cherry. Rumors reached my headquarters that McMillan was rewarded with a gift of $5,000.00. We never sought to confirm the report.

Jack Holt also openly endorsed Cherry.

AD SEEKS TO TIE ME TO MCMATH

Political ad for Cherry:
You're Safe in Judging the Future by the Past
The ad sought to tie me to the alleged mistakes of the McMath administration. Such tactics had a tendency to solidify the McMath support in my camp. Recalling their one-sided victory two years before the Cherry camp strategists were making the mistake of classifying all voters as anti-McMath and pro-McMath. The strategy failed because I had dozens of leaders and many followers who did not fall into these two groups. But when many pro-McMath voters were more or less pushed into my camp by the criticism of the Cherry forces it became a plus for me because I lost few if any of my other supporters.

August 5 — *Arkansas Democrat*

LANEY BACKS CHERRY FOR SECOND TERM

Former Governor Ben Laney, apparently without participating actively in the campaign, announced that he would vote for Governor Cherry for a second term.

FAUBUS HITS HIGHWAY POLITICS; COMMISSION ASKED TO INVESTIGATE
Eldredge Says "No Politics" in Department

Highway Director Herbert Eldredge had a meeting of all top supervisory personnel of the Highway Department at the agency's headquarters in Little Rock. He told those gathered that if Governor Cherry lost the system would change, and that it would be better to work under the new system than to go back to the old. Furthermore, he stated, if Cherry lost, a lot of people would lose their jobs and he, Eldredge, would be the first to go. The purpose of the meeting, which was supposed to remain secret, was clear: Get back to their areas and work for Governor Cherry. The first information on the purpose of this meeting came from Joe Smreker who obtained it from a confidential source.

At Van Buren in Crawford County, the people for a long time had been pleading for resurfacing of a section of state highway which also served as a city street. The Highway Department, suddenly galvanized into action, moved in full force during the runoff period and began work on the project. The crews even worked on Sunday. The move was so clearly politically motivated that dozens of people called me and my headquarters staff to inform us of the action. This was the old-time way of maneuvering for votes by use of the Highway Department although seldom were the actions so patently political.

These were the political tactics which Governor Cherry and the new "independent" Highway Commission were supposed to stop and which they had proclaimed were at an end. Because of this the hasty move into Van Buren probably cost them more votes than it gained.

I responded to the Palmer chain of newspapers editorial call to "withdraw now or suffer a humiliating defeat." My reply to the press was: "Mr. Palmer has never been my friend, nor lent me any support, and I don't know any reason why I should listen to any suggestion from my political enemies."

———

Political ad paid for by Leffel Gentry:

JUST OUT! OFF THE PRESS TODAY!
WHO IS THIS MAN FAUBUS?
GET YOUR COPY TODAY . . . FREE
16 illustrated pages

The booklets were available at the Cherry headquarters.
—0—
Citizens Speak for Governor Cherry — To-Night

This was a TV panel of Arthur E. McLean and Everett Tucker, both Little Rock businessmen.
—0—
Orval Faubus for Governor
A Reaction Against McCarthy-Like Smear Tactics

The political ad reproduced a letter from a resident of Mena who remembered me there and recalled that I participated in religious services with a youth group on a Sabbath in a nearby church.
—0—

ENDORSED BY PASTOR BOB JONES

A letter of endorsement and expression of full faith in my integrity and loyalty by my pastor, Robert W. (Bob) Jones of the First Baptist Church in Huntsville.

— — —

HIGH TEMPERS DURING THE RUNOFF

Following the Commonwealth College charges in the runoff, tempers of many supporters of both candidates rose to fever pitch. It was reported to me that Rufus Morgan, a war veteran friend in Morrilton, made a special trip to Little Rock "with blood in his eye" ready to take on all comers in my defense. My early supporters in Morrilton were Morgan; Sadler; Olen Fullerton, operator of the Church of Christ Children's Home there for orphans, and former fellow Highway Commissioner, respected by all his associates; road contractor Jeff Mobley, who gave me a $500 contribution early; Odell Yocum, a personal friend and former county agent of Madison County; and Ben Wilbanks of Plumerville, a war buddy. Sheriff Marlin Hawkins went along with the Cherry forces in the first primary, but joined forces with my friends in the runoff.

One morning in the Marion Hotel coffee shop a lone man entered, took a seat at the counter and uttered some strong imprecation against me. A man seated near the back arose from his table and without a word advanced on my condemner.

Noting the attitude of the approacher the man arose from the counter and the advancing man, with one blow, sent him sprawling amidst the tables and chairs. The fallen man arose and without a word left the shop through the doorway to the street. His assailant turned just as wordlessly and exited through the door to the hotel lobby.

Leck Owens, my long-time friend of Berryville and Fayetteville, then assistant Highway Engineer of the Batesville district, was directing work of a highway crew in a north central county. A Cherry supporter came by and stopped to campaign with the highway crew. The campaigning led to strong denunciation of me until Leck had had enough. With a blow of his big fist he sent the campaigner tumbling into the briers and brambles beside the roadway. As the man crawled out Leck said, "That man (Faubus) is my friend, and you can't talk about him like that to me. Now you be on your way." Without further words the man departed.

One evening when I was on television, Alta and some friends at the Marion Hotel wanted to see the telecast. Not a television set was available. Ben Shelley, the affable and friendly hotel manager, told them to go to the Gar Hole where a set was kept for the customers. The Gar Hole was a well-known Little Rock watering place where thirst was quenched mostly by beer. One of the group was Roy Riales, an early supporter from Mena, then a candidate for the State Senate. The group went to the Gar Hole and were seated at a table watching the telecast. Three men at the counter, evidently critics of my candidacy, began to expostulate against me in loud voices using some profanity. Riales went over to remonstrate with them, explained that the lady with him was my wife who wanted to see the telecast, and returned to the table. The three continued their loud remarks of condemnation, whereupon the manager admonished them. When they still persisted in their loud remarks, Riales arose with his male companions and took them on. The manager broke up the fight and ejected the trio. "They asked for it!" he commented, as he requested Roy and his companions to be reseated with Alta to view the remainder of the telecast.

Mack Sturgis at home at Dover began a conversation over a back fence with a neighbor about the campaign. The neighbor roundly condemned me in strong language. The angered Sturgis threatened to crawl through the fence and attack his neighbor physically; whereupon the conversation turned to other matters. On another occasion Sturgis invited a loud critic to go outside a downtown Russellville business house to contest their differences but the critic wisely declined.

A bread truck from Fayetteville making deliveries in Huntsville, put on his vehicle a sign in large letters: "DON'T SHOOT! WE'RE FOR FAUBUS!"

THE FAITH AND LOYALTY OF HOME FOLKS AND FRIENDS

The faith and loyalty of the people of my home county cannot go unnoticed.

The day after Cherry's attack of August 2, a statement was drawn up expressing full faith in my loyalty and patriotism and condemning Governor Cherry for his smear tactics used against me. The statement was circulated throughout the county and signed by hundreds of citizens. The signed papers were then mailed to Governor Cherry and to me.

As the Commonwealth issue grew in intensity hundreds of telephone calls began to come to Huntsville seeking information about me. If the caller knew someone in the area the call was placed to the acquaintance. However, the great preponderance of the calls were from strangers, many of them church leaders. Others were from business and civic leaders.

Perhaps a greater number of the calls were taken by my own pastor, Reverend Robert W. "Bob" Jones, than any other individual. A number of the inquiries were handled by the Methodist minister, and Arlis Coger, a prominent businessman,

received many of them. Officials of the Chamber of Commerce and other civic clubs, as well as officials of the Veterans' organizations and the Masonic lodge received and answered others.

The people who received these calls could speak of me from long personal acquaintance and official association. I was president of the Madison County Chamber of Commerce, past secretary-treasurer of the Lions Club, a member and past historian of the American Legion post, a 32nd Degree Mason and member of the Huntsville Lodge, a teacher in the rural schools of the county for ten years, a former county official, and at that time Huntsville postmaster and owner-editor of the weekly newspaper in the county, *The Madison County Record.*

There were others who expressed their faith in me whenever there was opportunity: one of my former teachers, Robert M. Reed of Combs, a teacher-minister in that area for fifty years; Rev. Alonzo Ledford, minister and school board member at Pinnacle where I first taught school, and his son, Reverend Basil Ledford; Reverend Claud Counts of Drakes Creek, and Reverent D. F. Taff of Mulberry, both of whom came to hear me speak at Van Buren; Reverend Charles Wages, a Methodist minister who formerly pastored in Madison County, then living at Forrest City where he introduced me when I spoke there before the first primary. These and dozens of others, many of them unknown to me, upheld my banner when the attack was made upon my loyalty as an American citizen.

Even the Republicans recommended me far and wide. Dalton Dotson, former Republican sheriff of the county, then had a district job with a federal farm program. As he traveled his area in northeast Arkansas he took every opportunity to spike the rumors of subversion being circulated about me. In Huntsville on election day his father, the grizzled, humorous Tom Berry Dotson, who never before had approached a Democratic polling place, went into the primary to vote for me and led some 70 of his rock-ribbed Republican friends to do the same. Mrs. Freda Hankins, wife of then Republican County Judge Howard Hankins, who had defeated me in the general election for that office in 1946, joined others in the Democratic primary to vote for me.

N. D. "Doc" Heathman, Republican representative from the county who had two years before defeated my ally, Rolla Fitch, for the office, was one of my strongest boosters. Earlier, as already mentioned, he had joined openly in the organizational efforts in my behalf.

Every state and district employee in the county, save two, were for me. A Highway Department district supervisor came to the county to verbally remonstrate with the county foreman, Frank Murphy. The aging Murphy, his tanned, work-lined face animated with his reply to his superior said, "Why, I don't need to talk for Orval; everyone here is already for him!"

Jewel Whitaker of Harrison, formerly Highway District Maintenance Supervisor for the northwest Arkansas area who had been terminated during the Cherry administration, was another strong advocate for me. Then operating a grocery store in the city he never missed an opportunity to recommend me. Whitaker, a dedicated, skilled, and honest employee of the Highway Department during the McMath administration, was one of the main reasons that no breath of scandal or wrongdoing was ever brought out about the First Highway District by the Highway Audit Commission. Some years later Whitaker was reinstated as District Supervisor and served until ill health forced his retirement some time after my administration ended. Upon his retirement a joint "Jewel Whitaker Day" and dedication of the new highway district headquarters was held in Harrison. Every speaker voiced words of praise for the job he had done. Knowing of his absolute honesty, a phrase that occurred to me as a spectator at the event was "The noblest work of God is an honest man!" Jewel Whitaker was one of those men.

Another strong advocate of mine was Albert Stephens of Sheridan, then Assistant District Maintenance Supervisor of the Highway Department in that area. Although he had to be circumspect, I heard a number of times of his recommendation of me. Albert was an honest, hard-working man who apparently did not have the desire and capacity to make money, with which his younger brother, Witt, was so highly gifted.

Another advocate in that area was the father of the Stephens' brothers, the venerable and respected A.J. "Jack" Stephens. A former legislator, he was in the small gathering which heard me speak at Prattsville early in the campaign and later gave a sizeable contribution to my campaign fund.

Another honest, dependable Highway Department official, admired and respected wherever he was known, was Walter Hicks, a construction supervisor in the Fayetteville area. He was my unwavering friend and advocate throughout my statewide political career and even until his death in later years at Camden.

Another Highway Department employee with friends at many points where he had headed survey crews for new construction projects, was Tom Wacaster formerly of Hot Springs. Tom, a constant friend since our first acquaintance in 1949, never missed an opportunity to recommend me in spite of the displeasure it caused some of his superiors in the department.

There were others like John Miller of Combs, Leo Hudson of Marble, Alton Farley of Siloam Springs, John Box of Rogers, Jeff Davis and Hilman Watkins of Harrison, whose faith in me was built on personal like and trust. Can there be a better basis for a lasting relationship?

BATESVILLE AND
HEBER SPRINGS APPEARANCES

On Friday, Governor Cherry and I both were in attendance at the White River Water Carnival at Batesville. Whether by design or coincidence, the arrangements by our leaders did not bring us together. At noon, while Cherry was at the Country Club with a group of the more prominent business leaders, I had lunch downtown with Democratic leaders including most of the members of the Independence County Democratic Central Committee. I was presented by Bill Headstream who had introduced me earlier for an address to a large crowd in front of the courthouse. The arrangements were made by Don Vaughn and Fred Livingston, Sr., two of the best county political organizers in the state. The closest Cherry and I came was at the airport. As I approached for departure Cherry and his party were ready to board for take-off. A reporter wrote that there were no waves or greetings. I seem to recall that there were.

From Batesville I flew to Heber Springs where the sound trucks had already arrived. This city had been placed on the schedule only the day before at the insistence of Fred Johnson who had become my principal leader there. We landed at the small grass-covered air strip which didn't appear too safe. I was using Jim Crain's plane and pilot, the best with whom I have ever flown. Mr. Johnson met the plane, took me downtown and turned me loose at the edge of the beautiful city park where the annual Old Soldiers Reunion was underway.

A long-standing regulation prohibited political speaking in the park. My sound system was set up just across the street from the park with a truck for a speaker's stand. There being yet ten to fifteen minutes before speaking time, I wandered slowly up through the park toward the pavillion where some program was underway.

There was a huge crowd in the park but as I slowly walked along I noted only two persons who showed any signs of recognition, and they didn't seem at all sure. As I neared the pavillion I could hear the voice of the emcee. I heard him bring the program to a conclusion and then announce that Orval Faubus,

a candidate for Governor, would speak at three o'clock across from the park. The time had already arrived.

The speaking site was downhill east of the pavillion. The crowd broke immediately down the slope many of them in a run. As I walked many of them brushed against me in their haste not knowing they had made physical contact with the man they were hurrying to hear.

I spoke in the full glare of the broiling sun as hundreds stood on the blistering streets and sidewalks. Others stood in the shade of trees in the park itself. I noted a number of overall-clad mountaineers standing or seated on the curb or on the fenders of vehicles adjacent to the speaker's stand.

The old-time mountaineers of the Ozarks and Ouachitas are a strangely impassive, undemonstrative breed. I have seen them sit quietly through a speech, showing no emotion, never moving, not even a facial muscle. However, when a speech is finished if they approach, shake hands, and say, "Young man, I'm fer ye," the speaker can put it down that he has a vote and have no further concern.

That day when I came to the part of my speech in which I recited the ills of the Cherry welfare program — how the department personnel spent hours investigating the old people who were trying to help themselves by raising a few chickens, milking a cow, making a garden, or canning fruit — of how their checks were reduced while those who did nothing to help themselves were given the biggest grants — I saw the old-timers stir. There were slight nods of their heads, sharp knowing glances at each other and sometimes quick nudges of elbows into neighboring ribs.

Those actions, I knew, were being real demonstrative for mountaineers. I was applauded a number of times by the audience but I don't recall seeing a handclap from the overall-clad group. However, I knew I was "selling," and when the speech was finished I knew I had done well. With every community and practically every home in Cleburne County represented in the audience I felt confident of the outcome in that county.

OLDTIME CHIVALRY NOT DEAD

When I had finished, Mr. Johnson told me that Mrs. Frank Dodge, whom we had dubbed the head of the Cadillac Brigade, was there. She wanted to speak for Cherry but had no equipment and had made no arrangements. I don't recall whether she requested to use my equipment or whether it was suggested by Mr. Johnson and my supporters. Anyway, I immediately gave instructions to my sound crew to leave the equipment set up and let Mrs. Dodge use it. This didn't make the crew including my son, Farrell, very happy. They had endured some long, hot days and long tiresome drives by both day and night. This was the last public speaking engagement of the week and they were anxious to get back to Little Rock for much-needed rest.

Taking off from the airport the pilot circled the town. I could see Mrs. Dodge standing in the back of the pick-up truck. The crowd had thinned to mere remnants of its former size.

Farrell and the sound crew reported to me later that Mrs. Dodge "jumped on" the audience, as they described it, for not applauding her as they had me.

The next day there was a small item in a Little Rock newspaper about my decision to let Mrs. Dodge use my equipment to speak against me for my opponent, to the effect that "chivalry was not yet dead."

o━o━o━o━o━o

Sunday, August 8 — *Arkansas Gazette*
Faubus Asserts Leffel Gentry is "Real Governor";
Challenger Declares That Cherry
Forces Use Pressure Tactics

Cherry Stacks His Own Record Against Faubus;
Says Manipulators Surrounding Would Scare Industry

Faubus Ad:
"To Crush McCarthyism" — was volunteered and paid for by Y.W. Ethridge of Hamburg.

On Saturday, August 7, I made a television speech at Ft. Smith. My supporters had to purchase an hour's time in order to obtain a half hour. I used the full hour and was still going fine when it expired.

Sunday, August 8 — *Arkansas Democrat*
   All-Time Record Vote Predicted for Runoff
   Pulaski Absentee Votes Indicate Heavy Turnout

CLOUDING THE ISSUES
Political Ad paid for by
Faubus for Governor Committee   4/54

The opposition early began the use of paid political cartoons against me. After the Commonwealth charge in the runoff primary, we came up with some of our own. The above was our version of Gov. Cherry creating a smoke screen of "false charges" and "smear attack" to hide "the real campaign issues."

CHERRY, FAUBUS MEET ON TV

On Sunday afternoon Governor Cherry and I jointly faced a panel of newsmen for questions and answers. The confrontation was arranged by Bill Hadley of Channel 7 with studios in both Little Rock and Pine Bluff. The program was held in the Little Rock studio with Mr. Hadley as moderator. It lasted a half hour and at the conclusion the station wanted to continue. I agreed but Governor Cherry declined, ending the session.

My friends thought I came out better than my opponent, not so much from what was said, but because of my seeming assurance and confidence in the handling the questions. At the conclusion Cherry and I shook hands, reaching across in front of the moderator who was between us. The handshake was shown in a front page photograph in the *Arkansas Gazette* the next day. At the time, I'm sure by chance, Governor Cherry appeared to be glumly looking downward while I was looking straight at the Governor in a friendly manner. Both Joe Martin and Doug Bradley, two of my leaders at Jonesboro, said the photograph was favorable to me and they thought it helped my cause. As I recall the Governor's demeanor was proper, not friendly but neither indifferent or antagonistic.

The story of the encounter the next day on page two of the *Arkansas Democrat* was headlined: "Candidates meet, but find little in common."

The appearance probably had the largest audience of any program for a single station in the history of the state up to that time.

The panelists were: Harry S. Ashmore, executive editor of the *Gazette,* Marcus George of the *Arkansas Democrat,* Leon Hatch of the *Associated Press,* and Bill Hughes of the *United Press.*

I was accompanied to the station by Rolla Fitch, John Reed of Judsonia, G.T. Harris of Huntsville and Richard Davis, my press liaison man.

THESE TWO MEN. . .
Political Ad paid for by
Faubus for Governor Committee   4/54

Gov. Cherry at his desk was squeezed between two of his most active supporters, Pulaski County State Senator Ellis Fagan and Cherry campaign manager Leffel Gentry. The aim was to tie all of them to the AP&L, whose highly unpopular rate increase had become an important issue in the campaign.

44

Cherry Ad:

> All Cherry Pickers Invited to Join the Big
> Victory Caravan to Searcy

Faubus Ad:

> To Voters of Arkansas
> There are four main issues: 100% Assessment, Utility
> Rates, Welfare, Feed, Seed and Fertilizer Tax

Monday, August 9 — *Arkansas Democrat*

> Election Day Weather Favorable
> to Record Turnout of Voters
> Cherry Set to Close at Searcy
> Faubus Says He'll Serve All the People;
> Jonesboro Rally to Climax Campaign;
> To Vote at Huntsville

LAST CAMPAIGN DAY; JONESBORO RALLY

On the last campaign day, August 9, I flew to Forrest City for a speech there. I was introduced by Methodist minister Rev. C. W. Stegall to a very good crowd.

Then I flew to Marianna to speak in the county seat of Lee County. My leader there was the respected A.C. (Angus) Mahan assisted by Bliss Yancey. Another who befriended me was a young up-and-coming man in politics, Paul Benham. W.L. "Bill" Ward, Sr., who for years had served his area in both houses of the legislature and was already a legend in his time, had, along with Mr. Mahan, greeted and befriended Alta when she visited the county earlier when I could not be there.

I was introduced by Al Presdige and spoke from the beautiful park in the city square to a large, attentive audience of both black and white listeners. However, I knew the prevailing sentiment in that county was for my opponent because of the considerable number of political leaders in that area who were his allies.

When I finished I walked through the crowd shaking hands. I encountered Mr. Ward who congratulated me on my speech — "One of the finest I've heard," he commented. He did not say how he stood in the race. My guess is he was for Cherry or remained non-committal because of the prevailing sentiment there. I know only that later he and his son, Bill Ward, Jr., became my strong allies and remained loyal supporters until their deaths.

I then encountered a younger man, apparently awaiting my approach, dressed in ordinary work clothes. We shook hands and he said "Do you know me?"

I searched my memory for some fragment of recollection. Perhaps it was his attitude that told me. I said, "I can't call your name but you're from the 'Old 35th.'"

"Yes," he responded, "I'm Archie Jones of Company F."

That company of the 320th Infantry Regiment was the original unit for both of us in the 35th Division of World War II. I had led Archie and other members of the company in training at Camp Rucker, Alabama. Of the 187 men and officers of Company F who crossed the English Channel on July 4, 1944, to enter the battle lines in Normandy, Archie was one of only four who was still with the unit at war's end.

That I had met and renewed acquaintance with my old combat comrade gave me a good feeling. Somehow I felt reassured as I took off for Jonesboro and the last engagement of a political campaign that had been as hectic, if not as serious, as the military campaigns in which we had engaged against the Hitler forces on the continent of Europe.

— — —

CLOSE OF CAMPAIGN AT JONESBORO

My leaders in Craighead County, Joe Martin, Doug Bradley, Attorney Jim McDaniel, Fred Carter, Sr., Maurice Rubenstein, Julian James and others, had arranged for me to speak at the Cole showgrounds on the outskirts of Jonesboro. We could not obtain the traditional site for political gatherings, in front of the Elks Club on the city square, because a rally for Governor Cherry was being held there with Boyd Tackett as speaker. News reports estimated Tackett's crowd at 2,500. When I drove through the area on the way to my rally the meeting had ended and the square was empty.

I found a huge crowd at the park. Hundreds were there from adjoining counties. Mississippi County was well represented, the number including my early leaders, Udell Newsom of Dell, A. O. Hudson, REA Administrator H. C. Knappenberger, G. O. Poetz and J. T. Sudberry, all of Blytheville. Sudberry owned and ran the radio station at Blytheville and gave my candidacy good coverage throughout the campaign. I had also enlisted the aid of two powerful leaders in Osceola, Ben Butler, Sr., and Frank Williams. These and other leaders had joined with Jim Crain's organization giving me a strong force in the large eastern Arkansas County.

My father, J. S. "Little Sam" Faubus, had come to Little Rock and went from there by automobile with others to the closing rally. On the way his party was halted briefly by road construction work. My father asked a highway employee standing by, "Who do you think will win the Governor's race?"

"I don't know," said the unknown worker to his unknown interrogator, as he wiped sweat from his face, "but I hope Faubus wins."

I was introduced by Jonesboro attorney Jim McDaniel, well known as a speaker for his eloquence and power. McDaniel was absolutely fearless as a political orator, sometimes to the point of being rash. When he mounted the flatbed truck which served as a platform that night, bearing in mind the main subject of the runoff primary, his first words to the huge assembly were:

"There sure are a lot of Communists here tonight!"

The crowd responded with cheers.

Following McDaniel's excellent introduction there was a five-minute ovation. When it subsided I began my remarks with some new lines I had written for the occasion during the flight from Marianna. They included these statements:

"I have not come to Jonesboro, the hometown of my opponent, to ask you to turn your back on a friend and neighbor. I have come to ask you to reject his candidacy because he has failed in his stewardship as Governor."

I then compared the situation to an employer engaging an employee. That employee might be a friend, a neighbor, even a brother. No matter his relationship, if the employee could not or did not perform adequately the tasks which were his responsibility, then it would clearly be in the best interests of all for him to be relieved.

"There need be no malice or condemnation," I said, "toward your friend or neighbor in relieving him from the position, but it would be foolish of you to allow him to remain in the position he cannot capably fill."

"Thus it is with your neighbor, whom I now oppose. He has failed in his stewardship and for the best interests of all should be relieved from his office."

I then proceeded to state the case for rejecting his candidacy and the reasons for supporting me. The crowd was enthusiastic. There were so many interruptions that my speech exceeded the allotted radio time, but nearly all stations throughout the state extended the time and carried the speech in full. When I finished the people crowded en masse around the truck to shake my hand. Those who couldn't get to me shook hands with any member of my family or staff who was available.

It was the largest political rally I have ever seen. Many estimated the crowd at 10,000 to 12,000. Sam Harris, the veteran political writer for the *Gazette,* had trouble convincing his editors of the size of the crowd. Finally Sam responded to their doubts with the remark, "No, we couldn't count them; we just measured them by the acre!" He and his editors finally agreed on a crowd estimate of 6,000 which appeared in the *Gazette* news report the next day.

My campaign, from a low point of only a week past, had ended on a definite upswing. My Craighead County leaders were elated with the success of the final rally.

━━0━━0━━0━━0━━

Wednesday, August 11 — *Arkansas Gazette*
FAUBUS LEADS BY NARROW MARGIN,
APPARENTLY WINNER OVER CHERRY
— — —

In the Associated Press tabulations Governor Cherry led narrowly for the first 59 minutes. Then I took the lead which was never relinquished. At 8 P.M. I had a 14,000 vote lead. When tabulations ceased with only 99 precincts unreported, my lead was reported as 4,100.

At one A.M. I issued the following statement.

> *The people of Arkansas have expressed their preference, and I am highly gratified to be acceptable as your choice for governor. I remain humble and shall seek the guidance of my Creator and the support of the good citizenship of our state.*
>
> *The returns are almost complete and my final message is not one of exultation, but that of gratitude to all those who have confidence in my ability and intense desire to provide leadership that will develop our state and improve the economy of our people. I shall not disappoint anyone.*

Judging by the phraseology the statement was prepared for me by Jim Bland.

Wednesday, August 11 — *Arkansas Democrat*

Faubus Wins by 6,988
Surprise Entry Gains Lead Early,
Holds to Slim Margin

George Douthit wrote:
Faubus Made Decisions, Kept Faith
Through Bitter Campaign
Then a headline told of a new development
Remmel May Oppose Faubus in November

RUNOFF PRIMARY NIGHT

On the night of the runoff primary, I took an early lead in the returns which climbed to a substantial margin. We expected a decline in that lead when there were more reports from the urban centers where Cherry was strongest.

However, it soon appeared that undue erosion of my vote was occurring in certain areas. The figures were not in keeping with earlier trends in the same areas and certainly not with the general trend state-wide.

On one of my rare trips through the hotel hallway that night I was accosted by *Democrat* reporter George Douthit. George

was a long-time observer of the political scene with extensive knowledge of politics in most areas of the state.

"Orval," he said, "it looks like they might be getting to you" (meaning "they" were "taking" some of my votes.) "One of the main places," he added, checking his vote figures, "is Hot Springs. There's just one thing to do, and that's get on the line and make some arrangements," he concluded.

I didn't ask George about what "arrangements" to make, and don't recall that he suggested any in particular. Anyway, my political leadership was so sparse in Hot Springs that there was little difficulty in deciding whom to call.

Jim Campbell, a former legislator and Speaker of the House in the 1951 session of the General Assembly, was one of my supporters there. I got him on the line and asked him to represent me at the Garland County courthouse where the returns were being received. He readily agreed. I directed him to make it perfectly obvious that he was there as my representative checking on the returns and recording them. I also asked him, if the opportunity afforded, to say to the right people that if "they" took any more votes from me, "they" had better take enough to win, for if "they" took any more votes from me and I won, "they" would suffer the consequences.

Mr. Campbell then reported to us throughout the night. While I was losing in Garland County there were no further dramatic departures from the general trend. Others of my staff were in touch with Raymond Clinton, another of my Garland County leaders who was well experienced in politics there. C.W. Mowery, Arkansas AFL president, was another adviser from Hot Springs.

Back at my desk in the headquarters facing the public shortly after my encounter with Douthit, another report showed a dramatic drop in my lead. Truman Baker was standing nearby with a happy attitude, his head high and his cigar at a rakish angle. When the report was read he looked at me and I nodded. He knew what it meant and took off immediately.

Ahead of time we had prepared for such a contingency. Telephones had been installed, secretly, we hoped, at a point outside the headquarters building. There experienced hands like Baker, Jim Bland, Orville Cheney and Bob Faust, along with Sid McMath, Henry Woods, Homer Adkins, and others, manned the lines to counties throughout the state to check for returns, and, if it were occurring, to halt, where possible, any undue erosion of our vote.

Whether this action was needed and, if so, whether it was effective, who can say? Anyway, we couldn't, in our judgment, afford to sit by and see a hard-earned victory slip from us by illegal vote changing, without attempting to halt it. From that point my lead declined more slowly.

I make no judgment as to whether the following is correct or incorrect, but I do know that it was widely "talked" in inner political circles following the conclusion of the Senate race, that in Eastern Arkansas "they took" enough votes from Paul Chambers to enable McClellan to win over McMath without a runoff.

I have always honestly believed that I lost a large number of votes in Pulaski County by miscounts in the 1954 campaign. The following is an example.

In one particular box — as reported to me personally by a lady election clerk who served there — following the voting the ballots were divided on an estimated equal basis for counting. The clerk participated in counting one portion of the ballots. In that particular portion I ran nearly even with my opponent, losing by a small margin. In the other half I lost by more than a three-to-one margin. The clerk who had helped to count the half where I ran nearly even, then tied those ballots in a bundle before placing them in the ballot box. The clerk who helped count the other half then untied the bundle and thoroughly mixed all the ballots together before the box was sealed.

0━━0━━0━━0━━0

THE WINNER
By Graham, Ark. Gazette   8/11/54

By deadline time for the Gazette cartoonist in the early morning hours after the runoff primary, the results did not clearly indicate the winner. Graham handled it in this unique way.

━o━o━o━o

WHEN VICTORY WAS ASSURED

In the early morning hours of August 11 shortly before dawn, when we were certain that victory had been won, Jim Bland arranged a breakfast for all staff members and workers who had watched with us through the night. After a prayer of thanksgiving, and for help and guidance in the future, we dined on scrambled eggs, ham and biscuits. A new face was present, Raymond Rebsamen, prominent businessman of Little Rock. Rebsamen was an old friend and associate of Bland from the days when they were leading figures in the Carl Bailey administration. A scrutiny of our campaign finances the next day revealed an $8,000 deficit. Mr. Rebsamen loaned us the money to meet the unpaid bills. Shortly thereafter sufficient funds were collected and I gave Mr. Bland a check with which to repay Rebsamen.

The final, certified election results days later were:

For Governor: Orval E. Faubus, 191,328; Francis Cherry, 184,509
For State Treasurer: Vance Clayton, 200,224; Sam Jones, 151,674

A news story said,

AP returns showed that Orval Faubus, 44, Huntsville publisher, had defeated Governor Cherry's bid for a second term in a tradition-shattering, vote-getting demonstration.

A turnout of 70% of the eligible voters in the runoff was unusually high

Remmel, now receiving great encouragement to run for Governor, said "If I get in, I'm in to win."

THE RULE HE FAILED TO FOLLOW
By Kennedy, Ark. Democrat   8/11/54

After the runoff primary, Gov. Cherry read an old political rule which the cartoonist indicates he failed to follow.

━o━o━o━o

ARKANSAS BUZZES WITH TALK
OF FAUBUS' UPSET OF CHERRY

This was the headline of a story in the *Memphis Commercial Appeal* of August 12, evidently written by Ken Johnson, the paper's representative in Little Rock.

The story said "Arkansas was buzzing with talk Wednesday as to the 'why' of Governor Francis Cherry's defeat at the hands of Orval Faubus. . ."

"In Little Rock and other communities," the story read, "building corridors and street corners were cluttered with persons asking what had happened to upset the state's tradition of giving an incumbent a second term in office."

"Each had his own version," the story said, "but to newsmen who covered the campaigns of both candidates. ., there appeared to be an ever-sharpening line-up between rural and city voters, in the closing days of the campaign."

"But," the story continued, "that was merely one aspect of the race. The Commonwealth College issue. . clearly backfired on the Governor."

The story then went on to list the alleged mistakes of Governor Cherry — 100 per cent tax assessment, utility rate increases, the welfare policies especially the "dead heads" statement and the aloof attitude of the highway department.

These, except for the last mentioned, I had all along contended were the main issues of the campaign.

The story concluded that "personalities undoubtedly played a part in the campaign" and said that I "developed a surprising flair for old time oratory and crowd-mingling that many voters liked."

"One man at a Forrest City rally commented on that after Mr. Faubus made a speech there to a small gathering last week," the story related, and then quoted an unidentified voter.

"Well, I don't know what's the real story on that Commonwealth College business, but he sure can make a speech."

LARGE CONTRIBUTIONS DECLINED AFTER VICTORY

As soon as our primary victory appeared assured I had a meeting with my principal campaign assistants.

"Now that we have won," I told them, "certain interests will be running to us with money. Do not take any of it," I instructed them, "for we want to remain free to make our own decisions as to policies and appointments. We won't be considered free to set our own course if we are hampered by large contributions from any source."

Roy Ritter recalls clearly the meeting and the instructions. He related to me that on the day following the meeting he was contacted by the representative of a large corporation which had opposed my candidacy and told, "I have a contribution of $78,000 to deliver to you now to help take care of your campaign deficit and other expenses."

"You're too late," Ritter told the agent. "The campaign is over and we have already arranged to take care of our deficit."

NOTHING LIKE A CAREFREE VACATION, By Kennedy, Ark. Democrat, 8/18/54

In such a carefree vacation, the problems kept intruding.

48

CHAPTER 4
THE GENERAL ELECTION, THIRD CAMPAIGN
OF THE YEAR. PREPARATION FOR OFFICE

MY FAVORITE HEADLINE

Following my primary runoff victory, Editor Brad Govan of the Melbourne weekly newspaper, taking his cue from the series of ads headed, "Who is this Man Faubus?" placed my picture on the front page and headlined:
"THIS IS THE MAN FAUBUS!"

CHECKED OUT AS POSTMASTER

On August 15, I was succeeded as Postmaster at Huntsville by a long time personal friend and former Republican County official, Taylor Hubbard of Huntsville. Inspector William Odell of Ft. Smith supervised the changeover. It was probably the only time in the history of America that a postmaster was checked out of a post office of the Second Class to become governor of his state.

CAMPAIGN STAFF DISBANDS; I GO ON VACATION

On August 14, heeding the advice of friends in Little Rock to get out of the way and "let things cool off," we closed the headquarters, and everyone took time to look after business or take a vacation. Bob Faust, a resident of the Capital City, was designated to look after our interests. In the face of rumors of vote-changing and other difficulties, he obtained the services of attorney Leon Catlett to represent me in any legal matters concerning the election.

After the trip to Huntsville to be checked out as postmaster I then with members of my family, using a car loaned by Little Rock insurance executive W. L. "Bill" Darby, drove westward out of the state into Oklahoma. We spent a few days at Pittsburg near McAlister visiting my aunt, Mrs. Ada Faubus McChristian, her husband, L. A. "Loddie" McChristian, a section foreman for the Frisco railroad and a strong union advocate, and their son, Tom Oral McChristian, a boyhood playmate.

INTERESTING ABOUT GOVERNOR CHERRY

Leaving there after a stay of about four days we headed at a leisurely pace for Colorado. One evening we drove into a fair-sized city which I noted was El Reno, Oklahoma, and I recalled that it was Governor Cherry's home town.

Proceeding through the town to the western outskirts we sought rooms for the night at the Phillips Motel. The operator was from Searcy County, Arkansas, and said he left there some twenty years or more ago.

As he was showing us to our quarters I asked, "Do you know the Cherry family?"

"Yes," he replied, and then related that he formerly saw them often but encountered them only occasionally since they moved downtown to a hotel. Then after a pause he added, "Old rock-ribbed Republican family."

I recalled without comment that during the campaign I had heard a number of times that Governor Cherry was formerly a Republican but dismissed the reports as irrelevant rumors. (Now, in these times of party-switching 25 years after the campaign, this fact seems relatively unimportant. But it then had much significance as many old-line Democrats would be most reluctant to vote for any candidate unless he had been long and strong in the Democratic faith.)

Without further prompting the motel owner continued. "There were three boys," he related. "Two left, one remained here. A few years ago the one who remained ran for the State Senate on the Republican ticket. It looked for a time like he would win," reported the motel owner. "Then he jumped all over his opponent, condemning him strongly. It reacted against him and he lost," he said. His last expression caused me to recall the recent runoff primary in Arkansas.

"One son went to Texas," he continued, "the other to Arkansas. The one who went to Arkansas ran for Governor two years ago as a Democrat, and got elected. You know," he added, "you can't get anywhere in politics in Arkansas unless you're a Democrat."

Then my informant concluded, "Some fellow beat him (Cherry) this last time."

Throughout the discourse I remained noncommittal, never revealing my identity. My name on the motel register, even if noted by the owner, probably meant nothing to him. We departed the next morning without seeing him. I don't know if our host ever realized that he was talking to the man who "beat him this last time" and that he was a guest at his motel.

From there we drove to northern New Mexico, passing through the beautiful mountain country and made our way north to Denver, Colorado. There we visited my aunt, Mrs. Minnie Joslin Johnson, her husband, J. S. "Jess" Johnson, and members of their family. We planned to extend our vacation but back in Arkansas Faust and Catlett had difficulty in getting the election returns certified. The Remmel boom, encouraged by disappointed Cherry pickers and those who placed some credence in the charges of subversion against me, was growing. I had to return home to protect my hard-won nomination and take measures to assure victory in the general election.

REMMEL CHANGES PLANS; TO RUN FOR GOVERNOR
INSTEAD OF CONGRESS

High interest continued in the political field following my upset primary victory. Ordinarily state political decisions for the year would have been settled following the primary results but not this time.

Although Cherry had carried Pulaski County by an overwhelming margin, there were highly publicized complaints about alleged election irregularities by disappointed Cherry-pickers. The Pulaski County Democratic Central Committee established an open door policy for all who wished to be heard. This had a settling effect on the complainers since they soon learned that I would more than likely be the gainer from any recounts or vote checks in the county.

As to the Governor, a headline read, "Cherry Leaves State; Keeps Plans Silent." Cherry supporters were urging the Governor to enter the field as an independent candidate and slated a rally for August 26 to drum up support.

In the face of these developments GOP Mayor Pratt Remmel, at the urging of friends and disillusioned Cherry supporters, changed his plans to seek the Fifth District

AFTER THE PRIMARIES, ORVAL FAUBUS RETURNED TO HIS BOYHOOD HOME.

Congressional seat held by Democrat Brooks Hays, and became the Republican nominee for governor.

On August 19 the Pulaski County GOP backed Remmel for governor or Congress. The next day the State Democratic Central Committee certified me as the official party nominee and Remmel said he would sound out Governor Cherry before reaching a decision on his political plans.

On the 22nd the Draft Cherry promoters stated their hope to organize a new party and Little Rock Jaycees at a meeting addressed by Remmel, encouraged him by shouting "our next Governor!"

On August 28 the state GOP confirmed Remmel as its choice for governor. The Mayor accepted the role as the Republican candidate for chief executive, announced the next day that a determined bid would be made and my third political race of the year had begun.

In other developments Senator Max Howell asked prompt action to investigate the state's utility laws and called for the elimination of rate increases under bond without a public hearing. The school people said 12.5 million more in school funds was needed, and Arkansas Education Association field director Forrest Rozzell was elected secretary of the organization to succeed Hoyt Pyle. The state's general revenues dipped $425,000 for July and August and employment hit the lowest mark since 1950.

THE CHERRY-FAUBUS CONTROVERSY

Letters to the People's Column of the *Arkansas Gazette* on the Cherry-Faubus battle in the runoff were said to be the greatest outpouring on any subject ever to occur. The *Gazette* published a number of the letters each day. On August 24 with the letters still pouring in the paper announced that it would discontinue their publication and the column would be devoted to other subjects.

At Walnut Ridge Jim Bland wrote an editorial for his newspaper, *The Times-Dispatch,* on "Who Is This Man Faubus." It was republished in the *Gazette* and other papers and helped to clear the air to some extent.

RETURN TO BOYHOOD HOME

After the primaries were over a request came for an interview by George Harmon, a reporter for the Memphis *Commercial Appeal.* He went to Huntsville and other points in Madison County to interview my long time friends and acquaintances, then asked to accompany me back to my boyhood home. The adjacent picture was snapped as I sat on a stone beside the spring which had been the family source of water before my father dug a well beside the house. In the background is the crude three-room dwelling made of rough sawmill lumber where I lived from about the age of one to 16. The room with the vacant window was the kitchen — the last addition to the residence. I was born in a pioneer log house about a mile distant across a valley to the west on a farm known as the Carroll Place. The photo showed I was lean from the rigors of the campaign. The necktie was loosened for the half-mile walk up the mountainside from the county road in the summer heat. Harmon's story appeared in the *Commercial Appeal* Sunday, August 22, 1954.

SOME ROUGH TIMES IN LITTLE ROCK

After my return from vacation, we moved into a modest dwelling just east of the State Hospital, courtesy of my friend, John R. Thompson. From there I sometimes walked alone across the Hospital grounds to War Memorial Stadium to attend football games.

While anyone who gets enough votes to be elected governor has many friends and supporters, there remained considerable bitterness and opposition in the capital city. My strength was greatest in the rural areas. I lost Pulaski County in the runoff to Gov. Cherry by 12,800 votes, and lost it in the general election to GOP Remmel by nearly 3,000. I also lost many of the major cities in the general election, such as Hot Springs, Ft. Smith and Fayetteville. I knew the only way to correct this disapproval was by the wisest selection possible of assistants, followed by good, sound administrative procedures by all concerned. This would take time. In the meantime the difficulties must be borne while pursuing a policy of making friends and building confidence in my new administration.

One unpleasant incident I recall clearly.

The Jaycees of Arkansas sponsored a Miss Hospitality Contest with entrants of charming young ladies throughout the state. The winner of the competition was scheduled to be crowned at War Memorial Stadium in Little Rock during the halftime intermission at a football game. I was invited to crown the winner, the new Miss Hospitality for Arkansas.

I had a strong feeling of what the reaction would be to my appearance on the field from a basically Little Rock audience in which the upper crust of business and the professions would be dominant. I wanted very much to decline the invitation, but how do you reject such a request from a group of hardworking young businessmen promoting a worthwhile undertaking? Also the charming young contestants from throughout the state had the right to expect the governor-elect to be present if he were invited.

I remember saying to myself, "All right! You asked for the position. You must have the guts to take the bad with the good. So go on out and do it!"

I accepted the invitation to appear and crown the new Miss Hospitality. During the ceremony other contestants were spotted at other points across the field. Appearing with me was President John Tyler Caldwell of the University of Arkansas and some Jaycee officials.

Announcements of other personalities and events were received with mild and courteous applause. However, when my name was announced, the stadium re-echoed with boos. The volume of disapproval seemed to me about three times greater than the applause. I noticed that Caldwell reddened with embarrassment. Miss Hospitality seemed puzzled. I proceeded with my part of the duties as if everything were normal, and then marched across the field back to my box on the sidelines. I had been seasoned for the unpleasantness of the occasion by my experiences in the war and by the last two campaigns.

I noted, without my awareness becoming apparent, that acquaintances nearby were visibly chastened by the unfriendly reception to me. Seated just to the left of my box were Jack East, Sr. and his son Jack East, Jr., the former an insurance executive at Little Rock, the latter a member of the legislature from Pulaski County. They appeared downcast and embarrassed. I evaluated their attitude as sympathetic toward me for having to endure the clear disapproval of the crowd. Although I never said anything to them then or later about the incident or their attitude, I acquired a warm feeling toward them which I still carry to this day.

I faced similar situations after that, but as the months went by the boos of disapproval gradually declined until they became insignificant or disappeared altogether.

About a year later I had occasion to appear on the same football field in a similar situation, again with President Caldwell. Again when I was presented the calls of disapproval arose, but this time the volume was only about a third of what it had been before.

"Governor," said Caldwell, looking at me with his ever present, friendly smile, "it's getting better!"

"Yes," I replied smiling more easily myself than before, and we marched off the field together.

INTERESTED ONLOOKER
By Kennedy, Ark. Democrat   9/1/54

It had been reported on at least four occasions that Pratt Remmel might run for Congress against Brooks Hays. Now an apparently better opportunity had opened up for the Republican Mayor to seek a major state office.

The day following his nomination for Governor, Remmel was out in the state getting acquainted and seeking votes. He had earlier begun county visits in the Fifth Congressional District.

Through circumstances I had done a great favor for Congressman Brooks Hays. Instead of a hard race for re-election against the popular mayor of Little Rock, he got by without opposition. However, I received no direct contact from Hays or his close advisers with offers of support. I lost Pulaski County to Remmel, the area which constituted the bulk of the voting strength in Hays' congressional district.

THREATS OF AN INDEPENDENT CANDIDATE

On September 2 the opposition floated a trial balloon to test the interest in an Independent candidate when Joe Cash hinted he would run as an Independent.

By that time I was back in the state and already working. News pictures showed me with Harlan J. Perryman, Salem, the Fulton County Democratic nominee for representative, and another showed Jim Bland, Mrs. Patsy Ellis and me as we opened an office in the Union Life Insurance Company building.

We now began to round up as many of those who opposed me as possible, company president Elmo Walker and most of the Union Life personnel being among the first to be brought into the Faubus camp. In this particular instance Mack Sturgis, a leading salesman for the company and one of my early supporters, was a good liaison man. I had earlier firmed up my relations with the Old Line Insurance Company when I accepted Company President W. L. "Bill" Darby's loan of a car for my vacation trip. In the meantime I had rejected the offer of a new Cadillac automobile as a gift. These alliances and others of similar nature were not all-important vote wise but they removed from the opposition important sources of financing and leadership.

I announced that Perry County Judge Carl Adams would be my main assistant in arrangements for the forthcoming Democratic State Convention. Then Carl was provided with much expert help from individuals like former governors Homer Adkins and Sid McMath, the experienced party officials as Harvey G. Combs, others like Henry Woods, Edwin Dunaway, Truman Baker, Fred Pickens, Joe Martin and still others including some prominent labor leaders.

I walked unannounced into the office of W. R. "Witt" Stephens for a personal conference, just as he had come unannounced to my room in the Marion Hotel some time before the campaign began. There was one great difference in the two conferences. He came to see me on an unfriendly mission; I went to see him to say that bygones were bygones; that he could be helpful to me and that I wanted his help. Witt responded affirmatively. I suspect that for him it was an entree with a new administration at less cost than at any time since he began to play a major role in state politics. As for me I had learned to like the big, slouchy-appearing financial wizard and desired his friendship.

POLITICAL WAGERS

Sometime after the runoff primary Truman Baker and I were seated in the Marion Hotel coffee shop. The affable and friendly Ben Shelley came by and after greetings had been exchanged, said to Mr. Baker, "Truman, you might as well come and get that money."

They invited me to accompany them to Shelley's office. There Mr. Shelley opened the safe and began handing to Truman several bundles of money. The bundles were the stakes in wagers made on the outcome of the election.

"My," I said to Truman, "you've sure got a lot of guts" to bet like that on the uncertain outcome.

"Well, you know how it is," he replied with evident great satisfaction. "They were waving that three-to-one money around, and I just couldn't turn it down."

I don't know how much Truman won — I didn't inquire — but it looked like a considerable sum.

Another, I learned later, who wagered extensively on the race was _____ Jackson, a fruit stand operator at Springdale. He covered all bets in the Springdale-Fayetteville area and then, so I was informed, covered the money that was sent from Little Rock, Hot Springs and Texarkana. Jackson remained noncommittal on any total amount or the odds but friends estimated he won from $30,000 to $50,000 on the outcome of the race. Possibly some of the wagers were made for other people.

FORD ASKS SCHOOLS TO CONTINUE SEGREGATION

Arch Ford, Arkansas Commissioner of Education, after meeting with Cherry's State Board of Education, in a statement on September 4 directed to 14 school districts with petitions to integrate, said: "There is a state law against integration . . . The State Board suggests local boards comply with state law in the absence of any decree from the U.S. Court."

DROUGHT CONTINUES

Conditions due to the drought continued to worsen in Arkansas. On September 4 I urged the federal government to dip into its stockpiles of surplus food and other items for outright grants to drought sufferers and to also establish work programs for the needy.

I'LL HOLD YOUR COATS
By Graham, Ark. Gazette   9/4/54

In a speech to a Little Rock civic club on Sept. 2, Joe Cash, Governor Cherry's State Labor Commissioner, said he was considering a race for Governor as an Independent candidate. He announced that 17 rooms in the Capitol Hotel had already been rented for his use as a headquarters and that he would make his decision known in two weeks. Remmel, who would profit from the contest, was ready to hold our coats.

GEORGE LISTS TEN "PROMISES"

Marcus George in his September 5 column, "Backstage at the Capitol," listed ten promises which he wrote that I had made, at least by implication. Contrary to George's inference, few, if any, were flat commitments. Some were problems which I discussed stating my viewpoint on them:
1. Repeal (Cherry-sponsored) Fiscal Code
2. Equalize property assessments with "standardized" values
3. Stop reductions in welfare checks whenever welfare recipients helped themselves
4. Stop gambling in Hot Springs
5. Hire only native Arkansans for state jobs
6. Exempt feed, seed and fertilizer from sales tax
7. Improve highways leading into Little Rock
8. Solve school segregation problems on local level
9. Get money to publicize the state
10. Reduce utility rates.

Number 4 was accomplished belatedly. Number 5 applied to residents of Arkansas and was not restricted to natives. It was accomplished with the exceptions that Rockefeller and the AIDC employed two out-of-state residents for the Industrial

program, and trained leadership was brought in for the Children's Colony. Number 8 was being followed until the Federal Courts and the Federal Army took over. With these three modifications, all promises were fully accomplished — and much more — before I left office.

FAUBUS IN WASHINGTON ON DROUGHT PROBLEM

I was joined on September 9 in Washington by Senator McClellan, Congressman Jim Trimble, State Senator Roy Riales of Mena, Roy Ritter and John Tyson, poultry growers of Springdale, and Kenneth S. Bates, Assistant Director, Agricultural Extension Service of the University of Arkansas, in conferences on the drought situation. I had taken my plea personally to the proper federal officials for the drought relief so desperately needed by many Arkansas farmers.

INTEGRATION PROBLEM

On the developing integration front, a plea to halt integration in the Washington, D.C. schools was turned down by a federal court.

In Little Rock a Negro group was assured by School Superintendent Virgil Blossom that the Little Rock schools would be integrated.

POLITICAL TUG-OF-WAR UNDERWAY
By Kennedy, Ark. Democrat   9/12/54

Except possibly for the year 1930, Arkansas suffered the worst drought in history in the summer of 1954. A prolonged heat wave burned pastures to a crisp and little grain or hay was produced. On the date of this cartoon, even before winter had set in when there should have been green pastures and abundant feed, some farmers could not keep their herds or work animals from starvation. I vividly recall a ten-day period during the primary campaign when the temperature each day ranged from 101 to 111 degrees.

From my farm background and campaign travels over the state I was well aware of the serious plight of the farmers. However, to be better informed I attended some farm meetings called to discuss their situation, one at Dardanelle to which I was invited by the late Fred Smith of that city. Then I hurried off to Washington taking with me some farm experts as advisers to intercede with the national administration for drought relief for the stricken farmers.

My Republican opponent, Pratt Remmel of Little Rock, perhaps because of his city background, was slower to realize the seriousness of the situation. However, he soon joined in the request for aid but because of my previously well-publicized trip to the Capitol his plea had a "me, too" ring. Still, he maintained that as a Republican he could more readily secure help from a national Republican administration than could a Democrat.

But that wasn't the way President Eisenhower worked. When not misled by his palace guard, he apparently made decisions on merit rather than pure political considerations. Drought relief was forthcoming for the state soon after the date of the cartoon.

Pratt and I both asked for the help because it was right, both aware, no doubt, that it was also good politics.

The President granted the relief for the same reason, perhaps equally aware of its political implications. Many farmers were saved from ruin.

SMITH RE-INSTATED

On September 17 Gene Smith was restored to his position as aide to Little Rock Police Chief Potts. He won re-instatement on a technicality and not on the facts of the case.

DROUGHT STATEWIDE

On September 18 Arkansas County became the 75th to lodge a plea for drought aid.

SELECTION FOR PARTY POSTS

On September 19 I made known my choices for the major positions for the State Democratic Convention: Mark Woolsey, attorney of Ozark, for Temporary Chairman and Keynote speaker, and Congressman Wilbur Mills for Permanent Chairman. For officials of the State Central Committee I selected Tom Harper, attorney of Ft. Smith, as Chairman; Mrs. Helen Riddick Wilson of Little Rock, Vice-Chairman; and Frank Robbins, publisher of Conway, Secretary.

Faubus to get unified support

Sen. McClellan and Gov. Cherry were scheduled to speak to the State Democratic Convention on Thursday afternoon. Sen. Fulbright and I would speak Friday afternoon, Sept. 20.

Former governors Adkins and McMath were on hand for the activities. Former Gov. Ben Laney stated in a letter that he would support the party nominees.

With work and organization things began falling into place to repel the GOP threat.

CHARLES "RIP" SMITH CHOSEN SPEAKER

Charles "Rip" Smith of West Memphis had obtained enough pledges to become Speaker of the House of Representatives.

Smith was a member of the Crittenden County political organization, then all-powerful in the county, headed by Sheriff Cecil Goodwin, W. F. "Bill" Ingram and Atty. James O. Hale. Goodwin was properly courteous when I visited the courthouse

during the primary campaign, but made no bones about how he stood. I was almost made to feel unwelcome. I noted that other officials and state and county employees were concerned to be seen talking with me. On meeting Ingram in West Memphis he was affable and friendly but told me I would get about 200 votes in the county.

I stopped to visit with Marvin Bird, a banker and fine man at Earle. He was friendly but asked about the leaders at Marion and West Memphis. I replied they were not for me. Whereupon he informed me that he would go along with them.

Two of my supporters were Cy Bond, Sr., an engineer and former county judge who had broken with the organization, and Royce Upshaw, postmaster at Turrell, a small settlement in the northern part of the county. There was no way to dent the strength of the political machine. My actual vote was 281 in the first primary. I did much better in the runoff when I had the support of a newly-organized group called the Good Government Committee, but still lost 3 to 1 — 3,288 to 1,108.

When Smith secured the pledges for Speaker, his fellow legislators fully expected Cherry to win a second term. It was traditional for the Governor to choose the Speaker, or at least for the Speaker to have his blessing. In the case of Governor Cherry, Smith fully qualified. He was one of Cherry's leaders in the House and a member of the Crittenden County political group that gave the Governor strong support.

Now the situation was drastically changed. There would be a new governor, the man "Rip" and his friends had strongly opposed, unless the Republican candidate should win which was not expected by the politicians in the state. This posed a new and unexpected problem.

"Rip" wanted very badly to be Speaker and came to see me. For some time we had been on a friendly basis personally, and for an even longer period Ingram and I had been personal friends. I told Smith that all I wanted from the Speaker was fair treatment, that he not be a member of a combine to oppose me politically and that he not use the position to block administration legislation.

"Rip" said that was fair and agreed to those terms. Whereupon I passed the word that he was acceptable to me and the matter was settled.

"Rip" Smith faithfully and honorably kept the agreement.

FACTION OPPOSES FAUBUS

A large ad ran in the September 22 issue of the *Democrat* signed by ten individuals, prominent citizens of Little Rock but none of them well known statewide. It was headed: "Democrats! This is a Call to Battle." The text called on delegates to block my nomination at the State Democratic Convention. If such a move failed, the ad suggested the support of the Republican nominee for Governor as an alternative.

Some Little Rock residents were so upset by the outcome of the Democratic runoff primary that they refused to accept the results. They urged publicly that the returns not be certified, although how certification was to be avoided was never specifically spelled out.

Feeling was so intense in Little Rock that close friends urged me and leading members of my campaign staff to leave town until things settled down. Citizens in my home county, where I had almost unanimous support, wanted to stage a giant homecoming at Huntsville in my honor but even this was discouraged and the idea was given up.

One group, thinking I was far too "leftwing" because of my background and the Commonwealth College affair, organized committees, wrote letters to newspapers, made speeches, appeared on TV and in every way possible opposed my candidacy. There were widespread rumors that I would never be permitted to qualify for the office even if elected.

After a time things began to quiet down. My hometown people, former associates, war buddies and others spent hours telling others about my family background, my boyhood, my role as a private citizen and as a public figure.

The Democratic State Convention had a unifying effect. All state and most national office holders in Arkansas attended. I had the unqualified support of my own Third District Congressman, J. W. "Jim" Trimble; Congressman Wilbur Mills took the role of Permanent Convention Chairman; both U.S. Senators, McClellan and Fulbright, were featured prominently as speakers; and Congressman Oren Harris gave both organizational advice and public support to my candidacy in his area.

Mrs. Ewilda Robinson, widow of former U.S. Senator Joe T. Robinson, the Democratic candidate for Vice-President in 1928, attended the convention for the first time in 17 years.

THEY WENT THATAWAY
By Kennedy, Ark. Democrat   9/24/54

Only in some urban areas were the extremist dissenters able to muster a substantial following against me and for the Republican candidate. Finally, the results were as portrayed by the cartoonist.

However, a solid Democratic front was still far from accomplished in Pulaski, Jefferson, Garland, Sebastian and Arkansas Counties.

0◄━0◄━0◄━━0◄━━0◄━0◄◄

DEMOCRATS OPEN DOOR TO NEGROES

September 25, 1954

At my recommendation the convention approved six additional members to the State Democratic Central Committee. The resolution of authorization made no mention of race but it was clearly understood that the six new members were to be blacks, one from each of the six congressional districts. It was the first time in the history of the state that black voters were made a part of the state Democratic policy making organization.

Later, in consultation with party leaders I made the selections. The six new members were: Pickens W. Black, a wealthy planter of Blackville (Jackson County); A. J. Pearson, Fort Smith; W. C. Mackey, Texarkana; all named soon after the convention.

The other three were named by the Central Committee in June, 1955, and were: Coy Franklin, Superintendent of Birdsong Negro Schools in Mississippi County; Fred W. Martin, a prominent political leader and later a city official of Hot Springs; and J. R. Booker, a prominent and respected attorney of Little Rock.

Two welcome headlines of September 30 were:

State welcomes first general rain since May 26

Cash not candidate for Governor; withholds endorsement

INTEGRATION MOVE ENDS IN DELAWARE

On September 21 an integration row closed two schools in Delaware. On October 1, a new school board, replacing one thrown out by the voters, rescinded the previous decision to integrate the schools and kept them segregated.

POPULATION LOSS HURTS, SAYS FAUBUS

Arkansas Democrat

Loss of population in Arkansas was deplored by Orval E. Faubus, Democratic nominee for Governor, in an address before the Conway Kiwanis Club yesterday.

Mr. Faubus said enough Arkansans are living in California to pay sufficient taxes to add 100 miles of hard-surfaced roads a year to the state system if they were back here, employed, and paying gasoline taxes and motor vehicle fees.

FAUBUS HEADS 35TH DIVISION ASSOCIATION

I was elected President of the 35th Division Association on October 2 at the annual reunion in Kansas City. I had progressed from fifth vice-president. Former President Harry S. Truman and I were the principals in the reunion parade and a number of other functions.

FAUBUS HEADS WAR BUDDIES; TRUMAN HAPPY

"Orval Faubus is a good man and will make a good governor," said Harry S. Truman. "I have known him for many years."

GOP TO TIP HAT AND TILL TO REMMEL

The GOP National Committee will buy radio and TV time in Arkansas during the campaign this fall for the first time in memory of anybody around here. — Washington, D.C. news story.

NATIONAL BATTLEGROUND IN OUR OWN BACKYARD

The projected construction of a giant steam plant near West Memphis by Dixon-Yates had become a boiling national issue. From Washington, D.C., came statement after statement on the matter from members of Congress, the President's Cabinet, leaders of both political parties and private power and public power advocates.

The national battle which centered over the state was between those who favored power development by privately owned utilities, led by the Republicans and conservatives, and those who favored publicly financed and owned power generation, led by the Democrats and liberals.

In Arkansas both Republicans and Democrats, conservatives and liberals, joined in supporting the Dixon-Yates project for two reasons. The plant construction would give a badly needed boost to the Arkansas economy and its completion would assure an adequate supply of electric power for the state's economic growth.

NO STATE BUDGET INCREASES; INTEGRATION PROTESTS IN WASHINGTON; DIXON-YATES POSTPONED

Because of limited state finances I urged the Legislative Council to limit budget requests of the various state agencies to amounts that could be met with available funds. This was bad news to many agencies which badly needed increases.

In Washington, D.C. demonstrations, mass meetings and school boycotts by pupils and parents protested the integration of the district schools.

The Washington politicians put off the controversy of the Dixon-Yates power plant at West Memphis until after the elections.

HIGH PERCENTAGE OF VOTERS IN MADISON COUNTY

In Madison County 6,036 poll taxes were paid thus qualifying a higher percentage of the residents to vote than any other county in the state.

For some reason attorney Robert R. Cress of Huntsville withdrew as the Democratic nominee for representative. The county Democratic committee named Roy Pettit of Delaney to make the race. A second Democratic nominee, Floyd Calico of Drakes Creek for county clerk, withdrew to continue as a teacher in the public schools. Charles Whorton Jr. of Huntsville replaced him on the ticket.

AP&L RATE INCREASE

Under the laws then on the statute books in Arkansas a utility could put a rate increase into effect by posting bond and publishing the new rates. Hearings on the matter would be held later.

The Arkansas Power & Light Company had acted under the existing law and put a substantial rate increase into effect in 1954, with the bills reaching the customers in the midst of the political campaign.

The rate increase became an important issue. I told the people that if elected I would recommend legislation to require hearings before the Public Service Commission, the agency which governed such matters, before any utility rate increase could become effective. The people responded by bringing their bills to my meetings for me to use as evidence, some holding them up in the audience while I was speaking.

The Power Company was hit with a number of verbal denunciations and protests.

One of its principal critics was a prominent banker in Little Rock, Arthur E. McLean, who had supported Governor Cherry in the primary campaigns.

My Republican opponent, related by marriage to a former AP&L official, was in danger of becoming known as the Power Company candidate. Even more credence was lent to the impression by the fact that during the Democratic primaries not a single prominent Power Company official was even friendly to my candidacy, and most, if not all, were solidly for Governor Cherry.

To avoid this growing danger to his candidacy, Remmel in early October made a startling political announcement. If elected, he said, he would appoint Mr. McLean, the rate increase critic to the Public Service Commission, the agency which would approve or disapprove the company's higher rates then being collected.

MAYBE THIS JUST ISN'T MY YEAR
By Graham, Ark. Gazette   10/8/54

Thus the cartoon with the Power Company portrayed as Reddy Kilowatt reading the latest unpleasant news of Remmel's announcement.

My recommendation to prohibit rate increases before hearings proved so popular that it was not necessary for me to present legislation on the matter. Senator Max Howell of Little Rock had already made known his dissatisfaction with the old method. Senator Clifton "Deacon" Wade of Fayetteville with others drew the legislation and introduced it early in the session of the General Assembly. I had merely to sign the bill into law upon its passage.

Thus the ill-fated AP&L rate increase of 1954 was the last to go into effect for a period of about 20 years, prior to a full and complete hearing.

The Power Company's problems at the time included the "Rate Increase Request" which was still not approved; "Stietenroth Defection" — Stietenroth, a high official of Mississippi Power and Light Company, resigned his position and issued critical statements of the power company's methods; "Speck Denunciation" — Jefferson W. Speck, the GOP nominee for Governor in both 1950 and 1952 denounced the rate increase; AP&L became involved in the terrific controversy over the Dixon-Yates Company plan to build a giant generating plant in Arkansas; the AP&L rate increase became an issue in the "Arkansas Primaries" and the Power Company's candidate lost; and "Polesitters" were picketing and interfering with the company's construction program. Then came the Remmel statement about McLean.

LITES HEADS DEMOCRATS-FOR-REMMEL

At a Pine Bluff meeting Offie Lites, Jr., was elected chairman of a Democrats-for-Remmel group with an estimated 200 present. Roland Remmel, speaking for his brother, the Republican nominee, said "Pratt owns one share of AP&L stock" and that his wife owned only non-voting stock in the company. T. P. Davis and Early Taylor took issue with Cecil Albright who had said he would seek to bar the Democratic bolters from future party primaries.

INDEPENDENT SUPPORTERS 'OUTLAWED' FROM DEMOCRATIC PRIMARY

An opinion from the Attorney General's office issued by Assistant Attorney General Claude Carpenter, Jr., said that those who supported Independents against the regular Democratic nominees were barred by party rules from participating in the Democratic Primary. The ruling also stated that a Democratic Committeeman who participated in the Independent movement would forfeit his position. The rules were clear. The opinion was correct. But the rules were seldom observed.

No Republican had been elected Governor of Arkansas since Reconstruction days, a period of 82 years. The Democrats were unalarmed and complacent. However, with the backing of his own party and many defecting Democrats it became apparent that Pratt Remmel would make a strong bid for the office.

TO RUN OR NOT TO RUN?
By Kennedy, Ark. Democrat   10/13/54

The question that arose in my camp was whether to ignore Remmel's efforts and work quietly, or to openly recognize the threat and mount a strong campaign. The situation gave rise to this cartoon, which was whether "to run or not to run?" against "Remmel's chances" in the November general election.

We worked quietly, mostly by telephone, with me making public appearances where requested. We opened no headquarters, hired no staff, printed no literature and ran only a limited advertising campaign.

FAUBUS HITS REPUBLICAN LEADERSHIP

In my remarks critical of Republicans I carefully distinguished between Republican leaders and the Republican rank and file. In Arkansas for years the leadership came allegedly from the Country Club set of Little Rock, which had little in common with rank and file party members. Besides, I knew that hundreds of Republicans in Madison County and Northwest Arkansas would vote for me in the general election.

This headline came from my remarks at Hot Springs the night of October 13th at a Democratic fund-raising event. County Tax Collector Ray Owen was master of ceremonies and I was introduced by Prosecuting Attorney-nominee H. A. Tucker.

That same day an Independent candidate had filed for Circuit Judge in Garland County against the Democratic nominee, C. Floyd Huff. As a result all the funds from the dinner were used locally with none reaching the State Democratic Headquarters in Little Rock.

The following night I spoke to an overflow crowd in Forrest City. At that time General Motors officials, prominent in the Eisenhower administration, were much in the news. I made the remark that the National Republican leaders were getting "general welfare mixed up with General Motors."

NO MORE REPUBLICANS NOMINATED

The deadline of October 4 for filing of Republican and Independent candidates passed without any further entries. It was the first time in many years that the GOP failed to file a candidate for any state office other than Governor, or for a congressional seat. The intent was clear. Stir up as few Democrats as possible and put all resources into the GOP effort, with the help of dissident Democrats, to elect Pratt Remmel.

INVESTMENT FIRM BUYS ARKLA GAS; W. R. STEPHENS BUYS UTILITY FOR $25 MILLION (OCT. 16)

Witt Stephens, self-described as a "country boy who came to town to get my mother a washing machine," was on his way to fame and fortune.

After the purchase a plea was made for a $3,640,000 rate increase for the gas company, which was eventually denied.

TEXAS BEATEN; BOSS CRUMP DIES

On October 17 the Razorbacks upset the Texas football powerhouse.

E. H. "Boss" Crump, benign and progressive political ruler at Memphis and a power in Tennessee politics for many years, passed away at age 80.

FAUBUS VISITS WITH ARKANSAS LANDOWNER

Governor Allan Shivers of Texas held a reception for me and a limited number of Texas and Arkansas dignitaries at the State Capitol at Austin before the Arkansas-Texas game. Among those present were Dr. John Tyler Caldwell, President of the University of Arkansas, and my executive secretary-designate, J. L. Bland. Governor Shivers told us he owned a tract of land on the White River northwest of Batesville.

REMMEL STEPS UP CAMPAIGN

Remmel on October 18 stepped up his campaign efforts, announced that he had sold his AP&L stock, and listed the reasons he expected to be elected.

ORVAL FAUBUS, THEY THOUGHT HE WAS JOKING, By Kennedy, Ark. Democrat, 10/17/54

In Arkansas a strong tradition prevailed that a first-term governor was easily re-elected. Only once in the history of the state had an incumbent governor been defeated while seeking a second term.

The cartoon showed that I had been a rural school teacher, editor, postmaster and now breaker of the second term tradition.

A story by George Douthit in the magazine section told how I had tried to get five other men to run for Governor, indicating that I might run if no other formidable candidate sought the office in opposition to Governor Cherry. The prospective candidates, according to Douthit, thought I was joking.

-leave us not get over-confident...

—FAUBUS DONS GLOVES FOR LIGHT WORKOUT AS 'SMALL CAMPAIGN' GETS UNDERWAY...

—REMMEL CONTINUES TO PLUG AWAY IN MOST VIGOROUS GOP EFFORT IN MEMORY TO TAKE GOVERNOR'S CHAIR.

THE POLITICAL TRAINING CAMPS
By Kennedy, Ark. Democrat   10/17/54

DEMOCRATIC PLATFORM

On October 20, we ran a political ad listing the eight points of the Democratic platform:

1. Defeat 100% Assessment
2. Exempt feed, seed and fertilizer from sales tax
3. Welfare program humanized and liberalized
4. Recognize rights of all people
5. Expanded highway program
6. Stop unwarranted utility rate increases
7. Acknowledge rights of labor
8. Maintenance of educational progress

CARROLL REPUBLICANS FOR FAUBUS

On the same date Carroll County Republicans formed a Republicans for Faubus group under the leadership of Lewis Stafford of Eureka Springs.

RAZORBACKS DEFEAT OLE MISS

On October 23 40,000 people jammed Little Rock for the crucial Ole Miss-Arkansas football battle. The next day the headlines read: Benson's Pass Chills Rebs, 6-0. The Razorbacks kept up their unbroken string of victories while toppling the Rebels of Ole Miss from the unbeaten ranks.

REPUBLICANS-FOR-FAUBUS MEETING AT EUREKA SPRINGS

On October 27th I attended a banquet in my honor at the Crescent Hotel in Eureka Springs sponsored by the Carroll County "Republicans for Faubus" committee. Lewis Stafford of Eureka Springs, chairman of the group, was assisted by Republican F. A. "Pat" Teague of Berryville, Carroll County Representative in the Legislature.

J. W. (Jefferson) Speck of Frenchman's Bayou in Eastern Arkansas, GOP nominee for Governor in 1950 and 1952, gave me a letter of support which I was authorized to use at the meeting.

The banquet hall that night overflowed with Republican supporters. Dick Simpson, a former Madison County office holder who had lived at Eureka Springs for several years, accompanied me to the meeting. We were the only Democrats present. Other Carroll County Republican sponsors were Mrs. Teague and attorney J. E. Simpson of Berryville and banker Ray Anderson of Green Forest.

OTHER REPUBLICAN SUPPORT

Besides the Carroll County group I had other Republican supporters in Northwest Arkansas. Among them were Lawdon Branscum of Marshall, M. N. "Mack" Graue of Fayetteville and Elmer Johnson of Springdale. Aubrey Hickenbottom of Harrison, Republican county judge of Boone County, was another GOP member who supported me openly.

WE MUST BE KIDDIN'
By Graham, Ark. Gazette   10/24/54

Arthur J. McLean, prominent Little Rock banker, had become one of the main critics of the Arkansas Power and Light Company, even criticizing the powerful utility in testimony before a Congressional Committee in Washington. C. Hamilton Moses, outstanding orator, powerful political figure and chief spokesman for AP&L, did an excellent job in the company's defense. Thus the bitter McLean-Moses contest.

As the general election approached, I warned of last minute smears (which, according to my information, were prepared for use). Remmel charged my forces with intimidation and fraud and made a great to-do in the appointment of poll watchers.

The Arkansas Razorbacks fought it out with Texas A&M in contention for the Southwest Conference title and a higher rating in the national polls.

The cartoonist was kidding with his "friendship" themes.

STATEWIDE ADDRESS

On the night of October 28th I made a state-wide television and radio address, the only one of the campaign.

PSC DENIES RATE INCREASE

On October 29 Governor Cherry's Public Service Commission denied the AP&L request for a rate increase and ordered a refund to the rate payers.

It was a good time for the decision if it were designed, as many thought, to remove the sting of the rate increase from the GOP candidate, regarded by many as friendly to the power company. Taking full advantage of the decision Remmel announced that if he were elected he would keep the Commission members. The AP&L appealed the ruling and the matter was postponed indefinitely.

● HUNTSVILLE TURNS OUT FOR REMMEL; THEY LISTEN AND SOME OF THEM INDICATE SUPPORT

Remmel had set out in the beginning of his campaign to visit every county in the state. He staged his Madison County rally, his 74th county to visit, in my home town of Huntsville on Saturday night, October 30. A large crowd gathered of both supporters and non-supporters.

I called a number of my friends there the day before and told them to see that Remmel had equipment and a place to speak, if arrangements had not otherwise been made. Naturally, this was unnecessary as the Republicans then controlled all county offices except one. I urged my friends to be especially vigilant to see that no act of discourtesy or rudeness occurred to my opponent while he was there.

Everything went well. Pratt told me many times afterward that it was the finest meeting of his campaign.

Remmel's political ad that day read:
"There is only one issue in the Governor's race. Which candidate can give Arkansas the most honest, the most righteous government."

Another ad for Remmel in the Little Rock papers read: "Here is why I'm changing after 60 years of voting the straight Democratic ticket." "Old machine and corruption."

Signed: Henry M. Rector, Sr.

I closed my campaign with a television speech over Little Rock Channel 4 TV directed toward Pulaski County and the Central Arkansas area.

HALLOWEEN 1954

It was Sunday, October 31, Halloween, the time to wear masks. The General Election was two days away, Tuesday, November 2nd.

The smiling, personable Pratt Remmel was the mask behind which the Republican Party was trying to fool the Democrats.

Remmel pledged to retain in office, virtually intact, the personnel of the Democratic administration which had just been defeated. The campaign strategy was an effort to elect a Republican governor without campaigning as a Republican.

The "Arkansas Democrats" were shown to be aware of the strategy being used by the Remmel supporters.

The trouble was that not enough loyal Democrats were aware of the strength of the Remmel effort. It was almost impossible to get many regular Democrats to do any extra work at all to help me because they could not be convinced that any threat existed.

Mayor Remmel's prospects were not altogether dim for a number of reasons. Among the causes were the keen disappointment of the Cherry forces at their candidate's defeat; the questions raised in the minds of many by the Commonwealth

College charges against me; my former connections with Governor Sid McMath, who was defeated by Cherry two years before and had just lost a bid for the U.S. Senate against Senator John L. McClellan; the absence of anything detrimental in the personal and public record of my opponent except the AP&L connection; and the popularity of the Eisenhower Republican administration.

YOU CAN'T FOOL ME!
By Graham, Ark. Gazette   10/31/54

On the other hand there were Remmel's clear connections with the Old Guard Republican organization in Arkansas and his assumed connection with the powerful but now unpopular AP&L group. There was McMath and his organization and the pro-McMath voters who were almost solidly for me. And I had strong Republican support in the traditionally strong Republican area of Northwest Arkansas. In such a situation the great imponderable was the assets weighed against the liabilities.

A "Clean Elections" group made up of Independents and some extreme conservatives announced its support for Remmel.

The *Arkansas Gazette* in an editorial urged support of the Democratic ticket and of my candidacy specifically.

The biggest comfort to me during the battle was the finding of my pollster, Eugene F. Newsom. He forecast that I would win by more than 60 per cent of the vote. However, it was the first time I had used Newsom's services and naturally I did not have the full confidence in the accuracy of his polls that I came to have later on in my political career.

Arkansas Gazette
Oct. 31, 1954

VOTE DEMOCRATIC—VOTE FOR FAUBUS

So there is a serious general election contest in Arkansas for the first time in many years — one in

which the Republican nominee must be regarded as a real contender. This does not mean . . . that the two-party system has come to Arkansas. Rather we have something approaching a no-party system — with the Republican candidate pledging to continue the policies of the Democratic incumbent . . . and even to retain all his Democratic appointees.

Actually . . . this amounts to a third primary race, with the only real change in the cast of characters. Mr. Remmel's . . . speeches, liberally sprinkled with quotations from the Bible, have been more in the nature of sentimental sermons than serious political discussions. . . .

. . .

How about the qualifications of the two men? Mr. Faubus is a veteran public servant who has held county office, and who by virtue of service as administrative assistant in the governor's office and as state highway director, may be assumed to be entirely familiar with the workings of state government. Mr. Remmel has served one and one-half terms as mayor of Little Rock, a position in which he has hardly distinguished himself for efficiency or for concrete accomplishment. . . .

Finally, there is the matter of party affiliation. Would it make sense to send to the statehouse a Republican governor to serve with a legislature whose membership is 98 per cent Democratic? . . .

Moreover, those who have not been blinded by prejudice or diverted by emotional appeals cannot fail to see in Orval Faubus qualities of courage, determination, and steadfast purpose which are essential to any chief executive. In many ways he typifies the people of the mountainous section of the state — a breed that has served Arkansas well in the past. Arising from a background of rural poverty, he has educated himself against great odds, distinguished himself in the military service of his country, and won the solid and sustained support of his friends and neighbors throughout his public career. These things speak well for any man, and they constitute the final answer to those who have sought to attack Mr. Faubus' character.

Orval Faubus won the Democratic nomination for governor the hard way, in a spectacular upset popular victory — while his opponent earned his place on the ballot by receiving the support of a hundred Republican politicians assembled in a hotel ballroom. Orval Faubus has earned the support of every Democrat in Arkansas — and of every thoughtful independent voter who is concerned about the welfare of his state in the years ahead.

Arkansas Gazette, November 1, 1954

On this day candidate Remmel wound up a hardworking political campaign in which he had visited every county in the state. After a visit to Desha County, his 75th, he returned to Little Rock and issued a statement claiming victory on the morrow. Remmel's campaign strategists used paid political cartoons as part of their advertising. In this last-day-of-the-campaign ad I was portrayed as the errand boy of Sid McMath. I had McMath's support in the election but I did not find it necessary to employ such a surreptitious manner in checking with him. Even though it was meant to be detrimental to my interests I liked the following cartoon. I thought the unknown cartoonist did an excellent job.

ERRAND BOY
*Political Ad paid for by the
Remmel for Governor Committee*   11/54

PUPPET SHOW
*Political Ad paid for by the
Remmel for Governor Committee*   11/54

A puppet, Faubus, dangled from strings manipulated by four figures, former Governor Homer Adkins, Jim Crain, Jim Bland, and former Governor Sid McMath. This cartoon may have been more help than harm. It showed I had some well known supporters, each of whom had a following.

FAUBUS-REMMEL JOINT APPEARANCE

On November 1 Remmel and I made a joint 30-minute TV appearance moderated by Bill Hadley. We were questioned by Miss Bobbie Forster of KXLR, Bill Hughes of AP and Ken Johnson of the Memphis *Commercial Appeal*. Our strongest disagreement was on the proposal to exempt seed and feed from the two per cent sales tax.

SUPPORT FROM RALPH UNDERHILL

In a letter in the column, "Our Readers Views," Ralph Underhill of Beebe pointed out that he was a member of the legislature when the first legislative investigation of Commonwealth College was conducted in 1935. Underhill stated that at the time the Legislature knew little about the college and that full disclosure came some two years or more after my visit there. He made the point that it was unfair to condemn me for my connections with the college at the time when the Legislature and the people in general had not learned of the true nature of the institution.

FINAL NOTE ON COMMONWEALTH COLLEGE

Some time shortly before the general election I received a letter from a Stone County resident about Commonwealth College and my connection with the institution.

The writer related how he had been attracted to the college by its literature and had made a journey to the institution to check on the possibility of enrollment.

Arriving at the college he encountered another young man from Arkansas already on the campus. He asked his fellow Arkansan, who proved to be me, about the college.

The writer then related how I told him that the college was unaccredited, and that it had some influences which were not in accord with our ideas and our philosophy of government. He wrote that I told him "This is not what you're looking for" as a means of continuing an education, and further stated that I told him I was leaving that day.

I had forgotten the encounter with the writer but the letter refreshed my memory. I recalled that I had encountered a new person near the entrance to the main building. The individual was easy to spot because he bore the unmistakable marks of the countryman, my kind of people, and, therefore, was quite different from the others. I approached the newcomer and spoke to him following which he told me his purpose. It was then, I advised him about the college.

I used the letter in my last campaign telecast from Little Rock.

The writer of the letter? It was signed James A. Morris of Timbo, Arkansas.

The writer of the letter who took my advice and did not enroll has since become successful and nationally famous in the music field under the name of Jimmy Driftwood.

— o — o — o — o — o —

The headlines on November 3 read:

GOP LOSES BIG CHANCE AS REMMEL GOES DOWN

FAUBUS WINS EASILY, BUT
REMMEL POLLS RECORD VOTE FOR GOP

Pratt Remmel was a most gracious loser. The day following the election he and his brother, Roland, came to my room in the Marion Hotel to congratulate me on my victory and to wish me well. Their attitude made a strong, favorable impression on me which I never forgot.

DEMOCRATS WIN CONTROL OF CONGRESS

On the National level the Democrats won control of both the House and Senate.

Among the new Democratic Governors replacing Republicans were Harriman of New York, Ribicoff of Connecticut and Leader of Pennsylvania. A new Democratic U.S. Senator was Alben Barkley of Kentucky.

John F. Simms, Jr., ex-Arkansan from Hope, was elected Democratic Governor of New Mexico. Kefauver and Clement were re-elected in Tennessee.

All Democrats won in Madison County and Joe E. Purcell was elected city attorney in Benton.

J. Strom Thurmond won a Senate seat as a write-in candidate in South Carolina, thus recording the first write-in victory for the U.S. Senate in the history of the nation.

RETURNS IN GOVERNOR'S RACE

The certified returns in the Governor's race were:

Faubus — 208,121; Remmel — 127,004

A headline on November 4 read:
COMBS WILL CONTINUE IN STATE POST
Harvey G. Combs, State Insurance Commissioner in Gov. Cherry's administration, remained loyal to the Governor in the Democratic primaries. However, once I was the Democratic nominee he supported my candidacy and agreed to go on television during the week prior to the general election as a member of a panel in my support.

While in the studio shortly before beginning the broadcast Combs was summoned to the telephone. The call was from Leffel Gentry speaking for Gov. Cherry and, according to my information, in Gov. Cherry's presence. Gentry demanded that Combs not appear on the panel in my behalf and emphasized he was speaking for the Governor.

Combs replied, "I have known that boy (Faubus) all his life and I went to grade school with his father. I'm a Democrat and I've always supported the Democratic nominee." Harvey and I were both natives of Combs in South Madison County. The Combs family moved to Huntsville from where Harvey left for Little Rock before I got to know them well.

When Gentry still insisted, Combs said that if the Governor wanted his resignation he would write it and drop it in the mail before going on the panel in my behalf.

Gentry persisted that Combs must not go on the panel, that Gov. Cherry was not supporting my candidacy and that if Combs insisted on going on the panel the Governor wanted his resignation.

"All right," replied Combs, "you've got it." He wrote his resignation, dropped it in the mail box and announced on the television panel what he had done.

Following my general election victory, some friends of Gov. Cherry remonstrated with him about Combs' dismissal. Combs had done a good job as Insurance Commissioner, they said, and had remained loyal to the Governor during the primaries. Furthermore, as a lifelong Democrat and former secretary of the State Democratic Central Committee longer than any other, Combs had a right to support the Democratic nominee. Gov. Cherry was further told, according to my information, that if he persisted in such tactics he was in danger of losing many of his remaining friends.

The Governor relented, declined to accept Combs' resignation and let him continue as State Insurance Commissioner.

SUPPORT OF WARREN OSGOOD

Another who appeared on the panel in my behalf was Warren Osgood of Little Rock. Mr. Osgood and I had become friends through our membership in the 35th Division Association and our attendance at the annual reunions. He was a close personal friend of both former President Harry S. Truman and the President's first cousin, Gen. Ralph Truman. It is said that Osgood was formerly the captain in command of a Missouri National Guard Company of which both Trumans were then enlisted members.

It turned out that Osgood, a former employee of the Ft. Roots Veterans Hospital in North Little Rock, was an old-time Republican and formerly an official of the party's Central Committee in the Little Rock area. The press questioned him closely about his party activity none of which he denied. In the race against Remmel the connection proved to be in my favor, a bonus of which I was unaware at the time Osgood agreed to appear in my support.

EARLY SUPPORT, PRIMARIES, GENERAL ELECTION

I entered the campaign for the Democratic nomination for Governor unfinanced, unknown and unsung, giving up the relative security of the life-time position of Huntsville postmaster.

My basic, early, sectional support against a Democratic incumbent seeking a second term, came from people in the poultry industry because of Gov. Cherry's veto of the bill exempting feed from the sales tax. Some of my first financial support, although weak, came from the area of Washington,

Benton and Carroll counties. Some Springdale supporters as Marty Stafford, Bob Sanders, Gus Eidson and Paul Condra, were among my early leaders. The old people on welfare, their relatives and friends, who felt they had not received proper consideration from the Cherry administration, became strong supporters in every section of the state. But it was an uphill battle against the second term tradition in the first primary.

In the runoff primary the charges of my association with Commonwealth College had to be overcome. The college, then defunct, was formerly located near Mena, Arkansas. Although it had been placed on the Justice Department's subversive list after my contacts with the school, the charges of my connection with the facility scattered my supporters with the force of an avalanche. I managed to rally them, and won the Democratic nomination by a small but safe margin.

After the turmoil of the primaries the Republicans decided to make a major effort to win the governor's office and nominated the second term mayor of Little Rock, Pratt Remmel, the first Republican to hold that office since Reconstruction days. With help from the National Republican (Eisenhower) administration and the backing of disappointed Democrats who refused to support my nomination, the challenge was formidable.

I won the race with 62% of the vote but the Republicans had made their strongest bid in decades.

Two days following the General Election the *Arkansas Democrat* ran Kennedy's cartoon.

LUCKY HE WAS A MOUNTAIN MAN
By Kennedy, Ark. Democrat   11/4/54

ORVAL FAUBUS AND THE TESTING AHEAD
ARKANSAS GAZETTE EDITORIAL, NOV. 4, 1954

A *Gazette* editorial on my battle with Remmel in the general election contained these comments:

> *Remmel's problem was to bolster the normal Republican vote of 55,000 with support from nominal Democrats who had backed Francis Cherry. He succeeded to the extent of some 60,000 votes, an impressive showing.*
>
> *. . . They were cast in protest against the candidacy of Mr. Faubus.*
>
> *. . . it is true that party loyalty, in the old sense, no longer has any meaning for our urban population.*
>
> *. . . Mr. Faubus goes to the statehouse under the most adverse circumstances any Arkansas governor has faced in many years. . . . There is the knotty basic problem of state finances. Declining revenues and rising demands for necessary improvements in services have created what amounts to a deficit of some $15,000,000. . . . Mr. Faubus' administration will be faced immediately with the dread prospect of asking for an increase in taxes.*
>
> *. . . Mr. Faubus will not enjoy the usual "honeymoon" session accorded a new governor by the legislature. His situation will be about that normally faced by a second-term governor, when the shadow of a coming election falls across all deliberations.*
>
> *But Mr. Faubus' greatest handicap is the distorted image created in the minds of so many Arkansans in the course of three bitterly fought campaigns . . . the suspicion and hostility will not diminish in the wake of victory . . . and it will undoubtedly be reflected by a sizeable faction in the legislature.*
>
> *The new governor does have, however, one considerable asset. . . . The fact is Orval Faubus entered the governor's race against the advice and without the support of any more than a tiny handful of professional politicians. . . . he single-handedly created his own bandwagon.*
>
> *We don't know how many commitments Mr. Faubus may have made. We do know that he had no reason to make any — that the professional support he received . . . would have come to him without any affirmative act on his part. And so we come now to the first significant test of his independence — his appointments, which will set the pattern for his administration.*
>
> *No one can predict at this juncture that Orval Faubus will make a great governor, or even a good one. But he has earned, in the ordeal of three campaigns, the right to try — and we wish him well.*

By co-incidence the *Gazette* editorial reflected my own thinking in the matter of appointments. I made a determined effort to select personnel based on qualification, integrity and loyalty. Of my first 15 announced major appointees, five had been against me in the primaries, five were known to support me, and I had no idea how the other five voted.

RETURN HOME AFTER FINAL VICTORY

It must have been Wednesday afternoon, when the returns were conclusive and Remmel had extended his congratulations, that I returned home to Huntsville. Accompanying me were possibly four or five cars with other Madison Countians who had worked in the campaign.

Reaching the intersection of Highways 23 and 16 at Brashears Junction I left the group without telling them and drove westward two miles to my boyhood home town of Combs.

There I turned north on the rough county road, forded White River — there was still no bridge of any kind — and shortly turned off on the narrow winding road leading to the community cemetery.

I went to visit my mother's grave. There I knelt to thank her for what she had been to me. I expressed my gratitude for the lessons she had taught me, for the molding of my character, for the principles and ideals of her life handed down to me, for the inculcation of faith that good and right must triumph, and for somehow giving to me the determination and patience to struggle on in adversity.

I arose and looked along the side of the mountain toward the site of the pioneer log house where I was born to a country girl of 17 who was married at 16. Then my eyes turned to the north to the outline of the mountain which always seemed to shelter the family homestead from the northern gales of winter. Faintly a mile distant across the mountain valley, there could still be discerned in the gathering dusk, the crude dwelling where mother "kept house" and with my father reared seven children.

There with never-ending toil "with the sweat of the brow," we tore from the rough mountain fields our meagre livelihood. There were never enough clothes to adequately protect us from the winter cold, and Sunday garments were often completely lacking. Sometimes food was sparce with which to feed her hungry brood. Luxury was a thing unknown in my mother's daily life, something far away enjoyed by others beyond her ken, or a fantasy in a story book.

I recalled with pain and regret that the circumstances of adversity always prevailed for my mother. She died (January 26, 1936) before the comforts of this affluent age became available in greater abundance to the mountain dwellers of her time, or the common people generally.

Following my election and inauguration as governor, I heard there was much talk of my mother among those who knew her. From her acquaintances there came, so I was told, a universal expression of regret that she did not live to experience the joy of my success. She would have been proud, I knew, but never haughty. She would have been glad to see me give the honest, struggling common people a better chance "to make it" in the game of life, and to help the unfortunate. She would have been most gladdened to see the new State Hospital, Blind and Deaf Schools and the Children's Colony.

Still she would have been hurt and saddened by the rough game of politics with its harsh charges and counter charges, and still further hurt by the false and slanted bad publicity.

Her friends could wish for her the joy of my success, and as I stood by her grave, I could regret that she missed so many of the comforts and pleasures of life. But do any of us often know what is for the best?

With the gratitude of my heart rolled out with the sorrow and regret, I turned in the gathering gloom from the lonely spot, to rejoin my companions.

I caught up with my group shortly after nightfall at the Whitmire Gap (always pronounced "Whitmore") on Highway 23 some 20 miles south of Huntsville. There the other cars were waiting. They had encountered and were held up by a long line of traffic. Soon I was spotted by someone who then took off to get to the head of the column of vehicles.

My friends and well-wishers had come out to escort me the remaining miles to my hometown. I can clearly recall that the long line of glowing red tail lights reached out of sight on even the longest stretches of highway with an unimpeded view.

Arriving at the town at or near the tail of the column I was directed to the courthouse. Waiting on the courthouse lawn was the Huntsville high school band under the direction of Miss Gayle Johnson. The band struck up a lively tune and preceded me through the hallway and up the stairs to a crowded courtroom. There I was presented by Mrs. Myrtle Clark Hathorn, one of my newspaper employees who had run the newspaper and looked after the business while I was away on the campaign. She had been dubbed by some reporters as my "Girl Friday."

Mrs. Clark presented me to speak to the crowd, but I was at a loss for words. In later times, remembering the occasion, I could think of a thousand things to say and of how I could have made a great speech.

The crowd was not demonstrative, but, it seemed to me, quietly happy. For the first time in 14 years all Democratic county candidates had swept to victory, and were very happy. I was pleased with their success.

Not everyone shared in the joy of the occasion. The Republicans, holding all offices save one, had been defeated. As I entered the courthouse behind the band, the sound reverberating loudly from the walls, I saw the Republicans gathered in the county clerk's office on the left, hastily retire to the county judge's office and close the door to shut out the sound. I remember having a tinge of regret that everyone could not be happy. Some of the defeated candidates I had known since the days when I didn't have 50 cents in my pocket and my only transportation was "Shanks Ponies."

N. D. Heathman, then Republican State Representative, was one of my strongest boosters. While opposed politically, many of the Republican candidates and I were personal friends. But in the competition of politics there have to be losers as well as winners. There is no other way.

The Democrat nominees for county offices defeated their Republican opponents making a clean sweep for the first time in 14 years.

Democrat	Republican	Office
Roy Pettit	N. D. Heathman	Representative
W. J. "Bill" Ledford	Ewell Boyd	County Judge
Noah Leathem	W. F. "Bill" Parsons	Sheriff & Collector
J. O. Fowler	Charles Samples	Treasurer
Rex Bowlin	Mrs. Norma Chancellor	Circuit Clerk
Charles Whorton	Esse Barker	County Clerk
J. B. Hathorn	J. C. Ewing	Assessor
Dr. Charles Beeby	Dillard Reeves	Coroner

I carried the county 3,474 to 1,469. The majority of 2,005 votes set an all-time record for a Democrat vs. Republican contest which still stands.

COMBS AND OTHERS NAMED

The PSC intervened in the sale of Arkla to Witt Stephens, although Stephens had supported Cherry's bid for re-election.

On November 22 I announced my selection of Harvey G. Combs for Insurance Commissioner in my administration.

LaFayette County Judge Brooks Parker succeeded Ouachita County Judge M. C. Reynolds as president of the powerful County Judges Association.

On December 1 I announced a hands off policy in a developing dispute over the highway director. There were complaints from legislators about some of the policies of Director Herbert Eldridge.

I CALLED ON SAM RAYBURN AT HOT SPRINGS

Sam Rayburn, soon to become Speaker of the House in Washington, vacationed in Hot Springs where I paid him a visit.

MASONS FILL EMERGENCY PRESCRIPTION

The Masons of Arkansas contributed $5,000.00 to the State TB Sanatoriums for the purchase of medicine when the state-supported institutions ran out of medicine and money.

ESCAPE HATCH
By Kennedy, Ark. Democrat   11/21/54

The Legislature and John Q. Public were in a flooded underground chamber with water "Financial Crisis" still rising. Three streams, "School Needs," "Salaries" and "Construction Needs," flowing into the chamber added to the "Crisis." An opening above, "Property Tax Equalization," seemed to offer the only way out for the Legislature. This was the beginning of the Democrat's propaganda campaign against any state tax for new revenue. It promoted property tax equalization as the solution for the state's financial ills.

JIM BLAND, OF WALNUT RIDGE, TO BE FAUBUS' EXEC SEC'Y.

I announced that J. L. "Jim" Bland of Walnut Ridge would be my executive secretary.

FLETCHER FEEDS CROW TO LOSERS

W. E. "Buck" Fletcher, Lonoke, was shown in a news photograph feeding crow to Senator Ellis Fagan, Rep. Charles "Rip" Smith, Sen. Max Howell, Sheriff Tom Gulley, Democratic leader Beloit Taylor and Sen. Artie Gregory as I looked on. All these except Fletcher had backed Cherry in the campaign. Fletcher killed a bunch of crows, had them cooked and served the meat to the losers at his farm home near Lonoke. So the old expression "had to eat crow" was literally true. All of us partook of the meat. It didn't taste bad at all.

Senator Joe McCarthy was censured in the U.S. Senate by a vote of 67 to 22.

I selected career employee Julian Hogan to oversee and advise on budgets for state agencies.

On December 3 I announced selections for three more key positions in my administration. Herman Lindsey, North Little Rock, State Police director for Gov. McMath, was named to the same position in my administration; Arch Ford, Conway, State Commissioner of Education, to continue in the same position; and J. Orville Cheney, former State Senator and store owner and operator of Calico Rock, for Revenue Commissioner.

FAUBUS NAMES HIS REVENUE COMMISSIONER--

J. ORVILLE CHENEY OF CALICO ROCK.

NATION HONORS 2 ARK. HEROES WITH ITS HIGHEST AWARD...

HIGHWAY COMM. GIVES SEAL OF APPROVAL TO DIRECTOR ELDRIDGE.

HEATED ARGUMENTS SPICE PSC GAS RATE HEARINGS.

HIGHLIGHTS OF THE NEWSWEEK
By Kennedy, Ark. Democrat   12/5/54

One of the first and most important of my selections of department heads, J. Orville Cheney of Calico Rock for Revenue Commissioner, met with opposition from a State Senator. Because of a previous political contest in which they were opposing candidates, the senator objected strenuously to the selection. However, Senate confirmation was not required. I declined to change my decision, but conferred a number of times with the legislator to show him that I did not wish to ignore his wishes in other matters.

Upon his appointment Cheney said he believed tightened methods of collection and closing of loopholes could increase the amount collected by $5 to $6 million per year. *Democrat* columnist Marcus George expressed doubt and wrote: "Come

January Cheney can start chewing that bite. Hungry schools and state institutions hope he can swallow it."

Cheney was right. The increase exceeded $5 million the first year of his tenure as commissioner.

The appointment of Herbert Eldredge of Texas as highway director was confirmed by the independent Highway Commission.

Two Arkansas soldiers, Sgt. Gilbert G. Collier of Tichnor and Cpl. Charles L. Gilliland of Yellville, were awarded the Congressional Medal of Honor posthumously.

A hot battle raged before the Arkansas Public Service Commission over an applied-for rate increase by Arkla Gas Company.

* * *

It was a time-consuming task to carefully consider and select all the board, commission and department head appointments.

In addition there were hundreds of job applicants 99% of whom wanted to see me personally. I worked day after day, early and late in the Union Life Building office but there was not enough time. No doubt many mistakes were made and many applicants overlooked.

The administration course in this field did not become smooth until some time after I assumed office.

THE DAY IS SET—

1955 JAN. 11 *Inauguration of Orval Faubus*

ARCH FORD NAMED TO STAY ON AS COMM. OF EDUCATION.

Just keep your seat ~

AMONG THE GIFTS OF THE WEEK:

a new car for O. Faubus

66

The day was set for my inauguration as governor, January 11, 1955.

The Razorbacks had won the Southwest Conference Championship and many Arkansas fans planned to go to the Cotton Bowl.

The State Board of Education, with my approval, announced that Arch Ford of Conway would continue as Commissioner of Education.

The SEC in Washington approved Witt Stephens' purchase of Arkansas-Louisiana Gas Company.

On a visit to Huntsville prior to the Christmas holidays I was surprised with the gift of a new car, a Mercury. The automobile was purchased by my friends in Madison County and 6 other Northwest Arkansas counties. The presentation was made by J. E. Dunlap, Jr., newspaper publisher of Harrison who was introduced by E. R. Stafford, the Springdale News publisher, in a ceremony in front of the American Legion Post Building. Later I received the keys from an old friend, Bruce Brashears, a business and political leader of Madison County for many years.

an electric organ for F. Cherry

'Aint a-gonna need this house no longer.'

At the Executive Mansion Governor Cherry received an electric organ from his aides and a Cadillac from friends.

-all I did was ask for a salary cut...

JOLT OF THE WEEK.

Orville Cheney

ALC

Guy "Mutt" Jones

SENATOR JONES BLASTS HIGHWAY COMM. FOR SPECIFICATIONS ON TOAD SUCK FERRY JOB--- TOO STRINGENT, HE MAINTAINS.

LT. GOV. GORDON HOTLY CRITICIZED FOR THREE PAROLE ACTIONS...

Revenue Commissioner appointee-designate J. Orville Cheney asked the Legislative Council to reduce the salary for the post to bring it in line with other department head salaries, from $8,500 to $7,500. The request was so unusual the Council fainted.

Senator Guy "Mutt" Jones protested the Highway Commission's stringent specifications for a Toad Suck Ferry road job.

The Democrat ran a feature story on J. L. (Jim) Bland. Ward Goodman was named chief engineer of the Highway Department to succeed Alf E. Johnson who left for a job in Washington.

Lt. Gov. Nathan Gordon was severely criticized for executive clemency granted while he was acting governor.

The preceding December news cartoons beginning with the Jim Bland caricature are by Jon Kennedy of the Arkansas Democrat.

A gas war in Little Rock and Conway dropped prices well below 30¢ per gallon.

INTEGRATION CAUSING UNREST

On December 13 Marvin Bird of Earle, member of the State Board of Education, said that integration was a matter of grave concern and was causing much unrest in many school boards of the state.

SIMPSON, CLINGER, PAGE AND CROOM

I announced that Dick Simpson of Eureka Springs would be appointed Arkansas Bank Commissioner.

Sherman T. Clinger of Rogers was designated to be Adjutant General of the National Guard and William "Bill" Page of Forrest City as assistant. Fred Croom of Russellville was named to head the Arkansas Selective Service Office.

DEATH OF AUNT MINNIE JOHNSON

Shortly before Christmas my aunt, Mrs. Minnie Joslin Johnson, my mother's only sister, died of a stroke in Denver, Colorado. I had visited with the family in August following the runoff primary. Our families had always been close and I was the first to be notified by Uncle Jess following the death.

Aunt Minnie as a young woman had lived for a time with my family while attending school at Combs, and also when she was my teacher at the one-room Greenwood (Greasy Creek) School during my first year of grade school.

With my youngest brother, Doyle, and my first cousin, Tom Joslin, I motored to Denver arriving on the 24th. A heavy snowfall in the area kept us snowbound on Christmas Day. Some Christmas cards were arriving in the mail. Aunt Minnie had always taken great pleasure in the greetings, sending and receiving many at the holiday season. Each one that came brought a pang of greater grief to Uncle Jess who finally said, "Don't let me see any more of them 'cyards'," — his invariable pronunciation of "cards."

We attended the funeral in ice and snow on December 26 and that same afternoon departed for home. We persuaded Uncle Jess and one of his sons, Bob, to return with us to Arkansas. Not far east of Denver we encountered greater amounts of snow and icy roads and stopped for the night. It was a wise decision. The next morning we saw many stranded and wrecked vehicles. If we had attempted to travel at night and suffered a mishap, we would have suffered severely for there would have been little, if any, chance of rescue.

The snow storm had traveled eastward and our progress was limited throughout the journey. One day in Oklahoma we were able to make only about 30 miles. The time required for the trip gave me the last opportunity for a visit with relatives unburdened with the cares of office and the weight of political decisions.

One day as we were driving along, Uncle Jess said, "It doesn't seem like you're Governor. It seems like you ought to be just Orval." The same thoughts had occurred to me.

Since we traveled only during the day and the nights were long, four of us engaged in some games of pitch with Uncle Jess an interested observer. All were skillful players. The competition was keen and the desire to win was great. It was the card game of my youth and early manhood. The mere mention of the game could conjure up a thousand memories of boyhood, family, friends and neighbors. As I look back, those were the last good games in which I participated with genuine enthusiasm, even though played under the shadow of grief and the impending role I was soon to play far removed from the circumstances and atmosphere of my life in the isolation of the hills. Yes, I played some games of pitch on occasion in later years but never with the zest and eagerness as before. It was more or less to be sociable and it didn't really matter whether I won or lost as in former times when, as Uncle Jess put it, I was just Orval.

CONFERENCE WITH GENERAL TRUDEAU

Arriving in Fayetteville I went immediately to an appointment at the Mountain Inn with General Arthur G. Trudeau and aides from Washington, an appointment of which I had been informed by telephone while still enroute in Oklahoma.

The General at the direction of the Army Chief-of-Staff, as I understood the matter, was handling the investigation of reports of alleged subversion in the armed forces. I was a major in the Army Reserve and my connection with Commonwealth College had been reported. For some months General Trudeau had been pursuing the investigation. His trip to Arkansas was to conclude the investigation by the interview with me.

When our interview on the matter was finished General Trudeau told of the intense interest, one might describe it as hysteria, that had developed in the wake of Senator Joseph McCarthy's investigations and public hearings in Washington on Communists in government. He related how many people, even before they were accused or mentioned, had come to him in fright, often in tears, to explain some connection in their past which might lead to the charge of subversion. Many people had been associated with individuals or groups, or had been members of organizations, later found to be subversive or to have subversive connections. Ofttimes, like myself, they had severed any such relationship. But the record of their association hung over them like a dark cloud threatening, in the wake of McCarthy's disclosures and accusations, to destroy them.

I have never been one to condemn Senator McCarthy for his efforts to root out the real Communists in government. His great mistake, in my view, was the failure to distinguish between the real subversives and those good Americans who in all innocence, had associated with subversives, or who had by mature judgment rejected Communism after such an association.

After all, we had fought WWII as an ally of Communist Russia. Roosevelt, Churchill and other leaders appeared on public platforms with Communist leaders in a spirit of cooperation. They sat in conferences with Russian Communists to plan war strategy against the Nazis. Constantly writers, commentators and movie makers extolled the virtues of the Russians. Without the size, the might and heroism of the Red Army and Air Force we might have lost the war.

Was it any wonder, then, that many naive, less well-informed Americans came to look with favor on the Russians? To them all Russians were Communists; therefore, for a time, they saw no harm in association with those who were friendly to Communists.

I had learned my lesson even before the war. To me dictatorship of any kind was alien to our system of democracy, free enterprise and our way of life. But others were not so well informed. Thus McCarthy made a great mistake in not distinguishing between real subversives and those guilty only of association.

I left the conference with General Trudeau with a warm gratitude for his understanding, genuine admiration for his knowledge of the problem and his ability and fairness in dealing with it. Neither the admiration nor the gratitude has diminished with the years.

From the conference General Trudeau departed for Washington and I took off for the Cotton Bowl game in Texas. I do not recall how or with whom I made the trip. I do clearly recall that in Dallas the coolness of the Cherry forces toward me and Mrs. Faubus was something to behold — and endure.

NUMBER TWO MAN OF THE YEAR

In the United Press poll for Man of the Year in Arkansas, I took the Number Two spot.

First place went to Bowden Wyatt, coach of the Arkansas Razorback football team.

Sen. Fulbright was third, and Remmel and C. Hamilton Moses of the AP&L were tied for fourth.

Others receiving votes were Governor Cherry, Sen. McClellan and T. H. Barton.

Wyatt was chosen because he had ended the long losing streak of the Razorbacks. He led the team to 8 victories against two defeats, and brought it a Southwest Conference championship and the honor of host team in the Cotton Bowl.

The editors picked me for second place, the news stories said, for three principal reasons, the first being that any man elected governor is, per se, a contender for recognition. But the editors also pointed out that I had been a man of great resourcefulness to overcome two severe handicaps. One was my opponent's attempt for the traditional second term which only once before had been denied a governor. The editors thought also that I handled with courage and tact the charges made against me for my alleged attendance at the defunct Commonwealth College.

I MAKE THE NUMBER ONE NEWS STORY
AND NUMBER TWO MAN OF THE YEAR

Unnoticed by me because of my travels, a hectic schedule and isolation by the storm, the media proclaimed that my victory over Governor Cherry upsetting the second term tradition was the Number One Arkansas story of the year. This was by United Press poll of its newspaper, radio and television editors.

In second place was the success of the Razorback football team which won a Southwest Conference championship and was the host team for the New Year's Day Cotton Bowl game at Dallas.

The Arkansas Power and Light Company's rate increase and its implications was the third biggest story.

The weather, in the form of a long, hot summer drought, was fourth.

Other stories in the top ten selected by the editors, ranked in order, were:

5. Republican Pratt C. Remmel's strong gubernatorial race in the November general election;

6. Arkansas prepares for impact of Supreme Court's decision on racial segregation;

7. Sen. John L. McClellan's leading role in Army-McCarthy hearings in Washington;

8. McClellan's defeat of McMath in bitter senatorial race;

9. Commonwealth College becomes most important issue in governor's race in Democratic primaries and general election;

10. Sen. J. William Fulbright's fight against investigative methods used by Sen. Joseph R. McCarthy.

SO ENDS THE YEAR

And so ended a most eventful year in my life and in the history of Arkansas politics. From some points along the way I could see at the same time on one hand the valley of degradation, dishonor, and defeat, and on the other the peak of victory, prestige, and success. There were many painful decisions, some of which could not have been made, and many problems, some of which could not have been faced and overcome, without a deep and abiding faith, coupled with compassion, courage and understanding. To the Power, to Him, who gave me that faith, that compassion, courage and understanding, all to Him is due.

GOV. ELECT FAUBUS GOES INTO HIDING
TO DRAFT INAUGURAL ADDRESS
By Kennedy, Ark. Democrat 1/9/55

The extreme press of conferences with many groups and individuals and the death of my aunt, made it difficult to find time to write an inaugural address. Finally, I gave a tentative outline to Jim Bland who wrote the address. I then secluded myself to put the speech in final form.

CHIEF JUSTICE ADMINISTERS OATH OF OFFICE

Chief Justice Griffin Smith administered oath of office to Orval E. Faubus as he became Arkansas' 36th Governor. The ceremony took place in the House chamber before a joint session of the House and Senate on January 11, 1955. The ceremony was repeated from the capitol building steps in the public program beginning at 12:30 p.m. and was followed by the inaugural address.

THE MAIN PROBLEM, *By Kennedy, Ark. Democrat, 1/9/55*

CHAPTER 5
INAUGURATION. CAREFUL TREADING;
NEW PROGRAMS, OTHER GAINS

1955 BEGINS

In the early days of January I proclaimed that new industry was the number one need of Arkansas.

Teachers' salaries were reported to be the lowest in the nation. The Legislative Council with the advice of Julian Hogan, my representative, pared all budgets for all agencies for 1955-56 to the level of 1954 in order to remain within the projected income.

In Washington Senator McClellan took over the committee post formerly held by Senator Joseph McCarthy.

MRS. ROOSEVELT VISIT

Mrs. Franklin D. Roosevelt visited Little Rock to speak in promotion of the United Nations. I was privileged to have dinner with Mrs. Roosevelt and a small group. I recall that she was quite reticent — not at all talkative. I related to Mrs. Roosevelt how the poor and suffering of the area where my family lived during the Great Depression came to my father to get him to write letters asking for help. The letters were not directed to the President, but to Mrs. Roosevelt. I distinctly recall that there was always an affirmative response, not just a reply to each letter, but some kind of action to aid the deprived people.

CLAUDE RANKIN DIES

On January 2 State Land Commissioner Claude Rankin died just 24 hours after taking the oath of office to begin his seventh term. He had served in some capacity in the Office of Land Commissioner since 1933.

On January 5 Governor Cherry appointed Jimmie "Red" Jones, Columbia County Tax Collector since 1950, to fill the vacancy.

The death of Rankin and the appointment of Jones created a legal tangle. By practice Rankin had always taken the oath of office on January 1 and again with the other constitutional officers on the second Tuesday in January, the second day of the new General Assembly. The question raised by the situation was whether Governor Cherry had the authority to appoint for the full new term, or the time remaining until inauguration day. If only for the short term the new governor would appoint a successor for a full term following the inauguration of all new constitutional officers. The family and friends of the deceased Rankin wanted his widow appointed, a request which Governor Cherry declined to grant, and they were already interceding with me.

MESSAGE TO THE PEOPLE

The *Arkansas Democrat* ran a special inaugural section in the Jan. 9 issue. In this section in a special personally signed message I asked for the cooperation and help of all unselfish and interested citizens in solving the state's problems with emphasis on the fields of education, development of natural resources and the establishment of new industry to provide jobs for the state's people.

FAUBUS COMMON TOUCH SEEN IN HOME TOWN

Arkansas Democrat, Jan. 9, 1955
—By Sy Ramsey (Democrat Staff Writer)

HUNTSVILLE — The "common touch" that helped Orval E. Faubus win the gubernatorial campaign is evident whenever he visits his home town of Huntsville.

It's an intangible quality, but folks in the rugged Madison County hills can spot it instantly. Mr. Faubus may be dressed in city clothes, but his unassuming gait and easy-flowing conversation mark him as part of the hardy pioneer stock in Northwest Arkansas.

"Victory hasn't gone to his head," a Huntsville friend remarked. "He's still one of us and he doesn't forget it."

The governor-elect spent about an hour touring the town square the other day before returning to urgent business in Little Rock. He shook hundreds of hands. His warm smile reassured the doubtful — as though telling them he was still Orval to them, a country boy who has made good but won't ever get stuffy.

The burden of future responsibility seemed to weigh on him even as he gazed with nostalgia at familiar town sites. It's a long jump from log cabin to state capitol.

Not everyone in town had been Mr. Faubus' supporter. However, all realize that vindictiveness has never been a fault of the future governor. Even among those who were not Mr. Faubus' friends, there is a small glow of pride that a local boy reached the top.

As a matter of history, Northwest Arkansas has contributed only one governor until the past election. More than one citizen of Huntsville felt that Mr. Faubus' victory might bring benefits to a region that had been "neglected" in state aid.

"Orval is still behaving like he's running scared," one Huntsville man commented after watching him tirelessly greeting townspeople.

The impression of an outsider is that the handshaking and back slapping is an integral part of Mr. Faubus' personality as well as the usual political ham-and-eggs.

* * *

The tide of enthusiasm for Mr. Faubus runs strong in this picturesque mountain country. And the few who are sulking or indifferent also understand that Huntsville has gained a place in the sun. It is the home of the man who will shoulder the hopes of Arkansas on Tuesday (Jan. 11).

———

In connection with the story the *Democrat* ran pictures of Frank Cannaday, Superintendent of Huntsville High School, Sheriff Noah Leathem, County Judge W. J. "Bill" Ledford, Albert King, former county official, J. F. "Jimmie" Coger and

Arlis Coger, druggists, Gordon Hawkins and Roy "Bus" Hawkins, tourist court operators.

Three of those filled important roles in my administration, Cannaday in the Reassessment program and the State Department of Education, King in the Comptroller's Office, and Roy Hawkins in both the Madison County revenue department and the welfare department. Hawkins was one of the most successful welfare directors in the state.

State revenues were very low at the time I took office. According to Budget Director Julian Hogan, the only way to keep up state services without a reduction, would be the use of the state reserve funds.

The three-year drought and the nationwide recession had caused a decline in tax collections. Consequently there was a great need for additional revenue, either from new taxes or an increase in already existing taxes.

Because of the time taken by the general election campaign there was not sufficient time to confer with legislators about a tax program, or with the interests to be effected, an exercise which cannot be overlooked in the successful promotion of any tax program sufficiently ample to meet overall needs.

The fact that a great majority of the legislators had supported an incumbent governor for a second term made the situation more complex. The traditional honeymoon for a first term chief executive did not prevail. Due to the difficult economic circumstances a strong anti-tax sentiment prevailed among the people.

Taking all this into consideration, coupled with an endowed sense of timing and a sense of what is possible under a given set of circumstances, I deemed it unwise to recommend the kind of program necessary for Arkansas' progress. While I went along with certain tax measures that were introduced, I made no strong effort to persuade the General Assembly to support them as such efforts would have been useless.

AND A NICE WARM THAW TO YOU, SIR.
By Graham, Ark. Gazette   1/11/55

A coolness pervaded the atmosphere as the new governor and the 60th General Assembly began their work. There was a courteous, friendly attitude, but without the warmth and "honeymoon" atmosphere usually enjoyed by a new chief executive.

ARKANSAS' CONSTITUTIONAL OFFICERS
FIRST INAUGURATION, JAN. 11, 1955

Nathan Gordon, Lieutenant Governor
C. G. "Crip" Hall, Secretary of State
Tom Gentry, Attorney General
J. Vance Clayton, State Treasurer
J. Oscar Humphrey, State Auditor
Jimmie "Red" Jones, Land Commissioner

LEGISLATIVE OFFICERS

J. L. "Bex" Shaver, Wynne, Legislative Advisor to the Governor
Charles F. "Rip" Smith, West Memphis, Speaker of the House
Nelson Cox, Clerk of the House of Representatives
Neill Bohlinger, House Parliamentarian
Archie Tipton, House Chief Sergeant-at-Arms
Lawrence Blackwell, President Pro Tem of the Senate
Jim Snoddy, Secretary to the Senate

ADMINISTRATION POSITIONS ALREADY NAMED OR APPROVED FOR SELECTION, INAUGURATION DAY, JAN. 11, 1955

J. L. "Jim" Bland, Walnut Ridge, Executive Secretary
Claude Carpenter, Jr., Little Rock, Administrative Assistant
Rolla Fitch, Hindsville, Administrative Assistant
J. Orville Cheney, Calico Rock, Revenue Commissioner
Arch W. Ford, Conway, Commissioner, Arkansas Education Department
Dick Simpson, Eureka Springs, State Bank Commissioner
Harvey G. Combs, Little Rock, Insurance Commissioner
Sherman T. Clinger, Rogers, State Adjutant General
William "Bill" Page, Forrest City, Assistant Adjutant General
Owen Payne, Jr., Berryville, Civil Defense Director
Herman Lindsey, North Little Rock, Director of State Police
Fred Croom, Russellville, Director of Selective Service Office
Frank A. Storey, Little Rock, Director of State Finance Department
Julian Hogan, Little Rock, Budget Director
Mrs. Charles (Patsy) Ellis, Little Rock, Receptionist in Governor's Office
Miss Elizabeth Fougerouse, Stenographer, Governor's Office
Miss Lucille Martin, Stenographer, Governor's Office
Miss Janice Colton, Secretary, Governor's Office
Mrs. Virginia Jenkins, Official Hostess, Executive Mansion

COLORFUL RITES AT CAPITOL START FAUBUS ON CAREER OF CAPTAIN OF SHIP OF STATE

All former governors and widows of former governors were invited to the inaugural ceremonies. Among those present were former Governors Sid McMath, Ben Laney and Homer Adkins, and the widows of former governors, Joe T. Robinson, George W. Hays and Jeff Davis.

0 ⬤ 0 ⬤ 0 ⬤ 0 ⬤

SIXTIETH GENERAL ASSEMBLY

January 10 to March 10, 1955

SENATE

Nathan Gordon, Morrilton, President
Lawrence Blackwell, Pine Bluff, President, Pro Tempore
Jim Snoddy, Alma, Secretary

• • •

Russell Elrod, First District, Benton and Carroll
Clifton "Deacon" Wade, Second, Washington and Madison
J. O. "Jake" Porter, Third, Crawford, Franklin and Johnson
J. E. "Pat" Garner, Fourth, Sebastian
Boss Mitchell, Fifth, Logan, Scott, Yell and Montgomery
Roy L. Riales, Sixth, Polk, Howard, Sevier and Little River
Gene Lee, Seventh, Pike, Hempstead and Nevada
Jack V. Clark, Eighth, Miller and LaFayette
Roy W. Milum, Ninth, Boone, Marion, Baxter, Newton and Searcy
Robert Hays Williams, Tenth, Pope, Conway and Perry
C. Van Hayes and Q. Byrum Hurst, Eleventh, Garland, Saline, Hot Spring and Clark
Dr. Edward Jones Byrd, Twelfth, Ouachita and Columbia
Marshall Shackelford, Jr., Thirteenth, Union
Guy H. Jones, Fourteenth, Stone, Van Buren, Cleburne and Faulkner
Ellis M. Fagan, Artie Gregory, Max Howell, Fifteenth, Pulaski
Oliver R. Williams, Sixteenth, Grant, Dallas, Cleveland, Calhoun and Bradley
Tom Logan, Seventeenth, Fulton, Randolph, Sharp and Lawrence
Y. M. (Milton) Mack, Eighteenth, Izard, Independence and Jackson
W. E. (Buck) Fletcher, C. E. Yingling, Nineteenth, White, Lonoke, Woodruff and Prairie
Lawrence Blackwell, M. Morrell Gathright, Twentieth, Jefferson and Lincoln
DeWitt Poe, Twenty-first, Drew and Desha
Gaither C. Johnston, Twenty-second, Ashley and Chicot
W. J. Hurst, Twenty-third, Clay and Greene
J. Lee Bearden, Marvin Melton, Fred H. Stafford, Twenty-fourth, Craighead, Mississippi and Poinsett
Fletcher Long, Lamar L. "Poppa" Rodgers, Twenty-fifth, Cross, Crittenden and St. Francis
Tom Allen, James P. "Doc" Baker, Twenty-sixth, Monroe, Lee, Phillips and Arkansas

HOUSE OF REPRESENTATIVES

Charles F. "Rip" Smith, Speaker
Nelson Cox, Chief Clerk

• • •

George O. Green, Arkansas
Glyn E. Sawyer, Ashley
Hugh Hackler, Baxter
Eli Leflar, Clayton Little, Benton
Vance Hickman, Boone
Carroll C. Hollensworth, Bradley
Harrell L. Johnston, Calhoun
F. A. "Pat" Teague, Carroll
Ben Bynum, Chicot
Jimmy Slack, Clark
Bryon J. McCallen, Clay
Winford "Smudge" Logan, Cleburne
Raymond L. Mays, Cleveland
Harry B. Colay, Columbia
Jim Bruton, Conway
Norman Wimpy, Charlie G. Johnston, Craighead
Milton Willis, Crawford
Charles F. "Rip" Smith, Lucien C. Rogers, Crittenden
James L. Shaver, Jr., Cross
L. Weems Trussell, Dallas
Frank Ross, Desha
Randell L. Williams, Drew
Russell C. Roberts, Faulkner
Jack Yates, Franklin
Harlin Jackson Perryman, Fulton
Ray S. Smith, Jr., Elmer Tackett, Garland

Jack Gwin, Grant
Hayes A. Triplett, Green
Talbot Feild, Jr., Hempstead
Dewey D. Stiles, Hot Spring
John Howell, Howard
Hubert J. Meachum, Independence
J. A. Rodman, Izard
Robert Harvey, Jackson
E. W. Brockman, Jr., Sam M. Levine, J. P. Walt, Jefferson
Robert C. Temple, Johnson
Pat Robinson, LaFayette
Paul M. Graham, Lawrence
W. L. Ward, Lee
R. C. Johnson, Jr., Lincoln
Marion H. Crank, Little River
A. M. McKennon, Jr., Logan
Joe P. Melton, Jr., Lonoke
Roy Pettit, Madison
Gordon Stanley, Marion
John W. Goodson, Miller
James J. (Jimmie) Edwards, E. C. "Gene" Fleeman, L. H. Autry, Kenneth S. Sulcer, Mississippi
John W. Kornegay, Monroe
W. V. (Shorty) Smith, Montgomery
Abner E. McGuire, Nevada
Quinton R. Clark, Newton
J. A. "Dooley" Womack, William S. Andrews, Ouachita
Paul Van Dalsem, Perry
Charles B. Roscopf, Marcus J. Howell, Phillips
Marvin "Pete" Austin, Pike
Guy W. French, W. H. "Bill" Thompson, Poinsett
Roy M. "Pappy" Haynes, Polk
Clyde Henry Kinslow, Pope
John P. Bethel, Prairie
Jim Coates, Jr., J. H. Cottrell, Jr., Jack East, Jr., Don Jones, Jr., R. W. "Bob" Laster, Joel Y. Ledbetter, Glenn F. Walther, Dave E. Thompson, Pulaski
Arlo Tyer, Randolph
Knox Kenney, Harold Wood, St. Francis
Virgil T. Fletcher, Saline
J. W. Black, Scott
Paul Jones, Searcy
Mel Phillips, Dan White, James S. Yarbrough, Sebastian
Winfred Lake, Sevier
A. M. "Dick" Metcalf, Sharp
Gerald V. Partee, Stone
Chadd L. Durrett, Melvin E. Mayfield, Union
Carl S. Whillock, Van Buren
Fred Starr, Charles W. Stewart, Jr., Washington
John S. Ferguson, J. H. Moody, White
Jack S. Oakes, Woodruff
W. C. Blackwell, Yell

THE INAUGURATION PROGRAM
Tuesday, January 11, 1955
10:00 A.M. HOUSE CHAMBER

The Star Spangled Banner led by Mrs. Ruth Klepper Settle

Roll Call of House and Senate

Invocation by Rev. Julian F. Anders of Warren, House Chaplain

Declaration of election results by Speaker Charles F. "Rip" Smith

10:30 A.M. Address by Gov. Francis Cherry

Oaths of Office by Chief Justice Griffin Smith to C. G. "Crip" Hall, Vance Clayton, J. Oscar Humphrey and Tom Gentry
Oath of Office by Chief Justice Griffin Smith to Orval E. Faubus

12:30 P.M. CAPITOL STEPS

The Star Spangled Banner by Walnut Ridge High School Band

Invocation by Dr. Nolan P. Howington, First Baptist Church of Little Rock

Declaration of Election results by Speaker Smith

Oath of Office by Chief Justice Smith to Constitutional Officers

Oath of Office by Chief Justice Smith to Orval E. Faubus

Address by Governor Faubus

Closing Number by Pocahontas High School Band

Benediction by Dr. Howington

The Huntsville High School Band under the direction of Miss Gayle Johnson provided music before and during the inaugural ceremony.

Informal Reception for the Public at the Executive Mansion, 3 to 7 P.M.

The Huntsville and Springdale B&PW Clubs were in charge of the reception.

AMONG THOSE NOT ABLE TO GET INSIDE
By Graham, Ark. Gazette   1/12/55

The weather is always cool and uncomfortable at inauguration time in January in the Arkansas Capitol. With few exceptions, ceremonies are held inside the building with the oath-taking and speeches in the House Chamber. The limited space is crowded to the maximum with the overflow in the hallways and other rooms of the Capitol building. The shivering figure new tax sources was unable to get inside for the inauguration.

One news report said the legislature wanted to hold the tax lines and look for school aid in a magician's hat.

THE LAST WORD AND THE FIRST
By Kennedy, Ark. Democrat   1/12/55

Gov. Cherry in his farewell address said no new taxes were needed. In my inaugural address, no new taxes were proposed, but I did not say they were not needed. The cartoonist said Arkansawyers applauded both speeches.

The anti-tax sentiment which prevailed with the general public was reflected in the legislature. Any request for additional funds by any agency, including the schools, would have to be justified in every way to have a chance for approval. It was clear that any proposed new taxes to meet any need would have the strongest opposition.

2 STATE LAND COMMISSIONERS SHARE OFFICE IN LEGAL TANGLE; FAUBUS APPOINTS MRS. CLAUDE A. RANKIN

On January 14 I appointed Mrs. Claude Rankin to the Office of the State Land Commissioner. Both officials, Jones and Mrs. Rankin, occupied the office on a friendly basis while they waited for the legal process to determine which would be the legal holder. A lawsuit had enjoined Jones from drawing any salary even before my appointment of Mrs. Rankin. I told Jones there was no personal animosity toward him in my action, but that I favored Mrs. Rankin. Also a legal determination was needed in the matter.

FAUBUS NAMES PRINTER TO HEAD LABOR BOARD

Clarence T. Thornbrough of the Little Rock Typographical Union, AFL, was named Labor Commissioner on January 23 and Bill Laney, Malvern, of the Steel Workers, CIO, was named Assistant Labor Commissioner. In making the appointments I was advised by C. W. Mowery, President of the state AFL, and Lee Tucker of the CIO. Also Sam Harris and Matilda Tuohy of the *Gazette* staff were strong advocates of Mr. Thornbrough, a *Gazette* employee.

CHERRY PICKIN' TIME
By Graham, Ark. Gazette   1/13/55

With my " '55" bucket I was ready to pick some of the cherries of the Cherry administration.

I asked the repeal of Gov. Cherry's state purchasing law, the feed and seed tax, the fiscal code and the harsh welfare restrictions including the relative responsibility law.

This latter law was in high disfavor. It required intensive investigation of each welfare applicant to determine if the senior citizen had a relative anywhere who could contribute to his support. If such a relative could be found anywhere, then the applicant was ruled ineligible for assistance. If the relative failed to lend assistance the needy old person went without help. The only way for a welfare applicant to remedy the situation was to file suit against the relatives in the state courts. If the litigant failed to get judgment against the relatives, or was unable to collect on a judgment rendered by the court, then the applicant became eligible for a welfare grant from the state.

To me this was a callous, heartless, unworkable piece of legislation. To set relative against relative in the courts as a means of determining the eligibility of a needy person for assistance was to me unthinkable. Besides, no provision was made for legal expense. If an applicant were so poor as to need a meager welfare grant, then as a practical matter, how could that person find funds for an attorney and court expenses?

The press had already labeled Cherry's farewell address as the opening gun of the 1956 campaign.

FAUBUS APPOINTEES TO GET CLOSE CHECK FROM BLOC IN STATE SENATE

By George Douthit, Democrat Staff Writer
Jan. 19, 1955

A bloc in the Arkansas Senate wants to give Governor Faubus' appointments to the Public Ser-
vice Commission and State Highway Commission a thorough public investigation. . . .

A proposal to change the Senate rules regarding confirmation of the appointments by the governor would make it more difficult to "rush" through appointments.

Opponents of the rule change are interpreting it as aimed at Governor Faubus.

* * *

An editorial in the *Arkansas Gazette* the next day said in part:

The move to revise the Arkansas Senate's rules on confirmation of gubernatorial appointments seems to be a political maneuver aimed at Governor Faubus.

. . . Under the proposed rules a small group of determined senators could block the key appointments of the governor and thereby force him into a trading position. . . .

As things now stand, Mr. Faubus is responsible for the men he puts in key administrative posts — a responsibility he has publicly acknowledged on many occasions. The Senate would be ill-advised to tamper with the system.

On January 20, the *Democrat* ran a story which said in part:

The appointment of Jim Crain, Wilson, to the State Highway Commission is scheduled to be handed to the Senate as soon as the upper house straightens out its arguments on confirmation. . . .

In the meantime, it was necessary for me to have a showdown conference with Mr. Crain and Truman Baker. They thought I was vacillating on the selection of Mr. Crain, which was not the case. I explained that the appointment was worthless without confirmation, and that the administration could not afford to lose a battle on such a crucial appointment. They agreed.

By the time the *Democrat* story broke, Jim Bland, Bex Shaver and I were ready for the Senate showdown. Mr. Crain's appointment went to the Senate that afternoon.

Two days later the appointment was confirmed, and the administration had thwarted the first major effort of opponents.

There was a rumor that I wanted to kick Miss Willie Lawson off the Highway Commission because she had actively supported Gov. Cherry in the Democratic Primary and then Republican nominee Pratt Remmell in the General Election. Miss Lawson had supported

Cherry and Remmell but we did not interfere with her commission status. Her term would expire in two years.

Jim Crain of Mississippi County replaced Dan Portis of Poinsett County on the Highway Commission. I liked Portis as a commissioner, but I had to appoint one of my supporters, and Crain was my number one choice.

The able Ham Moses spoke at a dinner meeting for legislators and business and industrial executives.

HIGHLIGHTS OF THE NEWSWEEK
By Kennedy, Ark. Democrat   2/6/55

I filled a peace making role between the Highway Department and the mayors who wanted a larger share of the road money.

We announced that the Governors Mansion would be open to the public every Tuesday and Mrs. Faubus was shown posting the invitation, "On Tuesday Y'all Come!" The policy was continued many months permitting thousands of Arkansas residents and out-of-state visitors to see the executive mansion.

FAUBUS LIKED 120-DAY BOND LAW

I signed into law a bill requiring a 120-day wait after application before any utility rate increase could go into effect. This gave the PSC time to hold hearings and make decisions on applications before the expiration of the waiting period. In my 12-year administration no major utility rate increase was permitted to go into effect without a full hearing and a decision by the Public Service Commission within the 120-day period.

———

This headline appeared on January 27: "Senate Votes to Repeal Welfare Law Requiring Relatives to Help Needy; News Brings Faubus Grin." I signed the bill with much satisfaction.

YOU JUST CAN'T HARDLY GET THEM KIND NO MORE
By Graham, Ark. Gazette   1/30/55

In an editorial with this cartoon, the *Gazette* bemoaned the absence of any progressive spirit in the Legislature, said that it was "proceeding without effective leadership," and that "with three weeks gone Governor Faubus has yet to make his first affirmative move."

To the *Gazette,* a progressive program and an affirmative move was a tax increase to support the public schools.

To the *Democrat,* a tax increase would be regressive and negative. It kept editorializing that while the schools needed money, the place to get it was in equalized assessments on property in the local school districts. Many legislators accepted this view or used it as an excuse to oppose any new taxes.

In this situation any effort to raise more revenue on the state level was hopeless, as the AEA discovered when, with all its influence, it could muster no more than 25 votes in the House to increase the sales tax. This figure was given to me by Representative Fred Starr. Other legislators confirmed the count.

As a practical matter, nothing could be immediately accomplished. It was necessary to wait, regardless of need, or editorials and cartoons. Even if the *Gazette,* in this case, were right.

The Ft. Smith Southwest American
February 11, 1955
By Clarence F. Byrns
Governor Orval Faubus' special message (on February 7) to the state legislature on finances was the high spot of this session to date.

The Governor's analysis of the state's present financial plight was both clear and specific. Surpluses accumulated from previous years of continuing rising revenues made it possible to set up a cushion fund of $9,030,000 at the beginning of the fiscal year July 1, 1953. Revenues did not continue to climb as they had done in previous years. Over the two-year period ending June 30, 1955, the cushion will be cut down from $9,030,000 to about $5,000,000. [That was the fiscal period covered by the appropriations made for the Cherry administration — OEF.] It will not be possible this year to provide out of current revenues from existing taxes enough funds to carry on state services at their present level. The shortage of money will be about four million a year.

Over a period of several months this column has repeatedly pointed out the financial puzzle which the governor described, and the decision the people of the state must make. It is higher additional taxes to hold or expand present services, or a reduction in almost every field of governmental service in the state. The time has now come to make the decision. What the people back home think about it will determine the outcome.

Editor and Columnist Byrns was a well informed man, a writer of ability and, even more important, of unquestioned integrity and fairness in his reporting.

The last sentence in his column was significant. Byrns knew and understood the democratic process and the workings of the legislature as did few people. He knew that no matter how great the need, the legislators would not solve the problem by enacting new taxes if the people back home said no.

The decision had to wait two years.

ARKANSAS HAS 'FOUR GOVERNORS'; SENATE ATTENDS DINNER HONORING CLARK

Texarkana Gazette, Feb. 15, 1955

Governor Orval Faubus of Arkansas, his official family and 28 of the 35 senators in Arkansas came to Texarkana Monday to be honored. A special honoree was Senator Jack V. Clark of Texarkana.

The visitors were greeted by Texas Mayor A. P. Miller, Jr. and Mayor Haskell Hay of Texarkana, Ark. The group lined up on Texarkana's State Line with someone quipping "we're used to straddling the line."

Under Arkansas' law of gubernatorial succession when the chief executive crosses the state line into another state, the next in line of succession becomes the acting governor with full power and authority of the office.

Thus, as I stepped across the state line followed by Lt. Gov. Nathan Gordon, then by President Pro Tem of the Senate, Lawrence Blackwell, each was governor in succession. While we were all across the line, Arkansas had a fourth governor back in Little Rock in the person of Charles F. "Rip" Smith, the Speaker of the House.

Later we were feted at the Country Club at a $25.00 per plate dinner. There, J. T. Mehaffey, editor of *Texarkana*

NEW CONCEPT
By Kennedy, Ark. Democrat   1/30/55

I made no major effort to influence the activities of the 60th General Assembly, except in the matter of legislation in which I had a specific interest. I said that I would wait for the Legislature's program which the cartoonist said was a new concept. It was my manner of maneuver to avoid a confrontation I might lose.

Gazette, was toastmaster and handled the whole affair in a masterful manner. I was seated by C. E. Palmer, owner of the chain of Palmer Papers. I had a nice visit with him and in my remarks to the audience, jested about his bitter opposition to my candidacy in the 1954 primaries.

I paid tribute to Clark for his work in the Senate, and to George Douthit, a former newspaper reporter at Texarkana, for his help and advice in the campaign as a reporter for the *Arkansas Democrat* at Little Rock.

Leon Kuhn, a Texarkana businessman, was general chairman of the whole affair and under his guidance everything went like clockwork.

W. J. "Bill" Smith of Little Rock said he attended this meeting, went through the receiving line and shook hands with me. This was our first personal contact but I have no recollection now of seeing Judge Smith at the time.

OLD CONFEDERATES IN NEW HOME

On February 15 the papers carried the news that the Confederate survivors, housed in the barracks at Camp Robinson, would move into their new $190,000 home on the grounds of the Blind and Deaf Schools.

INTEGRATION QUESTION ARISES

The integration question was first mentioned publicly on the floor of the legislature on February 8. On February 16 a bill was introduced to keep the schools of Arkansas segregated. It was a sensitive issue at the time which many wished to avoid.

Many legislators hoped to get through the session without controversy over the integration-segregation issue. That was also my hope since the attitude of the national administration and the federal government was yet unclear. Among the sponsors of the measures were Representative Lucien Rogers and Senators Fletcher Long and W. E. "Buck" Fletcher.

The proposals won quick approval in the House and were forwarded to the Senate. The only public opposition came from a few black leaders.

NO LIQUOR AT MANSION

On February 17 I announced that no liquor would be served at the Governor's Mansion. It should be stated that the ban was the continuation of a policy established by Gov. Cherry.

ALL EARS
By Kennedy, Ark. Democrat   2/6/55

I was scheduled to speak to a joint session of the General Assembly on Monday, February 7th as the members began their fifth week of deliberations. My subject was the sad condition of state finances and the impossibility of meeting the needs for adequate state services without additional revenue. Speculation on my talk was rife, the papers reported, with everyone anxious to hear what I had to say.

$10 MILLION INCREASE FOR WELFARE IS SEEN — FOOD PLAN WOULD UP AID FOR ALL

Working with Welfare Director A. J. "Red" Moss we formulated a plan whereby the State would receive surplus commodities (foods) from the federal government for distribution to the needy. To keep down state expense, the county judges were authorized to distribute the food with the counties paying the local costs of storage and clerical help. I requested the legislature to approve an appropriation of $100,000 for warehouse, office space, clerical help and trucking expense of the commodities to the counties. Thus, for that nominal state cost we were able to secure and distribute to welfare recipients more than $10 million worth of food annually. The value of the food was estimated at $10 or more per month to each person on welfare.

Howard Cain of Huntsville became director of the food program when it became operative.

FEED TAX EXEMPTION APPROVED

The feed tax exemption bill was approved by the Senate on February 17. A news headline read:

"Faubus Delivers on Campaign Promise — But Gets Financial Headache in the Bargain"

By dint of strong effort I secured approval by the Senate after prior passage by the House. The measure would have been beaten before I began my efforts late in the afternoon before the vote the next day. When the vote came it won approval 25 to 9 with 18 votes required for passage.

The Capitol press corps had polled the Senators the day before and confidently predicted defeat of the measure.

As soon as the vote was taken, the entire group came rushing to my office. As they came hurriedly through the doors Bill Hughes of the United Press announced, "Governor, this is all on the record."

I quietly answered their questions, grinned at them in a pleased manner and the session was soon over.

The state could ill afford to lose the revenue, estimated from $200,000 to one-half million, but could still less afford to lose the poultry industry. Other major poultry producing states had already exempted the feed from the sales tax.

Thousands more Arkansas citizens would have been forced to leave the State to seek employment if the poultry industry had gone under.

It was correctly argued that feed was a useless, dead substance until used to produce poultry and livestock which then went on the retail market where the sales tax was levied.

In one sense the event was a landmark in my career. I had more than delivered on a promise — a very difficult task in this case. Astute observers now knew I could be depended on in a pinch instead of taking an easy way out.

SORRY, BOYS — FOUND IT THERE WHEN I MOVED IN!
By Graham, Ark. Gazette   2/8/55

In my Feb. 7 speech I endorsed a sales tax increase as a solution to the state's financial needs. I was praised by two spokesmen for the public schools, Forrest Rozzell and Hugh Patterson. To the *Gazette* I had now made an affirmative move.

SO THEEERE YOU ARE - - - -
By Kennedy, Ark. Democrat   2/9/55

I had determined that $18 to $20 million of additional revenue was required if teachers salaries and welfare grants were to be substantially increased, and other state agencies moved above a bare bones operation. (Julian Hogan and Frank Storey, experts on state finances, spent hours of study with me on the state's financial problems. I had done my home work well by the time the speech was delivered.)

This cartoon was the *Democrat's* critical reaction to my Feb. 7 speech. To the editors I offered no proper solution at all. The *Democrat* editorial writer said: "Unquestionably schools do need money, but the place to get it is at their doors — in equitable property assessments."

ROAD FUND SHARE RISE FOR CITIES DEFEATED
ELDRIDGE PRAISES STAND BY FAUBUS

Arkansas Democrat, Friday, February 25, 1955

Arkansas Highway Director Herbert Eldridge, informed of the defeat of the municipal aid bill (HB 109) in the Senate yesterday, put in a good word for Governor Faubus' stand on the controversial issue.

Eldridge said he believed the governor's past experience in highway affairs had been an advantage to the Highway Department.

"He understands the problems we have," Eldridge said.

Mr. Faubus had more or less sided with the Highway Department from the time the bill was introduced.

DEATH CLAIMS SENATE'S POPPA RODGERS

Lamar Lucius "Poppa" Rodgers, age 73, State Senator from Crittenden County, died at a Memphis Hospital on February 26. The Senate in a body along with me and other state officials attended the funeral services at West Memphis.

THREE RING CIRCUS
By Kennedy, Ark. Democrat   2/27/55

The cartoonist said the 3% sales tax hassle provided a 3 ring circus at the State House. Arch Ford walked a tight rope; Van Dalsem in clown attire rode the "Filibuster" wagon; as lion tamer I attempted to get a reluctant lion, "AEA", to mount the stool, the 13-month sales tax plan. Revenue Commissioner Orville Cheney found that revenue was declining by $2 million per year.

Amidst intense maneuvering by both sides the 13-month sales tax increase was filibustered to death in the House in the closing days of the session. A delaying tactic by opponents of the bill called for the reading of the Journal of House actions for the previous day, a rule which is mandatory when requested. The reading went on for hours. Press reports said it was the first full reading of the Journal in 32 years.

y' gotta make him like it!

SCHOOL FORCES FEAR THEIR CAUSE IS LOST

A pill with a glass of water offered by an academic appearing person was rejected by a surly figure, the "public." The "School People" failed to convince the "public" that he should take the medicine — a tax increase to support the schools. According to my instructions the public must be convinced the pill is needed (more school revenue) before he will take it.

The general public was not convinced that an increase in taxes was necessary to give additional state aid to the public schools. The legislators believed that the folks at home were opposed to a tax increase for any purpose. No amount of persuasion or pressure from the governor, the United Committee for Better Schools headed by Hugh B. Patterson, or the AEA quarterbacked by Forrest Rozzell, could persuade a majority of the legislators to vote for any permanent tax increase.

The only program enacted beneficial to public schools was the property reassessment measure. It offered no immediate relief and the amount to be eventually obtained was problematical. Most legislators, in my opinion, voted for that program as a means of avoiding the immediate problem of a tax increase, and not with any genuine hope that property reassessment would be successful. (Three factors brought about surprising results in the program. My determination in pushing the plan, the diplomatic way in which we dealt with the matter, and my length of time in office, all combined to make the reassessment program eventually highly successful.)

The AEA Board in a prepared statement said, "It now appears that the General Assembly is not willing to levy the taxes necessary to finance the program recommended by Governor Faubus."

Patterson declared: "It doesn't look like there's a chance in the world for the income tax and the two-year sales tax."

No taxes were levied and no relief was offered for the schools. Many districts could not afford nine-month terms, cutting the school time to six, seven or eight months.

When the legislative session was over, I got with the school leaders and explained to them what I considered to be our major mistake. We had recommended a program which, although justified and needed, the legislature would not pass because the voters at home were not convinced of the need.

It was my recommendation that we formulate a program and organize a state-wide effort to develop fully the facts, present them to the people in every area and convince them of the need. The people in turn would then encourage, or at least consent, for their legislators to vote for the increased taxes that were necessary.

The adjacent cartoon explains my attitude and the idea.

Out of the discussions grew the Governor's Advisory Committee on Education (GACE).

FAUBUS TAX BILL IS READY

Having determined that the sales tax could not be increased to 3 per cent on a permanent basis (or for a 2-year period), I recommended in a special message to the legislature that the tax be increased to 3 percent for a 13-month period. Leaders of the school forces in both the House and Senate informed me the measure had a good chance of passage.

Enactment of the temporary increase would assure sufficient funds to carry on all state srvices without reductions and provide five million dollars annually for increased teachers' salaries.

LEGISLATURE ADJOURNS; BYRNS GIVES ANALYSIS

Arkansas Democrat, Wednesday, March 9, 1955

The current legislature may be rated most highly for what it did not do instead of what it accomplished, a veteran observer told the North Little Rock Lions Club yesterday.

Clarence Byrns, editor of Southwest American at Ft. Smith, listed two big achievements in the negative field:

1. Refusal to disrupt the highway department. "The governor, who everyone thought would try to wreck it, fought to preserve it," Byrns said.

2. Refusal to put a weight distance tax on big trucks. The newsman said such an act would have wrecked reciprocal agreements with most other states.

Although this general assembly is doing "an amazing job," according to Byrns, "there has never been one as devoid of leadership."

On the positive side, Byrns listed assessment reform and attempts to gain new industry as foremost achievements of the legislature.

However, the failure to provide new revenues is the greatest default, he said. But he didn't blame the lawmakers.

"The people of Arkansas have developed a hostility to state taxes and that is a serious thing," he said. "For 15 years we have managed without important new taxes, but that's at an end. You can't build a state by cutting budgets."

THE ONE THAT GOT AWAY
By Kennedy, Ark. Democrat   3/11/55

The fishermen left the lake, "1955 Legislative Session" and the "administration forces" had little to show in the way of accomplishment — see the string of small fish. But I told about the big one that got away.

The "tax increases" that got away was the recommended 13-month increase of the sales tax.

The recommendation brought Forrest Rozzell and Harry Ashmore to the Executive Mansion for a night conference. They objected to the temporary increase. Rozzell termed it "the damnedest booby trap" he had ever seen. They wanted to push for the permanent increase. I explained it could not be passed. The temporary measure was the only hope for new money.

They asked for more time to push the permanent increase. I finally acceded and agreed not to push the temporary measure until Rozzell gave me the word.

Their efforts for the permanent increase were fruitless. Finally, we had to move on the temporary increase bill. It was too late.

It might not have been for the best in the long run, but I will always believe the temporary increase would have passed if Ashmore and Rozzell had agreed to help and had not asked for the delay.

Anyway, although the cartoonist did not know it at the time, that was how the big one in the lake got away.

SIGNIFICANT ACCOMPLISHMENTS OF 60TH GENERAL ASSEMBLY

The March 10 three-column headline in the *Democrat* read: "Legislature Quits With One Top Achievement: Equalization of Taxes."

A one-column headline read: "Faubus Sees Hard Two Years Ahead." "Says maintaining present level of services difficult."

There were other significant accomplishments of the Legislature.

Sales tax exemption on feed which probably saved the poultry industry.

The new law regulating utility rates.

Repeal of relative responsibility law of the Welfare Program and the approval of the distribution of surplus government commodities, improving the old people's lot by about $14 million in benefits yearly;

Establishment of the Arkansas Industrial Development Commission;

Establishment of the Publicity and Parks program for advertising the state's scenic attractions and improvement of state parks;

Authorized Social Security coverage for all state and county officials and employees;

Authorized the Children's Colony;

Authorized construction of Justice Building;

Appropriated funds to complete the construction of the Medical Center at Little Rock.

TIGHTER!
By Graham, Ark. Gazette   3/13/55

With no new revenue measures enacted by the 1955 Session of the General Assembly, with the business recession still prevalent and, as a consequence, no appreciable increase expected from existing revenue sources, economy was the watchword during the early months of my administration. We used every possible way to save money in the operations of state government. One way was to leave vacancies in salaried positions unfilled as long as possible.

Another way was to eliminate non-essential services and jobs. A three-member committee of the State Board of Education, John Rye, Chairman, of Russellville, Dave McKay of Magnolia and Marvin Bird of Earle, spent a number of days at their own expense reviewing the administrative set up and operation of the staff of the State Department of Education. The Committee took its findings to the full board which voted to eliminate 26 positions and certain supplies and activities at a savings of $430,000 annually. The savings of Department expense was allocated to the schools for teachers' salaries.

GAZETTE DISAPPOINTED WITH LEGISLATIVE SESSION

The 60th General Assembly was shown in a cartoon in the *Gazette* as fiddling while the Capitol burned. An editorial admitted a few constructive accomplishments. It overlooked one of the most significant, the creation of the Industrial Development Commission.

The Session's Over, The Deficit Lingers On

Out of the disjointed, leaderless 60th General Assembly came a few constructive measures — acts dealing with the utilities, setting up a colony for deficient children, and establishing a new system of property assessment which at least holds out the hope of reform in this most neglected of tax fields.

There were substantial negative accomplishments, too. Some bad bills were done to death, and the new, independent Highway Commission survived this first legislative testing without serious damage.

MAKE ROOM FOR ARKY
By Kennedy, Ark. Democrat   3/18/55

Crawling onto the wall with the other states to talk to vacationeers about the "Tourist Millions" they spend, was the "Appropriation for Publicity" for Arkansas with the words — "Now, I can do some Crowing."

This new agency to improve state parks and promote tourism, was one of my programs for building the Arkansas economy. The legislation was handled by Senator Tom Allen of Monroe County.

PROBLEMS

With the Legislature adjourned I turned my attention to administrative problems.

Job requests by unemployed people, some desperate for work, constituted one of my most difficult tasks. We did the best we could but state employment scarcely made a dent in the problem.

It was reported that patients were sleeping on the floor at the State Hospital, a report which I quickly confirmed. There was insufficient room for beds for all patients in the ancient, obsolete structures of the state facility. The problem was met by placing mattresses on the floors of some buildings. Since the space was needed for other purposes during the day, the mattresses were taken up and stacked each morning by the patients themselves under supervision of hospital personnel. Then each evening the bedding was again placed on the floor for use during the night. This arrangement involved about 200 male inmates of the hospital.

Publisher Alex Washburn of Hope termed the sales tax exemption on feed an outrage and initiated a move by petition to refer the matter to a vote of the people.

Bitter cold on March 27 severely damaged the fruit and other early crops. The loss in fruit was estimated at $5 million.

In West Memphis a group was formed to promote a dog racing track in that city — a move which was to cause my administration difficulty in the months to come.

NOW HEAR THIS
By Graham, Ark. Gazette   4/1/55

At my recommendation a measure was passed setting up a new agency, the Arkansas Industrial Development Commission (AIDC), and money appropriated for its operation. The Commission's sole duty was to encourage industrial development in Arkansas.

It was my conviction that Arkansas would never have sufficient funds to adequately support its schools and pay for other state services unless the state was growing economically. It could never grow unless we had jobs for our people. The jobs must come from new industry or expansion of already existing industry.

The first commission members, appointed March 29, were Earl Harris of Rogers, Elmer Yancey of Searcy, W. R. "Bill" Smith of Lake Village, Leon Kuhn of Texarkana, W. P. "Will" Campbell of Forrest City, and Winthrop Rockefeller of Morrilton. Rockefeller, at my suggestion, was named chairman. The seventh member was Louis Hurley of El Dorado, president of the Arkansas Bankers Association, a position which changed yearly.

ENTER ALFORD AND LAMAN

Dr. Dale Alford was elected to the Little Rock school board and Casey Laman to the school board in North Little Rock. From these positions both men were to go on to greater prominence in public affairs.

YEP . . . SAME OL' TROUBLE, EYES BIGGER THAN YOUR STOMACH
By Graham, Ark. Gazette   2/2/55

Comptroller Kelly Cornett and Budget Director Julian Hogan were my principal advisers on all revenue expenditures and budget matters. The "assembly" had passed bills for more money than was available from current revenues. I had to remedy the situation by vetoing many appropriation measures.

BACKSTAGE AT THE CAPITOL

No Change of Mind, But Governor
Shows Real Political Courage in Veto
Of Controversial Legislative Acts

By R. B. Mayfield

Arkansas Democrat, Sunday, April 3, 1955

This is a "footnote" to last week's column, which was pitched on the angle that Governor Faubus had become an extremely cautious politician since assuming office.

This is not exactly a change of opinion, but an attempt to point out that the chief executive has shown some real courage in his veto of a number of controversial bills since then.

All in all, Faubus put his stamp of disapproval on 76 bills, to set a new record. Some were of a far-reaching nature.

A prime example was the governor's selection from two bills on unemployment compensation. The one he signed will help the laboring man by increasing maximum benefits and by extending the

period for which an unemployed man can draw benefits.

At the same time, the chief executive rejected a bill which would have penalized the working man. The measure would have denied benefits during a "cease-work" caused by a labor dispute.

Another choice was the veto of the so-called "loan shark" bill. This was another of the biennial efforts to get around the constitutional prohibition against usury.

The measure attempted to legalize a "time-price differential," which would have enabled dealers to charge what the traffic would bear on credit buying.

Liquor Veto Controversial

A third example in which the governor made a decision — in face of opposition — was in the rejection of the liquor export bill.

The measure was termed a "bootleg" bill by opponents, in that it would have legalized the export of liquor into dry Oklahoma and Mississippi.

Benefit Veto Sound

Another indication of courage on the part of the chief executive was in his veto of the bill to extend reitrement benefits to all state employees not presently covered.

Faubus turned the measure down on grounds that most employees were already eligible under the social security system. [Also, it did not cover all state employees; only those in the constitutional offices. — OEF]

This is true enough, and was a situation apparent to sponsors of the bill. But no one has ever made the claim that Social Security benefits were adequate to keep body and soul together.

The bill would have cost the state an estimated $400,000 a year, and we have a suspicion that is the real reason it was rejected.

ADDENDUM TO BACKSTAGE AT THE CAPITOL

I don't know how it escaped notice in the Backstage column, but I also vetoed the bill to legalize liquor stores along the state border in all counties which adjoined wet states. The measure had support from powerful interests and my veto brought great displeasure to some of my allies and legislative supporters.

In viewing the situation from this distance in time it is difficult to understand how many of those measures were lobbied to successful passage, or why, without receiving some indication of my attitude toward them. Someone must have purported to be speaking for me without my knowledge or consent, hoping I would be persuaded later, or that some of the measures would somehow become law without my notice. Such a development was a not-unheard-of occurrence with a new governor.

THE LOAN SHARK BILL

In the matter of the so-called "loan shark" bill, I recall that three groups were actively interested in promoting the measure — automobile dealers, department stores and appliance stores. Naturally there were other businesses which dealt in credit which also favored the bill.

After the bill was passed and the legislature adjourned, and it was found that I was not favorably disposed toward the measure, it was made known to me that a "consideration" of $10,000 was available to me "for my next campaign fund," if I could view the measure in a favorable light. I felt the "campaign fund" idea was merely a way to camouflage a deal wherein I could keep the full amount as "tax free" income if I wished.

The information of the "consideration" had no effect on my thinking. In the vernacular of the hills it could have been said, "It didn't even faze him."

One last effort was made which, it appeared to me, was designed to obtain my approval of the bill. On a Saturday morning I received a telephone call at the Mansion. Said the caller, "I have been designated as the keeper of this fund (the $10,000). I'm going to the races at Hot Springs and I need a safe place to leave it. Have you got a safe or someplace there (at the Mansion) where I could leave this?"

"No," I replied, "There is no safe here, and I wouldn't want it left here at all."

That ended the matter, and I never heard of the "consideration" again.

The following week I vetoed the loan shark bill along with a number of other controversial measures.

Years later I was visiting with State Senator Merle Peterson who in 1955 was an automobile dealer at Dumas. He recalled attending in Little Rock a meeting of sponsors of the price differential measure. During the discussion someone raised the question about my approval or veto of the bill. The questioner was assured, "Don't worry about that. Forget it." And the matter was not discussed further.

Days later Peterson, who knew nothing of the arrangement for the "consideration," learned that I had vetoed the loan shark bill. He knew then, he told me, that I was not controlled.

LIQUOR EXPORT BILL

In the matter of the approval or veto of the liquor export bill, I was told that if I would sign the measure "you will never have to grub again." Since I evinced no interest in avoiding any grubbing days in the future, no specific amount was ever mentioned.

DEDICATION OF
ACE COMB PLANT AT BOONEVILLE

I attended the dedication of the new Ace Comb plant at Booneville on April 6, along with AIDC chairman Winthrop Rockefeller and President V. T. Norton of the new company. We three were among the speakers and I was introduced by Rockefeller. When I arose to speak I looked out at the huge audience and said, "You must have come to see Rockefeller. I spoke here last summer (the '54 campaign) and there weren't nearly as many present."

On this occasion I heard Mr. Norton telling Rockefeller that they had more than enough applications for employment to staff the plant from former Arkansas citizens who wanted to come home. Mr. Norton was delighted with that development and I was more than delighted to hear the news.

I had stated that premise many times during the campaign, and afterward in speeches to civic clubs and members of the General Assembly. I was confident that enough former Arkansas citizens then living in other areas, were willing to return in sufficient numbers to staff any new industry in any average Arkansas town. The applications to the new Booneville plant by former Arkansas residents were proof that I was right.

DOGS, HORSES LEAVE FARMS;
FAUBUS HAPPY

Arkansas Gazette, April 12, 1955

Governor Faubus said yesterday that 53 privately owned dogs and 42 horses had been removed recently from the state penitentiary system's prison farms.

The governor said he received this information from "unofficial but reliable" sources after the state Penitentiary Commission made its investiga-

tion of Tucker and Cummins Prison Farms last week.

Mr. Faubus had charged in his request for an investigation that private stock and dogs were being kept at the prison farms. He said he had not received a formal report from the Commission, which decided after a trip to the farms that the penitentiary system was being run to its satisfaction.

"All governors have been plagued with requests for favors from the penitentiary setup that are, you might say, off-color," Mr. Faubus said. "It was my desire to make it clear that I would not be a party to that sort of thing."

He said he thought his charges and the resulting investigation had made his position clear and "removed the possibility of any such request coming from me."

The governor said that the Arkansas prison system was unique because the penitentiary could spend only what it earned from its farm operations.

"Our penal system is favorable because other states have to appropriate millions of dollars each year to operate their prisons," he said.

At the risk of being accused of immodesty I will say — it took guts to straighten out, as much as possible the corruption and defects of the state prison system. With the help of Mack Sturgis and the cooperation of Supt. Lee Henslee much was accomplished.

AND, WITH A TWINKLE IN HIS EYE
By Graham, Ark. Gazette   4/7/55

British Prime Minister Winston Churchill waved and gave the V for victory sign as he left the stage of British leadership for the last time on April 4. His sun was setting and the clouds were gathering. It was the twilight of the power and greatness of Britain and the British Empire.

A great nation which, with all its defects, spread a civilizing influence around the earth, saw its power diminish and finally vanish. Churchill presided over what was the last era of British greatness.

It is reported that the office of Governor Faubus is jammed from day to day; sometimes the crowd reaches out into the corridors and down the stairway. The object of the average caller is a state job. Mr. Faubus is probably being pestered by more seekers after jobs than any other governor since Carl Bailey. One man who has been out at the state house for years said it was the worst he had ever seen.

———

The news reports also told that 15,000 applicants were seeking the 450 jobs available at the new Little Rock Air Force Base at Jacksonville.

———

The "Obit of the Week": "McMath's Ol' Red", the Madison County coon dog presented to him by Madison County coon hunters, was reported killed while chasing a coon across a busy highway near the McMath home at Sheridan.

STATE PURCHASES McMATH BONDS; EFFECTS SAVING

The purchase of McMath highway bonds on April 27 with state funds was suggested and arranged by Frank A. Storey, Jr., head of the State Finance Department. The purchase saved the state more than $100,000 in interest payments.

———

WR BOOMS STATE

In a speech to New York bankers and business leaders, at a meeting in that city sponsored by the Chase Manhattan Bank on April 29, Winthrop Rockefeller extolled the virtues and opportunities of his adopted state. I was scheduled to address the meeting but was delayed in Las Vegas where I was waiting to see the postponed explosion of an atomic bomb. Jim Bland and others from Arkansas were in attendance in New York.

———

ARKANSAS' TAX INCREASE SETS A RECORD

Commissioner Cheney's report showed that March tax collections set an all time record.

MACK STURGIS NAMED STATE PURCHASER

To the recreated post of State Purchasing Agent, I named Mack Sturgis of Dover on April 24. It was a good appointment for the administration and the state. The post is a very sensitive and critical position.

I recall that in later months a reception was being held for former President Harry S. Truman while he was a guest at the Executive Mansion. Mr. Sturgis was one of those invited and I introduced him to Mr. Truman as the purchasing agent of my administration. The former president glanced at me then remarked as he greeted Mr. Sturgis, "I can tell you right now, Governor, this is the man who can make you or break you."

Mr. Truman was right. The office of purchasing agent is that kind of position. Not only must the official have good business judgement but he must be such that he cannot be bribed, pressured or overly persuaded. Fortunately for me Mack Sturgis did a good job for a longer period of time in that office than any other person in the history of the state.

MAN AND WOMAN OF THE YEAR AWARDS

The Arkansas Democrat's Man-of-the-year and Woman-of-the-year awards were made on April 24. The winners were:

W.E. "Bill" Darby, Little Rock, Man of the year for Arkansas

Mrs. Franklin Loy, Little Rock, Woman of the year for Arkansas

Rev. Msgr. James E. O'Connell, Man of the year for Little Rock

Mrs. Orval E. Faubus, Woman of the year for Little Rock

Colonel J. Carroll Cone, a former Arkansan, then Vice-President of Pan American Airways of Washington, D.C., was the speaker for the occasion with Democrat owner August Engel making the awards.

JIMMIE "RED" JONES STATE LAND COMMISSIONER

The State Supreme Court in a 4 to 1 decision on April 18, ruled that Jimmie "Red" Jones' appointment as State Land Commissioner was legal. The ruling was to the effect that the term of office began on January 1.

*CLOSE OF THE DOCKET
By Graham, Ark. Gazette*   4/30/55

On April 28 Chief Justice Griffin Smith of the State Supreme Court, collapsed while making a speech at El Dorado and died soon afterward. For some years I had known Justice Smith and counted him as a friend. I was glad to have such a respected jurist and public official administer the oath of office at my inauguration as governor.

To replace him as Chief Justice of the Court I appointed on Saturday, April 30, a long time friend and former chancellor, Judge Lee Seamster of Fayetteville. Judge Seamster was chancellor of the district of which Madison County was a part when I became Circuit Clerk and Recorder on Jan. 1, 1939. Along with then Circuit Judge James W. (Jim) Trimble, he gave valuable guidance and counsel to me as a new county official.

My selection of Judge Seamster met with widespread approval. I never heard any criticism of the appointment.

I arrived in Little Rock from Las Vegas, Nev., just in time to attend the funeral services for Chief Justice Smith. Later I made the appointment of Seamster and took off the same afternoon for Washington, D.C. where my engagements in the city were already due.

ARKANSANS IN WASHINGTON
NEED NOT WORRY, FAUBUS
ASSURES THEM, BUT HE HAS TROUBLES

by Sam G. Harris

Arkansas Gazette, Monday, May 2, 1955

WASHINGTON, May 1 — Governor Faubus told the senators and representatives of Arkansas today that they had no immediate political trouble back home.

But he added in the next breath that he expected opposition in next summer's Democratic primaries.

"I seem to be the only one with any trouble," he said.

The entire Arkansas congressional delegation and about 100 Arkansans residing in the Washington area heard the governor speak at a luncheon of the Arkansas Society.

Mr. Faubus said that "my own administration hasn't too much to brag about right now although we may before too long."

"But it is nice to be able to tell you that the state hasn't gone to hell since my administration took office."

The governor praised his department heads as men of ability and integrity.

He generated a great deal of merriment with a reference to defunct Commonwealth College at Mena.

He had referred affectionately to "my neighbor, Bill Fulbright," and commented that some of the first timber cutting he had ever done was for the benefit of the Fulbright Lumber Company of Fayetteville.

"The Fulbright Lumber Company must have done pretty good or at least better than I did," Mr. Faubus said. "They were able to send Bill to the University while I wandered off down to Commonwealth College."

The governor had to pause for the laughter to subside . . .

Mr. Faubus was introduced to the Society by President Lance C. Hooks as "the greatest governor in the country from the greatest state in the country." Hooks, formerly of Mount Vernon (Faulkner County) is with the Department of Agriculture.

Others on Program

Cmdr. Scott McCuskey of Stuttgart, World War II Congressional Medal of Honor winner as a Navy fighter pilot, was introduced as the next president of the Society. Commander McCuskey is on duty in the Naval Strategic Planning Division at the Pentagon with Captains Pat Henry of Monticello and Benny Bass of Thornton.

Governor Faubus and his party, and the Arkansas congressional delegation were the honor guests tonight at a party at the home of Pat Mathews of Humphries, now with the American Association of Railroads. Mathews is the son-in-law of former Representative Claude Fuller of Eureka Springs.

Tomorrow Mr. Faubus will attend the sessions of the National Governors Conference, which will be addressed by President Eisenhower.

He and his executive secretary, James L. Bland, also have an appointment with Labor Secretary James P. Mitchell.

'ARKANSAS PLAN'
FOR WELFARE COVERS NATION

By Sam G. Harris

Arkansas Gazette, Wednesday, May 4, 1955

WASHINGTON, May 3 — Criticism of Arkansas welfare policies made during the Democratic primaries last summer, has been converted into standard operating procedure for all states by the Republican-directed federal welfare program.

This was disclosed today at the . . . National Governors Conference where it was dubbed "The Arkansas Plan" to the delight of its author, Governor Faubus.

Mr. Faubus last summer flayed the state Welfare Department for discounting from routine welfare grants the efforts of welfare recipients to supplement their food budgets with home grown produce. If a client had a garden or a chicken flock, the food budget provided by welfare was lowered accordingly. Clients without such produce got bigger grants.

Premium on Laziness?

Mr. Faubus charged that this was putting a premium on indigency and penalizing the industrious.

Actually the system resulted from federal welfare regulations. When Mr. Faubus became governor, he and Welfare Commissioner Carl Adams put pressure on Washington welfare officials to change the regulation. They granted Arkansas an exception.

HEW . . . has relaxed the regulation nationwide and recommended that all states urge their welfare clients to plant gardens, keep chickens and, if possible, a cow to supplement their food needs and follow the "Arkansas Plan" of not reducing subsistence grants for such enterprise.

FEDERAL GOVERNMENT ASKS STATES TO ASSUME ALL RESPONSIBILITY FOR CIVIL DEFENSE

(Faubus Objects)

Arkansas Democrat, Sunday, May 8, 1955

I attended a two-day White House Conference on foreign affairs and National and Civil Defense in Washington on May 2 and 3. The conferences were so secret that even the executive secretaries, including my own, J. L. Bland, were barred from the sessions. There was an 18-minute coffee session with President Eisenhower during the conference.

Speakers at the general session included Secretary of State John Foster Dulles, Foreign Operations Administrator Harold Stassen, United Nations Ambassador Henry Cabot Lodge, Defense Secretary Charles E. Wilson, Gen. B. W. Childlaw of the Continental Defense Command and (National) Civil Defense Administrator Val Peterson.

The governors were told of a nuclear device capable of devastating an 80-square-mile area. We were told the device would create total destruction within a five-mile radius of the target site, and was described as capable of wiping out all living matter in the area.

The administration wanted to put the burden of civil defense on the governors and the states which were totally incapable of handling the problem. I stated these views to the conference, and later to the press, and was joined in my protests by other chief executives, two of whom were Gov. G. Mennen "Soapy" Williams of Michigan and Gov. Averill Harriman of N.Y.

FAUBUS SELECTED FOR MENTION IN HORATIO ALGER AWARD LIST

Arkansas Gazette, Thursday, May 12, 1955

Governor Faubus, who beat tradition and political odds to win the executive chair, is one of three persons receiving honorable mention in the Horatio Alger Awards this year.

The 10 award winners were announced at New York City Tuesday. The three honorable mention selections were announced at Little Rock yesterday by a representative of Mrs. Almon Faught of Jonesboro who nominated the governor. Mrs. Faught is ill at a Memphis hospital and was represented by Joe Martin, Jonesboro insurance agent.

The awards go to those persons selected in the balloting on the basis of attainments from modest beginnings in the rags-to-riches school of American ingenuity and free enterprise.

The others selected for honorable mention were John Milton of Lehman Brothers of New York, and Alvin Barker, president of the Barker Greeting Card Company of Cincinnati.

GRUBBS HIGH SCHOOL COMMENCEMENT SPEAKER

On Thursday, May 19, by invitation of the senior class of 19 members, Joe T. Rusnick, president, I was commencement speaker at the graduation ceremony of Grubbs High School in Jackson County. I had the pleasure of being with my long-time friends and fellow Madison Countians, Supt. Curtis Swaim and Mrs. Swaim.

SMITH DEFEATS MOWERY FOR AFL HEAD

Odell Smith, head of the Arkansas Teamsters Union, defeated C. W. Mowery of Hot Springs for the presidency of the AFL for Arkansas. Mowery had headed the organization for 12 years.

STATE GAINS JOBS FASTER THAN NATION

The state job situation was improving faster than the nation. The increase of jobs nationally was one per cent. In Arkansas the gain was 3.5 per cent.

U.S. SUPREME COURT RULING

The big news of May came on the last day. It was the awaited word, postponed at least twice, of the U.S. Supreme Court on the implementation of its integration ruling of May 17, 1954.

The *Arkansas Democrat* reported the ruling with a banner two line heading reaching the full width of its front page — the first such headline in many months.

The high court decision placed the segregation problems in the jurisdiction of the federal district courts. This was according to the pleading by state Attorney General Tom Gentry, in which he was joined by others, asking that the lower federal courts have jurisdiction and that time be allowed for implementation of desegregation orders.

Many local officials expressed satisfaction with the time allowed, consideration for local conditions and the fact that lower Federal Courts would have jurisdiction. But no one expressed approval of the integration to be accomplished except the leaders of the NAACP.

WEST MEMPHIS HAS ITS DAY; DIXON-YATES PLANT GETS UNDER WAY

A huge crowd gathered on June 3 for groundbreaking ceremonies at the West Memphis site chosen for the building of the $107 million Dixon-Yates power plant. Mr. Dixon and Mr. Yates, the heads of the financial combine formed to finance the construction of the plant, were both present and along with me wielded shovels in the ceremonial turning of the first soil.

AIN'T IT ORFULL, FORBUS?

This headline was for a story that related that my name was incorrectly listed in the Congressional Directory and the World Almanac. These publications spelled my name Forbus and said they had gotten the information from a source in Little Rock.

VOTING AGE OF 18 FAVORED

In an appearance before the American Legion sponsored Boys State at Camp Robinson, I recommended that the voting age be lowered to 18.

CHEROKEE VILLAGE

A new housing development and recreation spot was dedicated in North Arkansas on June 11. It was Cherokee Village near Hardy, the first of land developer John Cooper's highly successful projects. Cooper was a member of the tightly formed Crittenden County organization which was so effective against me in the primaries. I accepted an invitation to participate as a more or less minor luminary for the widely publicized dedication ceremony.

The weather was quite rough and it was with difficulty that we landed in a small National Guard plane at the new project's dirt and gravel airstrip. George Douthit covered the event and wrote, "Gov. Faubus listed only as the dedicatory speaker, became the one and only person to address the several hundred persons who sat in a steady rain for the festivities."

The other notable present, a Cherokee entertainer named Chief Evergreen Tree, didn't speak. I'm sure he was paid for the occasion.

The more notable celebrities as Sen. Fulbright, flew high overhead, went back to Memphis or Little Rock, or remained there in the first place. They never arrived for the occasion. One news report said I was the "only member of a big league line-up" who appeared.

HUMOR NOW AND THEN

It would be interesting if the humor of a campaign or an administration could be recorded. However, it seems that has never been possible.

One incident and remark amused me greatly and made an impression which never faded.

Joe Smreker of Little Rock, formerly of Ft. Smith, was a personal friend from the time of my service in the McMath administration and an early supporter in 1954. At that time he handled the construction machinery sales of a business in which he was associated with his relatives, the Youngs of Ft. Smith. He visited the governor's office quite often more out of friendship than any other reason for there was little if anything we could do for him in a business way.

After the governor's office affairs had become somewhat routine (they were never routine for long while I was serving). Joe would sometimes come in the office with members of my staff for a visit.

On this particular occasion he wss accompanied by Arnold Sikes, then my executive secretary. In the discussion of matters in general some subject arose on which it was agreed that some action should be taken. Joe suggested that certain actions be taken and inquired why they weren't being done.

"We can't," I replied with Sikes concurring, referring to rules which had to be followed and procedures which had to be observed and the bureaucratic red tape involved. "They won't let us," referring to those in key positions who were unwilling to change from old methods or who disagreed with new proposals.

"Hell," retorted Joe, half smiling and half serious as he looked at Sikes and then at me. "I thought we were **they** now!"

WASHBURN FILES PETITIONS

Alex Washburn, Hope editor, who led the drive to refer the bill exempting feed from the sales tax, stated that he feared the petitions would be hijacked by proponents of the bill and requested a State Police escort for the trip from Hope to Little Rock.

My comment was that I didn't think the conveyors of the petitions needed a police escort "any more than a hog needed a side saddle," but that the request would be granted.

Two State Police cars accompanied the vehicle which bore Mr. Washburn and other sponsors from Hope to Little Rock where the petitions were filed with Secretary of State C. G. "Crip" Hall.

OTHER SIGNIFICANT JUNE EVENTS

On June 23 Attorney General Tom Gentry ruled that the referral of the feed tax exemption was technically illegal. The ruling was a great disappointment to Alex Washburn and his supporters, but highly pleasing to the poultry producers. The feed tax exemption was now final and the matter would not appear on the ballot.

The CTC Bus Company in Little Rock got set on June 24 to operate with non-union labor in the face of the strike by union employees.

Winthrop Rockefeller announced a big gift to Arkansas colleges. The next day, June 25, he urged the editors and publishers in a speech to the Arkansas Press Association at Hot Springs, to do a selling job for the state.

On June 26 the Hoxie School Board said it had decided to integrate the district schools. The decision ushered in a period of turmoil which plagued the district for a long time and which proved disastrous for some individuals.

GOV. FUTRELL DIES

Former Governor J. Marion Futrell (1933-37) died at his home at Paragould on June 20 at age 84.

After an engagement in Northeast Arkansas I stopped in Paragould to attend the funeral services. Traveling by a small two-seat National Guard plane we landed in a field near Paragould shown on the map as an airstrip. The field, no longer in use as a landing strip was over-grown with tall grass and weeds. The takeoff was difficult and we barely made it. Once off the ground the pilot dodged a tree and skimmed over a passing freight train.

We were bound for Perryville where I was to speak to the REA Co-op annual meeting. There being no airport at Perryville, we landed at Conway and I went by car via Toadsuck Ferry to my destination. The delays were too great and I missed my speaking engagement much to the disappointment of Carl Adams.

PERRYVILLE CLINIC DEDICATION

The new health clinic at Perryville was dedicated on Sunday July 10. The program was well attended by figures prominent in the fields of education, medicine and politics. Listed as speakers were University President John Tyler Caldwell, Winthrop Rockefeller, then chairman of the AIDC, and me.

It seemed everyone dressed in his Sunday go-to-meeting clothes, including host Paul Van Dalsem, because Rockefeller would be present. The New York millionaire, now an Arkansas rancher, came dressed in his khaki shirt and trousers, cowboy boots and ranch style straw hat, and wore no necktie. Of course, the khaki clothes were not the ordinary run-of-the-mill garments by any means. They were probably more expensive than the Sunday suits worn by me and others.

The Perryville clinic was a new experiment in health care for the residents of rural areas sponsored by the University of Arkansas. State and federal funds for construction and operation were matched by a grant of private funds from Mr. Rockefeller.

Following the ceremony I rode back to Little Rock with Farrell in his new air-conditioned car. The vehicles I used were still without such comfort.

SAY WHEN - - - -
By Kennedy, Ark. Democrat   7/6/55

Officials and leaders in both political parties in Arkansas joined together in defense of the Dixon-Yates power plant. Pratt Remmel and I appeared at a huge meeting in West Memphis, along with city and state officials and business leaders in an effort to save the plant.

All efforts were to no avail. The heat on the president continued to grow. Whatever the merits or demerits of the plan, he cancelled the permit even after construction had begun.

WALTER GUY TAKES TOP POST IN SHRINE

Walter Guy, a printing company official of Little Rock, was elected Imperial Potentate of North America, the top post of the Shriners organization. I attended the installation ceremonies on July 14 at the Shriners Convention in Chicago. A news picture showed: Faubus, Guy, Raymond Rebsamen, Sen. McClellan and J. K. Shepherd.

As I write of this event I am now the only survivor of the group pictured.

REPERCUSSIONS SURE TO FOLLOW
HACKLER OUSTER

By Sam G. Harris

Arkansas Gazette, Sunday, July 17, 1955

There is a strong likelihood that there will be some more developments . . . in the wake of Joe Bill Hackler's ouster from the State Police Commission by Governor Faubus.

It is probable that one or two members of the Commission will resign in order to let loose a blast at Governor Faubus. . . .

The use of the Weights and Standards Division by the governor for patronage purposes had been a source of annoyance to members of the Commission who had been named by former Governor Francis Cherry and who had acquiesced, if not co-operated, in filling that Division with Cherry supporters when it was put under the State Police.

But the real cause of the blow-off was a disagreement over the location of the weight station at Springdale. The Commission at its June meeting had approved a site desired by Mr. Faubus' Springdale supporters. Two weeks later, the order for construction at that site was rescinded. . . .

The governor wasn't consulted. The first his office knew of a change in plans was when Springdale residents protested. Hackler had neglected to formally qualify on his latest appointment to the Commission. Invoking a statute which declares a vacancy exists if an appointee hasn't filed his duplicate oath of office within 15 days after the appointment, the governor replaced Hackler.

* * *

The Cherry-appointed Commission had not made much effort to establish a working arrangement with the governor's office. Its dealings with Mr. Faubus had been almost exclusively through Police Director Herman Lindsey.

* * *

One of Governor Faubus' glaring political oversights at the last legislature was not insisting that the State Police Commission be "reorganized" so that he could have named at least a majority of its membership. That is what other governors have done to avoid the very thing that slipped up on the present governor.

Many of the governor's friends have been impatient with him for not having forced a showdown before now with the Police Commission on a variety of matters. There are at least two more state agencies in the executive branch which are operating "independently" of the governor's office that are not doing him any good politically either. His friends would like to see him move in on them, if for no other reason than to show the public that there is but one administrative policy maker in the state government.

* * *

Since he has taken office, the governor has shown a marked dislike for controversy. . . . He has been operating on the theory that reasonable men can compromise their differences, regardless of political loyalties, for the good of the state. But he has learned also that you can't compromise if the other side involved is never available for discussions.

His easy-going manner in some of these things has given rise to a belief that the governor can be shoved around. Even some of his own close supporters have begun to think so too and are now trying to take advantage of him. They are in for a rude shock.

Governor Faubus is a politician — as skilled, if not more so, as some of his own appointees — and some of the state employees and board members held over from previous administrations. The present governor is the most patient man to sit in the executive chair for the past 25 years. He has just about reached the full and awful realization that his patience has been mistaken for weakness by his friends as well as his enemies. The reaction to that realization could be wonderful to behold.

* * *

Governor Faubus has been making considerable political hay this summer, especially in sections of the state where the majority looked on his name on the ballot last summer as something of an obscenity.

He has lost a few friends and supporters, which inevitably happens to a new governor who can't make everybody happy, but he also has picked up quite a few friends in some of the most unlikely places.

A MEMPHIS TRIBUTE TO OUR MR. FAUBUS

Arkansas Gazette, Friday, July 22, 1955

By Paul Flowers
in the Memphis Commercial Appeal

Sometimes little things disclose the most about character and personality. Now take Governor Orval Eugene Faubus, mountain-born governor of Arkansas, who has proved all over again that he was a good school teacher. He convinced participants in the recent Memphis State College Leadership Seminar that he has not forgotten how to put across his ideas before a class, and he kept about 100 listeners on the edge of their chairs for more than two hours.

* * *

It would be stimulating to meet some of those students he taught on Pinnacle Mountain or at Greasy Creek in the Ozarks and note the impressions he left on those students during his 10 years of teaching.

It was easy to visualize him making use of what resources came to hand in a mountain school, or improvising resources where there were none available.

As Perrin H. Lowrey of Blue Mountain, Miss., has said so often, "The aim of education is to make a man able to land on his feet in any situation." Orval Faubus lands on his feet.

His speech is delightfully typical of the Appalachian, Ozark or Ouachita mountaineer.

It is the English of the early settlers, the pioneers, the kings of the wild frontier; speech uncorrupted by New England, Brooklyn or Mid-Western influences. Speech such as must have been heard at the Mermaid Tavern or around the Globe Theater when rare Ben Johnson, Addison, Steel and even Walter Raleigh used the language in all of its richness. Speech such as was spoken, even by Daniel Boone and Davy Crockett; speech still current up around Cumberland Gap in Tennessee, along the Wilderness Road and at Pierce Carson's

Booger Holler in the Ozarks.

But his language was incidental except for the ear caressing qualities.

At one point the governor suggested that Detroit and California and other industrial areas might have saved themselves considerable time and money by investing in education in Arkansas and other Southern rural areas. . . . He suggested that these immigrants from Arkansas could have become much better citizens in far-away places if they had enjoyed more educational opportunities.

* * *

He went on to speculate that many of those Arkansans might have stayed at home to prosper in their own state and to bless their own communities if they had enjoyed more educational advantages. These comments came in private conversation after his address.

* * *

At one point during his talk, he grinned and quipped that school teachers in Arkansas are either leaving the state or getting into politics.

His command of his audience ranged beyond the students, graduate and undergraduate, many of them school teachers from Arkansas, who attended the seminar.

Joe H. Davis and Allen Morgan of the First National Bank leaned forward to soak up his every word, captured by his ability, charm and utter candor.

He is a man who can put excitement and adventure into the learning process. The art of teaching and the craft of newspaper editing are all the better today because Orval Faubus practiced them.

A headline on July 23 read: "Johnny Carson slated for stardom on TV."

Congress approved a $1 per hour minimum wage.

APPOINTMENTS, JANUARY 1955

Herrn A. Northcutt, Salem, Attorney for Revenue Department; James T. (Jimmy) Karam, Little Rock, Secretary for State Athletic Commission; Wm. M. (Bill) Berry, Stuttgart, to Public Service Commission; State Racing Commission: Robert M. (Bob) Roach, chairman, and J. E. Wright, both of Little Rock; June Gibson, Dermott; Laud Payne, Piggott; Lacy Lawrence, Texarkana; Allan Bryant, Malvern; Jim Evans, Yellville; Earnest Parker, Benton; Jeff Rowland, Paragould; W. P. (Penn) Davis, Newport; Dr. Edwin Dunaway, Conway (Carry over). J. Orville Cheney was Secretary of the Commission by virtue of his position as Director of the Revenue Department. W. B. McKay, Magnolia; John G. Rye, Russellville; Dr. John Cole, Malvern; Tom Cogbill, Jr., Star City; and Mrs. Edgar Dixon, Little Rock, State Board of Education. Dr. Ellis Gardiner, Russellville, to the Arkansas Tech Board of Trustees. Jimmy I. Latimer, Nashville; Gardner McNabb, Pocahontas; H. H. Howard, Leachville; and Rea Nelson, Berryville, to Burial Association Board.

APPOINTMENTS, FEBRUARY 1955

Ray Maxwell, McGehee, to A&M College Board at Monticello. Dr. John Sneed, Conway, and Sam Adkisson, Russellville, to Arkansas State Teachers College Board at Conway. John Chambers, Danville; George S. Neal, Russellville, Arkansas Polytechnic College Board at Russellville. Ray Bolling, Alma, judge at Oaklawn; Charles A. Greer, Biggers, Steward; Dr. E. K. Clardy, Hot Springs, track physician. Clyde Thomas, Gilham; Van Moseley, Camden, to Southern State College Board. Henry L. Dial, Pine Bluff; J. B. Wingfield, Prescott, to State Teachers College Board. Dr. Guy Smith, Little Rock, to board of Arkansas School for the Blind & Deaf. W. P. Ball, Little Rock, director of Parole Board, Loid Sadler, Morrilton, and O. W. "Oss" Fletcher, Paragould, members of Parole Board. Sadler elected chairman on motion of Mack West, Paragould, who relinquished the post. Other members were Clyde King, Marked Tree, and W. A. Bohnert of Crossett, Lee Henslee, Pine Bluff, retained as superintendent of state prison system. James M. Malone, Sr., Lonoke, to Public Service Commission giving my appointees control of the 3-member agency. The third member was Lewis Robinson of Little Rock who was retained. R. M. "Rob" Faust, North Little Rock, appointed head of the weights division of the State Police. Wendell D. Lee, Pine Bluff; Farris E. Madison, Alicia; C. E. Larrison, Wilmot, to Arkansas AM&N College Board. Lt. Col. Fred M. Croom, Russellville, assumed duties as Arkansas Director of Selective Service. John R. Thompson, Little Rock, Attorney for Public Service Commission. Max Poe, Pocahontas, to Arkansas State College Board at Jonesboro. Dr. L. E. Barrier, Little Rock, to McRae Memorial Sanatorium Board. Dr. Ralph E. Crigler, Ft. Smith, and L. L. Mitchell, Prescott, to State Tuberculosis Sanitorium Board. Charles Wilkins, Brinkley; J. G. Waskom, Jr., Marked Tree; Mrs. Floyd Bates, North Little Rock; A. O. Hudson, Blytheville; Rev. O. Sherman, North Little Rock; Anna M. Strong, Marianna, to Fargo Training School Board. Ted R. Christy, Little Rock, to Board of Review. Jim McDaniel of Jonesboro declined the position.

APPOINTMENTS, MARCH 1955

M. M. Zavelo, Camden; Theo Money, Waldron; John Tyson, Springdale, chairman to Alcoholic Beverage Control Board. Joe Bill Hackler, Mt. Home; Mike Berg, Camden; Everett Webb, Walnut Ridge; to State Police Commission. Representative L. H. Autry to be Governor's representative on the Legislative Council. Arch Tipton, Little Rock, as acting director of ABC Board. Mrs. H. P. Manley, Ft. Smith; Mrs. John Pruniski, North Little Rock, to Confederate Home Board. Hubert L. Burch, Fayetteville; Charles S. McNew, Pine Bluff, to Boys Industrial School Board. Dr. J. Max Roy, Forrest City; Dr. M. L. Harris, Newport; Dr. H. J. Hall, Clinton; Dr. G. D. Murphy, Jr., El Dorado; Dr. W. A. Snodgrass, Little Rock; Dr. Frank Burton, Hot Springs; Dr. Jeff Baggett, Prairie Grove; and Dr. C. H. Young, Little Rock, to Arkansas State Medical Board. Roy Ritter, Springdale and Dr. Preston Loyce Hathcock, Fayetteville, to University of Arkansas Board of Trustees. State Livestock Sanitary Board; C. F. Fitch, Hindsville; Harold Martin, Batesville; Curtis R. Vaughn, Hindsville; Buster Fraker, Springdale; W. E. Shaw, Jr., Marked Tree; Joe Ray, Danville; and Rupert Blalock, Walcott. Negro Boys Industrial School Board: Alfred E. Smith, Paragould; I. S. McClinton, Jeffrey Hawkins, both Little Rock; Claude Marsh, Searcy; and W. F. Pierce, Dermott. Dr. W. R. Brooksher, Ft. Smith, State Cancer Commission. Carl Adams, Perryville, Welfare director, A. J. "Red" Moss, Little Rock, Assistant Welfare director. Jim Bruton, Morrilton, Asst. Supt. state prison. Bruton resigned as Conway County representative to take the position. Dr. Joe Verser, Harrisburg, Secretary of State Board of Medical Examiners. Justice Building Commission: Jack Smallwood, Russellville, Chairman; C. G. "Crip" Hall, Little Rock, Secretary; Harry Parkin, Little Rock; J. V. Satterfield, Little Rock; and J. L. "Bex" Shaver, Wynne. Mrs. W. T. Dorough, Little Rock, reappointed to McRae Memorial T.B. Sanatorium Board. Fred Pickens, Newport, to University of Arkansas Board of Trustees. James R. Campbell, Hot Springs; reappointed James H. Ross, Monticello; and David L. Ford, Ft. Smith, to Claims Commission. Kelly Cornett, Huntsville, formerly of St. Paul, State Comptroller. Conally M. Henson, Little Rock, Deputy Revenue Commissioner. Craig "Jerry" Campbell, Little Rock, Transit Auditor, Revenue Department. Charles C. Tull, Little Rock, retained as Senior Parole Officer. Three new parole officers employed were Craig Holt, Bentonville; L. L. Buchannan, Prescott; Clarence Ransom of Denmark.

APPOINTMENTS, APRIL 1955

Geological Commission: Jim McDaniel, Jonesboro; John Morrow, Batesville; Rabie Rhodes, Harrison; V. S. Parham, Magnolia; Wayne A. Stone, Pine Bluff; Jack Pickens, Little Rock, reappointed; R. A. Young, Jr., Ft. Smith. Cosmetology Board: Mrs. Buna Linebarger, Mountain Home; Mrs. Mable Riggs, Ft. Smith; Miss Louise Jones, Ft. Smith; Miss Imogene Cox, Harrison; Mrs. Helen Grimmett, Batesville; Mrs. Ela Miles, Hot Springs; and Mrs. Judy Smith, Little Rock. John Sheffield, Helena, to State Publicity Commission. Sam E. Gearhart, Fayetteville, Chairman of State Publicity Commission. Earl Berry, Little Rock, former Marion County official, to head the Tax Division of the Public Service Commission. Five key division heads retained in Comptroller's Department by Kelly Cornett with approval of Governor: Aubrey McCasland, County Audits; E. G. Kizzia, School Audits; Herbert George, Municipal Audits; Charles Clerget, Chief Examiner; Julian Hogan, Budget Control; Mrs. Irene East, Social Security and Pre-Audit Division. Children's Colony Board (new): A. Nils Florentz, Little Rock, Chairman; Dr. Joseph L. Rosenzweig, Hot Springs, Vice-Chairman; Mrs. Fred McDonald, Brinley, Secretary; Mrs. Raymond Whittier, Little Rock; Miss Theodorah Marks, El Dorado; Mrs. Agnes Bass Shinn, Harrison; Harold L. Ohlendorf, Osceola. Bryan "Bill" Stearns, Little Rock, as acting director of State Parks Division (made permanent on July 1st). William J. Jernigan, Jr., Little Rock, Chairman, Board of Review; other board members, Odell Smith, Little Rock; Hoyt B. Marshall, Paragould. C. G. Mears, Hamburg; and C. R. Cole, Magnolia, to Oil and Gas Commission.

APPOINTMENTS, MAY 1955

Raymond Rebsamen and John Collins, both of Little Rock, to Merit System Council. Norman F. Williams, Little Rock, State Geologist, to Director of Geological and Conservation Commission. Commission on Alcoholism (new): Chester Bradley, Little Rock, Chairman; Rev. T. P. Devlin, Pine Bluff; Ike Murry, Dr. N. T. Hollis and Dr. Drew F. Agar, all of Little Rock; G. D. Smith, Star City, and Rudy Jones, Minturn. Miss Hermione Smith, Little Rock; Miss Frances C. Hart, Ft. Smith; Sister Mary Kevin Gallagher, Ft. Smith (reappointment), to State Board of Nurse Examiners. Mrs. Georgia Lee Russell, Little Rock, reappointed to Practical Nurses Division of Nurse Examiners Board. J. L. "Jim" Bland, leaves post of Executive Secretary to Governor to head the Employment Security Division. Luke Arnett, Acting ESD Director, was retained as the agency attorney. Arnold Sikes, North Little Rock, leaves post on Workmen's Compensation Commission to become Executive Secretary to Governor. Sherman V. Zinn, Sr., North Little Rock, Secretary to State AFL, to Workmen's Compensation Commission, replacing Sikes. Ralph O. Mott, Ft. Smith, to Arkansas State Board of Architects. Dean Y. Rowell, Pine Bluff, Administrative Assistant, as Director of Arkansas Boys Industrial School, to replace Felix W. Ryals who resigned to become Supervisor of Desha County schools. Anthony A. Shock, Pine Bluff, named Staff Supervisor. Arkansas Motor Vehicle Commission (new): James T. "Jim" Phillips, Fayetteville, Chairman; Frank W. Reeves, Helena; Stanley Wood, Batesville; Newt Hailey, Rogers; Searcy Wilcoxen, Hamburg; Henry Thomas, Little Rock; Charles Scarbrough, Pine Bluff.

APPOINTMENTS, JUNE 1955

Wiley Bean, Clarksville, to State Board of Public Welfare; Gaylon B. Price, Harrison, to State Apiary Board. A special Supreme Court to pass on legality of the plan to build a Justice Building: Ned A. Stewart, Texarkana, Chief Justice; Edward L. Wright, Little Rock; Surrey E. Gilliam, El Dorado; Harry L. Ponder, Jr., Walnut Ridge; John Mac Smith, West Memphis; J. G. Burke, Helena; and Harry P. Dailey, Fort Smith, Associate Justices. Rolla Fitch, Hindsville, leaves post as Administrative Assistant to Governor to head Alcoholic Beverage Control Board. Howard Cain, Huntsville, was employed as an enforcement agent with the agency. William P. "Bill" Rock, Baltimore, Md., named by Commission as Executive Director of AIDC. Gov. Faubus appointed Chairman of Committee on Industrial Development for Southern Governors' Conference by Gov. Lawrence Wetherby of Kentucky. Other members: Gov. Raymond Gary of Oklahoma; Gov. William C. Marland of West Virginia. Dr. William Paul Brown to head the Industrial Research and Extension Center of the U of A, Little Rock. Dr. David L. Harner, Springdale, to State Board of Optometry. Mrs. Mary Kathleen Ezell, Little Rock, to State Board of Psychiatric Technicians; reappointed were Mrs. Marie Nall, Oliver C. Henry and David J. Darma.

APPOINTMENTS, JULY 1955

Charlie Adams, Hughes, to Game & Fish Commission. Jay Dickey, Pine Bluff, to Stadium Commission. John H. Berry, Paris, State Mine Inspector. Burton Duggan, Little Rock, Abstractors Board of Examiners. Carl Thompson, Arkadelphia, Director of State Veterans Service Office. Joe Hearn, Bureau of Vital Statistics, State Health Department. Melvin Williams, Hot Springs Negro, appointed ABC agent by ABC Director Rolla Fitch with approval of Gov. Faubus. Williams was the first black to hold a state enforcement job in modern times. Faubus and 31 others initiated into 40 et 8 at Fayetteville. New State Tax Equalization Board: George Lyford, Forrest City, Assistant Director of PSC Tax Division; Gene Williams, Little Rock; Freedy Canaday, Little Rock; Frank W. Cannaday, Huntsville; A. H. Reed, Little Rock; John Cornyn, Mayor of Cammack Village; and Clay Cooper, Pocahontas, Field Supervisors; Mrs. Thelma Martineau, Little Rock, Clerk. State Publicity and Parks Commission (new): Sam B. Kirby, Little Rock, Executive Director. Members of the Commission: John Sheffield, Helena, Chairman; Ted Woods, Osceola; Tom Dearmore, Mountain Home; Ovid Switzer, Crossett, Vice-Chairman; Horace Fisher, Malvern; Lambert C. Dial, Brinkley; and George Reynolds, Petit Jean Mountain. William E. Ewald, Jr., Baltimore, Md., by the AIDC as Chief of Development. George E. Branigan, Fayetteville, and Leonard N. White, Little Rock, to State Board of Registered Professional Engineers. Carl Burger, Bentonville, to State Police Commission. Dr. Charles E. Oates, North Little Rock, to State Basic Science Board of Examiners. State Athletic Commission: Winston Chandler, Little Rock, and Dr. Garland Murphy, El Dorado, representing the American Legion; Marshall Blackard, Blytheville, representing the Disabled American Veterans; R. C. Hucheson, Ft. Smith, representing the AMVETS; William "Billy" West of West Memphis, representing the Veterans of Foreign Wars. Water Rights Study Commission: C. H. "Cy" Bond, Marion; Ewing Pyatt, Searcy; W. M. "Bill" Apple, Little Rock; Joe Hardin, Grady; Lewis J. "Red" Johnson of Little Rock, all named by the Governor, named by House Speaker Charles F. "Rip" Smith were James Reeves of Marion and James White of Helena; named by Lt. Gov. Nathan Gordon was Sen. Marvin Melton of Jonesboro. Water Compact Commission: J. J. Highfill, Springdale; John Faulkner, Mena; Sen. Russell Elrod, Siloam Springs; Donald Poe, Waldron; and Leonard D. White of Little Rock. Ralph O. Mott, Ft. Smith, reappointed to State Board of Architects. Fell Vaughn, North Little Rock, to State Contractors Licensing Board. Riddick Riffel, Little Rock, as Special Chancellor for Pulaski County district. Dr. Lawrence Davis, President of AM&N College for Negroes at Pine Bluff, to Board of Control of Southern Regional Education, a 16-state organization, to represent Arkansas. Other state members on the Board were Dr. Virgil Adkisson of Russellville and Representative L. H. Autry of Burdette.

CHAPTER 6
RACING CONTROVERSY DOMINATES NEWS
ADLAI STEVENSON VISITS ARKANSAS

LABOR VIOLENCE ROCKS LITTLE ROCK

Arkansas Democrat, Aug. 7, 1955

A strike of workers on the public bus system in Little Rock began on May 24. A compromise plan offered by Labor Commissioner Clarence Thornbrough was rejected. Inability of management and the striking workmen to negotiate a settlement prolonged the strike with increasing bitterness.

The company finally imported a number of armed drivers to assist in keeping the system in operation. The strikers in turn brought in some outside assistance and the situation threatened to erupt into open warfare.

The increased gravity of the situation caused the leaders of both sides to assume a more moderate stance and to strive harder for a settlement.

It is my belief that Odell Smith, Arkansas Teamster President and State AFL leader at the time, played a leading role in achieving a final settlement of the long dispute.

This particular strike problem was the closest Arkansas came to serious labor controversy during my tenure as governor. We tried to head off or avoid serious labor problems after the settlement of this dispute. I had good advice and help from Thornbrough and Bill Laney in the Labor Department, and labor leaders like C. W. Mowery of Hot Springs, Lee Tucker of Benton, Odell Smith, Bill Williams, Wayne Glenn and Eddie Jones of Little Rock, Charlie Forbess of Fordyce, and others.

GOVERNORS GATHER, TALK POLITICS FOR '56

The National Governors Conference was held at the Edgewater Beach Hotel in Chicago on August 9 to 12. Illinois Governor Wm. G. Stratton was host and Louisiana Governor Robert F. Kennon was the conference chairman.

While the conference was in session most of the Democratic chieftains made a pilgrimage to the nearby farm home of former Governor Adlai Stevenson, the 1952 Democratic presidential nominee. The Governors went in small groups as they were invited or inclined. One of the invariable subjects with their host was politics and the forthcoming Democratic Convention and presidential race of 1956.

I overheard Stevenson's conversation with two or three groups including my own. I thought he was much too coy about his own possible candidacy, saying, "Well, if the party wants me" — "if it is the will of the people" — "if it is the desire of the convention." To me he appeared indecisive.

Because of courtesy and a hesitancy to disagree none of the other governors of my hearing took issue with the former presidential standard bearer. Not so with me when it came my turn to speak.

"Gov. Stevenson," I told him bluntly, "No one is going to get enthusiastic about a candidate, unless that candidate is first determined and enthusiastic himself. The people don't want a man for president unless that man first has a desire to serve as president. To me, the whole question boils down to two simple facts. First, do you want to be president, and second, are you willing to make the sacrifice and the effort to make the race, and then to serve in the office."

The former governor was somewhat taken aback with my blunt analysis and made no comment. However, others spoke up in agreement with my viewpoint. One of those present was the quiet, modest-appearing new governor of Maine, Edmund

Muskie. I don't recall that he said anything but he looked at me with a grin and nodded his head.

About a week after I had returned home I noted in the news that Stevenson had dropped his coy attitude and announced that he would actively seek the Democratic nomination.

THE DEVELOPING INTEGRATION PROBLEM; GENTRY SAYS COLLEGES BOUND BY RULING

Interest in the developing integration problem gradually intensified.

On August 2 Attorney General Tom Gentry ruled that the Supreme Court decision applied to the institutions of higher learning. The news reports said the colleges were inclined to go slow on the matter of compliance.

Before the beginning of the 1955-56 school year in a conference in my office which was never publicized, I discussed integration matters with the presidents of the six white state-supported colleges. We were in agreement that the institutions would likely be faced with efforts of black students to enroll and that some decision should be made prior to school opening on whether to admit the applicants or reject them and face litigation. Lawsuits meant publicity and the possibility of demonstrations which could lead to disorder.

With the results fore ordained in any litigation before the federal courts, the presidents were inclined to accept the students, if there were not too many at first, and seek to avoid the litigation with its attendant publicity from which could grow contention and turmoil.

MY ADVICE TO COLLEGES

"If you follow that course," I said, "I want to advise you how to proceed."

"All right, tell us," responded President Alex Hull of Arkansas Tech at Russellville.

"Sometime on the first or second day of the term," I said, "some enterprising reporter will call you and want to know if any black students have enrolled. If you answer affirmatively and give the number, the news will make banner headlines, and you may have trouble."

"If you have any black students seeking to enroll, which I'm sure you will, receive them in a friendly and co-operative manner, but do not enroll them the first day," I advised. "Have them return at the end of the second day, or preferably on the third day," I continued.

"Then when the press calls on the first day, or perhaps the second, and inquires about enrollment of black students, you can truthfully say that none have enrolled. The interest of the newsmen will immediately decline or disappear altogether. Then if you have applicants," I concluded, "you can enroll them. You may get by for several days or weeks without publicity. By that time you will know if the other students and the residents of your area have accepted the situation without undue protest."

The situation developed precisely as I outlined it to the college presidents. Black students sought to enroll at five of the six white colleges. The situation was handled as I had advised. News of the enrollments was not publicized until September 16. By that time the institutions had been operating on an integrated basis for several days. During that time no incidents of any particular note had occurred.

APPRENTICE JOCKEY, By Kennedy, Ark. Democrat, 8/10/55

Woodrow Wilson Mann won the Democratic nomination for mayor by a narrow margin over Alderman
Franklin Loy, and was now the No. "1" jockey for the Democratic donkey for the November general election in
Little Rock.

Other election winners were Almon C. Perry for mayor of North Little Rock; Murray O. Reed for Little
Rock traffic judge; and James A. Griffey for Little Rock 4th ward alderman.

HOXIE DIFFERENT; CONTENTION GROWS BITTER

Quiet acceptance at the beginning of integration was not the case at the Hoxie public school. Publicity of the school board's intentions came even before integration began.

Hoxie is located in Northeast Arkansas two miles south of the larger county seat town of Walnut Ridge. A railroad town at the cross-roads of two major highways, it is in the cotton country where the level land from the east merges into the rolling hills to the west. Blacks were found in varying numbers to the south and to the east reaching all the way to the Mississippi delta where, in some counties, the black citizens outnumbered the whites. To the north only one county lay between the area and the Missouri border, while to the west the rolling hills and then the rugged mountains of the Ozarks stretched for 200 miles. There were few, if any, blacks in large sections of this region.

In some areas of the cotton country schools began in July or early August. Later in the year schools were discontinued for a month or more while the children, both black and white, assisted in the cotton harvest. This practice had been prevalent for many years and was especially helpful to the operators of family sized farms and to those persons in need of employment. Mechanized cotton pickers were not yet in wide use and most cotton was still harvested by hand.

Hoxie was one of those districts which still used the divided school term.

On August 4 the news reported that at a public meeting in the Hoxie district 150 patrons okayed a plan to boycott the integrated school. The next day it was reported that the boycott had started in the fight against racial integration.

On August 7 on another front it was disclosed that a lawsuit was readied to force integration of the Little Rock schools. The board was contending that the matter should wait until the 1957 school year.

In Hoxie by August 14 a full-fledged move to oust the school board had begun. Petitions asking the board members to resign were circulated and met with widespread approval. Among those speaking against integration at a rally of determined and angry people were Herbert Brewer, local leader of the anti-integration movement, Mayor Mitchell Davis of Hoxie, Paul Graham, Lawrence County representative in the legislature, Finos Phillips and Attorney Amis Guthridge, anti-integration leaders of Little Rock.

On August 16 it was reported that the Hoxie school board had decided to stick to its policy of integration even in the face of overwhelming disapproval of the district patrons. Petitions opposing the board policy circulated in the district bore 1,053 signatures while only some 25 patrons declined to sign, according to reports.

By the 20th the situation had grown so tense that the board summarily closed the schools. The board members, it was said, were seeking a way to calm the public furor over its admission of Negroes to the white schools.

"Hoxie becomes a town divided," one newsman wrote on the 21st, and the school board assumed a "no comment" attitude to its critics. The next day an integration opponent severely criticized the board for refusing to discuss the problem with school patrons as it had previously agreed.

On August 26, alarmed by the growing contention in nearby Hoxie, the Walnut Ridge school board announced that segregation would continue in its schools.

On September 7 a headline read: "Speaker vows continuation of Segregation Effort at Hoxie."

The anti-integration sentiment now began to surface at other points. On September 13 a Citizens Council sponsored meeting drew 400 people to a segregation rally at DeWitt in Central Arkansas. The State Board of Education at a meeting in Little Rock declined to delete the race question from school loan applications. An anti-integration rally was set for Dermott in Southeast Arkansas on the 19th.

On September 18 another well-attended rally at Hoxie heard the participants wildly cheer the foes of integration. Two new names appeared on the list of speakers, former state senator James D. "Jim" Johnson and Curt Copeland, both of Crossett in Southeast Arkansas.

On September 30 a large crowd at Hoxie waited in the rain to meet with the Hoxie school board. It was reported that the board avoided the integration protestors after previously agreeing to meet with them to discuss the problem.

COMMITTEE OF 100 APPOINTED

I appointed the members of the Committee of 100 to work with AIDC in the industrial program. Legislation authorizing the committee, to assure representation for each county in the industry seeking effort, was sponsored by Representative Virgil Fletcher of Benton.

OZARK STEAM PLANT HALTED

Plans for the construction of the Ozark steam generating plant by the Rural Electric Cooperatives received a setback when the pact with the Southwest Power Administration (SPA) was cancelled. The cancellation was a federal decision by the National Republican Administration.

MEMOIRS
By Graham, Ark. Gazette   9/24/55

Harry S. Truman, in Little Rock to attend the annual reunion of the 35th Infantry Division Association, September 23 to 25, reminisced with Arkansas Democrats about the good old days when he was president and the Democrats were in power in Washington.

Aside from the reunion activities I arranged a reception for former President Truman at the Governor's Mansion where he met and greeted several hundred leading Arkansas Democrats and members of my administration. Everyone enjoyed the occasion and the distinguished visitor seemed delighted, at one time rendering some numbers on the piano.

I had the pleasure of greeting my wartime comrades in Little Rock as president of the 35th Division Association and as Governor of the State. On the reviewing stand for the parade were President Truman, myself, Gen. Ralph Truman, Sid McMath, Mayor Pratt Remmel, Adj. Gen. Albert Sheppard of Missouri and Warren Osgood, General Chairman of the Reunion Committee.

W. E. "Bill" Kraemar of St. Louis succeeded me as Association President.

Gen. Truman, cousin of the former president, was grand marshall of the parade.

ASHMORE ON STEVENSON STAFF

Harry S. Ashmore joined the staff of Democratic presidential candidate Adlai Stevenson in Chicago, and Senator Fulbright, on a visit to Arkansas, made known his plans to seek re-election in 1956.

AIDC MEETS

The AIDC met at Winrock with Arkansas industrial leaders as guests of Winthrop Rockefeller and his fellow commission members, and outlined a program for acquiring industry for the state.

HINTON HEADS TAX EQUALIZATION PROGRAM

W. L. "Doc" Hinton, Jr., of Little Rock was named to head the Tax Equalization Program, thus assuming one of the most difficult jobs in state government. Mr. Hinton was formerly a wholesale liquor dealer and many people questioned the wisdom of his appointment. He sold his liquor business and applied for the tax position. I found he had years of experience in real estate dealing and property appraisal.

I decided to give him an opportunity in this difficult and sensitive position. It developed that Hinton was not only highly proficient in this field but was devoted, loyal and most diplomatic in his work. These qualities were important and Hinton's appointment proved to be one of the best choices I could have made.

THIS DOG TRACK STORY, By Graham, Ark. Gazette, 10/1/55

The public attempting to watch "The Dog Track Story" became confused as the greyhound racers — the controversy of the Southland dog race track at West Memphis — went around and around with no ending to the race.

The situation was confusing. The matter made the news almost daily as I kept saying there would be no permit for a dog track at West Memphis without an election at which the people voted in favor of its establishment. Yet the sponsors continued the construction of the facility just as if they were assured of success.

Looking back on the situation, perhaps the sponsors of the track had studied the law more closely than the opponents.

FAUBUS HELPS PAY TAXES FOR FRIEND IN HOLDING TO RULE

The rule, mentioned in this headline of Sept. 7, was that no request would be made to the revenue commissioner from the governor's office for any just tax bill to be forgiven or reduced.

At first, I was beset by dozens and dozens of these requests, but as everyone gradually learned that no unfair favors would be gained from the governor's office, the requests just as gradually declined. It took about a year and a half to get the policy of no undue favoritism established in the matter of tax collections and three years for it to be considered irrevocable. Then the work of the governor as well as the revenue commissioner was much easier, and tax collections much better.

In the particular case of this friend, he had paid for my advertising in his home town when I was unable to do so in the primary campaigns of 1954. I returned the favor by helping him to pay a delinquent sales tax bill.

The Revenue Commissioner had the authority to cancel the tax bill, but that would not have been strictly honest nor fair to other taxpayers.

* * *

GACE SPONSORED SCHOOL MEETING

My called conference on school needs on October 5 was attended by 600 people. Lee Roy Beasley, prominent fiscal official in the McMath Administration and now an oil company employee at El Dorado, gave the principal report, and the reaction was highly satisfactory. I asked the Committee (GACE) to continue its work and develop a program for submission to the 1957 General Assembly to improve the state's financial support of education and increase the meager salaries of the teachers.

I had months before become fully convinced that a progressive program for Arkansas was long overdue, and that it would require a major tax increase to be successful. I was equally determined to push such a program through the General Assembly if it were within my power to do so.

During the 1955 legislative session and following its conclusion, I bided my time until fully informed, both as to overall needs and new revenue sources, and how those revenues should be applied.

My thoughts and analysis of the situation were stowed in the inner recesses of my mind and I spoke no word of them to anyone, not even my closest associates. When the General Assembly of 1955 had ended I began my preparations for the program which I knew must come if Arkansas was to have adequate minimum state service and move forward.

Those preparations included the following tasks and activities: (1) endure the criticism of those who thought we had failed and enlist their help for a progressive program; (2) demonstrate ability as an administrator with improved efficiency in state government; (3) push to the maximum the new programs which had been enacted, as the AIDC and publicity and parks, to show the people the benefits of progressive legislation; (4) promote a statewide information program through the GACE and my own efforts to make the people aware of the needs and the benefits of an overall tax increase program; (5) become fully informed as to the most minute detail of the developed plan so that each question could be fully answered and every opposition viewpoint completely met; (6) secure the services of the most competent legislative adviser it was possible to obtain, see that he was fully informed prior to the convening of the General Assembly, and determine if his views were sufficiently in accord with the program to recommend it honestly and sincerely; (7) develop the program in consultation with my fiscal experts, department heads, key leaders

of groups to be benefited (as AEA), key legislators and my legislative adviser; (8) last, but not least, get re-elected so I could recommend the program.

My plan was now taking shape.

CHERRY NAMED TO $15,000 FEDERAL POST

Former Governor Francis Cherry was named October 6 by President Eisenhower to the Subversive Activities Control Board. The appointment was considered by many to be the former governor's reward for assisting Republican nominee Pratt Remmel in his race against me in 1954. The presidential appointment was subject to confirmation by the U.S. Senate. I informed the Arkansas senators that I had no objection to the appointment.

Pratt Remmel announced for re-election as the GOP candidate for mayor in Little Rock.

PEP SQUAD
By Kennedy, Ark. Democrat   10/16/55

A fund raising dinner for the National Democratic Committee was held in Little Rock at which Senator Fulbright, Congressman Wilbur Mills and I were speakers to 600 diners at $25 a head.

The fund raising affair was sponsored by the Democratic finance committee headed by Jack Stephens of Little Rock. The quota of $20,000 was exceeded before reports were complete from the counties.

FIRST SOUTHERN GOVERNORS' CONFERENCE

From attendance at the National American Legion Convention in Miami, Florida I went with my party to Point Clear, Alabama, to attend my first Southern Governors' Conference October 16 through 19, 1955. The host governor was James E. (Big Jim) Folsom, serving his second four-year term (1955-59) after being out of office for 4 years. The Chairman of the conference was Governor Lawrence W. Wetherby of Kentucky.

Harold Stassen, special assistant to the president and former governor of Minnesota, was the speaker for the State Dinner. Dr. Frank J. Soday, president of the Southern Association of Science and Industry, spoke on the progress in those fields in the South.

Other governors of the then 16-state conference, all present were: Theodore R. McKeldin, Maryland; Raymond Gary, Oklahoma; Robert F. Kennon, Louisiana; William C. Marland, West Virginia; George B. Timmerman, Jr., South Carolina; Marvin Griffin, Georgia; Luther H. Hodges, North Carolina; Allan Shivers, Texas; Thomas B. Stanley, Virginia; Hugh White, Mississippi; J. Caleb Boggs, Delaware; Frank G. Clement, Tennessee; and Leroy Collins, Florida.   McKeldin and Boggs were the only Republicans.

THEY'RE IN THE STRETCH
By Kennedy, Ark. Democrat   10/21/55

A real controversy developed over the establishment of the Southland dog track at West Memphis.

Under Arkansas law at the time, the applicant for a permit to operate a dog track must first construct a track facility, request inspection of the completed project, then ask for a permit to operate the track. The law was probably lobbied through the legislature to protect an already existing track, possibly the one that operated at West Memphis prior to World War II.

Of all the silly, unworkable legal arrangements of which I have ever heard, this one took the prize. Such a track was under construction at West Memphis at an announced cost of $1,600,-000. W.B. (Bill) Ingram, former Crittenden County Judge was the contractor. The owners were now pressing for an official inspection and action on their request for a permit to operate. Ingram was talking like a certain candidate for governor, possibly to apply pressure to me in an attempt to gain favorable consideration for a track permit.

Crittenden County opponents of the track had organized, were holding mass meetings, circulating petitions and sending delegations to Little Rock to make known to me their determined opposition. They had now gained statewide support from church groups.

A hasty view of the situation would lead anyone to the conclusion that no individual or group would spend that much money on such a project without some encouragement from the proper authorities, in this case the State Racing Commission appointed by the governor, or the governor himself.

There was a possibility, however, that the sponsors had sold sufficient stock in the enterprise on a nationwide scale to assure their profits whether or not the track ever opened. From the amount of stock sold, this could have been the case.

I had given no indication to any sponsor of favor for the track without a favorable vote at an election. The track permit had now become a problem of major interest, and maneuvering in the matter would soon come to a head. Someone, which included me, could be made to look like either a dumb cluck or a liar.

DOG RACES ARE OUT
FAUBUS SAYS BLUNTLY
FOR HIMSELF AND STAFF

Tells Desserters in Commission
To Resign Job

On Saturday, October 22, I went alone to the office where I wrote out a statement on the racing problems, typed copies for distribution, then summoned the press for a most unusual Saturday press conference. A picture by Gene Prescott in the *Gazette* showed me doing my own typing.

Following are quotes from the statement.

"A great deal of interest seems to have been generated . . regarding the possibility of greyhound racing at West Memphis. .

"It seems needful that I now must once again make known my stand in the matter.

"I have repeatedly stated, both privately and publicly, that there must be held a local option election in which the proponents of a track would poll a majority of the votes, before the matter of a permit would be considered by the Racing Commission.

"There has been no change in my attitude, nor has it varied at any time."

Election Prerequisite

"Without an election, the Racing Commission will not consider any application for a permit for dog racing at West Memphis or elsewhere.

"If there are any members (of the Racing Commission) whose views are not in accord with those expressed by me in regard to the dog racing question, then their resignations will be expected on my desk at the earliest possible moment."

As to Assurances

"I have also noted from the press that the promoters of Southland of West Memphis have indicated that they have certain assurances of a permit. I want to make clear that none of these assurances has come from me. My only word to them has been the same as to all others — no favorable election result, no consideration for a permit.

"It has been suggested by some of my advisers that the track sponsors plan to resort to court action to obtain the permit. I have all along realized that this is a possibility and have so stated publicly.

"As to the Oaklawn (Hot Springs) situation, the Racing Commission will handle the matter expeditiously and fairly as soon as litigation in the courts is completed . . .

". . . All problems must be met, and I'm saying now that the greyhounds are not going to run at West Memphis unless the courts rule that the law says they must."

DOG & HORSE RACING DOMINATE NEWS
By Kennedy, Ark. Democrat   10/23/55

The racing controversies dominated the week's news, while I was absent from the state attending the American Legion convention at Miami, Florida, and the Southern Governors Conference in Point Clear, Alabama. Kennedy showed me getting my information by telephone with the phrase "It wasn't too clear at Point Clear."

The 10-year franchise of Oaklawn for horse-racing at Hot Springs had expired early in my administration. Oaklawn's principal attorney, W.J. "Bill" Smith, was naturally unsure of his standing with the new administration since he had been one of Governor Cherry's principal advisers during the heated campaign of 1954. Therefore, Oaklawn had applied for renewal of its franchise for another ten-year period before the end of the Cherry administration and well before the expiration of its franchise. The application was made to the old commission which granted Oaklawn a new 10-year franchise before the expiration of the old. The terms of the Cherry-appointed Commission ended with Governor Cherry's term in office which was well before Oaklawn's old franchise expired.

A member of my newly appointed Commission, Jim Evans, had noted this procedure, or had it pointed out to him by some interested party, and had requested an opinion from Attorney General T.J. Gentry on the matter.

Gentry ruled that the procedure was irregular and the permit illegal. Thus the matter of a new franchise for racing at Hot Springs was open for bidding and approval by the new Racing Commission.

Oaklawn through Smith appealed Gentry's ruling to the state courts, the case eventually reaching the State Supreme Court. In a ruling on October 17 the court upheld Gentry's opinion. Thus the drawing "Supreme Court" "X-ing" out the Oaklawn Franchise with the remark, "T.J. is right." Smith asked for a rehearing which delayed a final decision for two or three weeks.

Southland Application

In West Memphis the Southland Corporation had virtually completed its dog race track. Its best known promoter, Cecil Ray Edmonds, said $900,000 had been expended, and that another $700,000 would be required to make the facility completely modern.

Thus the drawing of "Southland" with the greyhound knocking on the door marked "Racing Commission" with the thought, "Now for the franchise."

Legalized racing, which had been considered no problem, was suddenly approaching the decision stage which could be considered a crisis.

The attitude of the members of the racing commission, positions before considered largely as honorary, had now become of critical importance to the administration, to those interested in racing and to the people of the state at large.

— — —

NEW FACTORIES

In the industrial field Magnolia acquired a new plant by Firestone Company, and Pine Bluff got a new paper mill.

SAM HARRIS STORY

Sam G. Harris of the *Gazette* staff wrote a lengthy story on the background of the racing controversies which was published on October 23. His story began:

One of the biggest political dramas Arkansas has had in a long time is developing from the controversies about the dog track at West Memphis and the horse track at Hot Springs.

The cast of characters is growing daily. And mysterious is the word for many of the developments . . .

The tracks most likely will become an issue in next summer's primaries — . . .

Question Raised

The controversies are raising questions faster than they can be answered and generate speculation which becomes more involved daily.

Why did either start in the first place?

What is the interest of so many people — in and out of government — in these issues?

Where did the seekers after the West Memphis and Hot Springs franchises get their encouragement, if any?

Why were the issues raised at this time after 15 years of comparative tranquility in Arkansas's racing scene?

Governor Faubus answered several questions yesterday about the dog track only. He declined to answer any about the Hot Springs track because that issue — that the franchise of Oaklawn Jockey Club, Inc., is void — is still in litigation before the Arkansas Supreme Court.

Mr. Faubus has taken responsibility for what the Arkansas Racing Commission does in the West Memphis dog track situation — as long as the courts do not override him.

By the same token in the public eye he will have to take responsibility politically for whatever that Commission does or has done in the Hot Springs situation. And most likely his opposition will hold him accountable for what the racing commissioners have done as individuals.

* * *

Harris also wrote: Former Governor Sid McMath told the *Gazette* that he was not representing any of the parties of interest.

It was a tangled scheme of things involving both friend and foe, people I knew well and people I didn't know at all, people with good reputations and others thought to be close to the underworld, and figures noted as leaders in politics, business and labor unions.

Then on October 27, Sam G. Harris uncovered the information that my ally and former boss, former Governor Sid McMath, was representing the Eastern Racing Corporation. Eastern operated Suffolk Downs, a racing enterprise at Boston, and was bidding for the horse racing franchise at Hot Springs.

BAYING AT THE MOON
By Graham, Ark. Gazette   10/25/55

According to this drawing the matter of dog racing at West Memphis was out so far as my administration was concerned.

After my press statement, I went to work to determine what was going on. Why had so many prominent out-of-state figures come into the state, employed a number of prominent attorneys, gotten the Racing Commission and the Attorney General deeply involved and a large number of prominent labor leaders as well?

I soon learned that the dog racing matter was not settled by my statement, and that the Hot Springs track was involved in a well-laid plan of statewide proportions. I learned that any wishes of mine concerning Oaklawn were to be ignored, if they did not coincide with the scheme already devised and then being carefully firmed up.

A cartoon by Kennedy in the *Democrat* on October 28 showed the public trying to put the puzzle together with the thought "maybe some of the pieces are missing."

No one, not even the experienced press and political observers, could understand the developments. The puzzle to some was whether I was involved and if so how deeply.

By diligent investigation I finally fit the pieces together and made the picture clear when I took decisive action a few days later.

THE CONTINUING CONTROVERSY AT HOXIE

The school board at Hoxie continued to avoid any contact with its anti-integration critics although repeated requests were made for conferences. On October 4 Attorney Amis Guthridge filed a lawsuit against the board to compel it to meet and confer with the anti-integrationist group.

On October 15 the federal courts stepped in to the affray and banned the integration foes from all activity in opposition to the school board's integration policies. It was the first open intervention by a federal court into the affairs of a local school district.

The spreading state interest in the integration controversy saw a rally at Bearden in South Central Arkansas by determined segregationists. The Biggers-Reyno school district a few miles north of Hoxie announced it would not integrate. A segregation rally scheduled for Star City was cancelled, not for lack of opposition to integration but because some responsible citizens feared it would trigger racial strife in the area.

When the schools reopened at Hoxie on October 24, half the high school students did not appear and even more of the elementary grades were absent.

A suit was filed on October 29 seeking to integrate the schools at Van Buren. The NAACP announced it would step up litigation in integration suits throughout the state.

Briefs filed in the federal court on the Hoxie controversy were secreted by the judge.

LRAFB DEDICATED

The Little Rock Air Force Base was dedicated on October 10 by Donald A. Quarles, a high federal official and Arkansas native. An estimated 85,000 persons attended the affair.

NEGROES PROTEST DINNER

On October 14 some Negro leaders assailed the sponsors of a Democratic fund raising affair for not inviting them. It was a public affair to which all were welcome and no invitations were extended to anyone. The dinner had no connection with my own political organization.

STATE BUYS HIGHWAY BONDS

The state purchased some of its own highway bonds on October 26, thus effecting a saving of $48,380.

GOVERNOR ANDERSON A VISITOR

On the 28th Governor Victor E. Anderson of Nebraska was a guest at the Executive Mansion. He was inspecting our building in preparation to build a governor's residence in his state.

HIGHWAY WORKERS APPROVE SOCIAL SECURITY

The Highway Department employees voted overwhelmingly to approve Social Security coverage for all workers in the agency. The vote was 1,028 to 215.

The Highway Commission and the upper echelon personnel of the Department opposed coverage by the Social Security system, and fought hard against a favorable vote. I sided with the ordinary employees who wanted the coverage.

After the favorable vote by the highway employees the Commission took the matter to the courts where I fought the battle for the employees all the way to the Supreme Court.

After losing in the courts the Commission wanted to postpone the implementation date of the coverage. This would have deprived some older employees then ready to retire of coverage and reduced the amount of others. Again I contended with the Commission and won for the employees.

The Department retirement system benefits were greater for the higher paid personnel. Social Security was much better for the ordinary workers. For example, one long time employee, county foreman A. F. "Frank" Murphy of Huntsville, who worked until he was past eighty years of age, retired as soon as he had qualified with 18 months of Social Security coverage. His Social Security check was $120.90 and his Department retirement check, for which he had contributed much longer, was $21.50. Social Security also provided benefits for survivors while the Department system was for employees only.

I have remained very proud of the help I gave to the ordinary workers of the Highway Department in this matter and they were very appreciative of my support at the time.

VICTORY FOR THE MANN AND THE PARTY
By Kennedy, Ark. Democrat   11/9/55

Mayor-elect Woodrow Wilson Mann and the Democratic Donkey congratulated each other on "Victory for the (Mann) Man and the Party."

Mann defeated Republican Mayor Pratt Remmel in the general election by a vote of 10,000 to 8,872.

NEW PROGRAM BENEFITS AGED INMATES AND STATE HOSPITAL

On Nov. 6 we announced an Administration program in the fields of mental health and welfare which had been worked out by Director Carl Adams and Assistant Director A. J. "Red" Moss of the Welfare Department. It provided for the shift of 200 or more elderly inmates of the State Hospital to nursing homes. The program had three distinct advantages: (1) better care for the aged patients; (2) less cost in state funds — the state paid 100 per cent for care in the State Hospital, while in the nursing homes the federal authorities paid 50 per cent or more of the cost; (3) relieved the over-crowding in the State Hospital.

A DIM VIEW OF EACH OTHER
By Kennedy, Ark. Democrat   11/13/55

Gentry and Faubus viewed each other through colored glasses labeled "56", meaning we saw each other's actions in the racing controversy with the 1956 elections for governor in mind. Gentry was more and more mentioned as a candidate, but there was much more to the racing controversy than politics or political futures as events soon revealed.

DRAMATIC CLIMAX TO RACING CONTROVERSY

The two boiling controversies — whether a franchise would be granted to Southland for dog racing at West Memphis, and who would receive the franchise for horse racing at Hot Springs — came to a climax on Thursday and Friday, November 17 and 18, when the Commission members were in Little Rock for two scheduled meetings, one on each of those dates.

Ever since my statement of October 23, I had continued to seek information. During that period the following was confirmed or occurred.

1. On October 28, the day after reporter Sam Harris disclosed McMath's role as attorney for the Eastern Racing Corporation, the former governor was in my office early in the morning ahead of other arrivals, to inform me of his interests. I told McMath I recognized his role as attorney for the Eastern interests, and as an old friend and ally; that because of friendship and old times sake, I would like to help him. But I told him frankly, I could give him no commitment whatsoever until I had investigated fully and made a determination. Then, I told him, he would be the first to know my decision and attitude.

2. I began to accumulate a great deal of information, gathered on a confidential basis from Sam Harris and others,

about the background and connections of the controlling interests of Eastern Racing Corporation of Massachusetts. According to much of this information there seemed to be no doubt of their underworld connections and other unsavory associates in the East. Information also strongly indicated, although it could not confirm, that once these Eastern interests were firmly ensconced in the state with a legitimate enterprise, such as legalized horse racing at Hot Springs, others connected with the group would move in to set up, take control and otherwise run organized crime in the state. This was to include organized prostitution, illegal gambling and perhaps other activities.

John Pappas was the head public figure of the legal Eastern organization. In looking over a list of his close associates, some of them, including body guards, were found to have criminal records almost as long as the moral law.

The further my information gathering proceeded the more this type of information accumulated, until I reached the definite and irrevocable conclusion that to permit the Eastern group to gain a foot-hold in the state would be the worst possible thing that could happen in the whole controversy.

3. My decision made, I remembered my promise to McMath. I called him and he came alone to the mansion one morning before I went to the office. No one else was present at our conference.

My decision, I told him, had to be made on the basis of three factors: (1) what was best for the state and its people as a whole; (2) what was best for me and my administration, and; (3) what was best for racing itself if racing was to continue in Arkansas.

Based on these three factors, I told McMath, I could not favor his client but would oppose its application for the horse racing franchise. I disclosed none of my information about Eastern and its associates but confined my remarks to those explained above. "I'm sorry I can't go with you," I concluded, "but I hope you make a good fee."

McMath took my explanation and decision coolly and stoically and remarked, "I'm just an attorney in the case." Then he took his briefcase and departed.

Sometime during the period following my October 23 statement, a reporter had contacted Mr. Pappas in Boston and inquired if he were coming to Arkansas in the interest of his Hot Springs application. Pappas replied that he was not coming to the state on the matter unless he had a special invitation from the state administration.

Without any prior knowledge of this I was hit with a question on the matter by a reporter at a press conference. My reply was that anyone was welcome to visit Arkansas at any time, but that if Mr. Pappas was waiting for a special invitation to come to Arkansas to discuss the racing franchise, it would be a long time before he was here. He would not be invited by me, I told the press.

With that statement, plus my conference with his Arkansas attorney, I dismissed any possible visit of Mr. Pappas from my mind.

4. I then began to hear of frequent, informal meetings of certain members of the Commission at Briers Restaurant. Some of these meetings, according to my information, were attended by McMath. Brier's was a noted gathering place for members of many political clans and so I had many sources of information about the meetings there. (The restaurant was located about midway between the old Grady Manning and Marion Hotels. The old building has now been destroyed in the Little Rock urban renewal programs.)

5. Soon the pieces of information began to indicate the following: a combine of six commissioners, constituting a majority of the 11-member body, had been formed and certain pledges made to each other. The combine had reached an understanding with Eastern Racing Corporation or its representatives to grant to Eastern the horse racing franchise at Hot Springs. The understanding or agreement on this matter would remain unchangeable and unshakable no matter who disagreed, including the Governor.

I was still receiving contacts by Eastern representatives seeking my approval of its application. Apparently the members of the combine still entertained the hope that their decision would not meet with my disfavor, which explains the visit of Clyde Halk with me mentioned in the story by Sam Harris. If the decision proved to be sufficiently displeasing to cause their dismissal or resignation, then the group (before resigning) would grant the franchise to Southland for dog racing at West Memphis, as well as the franchise to Eastern.

6. Others were hearing variations of this story and other countless rumors. Jeff Rowland, Commission member from Paragould, a man loyal as the sun in its course and honest as the day is long, came to my office to recommend that I dissolve the Commission. I was approaching that conclusion at the time but gave him no indications of my thoughts. Friends sometimes unconsciously give away secrets by attitude, demeanor or otherwise.

On the day before the first scheduled commission meeting of November 17, I decided it was time to test the determination and resolve of the alleged combine.

7. One Commission member had been appointed almost solely on the recommendation of one of my political leaders at Newport, attorney Fred Pickens. I called Fred and asked him to confer with the commissioner, sound out his attitude and convey to him my suggestions on the horse racing franchise. My position on the dog racing permit was already a matter of public record and known to everyone.

A short time later, Pickens called back to say that the commissioner's attitude was contrary to mine and that he was adamant in his stand.

8. Another commission member had been appointed almost solely on the recommendation of State Senator Gaither Johnston of Dermott. It was rumored that this commission member would not attend the meeting because of illness, so I called Senator Johnston and asked if he could secure for me the commissioner's proxy for a vote at the meeting. The Senator expressed his readiness to help and indicated no concern about obtaining the proxy.

A short time later Johnston called back to report that he could not obtain the proxy and to convey to me his alarm at the attitude of the commissioner and his concern for me if the commissioner's vote was needed in determining the matter.

I thanked Senator Johnston for his help and asked him to observe and see if others came to see the commissioner who might want the proxy vote. It was not long until the Senator was again on the line to inform me that a car containing three persons whose descriptions fitted other members of the combine, had visited the commissioner's residence. After a short stay the visitors had departed returning toward Little Rock, the direction from which they had arrived.

It now appeared the "combine" in all likelihood, had the proxy which would maintain its block of 6 votes, giving it a 6 to 5 vote majority on the Commission. It was now equally clear that the combine would not easily be broken, and that any further contacts with these two commissioners, or other members of the combine, would only tend to alert them. Also further contacts could forestall the plan which I had already formed in my own mind for handling the situation. In fact, I decided it would be risky to contact any other members of the Commission. Further knowledge of the situation by loyal members might cause inquiries on their part which would complicate matters.

When Fred Pickens appeared at my office in the early morning before the first meeting on Nov. 17, to confer with me in person on the matter and express his concern, it was further confirmation that the combine was confident that it was in control and that I was not sufficiently alerted to threaten their plans. They, the members of the combine, were sure they would prevail in their aims at the second meeting scheduled for 1:00 p.m. the next day.

I met only briefly with the Commission before its session the morning of the 17th. Ten members were present. I reiterated briefly my opposition to a franchise for dog racing without approval of the people at an election. No such election had been held. However, I added, that matter could be handled at the meeting the next day. The Commission must first go and inspect the track as required by law and as the Attorney General had ruled, before any other official action could be taken.

Therefore, I told the members, Mr. Orville Cheney, secretary of the Commission, had made all arrangements for the inspection, including a chartered bus for transportation which was then waiting.

I then concluded, "Tomorrow you must also consider the matter of the franchise for horse racing at Hot Springs. I would like for you to come by my office about 15 minutes before the meeting so I can discuss the matter with you."

I then left the room, the Commission voted formally to make the inspection trip and took off for West Memphis to be wined and dined during the inspection tour.

Without giving Cheney full information on the scheme I had uncovered, I asked him to be observant for any information as to the attitude of individual members or the Commission as a group. At one point during the trip he pretended to fall asleep and overheard some bits of conversation which tended to confirm the existence of the scheme of which I had learned and the intention to carry it out.

Democrat reporter George Douthit wrote of the Southland inspection:

> *West Memphis Citizens put out the red carpet and gave the commissioners and visiting newsmen a royal welcome at the West Memphis Country Club, before the inspection was made.*
> *"Odds" Posted*
> *Afterward the entire crowd went to the race track where they watched eight greyhounds run a full-fledged race. The betting windows were manned, the tote board operated the "odds" and the results were posted. However, no bets went into the betting windows.*
> *Members of the racing commission admitted they were impressed by the big operation and felt that the track ought to be allowed to operate.*
> *Cecil R. Edmonds, president of Southland, played official host to the racing commission at both the dinner and the visit to the track. There were no speeches, only introductions. Mr. Edmonds told the DEMOCRAT that over $900,000 had been spent and that a total of $1.6 million would be laid out before the plant has "all the luxuries."*
> *Favors Meet in April*
> *One of the commissioners asked Mr. Edmonds: "If you received a permit to operate today, when would you start?"*
> *Mr. Edmonds replied: "It would be April before we could start holding races. I would like to hold races during April, May and June."*
> *The track's plans include complete air conditioning for hot summer nights near the Mississippi river. The track is only eight miles from Memphis and a potential 350,000 "customers."*
> *One member of the commission sighed: "I sure hate to eat this fine food when I know I've got to vote 'no'."*

> *Another said: "Arkansas is going to miss a lot of revenue if it doesn't let this track operate."*
> *The DEMOCRAT reporter, who accompanied the commission on the bus, asked one member point blank if he thought the commission would grant Southland a permit, if it weren't for the governor's opposition.*
> *"They'd do it in a minute and you know it, too," he replied. Then he added: "But I predict they will go along with the governor."*

* * *

PAPPAS IN LITTLE ROCK

After the departure of the commission and the transaction of some more business in the office, I took off hurriedly to fill some engagement. The appointments book kept by Mrs. Patsy Ellis reads: "Dedication of Highways 96-41 at County Line School" (Franklin, Logan and Sebastian Counties).

On the way out of town I grabbed a newspaper — the *Arkansas Democrat* which was already on the streets. As my driver wheeled the car over the Arkansas River bridge heading north, I unfolded the paper to be greeted by glaring headlines that John C. Pappas was in Little Rock. With his entourage from Boston, his Arkansas attorneys, McMath and Woods, and a number of big name labor leaders present, Pappas would hold a press conference that day, the news story read. The news story was the first I knew of Pappas' visit to Little Rock, which to me was entirely unexpected.

Somewhere I stopped the car, called a friend in Little Rock and asked him to check on the Pappas group and the press conference, and learn whatever was possible of the rapidly developing situation.

At the Pappas press conference a glowing picture was painted, which was window dressing for the decision expected from the Racing Commission the next day. Here is how the picture was described by *Gazette* reporter Matilda Tuohey in the morning paper of November 18:

> *A glittering package of sport, civic enterprise, jobs, stock and advertising was promised Arkansas yesterday if the Eastern Racing Association gets to operate a horse racing track at Hot Springs.*
> *The plush promises were made at a full-dress press conference by Eastern's president, John C. Pappas of Boston, and assorted persons who would be involved in constructing and operating the track.*
> . . .
> *Eastern's Offerings*
> *These are among Eastern's offerings to Hot Springs and to the state in return for a franchise.*
> *1. A modern plant costing about $3,000,000, to accommodate 25,000 or more players.*
> *2. Good thoroughbred horses for the 31-day meet and at least one $25,000 purse for a big feature race.*
> *3. An opportunity for Arkansans to buy up to 50 per cent of the stock in a new Arkansas corporation which would be formed.*
> *4. Jobs for 1,000 to 1,200 construction workers and for about 600 persons during the racing season.*
> *5. Use of the plant during the off-season by Hot Springs for civic affairs, plus racing days for charity.*
> *6. A publicity promotion within a 400-mile radius of the track to bill Arkansas as the "playground of the Southwest."*

McMath Is Emcee

Former Governor Sid McMath, who was employed by Eastern to represent its interests, was a sort of master of ceremonies at the conference.

. . .

Backing up all the assurances given were:

Mark Linenthal, a Boston architect and industrial engineer who drew the plans;

Al Harmon of Oklahoma City who had the contract for the construction;

Odell Smith of Little Rock, president of the Arkansas State Federation of Labor, who guaranteed the labor supply;

Two representatives of a bonding company were there to assure a performance bond (for completion of the track in time for a spring meet).

McMath said Eastern had cash assets of about $3,000,000 which it can invest immediately.

Ed Sullivan, Eastern's public relations man, said Suffolk Downs (operated by Eastern in Boston) does a lot of advertising and said the proposed Garland Park (at Hot Springs) would do the same.

McMath's law partners — Henry Woods and Leland Leatherman — attended the conference along with Clyde Halk, a Hot Springs businessman who has been looking after Eastern's interest for several months. A number of other persons in the room were not identified and stayed in the background.

Back in the executive mansion after a day's activity, I had a late night visitor. Jimmy Karam came to inform me of what was going to happen on the morrow.

"Governor," he said with vehemence, "do you know what they're going to do to you tomorrow?"

I indicated I wanted to know and he outlined the plans of the combine as I had previously learned them. Still I didn't divulge to Jimmy that I knew. In fact I questioned the accuracy of his information.

"Jimmy," I said, "I appointed all those fellows. I'm going to talk to them before the meeting tomorrow, and I don't believe they'll do that to me."

"Governor," Jimmy insisted with even greater vehemence, "they're already set. Nobody's going to change their minds because the agreement's already made. They're even betting money on it. One of them (a commissioner of the combine) has already asked me to bet a thousand dollars for him."

Then suddenly interrupting his chain of speech he inquired, "Do you have a telephone with an extension?"

I indicated that we did.

"Get on that extension!" he directed peremptorily, and immediately took the other phone.

In a moment a voice answered and disclosed his identity. He was one of the six I had mentally listed in the combine.

"_____," said Jimmy, calling him by name, "you asked me to bet a thousand dollars for you on who got the franchise tomorrow at Hot Springs. I haven't got your check yet and I just wondered if you're sure of what you're doing?"

"Well, I think so," the man replied, "I don't think there's been any change."

"I've got to know for sure," Jimmy emphasized, "I'm fixing to bet ten thousand dollars and I can't afford to lose that much."

"Well," the man hesitated, "I think it's all right but I'll recheck and let you know in a few minutes."

"You do that," said Jimmy, "and call me back," and gave him the number from which he was speaking.

In a few moments the phone rang, Jimmy answered it. The Commissioner said he had "checked with the boys," everything was all right and for Jimmy to go ahead and place the one thousand dollar bet for him, and to bet all he wanted for himself on the outcome.

Jimmy told the man to get his check to him, and the combine member said it would be there in the morning. The check came in the mail that night and Jimmy brought it to me the next morning. I quickly secured photostats of the envelope and the check and returned the originals to Jimmy. (The photostats are still in my files.)

I still maintained to Jimmy that I could dissuade the commission members from the plans set by the combine, disclosing nothing of my intentions. Jimmy departed shaking his head in perplexity at my stubborn (or stupid) attitude, and I made my way to the office.

There I selected a fast and accurate secretary and dictated a letter of resignation, and had a copy prepared for each commission member.

I then dictated a letter of dismissal for cause and had a copy prepared for each member.

I placed the documents carefully on my desk shortly before the commission members began to arrive in the outer office.

I had secured three uniformed state troopers from Chief Lindsey. As they arrived I instructed each one to place himself at a door to my office. After the Commission entered my office no one was to be permitted to leave the office until I indicated it was okay.

Jeff Rowland came shortly before the other commissioners began to arrive and I got the opportunity to tell him my plans. "That's the right thing, Governor," he said. "I'll go with you on it," he added, his face brightening.

I got the opportunity to merely warn two other commissioners of what was about to transpire. Then I informed Cheney and J. L. Bland of my plans as the remaining commissioners were entering the outer office.

Only Cheney, secretary of the Commission, was permitted to be present when the ten Commission members filed quietly into the inner office and were seated. I did not even take my seat. I walked back of the desk, explained briefly that the situation had become such that any decision that was made at that time on either of the racing matters would be subject to misunderstanding and misinterpretation; that it was my conclusion that the best course was for the Commission to resign. Then no decision could be made, and no legal action would be possible for some time because no commission would exist. There would be time to clarify the confused situation.

Rowland quickly spoke up saying, "Governor, I think you're right. I'll give you my resignation." I handed him the paper prepared for his signature and he took out his pen to sign it. Two or three others followed suit, among them Laud Payne.

By that time some members of the combine had begun to regain their speech and one of them said, "Well, I'd like to know why." (for the resignations).

I looked at him and replied, "I've just told you why."

Then another was aroused. "Well, I'm not going to resign! You'll have to fire me!"

I replied quickly but softly, "_____, you can have it either way you wish. Here's your resignation, and here's your dismissal for cause." I tendered the two papers. He took the blank resignation, and as he affixed his name he said threateningly, "This will make you another damned one-term governor."

By then those who had not signed were busy affixing their names. I do not recall that another word was spoken. I stacked the signed papers neatly on the corner of my desk, moved to one of the doors and had it opened by the trooper. The members, leaving more quietly than they had arrived, filed through the outer office and down the stairs and were gone before those who awaited them in the big reception room were aware of what had occurred.

I then nodded to Cheney who hurried out to the reception room to make an important announcement.

Now let the reporters' stories describe the scene there.

ENTIRE STATE RACING BOARD QUITS IN ROW OVER PERMITS

By George Douthit, Democrat Staff Writer

All 11 members of the Arkansas Racing Commission resigned at 1 p.m. today at the request of Governor Faubus over two controversial racing issues. The chief executive had received word of a rebellion in the commission against his wishes on the Southland dog racing franchise bid and the awarding of a franchise at Hot Springs.

The members of the commission went into the governor's office at 12:55. He had a prepared resignation for the members to sign and was prepared to dismiss those who declined.

It was a virtual firing over the rebellion.

Representatives of Southland of West Memphis, Oaklawn Jockey Club of Hot Springs and Eastern Racing Association of Boston, Mass., all concerned in the controversial issues had gathered with members of the press in the governor's reception room.

FAUBUS FIRES COMMISSION JUST BEFORE IT COULD DECIDE HORSE AND DOG RACE ISSUES

Crowd Shocked Into Silence By the Mass 'Resignations'

By Sam G. Harris and Matilda Tuohey Of the Gazette Staff

Governor Faubus fired the Arkansas Racing Commission yesterday, minutes before it was to have acted on dog and horse racing franchises at West Memphis and Hot Springs respectively.

The niceties of political protocol were scrupulously observed: Officially, the commissioners "resigned." But the typed resignations were waiting for their signatures when they were summoned to the executive chamber a bare 10 minutes before they were to have assembled in the main reception room to dispose of the two racing matters.

The governor declined to tell reporters anything except that 10 of the 11 commissioners at Little Rock for the scheduled meeting had "handed" him their resignations. He said that he had talked with them as a group five or six minutes before the mass resignations.

But Commissioner Laud Payne of Piggott told newsmen later that the governor merely called them in and as soon as they were seated, informed them that he would be happy to accept their resignations. All complied, Payne said, without protest. He said the request was unexpected as far as he was concerned. . . .

Ex-Commissioners Listed

Those resigning were Dr. Edwin L. Dunaway of Conway, chairman; Payne, Jeff Roland of Paragould, W. P. Davis of Newport, Jim Evans of Yellville, Lacy Lawrence of Texarkana, Joseph

Schmelzer of Little Rock, J. E. "Ed" Wright of Little Rock, Ernest Parker of Benton and Allan Bryant of Hot Springs.

The commissioner whose resignation wasn't received is June Gibson of Dermott, reportedly ill at his home.

All were original appointees of Mr. Faubus.

The governor, deftly parrying reporters' questions, declared that the resignations spoke for themselves, that they were free to infer or speculate whatever they desired, that he would name a new Commission in due time but was in no hurry to do so. . . .

There were reports earlier this week that the Commission was not unanimously in accord with the governor's sentiments on either West Memphis or Hot Springs. . . .

Apparently the governor felt there was a chance his wishes would be ignored on one or both points and that it was the kind of chance he couldn't afford to take politically in view of his previous statements.

Dramatic Surprise

The dramatic announcement of the Commission's resignation came as a thunderbolt, stunning the large crowd which was awaiting the Commission's appearance in the big reception room.

While the announcement was being read by Revenue Commissioner J. Orville Cheney, . . . the ex-commissioners filed out of the governor's small reception room and left the building.

Every seat except those reserved for the Commission was taken in the designated meeting place 10 minutes before the scheduled 1 p.m. meeting. John Cella of St. Louis, president of Oaklawn, and his attorney, W. J. Smith of Little Rock, were there. So was John C. Pappas, president of Eastern, with an entourage which included his Arkansas attorney, former Governor Sid McMath. Cecil Ray Edmonds, president of Southland, and his staff including Speaker of the House of Representatives Charles F. Smith, West Memphis attorney, were on hand as were some 100 to 125 others who lined the walls of the room.

Cheney, his face strained and tense, walked out of the executive offices, rapped for order and declared:

"There will be no meeting of the Racing Commission today. The Racing Commission has been dissolved."

There was not a sound in the room for a full minute. Then reporters hurried up to Cheney for an explanation and he read the full letter of resignation as advocates and supporters of the various applicants milled around.

McMath and Charles F. Smith both expressed surprise at the turn of events, saying that they were anxious to present their cases before any qualified commission. Craig "Jerry" Campbell, Southland's publicist, said that his employers were wholly unprepared for the development.

Pappas, in a prepared statement later, said he was sorry Eastern didn't have an opportunity to present its case yesterday but that it stood ready to do so and all Eastern "ever expected is a fair hearing." The statement expressed the view that the new Commission should open the Hot Springs bids "as quickly as possible."

Governor Sees Press

An aide from the governor's office walked into the milling group and told reporters that the governor would see them immediately if they wanted to talk to him. The aide said the governor was in a hurry to leave town to fill a speaking engagement at Fort Smith.

The governor handed copies of the resignations to each of the reporters, saying that the copies told the whole story.

He was asked if he had told the Commission his feelings on the two franchises under consideration during the brief conference before the resignations. He said he hadn't had an opportunity to impart such information to them and hadn't polled them.

When would he appoint a new commission? "I have plenty of time," he replied, adding that he had a rather busy schedule for the next several days.

Would he comment on events preceding the resignations? "No more than that it was signed here and delivered to me here — signed on this very desk."

Would he acquaint his new appointees with his feelings about the Hot Springs and West Memphis situations? "As I name a new Commission I will discuss the problems fully and I expect our views will coincide."

Six Applications In

Mr. Faubus said he had some prospective appointees in mind but declined to identify them. (Before he could get away for Fort Smith he had received requests from four individuals for appointment to the Commission and his secretarial staff had received two others.)

Would it be safe to speculate that the Commission had been fired? "I can't control the speculation of the press."

Could newsmen infer that he had learned the Commission was not in accord with his views? He smiled and said that any inference made would be at the writer's risk.

Does he think that chances are getting better for the passage of the "Baptist Amendment" — proposed Thursday by the Baptist State Convention to outlaw pari-mutuel and other gambling? "I certainly do."

Again, was he surprised at the Commission's action? "I am rather hard to surprise."

Will there be a racing meeting in the spring of 1956 at Hot Springs? "Everyone anticipates there'll be a racing meet at Hot Springs."

What effect will the resignations have on the three bids pending on the Hot Springs franchise? "That is a legal question I haven't looked in to."

The governor said there was no legal way now that his requirement for a Crittenden County referendum on dog racing could be met.

"It could have been held earlier under the cloak of legality but it can't be held under such a cloak now," he said.

Baptist Ministers Received

As reporters left the executive chamber, a delegation of Baptist ministers including Dr. Ben L. Bridges, general secretary of the Arkansas Baptist State Convention; Dr. Dale Cowling of Little Rock, Convention vice president; Dr. W. O. Vaught, Jr.,

of Little Rock, immediate past Convention president, and Rev. Russell Clubb of West Memphis, was ushered in along with the Governor's lunch.

Apparently they had assembled to attend the Commission meeting and called on the governor after the surprise announcement to pay their respects. They told him he was in their prayers and that they appreciated his firmness in meeting the dog racing "threat."

Payne said that so far as he knew there hadn't been any kind of poll of the commissioners concerning their stands on the twin controversies.

Payne, a Piggott publisher and former member of the legislature, expressed doubt that Southland would have received a permit "at this time."

How about Oaklawn's chances with the Commission, Payne was asked.

"That is what he (the governor) didn't know for sure," he replied.

Of the ten Racing Commission members who resigned, five were reappointed when the Commission was reconstituted on November 28. They were Rowland, Payne, Wright, Schmelzer and Dunaway, with the last named continuing as chairman.

Gibson, who remained ill, was not disturbed in his position. He was later admitted to a Little Rock hospital where he died December 14, 1955.

Individuals in public life, ofttimes inexperienced, are often exposed to powerful pressure and persuasion, and sometimes to strong inducements coupled with seeming justification for certain attitudes and decisions. Then there is the ever present human fallibility from which none of us is free, which leads everyone at times to make mistakes.

The five members who were reappointed continued as loyal and trusted members of the administration. Of the other five who resigned, all, except perhaps one, were again counted among my friends and supporters before my administration had ended.

The five newcomers to the Commission whose appointments were announced on November 28 were: R. A. "Bob" Young, Jr., of Fort Smith, Ned Stewart of Texarkana, Carl Hope of North Little Rock, James Bush of Helena, and Dr. Porter Rogers of Searcy. As the years have rolled by time appeared to reveal, after my administration had ended, that one of the new appointees had feet of clay.

Even after the Racing Commission was reconstituted, and it was clear that no real fault could be found with Oakland Park's operation for the more than twenty years past, the controversy was not ended.

Attorney General Gentry blasted my alleged domination of the Commission, and officially ruled that the highest bidder must be considered favorably for the franchise.

Research by *Democrat* reporter George Douthit revealed that Oaklawn's high bid had ranged from $5 to $100 over the past years of its operations. On the occasion of those bids there was no competition, as Douthit pointed out.

Now three firms, including Oaklawn, had submitted sealed bids in seeking the franchise. This, according to Douthit, made Gentry's ruling of great importance, as the opening of the bids awaited a formal meeting of the Commission to consider the matter.

On December 5 the Commission met, took from the locked safe the sealed bids and opened them for consideration. The bid for the secret firm of Kansas City was $1,150; Eastern represented by McMath bid $10,001; Oaklawn represented by Bill Smith bid $25,600. When the bids were read the losing attorneys silently folded their brief cases and quietly departed. Oaklawn received the franchise.

The Commission by unanimous vote denied a franchise to Southland for dog racing at West Memphis. The firm's attorneys immediately began preparations to appeal the decision to the Courts.

On December 31, I appointed Joe Lee McKennon of Dumas to the Commission to fill the vacancy created by Gibson's death. The crisis over racing at Hot Springs, which for a time threatened my political welfare and credibility as a public figure, had ended. Affairs at the horse racing track continued on a tranquil basis throughout the remainder of my administration.

The principal attorneys are mentioned in the news stories, W. J. "Bill" Smith being one of them.

To my recollection it was not until after the Oaklawn controversy was ended that I first met Smith, on or after December 5, 1955. About a year later he was to begin, at my request, the role as my legislative advisor.

In an editorial on Nov. 19 headed, It Was the Firmness of the Governor, the *Gazette* said: "Resignation of the entire Racing Commission in the middle of the dog and horse racing controversy testifies to the strength and sincerity of Gov. Faubus's convictions, particularly on the dog track issue."

LATE SCRATCHES
By Kennedy, Ark. Democrat   11/20/55

When an entry has been made in a race, the name is listed with all others on a sheet called a racing form. If for some reason the entry is withdrawn from the race, its name is scratched out. This cartoon appeared following the dramatic climax of the racing drama on November 18. From a racing commission form I scratched off the names of the Commission members who would not participate in the meeting scheduled for that day.

REL GRAY ELECTED BAPTIST PRESIDENT

Arkansas Baptists in state convention elected Rel Gray of Helena as state president, and endorsed the move to vote down all forms of gambling statewide.

THE INTEGRATION-SEGREGATION FRONT

On November 8 two Hoxie school directors who had opposed integration of the schools were overwhelmingly re-elected, clearly showing the sentiment of the people of the district.

On November 29 at a mass meeting in Pine Bluff a move was adopted requesting me to recall a state school delegation which was to attend a national conference on school affairs.

The racial issue was cited in the petition to me. I had nothing to do with the selection of the delegation nor the conference it was to attend. The petition was signed by Jim Johnson of Crossett and L. D. Poynter of Pine Bluff. Johnson had begun his skillful maneuvers designed to place me on the spot in the segregation-integration controversy, and to prepare the way for his candidacy for governor in 1956 as the state's leading champion of segregation.

RUMORS START AGAIN: IS SID CONSIDERING RUNNING FOR GOVERNOR?

Arkansas Democrat, Wednesday, November 30, 1955

> *The newest rumor around the state capitol today was that former Gov. Sid McMath would seek the governor's office again next summer. . . .*
>
> *The basis for the rumor, apparently, is the present controversy over the racing franchise for horse racing at Hot Springs. McMath is attorney for Eastern Racing Corporation of Boston headed by John Pappas. Eastern's bid was rejected.*

December 8 —

STEVENSON HUNTS, TALKS POLITICS IN ARKANSAS

Former Governor Adlai Stevenson of Illinois, the Democratic Party's 1952 nominee for president and again a candidate for the nomination, came to Arkansas for a visit and duck hunt as the guest of Dr. J. S. Rushing of El Dorado. The hunt was at the Rushing farm at Jerome in the extreme southeastern corner of Drew County.

Democratic Chairman Tom Harper met Mr. Stevenson at Memphis and the two flew by small plane to Greenville, Miss., where they were met by Dr. Rushing and Sen. Fulbright. They traveled by car to Jerome where other guests awaited, including Sen. McClellan, Congressman Oren Harris, Sen. John Sparkman of Alabama, Stevenson's running mate in 1952, and Sen. Russell Long of Louisiana.

A speaking engagement in Little Rock delayed my arrival at Rushing's palatial farm and hunting combine until the second day of Stevenson's three-day visit. On one night of the affair some 200 Arkansas political leaders were guests for dinner and a reception for Gov. Stevenson. The gathering looked like the Who's Who of Democratic politics in Arkansas. Dozens of newsmen also gathered and a press conference with the presidential candidate was arranged by Harry S. Ashmore, a Stevenson staff member who accompanied the former governor.

December 9—

STEVENSON TURNS FROM HUNTING TO POLITICS

The main guests, Stevenson, Senators McClellan, Fulbright, Long and Sparkman were reported to have gotten their limit of ducks — 4 each, the first morning of the hunt before my arrival.

On the second morning when I hunted with Stevenson, Fulbright, Rushing and perhaps two or three others, we waited in the cold for the ducks which did not come. The incident clearest in my memory was the belated arrival, after we were almost numb from standing in the cold water, of one lone, stray duck which plumped down near by. As it became alarmed and took off through the timber the guns of Stevenson and Fulbright roared in the stillness, followed by a mighty oath from Fulbright as the lone duck continued on its way. I felt happy with the duck's escape but I didn't note any evidence of compassion from others present. That was our duck hunting for the day. From such success, or lack of it, the turn to food and politics in the comfort of the lodge was a welcome change.

Stevenson spoke at the dinner but his remarks were not crowned with phenomenal success. His attempts at humor left his hearers unimpressed. He had a ready wit for certain times and places but his attempts to be a regular guy with such a group just didn't seem to go over. At such a time and place with such a crowd, there was an opportunity to "sew up" politically an entire state and send the word ringing across the South and beyond its borders. But the candidate just couldn't seem to go over, couldn't establish a rapport, was unable to strike while the iron was hot. He had the opportunity to knock the ball over the fence, but many felt instead of a hit his appearance was at best a walk. Many who appreciated the rare opportunity to hobnob with a potential president were more dubious of his candidacy after he left than before he came.

Certainly this was no fault of those who arranged for Stevenson's visit. No host anywhere could have done better with genuine hospitality, comfort and plenty for all his guests than Dr. Rushing. Those present, if properly impressed and inspired by the candidate, could have carried the state for the presidential seeker, for the nomination or for the office as the party nominee.

DINNER HONORING
CONGRESSMAN JIM TRIMBLE

The neighbors and friends of Jim Trimble staged a dinner in his honor in his hometown of Berryville on the night of December 21, 1955. I was invited along with Harry Oswald, executive secretary of the Rural Electric Administration Cooperatives of the state, to attend and participate in the program.

I accompanied Harry who drove from Little Rock.

That was the period when the "This is Your Life" programs were prevalent. After the dinner the affair, much to Congressman Trimble's surprise, was turned into a courtroom setting with Jim on trial and many relatives, friends and associates testifying to certain events in his life.

Judge Trimble had a most successful career in public service. He started in politics as a Carroll County official and had continued to rise, never having suffered a defeat. He studied law and earned his license. From his county office he ran for the district position of prosecuting attorney.

The district was then composed of the four counties of Washington, Benton, Carroll and Madison. The first two, more populous and prosperous, were the abodes and places of practice of some of the most distinguished members of the bar in Arkansas.

ADLAI COMES CALLING
By Kennedy, Ark. Democrat   12/8/55

Adlai Stevenson of Illinois, a candidate for the Democratic presidential nomination, was invited to Arkansas for a duck hunt. Adlai hoped to lure the ducks, mid-South support, to his section of water where he could bag them as delegates at the 1956 convention.

108

As it happened Jim drew two of the most able lawyers of those counties as opponents. They were great speakers as well. Fortunately for Jim they spent most of their time combating each other and referred to him as just a green country boy. It was a joint campaign, customary in those days, with all candidates appearing together and speaking from the same platform to the same audience.

In those days 95 per cent of the population was rural. Everyone knew about one-room schools, wood-burning stoves and cold wedges and wagon tires on frosty mornings. Everyone knew about tilling the land with horse-drawn plows, planting and cultivating crops and the ultimate harvest. Jim, of course, was most familiar with the rural way of life having been born and reared in a small mountain community in South Carroll County known as Possum Trot.

Mr. Trimble's two opponents made flowery, eloquent speeches, their oratory holding entranced their less learned listeners as it flowed out and around them. But the well educated speakers with their refined and well-honed eloquence didn't seem quite down-to-earth. The well-turned phrases didn't seem to find a secure lodging place in the breasts of those who were to make the decision on election day.

When Jim rose to speak his evident lack of experience and eloquence — he was never a great speaker — quickly established for him an empathy with his hearers. They were not, they realized, good speakers either but they understood life around them as Jim understood it. Jim readily accepted the label of "green country boy" placed on him by his opponents.

It was the practice then, when seed corn was plentiful and a "good stand of corn" was important, to plant more grains than were expected to grow to maturity. If the seed grains sprouted well the stand of corn would be too thick, and at the proper time the corn had to be thinned by pulling out the extra plants. What country boy hadn't heard his father say: "Pull out the others, leave the green stalks and let them grow."

Jim said to his hearers:

"When I was a boy thinning corn on the farm my father always told me to leave the green stalk, pull out the others, and let it grow."

That thought found a lodging place in the minds of the voters. They followed Jim's suggestion on election day. They pulled out the other candidates and left Jim to grow.

Prosecutor Trimble was promoted to Judge Trimble in the election of 1938, and later elected to Congress.

Jim assumed the judgeship on Jan. 1, 1939, at the same time I assumed the office of Circuit Clerk and Recorder. In many ways he was like a political father to me. I had come to the county seat as a green country boy as had Jim to his own county seat some years before.

There were many stories of Jim's boyhood and career, some touching, many humorous. I was called on to testify as to Jim's judicial record in Madison County of which there were many humorous and human interest stories.

It was a long program, but a pleasant and nostalgic one for Congressman Trimble. It must have remained one of the pleasant highlights of his career.

RESORTING TO SURGERY
By Graham, Ark. Gazette   12/9/55

The State Hospital Board was concerned with the condition of the physical plant of the facility. The buildings were old and obsolete, without airconditioning and other modern conveniences, and overcrowded with some patients sleeping on the floor.

The newest building, erected during Gov. Cherry's administration, was defective and not in use. Some contractor goofed and was not required to make good on faulty construction.

The ancient multi-storied brick structure housing the children had an ever widening crack reaching from top to bottom. Three different architectural and engineering firms were engaged for assistance and advice. Attempts were made to reinforce the defective structure with steel bands but the personnel of the firms would give no assurance that the building would stand. It might collapse within 24 hours with resulting death and injury to the small inmates.

Major reconstruction projects were needed to replace most of the ancient buildings. But there was little use in considering such a program unless the General Assembly approved new tax measures to obtain the necessary revenue.

RUMOR OF THE WEEK:

WINTHROP ROCKEFELLER URGED TO RUN FOR GOV. ON GOP TICKET.

AP&L PRESENTS CASE FOR $1 MILLION INCREASE...

we're hurting!

AP&L

P.S.C.

don't think it hasn't been charmin'

—outside of bein' a @#* republican, Pratt, you're okay.

PERSONALITIES ---

JOE C. HARDIN, NEW STATE MGR. FOR ARK-LA GAS...

REMMEL BOWS OUT AT LAST COUNCIL SESSION

WORK BEGINS ON MAMMOTH PAPER MILL AT PINE BLUFF.

HARVE THORN, TO SEEK ATTY.-GEN'L. POST IN '56...

HIGHLIGHTS OF THE NEWSWEEK, By Kennedy, 12/25/55
    RUMOR OF THE WEEK: "Winthrop Rockefeller urged to run for Governor on GOP Ticket." Many people were not aware that Rockefeller had not been in Arkansas long enough to meet the residency qualification to run for governor. Remmel bowed out of his last council meeting as Mann took over as Mayor on January 1, 1956. The AP&L pled poverty before the PSC as it asked for a still further rate increase. Work began on a mammoth paper mill at Pine Bluff which would provide many permanent industrial jobs in the area. Joe C. Hardin was selected by Witt Stephens to be manager for Ark-La Gas Company. Harve Thorn, former Speaker of the House, announced for Attorney General proclaiming himself an ardent segregationist.

A PENNY FOR GOV. FAUBUS

Oswald and I grew tired and sleepy on the return journey. To refresh ourselves we stopped at 2 or 3 o'clock in the morning at an all-night cafe in the northern approaches to North Little Rock. We were the only customers and the only attendant was a kindly, middle-aged lady.

The bill for our order was sufficient to qualify for the collection of one cent in sales tax — still two per cent then. When we stepped up to the cash register Harry inquired of the bill and the lady said pleasantly, "It's 40 cents and a penny for Gov. Faubus."

Harry cast a fleeting, involuntary glance at me but did not give away my identity. He paid the bill and accepted the change as I stood by close enough to reach out and touch the lady. When the transaction was finished I said to her:

"I'm glad to note two things. First, you're conscientiously collecting the tax for the state. And second, you pronounce my name correctly."

Then I stuck out my hand to introduce myself, "I'm Governor Faubus," I said to the lady.

She was so surprised and shocked that she became speechless. I don't recall that she recovered her composure sufficiently to say anything before we left the establishment.

ARK-LA REFUNDS

The Arkansas Louisiana Gas Company had delayed as long as possible the reduction of its rates and the making of refunds to its customers. The company, now controlled by W. R. "Witt" Stephens, announced on Dec. 21 that its rates would be rolled back and the refund checks would go out.

HOXIE SUPERINTENDENT RESIGNS

In the increasingly bitter integration controversy at Hoxie, Supt. K. E. Vance announced on Dec. 23 that he had resigned effective Jan. 16, 1956.

APPOINTMENTS, AUGUST 1955

Advisory Council to ESD: V. H. Williams and F. L. Call, Little Rock; Vernon McKimmey, Camden; George Ellison, Ft. Smith; and W. D. DeMers, Little Rock, representing labor. Joe Schmelzer, Little Rock; B. G. Adams, Conway; Floyd Sharp, Little Rock; Ray Kimball, DeQueen; and Rex Morgan, Corning, representing employers. Rev. Nolan P. Howington, Little Rock; Suzanne C. Lighton, Fayetteville; Henry Armstrong, Ft. Smith; J. G. Smith, Pine Bluff; and Joe Decker, Pocahontas, representing the public. Robert B. Roach, Little Rock, resigned as Chairman of State Racing Commission; Dr. Edwin L. Dunaway, Conway, was designated as Chairman; Joseph L. Schmelzer, Little Rock, appointed to Commission to fill vacancy. Marvin Melton, Jonesboro, chairman and Jeff Davis, El Dorado, vice-chairman to the Water Rights Commission. Carl E. Wright, Little Rock, to Water Pollution Control Board. J. Lester Booker, Little Rock, to Contractors Licensing Board. Forestry Commission: Fred Dierks, Jr., Hot Springs; C. F. Byrns, Ft. Smith; and Spencer Fox, Pine Bluff. On September 5, Melvin Dacus, West Memphis; and Beryl Anthony of El Dorado were appointed. J. M. Spicer of Stuttgart to State Plant Board.

APPOINTMENTS, SEPTEMBER 1955

Frank Cannaday, Huntsville, took position in Education Department. Ben Rankin, Little Rock, replaced Cannaday in Tax Assessment Co-ordination Division. Lt. Jack Rhea promoted to Captain — named Director of Highway Safety; Sgt. Mack Thompson to lieutenant, named state fire marshal. Dr. W. Marion Brown, Board of Dental Examiners. J. O. Mitchell, Jr., Board of Accountancy. Hospital Advisory Council. Reappointed Rev. John Kordsmeir, Dr. Marion H. Gray, both of Little Rock; J. A. West, El Dorado; Marvin A. Altman, Ft. Smith. Appointed Carlos J. R. Smith,

Helena; John Gilbreath, Little Rock; Dr. R. C. Dickinson, DeQueen; Mrs. Alice Lochbaum, Little Rock; and Rosa Lee Gilmore, Benton. Robert L. Rogers, II, Little Rock, to State Hospital Board to fill vacancy created by resignation for business reasons of Harold H. Hedges, Jr., who praised the administration. Frank T. Blackburn, Little Rock, to State Board of Pharmacy.

APPOINTMENTS, OCTOBER 1955

Dr. E. D. McKnight, Brinkley, State Board of Health, first appointed by Gov. Parnell in 1930. Raymond G. Clinton, Hot Springs, to Arkansas Motor Vehicle Commission to replace Charles Scarbrough who resigned. The Committee-of-100, appointed to aid the AIDC in the state's industry seeking effort, met and organized on Oct. 18; named to leadership positions were: Kohn Bray, Marked Tree, Chairman; Don Harrell, Camden, Vice-Chairman; Edwin Dunaway, Little Rock; A. P. Raney, Paris; L. L. Baxter, Fayetteville; L. L. Lipe, Eudora; B. A. Lynch, Blytheville; Searcy Elrod, Rison; W. W. Jones, Benton; J. K. Wadley, Texarkana; D. H. Thurston, El Dorado, all to executive Committee. Other members of the Committee-of-100 were: Paul Jones, Stuttgart; S. J. Wilson, Montrose; Wade Lahar, Mountain Home; Wallace G. Stone, Siloam Springs; Sam Doolittle, Bentonville; Claude H. Turney, Harrison; Joe L. Reaves, Jr., Warren; Clarence Johnson, Harrell; Ray Anderson, Berryville; Cecil Cupp, Arkadelphia; Lloyd Russell, Piggott; A. P. Stephenson, Heber Springs; Ray Howard, Magnolia; R. W. Morgan, Jr., Morrilton; M. S. Rubenstein, Lake City; Julian James, Jonesboro; Paul Alexander, Mulberry; J. C. Johnson, West Memphis; Whit Shaver, Wynne; Fred Thompson, Fordyce; Merl F. Peterson, Dumas; Bennie Ryburn, Monticello; M. L. Black, Conway; Eddie Anderson, Ozark; L. R. "Jack" Cochran, Salem; Frank Sweeney, Hot Springs; Garland Anthony, Hot Springs; Sen. Oliver Williams, Sheridan; C. Winston Mack, Paragould; H. M. Olsen, Hope; J. Carroll Cuffman, Malvern; R. J. Sain, Nashville; W. F. Headstream, Batesville; A. B. Whitfield, Calico Rock; P. L. Copeland, Newport; Wallace McGeorge, Jr., Pine Bluff; Stanley McNulty, Pine Bluff; L. H. King, Clarksville; Malvin Christie, Lewisville; W. A. Dowell, Jr., Walnut Ridge; Paul Benham, Marianna; Lynn Thomasson, Star City; James T. McGuyre, Foreman; Frank Carr, England; Harold Whitson, Huntsville; Gus McCracken, Flippin; William G. Fox, Manila; Ben F. Butler, Osceola; Albert L. Rusher, Brinkley; E. L. Sims, Mt. Ida; B. A. DeLamar, Prescott; H. T. Thurman, Jasper; B. T. Fooks, Camden; B. J. Sufferage, Perryville; Victor A. Juengel, Helena; Harry J. McCarty, Helena; Olen Hendrix, Antoine; S. C. Chapin, Trumann; Carl Barham, Mena; Sam Elwood, Russellville; M. J. O. Crowley, DeValls Bluff; Ben R. Shelley, Little Rock; Dave Grundfest, Little Rock; A. F. Crowell, Jacksonville; Earl Fewell, North Little Rock; Kenneth "Pat" Wilson, Jacksonville; A. J. Baltz, Pocahontas; T. E. Bostic, Forrest City; John T. Lanier, Sr., Forrest City; A. J. Flemmons, Waldron; Bill Seegar, Leslie; Roy Redmon, Marshall; Roy C. Martin, Ft. Smith; W. H. Carter, Ft. Smith; Ray Kimball, DeQueen; Harry Pollock, Ft. Smith; Web Long, Hardy; Ivan Williamson, Mt. View; Connie Fields, Shirley; Thurman Parsons, Springdale; R. Vernon Powell, Beebe; Dr. Porter R. Rogers, Searcy; James R. Sullivan, Augusta and Garrett Jones, Dardanelle. Sam Rorex, Little Rock attorney and prominent Legionnaire, to Chancellor in Pulaski to fill the vacancy created by the death of Judge Rodney Parham. Gordon Carleton, DeQueen, prosecuting attorney to fill vacancy created by the slaying of R. Coker Thomas.

APPOINTMENTS, NOVEMBER 1955

John R. Newman, Harrison newspaper owner and editor, to State Library Commission. A. J. Baltz, Pocahontas, to Forestry Commission.

APPOINTMENTS, DECEMBER 1955

L. A. Dhonau, North Little Rock to State board. John L. Wilson, Mayor of Hope, to State Board of Review, Kay L. Matthews, Little Rock, formerly of Calico Rock, and former aide to Tom Gentry, to head Board of Review. Job Education Study Group: Representatives at Large: Winthrop Rockefeller, Morrilton; Rabie Rhodes, Harrison; L. C. Baber, Little Rock; M. P. Jones, Searcy; and R. C. Hartlieb, Hazen. Representing Education: R. B. Chitwood, Lake Village; Roy Nelson, Hughes; Joe Slaven, Siloam Springs; James A. Jones, Little Rock; and Dr. Carl Reng, Jonesboro. Representing Agriculture: L. C. Carter, Stuttgart; Waldo Frazier, Little Rock; William J. Seeger, Leslie; Lewis J. "Red" Johnson, Little Rock; and Ernest Ott, Crawfordsville. Representing Labor: E. W. Wilkerson, Ted Brewer, Bitsy Simmons, Mrs. Lena Trimble and Harold Veazey, all of Little Rock. Representing Management: John Rye, Russellville; Chet Stinnett, El Dorado; James B. Simmons, Helena; Gene Smith, Little Rock; and J. T. Doughtie, Morrilton. Representing the Legislature: Senator Tom Allen, Brinkley; Senator Boss Mitchell, Danville; Representatives Marion Crank, Foreman; Clayton Little, Bentonville; and John P. Bethel of Des Arc, the last being the author of the legislation creating the study group. State Board of Registered Physical Therapists: Appointed Miss Ruth Burnett, Jacksonville; reappointed Ewing R. Guthrie, Jr., Little Rock. Herbert Holmes, Augusta; Avery Shinn, Russellville; and Carlton Mays, Fordyce, all reappointed to State Burial Association Board. C. F. Byrns, Ft. Smith; Harold Snyder, Dardanelle; and R. E. Jeter, Wabbaseka, to serve on the Arkansas River Basin Association representing Arkansas.

ALL QUIET, By Kennedy, Ark. Democrat, 4/22/56

Using the theme of my military experience in the infantry in WW II, the cartoonist showed me checking for opposition to my plans for a second term. The signs then read "quiet," but not for long. Soon my advance was being disputed by a number of candidates. I officially filed for a second term at 10:15 a.m. April 25.

CHAPTER 7
THE SOUTHERN MANIFESTO
THE HEATED CAMPAIGN OF 1956 WITH
JOHNSON, SNODDY, PROSSER AND PIPPIN

PROPOSAL FOR ROCKEFELLER

Governor Faubus asked today if he planned to attend the "Salute to Eisenhower Dinner" at $50 a plate January 20, said that he hadn't been re-invited "after I made them a proposition."

Multimillionaire Winthrop Rockefeller, a Republican, was named by Democrat Faubus to head the AIDC, and is also spearheading the Republican dinner.

Mr. Faubus a hill farmer and small county newspaper publisher said today:

"I made them this kind of a proposition. I told them I would go to their dinner and contribute to the Republican party in proportion to my wealth, if Winthrop Rockefeller would come to my Democratic dinner and contribute in proportion to his wealth. I haven't heard from them."

I heard Rockefeller was quite amused with my unique proposal.

VERY WARM FOR JANUARY
By Kennedy, Ark. Democrat   1/13/56

Attorney General Tom Gentry was after me again, this time on the gambling issue in Hot Springs. Pictures and headlines in the *Democrat* the day before alleged that gambling was rife in the spa. At a press conference on the morning of January 12, *Democrat* reporter George Douthit was late. By way of greeting I made some remark about his tardiness and he replied, "I've been busy cutting your throat."

Douthit had been getting pictures and statements from Gentry which appeared with banner headlines later in the day. The publicity gave rise to this cartoon.

Shortly afterward I countered Gentry's efforts by offering him, as chief state law enforcement officer, the full use of the State Police to raid any gambling establishments anywhere at any time he chose. Gentry was now in the position of "put up or shut up" since, according to his claims, he had the necessary information for such action.

The attorney general used the State Police in a couple of what appeared to be half-hearted raids. Then his interest declined. Without question, his statements and blasts at the administration were of purely political motivation. Gentry was being prominently mentioned as a candidate for governor in the Democratic primaries. However, he soon found the Hot Springs gambling issue could not be successfully used as a launching pad for a governor's race.

Soon his use of the gambling issue ceased and his vocal criticism of me likewise faded away. There were no personal animosities between us. I realized that his efforts were politically motivated. In later years we developed a friendship which remains unimpaired. At one time I appointed him circuit judge in Pulaski County.

—everybody likes a good steak!

$55,000 TO GOP. FUNDS

HAROLD SADLER FOR GOV.

TRIAL BALLOON.

McMATH SAYS HE WON'T SEEK OFFICE — *THIS YEAR.*

—I've got my hands full already!

ROCKEFELLERS' SALUTE-TO-EISENHOWER DINNER A HUGE SUCCESS --- 1,100 GUESTS.

abolition of poll tax

increase in work. mens compensation

START OF A NEW MOVE...

LET'S MAKE PEA RIDGE A NATIONAL PARK!

HIGHLIGHTS OF THE NEWSWEEK
By Kennedy, Ark. Democrat   1/22/56

The move to make the Pea Ridge Battlefield a National Park was instigated by my administration. A 78-member committee appointed by me and headed by George Benjamin of Little Rock, actively promoted the project. Ultimate success of the undertaking was due in large part to Benjamin's diligence and persistence.

McMath said he wouldn't seek office because he was attorney for two amendments to the state Constitution — abolition of poll tax and increase in workmen's compensation.

— — —

"Everybody likes a good steak," said Winthrop Rockefeller as he pushed along a wheelbarrow load of money — $55,000 to GOP Funds.

Many Democrats were among the 1,100 in attendance at the fund-raising dinner to hear Presidential Aide Nelson Rockefeller speak, with his two brothers present, Winthrop and Laurance. Not many Arkansawyers then ever got to see that many millionares at one time.

— — —

A trial balloon was floated for Harold Sadler for Governor in the Democratic primaries.

THE GROWING INTEGRATION PROBLEM

Court rulings on integration and integration problems dominated more and more the news and the thoughts of the people.

NO SEGREGATED RAIL TRAVEL

In Chicago the ban on segregated rail travel caused a rail mixup and delays in travel. In Arkansas the carriers, both rail and bus, made the change smoothly.

THE HOXIE INJUNCTION

In the Hoxie litigation the federal injunction was made permanent on January 9. Judge Albert L. Reeves of Kansas told three groups of anti-integrationists they were prohibited from "boycotting, picketing, trespassing on school property, or threatening school administrators and board members with bodily harm." Spokesmen for the three groups protested that the order violated their right of free speech, and enjoined them against acts which never had been committed. Many patrons of the district were now forbidden to visit the grounds of their own school. One principal in the meetings, protests and legal battles, Jim Johnson, was not included in the court ruling. The next day Johnson announced the order of Judge Reeves would be appealed.

NO INTEGRATION IN GEORGIA

On January 10 Governor Marvin Griffin of Georgia said there would be no mixed schools in that state, and the news was carried nationwide that Georgians were acting to keep segregation. At the same time Louisiana and Mississippi proclaimed defiance of court-ruled integration.

HOXIE BOARD APPROVES VANCE RESIGNATION

On January 11 the Hoxie school board approved the resignation of Superintendent K.E. Vance and selected Robert Wilson as his replacement. Prosecutor W.J. "Bill" Arnold criticized the departing superintendent for mishandling of school funds but no indictments were filed.

FT. SMITH AND VAN BUREN

On January 15 an integration hearing involving the Fort Smith schools was set, and the next day it was announced that an integration suit was nearing for Van Buren.

COLEMAN SAYS NO INTEGRATION IN MISSISSIPPI

Gov. J. P. Coleman of Mississippi announced his defiance of any effort to bring about any integration in his state.

BATES LEADS ENROLLMENT EFFORT
IN LITTLE ROCK

Negro students under the leadership of Mrs. Daisy Bates, state NAACP director, attempted to enroll in four Little Rock high schools on January 23. Their enrollment in white schools was refused by school officials with Superintendent Virgil Blossom as spokesmen, on the grounds the school authorities had not yet had time to make plans. The effort got big news stories with pictures and banner headlines, and caused the pot to begin to stew beneath the outward appearance of calm.

GOVERNORS CONDEMN COURT RULING

The Supreme Court order on desegregation was strongly condemned at a meeting on the 25th by governors George Bell Timmerman of South Carolina, Thomas B. Stanley of Virginia, J.P. Coleman of Mississippi and Marvin Griffin of Georgia. Luther Hodges of North Carolina attended as an observer.

INTEGRATION EFFORT AT WALNUT RIDGE

Three negroes attempted without success to enroll at Walnut Ridge on the 27th, but the effort made statewide news.

SENTIMENT AGAINST INTEGRATION
OVERWHELMING

On January 29th I made known in a press release the sentiment on integration as shown in a poll, the accuracy of which was without doubt. Prepared specifically for me at my request the survey revealed that 85 per cent of the people were opposed to court ordered integration and a majority of the remaining 15 per cent were undecided.

In an effort to quiet the rising concern of this overwhelming majority, I gave a statement to the press saying that Arkansas would not be bullied on the racial integration matter.

BYRD AGAINST FEDERAL SCHOOL AID

On January 30th Senator Byrd (D-Va.) voiced his opposition to federal aid to the public schools because of the increasing difficulties over the High Court's decision on segregation.

RACIAL BRAWL AT CHATTANOOGA

At Chattanooga, Tennessee an interracial brawl erupted in a mixed crowd at a concert. News of the violence there added to the rising concern across the South including Arkansas.

Editorial
Arkansas Gazette
SUNDAY, JANUARY 29, 1956

Governor Faubus made a sober and thoughtful statement on the school segregation matter when he replied to questions submitted by the New York Times. ... The governor's words will not satisfy extremists on either side but will appeal to persons of tolerance and good will in Arkansas ...

Mr. Faubus pointed out that school districts in Arkansas are independent, "virtually autonomous," and their policies are "determined by boards elected by the school patrons at open elections." He said further that the state govern-

ment "traditionally refrains" from intruding in the management of the local school districts.

The governor called attention to . . . good relations which exist between the races in Arkansas. He said that complete integration, if it ever comes in this state, "will be a slow process," and he added a truth which should not be lost in any quarter:

"It should be obvious that centuries-old customs, and regional traditions, cannot be changed overnight, even by court edict."

There is nothing simple or easy about the issue which has been raised in the South by the Supreme Court's decision. The governor of Arkansas, by well-considered and sincere expression, has put this state on record as wanting to follow a course that will be moderate, reasonable and practical.

FEED TAX PETITIONS DEFECTIVE

The State Supreme Court in a 4 to 3 decision ruled that the petitions to refer the sales tax exemption on feed were defective. The ruling meant there would be no vote on the measure at the 1956 general election. Thus an issue that could have been troublesome was removed from the coming campaign.

WR AND FAUBUS AT OZARK

Rockefeller and I attended a $5.00 per plate dinner at Ozark to raise funds for the AIDC.

MENCKEN DIES

H. L. Mencken, wit and dissenter and famed agnostic, who was a strong supporter of Commonwealth College as I had learned during my visit there, died in Baltimore, Maryland at age 75.

TIGHTER INVESTMENT LAWS

State Insurance Commissioner Harvey G. Combs and State Bank Commissioner Dick Simpson announced they would seek legislation to curb fraudulent stock schemes at the next legislative session. Both men had advised me that the laws were insufficient for control of actual fraud and fly-by-night insurance and investment schemes. Simpson began at that time to disapprove many charter applications for new investment firms, although legal grounds for such action were often questionable or lacking.

COFFELT AND TINNON FOR ATTORNEY GENERAL; OTHERS ANNOUNCE

During January Kenneth Coffelt of Jacksonville and Tom Tinnon of Mountain Home joined Harve Thorn as announced candidates for Attorney General. Guy Amsler of Little Rock announced for Chief Justice of the State Supreme Court. Former State Senator Lee Reaves of Warren was mentioned as a possible candidate for Governor; State Treasurer Vance Clayton filed for a seventh term; Pulaski County Judge Arch Campbell filed for a fourth term, and Sheriff Tom Gulley for a sixth.

LONG WINS IN LOUISIANA

In Louisiana former Governor Earl Long was nominated for governor in the first primary over four opponents.

— — —

LEGGETT APPREHENDED

Emment Earl Leggett was apprehended by Air Force police in a brutal attack on two sisters, and later admitted the slaying of the 14-year old King boy some time before. Leggett was pictured in the custody of Sheriff Tom Gulley and State Trooper Floyd Weaver. Each of the three was destined to play a part in or affect my political career in the months to come.

— — —

ROCKEFELLER MAN-OF-THE-YEAR

Winthrop Rockefeller was named Arkansas' man-of-the-year in the Democrat poll. Six new industries announced expansions or locations in the state.

JOURNEY'S END FOR AN ARKANSAS TRAVELER
By Graham, Ark. Gazette   2/4/56

The bazooka was hung up for the last time and was now silent. Bob Burns, 1890-1956, native of Van Buren, who moved to Hollywood and launched a highly successful radio program, made the raucous sounding instrument world famous as a part of his nationwide show. Every country boy and a majority of the city dwellers were long familiar with the name of Burns and the sound of his bazooka.

In my own particular area one of the big events of the year was the annual St. Paul Reunion held at the railroad town of the same name just five miles from my birthplace near Combs. In the heyday of the Burns' program people appeared at the Reunion from the mountain tops and valleys of the surrounding hills who were known as relatives of the great comedian. Usually they were "uncles" of whom Burns occasionally made mention on his program. Now Burns was dead at age 65 and the bazooka sounded its harsh notes no more. But a powerful anti-tank military weapon, named for the famous musical instrument, continues to speak.

BARKING UP THE WRONG TREE
By Kennedy, Ark. Democrat   2/12/56

Before the Campaign of 1956 had gotten underway and more than 18 months before the '57 Crisis erupted, the problem of integration was often the uppermost topic of interest in Arkansas.

There were those who said that integration, if peacefully accomplished, must come "gradually with public support." Others led by "pressure groups" advocated and demanded "immediate integration" regardless of the consequences. A great majority of the people agreed that these pressure groups were barking up the wrong tree.

There were others who said "Never" to integration in any form.

For political leaders interested in promoting progress for all people, the integration question was an unwanted problem.

STATE HOSPITAL PROBLEMS

The problems of the State Hospital were brought more and more to my attention. Often patients received inadequate care; rip-offs by private vendors selling food and other supplies to the institution continued; there were reports of discrimination in dealing with employees; and petty thievery by employees was rife.

Failing to obtain correction of these evils by quiet efforts, I let loose a blast at the hospital administration. Since these improper practices were not generally known the public wondered at my actions.

Soon the hospital board got involved, and then the Legislative Council. A full fledged investigation by the latter proved the accuracy of my charges of misdeeds and sloppy administration.

State property assessments were up $25 million showing the reassessment program was working.

State revenue collections in January set an all time record under the direction of Commissioner Cheney.

THE INTEGRATION CONTROVERSY

February 1956
INTEGRATION LAWSUIT IN LITTLE ROCK; CRENSHAW STATEMENT

On February 8th a lawsuit was filed in Federal Court in Little Rock to compel the school board to integrate the city schools. Sponsored by the NAACP, the suit contained the names of 33 Negro plaintiffs. The basis for the complaint was that these black children should be allowed to attend their neighborhood schools, or, in other words, the school nearest their homes.

Attorneys for the Negro plaintiffs were Wiley A. Branton of Pine Bluff; U. Simpson Tate of Dallas, Texas; Robert L. Carter and Thurgood Marshall, both New York.

A statement by the NAACP spokesman, Rev. J. C. Crenshaw of Little Rock, gave as a basis for the lawsuit for integration the following:

"We want all children, regardless of race, to go to the public schools nearest their homes. We seek an end to the hazards, inconveniences and discrimination of a system which now requires little children to pass each day several schools from which they are barred because of race, and travel nearly 10 miles to racially segregated schools."

That was a very good statement. But how does it square with busing for racial integration now?

STEVENSON STATEMENT

Presidential candidate Adlai Stevenson said in a speech at Los Angeles on February 7 that the use of troops would not solve the integration problem.

JIM JOHNSON ASKS
RESTUDY OF SCHOOL BILL

I was asked in a public statement by Jim Johnson on February 14 to call a special session of the legislature to reconsider an anti-integration bill that failed to pass in the regular session of 1955. When the legislation came before the General Assembly it passed the House but was pigeon-holed in the Senate. Many of the senators simply didn't want to risk inflaming the racial issue at the time.

Some senators almost lost their positions simply because they did not push harder for the segregationist measures. One of them was Tom Allen of Brinkley, a fine legislator, who barely gained re-election in 1956 when the issue was used against him.

Senators Fagan and Howell of Little Rock also had opposition. The segregationists with Jim Johnson emerging as their undisputed leader, had hold of a powerful issue and were using it quite effectively. Many prominent people, including most political leaders, did not yet realize what was happening or the intensity of the feeling of the people on this emotional issue.

Johnson's request for a special session of the legislature was a part of his political maneuvering in preparation for the 1956 campaign. The purpose of the request was to put me on the spot and place me in disfavor with the great majority of the voters.

— — —

ROBERTSON AMENDMENT

In Washington on February 6 Sen. Robertson (D.-Va.) authored a joint resolution legalizing either integrated or segregated schools. The next day Sen. McClellan and eight other senators joined Robertson in sponsoring the resolution. Three days later McClellan and others had withdrawn as sponsors. After mature reflection, McClellan said that under the

Constitution the states were granted jurisdiction over education, and that the proposed resolution would erode that right. The Robertson proposal died.

HOXIE ARGUMENT

The Hoxie school board agreed, or was forced, to meet with the patrons of the district to discuss financial affairs, including the mishandling of school funds and the employment of relatives. Press reports on February 15 said that finances gave way to integration as the main topic of discussion.

THE BIRD COMMITTEE

The Bird Committee of Arkansas went to Virginia to study the integration situation. It was reported at that time that the Old Dominion had come up with the best methods and plans to resist legally the federal courts' intrusion into school affairs. The committee headed by Marvin Bird, banker of Earle and chairman of the State Board of Education, included Bert Dickey, planter of near West Memphis; Charles Adams, planter, school board member and political leader of Hughes; J.L. (Bex) Shaver, attorney of Wynne and former lieutenant governor; and R.B. (Richard) McCulloch, prominent attorney of Forrest City. The group reported to me on February 25 on its return from the fact finding trip and an announcement came from the meeting that the state would resist "sudden and complete integration." The Bird Committee report was released to the press and the public.

JUSTICE DEPARTMENT INTERVENES AT HOXIE

On February 23 the Federal Justice Department openly entered the Hoxie dispute on the side of the integrationists. It was the first action by the Department anywhere to back up the U.S. Supreme Court ruling.

ROLAND SMITH DELEGATION

On February 24 I met by appointment in my office a group of Negro leaders, who urged me to carry out the federal court's integration order. The delegation's case was stated by a very eloquent and able spokesman, Reverend Roland Smith of Little Rock. I made no comment either way on the black leaders' request.

On the 27th the Negro leaders were silent when questioned about my stand with the Bird Committee.

FOLSOM OF ALABAMA

On the same day Governor Folsom of Alabama announced that he would maintain order at the University of Alabama where the widely publicized enrollment of Autherine Lucy had been ended by violent demonstrations. Knowledgeable observers said the Negro woman barely escaped with her life. On March 1 a federal court ordered the University to re-admit Lucy, and the next day the board of trustees expelled her on official grounds ending the affair except for the reaction to Folsom's statement about maintaining order. On March 11 integration foes blasted Folsom and called for his impeachment.

SEGREGATION RALLY AT ENGLAND

A segregation rally of enthusiastic attendants was held at England on February 24. Pat Henderson of England, general chairman of the gathering, sent out the invitations for speakers. Jim Johnson told an estimated 1,400 people that 300,000 signatures would be sought on his segregation amendment petitions to show how the people of the state felt about integrating the schools. Other speakers were former Governor Ben Laney of Camden, Roy V. Harris of Georgia, Robert B. Patterson of Mississippi and Attorney Amis Guthridge of Little Rock.

Three days later Johnson charged that state employees had been discouraged or forbidden to sign petitions for his constitutional amendment to compel the maintenance of segregation in Arkansas. The charge was false and I so stated to the press. State employees were completely free to exercise their own inclinations in such matters. It was a ploy on the part of Johnson to gain attention for his petition efforts, and gain still further publicity as he prepared to run for governor.

— — —

LITTLE ROCK BOARD ASKS DISMISSAL

The Little Rock school board asked for the dismissal of the NAACP sponsored integration suit, pleading that "hasty integration" would be "unwise."

SENATOR POE DIES

State Senator DeWitt Poe, age 62, McGehee, a most able legislator, died on February 23.

Faubus Says Facts Will Attract Money for Better Schools; Addresses 1,500 at School Meeting In Robinson Auditorium

This was the headline on March 2 for a rally sponsored by the Governor's Advisory Committee on Education (GACE) in Robinson Auditorium in Little Rock. The purpose of the meeting was to encourage support for an adequate financial plan for the improvement of education and other state services. With the advice of educators and other progressive citizens I had selected and appointed the first members of the Committee some time in 1955.

This Committee, working with me, the AEA, the ATA and the State Department of Education, performed in an outstanding manner in gathering and disseminating facts and information on the problems facing education in Arkansas, especially the low salaries of teachers in the public schools.

Two things about the Committee are worth mention. While primarily concerned with the problems of education, it kept in mind, at my urging, the fact that it would be difficult, if not impossible, to gain approval of a tax program to benefit education alone. Therefore the needs of other programs as welfare, the State Hospital, Forestry Commission, the State Police, the institutions of higher learning, the need for a children's colony for the mentally retarded, and other state services even including the State Livestock Show and state parks, all were kept in mind by the Committee members as they did their work.

Second it was a bi-racial committee containing a number of blacks as members, among them Lawrence Davis, president of AM&N college at Pine Bluff, Attorney J.R. Booker of Little Rock, and Cliffie Bond of Madison. With the rising tide of anti-integration sentiment there was a degree of risk in holding the rally, for it was an integrated meeting. However, with the sad state of Arkansas finances we knew we must have a progressive program or all in state government and public service, and those dependent on state service as hospitals, schools and welfare, would continue in their deprived condition, whether black or white. So we who had "set our hands to the plow" continued with our efforts without looking back and without any expressions of fear or misgivings. Although many extreme segregationists were beginning a drum fire attack on me and my administration because of the integration that had already been effected during my time in office, fortunately there was no strong criticism of my work with the GACE because of its integrated status. Perhaps the extreme segregationists failed to note the membership of blacks on the Committee.

The work of the GACE helped greatly in the implementation and the successful presentation to the next General Assembly of one of the most progressive programs in the history of Arkansas.

In recognition of the significant role of this Committee and its diligent and dedicated efforts, due credit is hereby given the original members for their contribution to a progressive educational program and an overall program for the progress of Arkansas in other fields.

GOVERNOR'S ADVISORY COMMITTEE ON EDUCATION

Lee Roy Beasley, El Dorado, Chairman
Mrs. Edgar F. Dixon, Little Rock, Executive Vice Chairman

James B. Abraham, Lonoke
Tom Allen, Brinkley
L.H. Autry, Burdette
Marvin Bird, Earle
W.C. Blewster, Magnolia
Virgil Blossom, Little Rock
Mrs. Cliffie Bond, Madison

Mrs. Virginia Bonds, Conway
J.R. Booker, Little Rock
Clarence F. Byrns, Fort Smith
John T. Caldwell, Fayetteville
Dolph Camp, Magnolia
W.W. Campbell, Forrest City
Claude Carpenter, Jr., Little Rock

R.B. Chitwood, Lake Village
LeRoy Christophe, Little Rock
Mrs. LeMon Clark, Fayetteville
T.C. Cogbill, Jr., Star City
Dr. John Cole, Malvern
R.H. Cole, Magnolia
Chris Corbin, Fort Smith

Lawrence Davis, Pine Bluff
Lonnie Etheridge, Weldon
A. W. Ford, Little Rock
Munn Forrest, Corning
Mrs. Helen Henderson, Imboden
Mrs. Charles R. Henry, Little Rock
Lewis "Red" Johnson, Little Rock

M.P. Jones, Searcy
Dr. W.J. Ketz, Batesville
R.A. Lynch, Tyronza
Dr. L.H. McDaniel, Tyronza
W.D. McKay, Magnolia
Mrs. Frances Neal, Little Rock
Hugh B. Patterson, Jr., Little Rock

Mrs. F.A. Poe, Paragould
H.R. Pyle, Little Rock
Lee Reaves, Warren
Rabie Rhodes, Harrison
Forrest Rozzell, Little Rock
John Rye, Russellville
Marshall Shackleford, Jr., El Dorado

Joshua K. Shepherd, Little Rock
Cecil Shuffield, Nashville
Mrs. J.R. Sink, Newport
Charles F. Smith, West Memphis
Silas D. Snow, Conway
Jack Stephens, Little Rock
E.S. Stevenson, Hot Springs

Garland Stubblefield, El Dorado
Paul Sullins, Crossett
Paul Van Dalsem, Perryville
Mrs. Carroll Watson, Osceola
Tom Whiteside, Siloam Springs
B.G. Williams, Little Rock
Thomas G. Wilson, Conway

NOW HEAR THIS!
By Kennedy, Ark. Democrat   3/7/56

At the Crater of Diamonds near Murfreesboro in Pike County, the only diamond mine on the North American continent, Mrs. Arthur Lee Parker of Dallas, Texas, on March 4, 1956, found a stone weighing 15.31 carats. Valued in the rough at $15,000.00 the diamond was named "Star of Arkansas." After being cut and polished its value was much greater. In early 1977 it sold for more than $100,000. Only one larger diamond than Mrs. Parker's trophy has been found at the Crater. It was the "Uncle Sam" of 40.23 carats discovered during commercial mining many years earlier. Operated as a privately owned tourist attraction the crater had 15,000 visitors in 1955 who found 107 stones. It is now a state owned facility being acquired from private interests during Governor Dale Bumpers' first term in office, 1971-1973, at a reported cost of $800,000.

THE SOUTHERN MANIFESTO
FORERUNNER OF RESISTANCE TO INTEGRATION

On March 8 to 10, I made a trip to the national capitol with a Camden delegation headed by publisher Walter Hussman to confer with Navy officials on a possible new use of the great

Shumaker Ammunition Depot near the city. The Navy had announced it would be closed and I was helping Hussman and his associates seek a new use for the facility which would keep the workers employed.

Soon after arriving in Washington I got an urgent request to meet with the Arkansas Congressional delegation. The document that was to become known as the Southern Manifesto, of which I had no knowledge, had been formulated, and was then in circulation for signatures among Southern Congressmen of both houses. The Arkansas delegation had the matter under consideration and wanted to confer with me about sentiment in the state.

Arriving at the conference site I found the members more anxious for news of the situation at home than any group I have ever encountered. All members were present, — then six house members, and two senators — except Jim Trimble who was ill in the Naval hospital.

There was little discussion of the Manifesto itself. Each member of the delegation knew the contents. The question seemed to be whether or not all members would sign the document, the doubtful signers being Hays and Trimble.

Most of the conference conversation centered on questions to me about the situation in Arkansas. There was much to tell them but, as I recall, I only answered their questions. There was growing concern as the U.S. Supreme Court continued to expand its original ruling; Hoxie had been torn asunder by dissension; even the *Gazette* reported 1,400 in attendance at a segregation rally at the small town of England where former Governor Ben Laney and former State Senator Jim Johnson were speakers; the proliferation of meetings across the state to which out-of-state segregationists were addressing large crowds; and eye-witness reports of Jim Johnson's segregation meetings where dozens of people fought their way to him with money in their fists to donate to the cause.

Some one asked, "What would you advise?"

"I'm giving you the best information I have", I replied, "but I don't think it's my role to advise you."

"Well, what is your opinion? You can express that can't you?" some one insisted.

"It is my opinion," I replied, "that if the delegation declines or refuses to sign the Manifesto that only one could survive politically in the coming primaries. That one would possibly be Jim Trimble because of the makeup of his district, and even he would have difficulty."

I am convinced that my expressed opinion had no bearing on the individual decisions of the members. Some one had a copy of the Manifesto and McClellan, Gathings, Norrell and Mills signed it there. Harris, who had contacted me for the meeting, had already made the decision to sign, but I don't recall whether he signed there or later at the hospital with Trimble. Fulbright, having heard that Laney might oppose his bid for re-election, had signed the document even before arriving at the conference.

The meeting concluded with Brooks Hays having not yet signed the document, Harris insisted that I accompany him and Hays to see Trimble. I wanted to see my own congressman any way so readily agreed.

Congressman Trimble was confined to his bed but was fully capable of seeing visitors and discussing any matter.

The subject of the Manifesto angered Trimble, one of the few times in our long association that I ever saw him exasperated to the point of sharp, angry words. He felt, as many others, that the matter should not have arisen; that public figures were being put on the spot with no advantage to any one; that the matter should have been permitted to remain quiescent.

I must confess that at that particular time I felt much the same about the matter as Trimble. With so many progressive improvements to make in Arkansas, I regretted to see the people and their officials distracted and divided by an emotional and explosive issue involving a problem that had existed for centuries.

But now, I think Trimble and others with the same feeling were probably wrong. Even if all had remained quiet it would have purchased only a little more time. The problem was there and sooner or later had to be faced. To remain quiet and expect the problem to subside was a vain hope and illusion.

To complicate matters many people believed the effort to bring about changes in racial relations was being attempted, not by legal and constitutional means, but by illegal and unconstitutional usurpation of the people's rights by illegal rulings of the U.S. Supreme Court. These illegal rulings constituted the heart of the protest of the Southern Manifesto.

It was argued that the surest protection for all groups over the long run was the observance of the Constitution. There should be no usurpation of power by the courts, it was contended, and changes in racial relations, or in other fields should be brought about in a legal and proper manner as clearly set out in the Constitution itself.

However, as Trimble and I soon realized, the voices of reason, speaking for law and proper means of change, were already being drowned out by the integration extremists and political opportunists on both sides. The matter soon became a purely political issue, and the main question for all officeholders faced with the problem was political death or survival.

When Congressman Trimble had subsided I briefly explained to him what I had told the other members of the delegation.

"You have a good chance to survive without signing the Manifesto," I told him, "because you know yourself that the problem is small in your district. "But" I added, "I don't think any other member of the delegation can survive if he declines to sign it."

I don't recall that Jim said another word after I started talking. While I was still speaking he silently reached for the document and attached his signature well before I had finished. Jim was practical, realistic and co-operative. I have always had the impression that regardless of his feelings, he didn't want to put the other members of his own delegation on the spot by refusing to sign.

The document was then handed to Congressman Hays and I must say he was in travail. His tone was plaintive and tearful as he complained of the matter. A callous critic would say he whined, but that would be too strong a term. As he talked he spread the document on a desk in the cramped hospital room, took from his pocket his pen and prepared it for writing. I shall never forget his last words, uttered in a most plaintive tone, as with head bent over the paper he signed the document.

"What will some of my good friends think of me now?"

I assumed that he had reference to some of his liberal colleagues in the Congress.

Leaving the hospital, Harris, Hays and I journeyed back into the city and went our separate ways. Some two days later the news of the filing of the Manifesto before the Congress made glaring headlines across the nation.

Now, as it developed, with every Southern congressman having signed the Manifesto except a mere handful, any state official or candidate back home who didn't join in the rising opposition to the court's illegal decision, would be completely lost and obscured in the political dust of the front runners. The proof was in what happened to the Southerners who declined to sign. All were disastrously defeated except one. Congressman Trimble told me the story of the survivor. He was a well known figure with great seniority and prestige in the Congress. When the sentiment in his district became clear, he completely reversed his field. "Yes," he told the voters of his district in a fighting campaign, "I didn't sign the Manifesto, but I didn't sign for only one reason. It wasn't strong enough!" With this reversal of position and the subterfuge about signing, he barely survived. (See May 28, 1956 item of Carolina Election)

(In later years I personally heard Brooks Hays say that he regrets signing the Manifesto and that his signing was a mistake. It seems to be popular to take the attitude which he now assumes. As to his signing at the time in 1956, I can voice the personal opinion that if he had declined, his congressional career would have ended sooner than it did.)

Without doubt, the Southern Manifesto was the fore-runner of the widespread, open resistance to integration which followed. The resistance led to clashes and violence. Yet the violence in the South did not approach in severity the violence and disorder which came later in other sections where there were no signers, as Watts, Detroit, Chicago, Rochester and Washington, D.C. itself. It was a situation for which no individual was fully to blame, nor one which any individual in public life could easily avoid.

The blame, many believed, lay with a run-away U.S. Supreme Court which had usurped the power which belonged to the states by entering into a field in which it had no legal authority. Many who believed the changes sought were desirable, contended the method was illegal. From this standpoint the signers of the Manifesto could justify their actions.

"Fireworks start when Congress gets Manifesto," read a headline on March 13. On that day Senator Wayne Morse of Oregon, whose state then had no racial problem, challenged the Manifesto in a speech in the Senate. The document, now with 100 signers — 19 senators and 81 House members representing eleven states — was formally presented to the Congress on March 12.

STATEMENTS IN THE SOUTHERN MANIFESTO

Here are Key Phrases from it:

"The unwarranted decision of the Supreme Court in the public school cases is now bearing the fruit always produced when men substitute naked power for established law.

"The founding fathers gave us a Constitution of checks and balances because they realized the inescapable lesson of history that no man or group of men can be safely entrusted with unlimited power. They framed this Constitution with its provisions for change by amendment in order to secure the fundamentals of government against the dangers of temporary popular passion or the personal predilections of public office holders. . . .

". . . parents should not be deprived by the government of the right to direct the lives and education of their own children . . .

". . . the Supreme Court of the United States, with no legal basis for such action, undertook to exercise their naked judicial power and substituted their personal political and social ideas for the established law of the land . . .

". . . It is destroying the amicable relations between the white and Negro races that have been created through 90 years of patient effort by the good people of both races. It has planted hatred and suspicion where there has been heretofore friendship and understanding."

GOVERNOR COLLINS OF FLORIDA
FIRES NEGRO ASSISTANT

Florida Governor LeRoy Collins relieved a Negro assistant state attorney of his duties on March 17 for allegedly boasting that his Miami office was integrated and that white stenographers took his dictation.

ARKANSAS DEMOCRAT
March 19, 1956
SEGREGATION CANDIDATES VICTORIOUS AT HOXIE
(BY THE ASSOCIATED PRESS)

A victory by segregationists at Hoxie was the biggest news in school district elections Saturday.

Herbert Brewer and Enos Nicholas, representing pro-segregation forces, gained positions on the five-man Hoxie School Board. . . .

Hoxie was one of the few districts to vote down a proposed increase in tax millage. The defeat of the tax was attributed to the integration controversy. . . .

AND NEXT ON THE PROGRAM
By Graham, Ark. Gazette   3/20/56

Tom Gentry, legal council for state agencies by virtue of his office, was critical of the State Racing Commission in its handling of the West Memphis dog track matter. The Racing Commission then announced its termination of his services. The Commission was pictured meeting to consider the dog track matter, inquiring for an attorney with the dogs as onlookers. Later Little Rock attorneys Warren Woods and Griffin Smith were selected to represent the Commission.

POLL TIME;
THE SITUATION, THE APPROACH

A political poll was being done by someone. It was not mine because it dealt with the standings in the governor's race of Faubus, Finkbeiner, Gentry and Ingram, with no mention of Jim Johnson. In my polls I directed that Johnson be checked because I had learned that he was developing powerful political strength because of the integration issue.

All the leading politicians discounted Johnson as a candidate, and dismissed the active organizers of the segregation movement as extremists with some political strength but not really a threat. My information did not bear out this evaluation by the political leaders.

Other than the members of the Bird Committee the first of my political leaders to apprise me of the extent and seriousness of the situation was Searcy Wilcoxen, banker and auto dealer of Hamburg.

Searcy had been of the same opinion as the other political leaders about Johnson and his movement, and privately made disparaging remarks about Johnson and his extreme followers. One day his wife remonstrated with him to be more cautious or he would be hurt in his business and suffer harm otherwise because of his attitude. She warned him that the segregation movement was wide spread and the members deadly serious.

A man of very good judgment, Searcy heeded his wife's warning and did some checking on the matter. Mrs. Wilcoxen's opinion and information were confirmed to the fullest. Searcy made contact with me to give me the information.

Shortly thereafter, following some checking and evaluations of my own, I called my pollster, Eugene F. Newsom.

"I want you to check four counties," I told him and gave him the names, Desha, Chicot, Drew and Ashley. The latter contained Hamburg, Mr. Wilcoxen's home town, and Crossett, the home town and base of operations of Johnson and his lieutenants.

"Well, I've never checked a small area like that," said Gene, "but you're paying me so I'll do it."

I told Newsom my prime interest and advised him of what I thought he would find — that I had already lost the two smaller counties, Drew and Ashley, and might be holding about even in the two heavier voting counties of Desha and Chicot.

"I don't believe a word you're saying," Mr. Newsom voiced confidently, "but I'll get on the job right now."

About a week later Gene called and, it seemed to me, a little disappointment and chagrin tinged his voice as he reported his findings.

"You're just as right as you can be!" he said. "I polled five counties instead of four," he added. I believe the fifth county was Bradley, also in the smaller category as to voting strength. "You're behind in the three smaller counties two to one, and leading in the two larger counties 4 to 3," my pollster informed me. "When I put them all together you and Johnson are dead even with virtually no undecided voters. No undecided this early in the campaign makes the situation phenomenal," he concluded.

And Johnson was not yet an announced candidate.

The information was no surprise to me, but it was now scientifically confirmed that my re-election to a second term was not a foregone conclusion. There was work to be done. Most of that work, planning, strategy and effort would have to be done by me and my supporters among the ordinary people - often referred to as the "little people," or the "common people." The business and professional people, as well as some political leaders, could not be made aware of the true situation or be convinced that a threat existed.

As has been the case so many times in history, those leaders and people with better education and greater financial means, moving in more genteel social surroundings, and thus inevitably detached from the masses with their greater hardships and harsher living conditions, were making an age old mistake. They were, both consciously and unconsciously, refusing to recognize a distasteful problem, even though it was so serious that it would shake the whole of society to its very roots and cause the very foundation of government to tremble.

Dreading and withdrawing from any personal involvement in the struggle this upper class, except for a certain number of zealots and crusaders, hoped that someone else would work the matter out. They ignored the problem in the vain hope that it would go away or never bother them. Even when, in the last analysis, they were forced to take some action, they failed to bite the bullet. They took refuge in palliatives and false remedies, as token integration, or participation in a couple of mixed gatherings, and assumed a public stance of compliance with the New Order. At the same time many were quietly looking for segregated schooling for their children and seeking, if necessary, to move to more exclusive neighborhoods.

As is the case in countless examples of history, the rich and the well-to-do are not the challengers of tyranny from established authority. They have too much to lose. They compromise, make accomodations, "go along." It remains for the poor, the down-trodden, the deprived, the workers, the sufferers of hardship, to challenge the encroaching tyranny of government.

I had, in the first place, been elected governor with my basic support coming from the working class of people. Only a small proportion of the rich and prosperous had lent me any encouragement or support. Harold Sherman in Little Rock on one occasion early in the 1954 campaign learned the results of a poll at a meeting of young businessmen in the city. From about 200 participants I received only two votes. An analysis of the returns from all three elections of 1954 showed clearly that my heaviest support came from the poorest areas. I received the least number of votes from those sections where dwelt the most affluent.

I had little or no ill will from the great mass of the common people. We had many things in common. These hard working citizens, both black and white, wanted more good roads and bridges. I was helping to build them for their use.

The school teachers, both black and white, wanted better salaries. I was on their side and working hard to get those improved salaries.

All citizens, both black and white, wanted an improved State Hospital with better policies for employees and better service for patients. I was fighting their battle at that very time.

The people of Arkansas wanted more industry for more and better jobs so they or their children could make a living without leaving home to seek employment. The industrial program which I had sponsored was quite successful and gaining ground. Already I could go to many points, step through a factory door and see hundreds of people, both black and white, at work who otherwise would be jobless or employed in other states.

All the old, poor people, the disabled and the blind, both black and white, wanted a better welfare program where they were treated with dignity and respect. They and their relatives knew that I understood their problems and their desires as well or better than any governor who had come along. They were solidly for me as the "best welfare governor" they had known.

These and other problems and hopes we shared in common. They were supporting me as I sought to attain at least a portion of our hopes and dreams for betterment.

But now another issue had arisen which to many, in fact to a majority of the people, transcended in importance any other problem, or all other problems combined. The issue was brought about by a court in the distant city of Washington which said that integration of the races would be forced upon the people regardless of their wishes in the matter. For 92 years previously, with some of the greatest jurists of the nation as members, the court had said that some separation of the races was permissable. Now a new court headed by an arrogant, pious, self-righteous, ambitious politician with little judicial experience, had said all the previous courts were wrong.

If the court for 92 years had been wrong, how could the people immediately have faith that all at once it was now right?

Few respected lawyers came forward to defend the court decision; many condemned it as unconstitutional. Among the common people who were affected, more than 85 per cent thought the decision was wrong.

The prevailing public opinion was that the decision would not be enforced if the people objected. After all did not the people have control of their own schools and was not this a country of majority rule?

When the push for actual integration of the public schools began, those who rose up in opposition found plenty of ready followers. At Hoxie where some 25 Negro students were integrated into a white student body of approximately 1,000, the resulting conflict tore the community apart. Hundreds of students stayed out of school, the superintendent resigned and left by mid-year, and in the school elections of 1955 and 1956 the school patrons overwhelmingly defeated those school board members who favored racial mixing and re-elected or elected members who opposed it.

The Federal Courts stepped in and forced continuance of integration in the school, but its power could not cure the bitterness and the conflict. Enmity built up between neighbors which was, or will be, cured only by death. Some families moved away to start life anew in distant areas. Discord was rife where once harmony prevailed.

By this time in 1956 the issue was being joined statewide The time of turmoil was at hand. Forgotten by many were industrial growth, good roads, increased teachers' salaries or a new State Hospital.

To talk to a man about a new industry for his town facing an integration problem was like trying to gain his attention while his city was being sacked and burned by an alien army.

To mention a program for better teachers' salaries to a family whose school was about to be integrated served only to infuriate its members.

To talk to a farmer who was facing the integration problem about a good road by his farm was like trying to interest him in a nice carpet for his burning house.

There was no enmity that I could detect at the time between the blacks and the whites, either as groups or individuals. To the contrary there was much good will, and blacks, through my administration, were increasingly welcomed into responsible positions in government and other fields. It was just that almost all whites and a considerable number of blacks, feared that the bringing of the races together in integrated schools by force would bring out the worst traits in both groups and increase animosity and conflict as well. The result would be a breakdown in discipline, decreased respect for each other, increased conflict, immorality and vandalism.

And what good would be accomplished? In the majority opinion, none.

There were other people, many of them not faced with the problem, who did not fear integration to such a great extent. Some even favored it - but objected to the court ruling on grounds that it was unconstitutional. They believed the Federal government had nothing whatsoever to say legally about the schools in any state. To them the rights of the states as guaranteed in the Constitution were just as important as the authority guaranteed to the Federal government by the same document. They were alarmed by the Supreme Court's usurpation of power belonging to other branches of government.

Anyway, a powerful wave of anti-integration sentiment was sweeping the state like a river in flood, and beginning to spill over the banks. The various segments and viewpoints were not yet unified politically, but they were ripe for organization. Many were literally seething to be organized, motivated and directed to action.

To sit still and become known as a do-nothing governor in the face of this tide of public sentiment, especially after the issuance of the Southern Manifesto, would be inviting disaster. If Jim Johnson with his zeal, eloquence and diligence, should attract some able and respected assistants, he could well be the full recipient of this strong tide of sentiment. If so, in many sections of the state, he would overcome any candidate supported by the sophisticated political leaders and the business community. In the South, in Central Arkansas and the Eastern

region he would smash even me like a sledge hammer hitting a drum. If I did nothing and the Johnson forces were well led, the Northern and Western counties would not be sufficient to pull me through. Even in those areas the people did not like federal dictation although most of them knew little of the racial problems.

After deep thought and intense study, I plotted my course. I would stand in defense of the constitutions, both state and national, which guaranteed the people the control of their own schools. In the Arkansas school system the people through their own school boards, subject only to broad state law, were legally the complete masters of their local schools. There was no word, phrase, law, regulation or otherwise which gave the Federal government, in either branch, any say what-so-ever over any matter pertaining to education.

In taking and defending such a position, one need not espouse or oppose segregation or integration. It could not be denied that we had both in Arkansas. One need only to defend the right of the people to run their own schools and support education as they saw fit, including the segregation-integration question. That right was set out, not only in the U.S. Constitution, but in every state constitution and in many of the admission acts of the states to the union. In discussing the problem the same speech could be made, taking the same stand, without the slightest modification or compromise, any time, to any group, any where in the union from Crossett to Chicago or Charlotte to Los Angeles.

The stand would be in keeping with the Federal Constitution and the Bill of Rights. It would follow the teachings of Thomas Jefferson, the advice of George Washington, the statements of Abraham Lincoln and the admonitions of such modern day statesmen as Senator William E. Borah of Idaho.

If the people should choose to give more power to Washington, they could do so by changing the Constitution. If anything were radically wrong, it could be rectified by changing the Constitution through the methods prescribed. But, as Jefferson and Washington said, let there be no usurpation of power by the central government for in that course lies eventual dictatorship and the destruction of the republic.

The journey to Virginia of the committee headed by Marvin Bird and its report to me were parts of the plan. The formulation of the laws by Richard McCulloch of Forrest City, recognized by all his colleagues as an attorney of eminent ability and integrity; the refining and revising of the acts in full debate and discussion; the initiation of the acts by petitions circulated among the people; and a vote on the measures by all the people at the general election, were all a part of the design to give full play to citizen participation and a free expression of the people's will.

We already had integration in Arkansas, in fact more than any other state with a comparable problem. We would continue to have it. There would be more as the people chose, by their own will, to accept it. I would not join the extremists who said never to any integration whatsoever. Neither would I join the extremists who said integration at all costs. I would defend the people's right to choose, and to control their own schools, which was according to the Constitution.

This stand would not satisfy the extremists on either side. If my stand were not sufficient to satisfy a majority of the electorate, and the extremists on either hand prevailed, then so be it.

THE GROWING PROBLEM; OTHER DEVELOPMENTS

The segregation-integration issue continued to grow in public interest throughout the month of March. News reports on the third said the issue had hit the libraries. The controversy was not over use of the facilities on a non-discrimination basis, but objections by blacks to certain books. In many areas of the nation in response to complaints, the books of Mark Twain were removed from the shelves.

The U.S. Supreme Court confirmed the expansion of its original ruling to state colleges and universities. In Arkansas the institutions of higher learning were already in compliance with the new ruling. Blacks had already been admitted to the state-supported institutions.

A segregation rally was held on March 20 at Jacksonville which was widely attended. The speakers, Amis Guthridge, Harve Thorn, England Police Chief Joe Foster and Reverend Jerry Shrieves, termed the integration moves as "political," and exhibited supreme confidence in the success of the segregation movement. The news said I signaled an early decision on administration policy on integration; a rumor circulated of petitions by legislators requesting me to call a special session of the Legislature to deal with the problem; an advisory committee on integration made the news from Hot Springs; and the month closed with a well publicized segregation rally at Conway on March 30.

State Representative Russell Roberts was billed as chairman of the planning committee for the Conway meeting with former Governor Ben Laney as master of ceremonies. The main speakers were Johnson and James C. Davis, a state official of Decatur, Georgia.

Commissioner of Education Arch Ford poured a little oil on the troubled waters when he said that few school boards planned integration for the school year.

The nationwide news contributed to the growing interest and agitation. Virginia added an anti-integration amendment to its constitution; President Eisenhower on March 9 announced a meeting to discuss Arkansas racial problems which never materialized, and of which I had no knowledge whatsoever; on March 14 the president called for moderation in the integration school disputes and on April 1 the news said "Ike may call Southern leaders to talk over race relations issue." The Mississippi legislators were facing a bill which would strip integrated churches of tax exemption. In Alabama there were calls to impeach Governor Folsom. To offset the growing criticism Folsom called on March 20 for states rights segregation action in his state and across the South.

On March 22 I made known my sponsorship of two measures recommended by the Bird Committee.

The most important was an initiated act to grant to the school boards of the various public school districts, full power and authority over the assignment of students for attendance to the various school facilities. This was no extreme measure which said "never" to any integration at all. Under its terms a school board could authorize full integration, limited integration or no integration. The measure would accommodate those districts with minor problems which had already integrated as Fayetteville and Charleston, the districts which wished to try either limited or complete integration and those where no integration was considered desirable. In short, the problem was left to the free choice of the people of each district, which was constitutionally sound.

The other measure was a resolution of interposition which had no binding effect, but which permitted an expression of the "sense of the people" as to the usurpation of their rights and the rights of the states by the federal government.

Once the measures were prepared with my endorsement, the people went to work. There were volunteers by the hundreds to circulate the petitions and then to work for the adoption of the measures. The measures provided a vehicle for the expression of the people's will. Naturally they did not satisfy everyone. One negro leader, I.S. McClinton of Little Rock, in a public statement strongly condemned the proposals. However, the great majority of people felt their interests should be considered.

Among the volunteers to circulate the petitions at his own time and expense was former state legislator Ralph Underhill

of White County. Underhill was returned to the House in the Democratic primaries of 1960.

KIWANIS CLUB RESOLUTION AT ENGLAND

To indicate the growing concern of the people with the integration problem the following news item of April 25 is reproduced.

LEGISLATIVE SESSION CALL WINS FAVOR

ENGLAND, Ark. — On motion of Paul Godsey, local automobile dealer, the England Kiwanis Club Friday went on record as favoring an early call for a special session of the General Assembly to enact legislation that will assist school boards desirous of continuing the operation of segregated schools.

The club voted unanimously to notify Governor Faubus of its position.

Godsey was one of my original supporters in 1954. Our acquaintance began when we were both McMath allies and members of the McMath administration.

SOUTHLAND GETS PERMIT; INDUSTRIAL GROWTH

In other developments the Racing Commission, in response to orders of the courts, granted a permit for the operation of the dog track at West Memphis. The tax equalization program was attacked in the courts. A new $16 million mill was announced by the Crossett Lumber Company; Manila got its first industry through efforts of the AIDC; and the Mohawk Tire and Rubber Company began operation at Helena with 700 employees.

AFL & CIO MERGE

The state AFL and state CIO merged on March 20 to form one labor council thus effecting the first state merger of the two great labor groups in the nation. Among the officials selected for the new group were Odell Smith, president; Charles M. Catton, treasurer; Wayne Glenn, executive secretary; and W.C. "Bill" Demers, vice-president. On March 25 a news headline read: "Labor's brightest spot in the nation: It's Arkansas."

My trip to Washington to help save the Camden ammunition depot for people of the area was successful.

POLITICAL DEVELOPMENTS

In politics members of the House filing for the State Senate were Robert Harvey of Swifton, and House Speaker Charles F. "Rip" Smith of West Memphis. Jack Shelton of Monticello also filed.

Pat Mullis announced for Congress against Congressman Norrell. On March 18 Jim Snoddy of Alma said he may run for Governor and that his feelers were "encouraging."

Attorney Lee Ward of Paragould joined the race for Chief Justice of the State Supreme Court.

200 HEAR FAUBUS, CRAWFIS EXCHANGE SHARP CHARGES AS HOSPITAL RIFT WIDENS

Two members of the Pulaski County Mental Health organization, or some such group, expressing interest in the State Hospital, came to my office posing as neutral arbiters but, as I later learned, were spies and allies of Dr. Crawfis. I showed them most of the information I had on defects and misdoing at the institution. They asked if I would meet with Dr. Crawfis and some of their members to discuss the matter and I, naturally, agreed.

The next thing I knew it was in the press that I would discuss the matter at a public meeting with Dr. Crawfis, - in other words a public debate. It didn't appear to me to be a proper manner in which to settle an administration squabble. But, I had been tricked into the matter and there was no graceful way out.

So on the appointed time I gathered up my material, went to the appointed place in the AEA building to meet Crawfis and his allies. To shorten an interesting story of a lively evening, I got the best of Dr. Crawfis and the schemers. When I got through some were angry and pale as ghosts, and others literally ran from the building in tears.

A number of hospital employees were on hand and cheered me repeatedly. Jimmy Karam was present and said it was better than my Pine Bluff speech, only in a different setting and a different manner. John F. Wells, one of my strongest and most consistent critics, conceded that I won the debate and attributed my victory to the superior debating skills I had learned at Commonwealth College.

A news headline soon afterward read: "Hospital Head 'Looking' for Job After Exchange with Faubus."

INTEGRATION, POLITICS, INDUSTRIAL GROWTH

The integration controversy and politics dominated the news as the filing deadline of May 1 neared for the Democratic primaries. A third subject, more promising and more pleasant

for the state, was very prominent also — industrial growth.

On April 10 the International Paper Company confirmed its plans for the construction of a $57 million plant at Pine Bluff. When completed the plant would employ 1,450 persons. Its annual output would include 130,000 tons of newsprint and 105,000 tons of bleached kraft board. When the plant went into production it was a source of supply for newsprint for the papers in Arkansas. Formerly the newsprint for my own paper in Huntsville bore the imprint on the package covers "made in Canada." After completion of this plant the newsprint came from Pine Bluff.

Four days earlier a new plant location was announced for Ft. Smith, which would use Arkansas-produced aluminum and provide 1,500 jobs.

On the 17th, North Little Rock received the welcome news of a new industry which would employ 90 people. On the 28th, a factory for the manufacture of gloves was announced for Mt. Ida.

UTILITY RATES ROLLED BACK

The refund checks on rolled back gas rates were being mailed by Arkla Gas Company and AP&L lost its appeal to the State Supreme Court to keep its higher rates.

INTEGRATION

In the integration controversy the news reported the displeasure of the NAACP with Little Rock Supt. Blossom's racial designation of the schools.

KITH AND KIN
By Graham, Ark. Gazette   4/17/56

Many of the people who left the state wanted to return home, and many at home who must leave to find work, wanted to stay. The only means to fulfill those desires was more industry for Arkansas to provide the necessary jobs. On this the AIDC and the homesick travelers from Arkansas agreed.

Adlai Stevenson, candidate for the Democratic nomination for president, said that integration was the law of the land. (Regardless of whether integration was right or wrong, how sad that so prominent a figure did not know the difference of the "law of the case" and the "law of the land.")

Negro leader I.S. McClinton of Little Rock called for the establishment of an interracial commission for integration problems. The proposal had merit but was most untimely and nothing could be done except to ignore it.

Representatives of segregation groups met in New Orleans and formed an inter-state citizens council representing eleven states.

On April 23, the U.S. Supreme Court still further expanded its anti-segregation ruling by outlying segregation on buses within the states. Its previous ruling applied to inter-state transportation, with which Arkansas had complied without difficulty. The next day the state NAACP headed by Mrs. Daisy Bates announced it would press for an end to segregation on the Little Rock bus system.

Some small bus lines immediately stopped any effort to maintain segregated seating, and by the 26th the Little Rock bus system had complied with the NAACP demands. The developments dominated the news of the capital city and now the headlines read: "No incidents reported as bus segregation comes to an end here" and "Little Rock's era on bus segregation fades out quietly."

Needless to say there were numerous small incidents which infuriated numbers of white people who still used the buses for transportation. It was not so much the end of segregated seating as the discourtesy and arrogance of some blacks. Others conducted themselves in a becoming manner helping to offset the acts of the discourteous. However, many citizens now abandoned public transportation never to use it again. (My personal observation while traveling in the South by bus during the war, was that the crowded conditions had already diluted segregation on the interstate bus systems.)

Nevertheless these developments cost me votes in Little Rock and provided still more grist for the rapidly grinding political mills of the extreme segregationists with Jim Johnson having emerged as their principal state spokesman. I remained a silent observer of the events involving the city bus systems. For Johnson the integration move could not have come at a more advantageous time.

Just previous to the bus system developments, Johnson on April 20 announced that a White Citizens' Council meeting would be held in Little Rock on April 30. It was not recognized at the time but this was to be the big event, the climax of Johnson's diligent organizational efforts. Then on April 23 Johnson said he may run for governor.

On April 25, Governor J.P. Coleman of Mississippi promised his people that he would hold the line on segregation. This was proof to many that the attitude of a governor could prove decisive in combatting the illegal Supreme Court decision.

Then Winthrop Rockefeller, in an inept and untimely statement made while on a visit to Washington, D.C., said that Arkansas's attitude of opposition to integration would scare industry from the state. Since Rockefeller as chairman of the AIDC was a member of my official family, Johnson immediately seized on the statement to his decided advantage.

Finally on April 27 a headline read: "Integration Stand of Faubus Hit." It was an attack on me by Senator James Eastland in a speech at Tupelo, Miss. The attack was no doubt

NOW, JUST A DOGGONE MINUTE
By Kennedy, Ark. Democrat   *4/15/56*

Businessman Chris Finkbeiner of Little Rock was a prime prospect as a candidate for governor in the Democratic primaries. He was being urged to enter the race with pledges of support by "anti-Faubus forces."

inspired by Johnson, a personal friend of the Mississippi senator with whom he often conferred on political matters.

POLITICS IN APRIL 1956

STATE AUDITOR HUMPHREY DIES

April 1: State Auditor J. Oscar Humphrey died. From Sevier County, serving his 13th term, he had held the office since 1929 except for one term, 1935-1936.

April 3: I appointed Humphrey's son, F. Nolan Humphrey, to serve out the unexpired term.

Jimmie "Red" Jones, Land Commissioner by appointment of Governor Cherry, and thus ineligible to seek re-election to that office, announced as a candidate for State Auditor.

April 4: William H. Donham of Little Rock said he would oppose Brooks Hays for the Second District Congressional seat.

April 8: B.E. "Bus" Friday of Little Rock announced for State Auditor, becoming an opponent of Jimmie Jones.

April 14: Former State Senator Lee Reaves of Warren said he would not run for governor, and Chris Finkbeiner of Little Rock said he may seek the office.

April 17: Representative J.A. "Dooley" Womack of Camden said he may oppose Harris for Congress.

April 19: Sid McMath said he would not seek the U.S. Senate seat of Senator Fulbright.

R.W. "Bob" Griffith of Little Rock joined the race for Attorney General making the fifth candidate for that office.

April 22: C.G. "Crip" Hall filed for a 11th term as Secretary of State.

Senator McClellan was in the news as a dark horse entry for president.

April 26: Possible candidates for governor, Finkbeiner, Snoddy, Johnson and Tom Gentry, were reported as undecided.

April 28: Ben F. Pippin, age 70, a Cherry administration appointee and retired employee of the State Police Weights Division, announced for governor.

April 29: Ben Rankin of Little Rock, brother of the late Claude Rankin, filed for Land Commissioner.

Chancellor Carleton Harris of Pine Bluff filed for Chief Justice of the State Supreme Court. He was pitted against Guy Amsler of Little Rock and Lee Ward of Paragould.

April 30: Newspaper readers were greeted by these headlines:

Segregationist Rally To Draw from 5 States;
Marvin Griffin of Georgia to Attend

Rally may be Springboard for Candidates;
Giant Segregation Rally at Robinson Auditorium

Johnson's organizational movement was building to a dramatic climax.

UNACCUSTOMED AS I AM . . .
By Kennedy, Ark. Democrat   4/26/56

In seeking renomination and re-election to a second term as governor, I was looked upon as the favorite. The cartoonist, with a great deal of truth, portrayed me as unfamiliar with the role. Usually I was fighting an uphill battle as the underdog.

ROLE OF
FAVORITE
IN
GOVERNOR'S
RACE

ROLE OF
UNDERDOG

FALL OUT!!
By Kennedy, Ark. Democrat   5/4/56

In Pulaski County Senators Max Howell and Ellis Fagan had opposition. Senator Artie Gregory, more widely known as a segregationist and states rights advocate, got by without an opponent.

May 1, from *Arkansas Gazette*

JOHNSON HEEDS CRIES OF SEGREGATIONISTS; SAYS HE WILL RUN

James D. Johnson of Crossett announced last night before a wildly demonstrative crowd of about 2,000 men, women and children that he would run for governor.

Johnson's announcement, expected for weeks, was made at a segregation rally at the Auditorium at Little Rock.

Johnson, 32, a former state senator, "agreed" to run after Herbert Brewer, a leader of segregation forces at Hoxie, came to the stage at the end of the program and "suggested" that Johnson run.

The suggestion touched off a demonstration that lasted more than 20 minutes. People streamed down the aisles to toss money into the orchestra pit to make up Johnson's $1,500 filing fee. They crowded onto the stage and milled around Johnson shaking his hand and wishing him luck.

"I'll run for governor", Johnson told the crowd, "If you'll support me!" His answer came in wild applause and cheering. . .

Last night's crowd was the largest at any segregation rally in Arkansas. The previous record was about 1,400 at a rally at England February 24.

Another participant in the rally was former Governor Ben T. Laney who acted as master of ceremonies. Laney read three telegrams in which he said Senator John L. McClellan, Representative W.F. Norrell, and other members of the congressional delegation at Washington, "expressed their regrets" at being unable to attend the rally because of the press of business. Although billed only as the emcee, Laney in a 25-minute talk urged the audience to send legislators to Little Rock who would support anti-integration legislation.

"How are you going to get state officials to take note of your views?" Laney asked. Then answered his own question, "Cut a few political throats! Look up the records," he said.

The headline in the *Arkansas Democrat* read:

*Integration Foes Pick Johnson for Governor;
Draw Up Battle Lines; Is Drafted
After Rally in Auditorium*

by Bill Butler, Democrat Staff Writer

Arkansas' newest candidate for governor, James D. Johnson, Crossett, will campaign on a platform based on complete segregation, a state old-age pension, a politics-free State Hospital, and industrial development of the state.

. . .Mr. Johnson revealed that he was ready for all-out political warfare. He said he was prepared for any sort of campaign his foes wanted to wage.

And he tuned the campaign fiddles by taking a verbal swing at Governor Faubus and Winthrop Rockefeller.

He lashed at the governor's "do-nothing stand on segregation" in Arkansas and said that the late announcement of Mr. Faubus on the question revealed nothing but "a political angle."

"Despite Mr. Rockefeller's statement on integration" he declared, "I feel that we can go forward with industrial development of our state without the advice of persons like Mr. Rockefeller who insists we can't have it (industrial development) without integration."

Mr. Johnson filed for the Democrat primary ballot today with money that was tossed into the Robinson Auditorium orchestra pit by supporters at the anti-integration rally last night.

A total of $2,269.18 was contributed by the wildly shouting persons at the rally.

The crowd streamed to the front of the auditorium and tossed money into the pit. In less than 40 minutes, a stack of bills and checks almost two feet high piled up in the pit.

Then Mr. Johnson told the crowd he would run for governor and appealed for the crowd's support.

The *Democrat* report estimated the crowd at 2,500. In a statement to reporters Johnson said, "The draft came as a complete surprise."

Of course he couldn't admit it at the time, and perhaps not even yet publicly, but the Johnson draft at the auditorium was a well conceived, well planned and well executed method of launching his candidacy. It was also quite effective, as I could tell immediately. It was no surprise to Johnson and his confidants, who even made sure there were plenty of one dollar bills in designated hands to toss into the pit. It would have been a surprise to Johnson and his lieutenants if the plan had not worked.

However I must say in all honesty, that the "Draft Johnson" movement was the only phony part of the program, and that part only to those who knew before hand. The devotion, the dedication, the determination, the willingness to sacrifice, work, and contribute funds to the cause even when necessary to borrow money to do so, were genuine enough. The movement with the necessary zeal and conviction was there. And now the movement had its candidate. All of which would not be easy to overcome. There could be no fumbling, procrastination or want of energy if I were to be sure of victory. This I understood, and acted accordingly.

TICKET CLOSES FIVE IN RING FOR GOVERNOR—

ORVAL **FAUBUS**...... defending champ, cagy infighter-- can take a lot of punishment.

JIM **JOHNSON** — outstanding darkhorse, has been training vigorously.

'STEW' **PROSSER** — out-classed.

JIM **SNODDY** — promising newcomer-- look for good effort.

BEN **PIPPIN**......... in for exercise.

JON KENNEDY

HIGHLIGHTS OF THE NEWSWEEK
By Kennedy, Ark. Democrat   5/1/56

LAST MINUTE FILINGS

May 1: Tom Gentry bowed out as a candidate for governor. The news said Snoddy or Finkbeiner would oppose me.

Guy H. "Mutt" Jones, Conway, filed for re-election to the State Senate.

(Senator Alben Barkley of Kentucky fell dead of a heart attack as he ended a speech to students at Lexington, Va.)

May 2: The deadline for filing was at noon with Mrs. C.G. Hall for the Secretary of State's office, and Frank Robbins of Conway, State Democratic Party Secretary, taking the last minute filings.

Snoddy and Johnson both filed for governor, proclaiming themselves as avowed segregationists.

Finkbeiner on hand to the last minute, declined to file.

S.K. "Stew" Prosser, Conway, filed at 11:40 to become the fifth gubernatorial candidate.

Sam Jones filed for Land Commissioner becoming an opponent of Rankin.

The news reported from Washington that the telephone informed Senator Fulbright, the first Arkansas signer of the Southern Manifesto, that he was home free without an opponent for the second time in 12 years.

In Pulaski county Robert L. "Bob" Laster and Floyd Fulkerson opposed Senators Ellis Fagan and Max Howell for re-election to the state senate.

Reports from Alabama brought encouraging news to the Arkansas segregationist candidates.

SEGREGATIONIST DEFEATS FOLSOM IN ALABAMA

Governor James "Big Jim" Folsom of Alabama, ineligible to succeed himself as governor, had filed as a candidate in the Democratic primary for the party post of Democratic National Committeeman. State Representative Charles W. McKay, Jr. filed as an opponent and charged that Folsom was "soft" on legal separation of the races. The unknown McKay sent Alabama's best known and most popular political figure down in crushing defeat. In some areas the vote against Folsom was 15 to 20 to 1 and he was trailing in 50 of the first 60 counties to report.

The *Gazette* recognized the danger of the integration issue in the campaign and in this editorial attempted to defuse it.

THE RACIAL ISSUE AND THE CAMPAIGN
Editorial
Arkansas Gazette
May 2, 1956

The campaign for governor will not be on the line of pro-integration and anti-segregation. Orval E. Faubus is opposed to integration as former State Senator James D. Johnson is. There is the difference that Mr. Johnson will apparently concentrate upon the racial issue and seek to ride an emotional wave that he himself has helped create. His candidacy would be a more logical one politically if another candidate were seeking to lead Arkansas into integration, but of course no other candidate is going to do that.

Mr. Johnson's candidacy may ignite inherent prejudices. But the racial issue is one that should be treated with calmness and sober spirit. Nobody has to be extreme or violent to hold firm convictions.

In his successful race two years ago, Orval E. Faubus made a tentative start toward injecting the racial issue into his campaign against Francis Cherry. The militant anti-integrationists' present candidate for governor made no mention of the racial issue in his unsuccessful 1954 campaign for attorney general. He did not promise to "do something about" the basic Supreme Court decision which had been handed down on May 17, 1954. That is an important date to remember in this context because it means that the Court decision came before the 1954 primary campaign was well under way. And a state attorney general might reasonably have been expected at the time to be able to do at least as much as a governor toward ameliorating the effects of the Court's ruling.

MORRILTON SCHOOL PROPOSAL BY ROCKEFELLER

The integration controversy continued prominent in the news. On May 5 the Arkansas NAACP leaders declared they wanted desegregation now. Rockefeller added to the complexity of the problem by a proposal to finance a "model" integrated school at Morrilton. The announcement made by George Reynolds, a Rockefeller associate, said up to $2½ million would be spent. The proposal made state wide news and, although efforts followed to minimize the integration feature of the school, the plan, coupled with the NAACP demand, added fuel to the fires being fanned by Johnson and Snoddy and certainly did not improve my political fortunes.

Over the years the operation of the State Hospital had been a problem to many governors. With obsolete buildings forbidding in appearance and overcrowded with patients, with inadequate funds, underpaid employees, slipshod business methods and considerable downright dishonesty and fraud, the hospital was for a time my "Number One Headache."

Hundreds of complaints came to me from employees, relatives of patients and others. I passed all this information on to hospital personnel hoping for corrections and improvements.

For some reason Dr. Ewing Crawfis denied the wrong doing at the institution and defended some of the guilty. As a result a public quarrel developed with the superintendent accusing me of political meddling.

The controversy became one of the key issues in the governor's race. Pressure was applied to me by resignations and critical statements, timed and spaced to obtain maximum publicity. But I did not yield an inch in my contention with the authorities in my efforts to clean up the administration of the state facility, and after about a dozen resignations, including Dr. Crawfis, things began to settle down.

After the resignation of Dr. Crawfis on May 9, a new superintendent was secured. With the fine cooperation of the board and the General Assembly, steady progress was made in the operation of the facility from then forward.

In the next few years as a result of extensive construction, - all with state money, - increased operating funds, trained personnel and honest administration of the business affairs, the facility became internationally known as one of the finest mental health units anywhere. All those who had a part in converting the State Hospital from one of the most inadequate facilities of its kind to the fine hospital it became, can be justly proud of their efforts and their accomplishments.

MANION AT EL DORADO

On May 24 to 26, Clarence Manion, Dean of the Law School of Notre Dame University, Southbend, Indiana, appeared in the state. After news conferences in Little Rock he spoke at a segregation rally organized and sponsored by Johnson at El Dorado. Manion, reputed authority on the U.S. Constitution, strongly criticized the trend to centralized government.

NON-SIGNERS OF MANIFESTO DEFEATED

On May 28 came news of the defeat of two North Carolina Congressmen, Thurmond D. Chatham and Charles B. Deane, because they failed to sign the Southern Manifesto. Governor J. P. Coleman of Mississippi pointed to their defeats as a warning to other officials of the South.

LOUISIANA FOR INTERPOSITION

On May 29 Louisiana okehed interposition, becoming the sixth Southern state to adopt this method of defense of states rights and state control of schools.

MORE RESIGNATIONS AT STATE HOSPITAL

CHARGES OF POLITICAL MEDDLING

SEARCH FOR REPLACEMENTS

ISSUE IN GOVERNORS RACE

STILL THE #1 HEADACHE!
By Kennedy, Ark. Democrat   5/18/56

ALL PRESENT AND ACCOUNTED FOR, By Kennedy, Ark. Democrat, 5/20/56

The Democratic candidates for governor were "all present and accounted for" on the "Anti-Integration Line," evidence to those who have forgotten that the "Line" was an important campaign issue some time before the '57 crisis. Two things about the cartoon are possibly noteworthy. Jim Johnson is shown to have a more "present-and-accounted-for" attitude than the others on the issue. Secondly, all the figures bear their last names, Johnson, Snoddy, Pippin and Prosser, except mine which bears my first name. Did this denote the common touch with cartoonists as well as with rank and file voters?

Jim Johnson's first campaign shot was made direct-ly at me.

The great Elvis Presley performed in Little Rock.

On the segregation issue I took my stand on two measures — a pupil assignment law, and a resolution of interposition. The measures constituted perhaps the mildest platform on the explosive issue of any candidate in the South at that time.

ADMINISTRATION PROGRESS

There were some pluses for my administration in May. We disclosed that food worth $14,700,000 had been distributed in the past year to needy welfare recipients.

A congressional committee okehed the establishment of Pea Ridge National Military park, moving it a step closer to final approval. A historian long before had rated the engagement as one of the 15 most decisive battles of the world.

A third paper mill was under consideration at Pine Bluff. My administration received an okeh from organized labor.

Collections by the Revenue Department indicated a record harvest of $110 million. Already collections had increased $8 million for the first eleven months of the fiscal year.

Sam Harris, veteran political writer and reporter for the *Gazette*, stopped covering the capitol, — but this was not a plus for the administration on political reporting.

LAKE DEDICATION AT SILOAM SPRINGS

Governor Raymond Gary of Oklahoma and I, on May 21, joined in the dedication of a new lake along the Arkansas-Oklahoma border near Siloam Springs. Many state and local civic and political leaders were present among them State Senator Russell Elrod of Siloam Springs, famed humorist Chet Lauck (Lum of Lum and Abner radio team) of Houston, Texas, columnist Clarence Byrns of Ft. Smith and John Brown University President John Brown, Jr.

Aside from recreation and flood control the lake provided water for municipal and industrial use.

JOHN BROWN UNIVERSITY

I joined President John Brown, Jr. and chairman of the Board John Brown, Sr. in groundbreaking ceremonies for a new Science Building at the University. Others participating were Lauck, Governor Gary and Dr. Lawsone of Dallas, Texas.

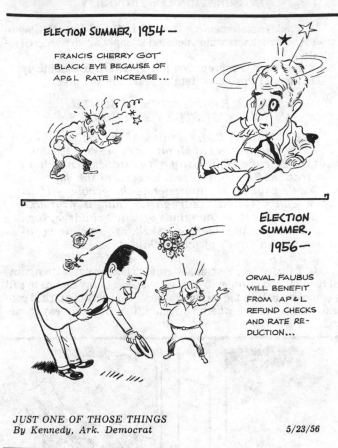

The Arkansas Power & Light Company's increased electric rates caused electric bills to skyrocket in 1954 and Gov. Cherry got a black eye. For two years we battl-ed the AP&L to roll back the rate increase. The company finally exhausted all avenues of resistance. The rates would be reduced and the company announced a refund of 9 million dollars to the rate payers. The announcement was made during the 1956 campaign and I was getting bouquets. An Arkla rate increase was also reduced and that company made refunds totaling $1,200,000 to its customers.

It wasn't, as the cartoonist indicated, "just one of those things . . .". It's all in how matters are handled, and sometimes whether you're right or wrong.

MED CENTER COMPLETED

The new University of Arkansas Medical Center at Little Rock was completed and held open house on June 9 — a big event for Little Rock and the University.

I hinted at new taxes to meet the rising demand for state services (in the midst of a campaign?!?!?!?)

At the joint recommendation of State Democratic Chairman Tom Harper and me, Wayne E. Glenn, Little Rock labor leader, was named by national party leader Paul Butler as Arkansas chairman for labor activities in the national campaign.

Tax collections by Commissioner Cheney gained $9.2 million and set an all time record for total collections of $112 million.

On June 30 I announced the selection of J. L. "Jim" Bland and Arnold Sikes to head my re-election campaign.

INTEGRATION CONTROVERSY

In a public statement on June 10 I offered financial aid to those school districts which decided to oppose court-ordered integration.

In Louisiana a segregation bill passed overwhelmingly.

On June 12 this news item appeared in the press.

RACIAL RESISTANCE IN SOUTH "SHOCKS" HISTORY AUTHORITY

Dr. William B. Hesseltine of the University of Wisconsin speaking at Memphis expressed "shock" at the extent and intensity of resistance to racial integration. He was amazed, he said, at the Supreme Court's psychiatric approach to the problem. If, as the court stated, segregation had a profound adverse effect on the minds of black children, then what about the effect, he asked, of forced integration on the minds of white children.

In Tallahassee, Florida, attempted bus desegregation caused turmoil and disorder. Violence led Gov. Leroy Collins to call a complete halt to the bus operations. This was in marked contrast to Little Rock where no such difficulties were experienced.

THERE GOES THE HOPE CHEST
By Kennedy, Ark. Democrat   6/13/56

Winthrop Rockefeller, after taking up residence in Arkansas and securing a divorce from Bobo Sears Rockefeller, was looked upon as the state's most enticing

bachelor. He had assumed the role of rancher, wearing cowboy clothes including ten-gallon hats and WR monogrammed boots, as he supervised his modern cattle ranch stocked with Santa Gertrudis. He often wore the same clothing as he traveled about the state on business trips or speaking engagements.

Then he married Jeanette Edris of Seattle, Washington. "Arkansas maidens fair" tossed away their hope chests which included such items as cowboy clothes, a lariat, a map of Winrock Farm, and a book entitled, "How To Manage Servants."

INTEGRATION QUESTION IN THE CAMPAIGN
Governor Laney Speaks

July opened with my opponents dominating the news.

In a speech at Pine Bluff to 1,000 people on July 1, former Governor Laney said, "The Federal government has no right to take state's business into its own hands," and got a standing ovation.

"NEVER" FOR INTEGRATION, SNODDY SAYS

Jim Snoddy opened his campaign with a blast at my administration in a television speech in Little Rock on July 2. Snoddy's TV presentation was poor and many observers thought it doomed his candidacy from that moment. Snoddy was one of those who agreed it was not good. Person to person and in the field he was a good campaigner.

Snoddy virtually ignored the integration issue in the television speech and dealt with it in a political ad and press release immediately afterward. This is a quote from his paid advertisement:

"I am definitely and absolutely in favor of segregation today — tomorrow and always. I am not — and never have been in favor of gradual integration."

"I will use all the facilities of the governor's office at all times to enforce the state laws regulating segregation!"

The AP&L rates came down July 1, refunds would begin soon, "$9 Million Dollars" was in the bag for the rate payers.

"Favorite Sons" in the News

A rumor from Atlantic City had me a possible favorite son candidate for president at the Democratic National Convention. The statement that McClellan and I were foes was erroneous. We were in contact and worked together during the convention in Chicago. We had experienced no differences since the campaign of 1954 and had worked in full co-operation on many projects for the state.

LOOK OUT FOR FLYING BOUQUETS
By Kennedy, Ark. Democrat   *6/20/56*

old folks

interpositionists

unions

Ark. Youths

ORVAL

FIRST PRIMARY JULY 31

teachers

civic groups

poultrymen

KENNEDY

My first term had been frugal, but we had been able to accomplish a great deal. What was equally important we had alienated no important group. There were some disappointed job seekers and some special interests who wanted to be unduly favored. The overall program for the progress of Arkansas had now been formulated in my mind, which enabled me to strongly indicate what could be done for many groups and many people during my second term.

THE PORTIA JULY 4 PICNIC

The Portia July 4 picnic in Lawrence County had been one of the most noted verbal dueling grounds for Democratic primary candidates for decades. Located scarcely a stone's throw west of the integration battleground of Hoxie, and within the school district's bounds, the candidates appearance there took on added significance with the integration issue dominating the early campaign oratory.

The headlines read: "3 Candidates Cross Swords on Integration" and "Faubus, Johnson Swap Verbal Blows on Segregation Issue."

I took advantage of the situation to make my first reply to Johnson's severe and effective attacks on me on the segregation issue.

I pointed out, and cited the record to show, that I recognized the importance of the problem two years earlier, and had taken a stand in the campaign of 1954. Johnson a candidate for Attorney General in the same campaign had never once mentioned the issue. The reminder to the voters was effective in blunting Johnson's attacks.

Johnson had also advocated a bill to remove 4,000 miles of unimproved roads from the state highway system during the

Cherry administration. I used this against him effectively in rural areas where improved roads were badly needed.

The order of the speakers at Portia that day was: Johnson, Snoddy, Prosser and me, followed by Sen. Estes Kefauver, a candidate for president.

PETITIONS FILED
SEEKING BAN ON INTEGRATION

Petitions filed by Jim Johnson initiated a constitutional amendment prohibiting integration in any form, anywhere. The amendment also made mandatory the removal from office of any state official who did not uphold and enforce the laws compelling segregation, and applied specifically to the governor. Had the amendment been in effect at that time, I could have been removed from office for permitting integration of the Hoxie, Charleston and Fayetteville public schools and the institutions of higher learning, or for permitting the integration of the public bus system in Little Rock and the coaches and waiting rooms of the railroads.

Snoddy's statement on integration and Johnson's amendment were so strong that to many people they had the effect of casting me in the role of a moderate on the explosive and emotional issue. In fact to many Johnson followers, I was an integrationist.

———

Faubus Hurls Fund Challenge at Opponents;
Crowd Whoops as Johnson and Snoddy Raked Over Coals.

Thus read one headline on July 7 about the official opening of my campaign at an out-door rally at Clarksville the night of July 6. I had a number of good organizers there including Armel Taylor, Harold Whitson, Wiley Bean, Sterlin Hurley, Chic Morgan and others. I could also draw from another of my strongest counties, Franklin, where three of the four major factions were supporting me, and personal friends like Eddie Anderson, Jim Owens and Champ Turner were active in my behalf.

———

Faubus Says His Record Trustworthy

Governor Faubus last night challenged his opponents to find his record not "trustworthy," as he opened his campaign for re-election before 3,000 people on the Johnson County Courthouse square at Clarksville. *He indicated he would try to get this campaign away from integration and onto other issues, but his best round of applause came when he said no school district would be forced to integrate against its will while he was governor.*

———

JAYCEE RALLY AT PINE BLUFF

In a speech at a Jaycee sponsored rally in Pine Bluff the evening of July 9 I said that integration was not an issue in the campaign. For the statement I received a chorus of jeers. I was cheered strongly for other parts of my speech, especially for my labor record and for combatting utility rate increases and my help to welfare recipients.

The basis for my remarks on the integration question was the fact that all candidates were opposed to court-ordered and enforced integration by the Federal authorities from Washington. Although the positions of candidates might be the same, it was an issue that could not go un-mentioned or un-noticed.

Johnson spoke that night in Camden in Ouachita County where we were attempting to halt his westward surge from his stronghold in the Southeast.

THREE TO MAKE READY
By Kennedy, Ark. Democrat   6/27/56

Snoddy led off with the first political ad of the campaign. Johnson had been organizing among the segregationists for months and now became more vocal in his attacks on me. Thus Snoddy and Johnson were shown preceding me on the diving board as we plunged into the fray of political battle.

134

FAUBUS STAND REPEATED

In a speech in the Marianna City park in Lee County on July 11, I repeated the stand I had taken against compulsory integration. The press correctly reported my statement: "No school district will be forced to mix the races as long as I am Governor of Arkansas."

However I gave no signal of retreat from the dangerous ground I had already occupied in permitting voluntary integration where the school officials and people chose to do so, or where they had yielded to federal pressure.

HAYS AGAIN ON A MANIFESTO

On July 13 the Arkansas Congressional Delegation was again in the news in opposition to usurpation of states rights. Brooks Hays said he deplored the civil rights bill then before Congress as a peril to the United States.

The delegation had signed a "second Southern Manifesto" deploring the (GOP) Administration's civil rights bill. Hays was not then proclaiming Southern moderation for which he later became known. His opposition to federal interference in states' rights was a matter of record - and of political survival. The federal government had no more constitutional authority to interfere with education in the states than it did to enter into the field of elections and voting, a matter Hays was here opposing.

HAYS' STATEMENT

"I have joined in the statement condemning the so-called civil rights bill because it is contrary to convictions which I have entertained throughout my life with reference to constitutional powers of federal and state government. The right to vote, with many other precious rights, must be protected, but the states are the best guardians of the rights. . .

The issue should not be identified with questions of race, it has nothing whatsoever to do with the Supreme Court decision requiring desegregation of public schools and it is unfortunate the civil rights statement is being construed by some as having this implication. . .

This conception of state responsibility carries with it, of course, a continuing opposition to unwarranted invasion by federal authority of control over elections. . .

Those who would exploit any difference between them (races) are rendering a great disservice (to their country.)

AIDC REPORT

On July 13 the AIDC issued its annual report on its first year of industry-seeking. The effort had been even more successful than we had hoped. The report disclosed that the state had gained 10,000 new jobs since the commission began functioning on July 1, 1955. Signed by Chairman Winthrop Rockefeller and the other members, the report helped to undo some of the harm done to my political fortunes by the Rockefeller statement in New York linking industry and integration.

GRAND JURY APPEARANCE

I surprised and disarmed my critics by volunteering as the first witness before the Pulaski County Grand Jury charged with investigating allegations of bribery in connection with racing in the state.

SNODDY ATTACKS STEPHENS

On July 14 Snoddy trained his political guns on W. R. "Witt" Stephens, majority stockholder in Arkla Gas Company, charging that he was my principal money raiser for the campaign. Later Snoddy alleged that the gas users of the state were paying tribute to Stephens.

CAMPAIGN GROWS HEATED

By mid-July the campaign had grown heated. On some occasions I trained my guns on a weak spot in Johnson's organization by attacking one of his lieutenants, former editor and publisher Curt Copeland. The Johnson aide, who was one of his campaign speakers, had published newspapers in Mt. Ida and Hot Springs, leaving both towns in high disfavor. For some time he had been engaged with Johnson in the publication at Crossett of a magazine dealing with the race issue which was so extreme and often in such bad taste as to be repulsive.

Headlines on the 17th read: "Governor bares knuckles to Copeland, and 2 Main Foes;" "Faubus Blasts Copeland; Says Snoddy Fishing" (on charges about Witt Stephens).

Then on the 19th Johnson vowed to kick Negroes from their posts in the Democratic party and said my first act was to put them in the party jobs. His statement about my actions was basically true. In 1954 I had recommended and the State Democratic Convention had created six new positions on the Democratic Central Committee to be filled by blacks.

Johnson stepped up his attacks, a headline on the 20th reading, "Johnson labels Faubus puppet of Rockefeller", and on the 21st "Johnson lashes at Faubus in racial talk at Texarkana."

Snoddy also speeded up his charges in the drumfire of attack on me and my administration.

Johnson once varied from the racial theme and in a speech at Pine Bluff alleged that I was destroying the non-political status of the Highway Commission. One of the Cherry-appointed commissioners lived in Pine Bluff as well as one of the authors of the amendment making the commission independent. The Johnson charge was ineffective because it had no basis in fact.

Snoddy plunged into Northwest Arkansas and claimed his efforts would split the vote in my home area stronghold. My reply was "the split will be about like a splinter from a saw log."

On July 23 I asked my two main opponents what they had accomplished for the people while serving in the State Senate. Each had served a four-year term. Their records were, to say the least, non-spectacular. On the same day Johnson leveled a new blast at the "race-mixers," and numbered me among them.

On July 25 a handbill quiz directed to me was distributed in the north by the Snoddy forces. It was quickly followed by leaflets strewn from planes over northern towns by the Johnson workers. The leaflets pictured me flanked by four black citizens, two on each side.

I held up one of the leaflets as I spoke in some of the areas.

"Now, ladies and gentlemen," I said, "Let's have this clearly understood. I am the servant of all the people in this state. I owe respect and courtesy to all my constituents, both black and white, and consideration for their problems. I have been photographed with black citizens and black leaders, and will be again. But, this photograph is a fake."

The photograph showed me in a white suit, the only one I had ever owned. I explained that I had worn it on only three occasions, all of which I specifically recalled. And on those occasions I was not photographed with any black people. "The point I want to make," I concluded, "is this. If the opposition will falsify, as they have in this leaflet, isn't it likely they will falsify other matters."

The headline and lead for a *Democrat* story on July 26 read:

*Faubus on Rampage in Greene (County);
Governor Lashes Two Top Opponents*

Faubus spoke to 4,000 at an outdoor theatre its use arranged by supporters, using a slambang, electioneering style for first time in the campaign.

———

On July 26 Tom Tinnon of Mountain Home, candidate for Attorney General, made the statement that segregation was not an issue in the campaign. He went down to defeat.

FORWARD WITH FAUBUS

A Paid Political Cartoon by Committee to Elect Jim Snoddy, *Arkansas Gazette*, July 29, 1956 (3/4 page ad) is shown below.

This cartoon was completely out of character for Jim Snoddy. Snoddy was a good citizen, a gentleman. Some time following the campaign we became warm personal friends. However, when a man gets into the hectic, hurly-burly activity of a governor's race, he cannot oversee everything that is done for him nor always exercise clear, calm judgment.

Among the cartoon characters pushing me forward and what each said were: Bob Young, holding a "$200,000 tire contract;" Truman Baker, "Get them truck deals ready, Orval;" "Indian Bay" Charlie Adams, "Don't let em scare you,Orval - do it or we're sunk;" a thugish figure, "Get them dogs running, Man;" Jimmy Karam carrying a $10.00 contribution, "We can Make a Million;" "Holy" Homer Adkins, "Don't worry, Orval. I've got the election fixers lined up;" Rolla Fitch, "Don't dare answer them 11 questions" (Propounded earlier); Witt Stephens carrying a $60,000 starter contribution, "Go on, Orval

FORWARD(?) WITH FAUBUS, Political Cartoon paid for by Committee to Elect Jim Snoddy, 7/29/56

136

— Don't be afraid — Wall Street and the money boys are behind you.'' (How come Jim Crain was omitted?)

Along with the exaggerations there were two misconceptions which were amusing to me. Jimmy Karam in those days didn't contribute even ten dollars to anybody's campaign, and any person who had the idea that any political contributor ever put up as much as $60,000 for any of my campaigns was sadly mistaken. Also '' country boy'' Witt's cigar was familiar but what about that silk top hat, bow tie and striped pants?

These figures pictured as my backers were pushing me on to a number of roads which the ad said were one way. Each road was labeled and marked with a sign post. The labels followed by the signs were:

Road to Integration: Gradual.

Road to Higher Taxes: 3% Sales Tax.

Road to $125,000 Bribes: Dog and Horse Racing Deals.

Road to Higher Gas, Electric and Phone Rates: Higher Utility Rates.

Road to Ruin for the Old Folks: Welfare Grants Now Less than 2 Years Ago.

Road to Ruin of Non-Political Highway Dept.: Faubus, "I'll Make Truman Baker Highway Boss."

Road of Broken Promises: To Old Folks, Teachers, Tax Payers and Own Crowd.

Road to Unsavory Influence: Remember He Saved M.L. Turner from the Chair?

Road to Fat Jobs for Ex-Criminals: Faubus' ABC Director and others too.

Road to Corrupt Politics: Remember Illegal Ballots - Madison County 1954?

One of the roads could later be correctly charged to my administration. In my second term I recommended and secured the passage of the 3 per cent sales tax.

The others had little or no basis in fact.

To some the ad was irritating; to others amusing. To me it was ineffective because it tried to say too much.

'STEW' PROSSER'S CANDIDACY

Probably no candidate ever had as much fun as Stewart K. Prosser of Conway in his campaign efforts. His newspaper ads were hilarious, and his personal approach to the voters was often equally as humorous. One of the planks in his platform was to ''reroute the Panama Canal across Arkansas,'' an idea which he advocated in deadpan seriousness in discussions with voters or members of the press. Prosser was more successful in creating laughs, causing comments and attracting attention than in getting votes. Note his slogans. Besides, he made no effort to take any votes from me.

COMIC RELIEF
By Kennedy, Ark. Democrat   7/15/56

FAUBUS TALK INTERRUPTED
BY FIST FIGHT — *GAZETTE*

This headline followed an altercation at Pocahontas where I spoke on July 26. The altercation was the final effort and the culmination of a very determined, planned scheme by a segment of the Johnson forces to heckle me during my speeches, to disrupt my meetings and, if possible, to actually drive me from the stump.

ON THE CAMPAIGN TRAIL —

I hate to do this, but —

Faubus

COPELAND

— I want no Negroes in Democratic party jobs!!

Johnson

It was well known that my stump speaking was perhaps my most effective means of campaigning. If by heckling, disturbances and other forms of interruptions my speaking could be made ineffective, or stopped entirely, it would leave that field virtually pre-empted by Jim Johnson, one of the most effective campaign stumpers in the history of the state. Snoddy, although a pleasant and effective campaigner otherwise, was not noted for his speaking ability. With some issues more volatile than in any political struggle for almost 100 years, the campaign oratory and persuasion in direct contact with the people took on a much higher degree of importance than ordinarily.

For some time I had been gradually growing aware of the escalating emotion and division among the people over the integration issue. I knew of the extent even before I visited Washington at the time the Congressional delegation signed the Southern Manifesto. But I was not aware of the extreme depth and bitterness, even fear, of many of the people over the issue until one day in Elaine in Southern Phillips County.

It appears from the office appointment book (the campaign schedules not available at this writing) that the date was July 12, shortly after I had opened my campaign.

I was a guest of Mayor Watson for some civic event, and then the guest of some fine people in their home. I had been invited to the town as governor to assist in some worthwhile civic enterprise.

FULL-BLOWN OPPOSITION

SECOND TERM TRADITION

GOV. FAUBUS

NOBODY BUT MYSELF TO BLAME
By Kennedy, Ark. Democrat   7/25/56

"Full-blown opposition" developed to my candidacy for a second term. The tradition that a governor could win re-election with little difficulty was no longer a strong shield to opposition. The holes in the umbrella "second term tradition" had been put there by me when I successfully opposed an incumbent governor seeking a second term. Thus the caption "Nobody but myself to blame."

But in my public appearance, my contacts with ordinary citizens and among the other guests at the home, I could sense that all was not well. On the streets and roads among the people the animosity, fear and distrust, some of it directed toward me, was amazing. It was not something easily seen and defined; it was more felt and sensed and "so thick you could slice it with a knife." There were no rude words to me or untoward acts of discourtesy. There was no discussion of the matter with me, nor within my hearing, which was significant. When I left Elaine that day I knew the situation was reaching the danger stage.

On some weekend in Little Rock I advised my aides that some kind of security should be arranged for my protection and my political meetings. My aides were not impressed. They were surrounded and living in the very midst of a friendly atmosphere and dealing with friends across the state, most of whom were as unaware of the situation as they.

But the word was passed and when I began the next campaign trek - Brinkley was one of the first stops - I noted that my camp followers were almost as numerous as the citizens attending the public speakings. However, at each meeting they grew less and by the third day, except for my driver and sound crew men, the latter mostly youngsters who were with me very little, I was again alone. The director of the sound crew was Wilson Matthews, then Central High School coach in Little Rock - later assistant Razorback coach at the University of Arkansas. Matthews was one of the calmest and most efficient men with whom I ever worked in any undertaking.

The intent of some of the Johnson forces became crystal clear when I spoke in Monticello one afternoon. That area was Jim Johnson territory and his followers were gathered in force. There they meant to disrupt my meeting and perhaps prevent me from speaking.

However the town had a strong and fair police chief, perhaps a friend and supporter. He had become aware of the situation and alert to what was transpiring before I arrived on the scene.

He told my opponents, "Yes, Faubus is billed to speak, and he is going to speak, and you (the Johnson people) are going to let him alone." "You (the Johnson supporters) can speak before he gets here and you can speak after he leaves, but you're going to be quiet while Faubus speaks."

The police chief's instructions included the opposition loud speakers rigged on mobile vehicles which were ballyhooing the city square when I arrived. The police chief told my crew where to set up, and I was hurriedly briefed by Matthews when I arrived.

I spoke to a good audience and was enthusiastically received. There was no disturbance but I noticed the prominence of the police chief, as well as the silent loud speakers of the opponents.

Dozens crowded around to shake hands when I had finished and I gave them my attention as usual. But in one corner of my mind I noticed and listened as the enemy loud speakers took over. They were announcing over and over that I was scheduled to speak at Warren that evening at 8:30 which by then would be nightfall, and urging all their followers to be there.

When I reached Warren I checked for some of my security force and could find no evidence of them anywhere. There was only Matthews and my youthful sound crew, including Farrell, age 17, and Billy Moore, a small but tough Razorback football player. The latter two were without fear and spoiling for a fight — in fact one of our difficulties was to restrain them - but a fight was what the enemy wanted and what I didn't want. That could disrupt and perhaps break up the meeting. My message would not get to the people and news of the disorder and the opposition would spread like wildfire.

I decided to call Little Rock. The headquarters was closed and I could reach no member of the staff. I decided I needed some one more appropriate for the occasion and dialed for Jimmy Karam. He answered and I briefly apprised him of the situation. "I'll be there!" he said without hesitation.

"I don't think you've got time to make it," I said. "I'll be there!" he reiterated and hung up.

For some reason Arch Tipton was around and came with Jimmy. I guess it was the wildest ride Mr. Tipton ever had for I'm sure Karam broke every speed law on the books. But he was there before I began to speak.

I asked him to let my youngsters show him the situation but to restrain them if possible and, if he could, to keep the enemy loud speakers quiet while I spoke.

"Fine, fine!" said Jimmy, "you do your speaking and leave this to us. We'll take care of it," he asserted with evident confidence, pleasure and anticipation.

Somewhere Jimmy had picked up a large curved, crooked club which he was using as a walking stick. When he slouched and his trousers hung low on his hips his sight was enough to make any troublemaker take a second look. That ungainly, club-like walking stick made his appearance even more ominous.

As I recall, the program had some preliminaries. Perhaps other candidates announced, I'm not sure. Then I was introduced — perhaps by Lee Reaves, I don't recall.

As I took the microphone to begin my speech, an opponent directly in front of me switched on his loudspeaker. Instantly he was surrounded by Jimmy, Farrell, Billy and perhaps one or two others.

Jimmy leaning through the window said, "Turn that thing off! The governor's gonna speak!" or perhaps Jimmy reached in and switched it off.

The man made a brief remonstrance saying, "It's a free country ain't it?"

"Not tonight, it ain't!" said Jimmy. "You turn that off and leave it turned off," and his tone was unmistakable.

The man was so impressed that he left his vehicle, went over to the nearby police station and, for his own safety, remained there with the policemen until the program had ended and we departed the town.

By the time I spoke other members of my security force, unknown to me, had appeared on the scene. They had spotted the trouble makers and were ready. I heard some heckling to my left which was quickly quieted. To my rear came the worst disturbance, but the shouting had barely begun before it was silenced. One of my security men posted behind the heckler, grasped him from the rear and, as described to me later, shook him "like a terrier shaking a rat". When he finally let go the heckler staggered away ill and vomiting.

All this I did not know, or ignored, and continued with my speech as if all were harmony and accord. After these brief incidents it was a peaceful meeting, and perhaps not over two dozen spectators knew of the planned disruption or what occurred.

After the Monticello and Warren engagements my staff, even in the safety and comfort of headquarters, agreed that some security and protection for the candidate and the meetings were essential. A small but well disciplined force was always on hand from then to the campaign conclusion. The small force was composed of men of large stature and when seen together was said by one observer to look like Roman Gladiators. In connection with the same situation, Jim Malone, Jr. — "Little Jim" as he was often called to distinguish him from his father, J.M. "Jim" Malone, Sr. - was not permitted to speak for me in Bearden and was virtually run out of the town. There were other incidents of similar nature across the state.

At Pocahontas, where I spoke in every campaign, the meetings were held at the Randolph County courthouse with

A.J. Baltz, one of my leaders there, usually making the arrangements. The speakers' stand was placed on the concrete floor at the head of the steps. The steps led down to an octagonal, sodded court yard area which sloped upward in stages away from the building. Sloping banks interspersed with shade trees lined the sides of the picturesque courtyard while a street ran atop the high embankment at the back.

On this particular day a large crowd was present and, as was customary, the spectators were scattered, some seated nearby on the courthouse steps and platform, some at the nearest points in the courtyard and on the sloping borders, and others farther back 200 feet or more from the speaker.

The Johnson supporters were there that day in considerable force and we had received word that another, and perhaps more determined effort would be made to disrupt my rally and stop my speech. A Johnson supporter by the name of Smith was on hand with a loudspeaker. With the volume full he had ballyhooed the town, then halted to speak to my gathering crowd just before my arrival. He had condemned me in such harsh and vitriolic terms as to repel many listeners.

When I reached the point in my speech where I mentioned the integration question, which was always dealt with briefly, I saw a man arise at a point near the back of the courtyard and heard him shouting. I saw people nearby begin to look his way but I continued my speech as if nothing whatever was amiss. The man continued to shout and gesture but when it seemed he could not gain my attention he began to advance at a quick walk down the northern edge of the courtyard toward me.

By then the protester was beginning to attract more attention but I continued my speech as if he were unnoticed by me. When the protester had progressed perhaps one-third of the way to the speakers stand, I saw a large man step from the spectators lining the bank and block his way. The big man's attitude was not threatening but I could easily tell that words were exchanged. The protester gestured angrily and then swung his fist at the man blocking his way. Whereupon the big man shot out his fist striking the protester in the upper body or head. The man of rather small stature was knocked backwards up the slope. The blow was effective for I distinctly saw his feet leave the ground and could see the soles of his shoes while they were still in the air before he landed on his back and shoulders.

Springing up he dashed through the line of people along the border of the courtyard. There, as I learned later, he ran past Farrell and Billy Moore who gave pursuit as he made for a pickup truck. They intercepted him as he opened the door of the vehicle and reached for a pistol. Moore struck him a blow in the side with a monkey wrench and he slumped down without getting his hand on the gun.

At that moment a law enforcement officer reached the scene. Billy and Farrell merged into the crowd, and their part in the affair did not become public knowledge.

The meeting continued peacefully without further interruption. However the encounter in the courtyard was seen by virtually everyone, including the press. It was almost immediately known that the protester was Herbert Brewer the segregationist leader and strong Johnson supporter, recently elected school board member at Hoxie, some 20 miles south of

FINAL WEEK OF FIRST PRIMARY CAMPAIGN TAKES ON ASPECT OF A MOUNTAIN FEUD...

FALSEHOODS
USE OF HECKLERS
OPPONENTS DESPERATE
'PAPER PLANS'
'DEAL' AT WEST MEMPHIS
FAUBUS

GOV. TAKING CREDIT FOR REFUNDS
'MIXING' AT MEDICAL CENTER
JOHNSON

'BIG TAX' GOVERNOR
SNODDY

I'll be glad to see the TV schedules get back to normal!
John Q.

MOUNTAIN FEUD, By Kennedy, Ark. Democrat, 7/29/56

The final week of the campaign was portrayed as a mountain feud. I fired away at my two main attackers with charges of "falsehoods," "use of hecklers," and "opponents desperate!" Johnson fired with "Governor taking credit for refunds" (from gas and electric rates), and "mixing at medical center!" meaning racial integration. Snoddy leveled charges of "paper plans," "deal at West Memphis" (on dog track), and "big tax governor!" John Q. Public seemed generally displeased with the controversy. But that was the cartoonist's idea.

Pocahontas. By the next day it was in the news that the man who stopped his shouting advance on the speakers' stand was Bob Baker from Nashville in Southwest Arkansas, and it was strongly suspected that he was at the meeting to protect me from interruptions or attack. It was not known publicly that a security force had been established to enable me to remain on the campaign trail, and that Baker was a member of the force.

Anyway, Bob Faust, very alert in such matters, immediately pulled Baker out of the security force and sent him back to work with the Weights and Standards Divison of the State Police, from which he had been on leave while on the road during the campaign.

After that only one other confrontation was attempted by the Johnson forces, and that was verbal. Curt Copeland, speaking through Sharp and Izard Counties invited his hearers to come on up to Mountain Home where he would meet me in my speaking engagement there in the late afternoon and "take the hide off me."

Reaching Mountain Home ahead of me was my security force which included "Buck" Mooney, a large, well-liked former game warden and enforcement officer in that area. Mooney encountered Copeland and his two or three cohorts in the corridor of the Baxter County courthouse. He told Copeland he knew he had a gun on his person, that he could have him arrested, or he, Mooney, could take the weapon from him and make him eat it. Instead, said Mooney, he would make with Copeland, knowing the purpose for which he was there, "a muscle bound" agreement. If Copeland and his crew would "Keep quiet while Faubus speaks," then Copeland and his crew could speak as long as they liked with no interference. Copeland agreed.

When I arrived at Mountain Home, traveling by air and late because of stormy weather, a large crowd was still waiting. Kay Matthews, accompanying me that day as he did much of the campaign, informed me of Copeland's presence and the situation as described by Mooney.

I noticed Copeland and his two or three companions seated just to my right on the courthouse lawn as I spoke from the high steps at the western courthouse entrance. After the regular part of my speech I took my text on Copeland — his record of misdeeds; quoted and showed pictures from the magazine he and Johnson were publishing. Without doubt I was more condemnatory of Copeland than any public figure I ever faced — he had placed himself in the position — and concluded:

"Always in the Ozark Mountains we have heard of two kinds of liars. One is a natural born liar, the other is self-made by practice, I'm telling you he's both, and there he sits right there," as I pointed him out.

I shall never forget Matthews' delight with the way I handled the situation. The crowd of townspeople and overall-clad mountaineers hung on every word.

The speech ended, the people crowded in to shake hands, and Copeland rolled his outfit up on the lawn to speak. No one was listening as they enthusiastically greeted me. When I had finished greeting the last voter and started to drive away in the gathering dusk, Copeland was holding forth. The courtyard and streets were totally empty except for the two or three Copeland had brought with him.

Some people now may wonder about the necessity of a security force to protect a public speaker at that particular time. Without such a security force in the campaign of 1956, I am convinced I would have been driven from the stump in many areas. Emotions were deeper and stronger on the integration question than on any other issue in my lifetime. It is also well to remember that it takes virtually 100 per cent of a crowd, be it civic, church or political, to maintain good order. A well organized effort by a determined few can completely disrupt and defeat the purpose of any public gathering of orderly citizens, unless there is a counter-force to maintain the peace by control of the disorderly disrupters.

TEXANS VOTED ON JULY 28

Texans voted in a governor's race and on a number of issues on Saturday, July 28.

U.S. Senator Price Daniel running as a conservative and moderate led a field of six candidates for governor. He went into a runoff with liberal Ralph Yarbrough, whom he defeated in the second primary.

Significantly, Texas Democratic voters approved a number of drastic measures in opposition to court-ordered integration before those same measures came to decisions in Arkansas. They gave 6-1 majorities to three referendums aimed at placing the state on record against the Supreme Court's ruling against segregation.

Approved were resolutions favoring school segregation, the doctrine of interposition and strong laws against racial intermarriage.

The Texas vote was indicative of the sentiment across the South and in other areas of the nation.

WHIRLWIND FINISH

On July 28 the news said Snoddy blamed me for the utility rate increases, yet all the raises occurred during the Cherry administration in which Snoddy briefly played a major role. Herbert Brewer filed suit against me and Bob Baker. Johnson made a 90-minute address to a wildly cheering crowd in El Dorado in Union County, one of his strongholds.

On the last campaign day, I flew across the state in a press described "Whirlwind Campaign Finish." Beginning the day by reviewing National Guard troops at Camp Chaffee, I then flew to engagements at Rogers, Harrison and Mountain Home, where occurred the confrontation with Copeland, and then to Jonesboro for my closing statewide rally. Flying around storms I reached my final engagement site at 7:55. A filmed telecast was shown on TV at Little Rock.

At Jonesboro, my original cast of able organizers had been joined by banker-businessman Herbert McAdams, one of the most capable civic, business and political leaders in the state. My Jonesboro organization could always be counted on to be efficient and effective.

––––

I CARRY MT. OLIVE AND LITTLE TEXAS

By noon election day July 31, two boxes had reported. The results from Mt. Olive in Izard County were: Faubus 12, Johnson 3, Snoddy 1. Little Texas in Scott County, Faubus 14, Johnson 1, Snoddy 0.

THE ELECTION RESULTS

The *Gazette* headline the day after the election read: "Faubus Sweeps to Victory; Margin Assures No Runoff."

The *Searcy Citizen* headlined: "Faubus Landslide"

I carried 67 counties, Johnson seven — six in the Southeast and St. Francis in the East Central area. Snoddy carried his home county of Crawford. Johnson carried the Hoxie area but I carried Lawrence County. Snoddy conceded but Johnson on August 2 made charges of fraud in the election, said he wouldn't give up and planned a third party movement. Prosser ran fourth with Pippin placing fifth.

Bruce Bennett, El Dorado, from segregationist Union County which Johnson carried overwhelmingly, won a clear majority over four opponents for the nomination for Attorney General.

State Senator Max Howell won re-nomination in Pulaski county without a runoff. Sen. Ellis Fagan faced a runoff with Bob Laster.

APPOINTMENTS, JANUARY 1956

Charles M. Traylor, Little Rock, Real Estate Commission. Carneal Warfield, Lake Village, School for Blind and Deaf. Walter Priest, Beebe, State Teachers College Board.

APPOINTMENTS, FEBRUARY 1956

Joe Steele, Springdale, State Police Commission. Dr. Frank Kumpuris, Little Rock, State Cancer Commission.

APPOINTMENTS, MARCH 1956

Fred Pickens, Attorney of Newport, reappointed to University of Arkansas Board of Trustees. Marvin Bird, Earle, banker and civic leader, reappointed to State Board of Education. Jim Phillips, Little Rock, formerly of Berryville, Assistant Business Manager, State Hospital. Dr. Ellery Gay, Little Rock, to post in Welfare Department. Mark E. Woolsey, Ozark, Special Justice of State Supreme Court. Van Dyke Chavez, Pine Bluff, to Boys Industrial School Board. Ed Keith, Magnolia, to Stadium Commission. Kay L. Matthews, Little Rock, Administrative Assistant to Governor. John V. Turner, Russellville, former Pope County Judge, to succeed Matthews as Chairman of Board of Review. Olen Hendrix, Antoine, State Hospital Board. Horace Fisher, Malvern, Publicity & Parks Commission. Harry W. Parkin, Little Rock, reappointed to Justice Building Commission. Harold F. Ohlendorf, Osceola, reappointed, Children's Colony Board. D. O. Talbot, Stamps, reappointed to Southern State College Board. C. R. Teeter, Star City, to A&M College Board at Monticello. Mrs. W. M. Davis, Jonesboro, reappointed to Girls Training School Board. Dr. R. M. Eubanks, Little Rock, reappointed to TB Sanitorium Board at Booneville. Asa Bohnert, Crossett, reappointed to State Prison Board. Rabie Rhodes, Harrison, reappointed to Geology and Conservation Commission. A. Curtis Goldtrap, Ft. Smith, appointed to Arkansas Tech College Board at Russellville. Russell Owen, Marked Tree, Arkansas State College Board at Jonesboro.

APPOINTMENTS, APRIL 1956

James J. Brennan, Hot Springs, to AIDC Staff. (R. B. Chitwood, Lake Village, elected president of AEA.) J. C. Mitchell, Little Rock, to Arkansas Merit System Council. Dr. R. D. Williams, El Dorado, to Livestock Sanitary Board. Robert Scott Campbell, Hot Springs, prosecuting attorney to fill vacancy created by death of Hiram A. Tucker.

APPOINTMENTS, MAY 1956

William P. "Bill" Rock, Little Rock, as chairman of Arkansas Nuclear Energy Committee and Sen. Marvin Melton, Jonesboro, as a member of the committee. Dr. John O. Miller, Brinkley, to State Board of Optometry. Dr. Robert C. Carnahan, assistant administrator, appointed director of State Hospital to replace Ewing Crawfis, resigned. Dr. W. E. Phipps, Jr., North Little Rock, to Conway State Teachers College Board. Gene Waldon, Ozark, to Arkansas Tech Board at Russellville to replace Jim Snoddy who resigned to run for Governor. Rufus V. Herndon, Jr., Hope, to Embalmers and Funeral Directors Board. R. B. Steed, Star City, to Arkansas State Board of Pharmacy. Yandell Johnson, Little Rock, Arkansas State Board of Architects. Harold L. Stephenson, DeWitt, to Henderson State Teachers College Board.

APPOINTMENTS, JUNE 1956

Nelson Cox, Camden, director, Game & Fish Commission to fill vacancy caused by death of T. A. McAmis; Trusten Holder, Little Rock, director of operations, G&F Commission; announcements made by F. M. "Swede" McCormick, commission chairman.

APPOINTMENTS, JULY 1956

Clovis Copeland, Little Rock, from Public Relations consultant, to assistant to State Publicity Director Sam Kirby. Riley N. Donoho, Ft. Smith, to Game & Fish Commission. Billie Dunn, Conway, American Legion, to State Athletic Commission. Max A. Mehlberger, Little Rock, and B. J. Rhinehart, Pine Bluff, to State Board of Registration of Professional Engineers.

CHAPTER 8
PREPARATION OF PROGRAM OF PROGRESS
INTEGRATION TURMOIL IN OTHER STATES
GIRLS' SCHOOL CONTROVERSY

THE NATIONAL DEMOCRATIC CONVENTION

On the morning of Aug. 12 after our arrival in Chicago, the Arkansas delegates were guests at a sumptuous breakfast hosted by Arkansas Committeewoman Mrs. Gressie Carnes of Camden, and Mr. Louis Reynolds of Virginia, an official of the Reynolds Metals Company. Gov. Averill Harriman attended the breakfast and visited with the delegates, accompanied by Gov. Raymond Gary of Oklahoma, who was supporting him. A news picture in the *Democrat* showed the three of us in a close chat.

Some time after Harriman departed former Gov. Stevenson came for a visit.

The next morning the delegation held a caucus, elected me chairman and voted to postpone endorsement of any candidate until the following day. This apparently was suitable to everyone except some of the Stevenson supporters. The Union Labor delegates, including Odell Smith, Henry Woods, Tom Gentry and others, were strong for Harriman but didn't have enough votes to control the delegation. Several delegates of North Arkansas, as J. E. Dunlap, Jr., of Harrison, Arthur Carter of Berryville and Ben Butler of Osceola, leaned toward Sen. Symington of Missouri. Four or five favored Kefauver until he made his "criminal" charge about the Dixon-Yates plant, which left him only two supporters, one of them a relative (unknown to me at the time), and the other Jim Brandon of Little Rock.

I was concerned with maintaining harmony and unity in the delegation. If we had attempted to make a decision that first morning, no candidate would have commanded a majority and the caucus might have developed into a squabble.

As for my personal inclination, I was secretly hoping for a deadlock between Harriman and Stevenson with the convention turning to some other candidate as Symington or Johnson. Frankly, I had no hope of victory with either of the major contenders as the nominee, and Kefauver, who was otherwise liked, had by his own public statements forfeited the support of the South.

Also, Sen. McClellan had privately conveyed to me his desire for a delay. In addition, in a personal visit with former President Truman and his cousin and my personal friend, Gen. Ralph Truman, I had learned of strong enmity toward Stevenson because of personal slights by the Stevenson forces. The Trumans were supporting Harriman.

By the next morning, Aug. 14, the situation was still unclear with intense pressure, persuasion, and maneuvering going on with the large delegations. It appeared that Stevenson had gained ground in spite of Truman's open endorsement of Harriman, but the issue was still in doubt.

On the way to the caucus that morning I walked with Raymond Rebsamen. He was aware of the possibility of a deadlock. We agreed that if the Arkansas delegation remained uncommitted it might exercise a greater influence on the outcome.

As soon as the caucus convened Rebsamen quickly made a motion to postpone for another day any decision on which candidate to support. There was a quick second, I put the motion to a vote and it carried. The caucus was quickly adjourned.

The Stevenson supporters were quite displeased with the postponement. Former Congressman Claude Fuller of Eureka Springs was quite vocal in his protests after the meeting.

Another very unhappy Stevenson advocate was Hugh Patterson. He said nothing to me but the following was related to me later by Mr. Rebsamen.

After the breakup of the conference Patterson accosted Rebsamen and remonstrated with him about his part in the postponement.

"Well, Hugh," said Rebsamen, "I didn't know it was personal. It's just politics to me."

"You damn right it's personal," Patterson replied. He then went on to say that the *Gazette* was the oldest and most influential institution in Arkansas; that the *Gazette* had a vested interest in the delegation and concluded, "The *Gazette* ought to say who this delegation goes for at this convention."

One evening at the convention I was invited to the Stevenson suite for a visit. The candidate was working with aides, one of them Harry Ashmore of the *Gazette*. Ashmore seemed to be finished with his work and was spending his time drinking bourbon with Patterson. It seemed to me to be a bother to the candidate for me to be there, and my presence a profitless venture for either of us. There was no talk whatsoever of my attitude, the attitude of the delegation or of convention activities. In fact, I hardly got to speak with Adlai while there.

On another occasion while the situation was still in flux, I was invited one morning to Sen. Lyndon Johnson's suite for a visit. When I knocked on the door a voice bade me "come in." I opened the door and there was the Senator walking across the room as naked as a jaybird. Evidently he had just had a bath and was preparing to dress. It was our first meeting.

After we had visited for a time, as I walked to the door for departure, he said, "Governor, meeting you has been the greatest thing that's happened to me at this convention."

I often wondered in the years which followed how large a role that sort of flattery played in his handling of the Senate as majority leader, or in getting his legislation approved by the Congress while he was president.

During the evening of the 14th it became quite clear from the behind-the-scenes information I obtained from Sen. McClellan, the Trumans, Gov. Gary and others, that the dam was going to break in favor of Adlai. It is said that the key to the break was when Walter Reuther and Mrs. Eleanor Roosevelt "put the britches" on Gov. G. Mennen "Soapy" Williams of Michigan. They virtually forced him to commit his large delegation of mostly Union Labor to Stevenson, instead of going for Harriman as the Governor wished to do.

When this word was conveyed to the Harriman supporters in the Arkansas delegation, they knew the drift was plain. This development made the situation of all other candidates — Symington, Johnson, Kefauver — hopeless and nullified the effectiveness of any favorite son holding operations.

In the caucus the next morning I recommended that the delegation commit to Stevenson. There was no dissent. After the caucus Mr. Patterson came around to assure me that a "good story" of my activities would go out to the *Gazette*. There was also a human interest feature about me to the effect that on my first trip to Chicago I had slept as a hobo in the park by the lake. Now I was back in the city as the Governor of my state and head of the Arkansas delegation to the National

Democratic Convention to select the Democratic nominee for president.

Arkansas was officially on Stevenson's band wagon before the convention outcome was clear. The Stevenson supporters were very happy and no one else in the delegation was unhappy. There had been no fighting in the Arkansas group and a feeling of unity, harmony and good fellowship prevailed.

ALONG THE OLD CAMPAIGN TRAIL
By Graham, Ark. Gazette   8/2/56

With a "no runoff" victory already in hand, I watched as Democrats, "Adlai" and "Estes" displayed a banner "Stevenson and Harmony." Kefauver had withdrawn from the presidential race and indicated his favor for Stevenson.

On the way home with all convention activities behind us, Claude Fuller, who was my good friend but was unhappy with some of my convention activity, was heard to remark to some associates, "Well, I didn't like some of the things he did but I'll say one thing. By God, he (Faubus) took charge of the delegation and run it."

News pictures back home included:

Henry Woods, Armil Taylor, J. E. Dunlap and Lacy Lawrence as delegates in Chicago; Hugh Patterson distributing copies of *Arkansas Gazette* delivered to Chicago especially for the delegation; John Kennedy shaking hands with Vernon McKimmey of Camden, with Joe Templeton of El Dorado standing by; Claude Fuller and Claude Carpenter, Jr., during a floor demonstration; Faubus and Gov. Earl Long of Louisiana in a discussion on the floor.

ANALYSIS OF JIM JOHNSON

Democrat reporter George Douthit in his Aug. 5 column, Backstage at the Capitol, gave perhaps the best analysis of Jim Johnson that I have seen.

He recounted then State Senator Johnson's political experience in which he campaigned for Francis Cherry in 15 counties in South Arkansas in 1952, all of which Cherry carried; his race for attorney general against Tom Gentry in 1954 in which Johnson lost; his campaign for governor in 1956 in which he was backed by two segregationist groups, White America Inc., and the Arkansas Citizens Council, a race in which he had just been defeated.

Then Douthit wrote:

"Mr. Johnson seems to be a man of changing political philosophies and may appear complex to a lot of people. But he isn't complex nor is he confused.

"Mr. Johnson is a clever young attorney whose political ambitions have him running forward at such a reckless speed that he doesn't pause long enough to survey his possibilities, or to study the question of whether his arguments are acceptable to the voters.

"This man has developed a fine oratory and probably could go places in the political field if his views were a little more rational and not so emotional. We found that on television he made an impressive appearance. But the voters became afraid of his philosophy."

Johnson never corrected the defects mentioned by Douthit. His zeal, audacity and oratory later won for him two great opportunities for major political office, but his failure to analyze public sentiment, and gather around him responsible lieutenants, denied him ultimate success.

SALVAGE IN MIND
By Kennedy, Ark. Democrat   8/3/56

A trade mark of Jim Johnson's campaign was the bucket passed through the crowds at his rallies for the collection of campaign funds. His successful use of the method was perhaps second only to James "Uncle Mac" Mackrell's use of the bucket in the primary of 1948. Although badly damaged by the primary defeat, Johnson contemplated its salvage for future operations.

A significant fact about Johnson's vote in 1956 has been consistently overlooked by most observers of Arkansas politics. Although it was a five-man race and the total vote was lower than in succeeding elections, Johnson's vote of 83,856 was the highest garnered by any opponent in my last five successful primary campaigns.

In the six-man race of 1962, McMath got 83,473, just short of Johnson's total, and Dale Alford received 82,815. There were 93,885 more votes tallied in the '62 race than in '56, while my vote was only 28,236 higher.

1956 DEMOCRATIC PREFERENTIAL PRIMARY

Faubus	180,760
Johnson	83,856
Snoddy	43,630
Prosser	1,653
Pippin	1,328

RUNOFF PRIMARY IN ARKANSAS

On August 14 while the delegation was in Chicago the Democratic runoff primary occurred in Arkansas.

Carleton Harris beat Guy Amsler for Chief Justice of the Supreme Court; Jimmie "Red" Jones won over Bus Friday for State Auditor; Sam Jones overcame Ben Rankin in a hairline finish for Land Commissioner; Congressman Bill Norrell overcame Pat Mullis and Brooks Hays had a victory over W. H. "Bill" Donham for re-nominations to Congress. Murray Reed won the Chancellor's office in Pulaski and adjoining counties over Riddick Riffel; Tom Gulley beat Sam Hallum for Sheriff; Ellis Fagan finally took a narrow lead over Bob Laster for re-nomination to the Senate and held on; Sen. Guy Jones of Conway defeated his run-off opponent for the Senate.

———

I GET APPROVAL
OF PRESIDENT TRUMAN FOR VEEP

A story in the *North Little Rock Times* on August 16 said that former President Harry S. Truman placed the stamp of approval on me as a suitable candidate for vice-president. The statement was made by Truman in Chicago where he was attending the National Democratic Convention. As a delegate there I was not aware of the former president's approval at the time.

THE VICE-PRESIDENTIAL NOMINATION

In the open battle on the convention floor for the vice-presidential nomination, the Arkansas delegation had not previously caucused. It appeared the two main contenders were Sen. Humphrey of Minnesota and Sen. Kefauver of Tennessee. The Humphrey forces chose Sen. Fulbright to make one of his nomination speeches.

The Fulbright speech failed to influence the Arkansas delegation. Too many of the state delegates felt Humphrey had been too vocal with his anti-South views.

Kefauver was in even more disfavor in Arkansas for helping to kill the Dixon-Yates plant, and even after the convention opened had again referred to the project as "criminal." Also he had refused to sign the Southern Manifesto, and upheld the illegal Supreme Court decision usurping from the states the control of their schools.

There was a lot of talk of Gov. Frank Clement of Tennessee, the keynote speaker of the convention, but his possible candidacy clashed with Sen. Kefauver of his home state. He had also spoken out against the Dixon-Yates project and was suspect in other states of the South on the civil rights issue.

There seemed no possibility of agreement in our delegation on either of these candidates, even though I was a personal friend of Clement. I suggested that we vote for Sen. Albert Gore of Tennessee on the first ballot. This the delegation did.

The first ballot was indecisive, but out of the voting came a new strong contender, Sen. John F. Kennedy of New York. At that time he was known neither as an extreme liberal or conservative. His father had been prominent in the Roosevelt administration, the name of which still bore much magic, and had made a fortune as a free enterprise American businessman. Sen. Kennedy was also a war hero and a brother had been killed in the conflict. In a quick poll of the delegates by Tom Harper and myself the decision was made to go for Kennedy. So far as I know we had not been asked for support, and no one in the delegation had been in touch with Sen. Kennedy or any of his supporters. We decided to support him because we thought he was a better candidate with which to win the election.

The roll call of the states was alphabetically and Arkansas, near the head of the list, led off with a solid vote for Kennedy. From that moment his candidacy began to accelerate. The other candidates faded in strength and the battle for the nomination narrowed to Kefauver and Kennedy. Several states passed and then clamored for recognition as the roll call proceeded.

There was strong dissension, it seemed, in the Tennessee delegation and there were rumors it would not vote solidly for Kefauver. The rifts were repaired and the vote was received with interest as the state gave the senator a solid vote.

I talked to Gov. Gary of Oklahoma about the race. It was his opinion that since the convention had already nominated a city lawyer from Chicago for president, the ticket now needed a running mate from a farm state. Therefore, he preferred Kefauver because he felt it would be easier to promote the ticket in Oklahoma and other farm states than with Kennedy, another official from a big city.

At one point Kennedy was, in my opinion, within 30 seconds to a minute of the nomination. It seemed a veritable stampede was developing in his favor.

Seated directly in front of Arkansas was the large California delegation. James Roosevelt, a son of FDR, was a member of the group. At one time from half to two-thirds of the delegates were on their feet clamoring for recognition. After passing on the roll call it seemed they now wanted to cast the California vote for Kennedy. Their clamoring was not seen or was ignored by the chair.

Then Roosevelt stood up and talked to the California delegates. "Take it easy!" he admonished. "Don't get excited. Let's remain firm." He quieted the delegation and kept it from going for Kennedy.

When Tennessee and Oklahoma voted for Kefauver followed by some key midwestern states, the tide swung back to the Tennessean and he won the nomination.

Later when Stevenson made his acceptance speech, he and Kefauver were joined on the platform by the losing contenders in a show of unity. I chanced to glance down the aisle to the rear of our delegation. There, alone in the middle of the aisle, looking somewhat neglected and chagrined, stood Sen. Jack Kennedy. Three or four of us from the Arkansas delegation went to him and urged him to go forward and join those on the platform. "You belong up there as much as the others," we said. After some hesitation he moved with us to the Arkansas location and then continued alone down the aisle toward the front. Observers will recall that Kennedy was the last of the contenders to join the group on the platform in the upraised hands of unity.

Another incident is worth recall. Before the winners appeared for the final speeches, Truman, who had fought Adlai saying he couldn't win (a sentiment which I secretly shared), said to the chairman, "Let me up there for a few words." He was permitted to speak and said, "Now there's some old man (meaning himself) around here who's been saying our candidate (Stevenson) can't win. Well, don't pay any attention to that. That's what they were saying about me in 1948 and we won then."

The speech met with most favorable response. I thought it was the best of the evening.

PREPARATION FOR ARKANSAS PROGRAM

The primary elections were over, as well as the National Democratic Convention, and there was no real threat from the Republican nominee for governor in the general election. I now began in earnest to get ready for a progressive program in the 1957 session of the General Assembly.

A progressive program meant a tax increase. That was where the real work lay — in selling the people, the civic and business leaders and the members of the legislature that the increase was needed. In fact it was necessary if teachers' salaries and welfare grants were to be increased; the obsolete buildings at the Blind and Deaf Schools and the State Hospital replaced; the Children's Colony built; a Vo-Tech (trade) School system started, and many other things that were needed including a more adequate State Police force and a state park system. In this preparation the GACE was to play a leading role, and the chairman on Aug. 20 began the appointment of committee aides in the counties.

NOW LET'S MAKE SOME MONEY

Some time after the successful campaign of 1956 was over, certain individuals in coming by the office began to suggest, "Now that you're elected to a second term, let's make some money!" Some of the people making the suggestion were friends and supporters. Others were not so close but knew how to wheel and deal with state business in a relatively safe manner when permitted to do so.

Two implications were clear. First, I had won the traditional second term which meant the end of the road politically because no third terms were considered possible in Arkansas. Therefore, I had no need to maintain a clean administration and a good administrative record as a help to re-election.

Second, now that I had no need to be concerned about a clean political record and a popular image, it was hoped I would turn certain individuals loose to make money from state business even if it meant bending rules and regulations and proper procedures. I would be cut in on the profits. Although these policies would be at the risk of bad publicity and possibly a scandal, it wouldn't be all important because with a second term already in hand, it was generally assumed I would not seek re-election.

I heard these suggestions most of the time without comment and without indicating my thoughts.

Then I contacted my key administration people, either as individuals or in small groups, and let them know, as my father was accustomed to saying, "how the land laid." There was to be no let down in standards of honesty and fair dealing, or in the observance of proper rules and procedures. As individuals in their own departments and collectively as an administration, they would be expected to do an even better job than they had previously done because they were now more knowledgeable and experienced.

These contacts with key people were followed by a general staff meeting of some 80 to 100 people composed of department and agency heads and key personnel. To all of them I laid down the challenge of a better record for my second term than for the first. I gave them credit as individuals and collectively for the success of the administration in service to the people. I praised them for their work and extended my thanks for their loyalty to the administration and the state. I invited their comments at any time on administration matters, and pledged my help and that of my staff whenever needed to solve agency problems.

The administration personnel responded well. There was no let down during my second term, and "we" didn't make any money.

THE MANSFIELD, TEXAS INTEGRATION CASE

On August 30 the news reported that Texans were guarding the schools at Mansfield to prevent integration. There was open talk of gunplay to head off any effort to mix students in the white schools.

On September 1 the school officials asked for a delay in school integration at Mansfield, but no action was taken by the federal courts or federal officials.

In the face of threatened mob violence and gunplay, Texas Governor Allan Shivers asserted state authority in the situation, and publicly said that if anyone was considered in contempt of the federal courts, for the federal authorities to see him.

Shivers was a strong states rights advocate, and Price Daniel, a conservative, had just been nominated to succeed him as governor, defeating the more liberal candidate, Ralph Yarbrough. Because of the Stevenson-Kefauver stand on the tidelands oil question and their anti-states rights attitude, Shivers had bolted the Democratic ticket and was openly supporting Eisenhower and Nixon for re-election.

When the integration controversy boiled over at Mansfield, Shivers sent a Texas Ranger to escort the Negro students from the white school back to their own school. Texas Rangers Captain Bob Crowder then announced that any Negroes attempting to enroll in the white school "will be transferred" back to their own.

In the face of this exercise of state authority by the Texas governor, the Negroes halted attempts to integrate the white schools. All disorder ceased and everything proceeded calmly and in good order in the schools and in the community.

SILENCE OF THE COURTS AND THE POLITICIANS

But the most noteworthy aspect of the Mansfield affair was the absolute silence from the Earl Warren Supreme Court and the national administration in Washington. There were no statements from Eisenhower, Nixon, or any member of the administration. There was not a peep from Attorney General Herbert Brownell or any member of the Justice Department. Silence likewise engulfed all the liberals of both parties of all sections.

And Adlai and Estes, who wanted a plank in the Democratic platform upholding the illegal Supreme Court decision, were evidently so "busy" with campaign plans that they "failed to note" the Mansfield developments, although the event commanded banner headlines throughout the nation.

Did someone suggest that there was no court order at Mansfield?

There was.

Whether or not a court order existed did not change the situation.

There was no court order at Hoxie, Arkansas, yet the Justice Department and the Federal Courts by their own initiative stepped into the case and assumed jurisdiction. School patrons were restrained from even visiting their own school and were threatened with imprisonment and the use of U.S. marshals on numerous points.

At Hoxie, Federal Courts and U.S. marshals were given supreme power over a school which, by every right, belonged to the people.

At Mansfield state and local authority through Texas Rangers ruled the day. There was no move by the Federal courts or any Federal authority, although a Federal court order was involved.

WHAT WAS THE DIFFERENCE IN THE SITUATIONS?

Mansfield was in Texas, a large state with a powerful bloc of electoral votes. The state had gone for Eisenhower in 1952, and now Democrat Shivers was openly supporting the GOP presidential ticket for re-election. The governor of Texas was a powerful figure and although he soon would retire from office, his influence and support must not be lost to the Republicans. It could make the difference in the Texas voting.

On the other side, if the Democrats criticized the federal courts and the Republican administration for not acting, it would so offend the states rights sentiment that they would not have the ghost of a chance to carry Texas. And they could lose other Southern states as well. Therefore, all of them — Adlai, Estes, Symington, Humphrey, Harriman — developed and maintained a strong case of lockjaw on the Mansfield matter.

But Hoxie, that was different. Arkansas was a small state and, what was even more significant, had voted Democratic for almost a hundred years. It was fully expected to vote Democratic again in 1956. There was nothing to be won or lost politically in Arkansas. Therefore it was the place for the courts to show their authority, to issue new rulings and reinforce those previously handed down.

Arkansas was the place for the liberal politicians of both parties to play politics, to condemn or praise the actions taken, not with an eye for Arkansas, or justice, but with an eye for votes elsewhere.

That was the difference!

ERUPTIONS IN TENNESSEE,
KENTUCKY AND WEST VIRGINIA

On Aug. 30 the news reported that blacks were seated in the high schools in Clinton, Tenn. Disorder occurred almost immediately and the second day police protection was necessary to get the black students to school and keep them there.

By the third day, Sept. 1, it was reported that a mob had taken over the town and city officials appealed for help to restore order.

The next day state troopers, ordered there by Gov. Frank Clement, and vigilantes had controlled the uprising. A violent storm quelled a segregation rally as tear gas was used to repel demonstrators.

However, the trouble was not ended. Hundreds of National Guardsmen using tanks were added to the forces of state troopers and local police to control the situation. Perhaps it was the first time that tanks were used in an American city against American people. The use of the tanks, tear gas and other weapons dispersed the demonstrators.

On the 4th, new violence flared in East Tennessee. Three citizens were injured as trouble occurred in Knoxville, Dayton and Oliver Springs. Guardsmen were called on to quell armed mobs as the race violence spread. Tanks were in use at Oliver Springs as well as Clinton.

On Sept. 5 it was reported that the black students went to school at Clinton under armed guard. A boycott of white students found 482 absent with 312 present including the blacks.

On the same date trouble erupted at Sturgis, Ky., and picket lines were set up around the school in opposition to integration.

A negro evangelist, W. D. Willet, speaking in Little Rock, urged the NAACP to go slow in pushing integration.

In Hot Springs, Arkansas, black students enrolled in one course in the public schools and there was hardly a ripple despite the tumult and disorder from Texas to West Virginia.

DEMOCRATIC STATE CONVENTION

The State Democratic Convention got under way in Little Rock with Wilbur Mills again permanent chairman. Newport Attorney Fred Pickens was the keynote speaker.

My nomination acceptance speech on the second day was praised as a great success. Former Congressman Claude Fuller, Sen. Fulbright and *Gazette* publisher Hugh Patterson urged that I stump across the nation for the National ticket.

The other Democratic nominees were: Fulbright for the U.S. Senate, Mills, Trimble, Hays, Gathings, Norrell and Harris for Congress; Nathan Gordon for lieutenant governor, C. G. "Crip" Hall for secretary of state, Vance Clayton for state treasurer, Jimmie "Red" Jones for state auditor, Bruce Bennett for attorney general, Sam Jones for land commissioner and Carleton Harris for chief justice of the Supreme Court.

INTEGRATION FUROR CONTINUES

By Sept. 6 Kentucky National Guard troops were on duty at a number of points to quell the disorder over integration of the schools. A near riot occurred at Sturgis as Guardsmen escorted black students into the school.

Guard rule was relaxed somewhat at Clinton, Tenn. but hundreds of white students were absent.

At Matooka, W. Va., whites staged a boycott against the mixed schools.

Eisenhower deplored the use of violence in the school crisis but said U.S. authorities would not intervene unless it became necessary.

On Sept. 7 it was reported that black students attended classes at Sturgis as the Guard held off a growing mob. The next day the students stayed away as martial law was readied in Kentucky.

The South, the press said, was tense and watchful in the wake of the mob violence.

On Sept. 7 a new point of trouble erupted at Texarkana, Texas. "Effegy, Cross and Gun Rise" read one headline. The trouble was at the Junior College where a ring of pickets turned back 3 black students seeking to enter. Another cross was fired in the border city. On the ninth, the blacks were again turned back by a tense mob at the Texarkana College. The situation was reported as "threatening."

On Sept. 8 my GOP opponent for Governor, Roy Mitchell, took a stand for integration, as he opened his campaign in Hot Springs, a Republican stronghold. He lost every county in the state.

The Pine Bluff school authorities barred integration until not earlier than 1958.

North Carolina voters backed a school plan to avoid forced integration by voting 4 to 1 for state funds for private school tuition.

INDUSTRIAL PROGRESS IN SOUTH
IS LAUDED AT SOUTHERN CONFERENCE

My report to the Southern Governor's Conference on September 9th to 12th at the Greenbrier at White Sulphur Springs, W. Va., on industrial growth in the South was one of the best received at the meeting.

Gov. William C. Marland was the host governor and the chairman was Gov. Frank Clement of Tennessee. Clement in an impassioned speech, gave a lengthy and detailed explanation of his use of the National Guard in the school troubles at Clinton. It was easy to see he was in trouble with his home folks and was on the defensive. He appeared to be suffering emotionally from the experience.

ARK. BOARD OF EDUCATION TO ASK $48,000,000 FOR SCHOOLS...

G.A.C.E.

I'm with you!

program calling for $18 million increase

The Arkansas Board of Education and the GACE decided to ask for $48,000,000 for schools which was an $18 million increase. At a GACE meeting in Little Rock I openly stated my favor for a tax increase to aid education and other state services. The AP&L appeared as Santa Claus with ratepayer refunds.

-here I come, ready or not.

AP&L

Consumer Refunds

CHRISTMAS IN SEPT.

-this might be the year---

VOTE FOR IKE & DICK and MITCHELL & HENLEY

STATE GOP LAUNCHES CAMPAIGN FOR GOV. and SENATOR... MAY SEEK MORE OFFICES...

The State GOP launched a campaign for Governor and Senator and said it may seek more offices. Note the sign on the GOP elephant.

Roy Mitchell of Hot Springs was the GOP candidate for governor, and Ben Henley of Harrison the nominee for the U.S. Senate. Bill Spicer of Ft. Smith opposed Trimble for Congress. Charles F. Cole of Batesville went against Bennett for Attorney General.

WELFARE BENEFITS INCREASE

On Sept. 20 we announced an increase in welfare grants.

The increase of $3 monthly effective Oct. 1, raised the grants to the highest point ever. The Democratic primary elections were long-since over; I had won renomination and was in need of no political help at the general election. This is noted because later on my critics over and over falsely accused my administration of increasing welfare grants for political reasons only at election time.

BROWNELL PRAISES HOXIE SCHOOL BOARD

On Sept. 17 the Hoxie school board was praised as courageous by Attorney General Herbert Brownell in Washington. He evidently had reference to the former board members for the board now was controlled by the segregationists.

ADLAI SAYS COURT RIGHT ON INTEGRATION; ASKS PEACEFUL COMPLIANCE; APPLAUDED IN LITTLE ROCK

Adlai Stevenson, speaking to a Democratic crowd at MacArthur Park in Little Rock on Sept. 25, said the Supreme Court was right on its integration ruling and asked peaceful compliance. When he made the statement perhaps a half dozen supporters clapped their hands and some others in the audience joined politely in the applause merely out of courtesy. Not five per cent of his hearers agreed with the statement, yet the press reported that he had been applauded for his defense of the court in Little Rock, Arkansas. That is how news can be slanted and grossly distorted by a biased press without telling an outright lie.

A later news report on Sept. 26 quoted Stevenson as saying he would follow but not force the court's decree.

WELCOME ADLAI

YOU EXPECTING A FRIEND IN TOO, I TRUST!

SEPTEMBER MORN '56
By Graham, Ark. Gazette   9/25/56

Governor Stevenson came to Little Rock for a campaign speech. The Democratic donkey expressed the hope that the general public viewed the presidential nominee as a friend — in other words, would support his candidacy. The cartoon expressed the viewpoint of the Gazette-controlling powers who were very strong for the nominee.

I was asked to introduce Stevenson. I presented him to a good-sized crowd of mostly administration people in MacArthur Park. A friendly press estimated the crowd at 5,000, but I couldn't count 2,000. I could not help but note that his hearers were more enthusiastic for the Democratic nominee before his appearance than after he had spoken. The attitude indicated that Stevenson, as a candidate, was a cold fish without the warmth so necessary for a successful campaign. He had a certain eloquence as a speaker, was well informed but sadly lacking in the common touch.

I had noted the same traits about Adlai when, as a guest of Dr. J. S. Rushing, he mixed and mingled with a select group of Democrats in Arkansas the previous December.

After Stevenson's MacArthur Park appearance, where he made statements that cost him votes in Arkansas, we went to work and carried the state for him in the general election. At the same time many Northern states whose delegations had been unfriendly to us at the convention, were lost. These states included Stevenson's home state of Illinois and the border state of Tennessee, the home of his vice-presidential running mate, Sen. Kefauver.

COURT BARS NAACP AID TO STUDENT

In an integration case in court it was revealed that the NAACP had offered and made available the sum of $11,000 to a student and the family to file the suit. A court decision barred the NAACP from promoting integration suits in this manner.

RAYBURN SPEAKS AT POCAHONTAS

On Sept. 26 Sam Rayburn appeared at Pocahontas where Congressman Mills and I joined him as he delivered his usual strong Democratic speech.

HAYS SAYS LITTLE ROCK INTEGRATION PLAN A PILOT RACIAL APPROACH

On Sept. 28 Congressman Brooks Hays lauded the Little Rock integration plan as a pilot or model approach to racial integration of the public schools. The statement was remembered to his detriment two years later.

HAM MOSES RETIRES FROM AP&L

HAROLD OHLENDORF OF OSCEOLA ELECTED ARK. FARM BUREAU PRESIDENT

LEARNING THE FACTS OF LIFE TOO LATE
By Kennedy, Ark. Democrat   9/5/56

Those who think the trouble over school integration began at Little Rock in 1957, should note this was a year before the beginning of the Central High School Crisis.

READIN', RITIN', AND INTEGRATION, By Kennedy, Ark. Democrat, 9/9/56

A CARTOON DEPICTING LITTLE ROCK 1957?

No, it was a year earlier in Tennessee and Kentucky. This drawing by Kennedy showing a youngster on his way to school with a helmet and gas mask as standard equipment, was prophetic. Note the mother's words of advice and warning.

Already, a year before the Little Rock Crisis of 1957, military forces using tanks and other weapons of war had been employed to quell disorders at schools facing integration under federal court orders.

TURMOIL ABATES IN PLACES, CONTINUES IN OTHERS ANTI-INTEGRATIONISTS WIN VICTORIES

Few white children were in school at Sturgis on the ninth and the situation continued tense for several days.

Louisville, Ky. integrated without undue incident. Serious trouble erupted 20 years later.

On Sept. 11 all white students, 590 in number, quit the Clay, Ky. high school. The next day the mayor asked for the ouster of the black students. The whites continued the boycott and on the 15th the Guard was still on duty to maintain 3 black students in the school. On that date the school board officially barred the black students. There was no integration in the Clay, Ky. schools that year.

On Sept. 23 the Kentucky governor withdrew the Guard units from Sturgis and Clay. The anti-integrationists had won victories, at least temporarily.

On Sept. 26 white Citizens called for a boycott of integrated schools at Henderson, Ky.

On Sept. 11 an unruly crowd again barred two black students from Texarkana (Texas) Junior College. President Eisenhower said intervention in the row was up to the federal judge.

In Little Rock on Sept. 12 Supt. Virgil Blossom told a PTA group that "integration depends on the public."

Georgia Governor Herman Talmadge who had declared his state would defy the U.S. Supreme Court ruling on integration, was elected to the U.S. Senate.

SCHOOL OFFICIAL CITES TROUBLES IN WASHINGTON, D.C.

After the integration of the Washington, D.C. schools, troubles increased to such an extent as to cause an investigation by a congressional committee. An official of the District of Columbia schools testifying before the committee said:

"It was necessary to call the police as many as 50 times a year where before no calls had been necessary; the danger of violence forced the cancellation of all social events formerly held; disciplinary problems so hampered the teachers that they could no longer do their jobs as instructors; gangs were organized which extorted lunch money and other valuables from many students."

Publication of this report increased the fears of mixing the schools and added zeal to the efforts of segregationists.

YALE LOCK CO. TO BUILD $4 MILLION PLANT AT FORREST CITY AFTER ACCORD WITH HWY. COMMISSION

It was necessary for a delegation of businessmen and civic leaders of Forrest City and officials of Yale Lock Company to come to the Governor's office to enlist my aid in gaining the cooperation of the Highway Department in order to acquire this great new industry. The delegation and the company officials wanted only to know the location of the future interstate highway, for which surveys had already been made, in order to properly select the site of the plant and begin construction. The company wished to avoid location of the plant on land that would later be used for the highway and thus find it necessary to move and rebuild.

Such lack of cooperation by the Highway Department led to difficulties for Director Herbert Eldridge with the legislators and other officials.

ARKANSAS ADDS 2 MOUNTAINS TO PARK SET-UP, MENA AND MT. MAGAZINE

On Sept. 30 the State Parks Commission at my urging, approved plans to add two mountain areas to the State Park System, Mena and Mt. Magazine. We were able to acquire the mountain near Mena and develop it as the Queen Wilhelmina State Park. However, we were unable to acquire the Mt. Magazine lands which belonged to the Federal Government.

FAUBUS ASKED TO HELP BLOCK MILLWOOD DAM

A group headed by Lewis Graves, a fellow publisher of Nashville, opposed the construction of Millwood Dam and requested my help in blocking the project. After listening to Graves' delegation I conferred at length with Peter Joers, official of the Dierks Lumber Company of Hot Springs, who also wanted to stop the large Millwood project. After considerable study, I supported a smaller Millwood Dam project with a much smaller flood plain, together with five smaller dams on the upper tributary streams in Oklahoma and Arkansas. The alternate plan was adopted by the Congress.

The smaller Millwood project has been completed and some of the smaller dams on the tributaries. One on the Cossatot River in Arkansas has been held up by litigation by opponents who want to preserve the river as a free-flowing stream. The free-flowing stream idea had not surfaced at the time I supported what was then known as the compromise plan. To publisher Graves the compromise plan was better than the original but he may have opposed any dam at all at Millwood.

From the time of our acquaintance Joers became one of my consistent supporters and quiet advisers throughout my administration.

STATE PROGRESS

Despite considerable turmoil within the state over integration, Arkansas continued to make progress.

A new industrial plant was announced for Lepanto on Oct. 6; I helped dedicate the Saunders museum at Berryville on Oct. 11; a date was set for the 4-lane highway to Jacksonville and the U.S. air base; on the 14th 5,000 new seats were okehed for the University stadium at Fayetteville; plans for the Yale Lock Company at Forrest City were underway; and $3 million in student housing was approved at the University of Arkansas. Fayetteville and Searcy got the richest plums each acquiring a new industry employing 350 and 250 workers respectively.

TAX INCREASE PLANNED

I confirmed my plans for a tax boost to finance a progressive program for Arkansas. With the GACE, the AEA, the Department of Education, the AIDC and other helpers, we began to round up legislative votes for the program.

COMMUNIST REVOLTS

The big world news in late October concerned the revolts against Communist Russian rule in Poland and Hungary, and the invasion of Egypt by Britain, France and Israel.

IKE SWAMPS ADLAI;
DEMOCRATS WIN IN ARKANSAS

President Eisenhower swept to a stunning victory over Stevenson, winning by a wider margin than in 1952. Democrats retained control of both houses of the Congress.

All Democrat candidates in Arkansas won overwhelmingly. The state went for Stevenson, one of the few in which he was victorious.

The city manager plan had a 2 to 1 victory in Little Rock, mainly because of the unpopularity of Mayor Mann.

BUS SEGREGATION ILLEGAL

The U.S. Supreme Court on Nov. 13 ruled bus segregation illegal, leaving no doubt in its decision in the Montgomery, Ala. case. Arkansas buses were already desegregated so there were no new difficulties in the state.

PEA RIDGE AND ARKANSAS POST
APPROVED BY FEDERALS

On Nov. 21 the Pea Ridge battleground was approved by the National Park Service as a Civil War National Battlefield Park, and Arkansas Post for a national historical shrine. Both projects were sponsored by my administration.

A STILLNESS AT OZARK
By Graham, Ark. Gazette   11/24/56

Some of the hardest fought battles in the Legislature during my tenure were over conflicting interests of the Rural Electric Co-operatives and the private power companies led by the AP&L. Twice the battle lines were drawn dividing the members of the General Assembly. Both times I sided with the Co-ops, not that I had any ill feeling toward the private companies which on the whole had done a good job in their field. I was con-

vinced the Co-ops were right, which made my decision easy. My political obligations lay with them from the beginning.

One controversy involved the plans of the Co-ops to build a steam generating power plant at Ozark as a source of power for their own use. Legislation was required and the AP&L attempted to block the move in the Legislature. A compromise was effected and the plant has for several years now been in operation, as well as a second at Augusta and a third plant at Camden.

The second battle was over territorial rights. There were cases where the Co-ops had brought electric service to areas adjacent to city limits after the private power companies had declined to serve the same sections. As those areas developed the city limits expanded beyond the Co-ops' lines. When this occurred the power company serving the city took the developed territory away from the REA without compensation. The Co-ops sponsored a law to prevent the loss of territory without their consent, and the battle was on.

The private utilities at that time wielded great political power. Suffice it to say that when I sided with the Co-ops in the fight, it took all the power and influence we together could muster to win.

This cartoon showed the prospect of peace between the Co-ops and the private companies in the struggle over the steam plant at Ozark. They agreed to join their efforts in constructing the plant (headline of 11-23-56). The conflict didn't end at that particular time, but later peace did come to the warring factions.

Now the power dispensers, both public and private, are working in harmony — a great relief to both governors and legislators. They help each other in service to their customers and territory can be exchanged only by mutual agreement.

—0—

I recall an interesting anecdote about the private utility — Co-op battles.

The evening before the next-day vote on one contested measure, the agents and lobbyists of the AP&L made their report to their employer. The matter was locked up, they said, with 26 votes in the Senate leaving only 9 votes for the co-ops.

"What about Faubus?" they were asked.

"There's not a damned thing he can do about it," the agents confidently proclaimed.

The next day when the tally was taken there were 18 votes for the Co-ops, just enough for victory.

But it sure took some doing.

MORE TROUBLE AT CLINTON, TENN.

With turmoil continuing in the integration trouble at Clinton, Tenn., federal help was requested on December 3. The next day violence occurred and the schools were closed.

A Federal judge then ordered the arrest of 16 persons and the following day Federal agents seized and handcuffed 15 individuals, both men and women.

On Dec. 9 it was announced the schools would reopen under surveillance of FBI agents and other police forces.

NATION EYEING ARKANSAS REASSESSMENT
PROGRAM WITH APPROVAL

Bert Luver, Des Moines, Iowa, city assessor, who was instrumental in ridding his state of a mired-down political assessment mess, in a speech in Little Rock on Dec. 8, said that "assessors all over the nation are watching Arkansas' reassessment program." The Arkansas program should be retained, he said, even if Arkansas' elected assessors were some day replaced by appointive "non-political" assessors. Mr. Luver evaluated the Arkansas program as one of the best in the nation.

CALLING THE HOGS, By Kennedy, Ark. Democrat, 11/9/56

This "Calling the Hogs" was not the pleasant diversion of urging the Razorbacks to victory on the football field. I was looking for sources of additional revenue to recommend to the Legislature.

As soon as the Democratic primaries were over I began work on a legislative program. It was one of the most intensive periods of work for me during my entire administration. The program had to be put together in detail well before my second term began, and before the meeting of the General Assembly. Legislators had to be informed, and many groups had to be persuaded to support the program. In meeting after meeting, day after day, I laid the facts on the line.

The GACE provided invaluable assistance in preparing printed material, informing people on the local level and persuading legislators to support the program.

Kennedy based his cartoon idea on the old-time practice of butchering hogs for the family meat supply, a task with which I had long been familiar. Here I called up the hogs (prepared tax proposals) to be butchered (enacted) by the legislature to provide meat (funds) for the family (state agencies) use.

However, those approaching hogs were not fat enough to butcher, which indicated I knew more about "hog-killing time" than the cartoonist. And another thing, "Soooie" is not used to call hogs; it's used to chase them away, — to make them run.

In the Razorback football call "woo-o-o pig" calls them up; "soo-o-o-ie" means get going — for a touchdown.

STEP RIGHT UP
By Kennedy, Ark. Democrat   11/25/56

The only source of substantial new revenue was the increase of the sales tax from two to three per cent. The GACE had calculated the new revenue that would be gained from the increase in each county, and the state funds that would be returned to each in increased teachers salaries, welfare grants, state employees salaries, etc.

Special literature for each county was printed giving these facts and other pertinent information. The poorer counties, it was shown, would have more money returned to them than would be paid out in increased taxes. This was a powerful factor in persuading the people of such counties to favor the program. Without such favor from the local citizens the legislators would oppose the tax increase.

The "GACE" had all the facts. The "Administration," the "Schools" and the "legislators" deferred to the committee.

I held my council about a detailed program until my inaugural address to the joint session of the General Assembly. Then I laid it on the line, recommending the increase in the sales tax, state income tax and all severance taxes. The program also included a $1.00 increase in the driver's license fee for a salary boost for state policemen, and to add new troopers to the State Police force.

I used all the power and influence I possessed as chief executive and every ethical artifice and method at my command to gain approval of the program. With a 3/4 or 2/3 majority of the full membership of both the House and Senate required on some measures, it was not an easy task.

HUNGARIAN REFUGEES

The Russian Communists using overwhelming military force, drowned the Hungarian freedom fighters in blood. Thousands were slain and thousands more herded onto trains bound for exile in Siberia. Other thousands fled the country before the borders were closed by the Russian military.

President Eisenhower raised the U.S. quota of refugees from 5,000 to 21,500. Later with the approval of Congress the quota was increased even more. Some of the refugees eventually reached Arkansas.

FAUBUS AND JOHN TYLER CALDWELL

Gov. Faubus and University of Arkansas President John Tyler Caldwell in the homecoming parade at Fayetteville, Arkansas prior to the football game Nov. 10, 1956. The photograph was through the courtesy of Secretary of State C. G. "Crip" Hall.

HOT POTATO
By Kennedy, Ark. Democrat   12/2/56

A controversy over management of the white girls school developed between me and the superintendent. The Board cast the problem back to me and I referred my information of alleged wrongdoing to the Saline County Grand Jury.

The Saline County Grand Jury report left me out on a limb but the training school board fired Mrs. Cogbill.

Judge Earnest Maner, presiding district judge in Saline County, had his troubles. A gambler represented by Atty. Kenneth Coffelt said he had given the judge money for some purpose that was not fulfilled. The grand jury absolved Maner of the charges and Maner cited Coffelt for contempt of court.

154

The State Supreme Court later dealt with the matter. Maner was reprimanded and Coffelt was cleared of the contempt citation.

The controversy involving Judge Maner evidently took precedence over a proper grand jury investigation of the Girls School.

WRONG GIRL
By Graham, Ark. Gazette   12/19/56

Supt. Cogbill resisted my efforts to make corrections at the Girls' School, and denied the wrongdoing that had been disclosed. Warned by some that it was dangerous to tangle with such an experienced politician, I nevertheless persisted. I was convinced the inmates of the school were being subjected to conditions which were as bad, if not worse, than those from which they had been removed when sent to the institution by local and district courts.

At her departure Mrs. Cogbill released 10 of the 14 inmates and said the other four would escape. For a time she had some favor in the controversy, but by the release of all the inmates she had gone too far.

We had anticipated Mrs. Cogbill's actions. Mrs. Blanche Martin, Little Rock, a former superintendent, had already been picked as the new head of the institution, a staff selected and plans made to take charge of the school. We waited for Mrs. Cogbill to complete her grand-standing and headline-making and vacate the premises. Soon the school was again full of inmates and operating in a more efficient manner.

━ ‣ ◗ ⬟ ◖ ⬟ ◗ ‣ ━

ALUMINUM BOWL

The Aluminum Bowl Game highlighted Christmas Season in Little Rock. Montana State College and St. Joseph's College of Indiana slithered to a scoreless tie in a downpour on a field of mud in a nationally televised game for the junior college football championship.

FEDERAL JUDGE CHALLENGES U.S. SUPREME COURT RULING ON INTEGRATION

In Dallas, Texas, on Dec. 19 a federal judge ruled against integration in the city schools. Federal Judge William H. Atwell, with a long and distinguished career on the bench, said in his decision that the U.S. Supreme Court ruling of May 17, 1954, was not based on law or the Constitution.

—0—

NEW INDUSTRY

During the month a $4 million industrial plant announced it would locate in Arkadelphia.

GAS LEAK
By Graham, Ark. Gazette   11/30/56

An "industrial customer" asked the PSC if it could smell — meaning the cutoff of gas by Ark La was a fake "pressure drop" for a "higher rate" and that it stunk (like a gas leak should.)

The standing of Ark La was at a low ebb, and the new owner and head mogul, W. R. "Witt" Stephens, wouldn't have won any popularity contests at the moment.

The temporary cutoff of gas to industrial users on the grounds that the fuel was needed by smaller commercial and residential customers, was thought to be maneuvering by Witt to coerce the industrial users to come to terms with his company on new rates in long-term contracts. There are provisions in the contracts of all utilities which permit the suspension of service to industrial users during periods of inclement weather when the gas is needed for homes, hospitals, schools, etc. Witt maintained that the cutoff was necessary because of weather conditions. Many of his critics were skeptical, as indicated by the cartoon.

HOT WATER BOWL
By Kennedy, Ark. Democrat   12/14/56

The Saline County Grand Jury, in its investigation of the White Girls School affair, heard 31 witnesses, including Mrs. Cogbill. However, according to news reports, the grand jury heard only four of the 34 witnesses interviewed by the State Police in its investigation. The jury returned no indictments and issued a report containing no severe criticism of the superintendent.

Thus, the cartoon showed me in the Saline Grand Jury hot water bowl, with hot water "invitation to give testimony," pouring into "report favorable to Mrs. Cogbill."

Mrs. Cogbill was noted for her ability to "politick" her way out of trouble. Although her tactics helped her elsewhere they were not effective with me.

I have always considered the abuse of authority to be a major transgression.

THE HAND OF EXPERIENCE
By Kennedy, Ark. Democrat   12/19/56

While bending every effort in preparation for a major legislative program, I had my troubles in other fields.

My wounds in the Girls School controversy, if indeed I suffered any injuries at all, healed soon after the superintendent was finally dismissed on December 10.

SATISFYING BACKWARD GLANCE
By Kennedy, Ark. Democrat   12/30/56

From 1956, looking back, and then forward to 1957, the happy figure saw "Solid gains all along the line," and said, "we're on our way!" Although opposing many of my policies, especially the tax increase I was promoting, the *Democrat* cartoon could be interpreted only as approval of state progress under my leadership.

APPOINTMENTS, AUGUST 1956

J. Thomas McIntyre, Supt. of Children's Colony in Arizona became adviser for Arkansas Colony Planning. Harry Stitt, Rogers, to Apiary Board.

APPOINTMENTS, SEPTEMBER 1956

Presidential Electors chosen at State Democratic Convention; Jess Taylor of Osceola; Mrs. Eunice O'Baugh of Pocahontas; Mrs. Virginia Fitch of Hindsville; William T. Jennings of Texarkana; Mrs. Joe T. Robinson of Little Rock; T. Stanley McNulty of Pine Bluff; Earl Wells of Helena; and Al Faubus of Elkins. David B. Ray, employed to head Arkansas Children's Colony. Knox I. Webb, Jonesboro, State Board of Accountancy. Dr. H. V. Glenn, Stuttgart and Dr. P. W. Lecky, El Dorado, to State Osteopathic Examining Board. R. M. Somers, Jonesboro, secretary, and Jack Lineback of Brinkley, member, State Board of Barber Examiners. Julian B. Davidson, Little Rock, State Board of Architects. Mississippi Roadway Planning Commission: Jim Crain, Wilson; J. Gordon Love, Hughes; Tom Faulkner, Helena; John Sheffield, Helena; F. N. Carnahan, Eudora; and Angus Mahan, Marianna.

APPOINTMENTS, OCTOBER 1956

Harlan J. Perryman, State representative of Salem, to become attorney for Labor Department. (Ray Thornton, Little Rock, deputy prosecuting attorney by Prosecutor Frank Holt) Dr. W. A. Richardson, Texarkana, State Board of Dental Examiners. Ben Butler, Osceola, Justice Building Commission. Dr. Bernard Paul, Ft. Smith, State Chiropody Examiners Board.

APPOINTMENTS, NOVEMBER 1956

Zan Jones, Little Rock, State Cosmetology Board. Dr. Granville Jones, Virginia, director of State Hospital, and A. C. Yopp, Kansas, administrator. Attorney Neill Bohlinger, Little Rock, to head the legislative probe of the State Hospital.

APPOINTMENTS, DECEMBER 1956

Dr. Charles E. Thompson, Acting Chief Vocational Counseling Services of Veterans Administration Hospital at North Little Rock. O. W. Holmes, Little Rock, and Sherman V. Zinn, North Little Rock, re-appointed to Workmen's Compensation Commission.

CHAPTER 9
PROGRAM OF PROGRESS APPROVED
NEW STATES RIGHTS LEGISLATION

DECSION TIME FOR ARKANSAS

The time was now at hand for decision on the plans which had been maturing in my mind since my first inauguration. The big question, bigger than any other faced in those early days of my administration, was — would the goal, which I had kept constantly before me for almost two years, be reached, or would we fall short?

I had decided on a tax program of three measures: (1) an increase in the sales tax from 2 to 3 per cent; (2) an increase in the income tax by a new method of computation worked out by Representative Clayton Little of Benton County — not an increase in the rate which would require a three-fourths vote of the Legislature for passage; (3) an increase in the severance tax on bauxite, timber, sand and gravel, oil, gas, coal and other minerals. The latter affected mainly the industrialists of the state.

It would be possible, I assumed, to reach general agreement among legislators and others on a program of progress. But could approval of the necessary tax increases be obtained in the Legislature? This was the key to the whole problem. Without more revenue the work on a progressive program would be an exercise in futility.

In promoting the tax program, I had the unstinting help of the Arkansas Education Association under the leadership of Forrest Rozzell, and the State Department of Education led by Arch Ford. These organizations also furnished guidance and information to the GACE.

Likewise, I received able assistance from leaders interested in the improvement of the AIDC program, State Hospital, Blind and Deaf Schools, the Arkansas Livestock Show, State Police, Soil Conservation and Forestry Commission, as well as those interested in the creation of the Children's Colony for the mentally retarded, and those interested in a system of vocational-technical schools.

The main obstacles were (1) the general anti-tax sentiment throughout the state, and (2) the fact that such a program had never been enacted during a governor's second term.

The best strategy, it seemed to me, was to have a program beneficial to all and good enough to justify the accompanying tax increase.

The GACE, active for several months, was most effective in educating the people and the legislators to the need of a program. The details were not spelled out. That was left for my determination.

After my renomination in July, I approached W. J. "Bill" Smith about becoming my legislative adviser. We met one Sunday at the Executive Mansion where, in a conference which lasted six hours or more, I revealed for the first time in detail my plans for the coming legislative session. Smith studied the matter and notified me of his acceptance of the post, expressing at the same time his agreement and enthusiasm for the program.

Then began our many private meetings, as well as conferences with fiscal experts, department heads and others. There began for me also the most difficult undertaking of the whole effort — meeting with opposition groups. At times I met with gatherings of 75 to 100 people among whom I had friends but not one single outspoken supporter of the program. For instance, I met with the Retail Merchants Association of which

my friend and early supporter, Clint Walden of Fayetteville, was president. All the members opposed the sales tax increase. Dave Grundfest of Little Rock was there and encouraged me privately.

There was continued fiscal and legal research. There were the necessary compromises, as with the border counties adjacent to states with lower or no sales tax, with the small oil well owners on the severance tax, and the mollification of the "big boys" on the adjustment of the income tax. Then there were the personalities with which one must always deal in public affairs. In all these efforts at reaching understanding or compromise, Bill Smith was of great help, displaying patience, tact and ability beyond any person with whom I have ever worked.

In looking back, I wonder what the course of my political history would have been if, impatiently and hopefully, I had rushed before the General Assembly in my first term in 1955 with such a program. Based on the history of the 1955 session, it would probably have failed. Would I, as a political figure, have then recovered from such a failure? And would the program, so important to the progress of Arkansas, have been delayed beyond the legislative session of 1957 to which it was now to be presented?

W. J. "BILL" SMITH

I persuaded Attorney W. J. (Bill) Smith to serve as my legislative assistant for the 1957 session of the General Assembly. He had served in this capacity to other governors (sometimes without title), and had also been Executive Secretary to Governor Ben Laney and a member of the Workmen's Compensation Commission.

Bill's knowledge of state govenment and legislative procedures equaled that of any one I have known. His ability to tactfully work with legislators, department and agency personnel, pressure groups and others was unexcelled.

In keeping with the theme of the cartoon I must remark, "Some Water Boy!"

I hope you do even better, kid —

10,350 NEW JOBS IN 1956

ARK.

1957

STATE PROUD OF GAINS AT YEAR'S END...

NEW JOBS IN 1956

The industrial program was more successful at an early stage than had been anticipated by most people. Winthrop Rockefeller had said it would be five years before the program was on a sound basis with full momentum. However, the program was enthusiastically received and supported by the people from the very beginning. It was a decided success by the end of my first term.

The budget requests of many state agencies were too high even with the hoped for revenue of my tax program. The reduction process was painful and difficult but invariably necessary.

EN GARDE!

SEN. FAGAN ALLOWS HE MIGHT LEAD OPPOSITION TO TAX INCREASES...

SENATOR ELLIS FAGAN

The able Sen. Fagan allowed he might lead the opposition to the tax increases and gave warning of his possible intentions.

On January 9 I met in the governor's reception room with officials of various statewide organizations. There were 70 or more in attendance and included women leaders as well as men. News reports said I received legislative support from the group.

Prior to this meeting, Sen. Van Hayes of Benton told me it would be difficult for him to support the tax program because the Benton Chamber of Commerce had unanimously adopted a resolution urging the Saline County legislators to oppose any tax increase. The resolution was sponsored before the civic group by a prominent Benton businessman who was also president of a statewide organization.

The businessman was in the group that met with me on Jan. 9 at the Capitol. I must have done a good selling job on the overall program, including the tax increase, for the businessman was converted. When he returned home he sought out Senator Hayes, told him to forget the Chamber of Commerce resolution and advised him to support the program.

Sen. Hayes conveyed the information to me with the word that he was now ready to give the program full support.

I knew we were making progress.

TRIP TO THE MONEY TREE
By Kennedy, Ark. Democrat   1/6/57

The Democrat *maintained an attitude of determined opposition to any tax increase. John Q. Public was shown in a state of fright as I approached with my baskets for more money.*

SIXTY-FIRST GENERAL ASSEMBLY
Jan. 14 to March 15, 1957

These new members together with those remaining from the 1955 session, constituted the General Assembly whose members "bit the bullet" in considering an overall program of progress for Arkansas which involved a general tax increase affecting all the people of the state. The members also had to consider the emotional and explosive segregation-integration issue, both at the regular session of 1957 and again at a special session in August 1958.

INTERESTED ONLOOKER, By Kennedy, Ark. Democrat, 1/11/57

Reflecting the *Democrat*'s editorial support of an independent, "non-political Arkansas Highway Commission," I was reminded the "public" would be watching my second appointment.

On January 14 I appointed Harry W. Parkin of Little Rock to replace Miss Willie A. Lawson, also of Little Rock, whose term had expired. There was no public criticism of my selection and no difficulty with confirmation by the Senate.

Others mentioned and recommended for the highway post were Raymond Rebsamen of Little Rock, Truman Baker of Searcy, Fred Pickens of Newport and John Rye of Russellville.

Baker was bitterly disappointed at not being selected but soon realized his appointment would have been untimely. He cooled off and continued in the administration in a tranquil manner.

Rebsamen, a very able man, was disappointed and I suspect never forgave me for failure to select him. He was the choice of Jim Bland who recommended him strongly. Rebsamen broke with Bland over the appointment but it was not Bland's fault that he was not chosen.

The new legislators for the 1957 session were:

THE SENATE

Nathan Gordon, President
J. Lee Bearden, President, Pro Tempore
Arthur Shirey, Secretary

Dan White, Ft. Smith, District 4, Sebastian, replaced "Pat" Garner

Robert Harvey, Swifton, District 18, replaced Y. M. Mack.

Jerry J. Screeton, Hazen, District 19, replaced W. E. "Buck" Fletcher.

Sam M. Levine, Pine Bluff, District 20, replaced Lawrence Blackwell.

Jack Shelton, Monticello, District 21, replaced DeWitt Poe.

M. A. "Mack" West, Paragould, District 23, replaced W. J. "Jack" Hurst.

Clarence E. Bell, Parkin, Charles F. "Rip" Smith, West Memphis, District 25, replaced Fletcher Long and Lamar L. Rogers.

THE HOUSE OF REPRESENTATIVES

C. W. "Charley" Woods, Crossett, Ashley, replaced Glyn E. Sawyer.

R. B. Webb, Mountain Home, Baxter, replaced Hugh Hackler.

Hardy W. Croxton, Rogers, Benton, replaced Eli Leflar.

Wilson T. Bethea, Hampton, Calhoun, replaced Harold L. Johnston.

J. E. "Piggy" O'Daniel, Waldo, Columbia, replaced Harry B. Colay.

Clay Brazil, Morrilton, Conway, replaced Jim Bruton.

Cecil B. Nance, Jr., West Memphis, Crittenden, replaced Charles F. "Rip" Smith.

Earl Willis, Monticello, Drew, replaced Randell L. Williams.

A. M. Ledbetter, Jr., Conway, Faulkner, replaced Russell C. Roberts.

Russell J. Benton, Glencoe, Fulton, replaced Harlin Jackson.

Dan Wolf, Hot Springs, Garland, replaced Elmer Tackett.

W. A. Branch, Paragould, Greene, replaced Hayes A. Triplett.

Don Steel, Nashville, Howard, replaced John Howell.

Thurston S. Kirk, Pleasant Plains, Independence, replaced Hubert J. Meachum.

Lonnie Etheridge, Weldon, Jackson, replaced Robert Harvey.

Knox Nelson and Carl Purnell, both Pine Bluff, Jefferson, replaced E. W. Brockman, Jr. and Sam M. Levine.

Abe King, Clarksville, Johnson, replaced Robert C. Temple.

A. C. Mowery, Jr., Huntsville, Madison, replaced Roy Pettit.

Gus McCracken, Flippin, Marion, replaced Gordon Stanley.

John O. Moore, Texarkana, Miller, replaced John W. Goodson.

H. H. "Buddy" Howard, Blytheville, Mississippi, replaced L. H. Autry.

George W. Stagg, Brinkley, Monroe, replaced John W. Kornegay.

Ode Maddox, Oden, Montgomery, replaced W. V. "Shorty" Smith.

E. H. "Ep" Weaver, Prescott, Nevada, replaced Abner E. McGuire.

E. L. "Van" Mosley, Camden, Ouachita, replaced J. A. "Dooley" Womack.

L. Landers Morrow, Mena, Polk, replaced Roy M. "Pappy" Haynes.

T. E. "Tom" Tyler, Gayle Windsor, Jr. and Sterling R. Cockrell, all Little Rock, Pulaski, replaced Don Jones Jr., R. W. "Bob" Laster and Dave E. Thompson.

Dr. Herbert H. Price, Pocahontas, Randolph, replaced Arlo Tyer.

B. S. Hinkle, Waldron, Scott, replaced J. W. Black.

Dewey L. Massey, Marshall, Searcy, replaced Paul Jones.

J. E. "Pat" Garner, Ft. Smith, Sebastian, replaced Dan White.

James A. Pomeroy, El Dorado, Union, replaced Melvin E. Mayfield.

Dr. H. J. Hall, Clinton, Van Buren, replaced Carl S. Whillock.

BOOTSTRAPS
By Graham, Ark. Gazette   1/17/57

I was trying to sell the people of Arkansas a pair of boots with giant boot straps, "$22,000,000 Tax Program," as the only way to pull Arkansas up to a higher level of state services and progress. Or so said the cartoonist.

TWO SUCCESSFUL 1955 PROGRAMS LEND FAVORABLE CLIMATE

The success of two programs, the Publicity and Parks Commission to promote tourism and the AIDC to promote industry, helped to lend a favorable atmosphere for my tax program.

On Jan. 5 Bryan "Bill" Stearns, state parks director, delivered to me a report showing the tourist program was paying off. The report revealed a $100 million in economic benefits to the economy during the past year in combined private and public business from tourists.

The industrial program's success continued.

On Jan. 10 a new glove manufacturing plant was acquired by Waldron.

On Jan. 11 Searcy secured another new industry, a bronze products plant that would employ 200 people.

160

On Jan. 15 it was disclosed that Mt. Ida would get a new glove factory.

On Jan. 20 a new industrial plant began operations at Clarksville.

On Jan. 29 I joined Hugh L. Clary, Rubinoff and his violin, local dignitaries and 600 people as we broke ground for the Clary Corporation plant at Searcy. Rubinoff was in the city for a concert and agreed to play his violin at the ground breaking ceremony. The weather was cold and miserable and the ground frozen, but it was a bright day for the Searcy economy.

None of the new industrialists coming to the state offered any objections to the (tax) program. Quite the contrary, Winthrop Rockefeller, chairman of the industrial commission and considered one of the state's biggest economic acquisitions, openly favored the program.

In Washington President Eisenhower reversed his stand and okehed the budget proposals for the construction of dams in Arkansas.

Adjutant General Sherman Clinger with my assistance secured federal funds for the construction of new National Guard armories at Ozark, Rector and Van Buren.

CIVIL RIGHTS FRONT

The fateful year of 1957 began with Governor Leroy Collins of Florida halting all bus service in Tallahassee because of integration violence. There was no trouble in Arkansas where all transportation service had been previously desegregated.

A black federal housing official, Earl E. Pruitt of Louisville, Ky., visited Little Rock and praised the housing projects constructed for blacks in the city, citing them as models for the nation.

POSSIBLE CANDIDATES FOR GOVERNOR

Two state senators, James L. "Doc" Baker of Helena and Marvin Melton of Jonesboro, were mentioned as possible candidates for governor in the next election.

Winthrop Rockefeller was awarded an honorary degree by the University of Arkansas, and was rumored as a candidate for governor in 1958.

CORRECTIVE PRESCRIPTIONS
By Graham, Ark. Gazette   1/19/57

The program worked out by my administration to place mentally retarded children in the planned Children's Colony and adult patients who were not severely ill in nursing homes, would greatly reduce the overcrowding in the State Hospital.

FAUBUS AND ROCKEFELLER AT HUNTSVILLE

The people continued to raise money for the industrial program. Rockefeller and I appeared at a $5 per plate dinner at Huntsville on January 7. The Republicans came to see Rockefeller, the Democrats to see both of us and the Masonic hall was packed. It was a successful and happy occasion. WR was the main speaker. At the conclusion, Gordon Hawkins, the dinner chairman, presented Rockefeller a check for the AIDC fund.

UP AT LEGISLATIVE MILL
By Graham, Ark. Gazette   1/23/57

My legislative program was the main topic of study and conversation following its presentation. I had much advice and counsel from legislators which was gladly received. An incident which stuck in my mind which I greatly appreciated, concerned the attitude of State Senator Jerry Screeton of Hazen.

A group which included the senator was discussing the program in the lobby of the Marion Hotel when Screeton proclaimed loudly for all to hear:

"Well, I'll tell you, if he (Gov. Faubus) has got the nerve to get on his white horse and recommend it, I've got the nerve to vote for it."

The bills were in the hopper and the legislative machinery was ready to roll.

161

READY FOR TAKE-OFF, By Kennedy, Ark. Democrat, 1/18/57

After a few days evaluation of my overall program there appeared to be a favorable attitude among the legislators.

PROGRAM WILL BE A LITTLE LONGER
THIS YEAR
By Graham, Ark. Gazette   1/25/57

The legislators recalled the short list of recommendations for the 1955 session, and contrasted it with the very long list of "proposals for 1957."

There was quite a contrast. In 1957 I presented my program for progress for Arkansas. I had spent months in its formation. I recommended it to the Legislature and to the people without hesitation or equivocation.

"Gov. Faubus Inauguration No. II" was quite different in the matter of legislative programs.

HIGHLIGHTS OF THE NEWSWEEK
By Kennedy, Ark. Democrat   1/20/57

VAN DALSEM PROMISES QUICK ACTION ON SALES TAX MEASURE.

I unveiled new plans for expanded state service and the "General Assembly" waited to check with the folks back home.

Van Dalsem, Chairman of the Revenue and Taxation Committee, held the rope that could tie up my program for a long time, but promised quick committee action.

Harry Parkin's appointment was the most noted of the week.

A bill to increase salaries of judges and prosecuting attorneys had strong legislative support — and was pleasing to the judges.

163

THE PROGRAM

My legislative program continued to be the principal topic of the news in Arkansas. A Senate committee approved the tax measures clearing them for early debate and a vote in the upper house.

In the House the program opponents authored seven revenue measures designed to cripple the program, and brought them to a vote. My forces defeated all of them.

The GACE sponsored a public meeting in Little Rock to promote the program. Among the prominent leaders present were: John Rye of Russellville, Vice-chairman of State Board of Education, Lt. Gov. Nathan Gordon of Morrilton, House Speaker Glenn Walther of Little Rock, Sen. J. Lee Bearden of Leachville, president pro tem of the Senate, Mrs. Edgar Dixon of Little Rock, vice-Chairman of the GACE, Robert Harris of Morrilton, president of Arkansas School Boards Association, Mrs. Carroll Watson of Osceola, state president of the Parents and Teachers Association, John Lookadoo of Arkadelphia, Executive Committee of the Boards of Trustees of State Colleges, and R. B. Chitwood of Lake Village, president of the Arkansas Education Association.

In the meantime I reached a compromise with the oil producers to exempt from the severance tax increase, small stripper wells producing 20 barrels or less per day. This removed a source of opposition to the program from South Arkansas. Since most of the small producing wells were soon phased out of production there was no appreciable loss of revenue from the change.

HEAVY, HEAVY - - - -
By Kennedy, Ark. Democrat   2/1/57

The Senate okay of the program severed one of the strings which kept the tax package from falling on the taxpayer's head. Only the House rope remained intact. The *Democrat* did not let up in its anti-tax propaganda.

HIGHLIGHTS OF THE NEWSWEEK
By Kennedy, Ark. Democrat   2/3/57

I gladly received the news of my program's passage in the Senate.

CLARY CORP. BREAKS GROUND AT SEARCY...

I joined the business leaders of Searcy and the Clary Corporation officials as we broke ground for the new Clary plant in inclement weather and frozen ground.

PROGRAM APPROVED BY THE SENATE

Under the able guidance of my leader in the Senate, Lee Bearden, the program was brought up for final debate and vote on January 30. The newspaper report tells the story.

The *Gazette*, Jan. 31, 1957:

FAUBUS TAX PACKAGE PASSES SENATE 25-10
$22 Million Plan Okayed in Two Hours
By Ray Moseley, Gazette Staff

"The Senate yesterday (Jan. 30) passed the biggest single tax increase program that has been proposed in Arkansas in 22 years after a mere two hours of debate.

Three bills sponsored by Governor Faubus that will cost the taxpayers about $22,000,000 a year got past the upper house by comfortable margins under the guidance of Senator J. Lee Bearden of Leachville (Miss. Co.).

The most controversial of all — a bill (SB 32) to increase the sales tax from two to three per cent — passed 25 to 10. The emergency clause, which puts it into effect as soon as it is signed by the governor, was adopted 28 to 6.

Then the opposition surrendered. It didn't even bother to debate the bills to increase severance tax-

es and lower personal income tax exemptions.

The income tax bill (SB 33) was passed 28 to 8 and the severance tax bill (SB 91) was approved 34 to 0.

A revenue stabilization bill of the governor's to apportion money for the various general revenue agencies also passed 34 to 0.

Now the bills go to the House of Representatives and a more prolonged and closer battle is expected there."

Sen. Ellis M. Fagan of Little Rock led the opposition to the tax program. Interest was intense. The Senate gallery was packed with members of the House, school people and others as opponents spoke against the sales tax measure. Most of the debate time was taken by opponents but the vote went the other way.

One of the few Pulaski County legislators to support the tax program was Senator Max Howell. He spoke for the measures in the Senate debate.

* * *

After passage of the tax measures in the Senate there was intense maneuvering in the House to block passage. A bill to remove the sales tax exemption on feed for livestock and poultry was beaten.

In the Revenue and Taxation Committee chaired by Van Dalsem the sales tax bill was voted out with a "do pass" recommendation by a margin of 11 to 9. The other measures were approved 14 to 6.

REA CO-OPS VS PRIVATE POWER COMPANIES

In the legislature the REA co-ops won a battle in the House to stop loss of their territory to the privately owned utilities without the co-ops' consent. The battle now moved to the Senate where the division of sentiment favored the private utilities.

The situation brought to my office a large delegation of REA representatives from all across the state, guided by their able executive secretary, Harry Oswald, and headed by my old friend, Afton Wheeler, then state president of the Arkansas Co-ops. Wheeler was a fellow Madison Countian who was county examiner when I took the examination to secure a teacher's license in March, 1928. He was a fine man and in the years which followed our first meeting we had become good friends.

The Co-op representatives had neglected in many instances to do their homework by failure to contact and inform their legislators before the legislature convened, and I told them so. They had come to ask for help with their territorial bill. The situation was difficult but I gave them the help requested. I was able to change enough votes to enable the co-ops to win by the minimum number — 18 — required for passage in the Senate.

APPEAL TO THE PUBLIC FOR PROGRAM SUPPORT

On February 3, with decision time approaching in the House, I went on statewide television in support of my tax program, using time purchased by the GACE. It was reported that I was the first governor to seek public support for such a program through television.

I explained the purposes for which the additional revenue would be used, named the principal agencies to be helped and the amount of new money each would receive.

There was also a measure before the General Assembly to increase the salaries of judges and prosecuting attorneys which had legislative favor. I also favored the measure but I again threatened to veto this bill unless teachers, welfare recipients and others also received needed increases in salaries or grants.

We were then ready for the vote on the program in the House which came on Feb. 5.

On February 6 the headlines and excerpts from the *Gazette* story read:

FAUBUS TAXES ENACTED WITH 71-27 MARGIN
By Matilda Tuohey, Gazette Staff

The House yesterday approved Governor Faubus' $22,000,000 tax program — the biggest single tax bite ever digested by the legislature.

Passage of the three tax bills by the House completes legislative action on them and they will go to the governor for his quick signature.

The House spent most of the day over the bill (SB 32) to increase the sales tax from 2 to 3 per cent — the hardest morsel for the members to swallow.

When the vote count on that bill tallied 71-27, the tax opponents collapsed and the bills increasing income and severance taxes whipped through with more than comfortable margins.

The administration had 20 more votes than it actually needed to pass the sales tax bill. And it had 10 more votes than it needed to tack on the emergency clause which will make the increase effective just as soon as Mr. Faubus sings the bill. [We made sure we had some extra votes for the emergency clause. — OEF]

The opponents knew from the beginning they were licked, yet they tried through amendments, pleas and warnings of political recrimination from the voters to stall or stop the inevitable vote.

Representative E. C. (Gene) Fleeman of Manila, Mississippi County, the governor's floor leader announced at the outset that the administration forces would make no effort to stifle debate on the measures.

The administration, sure of success, didn't want to risk the hard feelings which would carry through the remaining four weeks of the session if the opponents weren't allowed to speak their piece.

ALL AMENDMENTS FAIL

The sales tax bill was called up shortly after 11 a.m., and the first test vote of administration strength came about 30 minutes later when the House refused 25-72 to put the bill back for amendment.

Representative Marion H. Crank of Foreman, Little River County, one of the leaders of the fight against the bill, had made the motion for the first of a series of amendments to be presented.

Other amendments were:

Representative Ray Smith, Hot Springs, Garland County — to put a June 30, 1959, time-limit on the tax increase.

Representative Talbot Feild Jr., Hope, Hempstead County — two amendments — one to exempt grocery purchases up to $15.00; the other to exclude medicine from the tax.

Representative Carl Purnell of Altheimer, Jefferson County — to remove the exemption on livestock and poultry feed.

Representative Dewey D. Stiles, Hot Spring County — to strike the emergency clause so the bill could be referred.

DEBATE ON BILL ITSELF

None of these got anywhere and with the preliminaries out of the way, the House settled down to a discussion of the bill itself before packed galleries and a crowded Chamber.

Crank led off, pleading with the members that by voting the sales tax increase they would be ruining merchants in his county and others in the southwestern part of the state near Texas, which has no sales tax.

Other speakers against the bill were:

James S. Yarbrough of Sebastian, Winfred Lake of Sevier and Purnell.

Representative Jack Yates of Ozark, Franklin County, closed for opponents of the bill with the admonition that the tax measures would just "make the fat get fatter and the thin get thinner."

Speakers for the bill were:

Lonnie Etheridge of Jackson, W. L. (Bill) Ward of Lee, Jack S. Oakes of Woodruff, Russell J. Benton of Fulton, Charles B. Roscopf of Phillips, Paul M. Graham of Lawrence, Ben Bynum of Chicot and John P. Bethel of Prairie.

Freeman's closing argument (for the bill) was brief. He made this appeal to the House.

"We are here on our honor to do what we think is right. It is not right to deprive some working man's child of the education he is entitled to."

It was 4:07 p.m. when the roll was called on the sales tax bill. Then followed the crucial vote on the emergency clause with 67 votes required for approval. It received 77 votes.

The other measures were then called up for vote without discussion. When the legislative day ended the main body of my entire program had been approved.

Another story in the *Gazette* read:

FAUBUS BASKS IN SHINING HOUR BUT HIS FANS WHOOP IT
By William W. Hughes

Governor Faubus was calmer than his friends in his hour of triumph yesterday.

But he hailed the clearance of his tax program as "the most progressive and constructive step any legislature has taken in the past 25 years."

"Now," he said, "the state can move forward in all fields, as it should."

Mr. Faubus listened to the results of the House votes on his tax measures from a speaker system installed in his office. (I did not listen. Others did however.)

While his supporters and aides huddled around it, Mr. Faubus went into an adjoining office to sign some letters. He stayed there until the vote on the sales tax bill was completed, then came back to join the group.

There was an immediate rush of visitors (to my office) *as soon as it was announced that the emergency clause had been adopted.*

One man rushed up to tell him that "You'll be the first third-term governor since Jeff Davis."

Others representing state agencies that will benefit from the additional tax money were emotional when they thanked him for his efforts.

Mr. Faubus said he always was relaxed when the ballots were being counted, even during his two campaigns for governor.

But there was no denying that he was elated over his success as the first chief executive since the late J. Marion Futrell who was able to push across a comprehensive tax program.

Most observers credited the administration's success to Mr. Faubus' ability to get the agencies and departments together on needed taxes.

Mr. Faubus said he had realized that "you can't get a tax program passed by helping one or two agencies and leaving the others out in the cold."

* * *

On the day the tax bills were considered and before the votes were cast, Feb. 5, the *Democrat* in a strong editorial of opposition said,

"A vote for Governor Faubus' three-cent sales tax bill will be a vote to send much Arkansas business to neighboring states."

TAX BILLS SIGNED INTO LAW, 2/7/57

In the presence of my legislative leaders in my office I signed the tax bills into law on February 7. Standing left to right, Sen. J. Lee Bearden, Leachville; Representative E. C. "Gene" Fleeman, Manila; and Legislative Advisor, W. J. "Bill" Smith, Little Rock. In appreciation for his great ability and able leadership in the Senate, I used the pen of Sen. J. Lee Bearden, Leachville, to sign the tax measures into law.

In the Ft. Smith *Times Record* of Feb. 7, C. F. Byrns in his column, Off the Record, said:

A political miracle has occurred in Arkansas.

A second term governor has won decisive victory in both houses of the legislature for a $22-million-dollar increase in state taxes.

Second term governors normally have trouble holding what they have been able to do in their first terms.

. . . The program for new revenues was carefully developed, ably presented to the legislature and handled through the legislative process with skill that I have not seen matched in the 30 years I have been observing the proceedings at first hand. (Coming from Clarence Byrns I considered this a high compliment. — OEF)

The Searcy *Daily Citizen*, M. P. Jones, publisher, and Perrin Jones, editor, said on February 6:

The action . . . was the first major tax increase in Arkansas in more than 20 years . . . the first . . . of any kind since WWII. . . . Because of the need . . . and the fact this need had been unfilled for so long, our state legislators are to be highly congratulated for their action.

On February 6 following the final approval of my program by the House, I signed the bill giving pay raises to members of the judiciary. Looking on were Lt. Gov. Nathan Gordon of Morrilton, Attorneys James F. Hale of Marion and Leon Catlett of Little Rock.

SEGREGATION BILLS IN '57 LEGISLATURE

After the passage of my program the legislators turned to other matters. The subject uppermost in the minds of a majority of the people was resistance to court-ordered integration of the public schools in Arkansas.

Responding to this sentiment, four so-called segregation measures were prepared for consideration. Rep. Lucien C. Rogers of Crittenden County was a prominent advocate of the measures but he was by no means alone.

I was inclined to accept as sufficient the two measures which I had sponsored and which had been approved at the general election. Many others were not so inclined. I was not involved in the formulation or the sponsoring of the new measures, but the authors submitted them to me for my study and consideration before introduction. After a study of the measures with my advisers which disclosed them to be reasonable when compared to similar legislation being adopted by other states, I agreed to "go along" with the bills.

The four measures introduced in the House on February 11, within three days were passed overwhelmingly and sent to the Senate. A move in the upper house to delay the measures was defeated, and they were maneuvered toward a vote on Feb. 15.

Winthrop Rockefeller issued a statement in which he saw the danger of a Gestapo in the measure creating a state sovereignty commission. His statement had no effect on legislative sentiment.

On the 15th the Senate, in response to demands by zealous opponents, agreed to hold a public hearing on the measures. The hearing was set before the proper committee in the House chamber for the evening of Feb. 17. The public was notified and anyone who wished to be heard was invited to attend.

TEXAS SAYS HOORAY!
By Kennedy, Ark. Democrat   2/6/57

Arkansas border towns and cities were exempt from any sales tax where the border state made no levy such as Texarkana, or limited to the amount collected in the bordering state, such as Ft. Smith. Tennessee and Mississippi already had a 3% rate.

The cartoon was clever propaganda.

Texas now has a statewide sales tax of 4 per cent with a total of 7 per cent in some cities. Arkansas still has the 3 per cent rate.

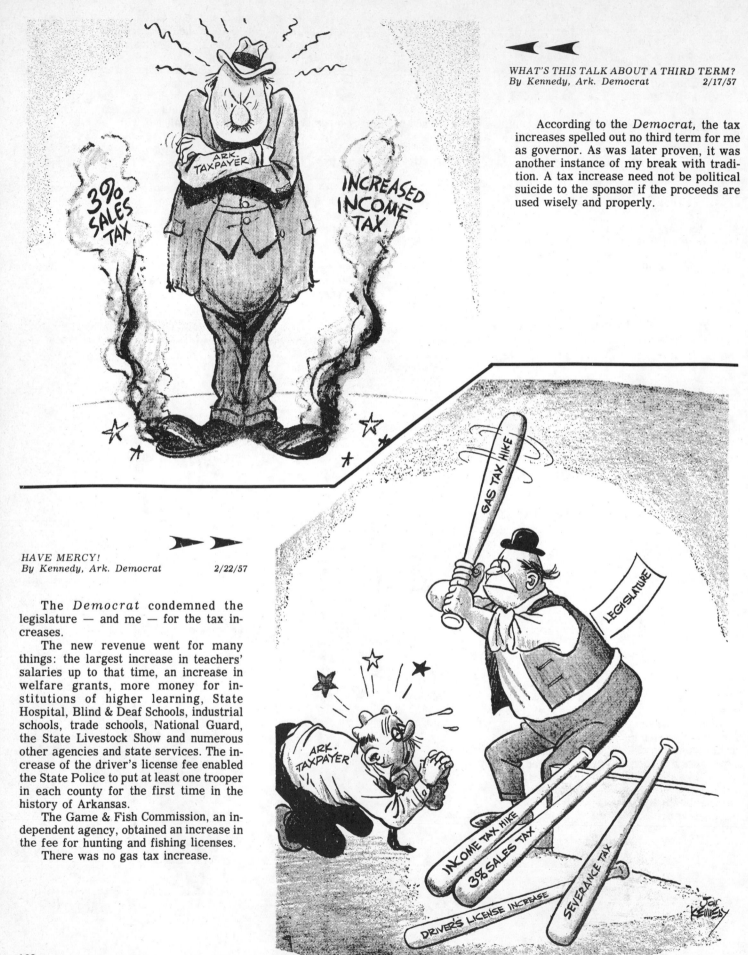

According to the *Democrat*, the tax increases spelled out no third term for me as governor. As was later proven, it was another instance of my break with tradition. A tax increase need not be political suicide to the sponsor if the proceeds are used wisely and properly.

HAVE MERCY!
By Kennedy, Ark. Democrat   2/22/57

The *Democrat* condemned the legislature — and me — for the tax increases.

The new revenue went for many things: the largest increase in teachers' salaries up to that time, an increase in welfare grants, more money for institutions of higher learning, State Hospital, Blind & Deaf Schools, industrial schools, trade schools, National Guard, the State Livestock Show and numerous other agencies and state services. The increase of the driver's license fee enabled the State Police to put at least one trooper in each county for the first time in the history of Arkansas.

The Game & Fish Commission, an independent agency, obtained an increase in the fee for hunting and fishing licenses.

There was no gas tax increase.

168

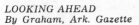

The cartoon had two basic errors. First, there was no federal law on integration, only a court ruling.

Second, the legislation was not mine. The two measures sponsored by me and my advisers had already been approved at the general election. The new legislation was drawn up by sincere legislators at the insistence of their constituents. The legislators most concerned with the measures constituted the bulk of the support for my tax program which had just been enacted. I could not now ignore them, because the program approved in the first half of the session could just as easily be repealed during the last half. In fact, a bill to reduce the sales tax from 3 to 2 per cent was introduced on March 4 by Gayle Windsor of Pulaski County. A majority of the Pulaski County legislators had opposed the program.

As I pointed out, the legislation was not radical. It did not prohibit integration, but permitted it to proceed where the people were willing and found it acceptable. No such moderate legislation was being enacted in other states, but measures much more extreme were being approved.

BLACK DELEGATION VISITS MY OFFICE

In the meantime a group of about a dozen prominent black leaders of whom I now recall only Mrs. Daisy Bates and I. S. McClinton, both of Little Rock, came to the capitol to lobby against the segregation measures. I was the only official to receive them and give them an audience. Others, including formerly friendly legislators, avoided them or turned them away. Two or three members of the group returned later to my office to report what had happened.

"Governor," said one, referring to efforts to halt the measures, "things have changed. There's nothing that can be done. Even if you tried, you couldn't stop them."

The Senate Committee hearing on the measures was held before a packed House chamber. The zeal of opponents and proponents was described to me later by Bex Shaver as "somewhat frightening." Opponents centered their fire on the sovereignty bill citing specific language which they termed particularly objectionable. One of the spokesmen for the measures was the aging but eminently able attorney, Richard McCulloch of Forrest City. In his calm and imperturable manner he demolished the arguments of opponents by reading the language to which they objected, followed by the reading of the same language in the civil rights bill then before Congress. The wording had been lifted word for word from the Congressional measure written and sponsored by U.S. Attorney General Herbert Brownell.

To the extreme "liberals" the language was "good" in Washington but "bad" in Arkansas.

Three days later opponents failed to delay a vote in the Senate and the measures were approved overwhelmingly.

I signed the bills into law on February 26.

In Washington on Feb. 16 Brownell was grilled for the third day by a committee probing the civil rights bill. (See Behind Washington News by Bascom N. Timmons in the *Democrat*, Oct. 3, 1957)

MILUM ROAD BILL

I signed into law a bill sponsored by Senator Roy Milum of Harrison, adding 900 miles of the most highly traveled county roads to the state highway system.

NEW INDUSTRIAL MEASURE

I recommended and the legislature approved a constitutional amendment authorizing local units of government to issue industrial bonds for the acquisition of land and construction of new industrial plants. The people approved the amendment at the next general election.

The construction program authorized buildings for the following: the new Children's Colony at Conway, a new Vo-Tech (trade) school intended for Pine Bluff, new structures at the State Hospital, the Blind and Deaf Schools, the four Training Schools which confined juveniles, National Guard armories, the State Livestock Show grounds and the district fairs, creation of new state parks and improvements at both old and new parks. The measure also contained funds for the purchase of land at the Pea Ridge battlefield in Benton County and at Arkansas Post in Arkansas County, the land to be given to the U.S. National Park Service for the creation of federal facilities.

GRADUATE INSTITUTE OF TECHNOLOGY

The Graduate Institute of Technology was established in Little Rock as an arm of the University. Using the facilities of the old Medical Center this new educational facility proved highly valuable in the technical and highly specialized training of top flight skilled personnel for industrial plants. This proved to be a great help in the acquisition of new industry.

DRAGGIN' IN
By Graham, Ark. Gazette   3/9/57

Several members of the legislature opposed all the way the overall tax program I had proposed. After the measures were passed over their opposition and additional revenue was assured, these program opponents came up with proposals to give certain agencies and groups even more.

One such proposal was a teachers' bonus, which would be in addition to the largest teachers' salary increase in the history of the state. Some school teachers fell for the bait as certain legislators sought to regain the favor they had lost by their opposition to the program. If these opponents had succeeded in defeating the program there would have been no teacher salary increase, not to mention a bonus.

Enough legislators felt constrained to vote for the bonus to pass it. I did not attempt to prevent passage but promised a veto.

STAND BACK BOY ... Y' BOTHER ME!
By Kennedy, Ark. Democrat   3/17/57

For years, according to many political observers, the Old Guard, headed by members of the Country Club set in Little Rock, had controlled and directed Republican affairs on the state level in Arkansas. Republicans on the county level had to clear everything with these state leaders.

Some Northwest Arkansas Republicans with Rep. F. A. "Pat" Teague of Berryville as their spokesman, sought a greater voice in state party affairs. The cartoon showed the reaction. Teague introduced and secured the approval of a law compelling the Republican Party to conduct statewide and county primaries thus changing greatly the situation.

Teague, a Carroll County Republican, was elected three times to the House of Representatives on the GOP ticket, (1953, 1955, and 1957), and attended a National Republican convention as a delegate.

He then switched to the Democrat Party and was elected to the General Assembly four more times, and attended a national Democratic convention as a delegate.

No other man in Arkansas attained this record. In this cartoon Teague was still a Republican but switched when Eisenhower sent federal troops to occupy Little Rock later in the year.

CONSTRUCTION PROGRAM

My program safely approved and signed into law and the explosive anti-school integration measures behind us, I laid my construction program before the legislature.

The program called for the expenditure of $7 million, the largest amount in the history of the state without a bond issue. The funds would be obtained by the collection of the new taxes from the effective date of my signature until July 1, when the new budgets became operative.

POLLUTION CONTROL

A pollution control commission was established, one of the first in the nation. This was some time before the federal government became interested in the problem.

REASSESSMENT PROGRAM SAVED

An effort was made to kill the property tax equalization program by defeating the appropriation of $366,000. House Speaker Walther, on the third try at passage, cast the 75th and deciding vote. This narrow victory for the program explained my modification of the plan earlier in the session for which I was criticized by the *Democrat*. The compromise probably saved this progressive program.

STATE RETIREMENT SYSTEM CREATED

A measure was passed setting up a state retirement system for all state employees. The bill was authored by Senator Sam Levine of Pine Bluff. At that time state employees had only Social Security coverage. Two years before state employees had no retirement benefits whatsoever except for two agencies, the State Police and Highway Department.

Later the state retirement system was expanded to include all county and city employees and non-teaching personnel of the education systems.

MEDICAL CENTER FUNDED FOR OPERATION

The great new University of Arkansas Medical Center in Little Rock begun six years previously was adequately funded for operation and would open its doors on April 25.

SALARY INCREASES; ROADS AND BUILDINGS CONSTRUCTED

With this progressive program the benefits were many. With more adequate funds for operation than ever before, underpaid state employees received needed salary increases. The increases ranged through the whole field from forest rangers, park personnel, state police and clerks in offices to school teachers and college professors. And to all of these the retirement system was a welcome benefit.

New roads and bridges were built, new state parks, new institutions as the Children's Colony and trade schools were created. And nowhere were improvements, both operational and physical, more needed or welcome than at the State Hospital.

Perhaps the most underpaid of all state personnel were the forest rangers who drew $70 per month and furnished their own vehicles and paid their own expenses.

WELFARE INCREASE

On March 20 the Director of the Welfare Department announced that all grants would be increased $10 per month on July 1, and it was not an election year.

SALARY EQUALIZATION OF BLACKS AND WHITES

More adequate funds meant a big jump forward in another field where improvements had already begun — the equalization of salaries of black and white employees in comparable work. The move toward equalization applied to state institutions, the public schools and institutions of higher learning.

It must be borne in mind that only influence could be used with the public schools as each school district was a governmental entity all its own.

GUESS WHO GOT IT IN THE END
By Kennedy, Ark. Democrat   3/13/57

It was my opinion then, and still is, that the approval of the overall tax program by the 61st General Assembly was the greatest forward step taken in Arkansas in my lifetime.

However, not everyone agreed with the viewpoint. The *Democrat* said the 61st General Assembly, dominated by vote trading, spending pressure and special interests, had run over and flattened the Arkansas taxpayer.

APPROVAL AND DISAPPROVAL BY GAZETTE

An editorial in the March 16 *Arkansas Gazette* said:
Governor Faubus will be remembered as the candidate who delivered on his promise to 'do something' about such biennial vote pullers as teachers' salaries, welfare grants and the State Hospital. Other . . . governors have tried . . . Orval Faubus has accomplished the most.

In the same editorial the *Gazette* criticized me on three points: for not stopping the State Sovereignty bill, the resolutions on the national amendments, and verbal pot shots by legislators at the independent Highway Commission. To stop the first two would have been like trying to halt a slowly sliding mountain that could accelerate its movement at any moment. Many were not yet aware of the gathering storm involving states rights and the racial issue.

A rising tide of bitter conflict over court-ordered integration was becoming apparent to close observers. The fiery debate at the public hearing on the sovereignty bill, divisions in the school elections, sermons in the pulpits, letters to the newspapers and an unprecedented deep animosity in the Democratic primaries of 1956 — all were signs that a pot was boiling and could boil over.

No candidate for school director anywhere in the state stood publicly for integration, except possibly at Hoxie where they were decisively defeated.

On the third point, much of the criticism of the Highway Commission was justified. Any agency of government, no matter the degree of independence, has an obligation to keep up its public relations. The controversy was over honest differences. Anyway, it would have been impossible for me to keep legislators from speaking out on the matter.

TERRA FIRMA, TEMPORARILY
By Kennedy, Ark. Democrat   3/15/57

The cartoonist indicated the enactment of my programs at the '57 session was not a sweet ride for Arkansas.

HIGHWAY DEPT. AND BUDGET COMMITTEE REACH QUICK AGREEMENT ON WAGE SCALE, PAVING WAY FOR GOVERNOR TO CALL LEGISLATURE BACK MONDAY.

WELFARE DEPT. OFFERS MED CENTER $2,000,000 YEARLY TO CARE FOR INDIGENT PATIENTS...

NO HIGHWAY APPROPRIATION

In a last-minute dispute the General Assembly adjourned without approving an appropriation for the Highway Department. The matter of contention was the inadequate compensation to highway workers out in the counties — the ones who really did the work of maintaining the roads.

An amendment was attached to the appropriation bill in the House by Representative Ode Maddox of Montgomery County, calling for a minimum wage of $1.00 per hour for the maintenance workers, upgrading two other low-wage categories, and providing per diem expense to workers on jobs outside their own counties.

The Senate declined to concur in the amendment, and the House refused to remove it. Thus no bill was passed in final form.

The failure to reach agreement was possibly connivance by a number of legislators who considered the action a good way to show the aloof Commission and Department that some cooperation with the Assembly members could be helpful.

The Highway Department and the Legislature quickly ironed out their differences and on March 21 I called a special session for March 25 to approve the appropriation bill. The Maddox amendment was included in the compromise.

With the help of Carl Adams and A. J. "Red" Moss of the Welfare Department, we worked out a plan to match federal funds and pay up to $2,000,000 annually to the Medical Center for the care of indigent welfare patients.

AND SO, AS THE SUN SINKS SLOWLY IN THE WEST
By Graham, Ark. Gazette   3/29/57

Two versions of the highway appropriation were approved at the Special Session. One authored by Perry Representative Paul Van Dalsem and Sen. Guy Jones of Conway, authorized the Department to purchase and operate the small, privately owned Toad Suck Ferry, with $25,000 for the purchase price. The other bill was identical except for the ferry provisions.

Toad Suck Ferry provided a crossing of the Arkansas River between Perry and Faulkner Counties, with the most direct link between Conway on the east side and Perry, Perryville and smaller settlements on the west. There was no other river crossing in the 70 miles between Little Rock and Morrilton.

The *Gazette* cartoonist showed three figures homeward bound following the end of the special session. ''Toad Suck Ferry'' was ''Putt-Putt-Putting'' along; the ''highway department appropriation'' was okeh; and ''criticism reprisal'' of the Highway Commission had ''sput-sput-sputted'' out.

HIGHLIGHTS OF THE NEWSWEEK
By Kennedy, Ark. Democrat   3/31/57

I pointed out the mistakes of the Highway Department to the special session, and got the legislators in the mood to act quickly. Reporter Bobbie Forster listened to my speech and told me I was becoming a statesman.

The Legislature left me to choose between two highway appropriation bills. The members reacted to John Sheffield's criticism of the legislature by calling for his resignation.

ONE GOOD TURN DESERVES ANOTHER
By Kennedy, Ark. Democrat   3/29/57

Veteran Perry County Representative Paul Van Dalsem had for years been recognized as the most effective opponent of tax increases in the legislature. He helped maneuver to death the 13-month sales tax increase proposal in the 1955 session. He had done the same to tax measures during the McMath and Cherry administrations.

Van Dalsem was also a chief proponent of economy. Year after year he led the economy forces, holding down salaries of top bracket employees, reducing operating costs and generally cutting the fat out of agency budgets.

With long and earnest effort, by supplying full information on even the smallest details of the tax proposals and the benefits, the veteran legislator was finally persuaded to support the 1957 tax program. His skill and persuasion were most effective in the House where the greatest resistance was encountered. His support was even more important in obtaining the three-fourths majority for the appropriations and the two-thirds vote for the emergency clause.

I had anticipated that sales tax opponents would refer the sales tax increase to a vote of the people. This proved correct. Without the emergency clause the referral would have postponed effectiveness of the measure until the 1958 general election. The increases in teachers' salaries, welfare grants and all other budget improvements would have been nullified until the election of November 1958. Without the benefits being apparent the people might have voted down the tax increase.

The cartoonist said Van Dalsem had taken a bitter pill by supporting the ''Faubus Tax Program.'' I was obligated to approve the bitter pill of ''Toad Suck Ferry Purchase.'' I did.

There was a happy aftermath of the Toad Suck Ferry matter. In the construction of the great Kerr-McClellan Navigation Project, a dam was built at the site of the ferry crossing. Since a state facility, the ferry, would be destroyed by the construction of the dam by federal authorities, it was maintained that the federal government was obligated to replace the facility. Taking this as their cue Sen. McClellan and Cong. Mills secured an additional appropriation of federal funds to construct a new bridge at the site. The State Highway Department built the approaches to the structure — a small price to pay for such a fine new bridge.

Without the efforts of Van Dalsem and Sen. Guy "Mutt" Jones in passing the Toad Suck Ferry bill, with my subsequent approval of the measure, followed by the help of Mills and McClellan, the bridge across the Arkansas River would not be there today. It might never have been built.

The completed structure was dedicated in 1971, the first year of Governor Dale Bumpers' administration, with Governor Bumpers, Van Dalsem and Jones as honored guests.

I VETO THE LOYALTY OATH BILL

A bill requiring a loyalty oath and a statement of non-affiliation with any subversive group by all state employees, including teachers, was introduced in the Senate by Artie Gregory of Pulaski County. It passed both houses of the Legislature by overwhelming majorities.

The principal objections to the measure came from a small group of professors at the University at Fayetteville, and the editorial writers of the *Arkansas Gazette*. The measure was not considered as stringent as the federal government oath required for federal employees.

I vetoed the bill on March 31. I did not think it was possible to obtain loyalty through such measures.

SUPT. BLOSSOM'S VISITS WITH ME

Soon after the close of the legislative session School Superintendent Virgil Blossom began frequent contacts and visits with me. I began listening to his oft repeated expressions of concern about the coming integration of the Little Rock schools. As the time for school opening drew near his concern grew to alarm and even fear. He told me of growing opposition and then of reports of organized resistance to the court-approved plan of the school board. He was so concerned, he said, that he was making arrangements to send his children to another school.

Some time after the close of the legislature Sen. Marvin Melton of Jonesboro, a brother-in-law of Supt. Blossom, had occasion to confer with me on some problem. I invited him to the Executive Mansion where we met in the evening. At the conclusion of our conference the Little Rock integration problem was mentioned and I remarked about Blossom's concern and his many contacts with me.

"Yes," said Sen. Melton, "Virgil's awfully worried. He's already made arrangements to send his children to stay with me and attend school at Jonesboro."

NEW INDUSTRIES

On March 1 Little Rock welcomed the news that a blue chip industry would locate in the city. The Teletype Company would employ 1,600 people when completed.

A new factory announced its location at Magnolia on March 7.

Helena bagged another new industry, a luggage plant on March 16.

On March 29 it was disclosed that the small town of Foreman would get a new $15 million cement plant. Representative Marion Crank of Little River County, where the plant was to be located, came to my office with Senators Marshall Shackelford of El Dorado and Roy Riales of Mena, where the four of us jointly announced the new plant to be built by a sub-

sidiary of Ark-La Gas Company. The power behind the plant construction was W. R. "Witt" Stephens, president of the gas company.

SCOTCHED?
By Kennedy, Ark. Democrat   4/14/57

The decennial census had shown a decline in the overall population of Arkansas in 1930, 1940, and 1950. In some of the small rural, mountain counties, as Madison and Newton, the sharp decline in population began prior to 1910.

It was hoped Arkansas' industrial program would halt the population loss by providing jobs which would keep Arkansas people at home and lure others to the state.

The cartoonist raised the question: has the population decline been scotched by new industry?

According to the University of Arkansas' Department of Economic Research, the answer was yes. Although the 1960 Census showed a slight loss since 1950, the University said the decline stopped during 1957 and that the state gained from that date to the next census in 1960.

The 1970 Census showed an overall gain from 1960.

I am convinced the industrial program was a major factor in halting the population decline, and for the gains made since 1957.

The following story taken from the files of *The Madison County Record* of Dec. 19, 1957, showed the severity of population loss in the rural areas of the state. Losses prior to the period covered in this survey were just as great, if not greater.

"Where Are Our Alumni" of Madison County
A study on "Where are our alumni?" from 1952 to 1957 has just been completed by the Senior American Government class of the Huntsville High School. Similar studies are underway in the Kingston and St. Paul schools.

This survey was to determine percentage of graduates leaving Madison County and Arkansas after graduating.

The results of this study are as follows:

Number of boys stayed in Madison County	23—10.0%
Number of boys stayed in Arkansas	84—39.8%
Number left Arkansas	104—49.3%
Number of girls stayed in Madison County	31—13.5%
Number of girls stayed in Arkansas	88—39.1%
Number of girls left Arkansas	106—47.1%
Total number graduated in 6 years	427
Total percent stayed in Madison County	13%
Total percent left Madison County	87%

Those commended for the excellent work done on this study are: Silver June Doss, Barbara Sparks, Wanda Usrey, Erma Jones, and the class sponsor, Mrs. Idelle Garcia. Miss Gayle Johnson also gave valuable assistance in locating former graduates. The loss was even greater in the Kingston and St. Paul high schools, but the figures were unavailable.

APPRECIATION FOR LEGISLATORS

The Department of Classroom Teachers on March 2 sponsored an affair honoring the legislators and their wives in appreciation for the legislation beneficial to the teachers and the schools. President T. G. Bratton presided with talks of appreciation by incoming President Mrs. Martha Bigley of Magnolia and past president Mrs. Helen Henderson of Imboden.

WHITE, NEGRO TEACHERS SALARIES CLOSER THAN EVER IN 1955-56

A report on April 5 gave these average annual salaries for black and white teachers: $2,375 for whites; $2,103 for Negroes.

I exercised all the influence and persuasion I could bring to bear from the moment I took office to equalize the salaries as soon as possible. Since teachers' salaries were completely in the hands of the local school boards no orders or directives could be given from the Governor's office.

I was able to obtain appreciable progress through the Department of Education — Arch Ford and Ed McCuistion cooperated fully — the AEA and ATA, and my personal contacts with school superintendents, school board members and political leaders.

In other fields where I could exercise authority the process of equalizing salaries continued, as the State Hospital, the TB sanitoriums, the industrial schools and other state agencies where black and white state employees were doing the same or similar work.

LORCHES IN LITTLE ROCK MAKE THE NEWS

Lee Lorch, 39, Little Rock mathematics professor, formerly of Dayton, Ohio, was charged and tried in federal court on eight counts of contempt of Congress for refusing to answer eight questions about alleged Communist activities while a witness before a House Un-American Activities Subcommittee at Dayton in 1954. Lorch left Fisk University in Nashville, Tenn. when his alleged Communist connections and activities became known and came to Philander Smith College, a Little Rock Negro school.

His wife was listed by the FBI and anti-Communist organizations as Grace Lonergan who had once served as a delegate to an official state Communist convention in Massachusetts.

Later, in official investigations of Communist activities by a Senate subcommittee, Mrs. Lorch created disorder and turmoil by refusing to be orderly or answer questions about her alleged Communist affiliation or activity.

Lee Lorch in a statement on April 7 laid his trial for contempt to his fight for integration.

Lorch's alleged contempt of Congress was committed in Dayton in an investigation which had nothing to do with the segregation-integration issue. A decision had not yet been rendered in his trial before Judge Lester L. Cecil. Lorch said if he was convicted it would be because he decided "witchhunters had been riding high, wide and handsome long enough," and he was opposing the practice.

It was an old Communist trick for a person accused of subversion to tie himself to an unpopular cause and claim he was being persecuted. At that time integration was sufficiently unpopular in Arkansas, but there is no indication that public sentiment or the integration issue had any relation to Lorch's alleged offenses in Dayton.

NEXT QUESTION: WHO'S TO RUN FOR GOVERNOR? TIMES NOT SHORT BUT NEITHER IS LIST OF NAMES

Among those listed on April 14 were Sid McMath, Chris Finkbeiner, Dean R. Morley, J. Orville Cheney and Frank Holt, all of Little Rock, Fred Pickens of Newport, Bruce Bennett of El Dorado, Marvin Melton of Jonesboro, James P. Baker, Jr., of Helena, Jim Johnson of Crossett, Lawrence Blackwell of Pine Bluff, Hardy Croxton of Rogers, and me. It was not traditional for a governor to seek and win a third term but the article said "Faubus is not bound by tradition." A little later W. J. "Bill" Smith of Little Rock was added to the list.

* * *

GOVERNOR? HE JUST WENT THATTA WAY
(Headline for story in Gazette)

I flew back from the Little Rock C of C Goodwill tour to Louisville, Ky. for an engagement at Arkadelphia on the 24th; other engagements, the list probably incomplete: U of A Medical Center April 25 for dedication, Dr. Lewis Webster Jones the speaker; Pleasant Plains school commencement evening of April 25; Forestry Day at Southern State College, Magnolia, April 26; Hot Springs Wild Life Conference April 27; Earle Rotary Club April 29; Groundbreaking Forrest City Hospital and Des Arc fish fry May 1; Fayetteville banquet May 3; another Fayetteville meeting May 4; Charleston school commencement May 6; Oden school commencement, Ode Maddox, superintendent. May 9; Huntsville school graduation May 10; Greenwood high school graduation, Means Wilkerson master of ceremonies, May 11; Holly Grove May 13; Southern Governors' Conference at Atlanta, Ga. beginning May 16; followed by dedication of Atkins Lake in Pope County; commencement at Arkansas Tech at Russellville May 19; graduation at St. Paul high school on May 24.

INDUSTRIAL PROGRAM GAINS CONTINUE

Our industrial program continued to gain momentum. During this week I attended groundbreaking ceremonies for the new Tectum plant at Arkadelphia. The ground-breaking and dedication ceremonies were happy occasions for everyone.

HIGHLIGHTS OF THE NEWSWEEK
By Kennedy, Ark. Democrat   4/28/57

Other highlights were: Pine Bluff okayed bonds for a new hospital and North Little Rock was waiting; the new State Medical Center at Little Rock, begun six years ago, was dedicated.

BRANDING TIME AT THE BAR NONE RANCH
By Kennedy, Ark. Democrat   4/28/57

Revenue Commissioner Cheney's efficiency continued to increase the collection of taxes. By non-interference and cooperation of the governor's office, tax collections in all categories under Cheney's jurisdiction had continually improved. He announced an even more stringent search for tax dodgers in the months ahead.

GOV. FAUBUS RECEIVES DOCTOR OF LAWS DEGREE
By Kennedy, Ark. Democrat   5/5/57

The University of Arkansas on May 1 awarded honorary degrees to Miss Alma Futrell of Marianna, Congressman Wilbur Mills of Kensett, James H. Penick of Little Rock, Dr. Paul Bigelow Sears of Yale University and me.

◦━◦━◦━◦━◦

PROPERTY TAX REASSESSMENT

The implementation of the reassessment or Property Tax Equalization Program enacted by the 1955 General Assembly was the most difficult undertaking of my administration. To bring a semblance of equity to the unequal and highly defective property tax system was a gigantic problem and fraught with the greatest political peril to the administration.

An attempt during the McMath administration had failed to make appreciable progress in corrections to the system. At times agency employees were virtually run out of town by irate local officials and taxpayers.

Gov. Francis Cherry, recognizing the need to remedy the situation, recommended the 100% property assessment act with reduced millage rates. The act was a contributor to his defeat when he sought re-election.

Realizing in 1955 that the legislature was determined to enact some kind of equalization program as a substitute for any increase in the sales tax or income tax, I attempted to guide its efforts. Legislative sponsors of the program wanted to vest final authority in a state agency to equalize assessments when the county governments failed to do so. I knew that if this were the case the local officials, facing the heat from local taxpayers, would do virtually nothing. They would simply leave the unsolved problem to the state.

Therefore I rejected the idea and insisted that the state responsibility would be to act only in an advisory and assistance

176

role. The authority to initiate the program was placed squarely on the local units of government.

The level of assessments was set at 20% of true market value. A provision authorizing the state to withhold state turn-back funds when the local government did not meet the required level was inserted in the measure. Some flexibility was allowed by a provision that no funds would be withheld if the local government reached 18% rather than the goal of 20%.

For example, if a county reached the 15% level, it would receive three-fourths of its turnback funds and one-fourth would be withheld. The amount withheld was set aside, to be released to the county if it reached the required 18% to 20% level within one year.

Also, the law was amended at the 1957 regular legislative session to allow more time for compliance.

The fact that all revenue from the property tax remained with the local units of government — county, city and school district — with none of the revenue coming to the state, was a major selling point with local authorities.

With constant urging and reminders to the local governments that they were helping themselves — that equalized assessments were fair to everyone in every way — with continuing patience, understanding and never-ending effort on the part of the state agency — headway was made with this most difficult problem.

BEGINNING TO SHAPE UP
By Kennedy, Ark. Democrat   5/8/57

This cartoon gave just credit to the assessors, members of the boards of equalization and other local officials for their efforts in the progress that was being achieved.

By May 1957 a two-year revaluation of assessments statewide had increased the property value on the tax books by approximately $500 million, a jump of 100 per cent. W. L. "Doc" Hinton, Jr., director of the state program, said $100 million in new property was "discovered" and placed on the books.

LANEY EMPLOYED BY ROCKEFELLER

Former Governor Ben Laney was employed by Rockefeller to manage his newly purchased rice farms in the Lonoke area.

A FACE IN THE CROWD, Source unknown

"A Face in the Crowd" was a movie, made in Arkansas by Director Elia Kazan, with the filming done at Piggott. The producers invited me to New York, expenses paid, to help promote the premiere. I appeared on a number of TV shows — quiz programs including "What's My Line" and "Strike It Rich."

I was accompanied by my son, Farrell, and Jimmie Karam. Wm. P. "Bill" Rock, AIDC director, joined us there. I helped my nephew, Jerry Faubus, to secure leave from his Air Force station at Syracuse, N.Y., and he joined us for three days. We had lunch with New York Governor Averill Harriman and Mrs. Harriman at their New York residence, and then accompanied them to a big league ball game.

Karam obtained reservations for an evening at the Stork Club which, at my request, he cancelled under protest and we all attended Billy Graham's crusade at Madison Square Garden. Afterward we saw a Broadway play, and then had dinner with Mr. and Mrs. Morris Miller who had located an industry in Arkansas and planned to locate another.

Bill Rock and I spent one whole day going from industrial prospect to prospect and were quite weary at day's end. Just before leaving for home we put Jerry on the bus for return to his base from which he was to leave for overseas duty.

Weather monopolized the week's news at home as the state was struck by violent storms. The Arkansas River levees broke at Dardanelle flooding thousands of acres of farm land. I called units of the National Guard to duty to assist at several points along the river.

NEW INDUSTRIES

Jonesboro on May 1 landed the new $800 thousand Colson Corporation plant, and followed 12 days later with the acquisition of a glass factory that would employ 75. A new plant announced its move to Russellville on May 31. Hoerner Boxes, Inc. on May 23 announced a new plant would be constructed at Little Rock.

SEN. McCARTHY DIES

On May 3 death claimed Senator Joseph R. McCarthy of Wisconsin at age 47.

SUPT. BOREN LOSES JOB

Victor Boren, superintendent of schools at Morrilton for 27 years, lost his position in a dispute with Winthrop Rockefeller over terms of the model school to be built by the millionaire. Boren later obtained employment at Booneville.

GACE CONTINUES

In a meeting on May 8 I called the GACE to continued effort to protect the newly enacted tax program and for further efforts to improve the schools.

AP&L GETS INCREASE

The AP&L finally got a rate increase approved by the PSC, $1,779,093, amounting to about 20 cents per month for household bills.

THORNBROUGH AND HAYS HONORED

Clarence R. Thornbrough, my Labor Commissioner, was chosen president of the Little Rock Religion and Fellowship group; Congressman Brooks Hays was elected president of the giant religious organization, the Southern Baptist Association.

ARKANSAS LAUDED AS EXAMPLE

Dr. Howard L. Bevis, chairman of a presidential committee for the development of scientists and engineers, praised Arkansas for its program to alleviate the critical shortage in these fields. The praise came principally for the establishment of the Graduate Institute of Technology (GIT) in Little Rock.

WASHBURN OPPOSES SALES TAX

Publisher Alex Washburn of Hope, heading the movement to refer the sales tax increase to a vote, journeyed to Ft. Smith to call on residents to sign his petitions. A few days later he opened a Little Rock office from which to direct the referral effort.

APPOINTMENTS, JANUARY 1957

John L. Sullivan, Little Rock, as Traffic Judge. Bernard Frazier of Warren and Lloyd Russell of Piggott, to the Burial Association Board. J. H. Smith, Birdeye, to Arkansas State College Board at Jonesboro. Harvey G. Combs, Little Rock, reappointed as Insurance Commissioner. (The Commissioner was a native of my home community, near Combs in South Madison County, moving to Huntsville and then to Little Rock. He was a school mate of my father and later a teacher in the first school established in the Greenwood District [Greasy Creek]. The first school was a log structure, replaced by a frame building in 1906 which is being preserved by the Orval E. Faubus Foundation.) John V. Turner, Russellville, former Pope County Judge, to Board of Review. J. M. Malone, Sr., Lonoke, reappointed to Public Service Commission. Glenn F. Wallace, Nashville, selected as chairman of the Highway Commission by his fellow members. Sam Harris, Little Rock, to State Hospital Board. Ovid Switzer, Crossett, reappointed to Publicity and Parks Commission.

APPOINTMENTS, FEBRUARY 1957

Dr. Ellis Gardner, Russellville, to Arkansas Tech College Board at Russellville. Clyde King, Marked Tree, reappointed to State Prison Board. Shaffer Haley, Pine Bluff, to Real Estate Commission. Hugh Kincaid, Fayetteville, to AM&N College Board at Pine Bluff. Paul Godsey, England, A&M College Board at Monticello. Ray Martin, Rison, Henderson State Teachers College Board. Dr. W. D. Halbrook, Conway, to State Teachers College Board. Mrs. Dorothy McDonald, Brinkley, Children's Colony Board. Dr. D. J. Webster, North Little Rock, and Dr. Floyd Brown, Pine Bluff, to Fargo Training School for Negro girls. A. C. Neal, Morrilton, Forestry Commission. Mrs. Marjorie Crabaugh, Russellville, Training School for white girls. Ben Butler, Osceola, Justice Building Commission. Mrs. R. C. Dickinson, DeQueen, Cancer Commission. James Robertson, Wynne; Dr. D. D. McBrien, Arkadelphia; Mrs. J. L. Taylor, Corning; Lawrence Blackwell, Pine Bluff, all to Commemorative Commission. John Collins, Little Rock, Merit System Council. Hubert Mayes, Little Rock, State Police Commission. Mrs. William Nash, Little Rock, Southern State College Board. Thomas Hall, Delaplaine, Booneville TB Sanitorium. Gus Pugh, Portland, Board of Public Welfare. J. D. "Jeff" Wood, Cabot, State Prison Commission. John D. Ward, North Little Rock, School for Blind and Deaf. Dr. G. W. S. Ish, Little Rock, and Mrs. Aris Cox, Helena, McRae TB Sanatorium Board. E. G. Pringle, Pocahontas, Boys Industrial School Board. Harold Martin, Batesville, Livestock Sanitary Board.

APPOINTMENTS, MARCH 1957

Sovereignty Commission: By terms of the Sovereignty Commission law, Ex-officio members were: Governor Faubus, Lieutenant Governor Nathan Gordon, Attorney General Bruce Bennett and Speaker of the House Glen Walther. The State Senate appointed two members. Senators Q. Byrum Hurst of Hot Springs and Charles F. "Rip" Smith of West Memphis. The House chose three, Representatives Lucien Rogers of Marion, Talbot Feild of Hope and Russell Benton of Salem. The commission would be complete when I appointed three members. Tom Bill Rogers, Harrison, State Bank Board. Earl Wildy, Leachville, and Dallas P. "Pete" Raney, Little Rock, to University of Arkansas Board of Trustees. Ervin Beisel, Helena, State Forestry Commission. Rabie Rhodes, Harrison, State Board of Education. Mrs. Lee Martin, Little Rock, State Library Commission. State Liquified Petroleum Gas Board: L. L. Rambo, Ozark; Ottis Cash, Warren; Roy A. Martin, Rison; Kohn Bray, Marked Tree; Alex Hill, Blytheville; Preston Grace, Batesville; and B. T. Harris, Little Rock. J. D. Hamilton, Paragould, Stadium Commission. Robert L. Rogers, Little Rock, State Hospital Board. Mrs. Clara Mae Speaker, Conway, Training School for Girls Board. Billie Dunn, Conway, State Athletic Commission representing the DAV. Lewis "Red" Johnson, Little Rock, Pollution Control Commission. Commerce Commission, a new agency: William "Bill" Berry, Stuttgart, Chairman; Kay Matthews, Little Rock, and Arthur Shirey, Lewisville, members. John R. Thompson, Cabot, to Public Service Commission to fill Berry's vacancy. Thompson was attorney for the PSC. Mrs. A. N. Nielson, Mulberry, Training School for Girls Board.

APPOINTMENTS, APRIL 1957

James A. Ross, Monticello, reappointed to State Claims Commission. Marshall Blackard, Blytheville, reappointed to State Athletic Commission. Olen Fullerton, Morrilton, to State Hospital Board. U. S. Branson, Blytheville, State Board of Architects.

APPOINTMENTS, MAY 1957

O. C. Bailey, El Dorado, reappointed to Oil and Gas Commission. Claude Carpenter, Little Rock, attorney for PSC. Tommy H. Russell, North Little Rock, administrative assistant to the Governor. Neill Bohlinger, Little Rock, hired as legal aide to Highway Director. R. B. "Dick" Winfrey of Oklahoma, formerly with Arkansas Highway Department during McMath administration, employed as state maintenance supervisor of Highway Department. R. S. Warnock, Magnolia, to State Bank Board.

APPOINTMENTS, JUNE 1957

Jeff D. Wood, Cabot, State Prison Board. Mrs. Dorothy Martin, Hot Springs, superintendent of the white girls training school. Automobile Commission reappointed: James T. "Jim" Phillips, Fayetteville, Chairman; Frank W. Reeves, Helena; Stanley Wood, Batesville; Newt L. Hailey, Rogers; Searcy Wilcoxen, Hamburg; Fred Poe, North Little Rock; Raymond Clinton, Hot Springs. An Advisory Board was also named to work with the Commission: A. C. Mowery, Huntsville; J. A. Rodman, Melbourne; R. B. Webb, Mountain Home; Curtis Blankenship, Warren; and Woodrow Hill, Perryville. Insurance Code Commission, to recommend reforms in state insurance laws: Edwin F. Jackson, M. J. Harrison, James I. Teague and Louis Rosen, all of Little Rock, Harvey G. Combs, State Insurance Commissioner, was ex-officio member. Rev. T. P. Devlin, Pine Bluff, Commission on Alcoholism, and Dean R. Morley, Little Rock, on same commission to succeed Ike Murry. Mrs. Nadine Ball, Batesville, Practical Nurses Examining Board. Mrs. Wilma Origer, Ft. Smith; Miss Frances Bruehl, Fayetteville; Mrs. Evelyn Smith, El Dorado, to Registered Nurses Examining Board. Dr. C. G. Melton, Fayetteville, to State Optometry Board. Commission on Uniform State Laws: Joe G. Barrett, Jonesboro; Robert A. Leflar, Fayetteville; and William Nash, Little Rock. Pea Ridge National Park Commission: This commission had the duty of obtaining the necessary lands, at state expense, for the establishment of the national military battleground park. The members were: Max Walker, Pea Ridge; Carl H. Brown, Harrison; Hugh Park, Van Buren; Homer Fleeman, Rogers; and Neill Bohlinger, Little Rock.

CHAPTER 10
WILLIAMSBURG CONFERENCE; EISENHOWER SPEECH
CIVIL RIGHTS DEBATE IN CONGRESS;
PRE-1957 CRISIS DEVELOPMENTS

ROCKEFELLER AT THE WILLIAMSBURG CONFERENCE

Winthrop Rockefeller, then chairman of the Colonial Williamsburg restoration project, the site of the National Governors' Conference, played a prominent role as a participant in the conference activities. He was the host of some social functions, and presided over a meeting in the restored House of Burgesses structure where Patrick Henry made his immortal "Liberty or Death" speech. The governors and a few others crowded into this small, historic building for the ceremony.

Rockefeller acquitted himself quite well in the affairs of the conference, both as a host, a member of my administration and an adopted citizen of Arkansas. The great wealth of the Rockefeller family had been used to create the restored Colonial Williamsburg, a great contribution to the preservation of Colonial history.

The night following the State Dinner at which the President spoke, Winthrop called me and we slipped in the back way for a private conference with Mr. Eisenhower which lasted for perhaps half an hour. Winthrop and the President discussed a few problems but the conversation was mostly pleasantries.

The governors noted the great work that had been done at Williamsburg by the Rockefellers and, through reports and Winthrop's prominent role at the conference, they learned also of the success of our industrial program in Arkansas. At one of the working sessions some governor remarked that "What every state needs is a Rockefeller."

Whereupon, I replied that the idea appeared to have merit, and I had no objections to any chief executive attempting to secure a Rockefeller, **except I** wanted to serve notice on all the governors then and there to "leave my Rockefeller alone."

Virginia Governor Thomas Stanley was both host and chairman of the conference.

FLORIDA SOVEREIGNTY COMMISSION

On June 30 Florida named a Sovereignty Commission to guard the rights of the state against federal usurpation.

A national news story said the acts of the Supreme Court were creating a constitutional crisis.

THE NEW YORK SEGREGATIONIST

New York segregationist John Kasper came to the South, uninvited and by his own initiative, to join in battles against integration. Portrayed in the press as a repulsive rabble rouser, he engaged in anti-integration activity at Clinton, Tennessee. He was charged with a large measure of the blame for the trouble there.

Kasper was one of those cited for contempt of the integration court order at Clinton and was one of 15 persons seized, handcuffed and jailed. Prior to that arrest he had been convicted on a previous charge of contempt of a federal court.

Kasper continued as a prominent figure in the school-mixing controversy.

SEN. JOHN KENNEDY OF MASS. ADDRESSES BAR ASSN. AT HOT SPRINGS.

HIGHLIGHTS OF THE NEWSWEEK, By Kennedy, Ark. Democrat, 6/19/57

"Visitor of the week" Sen. John Kennedy of Massachusetts addressed the Bar Association meeting at Hot Springs. Accompanied by Democratic State Chairman Tom Harper the Senator visited me in St. Joseph's Hospital. The nurses and other personnel were quite excited to see him.

Publisher Alex Washburn got sufficient petition signatures to refer 3% sales tax.

Shumaker Depot at Camden dismissed 1,000 workers.

"Orval" was in St. Joseph's Hospital after minor surgery, marked "Out of order."

179

ANOTHER DAISY IN THE ACT, By Kennedy, Ark. Democrat, 6/6/57

The 3 per cent sales tax was referred to a vote by petition by its opponents led by Hope publisher Alex Washburn. The voters might not accept the tax increase at the 1958 general election. Also, I might seek a third term.

-go easy on the house trailers--I'm trying to bring industry in, not chase it off!

GOV. RETURNS TO OFFICE, PREPARES TO SHOVE OFF FOR U.S. GOVERNORS' CONFERENCE.

I intervened with the State Police to allow 10-foot wide mobile homes to be moved on Arkansas roads thus saving three manufacturing plants for the state that were prepared to move elsewhere.

we want a two-party system, and two seats in congress!

OPERATION ARKANSAS

The GOP said, "we want a two-party system, and two seats in Congress." (The GOP finally won the two seats, in 1978.)

FARRELL MOVES TO MAKE ROOM FOR THE PRESIDENT

My 17-year-old son, Farrell, had to move out of his hotel quarters to make room for President Eisenhower at the conference the night of the state dinner.

The President addressed the conference and with a change in plans decided to spend the night. After some quick rearranging of hotel assignments Farrell shifted to a motor court.

COURT ACTION SCORED BY ATTORNEYS GENERAL

At a convention of state attorneys general at Sun Valley, Idaho on June 24, the actions of the U.S. Supreme Court were severely condemned in both speeches and resolutions. Attorney General Louis C. Wyman of New Hampshire led an attack on the court for illegal "law-making" actions, and its lack of judicial self-restraint.

The Court was under attack from leaders and groups throughout the nation, and not just from Southerners. Its decisions were severely criticized by Congressman Donald L. Jackson of California.

MEDICAL WELFARE PROGRAM

A new program of medical benefits for the state's elder citizens was established by the Welfare Department. This program, along with the increased grants and the multi-million dollar food distribution program, made the plight of the elderly far brighter than it had ever been in Arkansas.

CIVIL RIGHTS BILL

The battle over the Brownell civil rights bill continued in both houses of Congress. As the measure was studied and debated its extremely punitive provisions became more and more apparent.

A U.S. Supreme Court ruling on June 18 said "preaching" overthrow of the government, even by force and violence, was legal.

INTEGRATION PROBLEMS SURFACE IN ARKANSAS

As the month of June drew toward an end, integration problems began to surface in the state.

On June 23 the North Little Rock school board announced plans to integrate the 12th grade by attendance areas by the admission of 29 senior Negroes.

The Ft. Smith District said on June 25 that school mixing would begin there in the fall.

On June 28 a group headed by Attorney Amis Guthridge and Rev. Wesley Pruden of Little Rock, submitted several questions to the Little Rock board about a number of school policies if and when its plans for integration went into effect. The questions included the sensitive area of school social functions. The board procrastinated in supplying the answers.

DOING A TWOSOME
By Ficklen, Dallas Morning News   6/23/57

Partisan Republican politics danced all the way with the Brownell civil rights bill. Politics seemed to be the sponsors' main concern. Some of the Democrats were equally political in dealing with the matter.

CENTRALIZED GOVT.

HE'S NOT GETTING ANY SMALLER!

STATES RIGHTS

AND RESPONSIBILITIES

GOVERNORS

IKE

A WORD TO THE WISE
By Kennedy, Ark. Democrat   6/26/57

President Eisenhower in his address at the June meeting of the National Governors' Conference in Colonial Williamsburg, Virginia, made one of the strongest states rights speeches I have ever heard. He warned the governors of a growing centralized national government that was eating up the rights and responsibilities of state and local governments.

Unless the trend was halted, he said, some day the states would have no rights left at all. They would be mere vassals of an all-powerful central government with all decisions and administration of affairs emanating from Washington.

SEN. ANDERSON

SEN. O'MAHONEY

SEN. MORSE

IKE

CIVIL RIGHTS INSURANCE POLICY

BROWNELL AGENCY

SEN. MUNDT

OH, I DIDN'T SEE THE FINE PRINT . . .
By Baldy, Atlanta Constitution   7/18/57

Senators Mundt, Morse, O'Mahoney and Anderson — along with President Ike, found Brownell's civil rights bill much more severe than they had thought.

The measure, a Brownell product, was punitive, extreme, unfair, and patently unconstitutional in many respects, one being the deprivation of citizens of the right of trial by jury, and another that it applied only to a certain region — the South — and finally only to certain states in the South. The bill authorized the use of federal troops to enforce federal court orders, which was strictly forbidden in the Federal Code.

Mayor Woodrow **MANN**

continues drive to raze un-safe buildings in L.R.

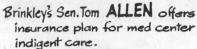

Brinkley's Sen. Tom **ALLEN** offers insurance plan for med center indigent care.

Sen. **M⁺CLELLAN** —

addresses Legion Convention.... receives highest Legion award.

Segregationist Amis **GUTHRIDGE**

suggests 'small building' for students wishing to integrate at Little Rock.

Arch **FORD**

had to wield economy ax on state school budget.

Bruce **BENNETT**

'discovered' $3,000,000 fund for highway dept.

Gov. **FAUBUS**

his views made news on many subjects — road crisis, segregation, med center, Pine Bluff's future, etc.

Chancellor Guy E. **WILLIAMS**

signed injunction against med center 'quota system'.

Jerry **SCREETON**

asked special session for road dilemma.

WHO'S DOING WHAT IN ARKANSAS! By Kennedy, Ark. Democrat, 7/21/57

MORE NEW INDUSTRIES

Towns where industries announced new locations in June were England, Clarendon and Springdale.

State tax collections were up $7 million for the past fiscal year.

TIME TO BREAK IT UP!
By Kennedy, Ark. Democrat   7/10/57

By failing to fill the vacancy created by the retirement of Federal Judge Trimble, the Eisenhower administration allowed a great backlog of cases to build up in the federal courts. This gave Brownell opportunity to send northern federal judges into Arkansas at will.

TEXAS BAR CRITICIZES COURT

In a resolution the Texas Bar Association urged the appointment of experienced judges and lawyers to the Supreme Court and deplored "the tendency of the Supreme Court to depart from judicial precedent in interpreting the Constitution."

On July 16 Sen. Harry Byrd (D-Va.) severely criticized Chief Justice Earl Warren and likened him to a Reconstruction era type lawyer.

On July 17 this news item appeared:

IKE RULES OUT
TROOP-FORCED DESEGREGATION

President Eisenhower said today he can not imagine any circumstance which would induce him to enforce desegregation through use of troops.

On July 27 former President Truman in a statement on Herbert Brownell said bluntly, "He's no good."

FOUR AREAS OF CONTENTION OR TROUBLE

Four continuing problems, all related, completely dominated the news in Arkansas during the month of July. They were (1) the integration problems in Arkansas and across the South, (2) the Knoxville, Tennessee trials of 16 citizens charged with contempt of federal court orders in the anti-integration demonstrations at Clinton, (3) racial troubles including violence in areas outside the South, (4) and the battle in the Congress over the Brownell civil rights bill.

FATAL FASCINATION
By Kennedy, Ark. Democrat   7/21/57

"Vote seeking" was the main idea when Brownell wrote the civil rights bill and conned the President into supporting it in the Congress. Other than measures proposed during the Reconstruction era following the Civil War, the Brownell civil rights bill was considered by many to be the most severe and unfair piece of legislation ever given serious consideration by the Congress.

THE CIVIL RIGHTS BILL; FULBRIGHT OPPOSES

In the civil rights struggle the House passed the bill as written by Brownell. When it reached the Senate it was subjected to closer study and more determined opposition.

A headline on July 10 read: "Fulbright Barrage Opens Senate Fight on Civil Rights Bill." Senator Fulbright said in his argument that the Constitution in four different places sought to guarantee the right of trial by jury, and that Congress was being asked to give up this right for the South.

The Arkansas senator stated that the GOP bill was designed to apply to only certain states in the South, which made it not only unconstitutional but patently unfair.

Senator Richard Russell of Georgia, long recognized as an authority on the Constitution, conferred with President Eisenhower, hopeful for changes in the measure. Others called for compromise but the supporters of the measure labeled the calls "premature."

Senator Karl E. Mundt (R-S.D.) joined Russell in a move to restrict the civil rights enforcement provisions by removing the authority to use the armed forces equipped with tanks and bayonets.

Senator McClellan attacked the bill as a "concealed device" to force racial integration. He termed the measure the "most blatant example of legislation by subterfuge ever presented to the Senate."

The Southerners were joined by other Senators outside the region who could see the dangers in the extreme provisions of the measure. The liberal Senator Clinton P. Anderson (D-N.M.) said the bill was too stringent.

The liberal Senators O'Mahoney (D-Wyo.), Church (D Idaho) and Kefauver (D-Tenn.) sponsored the amendment to remove from the bill the denial of a trial by jury, and the progressive Senator Henry Jackson (D-Wash.) agreed to back the amendment.

McCLELLAN PROPOSES BILL APPLY TO COMMUNISTS

In the debate on the jury trial amendment Senator McClellan proposed that if it were not adopted and the jury trial denial remained in the bill that it also apply to Communists as well as Southerners. Supporters of the bill opposed the McClellan proposal thus truly proving their hypocracy. They would deny the right of a trial by jury to loyal Americans charged with contempt of a federal court ruling, but guarantee the right to Communists who would destroy our form of government with all its rights and the nation itself.

President Eisenhower said he opposed the jury trial amendment. Many were now convinced he was merely issuing statements handed to him by Brownell.

As the month ended the opponents of the punitive provisions of the Civil Rights Bill were gaining but the battle continued.

JULY 4 ARKANSAS PICNIC, FULLERTON, CALIF.

From the National Governors' Conference in Virginia we traveled by automobile to Little Rock where I conducted affairs of the governor's office for several days. Then with others I drove to Fullerton, Calif. to attend the Arkansas July 4 picnic.

Attending the picnic were some relatives and many friends, former associates and acquaintances from my school teaching days and service as a county official at Huntsville. Many of them lived in the Fullerton area but others had driven long distances to renew acquaintance with me. It was a pleasant visit with many of them.

During all this time it was difficult to remove from my mind the problem of those on death row in the Arkansas State Prison whose death sentences must soon be finally determined by me. And there was approaching the opening date of Central High School in Little Rock with the impending potential of violence which could result in property destruction, injury to individuals and possibly death to more individuals than were involved on death row.

During this time I was suffering periodically from internal pain. Even before departing from Virginia I had left a conference session one day to seek relief from a physician there. The medicine he prescribed was not effective.

On the journey to Little Rock from Fullerton the internal pain became intolerable, and we telephoned to Little Rock for a private plane to meet us. I flew into Little Rock arriving at night, and the next morning entered the Baptist Medical Center under the care of Dr. T.J. Raney.

Extensive tests were conducted but no internal ailment was disclosed. No reason for the severe, internal pain could be found.

My legislative adviser, Bill Smith of Little Rock, visited me in the hospital. He later related that I said to him "Bill, they can't find anything wrong with me. I guess there are just too many people in the death house at the prison."

Although not completely aware of the circumstance at the time the statement was basically true.

VISIT TO THE FOWLERS AND THE BUFFALO RIVER COUNTRY

After leaving the hospital we accepted the invitation of Bill Fowler to visit in his home in the rugged mountains of western Newton County and "get away from it all" for a time. He had a beautiful six-acre mountain top lake stocked with fish, he said, where we could fish and relax as long as we liked.

The Fowler home is located under the shadow of a looming mountain beside the upper reaches of the Buffalo River. There could be no exaggeration of the wild beauty of the region. Bill's wife, the former Nina Lee Duty, was a fine hostess and an excellent cook. Bill's parents who lived near by were the old time, friendly, neighborly, helpful, independent mountaineers, the last representatives of a declining breed without which the mountains will never again be the same. Mrs. Fowler's widowed mother, Mrs. Orpha Duty, lived nearby and came to visit and help her daughter with the duties of hostess. She herself was the daughter of a one-time powerful political leader who had served the county as a state senator and was likewise known as an intellectual of the mountain region.

There were four of us in the visiting party including Mack and Irene Sturgis. I learned later they had all agreed to be cautious about food so I would partake of nothing that would hurt me. I think most everyone was convinced that I had some serious as yet undiscovered internal ailment.

We arrived at the Fowler home in the late afternoon. The next day when the others arose I was still sleeping in the cool of the morning. They quietly had breakfast and departed for the lake. When I awoke instead of feeling gratitude for their consideration of my welfare I was angered that they had left me. (I guess it's that prevailing fisherman's urge to be in the lead or at the least with an even start in a fishing endeavor).

I went to the lake, was put in a boat and, for the first time in my life began to use a fly rod. With Sturgis instructing from the nearby bank I fished along a wooded shoreline. Soon I got a strike. I jerked with such force that the small sun fish came flying out of the water and high over my head, landing the length of my line to the rear of the boat.

Mack Sturgis almost collapsed with laughter at my effort, which didn't detract from my foul mood. I recall having the thought that it was good he was on shore as he might have fallen overboard from a boat. When he could settle down, Mack instructed me further in the use of the fly rod — the proper wrist and forearm action rather than the use of the entire arm and body.

In the weeks to come I became almost as skillful in the use of the fly rod as Sturgis himself, who was one of the best amateur fishermen I have ever seen.

We remained with the Fowlers for three or four days, visiting Bat Cave, exploring the upper reaches of the Buffalo River and picnicing in Lost Valley. The whole area had a pervading quiet, calm and tranquil atmosphere and was indescribably beautiful. Although I was supposed to be on a careful diet because of my internal pain, before the stay was ended I was consuming biscuits and gravy, fried chicken and corn on the cob without any ill effects.

From that time I began the diagnosis of my ailment. The inner pain, indigestion and dialation of the stomach was brought on by prolonged tension. If I could get away from the problems and the boiling turmoil of official decisions, to a quiet, tranquil place next to nature with a few compatible friends, the tension would go away, my intestinal tract would relax and I would be at ease at peace with the world.

It was about this time that Sturgis and Tandy Rush, a Game & Fish Commission agent, introduced me to the float trips on the middle and lower reaches of the Buffalo. Tandy was an expert with a canoe. So on my first trip I was put in one of the light craft with him. As I soon learned he was famous for his almost continuous soothing comments to his companion and his calm approach to the rapids as he dexterously guided the craft on its smooth downstream journey.

As our canoe entered the first rapid Tandy commented about a large boulder which protruded above the foaming water. "See that boulder to your left? I'll bet it has upset many canoes. It could sure turn us over if we should hit it." It appeared we would pass safely to the right when the current somehow plunged the canoe against the protruding stone. The next instant we were in the swift, foaming stream, the canoe was filled with water and much of our fishing gear scattered. In some manner, I don't know how, I landed on my feet and got wet only to the waist. We frantically grabbed for floating items of gear and then guided the canoe to the shallows where we emptied it of water. We tried to get this done before being seen by the others but some of the party rounded a bend and observed us before we could get re-floated.

Later when we were having a mid-afternoon lunch Mack said, "Tandy, I know I told you to turn him (meaning me) over, but I didn't think you'd do it on the first shoal." After that first mishap, Tandy and I never had a canoe upset again.

I noticed that Tandy was not amused and his face wore a look of concern. Later he remonstrated with Mack about the remark. He feared that I would believe Mack and think the upset was intentional. After all, it was our first meeting and he didn't want to begin our acquaintance with a bad impression on my part.

In the years which followed, in my many trips to the Buffalo I seldom visited the beautiful valley without Tandy Rush as one of my companions. I grew as accustomed to his pleasant, inoffensive chatter as to the calming murmur of the stream. Tandy seemed as peaceful in temperament and spirit as the tranquil, smoothly flowing river. Somehow the man and the river seemed to go together, and all others were visitors.

The Buffalo River became my medicine, my physician, my healer in the turbulent months which followed for me in the governor's office. It would be difficult, if not impossible, to describe the pleasures or the benefits to me of the hours spent with my companions in negotiating the quiet stretches and the rushing rapids, or asleep on the quiet banks with the stream's murmur broken only by the call of the whippoorwills and the occasional hoot of an owl.

HIGHWAY DILEMMA

In late July 1957 my administration faced several major problems.

The Highway Department claimed a shortage of funds and talked of cancelling contracts and stopping work on road projects already under way. A close examination of Department finances disclosed the problem was not serious and it soon faded away.

Criticism arose over my delay in making appointments to the Sovereignty Commission. The appointments were made and that matter was settled.

The anti-integration pressure was a more menacing problem. Meetings had been held throughout the state to organize resistance to federally ordered integration. In some rural communities with racial problems, almost the entire white population turned out and cried for resistance with a zeal unmatched in the state's history.

THE PRESSURE IS ON
By Kennedy, Ark. Democrat   7/28/57

Twenty two years after "the pressure was on Orval" in the summer of 1957, the pressure has shifted to Boston, Detroit, Louisville, Cleveland, Chicago and other places, many of them outside the South.

SHEATHING THE BAYONET
By Graham, Ark. Gazette   6/24/57

FEDERAL TROOP USE PROHIBITED

By a vote of 90 to 0 the U.S. Senate removed from the Civil Rights Bill the "Reconstruction language" which authorized the use of troops to enforce federal court orders.

The action was taken, the amendment sponsors said, to "remove the fear of Southerners of the use of bayonets" in their region.

Months before the Little Rock crisis erupted Brownell had written this bill with the extreme provisions, one for the use of troops in the South and another depriving Southerners of the right of trial by jury. The U.S. Senate removed both provisions.

✳ INTEGRATION PROBLEMS IN ARKANSAS

The integration problems in Arkansas now began to surface at a number of points.

On July 1 I was faced with a demand from the Citizens' Councils for continued segregation. The demand was based on the laws of the state and the provisions of the state constitution requiring separation of the races in the schools and other facilities. Two sections of the constitution required the separation, one in the original 1874 Constitution, the other the Johnson Amendment adopted at the general election of 1956.

None of the state segregation laws had been specifically declared invalid by any court, and the constitutional provisions were still unchallenged by any litigation.

From the legal standpoint of state law the segregationists had an unassailable argument. Almost daily I was now faced with the question, by personal query or letter, "Are you going to uphold state laws and the state constitution, or yield to illegal federal court rulings when Congress has passed no law in conflict with our own?"

The U.S. Supreme Court had based its integration decision on the 14th Amendment. However people familiar with the amendment could cite language from it which said, "Congress shall have power to implement this amendment by legislation." The Congress had not acted. Therefore, contended the states rights advocates, the state laws still prevailed, and the invasion of the rights of the states by the federal courts without prior sanction of the Congress was entirely illegal.

Truly it was a sorely perplexing position in which I found myself. I was caught between the rulings, legal or illegal, of the powerful federal courts backed by an all powerful federal government on the one hand, and on the other the clear provisions of state law and the constitution backed by an overwhelming majority of my constituents.

My policy of permitting integration of local schools, and of privately owned publicly operated facilities as bus and rail lines, was already established and well known. For this I was severely attacked by my major opponents in the 1956 campaign. Clearly my opponents were right in charging that this policy was not strictly in compliance with state law.

However, in facing the realities of the situation — the changing times, the diversity of the state, the anti-South sentiment in some sections, the power of the federal courts and the national government — reasonable people understood that under such circumstances my position was perhaps more acceptable and defensible than the extreme position of the die-hard segregationists.

The situation contained another factor of no little significance. On the national level President Eisenhower was a layman of no great knowledge of law or the Constitution. Consequently he was subject to misuse by unscrupulous advisers. Unfortunately his legal advisor, Attorney General Brownell, seemed to have no concern for the law, the Constitution or the sentiment of the people. As the legal questions developed to great importance, it became clear that Brownell's motives were solely political. His purpose was to do something, legal or illegal, to capture for the Republicans the minority bloc vote in more than a dozen key Eastern and Northern States. His ultimate motive was to assure a political victory for the GOP in the next election.

It was on that basis that the Attorney General was even then mis-advising a trusting and perhaps well-meaning president on the civil rights bill.

As to my position on the integration question in Arkansas, it was perhaps more philosophical than legal so far as state law was concerned. I believe with Thomas Jefferson when he wrote:

"The way to have good and safe government is not to trust it all to one, but to divide it among the many, distributing to every one exactly the functions he is competent to. Let the national government be entrusted with the defense of the nation, and its foreign and federal relations; *the State governments with the civil rights, laws, police, and administration of what concerns the State generally; the counties with the local concerns of the counties, and each ward direct the interests within itself.* It is by dividing and subdividing these republics from the great national one down through all its subordinations, that all will be done for the best. What has destroyed liberty and the rights of man in every government which has ever existed under the sun? The generalizing and concentrating all cares and powers into one body."

According to Jefferson's philosophy the people should have the right to choose for themselves as to local issues and the right would include the control of local schools.

I believe with Abraham Lincoln when he wrote:

"My faith in the proposition that each man should do precisely as he pleases with all which is exclusively his own lies at the foundation of the sense of justice there is in me. I extend the principle to communities of men as well as to individuals. I so extend it because it is politically wise, as well as naturally just: politically wise in saving us from broils about matters which do not concern us."

Certainly in these utterances Jefferson and Lincoln had in mind school districts as well as states. It is equally certain that neither great man ever envisioned the day when a bureaucrat in Washington or a distant federal judge would direct the most minute details of a school district's affairs thousands of miles away.

OTHER INTEGRATION DEVELOPMENTS IN JULY

On July 2 the Ozark school board announced its intention to integrate the high school at the beginning of the new term.

On July 9 I was criticized for delay in naming the three remaining appointees to the Sovereignty Commission. On July 26 a law suit was filed by two known segregationists to force me to make the appointments.

Attorney Amis Guthridge, representing the Citizens' Councils, made a request of the Little Rock School Board on July 10 for a school for white students. He followed up with a proposal that the Board establish three types of schools as to race — for blacks, for whites, and the third racially mixed for those who wished, or had no objection, to attending an integrated school.

Guthridge contended that under the Blossom plan the black students had a choice while the white students were trapped without a choice.

On July 28 the school board rejected Guthridge's proposal. Guthridge replied, "While the school board and its lawyers are writing to me the explicit statement that no new segregated school could be established, they are establishing one right now, the new all-white Hall High School in the Pulaski Heights area." Many district patrons agreed with Attorney Guthridge's statement.

—0—

HOFFA ACQUITTED; PALMER DIES; HAYS MENTIONED FOR FEDERAL JUDGE

Other news reported the acquittal of James Hoffa in a trial in federal court in Tennessee, and that he would probably become national president of the Teamsters Union.

C.E. Palmer, prominent newspaper owner and publisher, whose newspapers had called on me to withdraw from the 1954 campaign, died in Texarkana.

Brooks Hays was reported in the running for appointment as a federal judge.

—0—

RACE RIOT IN CHICAGO

Race riots flared in Chicago on July 28 in which 20 were injured in the first day's fighting. The injured numbered 42 on the second day. Then on the 30th a task force of hundreds of police and other enforcement officers moved into the area to control the situation.

—0—

RIGHTS BILL AIM TO GET NEGRO VOTE
by Charles O. Gridley
(Washington columnist)

(Arkansas Democrat, Aug. 18, 1957)

The dimming prospects for a civil rights bill at this session of Congress does not obscure the fact that the bill itself has become a political pawn.

It has been clearly revealed that the Eisenhower administration planned it that way, in a calculated bid for Negro votes in 14 Northern states with large Negro populations.

Only the fact that a number of GOP senators refused to go along with the proposal in its original form prevented final approval of the House version, which was drafted by the Department of Justice (Brownell).

(The House version contained the "bayonet use" provision and no trial by jury.)

* * *

APPOINTMENTS, JULY 1957

Truman Baker, Searcy, to Game and Fish Commission. Don Montgomery, El Dorado; and James D. Reynolds, Camden, to Oil and Gas Commission. W. D. Howard, Springdale, Municipal Judge. W. L. "Bill" Ward, Jr., Marianna, Municipal Judge. Rocky Dunn, Conway, Athletic Commission. Council to advise on Vo-Tech Schools: Sen. Boss Mitchell of Danville; Representative John P. Bethel of Des Arc, author of the act creating the trade school program; Lewis J. "Red" Johnson, Farmers Union leader of Little Rock; Mrs. Dorothy Meyers of Monticello; Stanley McNulty of Pine Bluff; Ray Howard of Magnolia; and Bill Williams, labor leader of Little Rock. Sovereignty Commission: J. L. "Bex" Shaver, Wynne, prominent attorney and former lieutenant governor; Dr. Joe Rushton, Magnolia, prominent physician, businessman and civic leader; Connie Fields, Shirley, merchant, REA co-op director, former big league baseball player.

TIME TO SURVEY THE FENCE LINE
By Knox, Nashville Banner   8/7/57

The fear that Thomas Jefferson expressed — the usurpation of power by the federal judiciary thus throwing out of balance the division of powers between the three branches of government — is here vividly illustrated.

The U.S. Supreme Court has usurped authority clearly reserved to the states by the Constitution. The Court has forbidden the states to exercise authority over education including Bible reading and prayer in public schools, and also over capital punishment, pornography, disorderly demonstrations, abortions and subversion.

Millions of people believe it is time to resurvey that fence line, if there is ever a Congress with guts enough to defend its own property and the rights of the states.

MISCELLANEOUS

Harold Jenks of Piggott was hired by the Democratic National Committee to do party work. My friend and early supporter, John C. Sheffield, was elected mayor of Helena; Conway was selected as the site for the new Children's Colony for the care and training of mentally retarded children; a lingerie manufacturing plant decided to locate at Ratcliffe, a small crossroads settlement in south Franklin county, where it could draw its 400 employees from eight neighboring towns and the rural country side.

Casey Laman defeated Reed Thompson in the runoff primary for Mayor of North Little Rock and went on to become the city's most progressive long time leader. Mayor Almand Perry was eliminated in the preferential primary and later joined my administration.

SOME ARE STILL WAILING, By Knox, Nashville Banner, 8/9/57

The U.S. Senate amended the civil rights bill by removing the extreme provisions for the use of federal troops to enforce court orders, and the denial of trial by jury. The action provoked the outcry from the Northern liberals.

The House in Washington boosted postal rates from three to four cents for first class mail; Pulaski County real estate tax assessment value was boosted 50 per cent in a reappraisal with the assistance of the state reassessment agency; ground-breaking was held for a new plant at Clarendon with dirt being turned by Mayor Flynn Chivers and me; Jonesboro got the new Colson industry.

Press reports said Brooks Hays, president of the Southern Baptist Association, was eyeing a mission to Red Russia.

———

WHO ME?
By Knox, Nashville Banner   8/9/67

For years all civil rights measures enacted by the Congress were aimed at the South.

Any civil rights bill applicable to all sections of the nation never got past the inconsistent Northern liberals. Among the few exceptions among the liberals was Senator Abraham Ribicoff of Connecticut who, although not on the scene at the time, later openly advocated that such laws be nationwide in application. His pleas for fairness went unheeded.

SOUTH MUST ACCEPT RACIAL INTEGRATION, CHANCELLOR ASSERTS

Chancellor Lee Ward of Paragould on August 20 in a speech to students at Arkansas State College at Jonesboro, asserted the South must accept racial integration.

Ward was an excellent speaker, well-informed on public affairs and prominent in veterans affairs. He was a past Arkansas Department Commander of the American Legion.

Press reports left the impression that Ward meant the South must accept because integration was now the "law of the land" by virtue of the Supreme Court ruling. Critics said he ignored the 9th and 10th amendments of the Bill of Rights, and the admission acts of the states to the Union. The press reports also indicated that Ward favored integration.

The speech was widely covered in the news. Though an able man, Ward never won another election. He was defeated in races for the Democratic nomination for governor, for renomination as chancellor and for nomination to Congress.

RIGHTS BILL TANGLED UP IN CONGRESS
by James Marlow,
Associated Press News Analyst

(Arkansas Democrat, Aug. 20, 1957)

This is an ABC on how the civil rights bill got caught in a political wringer. It will be lucky if it comes out alive.

The House debated it 14 days, then the Senate a month before passing it. The House voted the kind of a bill the Eisenhower administration asked for. The Senate made drastic changes.

In the House an overwhelming number of Republicans, with a majority of Democrats, put it over against the opposition of Southern Democrats. From a political standpoint this was good business for the Republicans.

With both parties anxious for the Northern Negro vote in the 1958 and 1960 elections, Republicans could rightly say after the House vote: "We far outnumbered the Democrats in getting this bill through."

The Republicans got the jump on the Democrats in the Senate, too, by leading the way to consideration of the bill. But there one of the bill's main sections — No. 3 — was knocked out.

This section would let the government step into all kinds of civil rights cases, not just those involving voting rights. A majority of Democrats voted for this, a majority of Republicans against.

Republicans could argue rightly the Democrats had weakened the bill. The water gets muddy here . . .

CIVIL RIGHTS BILL AIMED AT
GETTING THE NEGRO VOTE
column by Stewart Alsop, August 22, 1957

Behind the shifting, complex, often fascinating drama of the struggle over civil rights, there is one simple political reality — the Negro vote in the key industrial states in the North.

That is, of course, in hard political terms, what the fight has been all about.

WHAT IS HARLEM'S REACTION
TO THE CIVIL RIGHTS BILL?
by Stewart Alsop

(Arkansas Democrat, Aug. 24, 1957)

This enormous Negro city-within-a-city is now in the process of making up its collective mind on the following question: Which party, Republican or Democratic, deserves most credit or blame for its role in the civil rights fight?

An increasing number are giving credit specifically to Vice President Richard Nixon. The new popularity of Nixon among the Harlemites was, indeed, the phenomenon which most impressed both Harris (the pollster) and this reporter. . . .

Of all the people we talked to, in all our weary hours of doorbell pushing, there was exactly one who had the slightest interest in, or understanding of, the disputed jury trial amendment. . . .

Civil rights is not the only issue which will determine how Harlem makes up its mind.

Especially in the tenements, there are many people who hardly bother their heads about civil rights, and who wax passionate instead about such matters as housing, rents, and above all, rising prices.

It was now becoming clear that Brownell and his fellow architects of the Reconstruction-era type civil rights bill had failed in their efforts to capture the Northern Negro vote by their sponsorship of the measure. The Democrats were now gaining the upper hand by calling for the passage of the amended bill, while the Republicans were threatening a presidential veto if it passed.

In such a situation, smarting from their defeat and frustrated by their failure to gain the Northern Negro vote by the use of such legislative tactics, would not Brownell and his allies welcome an opportunity to accomplish their original aim by some more dramatic move, even though illegal, if the opportunity presented itself?

⋆━◦━━◦━━◦━⋆

FAUBUS NOT TO HEAR GOVERNOR GRIFFIN

Governor Marvin Griffin of Georgia, and States Rights leader Roy V. Harris, also of Georgia, were scheduled to appear at the Capital Citizens' Council $10 per plate fund-raising dinner at the Marion Hotel August 22.

I had three engagements already scheduled for that day. One meeting, arranged by Assistant Adjutant General Bill Page and County Judge Paul J. Daugherty of Monroe County, was scheduled at the same time as Governor Griffin's speech.

I gave this information to the press and told them I had invited the Georgia Governor and his party to be my guests at the Mansion for the overnight stay, that the Governor had accepted and arrangements had been made to meet him and his party on arrival. I would return to the Mansion that night and would have breakfast there with Governor Griffin and Mr. Harris the next morning.

I had twice been in touch with Governor Griffin. I called him once to apprise him of the delicacy of the sensitive situation developing in Little Rock, and of the increasing rumors of possible disorder.

I then cautioned the governor about any remarks in his speech or press conferences that might unduly inflame the situation. The Governor replied, "We're just going to feed 'em the Constitution, Governor."

I called Governor Griffin later to explain that I could not meet him on his arrival, but that my aides would be there to accompany him to the Executive Mansion.

⋆━◦━━◦━━◦━⋆

Griffin Vows to Maintain Segregation
by Jerry Dhonau
(Arkansas Gazette, August 23, 1957)

Governor Marvin Griffin of Georgia vowed to segregationists at Little Rock last night that the public schools of his state would not be integrated as long as he was governor.

He said that constitutional government . . . would be dead "if the South surrenders her schools to the operation of the federal government."

"This issue," he said, "is the issue that overshadows all other questions" in the controversy over integration.

He described the Georgia plan for preventing integration to . . . an appreciative audience which numerous times interrupted with applause, rebel shouts and "Amens."

PARK CAN SPONSOR PETIT JEAN AIRPORT, ATTORNEY GENERAL RULES

Winthrop Rockefeller wished to construct an airport near his farm on grounds of the state-owned Petit Jean State Park. If the State Publicity and Parks Department would sponsor the project, half the cost of the project would be met with federal funds. Rockefeller would put up the other half for construction and then maintain the airport. The state would get at no cost, a modern airstrip capable of handling jet aircraft. Rockefeller would get a modern airstrip and other facilities at half price and could charge off for tax purposes the amount he spent as a contribution to the state, and pay no taxes on the airport facilities because they were owned by the state. I thought it was a very good arrangement for all concerned and approved the project. However, I didn't fully agree with those who praised Rockefeller for his generosity in the matter. The arrangement greatly reduced his expense for airport service at his mountain residence.

Attorney General Bruce Bennett ruled on August 3 that the plan was legal.

⋆━◦━━◦━━◦━⋆

STICKS TO TEXT

Mr. Griffin deviated little from his prepared text. . . .

He said that Georgia's Private School Plan had been established after the state legislature recently adopted an amendment to the state constitution to allow the legislature to regulate schools through control of school funds.

"Under this program if, as, and when the federal government prohibits operation of the public schools in a particular school district in accordance with the present homogeneous method of separate education, all authority to continue public schools in that district is abolished," Governor Griffin said.

GRANTS TO PARENTS

The Georgia legislative program provides for "an adequate system of grants" from state and local funds to the parents of all children, on an equal basis, for the education of their children, Mr. Griffin explained.

He said that under this legislation the education "will be committed to the people themselves." The system, he said, "will continue as long as the people desire" and "the integrity of the two races in Georgia will be maintained."

The governor called the 1954 Supreme Court ruling an "unconstitutional, unlawful decree." Its effect has not been felt in Georgia yet, he said, and "that fact is no mere accident."

"The determined and cooperative efforts of a dedicated people, a steadfast General Assembly and an administration committed unequivocally toward preservation of our cherished institutions — all of these working in concert have stemmed the tide," Mr. Griffin declared.

Governor Griffin's hearers confidently believed the plan of tuition grants to all students on an equal basis outlined by the Governor, was clearly legal, constitutional and within the right of Georgia to adopt and operate. If it were necessary they believed Arkansas could adopt the same or a similar plan that could be successfully used to thwart court ordered integration.

The Supreme Court later ruled otherwise but Griffin's hearers did not know then that it would.

HOW THEY DO US FAVORS
By Knox, Nashville Banner   8/14/57

The source of federal taxes is the people in the local communities. The money is drained from the people to Washington and then is handed back as federal aid funds. With federal funds, giving back to the people their own money - come federal rules and regulations often contrary to the people's wishes and best interests. The process is also expensive because of the increased cost of administration.

INTEGRATION RESISTANCE IS URGED
Arkansas Democrat, Aug. 23, 1957

The South was called upon to resist integration decisions by "every legal means" and to take "full page advertisements in all national magazines to sell the nation on the correctness of our stand and our way of life."

The challenge came . . . from Governor Griffin and Georgia publisher Roy V. Harris . . .

Griffin declared that the integration decisions of the U.S. Supreme Court were not "expressions of law and order but an attempt by naked force to destroy our government itself. It is anarchy."

. . . Governor Griffin said, "I think it is poor taste and bad judgment for states without the [racial] problem to tell us how to solve it. I say to them that they may catch it next on some other issue. They're trying to do it to us this time, but they probably will be next."

VOTES, NOT RIGHTS, . . . THE REAL CONCERN
By Paige, Source unknown   8/23/57

While Ike golfed the Republicans fished for Negro votes by sponsoring the Civil Rights Bill.

A significant fact about the voting rights bill should not be overlooked in relation to Arkansas. The new law which sent federal voting registrars into certain states did not apply to Arkansas. The state's record of permitting, even encouraging the exercise of the voting franchise by all citizens, made it exempt from the provisions of the new civil rights act.

"Constitutional government," he went on, "is being attacked on every front. Our rights are being destroyed by ruthless decisions of the supreme court which have, I believe, deliberately ignored the constitution."

The court decisions, he maintained, "ignored state constitutions and laws and 123 long established precedents of appellate courts. Instead it based its ruling on opinion of individuals, modern authorities in psychology, sociology and anthropology."

Both races, in Governor Griffin's opinion, "must preserve their integrity and identity." . . .

"We won't close our schools," he told the audience. "They will be closed by court order. If the public schools in Georgia are destroyed, the onus will be on the federal court and not on the people or state of Georgia."

He called it a time for "courageous action, because the liberties of men have never lasted long under a government of total power."

Draws Rebel Yells

Governor Griffin — whose speech brought the audience to its feet with rebel yells at several points — said that he was "talking out of my heart before this courageous group of Arkansas patriots who are fighting a dedicated battle to preserve the rights of states as set out in the constitution."

He expressed appreciation for the hospitality of Governor Faubus, who was absent because of a previous engagement. . . .

Mr. Harris declared that Governor Griffin is "ready with money and an organization" to begin advertising the position of the South in magazines with national circulation. . . .

Last night's audience represented many sections of the state including McGehee, Crossett, Hope, West Memphis, Scott and other cities.

*Jubilant Council Throng
Applauds Griffin for Speech*

(Arkansas Gazette, August 23, 1957)

About 350 handsomely dressed Arkansas segregationists gathered at Little Rock last night . . . at a $10-a-plate fund-raising dinner and the main speaker was Governor Griffin. . . .

. . . The meeting was slickly handled from start to finish, beginning with the distribution of literature in the lobby to Griffin's rousing remarks at the end.

The governor got a long standing ovation when he walked into the flag-draped ballroom. . . . Organist Tommy Scott of Little Rock struck up "Dixie."

. . . Before the heavy speaking started, Rev. L. D. Foreman, . . . master of ceremonies, introduced the president of a newly-formed organization, the Mothers' League of Central High School.

Mrs. O. R. Aaron . . . the president, went to the microphone and invited those attending to be at a rally at 8 p.m. today at the Hotel LaFayette.

Mrs. Aaron described the Mothers' League as an organization founded to "find ways and means to prevent integration of the races at Central High School and to provide a rallying-point for all parents who are like-minded."

. . . Rebel yells and applause greeted Griffin again when he arose to speak. His remarks were applauded at 18 different times, a couple of them standing. . . .

. . . Well-known pro-segregationists were in the crowd.

They included Charles F. "Rip" Smith, state senator from West Memphis; Joe Foster, chief of police at England; Herbert Brewer, who led the fight against the Hoxie School Board; and Robert Ewing Brown, president of the Capital Citizens' Council at Little Rock.

A familiar figure at the exit door when it was over was Jim Johnson of Crossett. . . .

Johnson tried to shake hands with everybody as they passed through the door. Phil Stratton of Crossett, his aide during (Johnson's) gubernatorial campaign, was standing nearby.

Stratton was asked if Johnson were "running again."

"He hasn't stopped running," Stratton said. "He knows how to win now." . . .

The head table at the dinner included Foreman, Little Rock Antioch Baptist Church Pastor, and Mrs. Foreman; Mrs. Aaron; Mr. L. D. Poynter, Pine Bluff, President of Citizens' Council of Arkansas; Reverend Wesley Pruden of Broadmoor Baptist Church; Mr. Harris; Major John King, Governor Griffin's executive aide; Travis Stewart, Governor's press secretary.

Griffin praised the Georgia and Arkansas U.S. Senators and Representatives — Brooks Hays was not excluded — for fighting the civil rights bill then being debated in Congress, and for their signing the Southern Manifesto. "Let's give them a big party when they come home," he said.

In speaking of some federally-supported programs, such as the school hot-lunch program, Griffin said: "If they [the Feds] try to tell us then to integrate the races, I will be compelled to tell them to get their blackeyed peas and soup pots and get out of Georgia." For this statement he got a standing ovation.

THE BREAKFAST AT THE MANSION

At the breakfast at the Mansion on the morning of August 23rd, the conversation was small talk. I recall that we discussed quail hunting in Georgia and Arkansas and duck hunting in Arkansas.

The Governor's speech and the meeting were not mentioned. Neither was the subject which was on everyone's mind — the segregation-integration problem. Mr. Harris later stated, "We thought Governor Faubus was on the other side, and we didn't want to embarrass him."

This is contrary to later speculation about the subjects discussed during Governor Griffin's visit. The speculation was completely erroneous. No strategy was discussed and neither of us was persuaded toward any course of action by the other. Therefore there were no plots, schemes, plans or conspiracies affecting the situation or the federal authorities, as was so often inferred by my critics in the months to come.

When our pleasant breakfast and small talk ended, Governor Griffin and his party were transported to the airport for the return flight to Georgia, and I returned to my usual duties.

SANCTUARY FOR REDS AND CRIMINALS, *By Knox, Nashville Banner, 8/26/57*

Many Americans believed the U.S. Supreme Court decisions had become a shelter for Communists and other subversive elements.

On August 24 the conviction of seven Communists had been overturned by the 10th Federal Circuit Court of Appeals at Denver. The Court said advocating overthrow of the government, even by force and violence, was not illegal.

IMPACT OF THE GRIFFIN SPEECH
ON THE STATE

The newspaper reports of the Citizens' Council sponsored meeting are quoted extensively because no one later could visualize the terrific impact of the Griffin speech and the meeting on the people of the state, without knowing what was said and the response.

The people learned that not a dent had been made in the long-established segregation patterns in Georgia. The effect of the so-called unconstitutional 1954 ruling of the U.S. Supreme Court on segregation had not been felt there and, Griffin told the audience, "that fact is no mere accident?"

The determined efforts of the people of Georgia, a steadfast General Assembly, and a state administration committed to the "preservation of our cherished institutions — all these working in concert have stemmed the tide," Griffin declared.

The facts, reasoned the anti-integrationists after hearing the speech, were clear. If the people worked together, as they had in Georgia, with the support of the Arkansas General Assembly, and an elected governor, the fight against court-ordered integration could be successful. If the lower federal courts persisted in pushing the illegal Supreme Court decision, then a system could be adopted, as it had been in Georgia, to provide tuition money to each student, making possible a system of education where each family would have control of the schooling of its children.

The segregationists also remembered, or were reminded by their leaders, that resistance by mass demonstrations to attempted integration a year before had been successful at Mansfield and Texarkana, Texas, Sturgis and Clay, Kentucky, and a number of other places. Success at some points had been achieved without the support of state authorities.

The segregationists were additionally encouraged by the violent demonstrations then underway at Levittown, Pa., against integrated housing. Many in the North, they reasoned, also had a dislike for the court ruling and would be sympathetic in their attitude.

The people also remembered that the entire Arkansas Congressional delegation had signed the Southern Manifesto, and had helped at that very time to remove the punitive provisions from Brownell's Reconstruction Era type civil rights bill. At that moment there was serious doubt that any civil rights bill at all would be passed in Washington. For their actions in both fields the Arkansas senators and congressmen, including Fulbright and Hays, were praised by Griffin in his speech.

The meeting attendants from all across the state went away with renewed confidence and renewed hope of success in resisting forcible integration. They carried Griffin's message to their friends and neighbors. The newspaper, radio and television reports carried the message to thousands more.

The news coverage included pictures of Griffin and Jim Johnson entering the meeting hall side by side.

What was the impression — even the conviction — that stemmed from the Griffin appearance in Little Rock and other events at the time?

It seemed crystal clear that where the people stood in determined opposition to the illegal Supreme Court decision, and had the support or co-operation of their elected school board, legislature and governor, they could be successful. If they — the people — did not have a school board, legislature or governor who would stand with them, they could obtain such through the ballot box. Then they could successfully oppose the federal court's illegal mandates.

Subsequent events revealed this not to be the case, but those events had not then occurred. With the overwhelming anti-Supreme Court sentiment prevailing at the time, together with other anti-integration developments, the great majority of people were ready to act — to resist.

The situation was not that clear to me, but I could read public sentiment and events.

These important questions were now raised in the minds of many people in the state who did not belong to the Citizens' Council. The council meeting in Little Rock and Governor Griffin's speech only served to highlight the questions and the problems.

NORTHERN JUDGE
ARRIVES FOR COURT TERM

Federal Judge Ronald N. Davies of Fargo, North Dakota, arrived in Little Rock to preside for an interem period on the federal bench. He would stay in Arkansas, it was announced on August 26, even if his own court term in North Dakota had to be postponed in December until the following year. Later events raised the question of whether or not the Justice Department was, by the announcement, trying to tell the people of Little Rock something in an indirectly intimidating manner.

STATE HOSPITAL PAY EQUALIZED BY GOVERNOR

A news story on August 1 reported that I had succeeded in my efforts to equalize the pay for employees of all races at the State Hospital.

_____

NEW MILITARY CHIEF

Major General Edwin A. Walker, assumed command yesterday (August 1) of the U.S. Army Arkansas Military District with headquarters at 417 West Second Street. He came to Little Rock from Hawaii where he had been artillery commander with the 25th Infantry Division. He held several commands in World War II and the Korean War. He succeeds Colonel D. A. Poorman, who became deputy chief of the Arkansas District.

This appeared to be an ordinary announcement of a routine change of station for a military officer. Was there more to the change than met the eye?

_____

CIVIL RIGHTS BILL CONDEMNED BY EDITORS; AMENDED AND PASSED BY SENATE

A gathering of editors from across the nation criticized the "secrecy" of the sponsors of the civil rights bill and condemned the measure as a definite step into autocracy. By a senate vote of 51-32 the bill was amended to assure a trial by jury. The amended bill was passed and sent to the President.

The big argument among liberals then became: who was entitled to the most credit with the minority bloc voters for passage of the measure, the Republicans or Democrats.

—0—

LITTLE ROCK INTEGRATION BECOMES MAIN NEWS INTEREST

Now the Little Rock integration-segregation controversy began to dominate the news.

On August 27 School Superintendent Virgil Blossom announced the entrance of Negro students in Central was delayed while the students awaited a briefing by him.

—0—

THE THOMASON CASE IS FILED

On August 28 a suit by Mrs. Clyde Thomason was filed in the court of Chancellor Murray O. Reed by her attorneys, Griffin Smith and Arthur G. Frankel. It requested a temporary injunction against the school board and Superintendent Blossom to prevent integration of Central High School. A news report in the *Gazette* said that if the temporary injunction were granted it "would be in effect until a ruling is made on the state's segregation laws."

Supt. Blossom revealed that "a meeting to discuss protection for Negroes entering Little Rock high schools" was to be held. Blossom said Mrs. Jo Ann Harrison, a member of a five-person Negro Parents Teachers Council Committee organized Sunday, had contacted him about such a meeting.

The Committee asked to meet with Blossom, Little Rock Police Chief Marvin H. Potts and Pulaski Sheriff Tom Gulley.

—0—

JOHN KASPER AGAIN

On August 29 the news said John Kasper, the trouble-making New York self-proclaimed segregationist, then free on bond at Nashville, Tenn., announced that he was coming to Little Rock. Immediately Citizens Council president Amis Guthridge said he was not welcome. L. D. Poynter of Pine Bluff said Kasper was not wanted in Arkansas. I issued a statement saying a Kasper visit to Arkansas would be "definitely detrimental."

The integrationists, or self-proclaimed "law of the land" leaders were silent.

—0—

GROUNDBREAKING FOR FARGO NEGRO GIRLS SCHOOL

On Aug. 29 I attended ground breaking ceremonies for new buildings for the Fargo Training School for Negro girls near Brinkley.

—0—

INTEREST IN LITTLE ROCK GROWS WIDESPREAD
The Premature Success Statements

Now newspaper editorials and news stories, statements of public figures and decisions in the Courts continued to spread the interest in the success or failure of integration at Central High School far beyond the district boundaries, far beyond the city in which the school was situated and even beyond the borders of the state.

Already Congressman Brooks Hays had stated earlier that Little Rock could become the pilot program for Arkansas and even the whole South in achieving school integration. There were many indications that Supt. Blossom, members of the school board and other promoters of integration had expected to become overnight heroes with immediate success of the Blossom plan. Now public comments and behind-the-scenes activity indicated they were not so sure of success.

But the movement that they had helped set in motion could not now be easily halted or delayed. It was bigger than any individual or group. Too many had become involved before the magnitude and gravity with attendant dangers became apparent to the little schemers as their dreams of glory engulfed their restricted view.

The black people, many of whom had been pushed and pulled into the integration scheme by other black leaders and the white advocates, would not now easily be denied. They could not be justly blamed. Not only had they been encouraged; they had been given flat, unequivocal promises of success. They now had every right to expect fulfillment of those commitments, not by the opponents of integration but by those white advocates who had induced them into the situation.

On August 30, the *Southern Mediator Journal* of Little Rock, a newspaper for black people published and edited by E. H. Jones, said in a front page editorial:

> "The integration of Negroes in the twin city high schools this fall, . . . will in all probability be the crucial test of integration and it will also set the pattern for Arkansas and possibly the entire South."

> "[The] Little Rock School Board is definitely committed to go forward with the program of gradual integration. . . ."

> ". . . Negro students will enter Central High School this fall because . . . the Federal Government has spoken."

The banner headline in the *Journal* stretching all the way across the front page read: "Anger and Threats Mar School Opening. Police Protection Asked Against Possible Violence."

In reference to this danger Editor Jones wrote in his editorial:

> "It is the responsibility of those in high office and high places including the School Board to see that we have peaceful and orderly integration. We have been promised that protection. We want it."

> "Little Rock is the testing ground for integration in the State, and if we fail here, it could have serious repercussion upon the general program of integration."

An editorial in the same issue of the *Journal* by Fred C. Byrd, quoted Supt. Blossom as he spoke to a group of black citizens the previous Sunday. Although there was no real reason to do so, Blossom had kept his attendance at the meeting a secret. Byrd quoted Editor Ashmore in his writing, and went on to give some very sound advice to his black readers pertaining to the school integration situation. He recognized the situation was of greater significance than Central High School when he wrote:

> "The world watches, the region waits, our

neighboring cities wonder — the pivotal point is how we do our part."

The black leaders honestly recognized both the significance and gravity of the situation. The white advocates, including the federal judge, continued to delude themselves and falsify the situation.

DALE ALFORD TAKES PUBLIC STAND; SAYS INTEGRATION SHOULD WAIT

For the first time Dr. Dale Alford, a member of the Little Rock School Board, took a public stand on the segregation-integration issue. He said that to "preserve the domestic tranquility" and the "public school system," integration should wait.

School board president Dr. William G. Cooper, Jr., said "There is nothing we can do." Wayne Upton replied, "It's in the hands of the courts." Blossom said, "No comment." R. A. Lile said that "we are abiding by court decisions." Henry V. Rath and Harold Engstrom, Jr., had no comment.

News reports quoted Alford as saying "I have always believed that segregation in our elementary and secondary schools was far better for the Negro and white children in this section of our country. My belief in this matter is still the same."

"The people of our sovereign state passed laws regulating our conduct in regard to this question. I will have to abide by the laws as voted by the people of Arkansas."

Alford also stated that a very explosive situation prevailed in the community over the integration controversy, which was another reason the matter should be delayed, as well as the conflicting state and federal laws.

August 31, 1957

U.S. WILL NOT HELP PRESERVE ORDER IF VIOLENCE BREAKS OUT AT CENTRAL HIGH, FAUBUS SAYS

by George Douthit, Democrat Staff Writer

Governor Faubus charged today that the federal government is unable or unwilling to help preserve order at the integration of Central High School here Tuesday.

". . . They are going to make us handle the enforcement of their own orders," the chief executive said hotly.

He said about a month ago he asked the Department of Justice to send someone to talk to him. This past week the agent, Arthur B. Caldwell, a former Arkansan, called on the governor. . . .

"I had about an hour's conference with this man," the governor said. "My main concern was to find out what, if anything, could be expected from the federal government in the way of assistance if disorder occurred."

"He (Caldwell) reviewed the court procedures and ended up by saying . . . there was nothing they could do to help, except issue court decrees." . . .

The governor said the Justice Department . . . had asked him to keep the discussion confidential. News of the conference . . . leaked out but neither would talk to the DEMOCRAT on the record.

TIMES STORY

Today, however, the NEW YORK TIMES . . . revealed that Caldwell had been conferring with the Arkansas governor.

Last Thursday, the DEMOCRAT met Mr. Caldwell at the capitol and learned that he was in Little Rock at the invitation of the governor, but Mr. Caldwell said "I can tell you nothing for the record."

On Friday, the DEMOCRAT asked Governor Faubus about Mr. Caldwell's visit and Mr. Faubus went into some detail but again off the record "because they asked me to keep it confidential; if they disclose it, I'll tell you everything about it."

Today, the DEMOCRAT read the . . . dispatch, quoting the TIMES, over the phone to the governor at the mansion.

ATTITUDE OF THE JUSTICE DEPARTMENT

Some four weeks before the beginning date for school in Little Rock, I called the Justice Department in Washington on my private line and asked to speak to the U.S. Attorney General, or one of his aides who could speak for him.

By that time I had obtained sufficient information about the developing Little Rock situation to be seriously concerned about events at the time school opened. Much of my information of impending trouble had come from Virgil Blossom, who, I assumed, was speaking for the school board and conveying the information to me with the board's knowledge and consent.

Since the plan to integrate Central High School was now in response to and by the direction of a federal court, I was sure the federal authorities had devised some procedures and formulated some plan of action to be followed in view of the difficulties, disorder and violence which had already occurred in various places from the Atlantic seaboard to Texas, and even in border and northern states like West Virginia, Kentucky, Missouri and Illinois. I wanted to discuss the Little Rock situation with some knowledgeable person in the Department, to be informed on their plans and preparations, and be assured that violence and disorder would not result in destruction of school buildings, and the injury or death of students, school personnel or others.

I could not contact the Attorney General or talk to anyone in the Department except a secretary or clerk. It was difficult to understand the refusal or failure of the Attorney General to return the urgent call of the governor of a state about the matter. But that was the case. I never heard from the Attorney General.

Finally, during the week before school was to begin, a representative of the Justice Department appeared in Little Rock. He was Arthur B. Caldwell, who asked to see me secretly on a confidential basis.

I agreed, and he was slipped into my office through a side door during a quiet period. I had my receptionist, Mrs. Patsy Ellis, hold all telephone calls and visitors and Mr. Caldwell and I conferred for perhaps two hours.

I asked Mr. Caldwell what could be expected from the Justice Department and the federal government in general, in the implementation and enforcement of its own court order on school integration. I inquired what action the federal government would take, what agents and enforcement officers would be used to determine the possibility of violence, what would be done to head off trouble, what would be done, how and by whom, in case of disorder and what could be expected to help restore order in case extensive disorder developed.

In response to my inquiries, Mr. Caldwell carefully outlined the policy and procedure of the Justice Department. When he had finished, to sum it all up, it was nothing. In the case of Little Rock, not even an alert had been given to the local U.S. marshal or the FBI agents assigned to the area. In other words, the federal government and all federal officials continued in an unconcerned manner in their ordinary pursuits as if no federal court orders were involved. This studied, deliberate disinterest was in spite of the fact that the implementation of such court orders had caused extensive disorder, rioting, destruction of buildings, injury and grave danger of death in various places across the country.

I was amazed to learn of this attitude and policy of the federal government in relation to its own court orders. It was with utter astonishment and some consternation that I learned that the federal authorities would do nothing about any disorder and mob violence that might be created solely by reason of its own actions — the implementation of federal court-ordered integration — when without such orders all would have been completely tranquil, peaceful and orderly in the community.

Mr. Caldwell's closing words still ring in my mind:

"Governor, we can't do a thing until we find a body."

This is phraseology or a figure of speech, often used by members of the legal profession, meaning that no move can be made against any person until an act has been taken. But I could not escape the thought that if no one did anything at the crucial time, which was shortly to arrive, that the statement might prove to be more than a figure of speech. There might actually be a dead body, and possibly more than one.

The conference with Mr. Caldwell was to me an amazing revelation. I was astounded to learn the federal authorities had no intention to do anything to implement its own order. I reserved judgment on the information, thanked Mr. Caldwell for his courtesy and helped him leave the office undetected.

I then began to seriously reconsider the entire situation. In the activity of a busy schedule in succeeding days, the matter never left my mind.

The more I thought about the whole matter, the stronger became the conclusion that the attitude and policy of the federal government were both extremely cowardly and hypocritical. The national administration meant to avoid the unpleasant, unpopular, politically disastrous consequences of its own policies — policies for which it was solely responsible. It meant to shift to others the "dirty work" entailed by the enforcement of its almost universally disfavored orders. Such "dirty work," included the bludgeoning of honest citizens with billy clubs; the use of pistols, rifles, bayonets, and tear gas, against otherwise good, moral people. It included their arrest, imprisonment and trial. Now all this burden was to be borne by local officials and all the expense by the local and state governments, while the federal government incurred no cost, and the idle hands of the federal minions remained unstained and unscarred.

I recalled the impassioned, pleading speech of Gov. Frank Clement of Tennessee at the preceding Southern Governors Conference, as he sought to explain his use of the National Guard to restore order and implement the federal court order to integrate the schools at Clinton, Tennessee. Gov. Clement was suffering greatly from that action, both emotionally and politically, and his speech was an attempt to explain away a part of the blame he was bearing from his own people.

The longer I studied the federal attitude the more I became convinced that it was 100% political. I also concluded that it was the most contemptible, cowardly, hypocritical brand of politics I had ever encountered.

I tried to mentally place myself in the position of the Attorney General (the federal government) in relation to the problem. I could envision only how ashamed I would be of such a cowardly policy if I were its author.

On the other hand, I tried to envision an Attorney General of knowledge and courage with a willingness to bear his just responsibilities. There was no need to think of the president in that respect. He appeared to be a good man who wanted to be fair in his dealings with the people. Unfortunately, he knew no more of the law and the Constitution than the average unlearned layman. His lack of knowledge in such matters placed him at the mercy of his small circle of advisers, and his statements and speeches contained only what was prepared for him by Brownell, Adams and Hagerty.

An Attorney General with the qualities of courage, legal knowledge and political responsibility could have called the governor of a state and said something like this:

"Governor, we have court orders to integrate some schools in your state. I know the Congress has passed no such law. These are only court decisions, but it is my duty to enforce them.

"Now, I know these orders are contrary to your state constitution, your state laws and the will of a majority of your people. So I'm going to instigate immediately lawsuits challenging that portion of your state constitution and your state laws on the subject, and litigate the cases to conclusions as quickly as possible. We hope the conclusions will have a settling effect on your people.

"Then, in places where the court orders are not accepted peaceably, I'm going to move in with the proper federal agents in sufficient force to obtain compliance. We know these federal orders are not your responsibility. They are our problem and we will handle them. We merely want you to continue the administration of state affairs and the enforcement of state laws, and not cause us any trouble in our difficult task if you can avoid it."

However one might have disagreed with the court orders or their illegal origin, one could have had respect for such an honest and courageous attitude on the part of the enforcers. However, in such a case, they would have had to do the dirty work; they would have been the unpopular villains, the enemies of the people, the butt of the epithets and invective, the ostracized bearers of the abuse and wrath of the great majority of the people who opposed the enforcement of the orders. This Brownell and the Palace Guard sought to avoid.

Therefore, they adopted the cowardly policy of calling on the state and local authorities to enforce federal court orders — a request never before made in the history of the republic.

I came to regard with utter contempt the authors and promoters of such a policy. I also resented the fact that they intended for me to do their dirty work for them.

I bore no malice toward Mr. Caldwell. He was properly considerate of the difficulty of my position. He was an underling, an employee of the Justice Department policy-makers and had no choice in the matter. At that time his father, John H. Caldwell, lived in Little Rock and was librarian for the State Supreme Court. I saw him often about the Capitol. In the months which followed I had no stronger supporter on the stand which I took than the distinguished and scholarly elder Caldwell.

In the several days that followed my conference with the Justice Department representative, I often hoped that conditions would not require any action on my part. However, I knew that if violence and disorder were a probability with possible injury or death to someone, either white or black, I would not stand aside.

So I waited and watched, not knowing what my decision or course would be.

MOTHERS MEET, PETITION GOVERNOR; JUDGE REED GRANTS INJUNCTION

At a meeting the evening of August 27, the League of Central High Mothers adopted a petition asking me "to prevent forcible integration of the Little Rock schools." League President Mrs. O. R. Aaron appointed a committee to present the petition.

The petition said "the overwhelming sentiment is against integration. We know that you respect the will of the majority of the people. We ask that you take "measures in accordance to the laws of the state" to prevent "forcible integration."

The meeting place was crowded and all those present could not get into the room. North Side President Mrs. Vernon Davis headed a delegation of 50 members of the Mothers League of North Little Rock.

At the end of a question-and-answer period a young man stood at the rear of the room and asked how many persons present would be at Central High Tuesday morning to "push back" any Negroes who try to enter as students. "And I imagine there are a few shotguns in Little Rock, too," he said.

The audience met the outburst with silence and a few moans.

Mrs. Aaron quickly told the man that the mothers were "trying to keep down violence."

Attorney Amis Guthridge took the floor to emphasize that the Citizens Council was opposed to violence.

The surprise of the meeting, according to reports, was the 30-minute speech by W. R. Hughes, a Dallas attorney of the Citizens Councils of Texas.

Rev. Wesley Pruden, pastor of the Broadmoor Baptist Church, asked the League to oppose integration "in a Christian way." He asked the audience to attend hearings on the two lawsuits the next day and the following Friday.

Others on the speakers platform were Mrs. Margaret Jackson, League vice president, and Mrs. Clyde Thomason, the recording secretary.

PETITION PRESENTED

A very large delegation of Central High mothers presented the petition to me the next day, August 28. I told them I would do everything possible to prevent violence.

JUDGE REED ISSUES INJUNCTION

On August 29 a hearing was held on the petition of Mrs. Thomason in the court of Pulaski Chancellor Murray O. Reed. Witnesses were Mrs. Thomason, Supt. Blossom and me. After a two-hour hearing Judge Reed enjoined Little Rock school authorities from enrolling the Negro students in all-white Central High School.

Mrs. Thomason's attorneys, Griffin Smith and Arthur G. Frankel, both subpoenaed me because of the violence possibility, according to the news reports. Reed said that in view of testimony that there is a possibility of violence he felt he should grant the order.

Press reports said about 20 Negroes had been scheduled to enroll.

In my testimony I said that "a number of revolvers have been taken from students, both white and colored." One news report said "Attorneys representing the school board did not cross-examine him on this point." The *Gazette* report said "The school board attorneys did not question him on the point. Nor did they call any witnesses to refute Faubus' assertion."

I testified that I believed it was a "most inopportune" time to start integration, and that if I felt Little Rock residents were ready for integration, I would have no objection. I stated I did not believe that was the case at the time, and that I feared violence could develop if Negro students attempted to enroll on September 3.

Supt. Blossom when asked about violence testified, much to my surprise, that he had "not given it a thought." The *Gazette* wrote that he testified that he "anticipated no violence."

As I walked into the courtroom during the course of the trial, an unidentified young mother rushed up to me and begged, "Please, Governor, see to it there is no violence."

The *Gazette* reported that Mrs. Thomason testified the mothers were "terrified" and were afraid to send their children to school.

Blossom said he had been assured by Police Chief Marvin

H. Potts that there would be no violence but that Potts had not told him of any plans to prevent disorder. He said all local authorities had been alerted.

In attorneys' arguments before Judge Reed, school board attorney A. F. House said that an allegation that bloodshed will occur doesn't make it so. But Smith raised a question — "There is the consideration of ability. There is fear that violence may erupt. It's not imagination. It has happened in a number of communities. We don't want to take the chance that it will happen here."

Thunderous applause broke out in the courtroom when Judge Reed announced his ruling.

In response to the press I said afterward that I was "gratified" by the injunction because it would give time to litigate some questions which should be litigated.

SCHOOL BOARD GOES TO FEDERAL COURT

After Judge Reed's ruling attorneys for the school district immediately rushed to Federal District Court and filed a petition asking for an injunction to prevent the plaintiffs (Mrs. Thomason and others) from "interfering" with the courts. Federal Judge Ronald N. Davies set a hearing for the next day, August 30.

Press reports said that when House went to Federal Court to file the petition, Judge Davies called him into his office. The Judge also talked with Wiley A. Branton of Pine Bluff, an NAACP attorney who represented the Negro plaintiffs in the original suit against the school board.

Blossom said that he would "tell Negro students" what to do after he found out himself.

Under the school integration plan, an estimated 15 Negro students will be enrolled in Central High. (Report of George Bentley and Ernest Valachovic of the *Gazette* staff.) Under the system of voluntary transfers, Hall High School is expected to be without Negro pupils, and Horace Mann is expected to be all-Negro.

JUDGE DAVIES GRANTS INJUNCTION

In the hearing in Federal District Court on August 30, Judge Davies ordered the School Board to proceed with integration, and nullified Judge Reed's injunction to delay the scheduled integration. Then Davies issued an injunction of his own to prevent any interference with the school board plan.

Judge Davies enjoined Mrs. Thomason and "all others" from using the Chancery Court order to stop the Board plan, and said they must not take any legal action which would lead to the Board's being placed in contempt of the Chancery Court. Any violators were threatened with contempt of Judge Davies' court.

At the hearing Attorney House said that the federal court had superior and prior jurisdiction of the case. Attorney Griffin Smith defended Reed's order as sensible and said the Chancellor acted in the interest of the public.

The entire hearing lasted one hour and 5 minutes. (*Gazette* report of Valachovic.) Judge Davies read his decision in 62 seconds.

THE THOMASON CASE AND THE TURN-AROUND

There is an unknown story behind the lawsuit of Mrs. Clyde Thomason, which has never been made public in detail. But let me begin at an earlier time.

Soon after the original U.S. Supreme Court decision of May 17, 1954, the Little Rock School Board and Supt. Virgil Blossom announced they would integrate the Little Rock schools. It was as if they welcomed the opportunity to try the new social experiment.

Frankly, I think that was the attitude of William G. Cooper, Jr., president of the board and an immigrant to Arkansas from the North. Some other members of the board may have shared his views.

However, as time went on and the disorder and division developed at Hoxie, where the racial problem was minor compared to Little Rock, the Board and Supt. Blossom became more cautious.

Then came the campaigns and elections of 1956. In the Democratic primaries my major opponents, Jim Johnson and Jim Snoddy, proclaimed themselves strong segregationists. Snoddy came out squarely against any integration whatsoever, token, gradual, or otherwise. Johnson went even farther, pledging to do away with any integration that had already been implemented, even in the institutions of higher learning.

Johnson initiated a constitutional amendment which was considered by many, even some segregationists, as extreme. It made mandatory the removal from office of the governor or any other public official who failed to uphold and enforce all segregation laws. He had no difficulty in securing ample signatures to place the measure on the ballot. (See news story of Feb. 25, 1956, of the meeting at England.)

Although classified as a "moderate" or an "integrationist" by some, because I had already permitted more integration in Arkansas than in any other Southern State (in fact, more integration at that time than in eleven other states combined with a comparable problem), I survived the primary. A good, tight administration and progress in other fields helped me win, but I had to take a stand against integration by force and to pledge the legal assistance of the state to the majority when opposed to court-ordered mixing in the schools.

In the November general election all these anti-integration measures, including the Johnson Amendment, were approved by wide margins notwithstanding the fact that thousands of electors vote against all such measures on the ballot simply because they haven't had the time to familiarize themselves with the proposals.

That was not all. In the General Assembly of 1957, once my program of progress was approved, the members turned to more segregation measures. In the face of strong editorial opposition and criticism by the *Arkansas Gazette,* opposition by the NAACP and certain integrationist ministers such as the Rev. Dunbar Ogden, the measures were overwhelmingly approved by the legislature. One of the new laws was the State Sovereignty Act.

When the NAACP pushed for integration in the Little Rock schools in 1956, the Board and Supt. Blossom told them to wait because, they said, "it would take a year to get ready." A part of that getting ready was the construction of a new school facility in the western part of the district. The new school named Hall High, turned out to be a refuge for the rich and well-to-do, some of whom "preached" integration or "law of the land," but didn't want any part of the practice for themselves.

The NAACP filed a lawsuit to compel integration and the Board was forced to submit a plan. By now it was apparent that integration in the Capital City would not be a mere formality. There would be difficulties. So the Board came up with a plan that called for mere token integration at first, which even most opponents recognized as tolerable, with full integration to be implemented gradually over a period of years. Also, a large part of the district, where lived the nabobs of commerce, the professions and industry, would not be affected. Their children, or at least those who attended public school, would go to segregated Hall High, which, according to estimates, would remain so for at least 25 years.

Judge John E. Miller approved the school board's plan and the NAACP appealed his decision to the 8th Circuit Court of Appeals. The NAACP's appeal was looked upon by some as partly "window dressing" opposition to justify and protect what was rapidly becoming in the public mind an integrationist school administration.

Even before the Miller decision was upheld by the higher court Supt. Blossom had begun a series of meetings throughout the district to explain and attempt to sell to the people the school board plan. The main selling points were the small number of Negro students to be admitted to Central in the beginning (token integration), with none to Hall High, and no whites forced to go to the new modern Negro facility, Horace Mann High School.

The second point was the gradual implementation of the plan which was represented to require 12 years — one additional grade each year. However, this part of the plan turned out to be indefinite and uncertain. It began to be talked of as a ten-year plan, and then in Judge Miller's ruling it came out as a six-year plan.

However, some patrons of the Central attendance area who could not obtain transfers to Hall kept coming up with the troublesome questions to Supt. Blossom about the length of time for token integration, and what would be the ratio of Negro and white students in Central when the plan was completed. The answer was evaded, avoided, and suppressed whenever possible, but when an answer to the ratio question was given it was "about 50 percent of each." (In 1976, it was 53% black and 47% white students.)

To those who sincerely opposed integration and were convinced it would destroy discipline and quality education, this was unacceptable. It was like being robbed a little at a time, or having a farm taken away acre by acre until all was gone.

There was a "make-believe" attitude on the part of Mr. Blossom, the school board, the ivory-tower dwelling *Gazette* editors and a few others, that the plan was being "sold to the people" by the meetings, and that it would be accepted. Such was not the case and Supt. Blossom was one of those who eventually recognized that the plan was not being accepted.

Some Little Rock businessmen deluded themselves with the idea that token integration — the small number to be admitted — would suffice to satisfy the black people. Since token integration was tolerable and no great harm could come from it, as almost everyone agreed, they argued that the Blossom plan should be accepted. The problem would be solved, they said, and the trouble and controversy would all be over. However, these deluded people were thinking only of the first year of integration at Central, and avoiding thought of the time when the ratio of black to white students would become virtually equal. They were likewise ignorant of the fact that in some of the lower grades black students would outnumber whites from the moment integration was implemented. Most, if not all, of those who argued for the plan's acceptance lived in the Hall High area which was expected to remain segregated indefinitely.

(At that time no one had ever dreamed of the extreme practice of busing to obtain school racial integration.)

Some five or six months before the school opening date, Blossom began to contact me and talk about the matter. His contacts became more frequent until it could be said he dogged my footsteps. He seldom came to the office because it was public and very busy but accosted me in hotel lobbies, downtown coffee shops, in parking areas and came often to the Mansion. His visits to the Mansion on week-ends and after work hours during the week became more and more frequent.

Once in the parking area of the old garage on Markham Street that was my first headquarters, he was relating to me and Harry Parkin the increasing difficulties and his growing concern. Harry had to go and as he moved away he remarked, "All I can say, Virgil, is you better stick close to this man," indicating me.

"Oh, I'm doing that, aren't I?" he replied turning to me, "and I'm going to continue," he said to Harry, nodding his head vigorously.

I of course confirmed his statement because at that time, with school opening not too far distant, I was spending more time listening to Mr. Blossom than anyone else in the state.

I learned that his concern was so great that he had arranged to send his children to Jonesboro to live with his brother-in-law, Sen. Marvin Melton, and attend school there.

He told me of reports of organized gangs of youths, both black and white, who were arming for possible conflict when integration began.

Mr. Blossom was my source of information on the confiscation by school authorities of 18 pistols from both black and white students. He said the guns were obtained by the students from a pawn shop in Benton to which they were returned after being taken from the youths.

Secret meetings were being held, Blossom informed me, in Little Rock and other points in the state to organize opposition to the integration of Central High School. To me the plans of opposition to integration discussed quietly by small groups at these secret meetings constituted by far the most alarming news of all the anti-integration activity. Then as the time drew near, he began to report the formation of caravans of integration opponents who were to converge on Central High School at the proper time. He grew concerned about the welfare of his family, the security of his home and his own personal safety. I assured him that when he felt the efforts of the Little Rock police were inadequate for his security I would give him additional protection by the State Police.

As his concern grew his visits to the Mansion, often unannounced, grew more frequent. Then he began to wonder, and then to hope, that something would be done to halt the Central High School integration planned for Sept. 3.

I once told him, "Well, Virgil, it's not my problem. I didn't get you into this. You know I'm not planning to push integration on to you. I have no authority in running the schools. My responsibility is to preserve order. If nothing happens, if there is no disorder or real threat of disorder, I won't have any problem and won't do anything."

Then Blossom asked if he could bring some school board members with him to the Mansion to discuss the matter with me. I agreed.

The next time he appeared he was accompanied by Wayne Upton, secretary of the Board. We spent some three hours that evening discussing the matter. Upton didn't say much, but he seemed in accord with Blossom's expressed concern. However, it did seem that Blossom wanted me to impress upon Upton the gravity of the situation. This I made no special effort to do but agreed with Blossom that there was cause for concern.

Within a few days following this meeting Blossom was back at the Mansion again with Upton. Again we had to listen to Blossom's new information, indicating trouble at the school and his repeated expressions of concern.

Then he wanted to know if I was going to do anything, or if I knew of anything that would be done by duly constituted authority in an attempt to halt the planned integration. Of course I didn't, and told them so. The Sovereignty Commission had not yet even been convened nor had an attorney been chosen, and I didn't know if it would act in the Central High School problem.

Upton seemed to second Blossom's fears of trouble and his desire that something be done.

I turned on them and said, "You are the ones who have the problem. You are concerned. Why don't you do something about the situation? It's more your problem than mine!"

They were somewhat taken aback by my abruptness, but finally Blossom asked, "Well, if we get a lawsuit prepared will you get it filed?"

"Why should I do that?" I asked, "why don't you get it filed?"

Well, they were on the spot, they explained, and besides they felt it would be better if the lawsuit came from the known opponents of the integration plan.

So I told them I would see what I could do if they brought me a proper, written complaint.

A few days later the all-star high school athletic events were being held at the Coliseum at the Livestock Show grounds. Coaches from throughout the state were in Little Rock with their teams. We had a reception one evening at the Mansion for the coaches and a few people from the State Department of Education. While these people were circulating and visiting throughout the house, Blossom appeared at the door.

I met him and as we paused in the hallway he quietly informed me he had the necessary papers we had discussed.

Prior to the arrival of our guests and Blossom, J. L. "Bex" Shaver of Wynne, one of my appointees to the Sovereignty Commission, and Richard McCulloch, an attorney of Forrest City who later became counsel for the Commission, had arrived for a conference with me. I took them upstairs to my study where they conferred while I fulfilled my role as host to the coaches and other guests. I told Blossom they were there and immediately escorted him to the study to join them. He explained to them the purpose of his visit and gave them the complaint.

When our guests and Blossom had departed, I joined attorneys Shaver and McCulloch in my study where we discussed the situation.

As to the lawsuit or complaint, complete except for the names of plaintiffs and attorneys, which Blossom had delivered, my companions said they could see nothing in it, in their hasty perusal, which should be changed, and said it might do some good. Of course they knew nothing of the matter. The only reason they were consulted was the coincidental circumstance of their presence when Blossom delivered the complaint to me. He stated that the lawsuit was prepared by "our people," meaning Blossom and his associates. Other than that phrase he did not identify those who drew up the complaint. But it was clearly understood that he and at least some of his associates identified with the integration plan, including members of the school board, wanted the lawsuit filed and hoped it would be successful in halting the integration plan.

Anyway, very shortly I placed the complaint in the hands of one of my confidants — I cannot now remember whom — and requested that the complaint be gotten into the hands of someone who would secure an attorney and get it filed.

To the best of my recollection that was the last I heard of the matter. However, I am positive that the complaint filed by Mrs. Clyde Thomason in Judge Murray O. Reed's court was the same or a revised version of the one delivered to me at the Mansion by Blossom on the occasion described above.

By the time for the hearing on Mrs. Thomason's complaint in Judge Reed's court on Aug. 29, I had done a lot of checking and information-gathering on the possibility of disorder at Central High School on school opening day. Trouble was brewing and appeared to be serious. Blossom was even more strongly convinced that trouble was imminent and expressed great concern for the safety of the Negro children.

Under these circumstances, I was quite ready to respond to the subpoena to testify in Judge Reed's court. I confidently expected my testimony to back up Blossom's stronger evidence and the extensive information he had obtained as to impending opposition that could lead to disorder. I expected my testimony to bolster his genuine concern and fear for the safety of the Negro students, as well as his concern for the welfare of himself, his family and others.

I arrived at the hearing about 30 minutes after it had begun and thus missed the testimony of Mrs. Thomason. Blossom was on the stand as I took my seat to one side and listened. Almost immediately I noted and was puzzled by his extremely evasive attitude in response to questions about possible difficulties. Then he was asked that all-important question about his viewpoint, knowledge, or opinion of violence in relation to integration.

With considerable hesitation accompanied by nervous body movements and erratic nodding of his head he finally responded, "I've never given it a thought."

At first I thought I had not heard right. Then as the testimony continued, I realized that I had. I was completely astonished — and astounded. I remember having the thought, "This can't be!" followed by the thought, "This must be a part of some strategy of which I am uninformed and which will later be explained to me." I entertained that hope during my testimony although I could envisage no way that it was possible.

Blossom was soon finished and I took the stand. I quickly discovered that Mrs. Thomason's attorneys were uninformed on the situation and thus unprepared to elicit by their questions the evidence that was available and needed. I had to volunteer much of the pertinent evidence. Part of it was the information about the pistols taken from students. If one of the plaintiff's attorneys had merely asked, "Governor Faubus, could you tell us where you obtained that information?" I would have answered, "From Virgil Blossom." The evidence would have been devastating to Blossom and the school board attorneys.

Or even before I testified if the plaintiff's attorneys had asked that question of Blossom himself, I do not believe he would have lied. He knew I was coming on the stand later and that he had told me about the pistols more than once. In fact a dozen witnesses, perhaps a hundred, could have testified that Blossom had related the matter to them.

The school board attorney — the frozen-faced A. F. (Archie) House — did the cross examination and carefully refrained from questioning me about the confiscated pistols. This was not by oversight; it was deliberate. The school board attorneys knew about the incident and they knew the source of my information. My cross-examination by Mr. House was brief and most carefully handled and, in my opinion, was conducted only for the sake of appearance.

I hesitated to volunteer information which would expose Blossom because of the thought that his attitude and testimony had some purpose unknown to me which would later be explained.

I left the court after my testimony and did not hear the closing arguments or the judge's decision granting the injunction. I felt as though I was in a daze for the remainder of the day as I pondered the attitude and testimony of Blossom and what I had heard and observed from the school board attorneys. I could only wait for further information and any possible explanation.

I noted the presence in the court of the Justice Department representative, Arthur B. Caldwell, where he was a close and interested observer.

That evening Virgil Blossom appeared at the front door of the Mansion. As I admitted him, he entered, his hand outstretched for mine, shaking his head from side to side and nodding in the utmost gravity as he said, "Oh, I want to thank you! I'll never forget you! I'll do anything for you! Just let me know when you need me! I'm forever in your debt!"

He uttered all this in the most serious mien. I realized he was thanking me for not exposing him in my testimony earlier in the day.

I realized then that strategy did not explain what occurred that day. Instead of backing up their own lawsuit, which they had prepared and requested my assistance in filing, the school board, their attorneys and, to my utter consternation, the superintendent, had taken a completely contrary position. Instead of bringing out in court the evidence and information of growing opposition to their integration plan, they had denied the facts by deliberately obscuring and suppressing the evidence.

I asked Virgil why he did not testify to what he had told me.

"Governor, all I can say," he replied, "I just couldn't!"

I inquired why he couldn't, and he was evasive, shaking his

head in the pronounced manner so familiar to those who knew him well. He finally said, "You know who I'm with," and would not elaborate further. His stay on that occasion was more brief than usual. It was the last of our many private, friendly discussions.

After his departure I pondered the situation. Instead of my testimony largely corroborating the evidence of the Superintendent and the school board about resistance to integration, I found myself as the leading witness for that position. Those whom I intended to assist took a completely opposite position.

It now dawned on me that the school board, their attorneys, Blossom and their integrationist allies had determined or the determination had been made for them, that the integration plan must go forward regardless of the consequences. To conceal opposition to the plan it was necessary to practice gross deception. The deception was practiced by deliberately and carefully evading, ignoring and suppressing the evidence of unmistakable opposition to court-ordered integration which was surfacing everywhere. This was well known to Blossom who felt compelled to give false testimony under oath, and in my opinion, was known to Attorney House who directed the course of the hearing for the school board.

It was now clear to me that I had "been had." I had been doublecrossed and betrayed by those I had dealt with in good faith. It was bitter disillusionment, to say the least.

However, I could never bring myself to believe that Virgil Blossom was guilty of such perfidy of his own free will and accord. Someone or some group, I am convinced, took mental and verbal control of Virgil Blossom, assumed complete domination of his actions, gave him a 180-degree turn and set him on the course which became apparent in his testimony. He was never permitted to deviate from that course during his remaining months in Little Rock.

"I never gave it a thought," he said under oath on that occasion when asked about possible violence at Central High School. Literally dozens of his friends and associates knew that the possibility of trouble and violence was his dominant thought for months before he made that statement.

When I learned the next day that attorneys for the school board, immediately following Judge Reed's decision, rushed quickly into Federal Judge Davies' court to ask for the nullification of the Chancery Court ruling, the thought occurred to me that I may have been used in the matter. Did the school board and its integrationist allies want a ruling from a state court, based on a weak case as the Thomason verdict turned out to be because of the failure to present sufficient hard evidence, in order that the matter could be taken into federal court? Once in Judge Davies' court the overruling of the Chancery Court decision would be a foregone conclusion. Then the federal judge could enjoin all opposition to the integration order. Following the injunction any citizen could be arrested and imprisoned at the judge's direction for writing a letter of opposition to a newspaper, carrying a picket sign, pointing a finger, speaking a protest or appearing on the school grounds. In fact, members of the General Assembly could be enjoined from legislating on the matter and imprisoned by the judge if they disobeyed the injunction.

When House went to the federal court to file the pleading for the school board he was called by Judge Davies into his chambers for a long secret conference, and so was Wiley Branton who represented the Negro plaintiffs. This gave the appearance of collusion between the presiding judge and the pro-integrationists. No one ever heard of a conference in chambers by Judge Davies with any attorney for the other side.

In the injunction granted by Judge Davies, everyone was enjoined from opposing in any way the integration order. The only exception was the General Assembly which was not enjoined from legislating on the matter perhaps because it was not in session. (However, orders of federal courts in other states enjoined senators and representatives from legislating in opposition to integration.)

If such a scheme were used to get the matter into federal court, was Blossom a conscious, knowing participant in the trickery, or was he, like I, an innocent participant acting in good faith being used by more clever and perfidious plotters?

If such a plot did exist it was a decided success. But it is difficult for me to believe that Blossom was a willing part of such deceit. There were those behind him, however, whom I believe were quite capable of planning and carrying out such a scheme.

If the school board wanted an injunction forbidding interference with its plan of integration the honest way would have been to go into federal court and submit the evidence of impending trouble that was being related daily by Blossom. At the same time a request could have been made for the assistance of U.S. marshals and FBI agents to prevent or control any disorderly opposition. However, that would have been contrary to the false claims being made that the plan had obtained peaceable acceptance. Also it would have been contrary to Justice Department policy as explained to me by Mr. Caldwell when he said, "We can do nothing until we find a body."

Following the hearing in Judge Reed's Court and the preceding events with their attendant publicity, anyone in Little Rock who wrote, stated or swore that no disorder or violence involving the integration of Central High School was possible or imminent, was so ignorant as to be of no consequence, or that person was a party to the course decided upon by the Justice Department and carried forward by the school board and its attorneys at least partially through perfidy and deceit.

CONFERENCE WITH THE SCHOOL BOARD

On Friday night, August 30, following Judge Davies' decision overruling Judge Reed's state court injunction, and Davies' issuance of the federal court injunction, the members of the school board and their attorneys held a special meeting in a downtown hotel. After they had convened, I received an urgent request at the Mansion to confer with them.

In looking back, possibly I should have declined. Or I should have summoned at least two of my aides, including one attorney, to be present during the meeting. That would have taken time. Anyway, the thought did not enter my mind. I responded to the request and, as I recall, drove alone to the meeting place and met the group in the conference.

It must be recalled that within the past week I had been through the disappointing conference with Mr. Caldwell, who had explained the politically motivated, cowardly, and hypocritical policy of the Justice Department. I had only the day before been misled in the Thomason trial in the grossest fashion after months of conferences in good faith with the school board's representatives.

With all this in mind, I waited coolly after my arrival to learn the reason for the conference.

After several unsuccessful attempts by indirect comments and questions to learn my attitude and intentions, it was finally stated bluntly. "We've got to know what you are going to do," referring to actions I might take in reference to school opening the following Tuesday. As I recall, it was Blossom who inquired in the form of the blunt statement for the group.

I was not surprised, but I was chagrined by the nature of the inquiry. They must have thought they were dealing with a country bumpkin, a coward, or a vacillating weakling. There was no finesse in their approach or method of inquiry. They could have said:

"Governor, we have a difficult problem. We know your situation is difficult too. It might be helpful to us if you could give us any information which we might not have. It might be very helpful if we could have your thinking on this problem, as well as any plans you have formulated, if any, to deal with the matter."

But there was no such approach. The group's attitude was more one of disdain than hospitality although I was a guest at the members' request.

I looked the members of the group over very carefully. Dr. Cooper, the immigrant Northerner, bore an attitude of aloof superiority; Brick Lile, whose expression of indifference toward others was sometimes mistaken for arrogance, had an inquisitive look. He may not have cared one way or the other about integration or segregation. However, he had become a business associate and satellite of Winthrop Rockefeller, and Rockefeller was an honest, open integrationist. Therefore, Lile's attitude on the matter of integration was pre-determined. Wayne Upton appeared nervous, his eyes shifting about in his pallid features. Alford's usual friendly, smiling air was more subdued. However, I seemed to detect from him a feeling of sympathy toward me that evening. Blossom was nervous and hesitant, and neither friendly or unfriendly. After the events of recent days I wondered if all the board members and the attorneys knew of his many visits with me, as well as Upton's. I wondered if they all knew of the lawsuit which had been prepared and delivered to me, and which one of them prepared it; or, if not, did they know who did. Or were certain members of that group playing games with each other as had been played with me? I did not form, or at least I did not retain any definite impressions of Rath or Engstrom. (The latter was my appointee on the State Board of Professional Engineers.)

I regarded the group as coolly as I have anyone. Cooper later swore in court that there would be no disorder upon integrating Central High School. Therefore, his attitude would have been no different then. It was plain that he was either ignorant of all the information Blossom had been giving me, or he was a member of the group that had determined to push integration at any cost.

Blossom, in evasive, sworn testimony in court, had just reversed his role, his attitude and his stories, which were known to dozens of people city-wide. Therefore, I could not then trust him in relation to the problem at hand. On the same occasion of Blossom's testimony I had observed House as he deliberately sought to avoid disclosure of evidence in Judge Reed's court. I answered their blunt inquiry carefully and truthfully. "Gentlemen," I said, "it is your contention that there will be no trouble. That is evident by the testimony of your superintendent in both state and federal courts in the past three days, as well as the statements of your attorney and your pleadings in federal court. If that is the case I will do nothing, for there will be nothing for me to do."

"I have no authority in the affairs of your school district. That is your problem and your responsibility."

"My problem is the maintenance of law and order. I do not want any disorder or rioting in this city with damage to property and injury to people as have occurred for the past two years in other sections of the nation, and which are occurring now as all of you know."

"Strong opposition has developed in Little Rock and all across the state to the integration of Central High School. This is because of the wide publicity that has been given, and the pronouncements that the Little Rock plan is to become a model for all of Arkansas and for the South.

"My information, which I have carefully and diligently gathered over the past several days, is at variance with your pronouncements and testimony in court as to the possibility of trouble. Many of these opponents feel very strongly about this matter and I have reports that determined efforts may be made to prevent the carrying out of your integration plan. As I see it now, there is a good possibility of trouble."

At this point Lile said, "If these people could see the determination of that Judge (referring to Davies) they would change their minds about the matter.''

I did not argue that point, but I thought "How wrong can you be?" I knew that a group of sincere, determined Arkansas people were not going to be cowed by the utterances of a federal judge, especially when he was a Northerner from a distant state with no racial problem. North Dakota had fewer Negroes than any other state in the Union, and Judge Davies was regarded as knowing less than nothing about the problem.

After Lile's statement I continued: "I hope you are right in your public attitude and that there will be no trouble. Then I will have nothing to do. However, if that is not the case, and there is disorder or the dire threat of disorder and violence, then I will use my best judgment based on the best information I can obtain, and act accordingly."

"I can't tell you what I'm going to do, because I have no way of knowing now myself. My actions will be determined by developments, whatever those developments may be, and my evaluation of the situation."

Nothing more was said. My part in the conference was concluded.

The next day, Saturday, Aug. 31, the board issued a two-paragraph prepared statement signed by all six board members which was distributed to the press by Blossom.

The statement, as reported by Bobbie Forster in the *Arkansas Democrat*, read:

> As a result of the Aug. 30, 1957, decision (Aaron vs. Cooper et al) in the U.S. District Court . . . the Board of Education of the Little Rock School District is now required to proceed on Sept. 3, 1957, with the court-ordered plan of gradual desegregation of schools.

> Further, the federal court held that the injunction issued by the Chancery Court of Pulaski County is null and void. In view of these federal court orders, the Board of Education is compelled to proceed with the first phase of desegregation of the

schools. We earnestly solicit and confidently expect the understanding and cooperation of all students and adults in the peaceful solution of this difficult problem, in order that the best interests of all may continue to be served.

Arkansas Gazette, Aug. 31, 1957

THE SOVEREIGNTY COMMISSION

The Arkansas Sovereignty Commission held its first official meeting at the State Capitol on August 30. The members were all present except one. Mrs. Patsy Ellis [of my staff] served as secretary. Dr. Joe Rushton of Magnolia, a member, was absent on a trip to New York City. On the recommendation of J. L. "Bex" Shaver the Commission voted to employ R. B. McCulloch, Sr. of Forrest City as its attorney.

CHAPTER 11
THE CRISIS BEGINS; LITTLE ROCK
BECOMES WORLD WIDE NEWS

FAUBUS SHOWING STRAIN
FROM 2 TOUGHEST ISSUES

Arkansas Democrat 9-1-57

—By George Douthit,
Democrat Staff Writer

Governor Faubus came into office on a wave of controversy and has managed to move from one public dispute to another. He seemed to enjoy them for the first two years . . . but they apparently are taking their toll now.

The chief executive is showing the signs of strain from the two biggest problems he has faced in his public career — the death sentence of Emmett Earl Leggett and integration of the Arkansas schools. Both hit their peak during the last week.

Born in the North Arkansas hills, having had a rather tough existence and having experienced 300 days or more of combat with the infantry in World War II, Mr. Faubus would hardly be expected to run from a fight. . . .

But in the Leggett case he has taken what appears clearly to be the minority side against public opinion that the youth should be put to death for his crimes; and in the case of integration, against the U.S. Supreme Court. . . .

He fought the administration of the State Hospital . . . He fired the superintendent of the Girls Training School . . .

On the subject of integration, the governor was mute for many months early in his administration. Integration was closing in on Arkansas steadily, yet Mr. Faubus would not comment at his press conferences.

Then one Saturday, without warning, the governor's chief aide, Arnold Sikes, walked into the newspaper offices here and handed a prepared set of answers on integration the governor had given to the NEW YORK TIMES.

SURVEY MADE

He said he had made a survey of the state and found 85 per cent of the people favored segregation. This was not surprising, . . . but it was his first utterance on the subject.

As he approached the campaign for his second term, Mr. Faubus sought to keep integration from being an issue. But from down in Crossett came Jim Johnson, who made it his platform for governor, and Mr. Faubus had to come out with a stand.

He took the position that no school district would have to integrate against its will and won a second term. . . .

. . . an eastern Arkansas group was not convinced that the high court's ruling couldn't be circumvented, and a movement was begun to enact two laws to fight integration. Mr. Faubus had to go with them or against them. He went with them.

In the general election, the voters expressed their feelings in favor of segregation in adopting these laws. . . .

But that wasn't the end. The 1957 legislature spelled them out more plainly . . . Now the fight is on, led by Mr. Faubus.

We are firmly convinced that the governor wanted no part of this integration fight. But, as we said, he has never run from a scrap and the fact that the highest court in the land is on the other side doesn't stop him.

But don't think it doesn't bother him, because it does. He is feeling the effects of these deep issues. We believe that they will determine whether he wants to try for a third term and wrestle with more of them or let some other citizen have them for the next two years while he runs his Madison County newspaper and enjoys the relaxation of his wonderful hills.

Arkansas Gazette, Sept. 1, 1957

An Editorial

A TIME OF TESTING

In his clear and forthright ruling in the Little Rock school case Judge Davies has swept away the legal confusion generated by the apparent conflict between state and federal laws.

The judge ordered the Little Rock School Board to proceed, . . . and he enjoined "all persons, in any manner, directly or indirectly, from interfering with the plan of integration." . . .

This means that on Tuesday some 15 Negro children will be enrolled . . . We have no doubt that our law enforcement officers can and will preserve order.

This is a time of testing for all of us. Few of us are entirely happy over the necessary developments in the wake of changes in the law. . . .

We are confident that the citizens of Little Rock will demonstrate on Tuesday for the world to see that we are a lawabiding people.

This editorial, Judge Davies' injunctive ruling and the statement that FBI agents would be on hand, were clearly designed to intimidate the opponents of integration. The persuasive effect was nil, and the efforts at intimidation were ineffective.

The editorial referred to "changes in the law," and the people asked, "What change in what law?" Congress made federal laws, not the Supreme Court. Judge Davies could make no law.

As the people saw the situation, a call for "law and order" was a hypocritical way of calling for integration. So, to the segregationists, "law and order," as proclaimed by the *Gazette* while refusing to integrate its work force, and as called for by the hypocritical ministers who refused to integrate their churches, meant the same as "integrate the schools now."

Therefore, these proclamations and editorials and the prayer sessions which came later, had no influence in cooling the anger of the people or in clearing the air of confusion.

I PREPARE TO USE THE GUARD

While spending a restless night at the Mansion on August 31, I received some calls and messages there about the Central High School situation.

The next day, Sunday, September 1, I was scheduled to go to Prairie Grove to participate in ceremonies commemorating the preservation of the Prairie Grove battleground. I wanted very much to attend the function for I had assisted the legislators of the area led by Clifton Wade and Russell Elrod, secure the state funds to aid in the development.

However, the information I had received about possible trouble in Little Rock led me to stay where I could receive further reports. I informed my friend Judge Lee Seamster of Fayetteville and state Parks Director Sam Kirby, and asked them to represent me at the celebration.

About noon I went alone to the office where I made some calls, received reports, and evaluated all the information.

I decided I had better be ready in case of need and tried to find my lawyer, W. J. "Bill" Smith. I had already alerted State Police Director Herman Lindsey and Adjutant General Sherman T. Clinger, but their directions were merely to remain available for further instructions.

I finally reached Smith on the golf course. When Bill arrived at my office I said, "I want you to write for me an official proclamation mobilizing certain portions of the National Guard for use at Central High School. My information indicates probable violence and disorder when integration is attempted or implemented at school opening on the morning of Sept. 3. I want the mobilization order written to be effective on Sept. 2 so the Guard can assume control of the school grounds on the evening before. Thus, security and order can be better assured. I haven't reached the positive decision as yet to use the Guard, but from the reports I am receiving it is probable. I want you to write the order to be sure and certain that it is in proper form and legal in every respect."

Bill looked at me for a moment before saying anything. He was usually calm and collected with serious matters and in a crisis. His decisions and reactions could be swift especially at a hectic time in dealing with the legislature, but on this occasion his reaction and his speech were very deliberate.

"Governor," he inquired, "are you thinking of putting the Guard on duty at Central High School before anything happens?"

"Yes, that is right," I replied.

Bill didn't exactly remonstrate with me, but he pointed out how that course of action could lay me open to charges of bad judgment and put me in an almost indefensible position before my critics. They could accuse me of hasty action, which they could contend was unnecessary, and allege improper motives on my part.

"On the other hand, if you wait until something happens, you can act and your position will be defensible in every way," he advised me.

I remember looking at Bill thoughtfully and carefully before replying. "Bill," I said, "I've thought of all of that. What you say is true. I know you're speaking for my welfare and advising in my best interests.

"Now, on the other hand, if I am convinced of probable violence at the school, and I wait until it occurs in order to justify my actions before my critics, and in that violence and disorder buildings are destroyed and some students killed, then the justification will be small comfort to my conscience.

"Suppose a mother, black or white, comes into this office and sits across the desk from me where you are sitting now and inquires of me, 'Governor, you testified in court that you had heard of possible violence at the high school. Did you believe there was going to be trouble?'

"Then if my reply is 'yes,' which it appears now it would have to be, that mother can reply, 'Then why didn't you do something to stop it? If you had acted my child would still be alive today.'

"So, Bill, I appreciate what you have pointed out to me. It is responsible advice to your client. However, I have decided that if I act in this matter, I will act in the most responsible manner. You know the adage, 'A stitch in time —'

"While I appreciate your attitude and information, I didn't call you here to discuss the matter. My decision is already made. I will use the Guard if I judge it to be necessary. I called you here to write the proclamation for me. If I get into trouble, you will bear no part of the blame for you have had no part in the decision."

While Bill and I were having this exchange my private telephone rang. It was Virgil Blossom. He was more excited and agitated than I had ever heard him and we had conversed dozens of times personally and by telephone.

Blossom expressed his alarm at the reports he was receiving. He told of caravans that were converging or would converge on Little Rock and Central High School from Texarkana, El Dorado, the Crossett-Monticello area, eastern Arkansas, and concluded, "One group has already arrived from northeast Arkansas and a number of them are now at the Marion Hotel."

"Virgil," I asked, "do you think you need protection?"

"Yes, I do!" he replied emphatically.

I recalled his complete about-face in his testimony in Judge Reed's court from what he had told me previously.

"All right, Virgil," I replied, "you write out a brief statement to that effect. It need not be long. Just state that in view of the reports you have received of opposition to integration which may lead to disorder, and which may jeopardize your safety and the safety of your home, that you feel you need protection. A brief statement to this effect will be sufficient. I will dispatch a State Police officer immediately to your home to pick up the note. You can have it written by the time the officer arrives. He will receive the note from you, deliver it immediately to me, and I will provide you with all the police protection that you need."

There was a pause at the other end of the line. Then Blossom said, "I'll call you back!"

"All right, Virgil," I answered, and he hung up.

Bill Smith was sitting by and heard all of my conversation and I'm sure a part, if not all, of Blossom's end. A voice from the private line carried well in the room.

As we worked, we waited for the superintendent's callback. It never came.

I wonder, had I supplied State Police protection as he asked, without a written request, would he have denied making the request if he had to testify in court later? That was the kind of double-dealing I encountered from the school authorities throughout the Little Rock crisis. Someone, I am convinced, directed or ordered Blossom not to make the request for protection to me in writing. It would be evidence contrary to their false claims of "no evidence of disorder or violence in opposition to integration of Central High School."

Bill Smith agreed to prepare the Guard mobilization order for me. I waited for further reports and developments before making a final decision.

And what of the federal authorities in the situation?

I received no word and could get no assurance that any U.S. marshals or FBI agents would even be present when school opened. They offered no protection to Blossom, (the city police, I later learned, sent five cars and officers for his protection), the Negro students, the school, or any other person or property involved. Supposedly, it was FBI policy to avoid involvement in any local situation. But there were U.S. marshals available.

The U.S. marshals, as Mr. Caldwell had explained to me, could do nothing until "a body was found." Under that policy, dozens of people could be killed and injured and school buildings destroyed while the marshals remained inactive. There was no federal policy of preventing or controlling violence, and no enforcement of its own court orders. What a cowardly default of responsibility!

HARDISON HONORED

I was shown in a news photograph with Mrs. T. W. Hardison viewing a plaque honoring her late husband, T. W. Hardison. We were joined by Winthrop Rockefeller, George Reynolds, Sam Kirby and others at Petit Jean State Park in a ceremony in memory of Dr. Hardison for his efforts in initiating the state park system.

CONFERENCE WITH ROCKEFELLER

On Sunday, September 1, Winthrop Rockefeller called me and urgently requested a conference. The site was designated in a downtown Little Rock hotel at about 8 p.m. Rockefeller stated that Louis Hurley of El Dorado would also be present, and perhaps others.

Hurley was president of the Arkansas Bankers Association in 1955 and had served on the Industrial Commission (AIDC) with Mr. Rockefeller during its first year of operation. They became very close associates and also partisan Republican allies.

On the day of the meeting the weather was very bad. Rockefeller could not fly from his mountaintop airport and was forced to drive to Little Rock, and Mr. Hurley, who had planned to fly, could not get to the meeting.

The only other person present was William E. "Bill" Ewald, a member of the AIDC staff brought to Arkansas from Baltimore, Md., by Rockefeller shortly after the implementation of the industrial program in 1955.

After preliminary greetings and the explanation of Hurley's absence, I found Rockefeller wanted to discuss the forthcoming integration of the Little Rock schools. Rockefeller wanted me to use my office and state powers to implement the federal court order.

I spent 90% of the time listening to Rockefeller's arguments, which sometimes seemed halting and uncertain, interspersed with Ewald's occasional interjections. At one point I countered with the question, "How can I assist the federal authorities when they are unprepared to do anything and whose official policy is to do nothing?"

Mr. Rockefeller found himself at a loss to reply to the question and expressed himself as "not quite in agreement" with this federal policy.

However, this did not deter him from his original position that I should use my office and state forces to implement the order. He emphasized the futility of opposing the federal government because of its overpowering might. From Rockefeller's argument the main thing to consider, it seemed, was the strength of the contending forces rather than what was legal or right.

Finally, I explained briefly, since it was already generally known, my policy on integration matters. I pointed out that integration had progressed further in Arkansas than in any other Southern or border state: all institutions of higher learning, more public schools, all transportation systems, the political party organizations, the work forces of many state agencies and my staff meetings had already been integrated. However, in none of these had disorder been sufficiently great to require the use of force to maintain order.

I told Rockefeller I hoped the situation would be the same at Central High School and that no action would be required on my part. However, I candidly added that my information strongly indicated the situation might be otherwise. I was keeping in touch as closely as possible and checking constantly on developments.

I concluded my explanation with the emphatic expression that I did not want disorder, violence and destruction of property in Little Rock such as had occurred in other places. Therefore, my actions would be determined by my evaluation of the potential violence situation.

In addition, I reminded him that I was sworn to uphold state law and the state constitution. They were in conflict with the mere order of a federal district judge. Some of these state laws and the state constitution had not yet even been challenged in the courts, and none had been litigated to a final conclusion. My request to the federal authorities to help clear the air by litigating these matters to a conclusion in the courts had been ignored.

Rockefeller also appeared disconcerted by Virgil Blossom's activities and the alarm he had been constantly spreading over the potential violence.

While I did not say so to the former New York millionaire who was now Arkansas' wealthiest citizen, I'm sure he sensed that I was in no mood to pull the national administration's chestnuts out of the fire at my own political and physical risk without any help from it and while its forces sat idly by.

Of course, he was a close supporter and associate of President Eisenhower and possibly Brownell. I feel quite strongly that his conference with me was at White House request. (The *Gazette* later concurred in this viewpoint.)

When he insisted that my best course was to implement the federal court order with state forces, I made a reply which was later quoted in substance in the press as coming from "inside" sources about the conference. "Mr. Rockefeller," I said, "If I should do now what you are suggesting, soon after the next election you would be working for Jim Johnson and his lieutenants. You would be running the AIDC for him, if you were permitted to continue at all in a state governmental capacity, which would be very doubtful."

Mr. Rockefeller didn't seem to take that thought too seriously but he did not argue the point. Ewald, as I recall, disagreed. However, while he had his qualifications in some fields, politically Ewald was so naive and ignorant that he couldn't have qualified as a candidate for dog-catcher without advice.

I recall that afterwards Ewald was always my adamant enemy. On the eve of the Democratic primary election of 1958 he told one of my closest associates, Jim Bland, who he knew would tell me, "I wish him [Faubus] the very worst." Yet he continued on the AIDC payroll for several years thereafter as a part of my administration.

As for Winthrop Rockefeller, he was wise and tolerant enough to recognize there were viewpoints other than his own. Although he held to his own opinions and beliefs and never once in my presence hypocritically compromised them in conversation for expediency's sake, he did not fall out with others who did not see things his way. At times he remained silent on certain issues, which is the prerogative of any public figure.

Another surprising attribute of one so rich and powerful as Rockefeller: he could disagree openly with another and argue an issue without rancor or impairment of a friendship.

At least that was my experience with him. Some disagreed. One of his associates in a private conversation with me once termed him "savage" in his attitude. Others said he was dictatorial and tended to consume his close associates.

It is the fate of any public figure to have widely varying viewpoints expressed about him.

Anyway, when our conference ended and I stepped out into the stormy night to return to the Executive Mansion, Rockefeller was better informed than when the conference began. He, quite likely, had determined that I was not going to bear the burden for the cowardly and hypocritical default of the Justice Department in its refusal to enforce its own court order, as well as its refusal to help prevent disorder in the face of whatever difficulties that might arise.

Rockefeller did not know what action I would take, for I myself still did not know. Although National Guard and State Police Commanders had been alerted and a proclamation for use of the Guard was being written, I still hoped that the use of these forces would be unnecessary.

PRAIRIE GROVE MEETING

The Prairie Grove event drew 3,000 people at which I was represented by Seamster and Kirby. Master of ceremonies for the affair was Circuit Judge Maupin Cummings, chairman of the Board of Trustees of the Prairie Grove Battlefield Memorial Foundation.

Speakers included Dr. Robert R. Logan and W. J. Lemke of the University of Arkansas, and Fred McCuistion, a Foundation member of Prairie Grove.

Seamster told the audience that I had decided to remain at Little Rock "because of a problem over which the battle of Prairie Grove was fought."

"Unless cooler heads prevail there is danger of bloodshed on the forced integration issue," Seamster declared.

Ernie Deane, *Gazette* writer, reported the event for his newspaper.

—0—

9/2/57

I PLACE THE NATIONAL GUARD ON DUTY

On Monday, September 2, I mobilized certain units of the National Guard, totaling 270 men and officers, to prevent violence at Central High School. Here is the text of the concluding part of my speech announcing my action:

I have therefore taken the following action:

"Units of the National Guard have been or are now being mobilized with the mission to maintain or restore the peace and good order of this community. Advance units are already on duty on the grounds of Central High School.

"I have briefed the commanders as to the situation and they already have or are now briefing the members of their commands.

"I have informed Chief Lindsey, Director of the Arkansas State Police, of the developments and he is now mobilizing a force to act as an arm of the State Militia in maintaining or restoring the peace and order of the community and to act in every way possible to protect the lives and property of the citizens of Pulaski County."

MANY DEVELOPMENTS AS GUARD PLACED

After my TV speech announcing the placing of the National Guard at Central High School and affirming that order would be maintained, the following was reported by Bobbie Forster of the *Democrat*.

The school board asked the Negroes not to try to enter Central until the dilemma is "legally solved."

In the federal building, the judge conferred with district attorney personnel.

Wiley Branton, Pine Bluff attorney representing the 35 or so Negro students said, "I have had no talks with my clients this morning."

Daisy Bates, president of the NAACP . . . said that

"events have moved so fast we haven't had time . . . to formulate any statement."

Maj. Gen. Sherman T. Clinger, Arkansas adjutant general, came to the school and said he was glad to see the crowd so orderly.

Bob Troutt Reports

Democrat staff writer Bob Troutt reported from the school:

Classes . . . began promptly at 8:45 a.m. . . . No Negro students showed up.

The only Negro at the scene . . . was L. C. Bates, publisher of the *State Press*, Little Rock, who said . . . he was a spectator.

The crowd of about 300 persons stood across from the main entrance to Central but no sign of violence was displayed.

The Guardsmen numbering 270 were equipped with arms, . . . all unloaded.

No one crossed the lines except students, teachers, school officials and newsmen.

Air Guardsmen of about 100 men commanded by Col. Frank Bailey were placed under orders of Lt. Col. Marion Johnson, troop commander.

George Douthit Reports

Democrat staff writer George Douthit reported from the Capitol that I was greeted by a record number of reporters, photographers and television cameras for a news conference. I said I was prepared to keep National Guardsmen and state troopers at Central indefinitely to keep peace and order. I was asked if I had changed my policy of permitting integration, and replied:

"Negroes enrolled at Ozark this week. There were no threats and integration was accomplished. Where people in a community are ready to accept it in good order, . . . I will not interfere. Ozark was ready."

I said that reports gave indications of violence in the Little Rock schools. I reported that Supt. Blossom asked for protection on Sunday. I learned that five city police cars were sent to give him protection.

A news item about Mayor Woodrow Mann appeared.

MANN SAYS CITY WILL COOPERATE

Mayor Mann issued a statement today promising cooperation in maintaining the peace and order of all citizens and "abide by the law as finally determined."

Mann noted that he had ordered all police vacations and days off cancelled yesterday afternoon.

"It had nothing to do with the governor's actions," Mann said.

Mann's order to city police occurred early Monday before it was known that Guardsmen would be on duty Tuesday morning.

Another news story said I anticipated there would be litigation of all laws pertaining to "forced" integration. Such litigation was needed to clarify the situation but no such legal action was initiated by the federal authorities.

Among the federal officials in conference in Little Rock were J. J. Casper, FBI agent in charge; U.S. District Attorney Osro Cobb and his assistant, James Gallman; Arthur B. Caldwell of the Justice Department; and Judge Davies.

NEWSMEN FLOOD LITTLE ROCK

A news item said newsmen from all sections of the nation jammed into my office for the Tuesday press conference. There was insufficient time for many of them to have gotten to Little Rock in response to the use of the National Guard.

Many of the reporters, especially the representatives of the "liberal" press, had been previously alerted to be present to report Little Rock's great success story on integration, and to hail a new set of national heroes for solving overnight a difficult problem which had never been, and is not yet, easily and completely solved. In fact, some stories to that effect were filed prior to the school opening date.

Many of these early arrivals of the press came to report one story. They remained to report a different story.

SCHOOL BOARD RETURNS TO FEDERAL COURT

In the afternoon of September 3 the School Board returned to Federal Court with a pleading, asking for further instructions. Judge Davies ordered the Board to come before him to show why it should not be cited for contempt.

At the hearing, attorney House said the Board stood ready to do whatever the judge said.

Davies then ordered the Board to "put into effect forthwith" its integration plan. The order was announced by Davies after a hearing that lasted four minutes.

Attorney General Bruce Bennett indicated that the interposition of state power against the authority of the United States Government could touch off a far-reaching states rights case. "The governor was within his rights to call out the Guard to preserve public peace," Bennett said.

Cobb declined to speculate on the states rights question.

DAVIES EXPANDS THE ORIGINAL ORDER

Democrat Reporter Bobbie Forster examined Judge Davies' decision and found that it ordered "all senior high schools" in the Little Rock district to integrate classes "forthwith." The all-inclusive order from the four-minute hearing applied equally to Central, Hall and Horace Mann High Schools.

Forster wrote that a three-line statement issued by the School Board after a one-hour closed door session also applied to all three schools.

This was a major revision of the original order which called for the integration of Central only the first year. On what evidence obtained in the brief hearing did the judge base his decision for this major revision of the original plan?

Was this expansion of the plan an attempt at intimidation of the opponents of the federal court order?

NEW ORDERS TO THE GUARD

At a conference with Gen. Clinger at the executive mansion shortly before midnight, September 3, I gave him new orders for the Guard.

After the "integrate forthwith" order of Judge Davies it was anticipated that those in charge of the black students would now attempt to enroll them in Central High School. If this occurred the Guard would need more specific orders than to "preserve the peace."

Based on reports from the Guard, the State Police and other sources, and an analysis of the crowd that gathered the first day, it appeared there would be great difficulties in preserving order, and grave danger to the black students if they were admitted. No agents for keeping the peace or for assistance in keeping the peace, or for protection of the students, were forthcoming from the federal authorities.

Since it was a federal court order, and the federal agents were accepting no responsibility for its enforcement, it was difficult to see why the lives and welfare of state officials, state citizens and Arkansas students should be jeopardized in enforcement of the order. I felt it would be easy to maintain order and protect everyone, including the black students, if they were denied entry to the school.

And the secret groups of integration opponents were still around with the danger they presented.

I gave Gen. Clinger orders to turn the black students away if they should appear. Additionally, I urged that great care should be taken to protect the students if the need should arise while they were in the vicinity of the school.

We anticipated the students would come in a group, or in small groups accompanied by adults. The appearance of two students, each coming alone, was not anticipated. I did not then suspect that the Communists would have a hand in the strategy.

My judgment of the reaction of the crowd participants was correct. Except for catcalls and heckling of the lone girl student, everything was calm and peaceable as the students were turned away.

▶ ◉ ◀━◉━◉ ◀━◉ ◁

9/4/57

Following are accounts by three different reporters which shows there was no violence and only slight disorder:

Report by George Douthit
Arkansas Democrat, September 4, 1957

> Nine Negro students . . . were turned back by National Guardsmen "on orders of Governor Faubus."
>
> There were no incidents except for some catcalls as a crowd followed a lone Negro girl who walked the length of the front of the school in advance of the main group of seven which was halted some minutes later. . . .
>
> Negro leaders accompanying seven of the students asked a National Guard officer if he were preventing their entering the school on the orders of the governor. The officer replied: "That is right."
>
> The Negroes, delayed only for names and photographs by a squad of photographers and reporters, retraced their steps.
>
> The group of seven Negroes was led by a well-dressed white man . . .

LONE GIRL

> Some minutes before 8 a.m., a lone Negro girl got off the bus at 14th and Park and walked to the school corner. A National Guardsman motioned her away.
>
> . . . She started walking as a crowd gathered around her. . . .
>
> Many white students . . . waiting for classes, started following her, and half way down the block some 100 to 200 persons, mostly students but some white adults, began calling to her.
>
> They said: "Send her back. You've got a better school of your own."
>
> The girl kept walking until she reached 16th and Park, a bus stop, where she sat down on the bus waiting bench.

When the group of Negro students started slowly marching the block to the school corner, there were white students several feet in front of them and some several feet behind, but they paid no obvious attention. . . .

LONE BOY

By this time the lone Negro student had arrived at 16th and Park . . . Most of the crowd was at the spot, along with many photographers and reporters. As a result the main Negro delegation came and went at the other corner with only 25 or 30 adult persons standing around and only a handful of newsmen.

There were no calls from the spectators. The few curious persons stood back and watched the event take place. . . .

YOU SURE OF WHAT YOU SEE OUT THERE GOVERNOR?
By Graham, Ark. Gazette   9/4/57

The *Gazette* cartoon questioned my "evidence of disorder" in the face of integration of the Little Rock schools. A few days later my expressed fears of disorder were confirmed. Fears of disorder were later confirmed in hundreds of cities in every section of the nation, from North to South and East to West.

The Arkansas Democrat
—by Robert Troutt

A 15-year-old Negro girl approached the National Guard line . . . attempting to gain entry, . . . but was refused . . .

Elizabeth Echford, wearing sunglasses and a white dress with broad checkered trim on the skirt, and carrying a small green notebook, then calmly walked the length of Park to 16th and sat on a bus

stop bench while a crowd of some 150 whites formed a circle around her and jeered. There was no violence.

Soon after the girl alighted on the bench . . . a second Negro student walked up Park toward 16th and stopped before a group of Guardsmen . . . He gave his name as Terrance Roberts, 15. He talked freely to reporters.

Terrance told the DEMOCRAT that he had been to several meetings recently with other Negro students who were called together with their parents by the school superintendent and other school officials. He said there was no meeting yesterday.

FOLLOWS ORDERS

The Negro student said they had planned their entry to Central High and were told to walk up to the lines of National Guardsmen and if they were not admitted to walk away and go home.

The boy, a former student of Horace Mann High School, said that the school officials had told him not to return to Horace Mann under any circumstances . . .

Although a large crowd again gathered when he arrived, no names were called and no violence occurred. Terrance said that he was "not afraid."

. . . During the entire proceedings white students remained behind the National Guard lines on school grounds and were told to stay off the sidewalk by the guards.

1,000 GATHERS

The crowd, before the incidents were over, had grown in number to nearly 1,000.

The National Guardsmen remained on school property, except for a few officers who drifted near the two Negro students at 16th and Park to assist State Police officers to keep the crowd in check. . . .

ECHFORD ASSISTED BY GRACE LORCH

(A lengthy story by Jerry Dhonau in the *Arkansas Gazette* contained the following information.)

Elizabeth Echford alighted from a public transportation bus at Thirteenth Street at 7:53 a.m. and walked a block to Park and Fourteenth Street.

She approached the Guardsmen on the corner, . . . [then] crossed the street and walked south on Park Avenue through a heckling crowd and sat down on a bus stop bench.

GUARD DISPERSES CROWD

She told newsmen she had "nothing to say." The abusive shouts from the crowd continued. A Guard officer told the crowd to move back from the bench and it complied.

Ten minutes later the second Negro, . . . Terrance Roberts, 15, approached the Guard line across Park Avenue from where the girl was sitting. . . .

Roberts said he had not registered and that . . . he was one of eight or nine other Negroes who were to enroll at the school.

Roberts then approached the Echford girl and spent some time in her presence.

A PLEA FOR ORDER

As heckling continued, Rev. L. D. Foreman, a Little Rock white minister and segregationist, tried to quiet the crowd by asking "Let's cooperate with them."

Roberts did not talk to the Echford girl, but it was then that she consented to give her name and age to newsmen.

Roberts then walked away along south on Park Avenue. . . .

. . . a white woman who identified herself as Mrs. Grace Lorch stood behind her [Elizabeth] at the bench. Mrs. Lorch said she "thought I would stay with her." . . .

ABUSED VOCALLY

Mrs. Lorch became the object of vocal abuse from the crowd of other whites. Two white women . . . asked for her name and address, but Mrs. Lorch refused to tell them.

At Mrs. Lorch's suggestion she accompanied the girl across Sixteenth Street to another bus stop.

A bus came and Mrs. Lorch boarded it with the girl.

7 NEGROES STOPPED

It was during the time Mrs. Lorch was with the girl that the seven prospective Negro students made their effort to cross the line. . .

The Negro teen-agers, Jefferson Thomas, Carlotta Walls, Gloria Ray, Jane Hill, Ernest Green, Thelma Mothershead and Minnie Jean Brown, were accompanied by several adults, including Rev. Henry Bass, a Little Rock Negro minister, and Rev. Will Campbell of Nashville, Tenn., a representative of the National Council of Churches.

The integration attempt resulted in no violence. All of the school's 27 Negro employees were on the job.

LORCHES INVOLVED

A *Democrat* photo on Page 2 showed two women members of the crowd present at Central High School, engaged in a heated discussion over the question of integration or segregation and my action in calling the National Guard to the scene.

Although unidentified at the time one of the women was Grace Lorch, who with her husband, Lee Lorch, both known Communists, played a leading role in the controversy.

—0—

COMMUNISTS STAGE COUP

On the morning of September 4, after careful planning and instructions, Elizabeth Echford, age 15, was placed on a city bus and directed to alight at Thirteenth Street and Park Avenue. She was then to walk the one block to Park and Fourteenth Street, where she would encounter the line of National Guardsmen surrounding Central High School.

She was to approach the line of Guardsmen to see if she could enter the school. If turned away, as anticipated, she was to cross the street and walk south on Park Avenue which ran in front of the school. Along that route would be the dozens of television news cameramen, photographers, reporters and observers.

She was instructed to again approach the line, and when turned away to continue south along the line of Guardsmen for the full two blocks in front of the school, through the spectators, students and newsmen.

At the end of the prescribed route, she was to cross Park Avenue and sit on a bench at a bus stop. Mrs. Grace Lorch, one of the alleged Communists who were the central figures in developing this strategy, would precede the Echford girl to that point and wait for her there.

The Echford girl followed these directions to the letter, and the success in reaping publicity was phenomenal.

At the bus stop the Echford girl was seated. A crowd which had gathered, started to heckle her. The hecklers were driven away by National Guard officers and members of the State Police. Another who protected her was the Rev. L. D. Foreman, who was known as a segregationist.

Mrs. Lorch, who was given credit in the press for "befriending" the Negro student, actually inflamed the situation by engaging in heated arguments with other women bystanders.

Ten minutes after Miss Echford was seated, the second lone Negro youth approached the Guard line. He was Terrance Roberts, a talkative boy, apparently quite calm. He talked freely to newsmen and said he was one of eight or nine other Negroes who were to enroll at the school.

When he related this bit of information, newsmen opened ranks for Roberts to approach the Guard line where he paused while photographers and cameramen took plenty of pictures.

Roberts then turned back, continued to converse freely with newsmen, and then went to the bench where the Echford girl was seated.

Lee Lorch, the alleged Communist, then under a congressional contempt citation for refusal to answer questions of a congressional committee at Dayton, Ohio, may have been the behind-the-scenes guide for Roberts. Lorch's contempt citation was then on appeal to federal court. He was not identified by newsmen as a participant in any of the activities, although a number of times a "well-dressed unidentified white man" was mentioned.

After obtaining maximum publicity, Roberts said he was "going back home to wait for further instructions." He departed alone and unmolested.

Shortly thereafter, Mrs. Lorch took the Echford girl to another bus stop where they boarded a bus together.

While Miss Echford and Terrance Roberts were the center of all this attention, as planned by their instructors, the other seven Negro students came quietly under the direction of several accompanying adults, both black and white, to another point, 13th and Park Street. There they asked the Guard troop commander about entering the school, were told that they could not, and quietly departed. As the news reports related, no voice was raised nor any unkind remark made in the presence of the seven students and their adult escorts.

COMMUNIST METHODS AND PLANNING

A part of the training of all dedicated Communist leaders is how to obtain publicity favorable to their cause and unfavorable publicity for their opposition.

Roberts and Miss Echford did not try to enter the high school alone on their own initiative. Their individual approaches were planned carefully to the last detail, as to locale, time, attitude, and even dress and what to say.

The planners of the publicity stunt chose the students well. While Roberts was the more suitable for interview — he was talkative and handled his speech well — the Echford girl stole the show. She was a fine-looking girl attractively and tastefully dressed, sufficiently shy, and her demeanor and general appeal could not have been better. Her long two-block walk through students, spectators and reporters, her two attempts to cross the Guard line and her 35-minute stay on the bus bench were perfect set-ups for newspaper and television photographs which were taken by the hundreds.

The news stories and the photographs of Miss Echford, the guardsmen and some of the shouting whites — who would have been wiser to keep quiet — went ringing around the world. The lone, shy, well-mannered Negro girl, notebook in hand, turned back by lines of armed Guardsmen and ringed, temporarily at least, by heckling whites — what more appealing picture could be portrayed to gain the desired sympathetic publicity.

How was the public to know that the actions, movements and statements of the two students had been carefully planned and executed for the sole purpose of achieving the notoriety they had now gained? If their main aim had been to enter the school, the attempt would have been made in the company of the other seven students. This point cannot be stressed too strongly.

When I saw the newspaper and television reports of the morning's events, I knew that a dramatic and successful publicity coup had been staged. When I saw Mrs. Lorch's name, I knew who had planned the coup.

The purpose of Communists in any free country is to espouse any cause, oppose any program and engage in any disruptive activity which will create turmoil and disorder, and which will weaken the government and the nation.

In America at that time their principal weapon was racial strife. Everywhere that trouble in this field occurred Communist agitators were deeply involved, although their efforts were most of the time unknown to the great majority of others engaged in the struggle.

It is possible the school officials in Little Rock did not know of the publicity plan. Even if they knew, they were simply caught up in a situation and it did not mean they were Communistic in any sense. I regarded people like Virgil Blossom and "Brick" Lile as American as apple pie.

As to newspaper publisher L. C. Bates, there never seemed the least taint of subversion in his attitude or philosophy. His wife, Mrs. Daisy Bates, was known to have had some Communist connections in the past.

When Henry Wallace, former vice president and cabinet member under Franklin Roosevelt, whom I had always greatly admired as a progressive and an idealist, ran for President as an Independent in 1948 his main organizational backing came from the Communists.

Wallace visited Little Rock during his campaign where he was photographed with Mrs. Bates and a man later identified as a known Communist.

But that circumstance did not by any means make Daisy Bates a Communist. After all, I was at Commonwealth College with known carriers of the Red Card and that did not make me subversive.

There is no doubt in my mind that both Lee and Grace Lorch were long-time dedicated Communists who had risen to high positions in the Communist apparatus.

I was provided with information by the dean of the Law School of Notre Dame University of South Bend, Indiana — information which, for the most part, purportedly came from FBI investigations. A part of that information was as follows:

Grace Lonergan Lorch was identified in Boston as a member of the Communist Party in 1950; she attended the Massachusetts State Communist Party convention in 1948; was invited to the National Convention of the Communist Party of the U.S.A. in 1943; and was a member of the New England District Communist Party.

She wrote letters attacking the prosecution of the Rosenbergs, the atomic spies, and was in close touch with Junius Scales, the Southern Regional Director of the Communist Party.

Both the Lorches were at Fisk University in Nashville, Tennessee, which they left to come to Little Rock, where Lee Lorch obtained a position as a professor at the Philander Smith Negro College.

There was an equal amount of information available on Lee Lorch's Communist connections and activities.

Perhaps other Communists were involved in the Little Rock Central High School controversy. Certainly there were a number of fellow travelers. The latter are sometimes more effective in assisting actual Communists in their endeavors because they bear an aura of respectability in the community and are less susceptible to attack by anti-Communists.

In fairness to Philander Smith College, it should be stated that the Lorches departed from that institution soon after the Memphis hearings by the U.S. Senate Un-American Activities Committee later in the year. Philander Smith had the reputation of being a very fine college — it was supported by many churches and a number of philanthropists in the state — and was not known for harboring known Communists on its faculty or in its student body.

As to the Lorches' departure, it was the policy of the Communist Party to move its operatives to new locations when their identity and party connections became exposed.

In connection with the appearance of the black students at the school, a significant circumstance should not be overlooked. That was the belief of the black people, the School Board members, the Justice Department officials and all the integrationists, including the Communist planners of the publicity seeking event, in my determination to prevent injury to anyone. Otherwise the display of the two lone black students in a possibly hostile crowd in an inflammatory atmosphere would not have been directed, or permitted.

Knowing of my attitude and the preparations to prevent violence, the promoters of the publicity effort felt they could safely use the two lone students in the manner which was done. This fact is borne out in a brief article by Miss Echford published in the May 1979 issue of *Southern Exposure,* a quarterly magazine put out by the Institute for Southern Studies at Chapel Hill, N.C. Excerpts of the article appeared in the May 17, 1979 issue of the *Arkansas Gazette,* page 2B, from which this quote is taken.

"She [Miss Echford] said she was nervous, but not 'too scared,' because she assumed the Guardsmen would protect her from the crowd."

That is quite an assumption for a 15-year-old girl student who probably knew nothing of the National Guard or Guardsmen, unless she had been instructed beforehand.

Knowing Communist methods and attitude I have a strong feeling that they would not have been unduly concerned if the students had been subjected to violence. From their viewpoint even more favorable publicity would have been obtained.

Anyway it was I, not the Communists, the Federal officials, the school board or the advocates of the Federal Court Order, who bore the burden of preventing harm to anyone and property damage in the area.

○━○━○━○━○━

Ft. Worth Star Telegram
September 4, 1957—

CLASH OF INTEGRATION AND PUBLIC ORDER

The governor of Arkansas . . . in anticipation of violence, surrounded Central High School . . . with armed militiamen. The school board, faced with that situation, advised against attempts to register Negro students in the school. . . .

Governor Faubus evidently was acting under . . . his police powers. . . . His tactics are a close parallel with those employed by Allan Shivers . . . in the integration attempt at Mansfield last fall. The salient difference, however, is that Governor Shivers sent in Rangers after violence had erupted. Governor Faubus has acted before the fact of violence — in anticipation that it would occur if he did not act. . . .

The issue thus becomes one of whether a state governor, under his police powers and to maintain order, can successfully block an . . . order of the federal courts. It is difficult to see how the federal authorities can proceed against such a situation, . . . without openly challenging the supposed sovereignty of the states.

It should be remembered that Governor Faubus, technically at least, is not challenging the so-called law of the land . . . What he has done is to nullify the effect of it . . . under his duty to preserve public order. . . .

. . . the question rather reduces itself to one of whether the public order is to be considered of more importance than integration. . . .

It remains to be seen what the federal government will, or can, do about it. In the case of Governor Shivers it did nothing, although he invited the federal courts to direct any contempt action at him. The constitutional issues here involved go far. . . . But when the United States Supreme Court overstepped the boundaries of state authority it made the present confusion inevitable.

TO KEEP THE PEACE

Editorial, Richmond News Leader
September 4, 1957

Virginia's J. Lindsey Almond, Jr., late yesterday said all that needs to be said on the crisis in Little Rock. The Democratic candidate for Governor . . . said:

"The first obligation of the Governor of any state, is to see that peace is kept and to preserve law and order. As long as the State does that, it's certainly no business of the Federal government."

LITTLE ROCK BECOMES NATIONAL AND INTERNATIONAL NEWS

Now the headlines glared in newspapers all across the nation and what became known as the Little Rock Crisis became the object of national and international attention.

Some papers took a completely anti-attitude toward my actions without the slightest attempt to learn the facts of the situation. Others more knowledgeable took a favorable view while still others waited to become better informed.

President Eisenhower denied any intent on the part of federal authorities to take me into custody. Reportedly, such a move was seriously discussed by federal officials in Little Rock.

Some sources in Washington, both official and unofficial, took an objective view. Their conclusion was that my motive in the use of the Guard was the key to the situation. If I had indeed used the Guard to prevent violence and to preserve order, then I was on sound ground both legally and morally, and was guilty of no defiance of the federal courts or federal law. On the other hand if the use of the Guard was solely to thwart the integration order of the federal courts, then I would be guilty of impeding federal authority.

I faced the reporters, some 70 in number from all across the nation, in a full dress press conference to answer dozens of questions.

In the meantime the circulation of petitions to oust Supt. Blossom from his position began in the city.

HOSTILE PRESS FINDS MOUTHPIECE

It didn't take long for the hostile members of the press and the federal power advocates, to find a public official to serve as their mouthpiece. To the *Gazette* and the hostile national press, this official was to them the same as "Charlie McCarthy" was to Edgar Bergen. On September 5th the Little Rock papers carried the following headline and story:

Mann Raps Action of Governor;
Mayor Says Faubus Claim of Violence
Is "Political Hoax"

Mayor Mann charged today that Governor Faubus' claim of threatened violence in the public schools is a "disgraceful political hoax," and said if it is not stopped "it could retard the state's progress by at least 25 years."

Mann said the situation here "at no time" has been anything that the Little Rock police could not control.

TEST OF STRENGTH IN ARKANSAS
By Knox, Nashville Banner   9/5/57

There were also many defenders of my position.

A "Judicial Dictatorship" (U.S. Supreme Court) was attempting to push down the pillars of "Police Powers" which sustain "Law and Order in a Sovereign State," just as the blind Samson destroyed the temple in Biblical days.

An editorial on the same page said:

. . . the Supreme Court, is attempting to force racial integration in violation of the Constitution and in the absence of Federal law.

If Congress had passed a school integration law that was constitutionally valid, Gov. Faubus' action

ORVAL AT THE BRIDGE, By Kennedy, Ark. Democrat, 9/4/57

Kennedy interpreted my use of the Guard as "Interposition." At the bridge I defended the city from attack from outside invaders, as did Horatius in the early history of Rome.

would be inexcusable. He would have no right to use his power as governor and his state authority over the National Guard to stand in the face of valid, though objectionable, law.

But Congress has passed no such law. The illegal aggressor is not the governor of Arkansas who seeks to maintain the status quo as desired by the majority of his people. The aggressor is a lawless Supreme Court bent on unconstitutional sociological reform.

. . . The weakness of the Federal position is not that there are no extreme measures the Federal Government may take but that the only measures left to it are extreme.

TO GET A PAIL OF WATER
By Dowling, N.Y. Herald Tribune   9/5/57

Now the cartoonists began having a field day, many of them at my expense. This was one of the first on the national scene.

A wall labeled "Orderly Integration Plans" held back a sea of "trouble," as I drove a spike through the wall to get a pail of water — "Gov. Faubus' political gains." At the time I could see no political gain for me in the controversy.

INFORMATION OF POSSIBLE VIOLENCE

Virgil Blossom's information of caravans of determined objectors to integration at Central High School were not erroneous. One group of three carloads of men, anti-integrationists from East Central Arkansas, stopped on the morning of Sept. 3 at the home of a man of like mind in a town 25 to 40 miles east of Little Rock. The men were heavily armed with repeating rifles, shotguns and pistols.

The arrivals were persuaded by their ally at the home to unload their weapons and leave them at his place.

"Well, hell," said one of the men to the home owner, "we thought you meant to stop this" [integration].

"Oh, we do," said the resident, "but hadn't you heard? The governor is placing the National Guard and the State Police at the school, and he said in his talk [by TV the night of September 2] that he was convinced all the kids had to go to their own schools.

"So, we're going on up there [to Central High School] but we mustn't take any weapons. We'll just stand around and look sad," he told the new arrivals. "We have to wait and see what happens and see for sure what the governor does," he added.

The weapons were taken from the three cars and stacked on the back porch of the house which, as described to me, constituted "a veritable arsenal."

These determined men, after leaving their weapons, were a part of the crowd which came to the high school the first day. I do not know about their presence during the day or on succeeding days, but the incident indicated the degree of violence that could have occurred had I not placed the Guardsmen at the school.

A well directed volley by these determined men, long skilled in the use of firearms, possibly assisted by others, would have resulted in any number of dead and wounded.

It was not the "shouters" who gathered at the school, nor the agitated members of the Mothers League, nor the speechmaking segregationist leaders that caused me the greatest alarm. My most pronounced concern was the possible violent reaction of members of these small groups of quiet, determined men who had vowed in secret meetings to stop the forcible integration of Central High School.

These men were not proclaiming publicly their intentions. It was of them that Blossom spoke when he told me of secret meetings being held to plan the blocking of court-ordered integration. These groups, said Blossom, were operating secretly in various parts of the state and in Little Rock.

These were the men Blossom feared would be in the caravans which he said were converging on Little Rock when he called me, thoroughly alarmed, while Bill Smith and I were in conference at the governor's office on September 1.

In my opinion Mr. Blossom had real cause for alarm. He had become widely known as the author of the integration plan for Little Rock, and thus the symbol of court-ordered or forcible integration. The success of the plan was to be a model, it was said, for the rest of the state. There were men who were determined that this would not be the case.

To the contrary, it was reasoned by some opponents, would not the elimination of the plan's symbol be a lesson to all those who, in the future, might think and plan along the same line? And if the blacks who were active participants in the plan were driven back, would it not be a lesson long remembered in other areas by those who might contemplate the forcible integration of other schools?

As to the Central High School situation, it had become a focal point of contention. There, it seemed, because of developments, both sides had determined to make their stands.

One determined opponent of integration, skilled in the use of firearms, could give way to emotion in a moment of frustration and anger, and wreak carnage with a repeating rifle. If others joined in the gunplay, as was possible or even likely once begun, who knows where the death and injury would stop?

Or, if the gunplay were carried out by those quietly determined to pull the trigger if necessary to stop integration, the result would be the same.

But this is not reasonable or logical, say the critics, to suppose that such could happen.

Was there any logic or reason in the killing of Charles Evers in Mississippi? Or the murder of the three civil rights workers in the same state?

OPPORTUNITY IN ARKANSAS, *By Jensen, Chicago Daily News, 9/5/57*

Along with this extreme cartoon appeared an editorial containing much criticism in which I was termed a "Sassafras Mussolini," with the expressed hope that I would be cut down to size.

The Negro students who sought to enter Central were leaving a much finer facility. Horace Mann was new and modern and was rated by the National Magazine of Architecture as fifth in the nation in beauty, design and utility.

Was there any logic or reason in the assassination of President John F. Kennedy in Dallas? Or Martin Luther King at Memphis? Or Senator Bobby Kennedy at Los Angeles? Or the shooting of George Wallace in Maryland?

Was there any reason or logic in the riots in Watts in which 38 people were killed, hundreds injured and property damage into the millions?

Was there any logic or reason to the looting and burning of whole sections of the nation's capital, a shameful spectacle witnessed by the people of the nation and the world?

In spite of the widespread criticism and verbal abuse which I endured, it was just such deeds, as well as rioting, property damage and injury and death to persons, which I sought to prevent in Little Rock, Arkansas.

History has recorded my success.

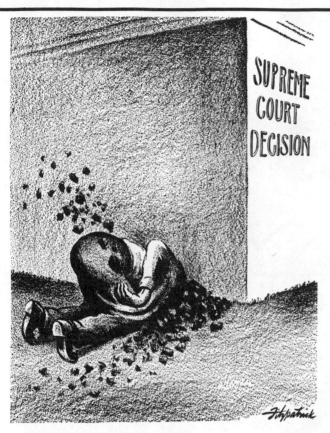

STATESMANSHIP IN ARKANSAS
By Fitzpatrick, St. Louis Post Dispatch   9/5/57

The political leaders of Arkansas were pictured attempting to undermine the U.S. Supreme Court decision. There was no recognition of the great constitutional question involved that divided the nation.

9/6/57

IKE AND THE CONSTITUTION

Editorial

Lebanon Daily News
Lebanon, Penna., Sept. 6, 1957

President Eisenhower has telegraphed Gov. Faubus of Arkansas asking him to abide by the Constitution of the United States. It might be well for Ike to read the Constitution, too. Here is what the First Congress of the United States under the Administration of George Washington wrote into the Tenth Amendment of the Bill of Rights:

"The powers not delegated to the United States by the Constitution, nor prohibited by it to the States, are reserved to the States respectively, or to the people."

It is simple language, easy to understand. Any graduate of West Point, or junior high school for that matter, should be able to understand it.

In Article III, Section 2, the Constitution says: "The Trial of all Crimes, except in cases of Impeachment, shall be by Jury."

When Ike was attempting to push his so-called "Civil Rights" bill through the last session of Congress, he made vigorous attempts to do away with jury trials.

Mr. Eisenhower and our degraded Supreme Court, not the Governor of Arkansas, should be forced to obey the Constitution.

SCHOOL DAZE
By Crockett, Washington Star   9/6/57

There were several "school daze" cartoons. This, one of the first.

GAZETTE "POWERS" OFFENDED

The personal incidents I experienced, or which were related to me were many, but there is insufficient space to relate them. Here is one.

Early in the Crisis of '57 Hugh Patterson was holding forth to some of his associates in the Little Rock Club. The club was a private segregated facility located in the downtown business section where some members drank bourbon and played poker at the noon hour.

"We can't let him get away with it! We can't let him get away with it!" Patterson exclaimed in a state of agitation.

"What do you mean, We?" inquired a listener (who was also my informer).

Patterson then modified his statement to explain, still in a vehement attitude, that the federal government couldn't afford to let my action go unchallenged.

My informer said Patterson regarded my action as a personal challenge to him.

It may well have been true that he so regarded the matter. I had long before discovered when the *Gazette* forces were supporting me politically, a propensity on the part of the *Gazette* hierarchy to rule without personal benefit of office. Except for the elderly J. N. Heiskell, I clearly detected a patronizing attitude on the part of Ashmore, Patterson and others toward me and "their men in office." They had an overweening desire to dictate the decisions and policies of state government through "friendly advice" to state officials. Those who followed their instructions were then rewarded with good publicity and friendly editorials, although, even then, they must submit at times to some chastisement from the pens of the benevolent, wiser and superior, as they regarded themselves, *Gazette* policy makers.

It was now abundantly clear that I was not controlled by the *Gazette,* and it was not dictating my decisions or my policies. The ego of the policy makers had been severely bruised. I'm sure my disregard of their viewpoint in the school controversy was taken as a personal affront.

READY WITH THE TOMBSTONE, By Knox, Nashville Banner, 9/6/57

The extremists were ready to bury the rights of a sovereign state and the powers and the duties of its elected officials.

The following editorials appeared in the *News and Courier* of Charleston, S.C. on Sept. 10.

APPEAL TO THE U.N.

As the head of a sovereign state threatened by aggressive outside action, Gov. Faubus of Arkansas may have a good case to present to the United Nations. He was duly elected by the people of his state. He is not a dictator ruling with authority seized by force of arms.

Interference with the internal affairs of the State of Arkansas is the kind of thing Americans deplore when the Russians do it. The fate of Hungary is a reminder of what can happen to a small state under the merciless power of a big one.

Another editorial said:

'MENTAL UPSET' LAID TO GOV. FAUBUS AS INTEGRATION PROPAGANDA LINE

The integrationist press now is reporting that Gov. Faubus is "mentally upset."

For its lead front page story Sunday, The Charlotte Observer published a special dispatch from Little Rock that started like this:

"Many here see strong reasons to believe that Gov. Orval Faubus of Arkansas may be emotionally and mentally upset by the situation in which he finds himself."

"Mental sickness" is a favorite expression used by integrationists to describe people who want to separate the races. The OBSERVER's special writer at Little Rock is a member of the staff of the DETROIT FREE PRESS, another link in the Knight chain that owns the Charlotte newspaper.

Still another Knight newspaper is The CHICAGO DAILY NEWS.

THE DAILY NEWS and THE CHARLOTTE OBSERVER last week printed editorials attacking the governor of Arkansas for calling out the troops to guard the schools. The purpose of the troops, said THE CHICAGO DAILY NEWS on Thursday, "is to defy not only decent human behavior, but an order of a U.S. judge."

Echoing this sentiment two days later, The CHARLOTTE OBSERVER said: "Faubus cannot be allowed to win the Arkansas fight . . . The authority bestowed upon the federal judiciary by the U.S. Constitution and federal statutes cannot be flouted by an individual, be he private citizen or governor."

Nothing will stand in the way of the integrationists in their mania to force mixture of white and colored races. The suggestion of "mental sickness" implies readiness to lock up opponents.

THE OBSERVER said that since Gov. Faubus "retired to the Governor's Mansion Wednesday afternoon, he hasn't made a public appearance. Even his closest friends have been repulsed in their efforts to reach him . . . A former Faubus friend said he had personal and specific knowledge that tranquilizer drugs had been sent to the Governor's Mansion in a two-day period this week."

The strain on Gov. Faubus and others in Arkansas is obvious. Those who saw him on television Sunday night, however, would have difficulty believing that he is "mentally upset." He parried reporters' hostile questions with skill.

The quotes from news stories — not editorial viewpoint — appearing in the *Charlotte Observer* show how some editors can and do falsely slant the news.

The Communists imprison those citizens who disagree with them as "mental patients." The liberal authorities in the U.S. were, for a time, ready to use the same methods of suppression in this country, as indicated in this story, and the treatment of Gen. Edwin Walker later in the Ole Miss difficulties.

THIS IS AN EXPLOSIVE SITUATION
By Herblock, Washington Post   9/6/57

This extreme cartoon accused me of adding to an inflammatory condition. I was doing everything possible, both publicly and behind the scenes, to reduce the explosiveness of the situation. There would be less danger if the battle could be kept in the legal and political arenas.

9/7/57

EYES OF THE NATION

Only four days after action began in the Little Rock crisis, the eyes of the nation were on the Arkansas capital.

The *Gazette* was filled with news, viewpoints, speculation and comments to bolster its viewpoint. There were also editorials including one in defense of Dr. Benjamin Fine, reporter for the *New York Times*.

Fine was more interested in expressing his views, which were anti-South in everything, than in reporting what was happening. Consequently, he created some problems on the school grounds which had to be handled by Gen. Clinger and Col.

Johnson. This opinion of Dr. Fine was conveyed to me by many reporters who worked with him.

The distortion and actual falsehoods in Dr. Fine's reporting and public statements are vividly illustrated in the following quotation from "Little Rock and the Press" by Hoyt H. Purvis for the Degree of Master of Journalism at The University of Texas in June, 1963.

Recalling the incident with General Clinger, Fine said in July, 1962, that he had "gazed in amazement" as four or five hundred armed militiamen with naked bayonets, revolvers and rifles at ready, stood shoulder to shoulder in front of the high school. "A yelling, angry mob shouted foul obscenities against the Negroes. And I, with a stub of a pencil and secretary's notebook pad, was accused of inciting to riot." (pages 68 and 69 of Purvis paper)

Falsehoods in Fine's statement:

(1) The total number of Guardsmen mobilized at the time was 270 and all of them were never on duty at once. So Fine could never have gazed at "four or five hundred armed militiamen" as he stated.

(2) The Guardsmen never prepared bayonets for use, so Fine's statement about "naked bayonets" is a naked lie.

(3) Revolvers were never in evidence for use at the school.

(4) The black students came and were turned away on September 4. There were no shouts at the seven who came in a group. There were shouts at one of the two who came alone, but no "foul obscenities" were reported. However, the incident between General Clinger and Fine occurred at a later date. No black students were present, as Fine falsely states, at the time he was admonished by Clinger against inciting to riot. They appeared only once, on Sept. 4.

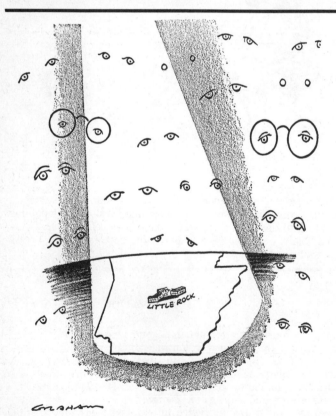

EYES OF THE NATION
By Graham, Ark. Gazette   9/7/57

IS THIS THE WAY TO SCHOOL?
By Dobbins, Boston Traveler   9/6/57

A good question!
Through the ranks of soldiers, U.S. marshals, state or city police, or armed guards employed by school authorities, is not the proper way to school for any child.

DISGRACEFUL STAND
By Goldberg, N.Y. Journal American   9/6/57

This cartoonist missed the point of the controversy. No one was attempting to deny an education to any student. The black

THE TOP ISSUE AT LITTLE ROCK
By Russell, Los Angeles Times   9/6/57

This cartoonist said federal law was pierced with the bayonet of states rights. Others had the opposite view, and no one could quote the law.

CHAIN REACTION
By Grant, Oakland, Cal. Tribune   9/6/57

The cartoonist sought to create the false impression that my actions had triggered a chain reaction which would cause dynamiting. To the contrary that was what I sought to avoid.

PAPER COVER IN DIXIE
By Hesse, St. Louis Globe Democrat   9/6/57

The papering over of the problem by court orders would not prevent an explosion of the integration bomb.

THREE "R"s IN ARKANSAS
By Justus, Minneapolis Star   9/7/57

The three Rs theme used the it's-good-for-Communist-propaganda angle. The people regarded all three Rs as false.

221

THIS IS MY RESPONSIBILITY
By Seibel, Richmond Times Dispatch   9/6/57

The rooster announced to the federal government eagle that Little Rock, Arkansas, was his responsibility.

PUT UP YOUR DUKES
By Kennedy, Ark. Democrat   9/6/57

No one in Arkansas, least of all I, sought any conflict with U.S. authority. A majority of the people believed the conflict was forced on the state by the illegal use of U.S. authority through the U.S. Supreme Court.

students chosen for the integration experiment were leaving a finer school than the one they sought to enter.

In this newspaper on the East Coast appeared a critical editorial exactly the same as appeared in the *Los Angeles Examiner* on the same day.

Was someone directing a nationwide propaganda campaign from a national headquarters?

9/8/57

FEDERAL, STATE LINE UNDECIDED

INTEGRATION CRISIS RECALLS IKE'S STAND IN TEXAS RANGER CALL

Sept. 8, 1957

Yet to be resolved in the Little Rock school situation is the question many feel to be the fundamental issue: the exact dividing line between state and federal authority.

Governor Faubus called the . . . Guard to duty . . . with the expressed purpose of preserving "public peace and preventing violence." He has interpreted his order to the guardsmen to turn Negro students away to be in the best public interest.

. . . Constitutional authorities have declared that the governor's "sincerity" and "motive" are the key as to whether he is within his constitutional rights. . . . if he acted in good faith . . . he is on sound constitutional ground.

Almost a year ago to the day — Sept. 5, 1956 — President Eisenhower was quoted at one of his press conferences, attended by 191 reporters.

From page five of the press conference transcript came these words:

"The President: Well, in each case I think the local governments have moved promptly to stop the violence. . . . Under the law the federal government . . . cannot move into a state until the state is not able to handle the matter."

"Now, in the Texas case there was the attorney for the students did report this violence and asked help, . . . But before anyone could move the Texas authorities had moved in and order was restored so the question became unimportant."

"Sarah McLendon, El Paso Times, reminded the president that:

"In doing so, Governor Allan Shivers sent Rangers to defy the court order, re-assign out the Negro pupils and said in a public statement which was carried in the newspapers: 'I'd defy the federal government.' He said, 'Tell the federal courts if they want to come after anyone, to come after me and cite me in this matter.' I wonder if you have discussed this with anyone in the Department of Justice?"

"The President: I have not discussed it because you are quoting both an order that I have not read and a statement that I have not seen. . . . Now, just exactly what Governor Shivers said I don't know. This is the first I have heard of it."

Evidently Brownell, Adams and others did not wish to challenge Gov. Shivers, governor of a large state, who was supporting Eisenhower against the Democratic nominee, Adlai Stevenson, in the campaign of 1956, at the very time of the Mansfield affair. Therefore, the president was purposely, it appears, kept in complete ignorance of Gov. Shivers' open defiance of a federal court order when he stopped the attempted integration of the schools at Mansfield, Texas.

There could be no clearer example of the political motivation and hypocrasy of the national authorities involved than the cases of Texas and Arkansas.

Texas was a large state with a powerful governor not bound to either party, with a large number of electoral votes that could be numbered in either political column. The defiance of the federal court order at Mansfield occurred while a campaign for the presidency was under way. Therefore, Brownell, the Justice Department, the President and the national administration made no response to the outright defiance. National liberals, including the Democrats, developed a universal case of lockjaw on the matter.

Arkansas was a small state with a governor supporting unequivocally the Democratic nominee for president in 1956, and a small number of electoral votes already counted in the Democratic column. Therefore, Hoxie was a good place for the Justice Department to inject its authority, Brownell to show his colors and the national Democratic liberals to make statements, even though no federal court order was involved.

Little Rock was advantageous in 1957, all for the same reasons, and all concerned could play national politics with the situation without restraint.

But, not so with Texas.

WATCHFUL WAITING

News stories reported that Ike had been advised to federalize the Arkansas National Guard, and that a closed meeting of the Joint Chiefs of Staff was held in the Pentagon; that Eisenhower was on the spot and silent after Judge Davies' ruling; that I remained firm with no change in course.

Mrs. Daisy Bates said the Negro students would not try to enter Central on Monday, that they awaited "safe passage."

Mayor Mann announced he would ask me to recall the Guard from duty at Central, and Attorney General Bruce Bennett gave an opinion on police powers of the state.

ARKANSAS LEADS IN INTEGRATION

Democrat staff writers Robert McCord and Larry Williams wrote a long story headed: Arkansas Leads South in Integration. The story was factual, revealing that far more integration had been effected in all fields in Arkansas than any other Southern state, and more than most of them combined including the border states.

PEOPLE SUPPORT MY STAND

A prominent news picture showed Bill Clements, owner of a North Little Rock supermarket, presenting to me a petition many feet in length, containing the names of unsolicited signers backing my stand in the integration controversy.

CAMDEN DEPOT TO REMAIN OPEN

A bit of good news was the announcement that the Shumaker Depot at Camden would remain open thus preserving jobs for many workers, both black and white.

Karr Shannon had this item in his column.
If the federal courts continue to increase their jurisdiction in the Land of Opportunity, state courts may have so little business as to be compelled to emulate the theatres — sell popcorn.
States Rights — The right to a hearing in a federal court.

ARKANSAS TRAVELERS
By Werner, Indianapolis Star   9/6/57

Two travelers equipped with Federal interference in states' rights and bigotry, advanced on the Little Rock high schools. An intrusion by such forces into the South while similar problems in the North were ignored, was bound to create sectional divisions and controversy.

And this was indicated by a Northern newspaper.

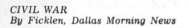

CIVIL WAR
By Ficklen, Dallas Morning News   9/5/57

A grave question of federal military force vs. state military force, was raised by the cartoonist. An editorial on the same page said:

It is the Governor's position that blood will flow if he withdraws the troops and he is not willing to permit that eventuality. It is his job to preserve the peace, school or no school, according to him. He is not opposing the court, but if the court insists upon a situation which results in a breach of the peace, or is about to result in violence, then it is his job to act. And he has acted.

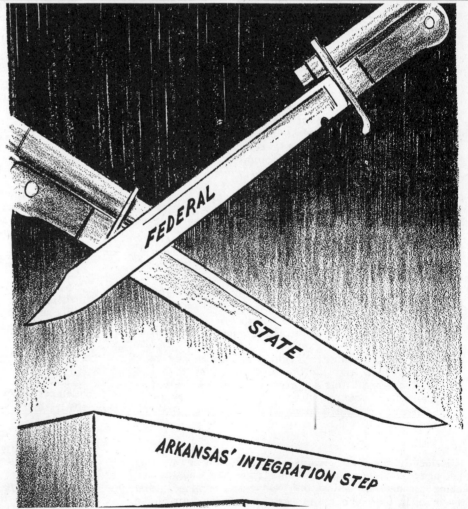

THE LITTLE ROCK SCHOOL ISSUE
By Little, Nashville Tennesseean   9/8/57

This cartoonist saw the Little Rock School Issue as merely an ineffectual effort by a tiny midget governor against the Gulliver of Uncle Sam.

LITTLE ROCK
By Ivey, St. Petersburg, Fla. Times   9/8/57

The cartoonist said the wheel of race relations progress struck a Little Rock. Was it racial progress or racial controversy?

FAUBUS KEEPING PROMISE ON ISSUE OF INTEGRATION

—By George Douthit
(*Arkansas Democrat*, Sept. 8, 1957)

While not entirely accurate, this column contains information, background and insight about matters which were largely forgotten by supporters, and deliberately and consistently ignored by critics.

"This . . . integration situation came to a climax last week, but it really had its inception in last summer's primary election when Governor Faubus said: "No school district will be forced to integrate against its will as long as I am governor."

Now when a politician makes a flat promise like that, he had better do everything he can to keep it — unless he is planning retirement. . . .

Also, no one expected that the governor, in trying to keep that promise would go as far as he went last week in calling out the . . . Guard . . .

But let's go back to the governor and his race for a second term. He had expressed the hope that segregation in Arkansas would not become an issue in the elections because it was a Southwide problem and not just an issue in this state.

Then along came . . . Jim Johnson, Crossett, running for governor on a segregationist platform. Mr. Faubus sized up the situation, saw the following Mr. Johnson was getting and learned he had to make a statement on segregation.

The governor did not want to come out all the way and say he would block integration in Arkansas because this state already was being integrated and Negroes already were in a number of schools . . .

NOT AGAINST WILL

So he made the promise: No integrating against your will. This satisfied eastern Arkansas segregationists, . . . and they gave the governor voting support. Consequently, he won over Mr. Johnson by a big majority.

Eastern Arkansas segregationists didn't let go at that. They evolved a set of constitutional amendments, including interposition, and put them on the November general election ballot.

The people, given their first chance to express themselves on the integration issue, voted for every one of them, including one placed on the ballot by Mr. Johnson. . . .

Now let's connect the governor with the Little Rock situation. Supt. Virgil Blossom presented a "slow segregation" program that was approved by the federal courts. . . .

. . . All during the "delay" period Mr. Blossom received lots of applause for his program, simply because he had managed a year's delay. Therefore, we thought the people of Little Rock were ready to "accept the inevitable."

WHY FIGHT?

Even before the summer we got a hint that some of the people were not so acceptable. A friend asked us what we thought of Central High integrating this fall. We gave the usual "inevitable so why fight it?" reply.

This friend told us there was trouble brewing, but that was all he would say. This was before school was out last May. Parents already were discussing what the situation would be this fall.

'idn't know that. In fact we were surprised
        school mothers held their big meeting . . .
    week. That meeting revealed what the friend
had been talking about. . . .

A delegation reminded the governor of his
promise: No school district will be forced to integrate against its will as long as I am governor.

MOVE NEEDED

Mr. Faubus felt he had to make a move. We
don't know how much evidence, if any, he had that
there would be violence. But we do know that a
crowd was going to gather at the high school. We
also know how quickly a heckling mob can become
a violent mob, when one member makes one wrong
move.

It never entered our mind that the governor
would go so far as to block integration. . . .

Then we learned a new angle to the situation.
The governor had asked the U.S. Justice Department in Washington to send an agent to explain
what could be expected in the way of enforcement assistance from the federal government.

Mr. Faubus said they told him they couldn't
put any agents here to prevent violence . . . It is
our opinion that it was at that moment that
Arkansas' governor got really teed off.

It was possibly during the next few hours that
he made the big decision to stop integration by
force. He gave us no hint of his plans.

. . . he called out his National Guard and the
state troopers and using threatened violence as a
reason, or an excuse, he stopped the integration.

To say he caused consternation among federal
officials is putting it mildly. . . . He also revealed
that the federal officials had not actually prepared
themselves to enforce the integration orders.

Knoxville Journal, September 8, 1957—

CAREERS OF IKE, FAUBUS
CROSSED BEFORE, BART SAYS

The careers of Dwight D. Eisenhower and of
Orval Faubus crossed more than a decade ago in
France, and a racial issue was involved then as it is
now . . .

Roles, however, were a little different. At that
time it was Gen. Dwight D. Eisenhower, commander of the Allied Forces invading Western
Europe, and Captain Faubus of the infantry. The
racial issue, too, arose under quite different conditions. . . .

Narrator of this tale, and a party to the experience, is Morris Bart, Knoxville builder, then a
lieutenant of artillery who shared sleeping quarters
in an abandoned French stable with Captain
Faubus, and who became and is a great admirer of
the now governor of Arkansas.

. . . he believes in Governor Faubus deeply as a
man and sent him a telegram Friday expressing his
confidence in "your high moral ideas and purposes," and notifying him that "my prayers and
best wishes are with you."

Rather his mind goes back to those days when
they slept together in the abandoned stable and
talked out their souls to each other during the long
winter nights when the war was very real and very
close.

"Captain Faubus was appointed trial Judge
Advocate and I was appointed defense counsel," to
dispose of a number of cases of Negro soldiers "who
had languished in the stockade for many months for
minor infractions," Bart recalled.

It turned out that a great many were released,
so many that it "came to the attention of higher
headquarters which expected convictions instead of
acquittals in ordinary Army policy. Captain
Faubus and I were both called to headquarters and
severely reprimanded on orders from Rheims
because we had given too much assistance to these
colored soldiers who were in legal difficulty."

That headquarters at Rheims — it also was the
headquarters of General Eisenhower.
. . .

These long talks in the stable "stripped bare
any superficial appearance," Bart said, adding
that "I can vouch for Orval Faubus as being one of
the great living Americans today."

9/9/57

HOW ARE THINGS WORKING OUT UP THERE?
By Knox, Nashville Banner   9/9/57

One of Knox's most prophetic cartoons.

The critics outside the area were all too ready with instructions for the South and cries of "Force integration now." Later
the growing Northern and Eastern race problems kept these
same areas quite busy. When Watts, Calif., was virtually
destroyed in a race riot, as well as large sections of Detroit,
Cleveland, Chicago, Rochester and Washington, it became
proof-positive that the problem was not just of the South, as the
finger-pointing politicians and editorialists had indicated.

THE TWO VIEWPOINTS, By Kennedy, Ark. Democrat, 9/9/57

SEPTEMBER MORN
By Hungerford, Pittsburgh Post Gazette   9/8/57

A version of the September Morn cartoon theme. In reviewing the events of the controversy, I can find no reason for a personal rescue plea at that particular time. The cartoon idea escapes me.

INCIDENTS QUELLED; ORDER MAINTAINED

State Police Director Herman Lindsey delivered to me personally several reports of possible violence.

One was of a man of more than middle age who lived a short distance west of Central High School. He vehemently opposed integration of the school and possessed a pistol.

The man said he was not in good health, that he wouldn't live too much longer. So he was going to take his gun and go down there and see how many he could get before he was stopped or before they got him.

Chief Lindsey heard of the report and interviewed the man. He reported to me that, in his opinion, it was not an idle threat, and that the man could do what he said.

I instructed Lindsey to keep in touch with the man, to tell him we were doing the best we could and that any violence would only hurt our efforts.

Chief Lindsey talked to the man and later reported that he was kept under constant surveillance whenever he came near the school grounds.

PRAISE FROM THE LEGION

A resolution adopted by some 175 members of the American Legion in a meeting in the Fifth District, Arkansas Department at Lepanto praised me for my actions in the use of the National Guard at Central High School.

A BAD CASE OF DIXIE JITTERS
By Hungerford, Pittsburgh Post Gazette   9/9/57

It is difficult to see how some of Hungerford's drawings applied to the situation. I never felt the need of any of Uncle Sam's "integration tranquilizers."

The Atlanta, Ga., Journal
September 9, 1957

TAKE A BOW, CHAMP

Gov. Orval Faubus' stand at Little Rock illustrates the conflict of the old and inherent powers of the states versus the recently assumed ones of the federal government.

Via the press, television and radio the governor has explained his position. It is simple. As chief executive of Arkansas it is his responsibility to maintain the peace. . . .

That the governor is on sound ground and fully within his rights is something that never could have been disputed until May 1954, when the Supreme Court handed down its decision against segregation in the public schools.

Under this new dispensation the federal government presumed enormous, additional powers. It entered a territory never surrendered by the states when the federal compact was formed. Attempts to resist largely have been wrecked by demagoguery and intemperance . . .

But in the governor of Arkansas the states have found a deft champion, one who can box and fence with the shiftiest of the federalists.

May his cause and the cause of the states prevail for today they are the same. . . .

THE FBI REPORT REQUESTED BY DAVIES

·The following news items appeared in reference to the FBI report on which FBI agents had been busy for days in Little Rock and throughout Arkansas.

FBI Investigation

Atty. Gen. Brownell advised Eisenhower, in a telephone conference, that an FBI report on the facts in the Little Rock case almost certainly would be filed with the U.S. District court there today. [Sept. 9]

Judge Davies requested the report after Governor Faubus called out National Guardsmen.

FEDERAL JUDGE TURNS DOWN BOARD'S PLEA TO DELAY INTEGRATION AT CENTRAL HIGH

Quotes from Judge Davies' ruling: (Sept. 7)

. . . Only the testimony of the Little Rock superintendent of schools was offered, . . .

The testimony and arguments this morning were, in my judgment, as anemic as the petition itself; . . .

. . .

The chief executive of Little Rock (Mayor Mann) has stated that the Little Rock police have not had a single case of interracial violence reported to them and there has been no indication from sources available to him that there would be violence in regard to this situation.

. . .

The petition of the Little Rock school district directors and of the superintendent . . . for an order temporarily suspending enforcement of its plan of integration is in all things denied.

Court is dismissed.

———

The school authorities and their attorneys made no effort to show the dangers of the situation. Their plea appeared to be anemic by design.

Naturally, Blossom could not then give his real information about the possibility of violence. Such information would have contradicted the sworn testimony he had given in Chancellor Reed's court, and later in federal court.

Since the Board went into Court with a plea for delay based on allegations of impending disorder and violence, and then in the 15-minute hearing produced no concrete evidence to back up the allegations, most people believed it was a "put-up job," a farce, an effort not in good faith, designed to be unsuccessful. Many thought the real design of the board's plea was to mislead the people. The board wanted the people to think it was seeking to avoid integration, but was actually making it easy for Judge Davies to overrule its pleas and then order it to proceed forthwith to execute the court-ordered plan.

If the school board plea was a "put-up job," one cannot, on the face of it, easily accuse Judge Davies of knowingly being a party to the deception. He was a stranger being mis-advised by those who had his ear. Furthermore, on the basis of the evidence submitted to support the board's plea, which was none, he could hardly have found otherwise in his decision.

However, his biased attitude in the matter having become apparent, one cannot escape the thought that he would have diligently sought more information, as federal judges have been known to do, had the situation been just the opposite. Judge Davies made no effort officially to learn the truth. Thus if not guilty of prejudice and malfeasance, he could at the very least be accused of negligence and bad judgment in the conduct of the case.

His acceptance of Mayor Mann's press statements as evidence without calling the mayor as a witness under oath, was improper for any magistrate.

THE PROPOSITION; ENTRAPMENT?

On one occasion some time after the crisis was well underway, but while the Guard was still in control and the schools were peaceful, an acquaintance came to me with a proposition.

"Governor," he said, "They (my critics) keep saying that there is no trouble or violence and that there would be none, and that your use of the Guard is just a farce.

"Now I know a gang of seven young toughs. They say if you want some trouble that they can get it going. They wanted me to find out from you if you wanted them to do it. And they know how," concluded my visitor.

I said, "You go back and you tell those fellows that I want no creation of any trouble whatsoever. I've been working night and day with my forces to keep down trouble.

"Tell them further, and make it plain, that if I hear of them, or any one of them, creating any trouble anywhere, I'll have every law officer I can get in their pursuit. I'll see that they are caught and prosecuted to the fullest extent of the law.

"And since they are now marked, they better be very careful where they go, whom they are with and what they get into."

"'Okay,' answered my acquaintance, "I'll deliver the message. But they thought you might need some trouble to discredit your enemies."

My message must have been effective for there were no instigated disorders by any such group.

I never thought of it at the time, but in the years since I have read often of the sometimes questionable tactics of enforcement officers who join up with law violators as seeming associates. They encourage the criminals to commit law violations and thus are able to catch them in the act, or obtain enough evidence to secure convictions in the courts. When such tactics go too far they become entrapment. This may well have been an attempt at entrapment by my enemies.

In all my conjecture, there are two officials I never suspected of any unfair tactics; Attorney Osro Cobb and Marshal Beal Kidd. I'm convinced they wouldn't stoop to such methods. Also, I'm sure they knew enough of the situation, and of me, to know that I would never be a party to such a plot.

During the 1957 crisis, there were many cases of threatened disorder, violence or conflict. We worked constantly through many avenues to quell the incipient incidents and to keep the lid on in the community and the area.

The state troopers, under the leadership of Chief Lindsey with the cooperation of all officers of the command, were very effective. Never was morale higher in the ranks of the State Police than at that time. The same was true of the National Guard. The Guard and police members were praised everywhere in the state, and elsewhere when they traveled outside the state.

They walked with increased pride because they were recognized as friends of the people and not their enemies. When I attended the various governors' conferences and other affairs throughout the nation, my own State Police members related how their counterparts in other states vied for the privilege of being assigned to me and my group.

The increased pride among administration personnel was never completely dissipated throughout my lengthy administration.

GREAT CAESAR'S GHOST, By Jenkins, Los Angeles Examiner, 9/10/57

The cartoonist said I had delusions of becoming a Caesar. In the background were the ranks of the National Guardsmen with a banner reading, "Arkansas Nationalorium Guardensium." In one hand I held a staff which read "Faubus the First" and from the other I spilled the wine of power on the Constitution. According to many constitutional authorities the wine of power was spilled in Washington, while many in the states attempted to uphold the Constitution by opposing illegal edicts of the U.S. Supreme Court.

CHAPTER 12
THE STATE POLICE ROLE; THE NEWPORT CONFERENCE

THE STATE POLICE ROLE

The Arkansas State Police guided by Director Herman E. Lindsey and his commanders, acted in a most responsible manner in carrying out the assigned tasks of keeping order and preventing violence at Central High School. It would be difficult to speak too highly of the efficiency, diligence and devotion of the troopers assigned, as well as the exercise of good judgment in the performance of their duties. Operations in the area were established in excellent order by Director Lindsey and his aides.

Twelve stationary posts were set up around the school which operated from 6:00 a.m. (4:30 a.m. the first day) to 4:00 p.m. each day. In addition five roving units were assigned to constantly patrol the entire area on a 24-hour basis with instructions to observe all vehicles and persons of a suspicious nature in or about the school area. The roving units were constantly in touch with the stationary posts as well as the school command post and the regular State Police headquarters not far away.

The instructions to all these officers were:

(1) To regulate, direct and expedite the increased vehicular traffic in the vicinity of the school.

(2) Provide protection for students and school personnel and for the personal property and persons of the residents in the area.

(3) To seek, identify, search, seize and detain, if the circumstances warranted, all persons and equipment of a suspicious nature, found within or attempting to enter the school area.

(4) To assist the Arkansas National Guard in its function of maintaining peace and order in the area of the school.

To indicate the potential for trouble, and the effectiveness of the State Police for checking it, the reports revealed that 163 licensed vehicles, 30 from out of state, were checked by the troopers in the period from 4:30 a.m., September 3 to 6:00 a.m., September 4. The vehicles and occupants were checked for the following reasons. (1) The vehicle and occupants were of a suspicious nature; (2) the vehicle made repeated trips past the area; (3) the vehicle was occupied by 3 or more males. All this was in addition to control of normal traffic in the area.

If the officers were not satisfied with the on-the-spot check, the vehicle and occupants were taken to State Police Headquarters for further questioning. Where law violations were discovered those apprehended were booked at the sheriff's office at the courthouse in downtown Little Rock.

Reports were written on each day's activities and, in due time, delivered to me. They are much too voluminous to quote at length.

On the first day people began to assemble at 5:30 a.m., the number reaching 400 by 9:30 that morning. I had numerous reports that more people would have appeared had they not learned that the Guard was on duty and the situation presumably under control. No black people appeared except the school employees, who were all on duty, and some black reporters including L.C. Bates, publisher of a Little Rock newspaper, who said he was an observer. The crowd remained peaceable but all did not disperse until the school day ended.

Delegations from other counties were noted and reported to me. Present from one county were a town's leading businessman, the town marshal, a deputy sheriff and a number of businessmen and farmers. The delegation from another county east of the capital city included the county judge, a president of a school board, a superintendent of a school, the president of a bank, a president of a chamber of commerce, a mayor, a former mayor, and other prominent businessmen and citizens.

State Police Welcomed to the School Area

The residents in the school neighborhoods gave a warm welcome to the police officers assigned to the area. They were especially nice to the personnel of the stationary posts and in many ways made them feel welcome.

One resident temporarily away from his home left it unlocked for the officers' use. At another post breakfast was brought to the troopers on duty. At another a neighbor kept the troopers supplied with coffee and cookies throughout the day, saying it was the least he could do to show his appreciation for his safety and the protection of his property. A lady near another post supplied coffee and cookies and expressed great satisfaction with the officers' presence saying it made her "feel so much better." Chairs were brought for the officers' use at another point as well as coffee and cookies throughout the day. At the post near Quigley Stadium the employees of the maintenance shop built and set up a radio receiver and speaker for the troopers there. Sometimes the members of the roving units of troopers had opportunity to share the rewards made by the citizens to men of the fixed units. This extraordinary courtesy and consideration for the members of the State Police continued throughout the period of duty at Central High School.

The Second Day

On the second day the crowd began to gather about 6:15 a.m. The number reached 350 by 8:30 a.m. and later increased to 1,000 or more.

Early that morning Captain Alan Templeton was approached by a citizen of the area (name and address given in the report). He advised Captain Templeton that prior to the opening of school he had "seen some Negroes" at the school attempting to register. The man said he was "not going to see this happen," that he went back to his residence, got his gun, concealed it on his person and walked over to the school. He said if the Negroes had entered the building to register he would have "cut them down."

Captain Templeton advised the man he would have been very foolish and pacified him to the best of his ability. The captain then issued orders to the troopers that the man was to be watched very closely, and that any time any Negroes came to the scene attempting to enter school that at least one plain clothes policeman was to be assigned the sole duty of watching the angry man.

The report of the second day described the coming of the black students to the school; of how the Guardsmen gathered around Elizabeth Echford for her protection during her walk, and how one Guardsman with difficulty restrained an unidentified white female who attempted to grab the black student.

Guardsmen accompanied the Echford girl to the park bench where she met Mrs. Grace Lorch, the alleged Communist. There both Miss Echford and Mrs. Lorch were protected by Guardsmen and State Police.

The same protection was provided for Terrance Roberts when he appeared. Roberts was escorted to the park bench where he met the Echford girl. The Guard quickly broke up the crowd and later the black students departed unmolested.

Immediately after the crowd was dispersed Captain Templeton, Lieutenant Mack Thompson and Sergeant Robert Ward found a dagger "stiletto" type, 8 3/4 inches in length, and a pair of heavy lead knuckles in the shrubbery where the crowd had gathered around Terrance Roberts. Nearby a very sharp 12-inch butcher knife was found in the shrubbery by Sergeant L.E. Guinn.

Evidently the possible assailants of the black students had discarded their weapons after observing the determination of the Guardsmen and State Police to maintain order and protect the students as well as others.

Of the many persons checked that day six were detained and some charged with violations. In addition to the weapons found in the shrubbery the following were confiscated. A steel-handled, braided leather whip, a billy club, a length of rubber hose, a pellet pistol, a fish knife, a number of ice picks, switch blade knives and hunting knives.

A part of the report that day read:

"The crowd this day was very restless. The incidents of the day made the crowd more restless. The word went through the crowd that the U.S. marshals would attempt to escort the Negro children through the National Guard lines and into the school. This caused a great deal of tension in the crowd and kept them milling around all day. If some one would have taken the lead this day, there would have been a great deal of trouble."

There was a rumor widely circulated that if the Guard and State Police did not prevent the federal agents or marshalls from taking the black students into the school, then a group of citizens would form behind the Guard lines and forcibly take the students from the marshalls.

Sale of Weapons

In checking on the sale of weapons the State Police reported the following:

A business whose normal sale of "spring blade" knives was one per month, had recently sold twelve. All went to teenagers about equally divided between blacks and whites.

Another store had an unusually large sale of water pistols. An unidentified black male who said he was from Port Arthur, Texas purchased eleven at one time. He said the sale of the pistols had been banned in Port Arthur because youngsters had used them to squirt fire extinguisher fluid into other youngsters' eyes. The same store manager said the recent sale of spring blade knives increased so much that she became alarmed and removed the knives from the counters.

A check of drug companies revealed a sale of three gallons of acid in Benton just 30 miles west of Little Rock. Other areas reported normal sales. The acid could be used in water pistols to inflict great harm, even blindness if squirted in the eyes.

One business reported above normal sale of guns for July and August. Other firms reported sale of all weapons as normal or slightly above normal.

An agent of the FBI office in Little Rock requested the above information which was provided by the State Police.

Again as on the first day Benjamin Fine, reporter for the *New York Times*, agitated the crowd by his abrasive and antagonistic manner of interview. He was reprimanded by Colonel Johnson, the Guard troop commander on the scene. In the days which followed Fine so angered the crowds that he could remain on the scene only with the protection of the Guard and the State Police.

The Third Day

On the third day the crowd began to assemble at 6 a.m. and by 8:30 had grown to more than 1,000 in number. The increase was due to the rumors that the U.S. marshals would escort the black students through the Guard lines into the school.

The angry man again appeared and advised that he had two brothers in World War I, and two sons in World War II, that his daughter had graduated from Central High School; that he had a bad heart and his doctors had told him he had not long to live. He then advised that if the marshals appeared with the black students he would kill both the marshals and the students.

Director Lindsey took personal charge of the situation and advised the man that just such an occurrence was what the Guard and the State Police were on post to prevent, that this sort of violence did not have any part in the order of things. Lindsey then issued orders to Captain Templeton to keep close watch on the man at all times, and to be especially alert if a U.S. marshal should appear.

At 8:30 a.m. the Police received an eye witness report that Benjamin Fine had offered ten dollars to some boys to start a fight in the crowd.

At 10:20 a.m. five black males were detained in the area and taken to Police headquarters. Some were found to have criminal records.

More weapons were confiscated during the day, and some ammunition for shotguns, pistols and rifles.

The crowd was reported to be in a very restless mood.

The Fourth Day

The crowd began to assemble at 7:00 a.m. and by 8:15 had reached 200. A small storm scattered the gathering at 8:45. It was Friday the last school day of the week, and very few spectators returned.

At 8:15 Major Doug Shelton of the Guard received information that two newsmen, identified as Pete Harris and Sammy Gotlieb of the International News Service, had arranged for another newsman to bring a black person into the crowd to create a commotion. The purpose was to obtain photographs and a story, as they were late and so far had obtained neither story or photographs.

Both newsmen were put under close observation and it was soon noted that they were watching a certain street corner. Shortly they began to ease from the crowd and the other newsmen toward that point. Plain clothes policemen followed them with orders to apprehend the black man when he appeared, and take him to headquarters for questioning.

Before the arranged incident could be consumated, six Minnesota college students with a Little Rock acquaintance appeared on the scene, one of them going through the Guard lines posing as a photographer with an eight-inch knife in his pocket. The newsmen got their story without the use of the black man.

Another Minnesota student was apprehended in a car with the Little Rock resident. A sixteen-inch curved blade Philippine brush knife was confiscated from the vehicle. The other students were then taken in charge some of whom had switch blade knives which they had purchased after arriving in Little Rock. They said the knives were illegal in Minnesota and they had purchased them for "kicks." All were taken to headquarters for questioning and the weapons confiscated.

An intoxicated man was apprehended in the crowd and taken to the county jail.

The rumor of the U.S. marshal escort for the black students persisted.

Vehicular traffic in the area decreased.

The stationary police posts were discontinued for the weekend but the roving units remained on duty. Roving units were also dispatched to North Little Rock at the request of school and city authorities.

There were reports the Little Rock city police were making numerous arrests of people carrying concealed weapons on their persons or in their cars, but that this information was being suppressed on orders of Mayor Mann.

Monday, September 9

Seven spectators were on hand at 6:00 a.m. By 8:30 the crowd had grown to 600. State Police Sergeant Arthur Halsell was assigned to watch the crowd and reported it to be the most unruly that had gathered. Police officials considered it potentially more dangerous than on previous days.

Dr. Fine so angered the crowd that he had to retreat behind the Guard lines for safety. Spectators pursued Fine and Colonel Johnson ordered the Guard to push them back across the street. Police reported the Guard had considerable difficulty but succeeded without serious incident. General Clinger reprimanded Fine for inciting to riot and creating incidents.

At 8:00 a.m. Sergeant Maurice Gately received a report of a riot at the North Little Rock high school. Director Lindsey immediately ordered Captain Templeton and ten troopers to the scene north of the river to help bring the situation under control. State Police were required in that area for the remainder of the week.

Among the weapons confiscated on this day at Central was a calibre 38-55 lever action Marlin rifle. The purchase of the weapon outside the city by a black man was reported to the State Police making it possible to apprehend the owner before he reached the school area and confiscate the rifle.

Police noted and reported that on this day the crowd at Central High School was composed of almost entirely new people.

A new check of businesses in the city on this date showed that the sale of weapons of all types had dropped to near normal.

Tuesday, September 10

The crowd began to assemble at 6:30 a.m., reached 200 by 10:00 a.m. and declined to 100 by noon.

At 8:05 the Guard had to protect a Negro reporter from the crowd.

The Police checked 131 vehicles, 59 out of state, during the day. Some persons were detained and more weapons confiscated, but the number of detainees and weapons were declining.

A stolen automobile from California was recovered during the check.

Some incidents of group attacks by blacks on individual whites were reported in the city but no incidents occurred in the vicinity of the school.

During the day reports reached the crowd that I had accepted service of a summons by Marshal Beal Kidd in the injunctive process in federal court. After that the spectators declined to such an extent that Director Lindsey discontinued the stationary police posts, but kept the roving units on duty. It seemed that the whole controversy became for the moment a legal contest, a waiting game, and most people were content to await the outcome of the court case to determine the next step.

By now the State Police had checked many hundreds of potential trouble makers, many of whom now feared to be found again in the immediate area. Those possessing weapons were especially careful to avoid the area. This to a great extent defused the explosive potential of the situation.

General Edwin Walker Checked

Trooper Floyd Weaver of the roving patrol units on duty at Central High School, observed a car as it drove around the school grounds a number of times in an exploratory manner and then began an apparent check of the side streets and avenues of approach to the school. The vehicle with a male driver was pull-ed over for a check because of its suspicious activity.

The driver, a middle-aged white male, refused to identify himself, and attempted to persuade the trooper to let him go. Failing in this he protested vehemently that he could not be compelled to disclose his identity, and that because of his position, which was not revealed, it was not proper for him to do so, nor for the trooper to compel him to disclose his identity.

Trooper Weaver persisted, finally telling the man "you either tell me who you are and furnish evidence of your identity, or I will take you to Police headquarters where you will be held until we find out who you are."

The man then discontinued his protests and revealed his identity. He was General Edwin Walker, the recently assigned commander of the Arkansas U.S. Military district. Trooper Weaver then let him go.

The State Police attached no particular significance to the apprehension of Walker at the time, and the incident was not reported to me until later events lent significance to the occurrence. We knew later, naturally, that the General was making a personal reconnaisance of the area preparatory to the federal military occupation of the school which came some three weeks later.

According to information we later received, the special training of the 101st Airborne Division began at Ft. Campbell, Kentucky, about the same time that General Walker was found reconnoitering the grounds of Central High School.

More Than 1,000 Vehicles Checked

In the first four days of duty, September 3-6, the State Police checked 447 vehicles of a suspicious nature of which 114 bore out of state license plates.

On September 9 and 10, 240 vehicles were checked of which 100 bore out of state tags.

By the time the work of the State Police and the National Guard had ended, more than a thousand vehicles and the occupants, all of a suspicious nature, had been checked. In addition dozens of leads on potential violence had been run down, many weapons confiscated and inflammatory situations defused. In this period of just over three weeks that the Guard remained under my control, not a single piece of property was damaged, and not a single person, black or white, young or old, male or female, was injured to the slightest degree in any disorder in the vicinity of the Little Rock schools.

The diligence of the State Police and the National Guard, coupled with the plain determination of both to quell any disorder and prevent confrontations, prevented many acts, any one of which could have led to wholesale violence and riot.

This probability of unplanned violence (disregarding any planned opposition to integration that may have been formulated in the secret meetings) is borne out in interviews conducted by members of the State Police on September 13 to 16. Some 35 interviews were conducted with Central High School students, with parents whose children attended the school, and with pastors who worked with youth groups whose members were students at the school. All those interviewed, except two students, stated there would have been trouble the first day of school if the black students had been admitted and the National Guard had not been placed on duty. Most of those interviewed were emphatic in their belief that the trouble would have been serious.

Sale of Metal Tipped Umbrellas

An interview with an employee of the Gus Blass Company, located in downtown Little Rock, revealed that the sale of metal tipped umbrellas had been unusually high.

From September 7 to 13 the umbrella sales amounted to $235, and for all of September the sales totaled $392. By comparison, the books revealed that the total for umbrella sales for the entire year of 1956 was only $192.

The employee related that the sales were to Negro teenagers who came to the store in pairs. They always checked for the slender 4 to 6 inch metal tipped umbrellas and had no interest in other models. Most purchases were made with ten dollar bills and none were charged to accounts.

TEARS
By Herblock, Washington Post   9/10/57

I was portrayed urging moderation and expressing sympathy for the people in my speech, but stirring up racial discord by my actions.

The main theme of the *Gazette* editors and other critics was to promote the idea that there would have been no difficulty had it not been for my actions. Subsequent events in Little Rock, and throughout the nation completely disproved this theory.

I ACCEPT SUMMONS TO JUDGE DAVIES COURT

On September 10 I accepted a summons by the federal authorities served by Marshal Beal Kidd, to appear in Judge Davies Court on September 20. I met the marshal on the front lawn of the mansion to accept the paper in the presence of dozens of photographers and reporters who lined the fence. I declined to answer questions.

DIFFICULTIES AT CENTRAL

All was reported quiet at the North Little Rock schools where 65 city police aided by State Police patrolled the area.

It was becoming increasingly difficult to protect Negroes who appeared at Central High School. The area was placed off limits except to regular Negro employees and black newsmen, the latter accompanied by Guardsmen.

SCHOOL BLASTED AT NASHVILLE

In the Nashville, Tennessee, integration troubles a blast wrecked a school building with damage placed at more than a half million dollars.

VO-TECH SCHOOL AT PINE BLUFF

On the progressive news side: Pine Bluff was selected as the site for the state's first vocational technical (trade) school. The new facility would provide training for all races of all ages and both sexes.

BIRDS OF PREY
By Graham, Ark. Gazette   9/10/57

The vulture, perched on the tree "Defiance of Federal Government," spoke "Hate" as it looked over Arkansas toward the U.S. flag. No law passed by Congress was being defied. This favorite symbol of the pseudo liberals was used over and over to portray those with whom they disagreed.

Karr Shannon wrote:

Governor Faubus' initial tevee address relative to racial integration in Little Rock's public schools can be summed up in three words: Declaration of Independence.

The Evening Star, Washington, D.C.
September 10, 1957

ON IMPLEMENTING INTEGRATION
Enforcement Situation in School Issue
Held Different From That in Voting

by DOROTHY THOMPSON
The greatest achievement of this past Congress was its reconciliation of North and South on the

right of our colored citizens to vote in all elections on equal terms with whites . . .

The important thing is that the bill was worked out by agreement . . .

A measure undertaken under such conditions genuinely protects the colored citizen. It establishes his rights by the consent of the majority . . . That is much more than a mere legal right.

For no law can operate to achieve its desired ends if it runs counter to the existing state of consciousness and conscience of the community.

A law to be effective must be respected. To be respected the overwhelming majority must believe it to be right. Respect is not created by statute. No one can respect what he firmly believes to be wrong.

Where a law is in harmony with public standards, its upholders (the police) find allies in the people. Where the law is not thus in harmony, the police appear as public enemies. Then peaceable enforcement becomes impossible.

One can, therefore, reasonably anticipate that the right of qualified Negroes to exercise the franchise will not encounter serious opposition. . . .

But quite different is the ruling forbidding separate public schools for white and colored. In the South the overwhelming white majority give it no natural respect. They are all but unanimously convinced that the court's decision is an act of legislative usurpation; that it invades a domain constitutionally outside Federal jurisdiction; that mixed schools in communities with large colored populations will not improve race relations but exacerbate them; and that the net effect will not be to lift the education of the colored but to debase that of the whites.

There may be legal ways of settling the constitutional issue, but there is no way of determining the rightness or wrongness of the other objections.

This column is not arguing their rightness or wrongness. It is only recording that where the law is devoid of public consent it cannot be enforced without violent action and counteraction, unconducive to improving the happiness of white or colored. . . .

The enforcement of law against a whole community is war, and in war not even victory creates respect.

KASPER IN JAIL; COMMUNISTS IN HUNGARY

The New York segregationist, John Kasper, was held without bail in Nashville, Tennessee.

The Russian Communists announced that Red troops would remain in Hungary.

BIGGEST PRESS CONFERENCE

The Little Rock newspapers showed a picture of the biggest press conference in the history of the Arkansas statehouse as I met the reporters in the large reception room.

Ft. Lauderdale (Fla.) Messenger
September 11, 1957

The Messenger wired Governor Faubus its congratulations upon his courage in standing up for a state's right to control its own schools, and for a governor's right to preserve order in his own state. Such things are basic if we are to maintain any semblance of state government in the face of a growing, all-powerful Washington bureaucracy.

Northern Papers Back Faubus
September 11, 1957

INDIANAPOLIS — Indiana's two largest newspapers, The Indianapolis News and The Indianapolis Star, editorially stood behind Governor Orval Faubus in his showdown fight with President Eisenhower and the Federal government.

Both newspapers maintain that the racial issue is being propagandized to smother the real issue — states rights.

The Star said in a lead editorial:

"We believe the sovereignty of the states is far more important to the liberty of both the majority and the minorities of our people than the speed with which integration is carried out under the Supreme Court decision.

"We believe Governor Faubus of Arkansas . . . has the right and the duty under the state and Federal Constitutions to act to preserve peace."

. . .

. . . The Federal government has no right, under the Constitution, or under laws made pursuant to the Constitution, to hale a state government into court in this case.

ARKANSAS' VOLUNTEER
By Ficklen, Dallas Morning News   9/10/57

A volunteer was ready to help Arkansas in the Little Rock crisis. With his hat labeled CSA, his jug slung over his shoulder, his towel marked "Ark.," his Confederate flag tied to the ball bat he planned to use as a weapon, the volunteer was ready to take off for the scene of strife in his neighboring state.

MARK THESE DAYS, By Knox, Nashville Banner, 9/11/57

According to the cartoonist, historic days were occurring in Arkansas and the South.

In the same newspaper was the reprint of the following editorial:

TIME FOR SOUTH TO DEFY WARREN'S FALSE LAW

by James J. Kilpatrick
in the Richmond News Leader

Let us talk for a while of defiance.

Throughout the week end, the television channels buzzed with talk of defiance.

One by one network commentators came before the cameras: Men clean-cut, and sober, and handsome. They were garbed in the sincere ties of Madison Avenue; they enunciated their calumnies in perfect pear-shaped tones.

By Sunday night, if a lie could be sold, they had sold it; Governor Faubus of Arkansas, said these professional, positive, rueful men, had "defied" the United States. Something, they said, had to give. They smiled their crinkled, appealing, professional smiles; and they agreed that Faubus the outlaw, Faubus the anarchist, Faubus the exponent of "defiance," would have to go.

It is a feeble thing one attempts in attempting to reply to them. They speak to how many millions, over how many hundred stations? And this is being written on a rainy Sunday night, [September 8, 1957] with the city room dark, and the lie a-building across a once great country.

Yes, let us talk of "defiance!"

Orval Faubus, Governor of Arkansas, sensed (or thought he sensed it, it matters not) an active lawlessness, an incipient violence, in the city of Little Rock. Reports had been brought to him of guns sold, knives sharpened, tempers at the trembling, red-eyed point that comes before explosion. And because he is Governor of a State in the American Union; because there are powers and responsibilities vested in him to keep the peace, he called out the guard. He would have been derelict in his responsibilities had he done otherwise.

Was this in Mr. Faubus "defiance?" Mr. Faubus is condemned before the evidence in his behalf has been presented.

Who has defied what? Whence came the wheel that ground the knives?

If we would talk of defiance, let us talk first of May 17, 1954, when this awfulness began. Let us talk of a Chief Justice, Earl Warren, who wove his spell around the fellow incompetents on his court. Let us talk of Earl Warren and defiance!

On that black date in the history of the Supreme Court of the United States, Earl Warren and his associates took this country's Constitution, twisted it, shaped it, distorted it. They mocked the law of the land. They laughed, and slapped each other's backs, and cried: We are the Constitution! We are the supreme law of the land! We nine! And they did an evil, defiant, lawless thing. They corrupted the Constitution; they stole from the people the people's own; they said: We know that the power to maintain racially separate schools never has been denied to the State by the Constitution, but henceforth we will deny it — we nine! — by the powers we usurp this day.

Was this in Mr. Warren not defiance? It is contempt, we are told, to call it so.

From that evil seed has grown the evil harvest. And law-abiding men, who resist this lawless act, are denounced as law evaders. Men who defend the Constitution are charged with destroying it.

Mr. Faubus, we suppose, will lose in the end: The Federal government the States created has grown to overpowering size. But it may be that the South can gain a victory from his defeat, if the brutal insistence of our Federal masters, demonstrated anew in Arkansas, brings fresh strength to the South's determination to resist.

It is possible, too, that the whole country may gain from this affair. We may assume, hopefully, that many people, indifferent to "integration" as such, will look with suddenly thoughtful eyes upon Federal domination in Little Rock. If the ancient, inherent "police power" can be thus taken from a sovereign State and transferred to Federal judges, a judicial oligarchy will have made the clean sweep. Then, truly, State and local government becomes nullities.

Will a free people stand for it? They cannot, and remain free.

When a sitting Federal Judge from North Dakota can impose his will upon the people of Arkansas, overriding the best judgment of the Governor of Arkansas, an alarm bell sounds. If an indolent people ever can be awakened to the theft of their liberties, surely they must awaken now.

Who rules? Who is sovereign? The people, in their States? Or appointive Federal judges? To what do we owe obedience — to the fundamental law of this land, as ratified by the States? Or to the lawless usurpation of a few mortal men?

Yes, let us talk of defiance! And if there is to be defiance, let it come now. Let it come bravely. Let it come with a sureness of conviction that the South is right and our oppressors are wrong.

We do not conceive it defiance to hold to what is lawfully ours. We count it, rather, loyalty, fealty, obedience to law that was law before Earl Warren was born.

On that certainty, whatever the consequences may be, let us take our stand. And pray God, let us never surrender.

———

On May 12, 1974, near the 20th anniversary of the Brown vs. Board of Education decision, Kilpatrick wrote:

The Supreme Court's unanimous opinion of May 17, 1954, was the most important opinion of this century. And, ironically, Brown remains to this day very bad law.

In a single stroke [that] morning in May, the Court struck down the segregated schools of 17 states . . . Warren's opinion paved the way, and it created the strong foundation, on which an entire new structure of (court-made) law could be built. After Brown, the deluge. . . . The black child born 20 years ago this week, not only in the South but elsewhere, has known a far different America — and with all its imperfections, a far better America — than his parents knew.

As a matter of jurisprudence, Brown still seems to me wrong. In essence, the court looked at the institution of school segregation and said: This is immoral. Therefore it is unconstitutional. It was a monstrous non sequitur. The palpable fact is that when the sun rose on the morning of May 17, 1954, segregated schools were indeed constitutional. They had been constitutional for 86 years. Many Supreme Courts had repeatedly said so.

But if questions of jurisprudence can be put to one side, it has to be said that this way is better. It is not perfect. It is better.

L'IL NAPOLEON
By Wuekes, Cleveland Plain Dealer   9/10/57

Portrayed as Napoleon on a small island of stone labeled "Little Rock, Arkansas," I extended my hand to stop a giant wave labeled, "Federal Court Order."

SCHOOLING FOR THE LITTLE ROCK NINE

A news story said schooling for the nine Negroes who had attempted to integrate Central High was undecided. I received a secret report that they were being tutored by the alleged Communists, Lee and Grace Lorch, with the knowledge of the school board. I made no attempt to verify the report. Little Rock publisher John Wells later indicated in his book "Time Bomb," that the Lorches were tutors for the students.

From *New York Times*, September 11, 1957

FAUBUS ARREST ASKED

Communist Party Calls for Governor's Imprisonment

The Communist party called yesterday for the arrest and imprisonment of Governor Orval E. Faubus of Arkansas. A statement adopted by the national administrative committee of the party Monday referred to the Governor as "an instrument of a conspiracy to nullify the authority and laws of the Federal Government."

The statement asked that President Eisenhower and Attorney General Brownell apply the enforcement powers of the Government to punish the leaders of "anti-Negro terrorism."

Many people saw the situation as follows:

Eisenhower, Brownell, the federal government and "liberal" political leaders were all fighting on the same side with the Communist Party against millions of law-abiding Americans who sought to uphold the Constitution.

The issue was not segregation vs integration. The issue was observance or non-observance of the Constitution, or whether certain changes, desired by some, opposed by others, would be made legally or illegally.

CAREFUL, THE WALLS HAVE EARS
By Kennedy, Ark. Democrat   9/11/57

Kennedy portrayed the listening ears of "the whole wide world" beyond the walls, as a minority hotly condemned my actions and a great majority defended them. My unerring pollster, Eugene Newsom, showed 80% of the Arkansas people favored the action I had taken. The mail, in the tens of thousands of letters, ranged from 90% to 98% favorable with 60% coming from outside the South and border states.

TO MEET WITH IKE

The big news of September 12 was my agreement to meet with President Eisenhower to confer on the school impasse in Little Rock. There was widespread speculation in the press that the meeting was for the purpose of my surrender. Eisenhower issued a statement condemning the speculation.

A nostalgic cartoon portraying the joys and sorrows, the small heartaches and triumphs which once accompanied the school days of childhood in the neighborhood school.

A small boy is leaving his very own dog, at his own home in his own neighborhood, and going away on his own school bus, with his own driver, with his neighborhood playmates, to his own teachers, to his own neighborhood school. Peace and tranquility prevailed in the days when people were permitted the constitutional right to control their own schools.

No gross displays of prejudice, bigotry and malice; no strange teachers and strange school mates from distant neighborhoods; no groups of shouting, angry demonstrators; no policemen or armed troops to keep order; no drug pushers and users; no organized groups extorting lunch money; no armed guards in the class rooms, about the grounds or on the school buses. All of which are now prevalent since the U.S. Supreme Court became the U.S. Supreme School Board.

LITTLE ROCK
By Werner, Indianapolis Star   9/11/57

The giant, "federal dictatorship," Goliath, is challenged by the "States Rights" figure, David. In an editorial the newspaper recounted its efforts to end segregation in its city and state, but took a strong stand against the usurpation of the rights of the states by the federal government. "States Rights," said the editorial, "are more important than the speed of desegregation."

RIGHT INTO THEIR HANDS
By Grant, Oakland, Cal. Tribune   9/11/57

Another cartoon used the overworked, ineffective theme — the Little Rock affair was good for the Communists. Figures walked into a giant hand, Communist propaganda, carrying signs. The cartoonist made the people appear ignorant by misspelling a word in one of the signs.

Now that the Supreme Court has taken away the rights of the people, has Communism been curbed, or is it more widespread than ever?

THROWING LIGHT ON THE SUBJECT
By Ellinwood, Source unknown   9/11/57

This cartoonist made an effort to be objective. He considered the issue so explosive that it could be set off by an unwise act of an extremist on either side.

ARRANGEMENTS FOR THE NEWPORT CONFERENCE; EXCHANGE OF TELEGRAMS

Some two or three days prior to the exchange of telegrams setting up the Newport conference, I was approached by the man who became known as the intermediary between me and the federal government on the Little Rock crisis.

Congressman Brooks Hays represented to me that the President was interested in a conference on the Little Rock problem and would I be responsive to the wish. Naturally, if the President was interested in a conference on the matter, it indicated he was willing to receive information and suggestions and to consider the difficulties of my position. Of course I was willing to confer with the President, as any reasonable man would be.

However, I was told, if I were agreeable to such a conference I must publicly take the initiative and ask for the conference. I had no great objection to becoming the petitioner in the matter and agreed to that request. I was then told that the President must be permitted to dictate the wording of the telegrams — both my telegram requesting the meeting and, naturally, his reply.

I paused when I saw the wording of the telegram which I was to send as anyone who reads it now can understand.

Sent 12:33 p.m. September 11, 1957 —

I have accepted summons from the United States District Court, Eastern District of Arkansas, to appear before that court on September 20, to answer certain allegations in litigation affecting the high school in Little Rock. Recognizing that we jointly share great responsibility under the federal constitution, I feel that it is advisable for us to counsel together in determining my course of action as chief executive of the state of Arkansas, with reference to the responsibility placed upon me by the state and federal Constitutions.

The United States District Court has already entered an order relative to the integration of the high school in Little Rock and this order has been affirmed by the Circuit Court of Appeals.

All good citizens must, of course, obey all proper orders of our courts and it is certainly my desire to comply with the order that has been issued by the district court in this case, consistent with my responsibilities under the Constitution of the United States and that of Arkansas.

May I confer with you on this matter at your earliest convenience?

/s/ Governor Orval E. Faubus

Note carefully the wording of the second and third paragraphs. If the wording is not a preface for the object of surrender of my position, then it is difficult to understand the English language.

However, two phrases enabled me to adopt the telegram as my own and, in good faith, send it to the President — "Obey all proper orders of our courts" the key being the word "proper," and "consistent with my responsibilities under the constitution of the United States and that of Arkansas," the key word being "consistent."

Later I doubted that Eisenhower had anything to do with the idea or the arrangements. I doubted that he was informed that the demand had been made in his name that he, the President, be permitted to dictate my telegram, even to the last word and punctuation mark. However, it is possible he was told, but I am confident everything was developed by Brownell, possibly with the assistance of Adams, Hays and Haggerty.

Certainly, Brooks Hays had to know because he brought the request and the instructions. My biggest complaint of Congressman Hays' role in the affair is the fact that he did not warn me of the devious strategy of the White House and the efforts of entrapment. Some contend that Hays was a party to the strategy.

The publication of my telegram to the President brought another flood of telegrams and telephone calls from across the nation warning me to be careful, and urging me to hold my position and not surrender the rights of the states to the federal government. Some messages were sent to me in care of the vacation White House at Newport. I'm sure they were read with interest by the Palace Guard, but I feel equally sure they were not made known to the President.

My message to the President also brought a spate of speculation in the press about the approaching "surrender."

I had little time to read the hundreds of messages, or to consider the intense interest and great concern with my trip to Newport.

Telegram of Mr. Eisenhower at 3 p.m. to Governor's mansion—

I have your telegram in which you request a meeting with me. Would it suit your convenience to come to my office on the Naval Base at Newport either Friday afternoon, September 13, at 3 o'clock or Saturday morning, the 14th at 9 o'clock? If you would let my office know your method of transportation to the Newport area, my staff will arrange to have you met and brought to the base.

/s/ Dwight D. Eisenhower

FAUBUS AND HAYS TAKE OFF FOR HISTORY-MAKING SESSION WITH IKE; GOVERNOR IS OPTIMISTIC

George Douthit quoted me as saying it would be "improper" for me to discuss in advance what I would say to President Eisenhower in the history-making meeting on the Little Rock integration situation.

I was reported to be smiling and cheerful but that I grew serious when reporters tried to get me onto the subject of the conference. My only comment regarding it was that I was hopeful something good could come out of it.

I was accompanied by Representative Brooks Hays and Arnold Sikes, my chief administrative assistant.

A story by Relman Morin quoted Hays as saying the talks would affect all of the U.S. He made the statement while waiting at the Little Rock airport to take off with me for the President's vacation headquarters.

Hays said that he planned to spend the night in Providence, Rhode Island, and that he hoped to have a preliminary private talk with Sherman Adams.

If Hays had a private meeting with Adams, or any of the White House staff, which he probably did after our arrival at Providence, it was without my knowledge. If there was any such conference, even by telephone, he failed to inform me.

From the East news reports said President Eisenhower was profoundly hopeful that out of his meeting. . .with me might come a pattern for quieter solution of school integration troubles. . . . He would not set forth any new or startling formula . . .

The President attached so much importance to the session that he had instructed two top aides — Attorney General Brownell and . . . Sherman Adams — to fly from Washington for the meeting.

"THE WHITE HOUSE DIDN'T ORIGINATE A THING," SAYS HAYS

It was Adams with whom Hays had been dealing for the last several days in Hays' role as intermediary between the White House and me.

The eastern report also quoted Hays as saying in Little Rock that it was he who originated the idea of an Eisenhower-Faubus meeting.

"The White House didn't originate a thing," said Hays.

At the time I left Little Rock I did not know that Brownell and Adams had been summoned to the meeting.

VFW ENDORSES MY ACTION

The Arkansas Veterans of Foreign Wars endorsed my use of the Guard to preserve order.

SCAVENGER'S FIELD DAY
By Talburt, Washington Daily News   9/12/57

If the Communist propaganda scavengers had a field day in Dixie in 1957, what a feast they must have had later in those burning, ravaged cities of the North.

WHAT-THE-HELL! WHO CARES?
(Front Page Editorial)
Jackson (Mississippi) *Daily News*, September 12, 1957

Here's the ultimate in asininity.

An INS dispatch quotes an unnamed U.S. diplomat in Paris saying that the integration crisis in Arkansas "is hurting the United States in France."

Why, where, how and what-the-hell?

Who cares a whoop in hades what people in Paris may think about any domestic problem in the United States?

An unknown Embassy official is quoted as saying: "Little Rock is most damaging to our effort to convince the French that we solve our problems rationally."

Why is it necessary for our Embassy to feel it is necessary for its personnel to convince the French about anything? . . .

Of all the piffle and sloppy hogwash ever embodied in one press dispatch that drivel sent out by the INS is the limit.

. . . We have not enjoyed a high place in French esteem since we started pouring free money, food and clothing into the French nation. There is no gratitude . . . for the fact that the United States twice saved the nation from being conquered by Germany.

Insofar as the South . . . is concerned, French opinion about anything that may happen from now on concerning integration is of no importance whatsoever. However, we would like for the French to make at least a half-hearted effort to pay back the multiplied billions of good American dollars they owe us. . . .

Therefore, why should we worry because some sissified diplomat in the American Embassy at Paris — his name not given — says that "the integration problem is hurting us in France."

What-the-hell, what-the-hell and who cares?

. . . . *SHALL NOT RING!*
By Williams, Detroit Free Press   9/12/57

Another version of "curfew shall not ring tonight." Some mailed copies and urged me to hold on. Many versions of this drawing appeared during the controversy.

NATIONAL ANTHEM, ARKANSAS VERSION
By Grant, Oakland, Cal. Tribune   9/12/57

Unable to successfully argue their case on historical and legal grounds, many critics reverted to criticism of me personally.

The Supreme Court has now ruled that we cannot sing the true version of this song in our schools because it recognizes "Great God, Our King."

WHO GOES THERE?
By Williams, Detroit Free Press   9/13/57

A miniature soldier, "Governor Faubus," momentarily halts the challenge to state sovereignty by the giant intruder, the federal authority.

242

PULL UP A LIMB
By Kennedy, Ark. Democrat   9/13/57

I think Ike personally preferred a settlement of the controversy. His advisers changed his attitude. As for my position an impasse could not be avoided short of abject surrender so long as Brownell made the decisions.

A surrender, I was constantly advised by attorneys, officials, editors, writers and others all across the nation, would not involve just me and the Little Rock situation, but the constitutional rights of all the states, all state officials and all the people of the United States.

In this personally undesired and unforeseen legal and constitutional struggle, I had the able assistance of Attorneys W. J. "Bill" Smith of the largest law firm in Arkansas, Walter L. Pope, author of *Pope's Digest,* and Kay Matthews, all of Little Rock, Senator Richard Russell of Georgia, R. A. Young and Tom Harper of Ft. Smith, and, at times, the advice of Pat Mehaffy, head of the firm with Smith and who later became a federal judge on the Eighth Circuit Court of Appeals. Hundreds of others throughout the state and the nation gave advice and counsel by telegrams, telephone calls and letters.

THEY CAN'T DO THIS TO ME!
By Alley, Memphis
    Commercial Appeal   9/13/57

The conference between President Eisenhower and me was pictured by Alley as restraint of the "radicals and wild men" who would try to settle matters by dynamite and other forms of violence.

The Memphis, Tenn., Commercial Appeal
September 13, 1957

THE NATION AWAITS

Not the South alone but the whole nation waits in suspense the meeting tomorrow ... on the frightening situation growing out of a straight out showdown between state and federal authority.

The joining of the issue may have come from a federal judge's brusque order ..., but it has grown to such massive and grave proportions that the knotty problem of segregation falls temporarily into the background.

What may be settled, or at least set up for settlement, at the vacation White House, is nothing less than the ultimate fate of the doctrine of rights of the separate states to a sovereignty of their own in domestic affairs not to be usurped or interfered with by central government.

Going authoritarian as it went "liberal," federal government in the last quarter century has so nibbled away at the powers of the states that a really big bite at this time would take about all that's left. There would remain practically nothing for state determination in any field of action — not racial relations alone — that Washington might not seek to enter and control.

But that is not all. Municipalities and other divisions of government, as creatures of their separate states, might well come under the same authoritarian sway. The government at Washington would have become literally central to everybody.

There was no inclination on the part of the President and his advisers to discuss the broad issues so ably set forth in the above editorial. Therefore the opportunity was lost.

As to the immediate issue of Central High School when, in the discussion, the dogmatic Brownell refused to consider even a ten-day cooling off period suggested by the President, advising him wrongly that it "was not legally possible," advice which the President resignedly accepted, all hopes of compromise and cooperation by the contending parties were lost.

For me there were left only two alternatives, — continue to follow a course which would prevent disorder and violence in my own state, or adopt unconditional surrender regardless of the violence and bloodshed that might ensue.

However, to surrender unconditionally to arrogant federal authority, believed by millions to be illegally applied, was not as simple as it appeared. A further provision, it soon developed, was the demand that the governor guarantee complete non-interference with the federal court order from any and all sources. To have successfully lived up to such a guarantee would have required the enforcement by state authority of the federal order itself while at the same time attempting to maintain order, the prevention of property damage and injury to persons. Never before in the history of the Republic had a state been called upon to assume such responsibility in reference to a strictly federal court order or a federal law.

As to the editorial quoted, the words of the unknown author were prophetic.

The federal government now bypasses the states, dealing directly with counties, cities and school districts.

Truly, as the editorial author feared, the government at Washington has become central to everybody in all things.

The hopes expressed by this editorial writer and cartoonist Alley, that some of the sovereignty and authority guaranteed to the states by the Constitution could be retained by them, were in vain.

NEUTRAL GROUND
By Maples, Ft. Worth Star Telegram 9/13/57

Maples had the "Eisenhower-Faubus talk" on neutral ground, the "9" hole of the golf course.

ONE POINT OF AGREEMENT
By Crockett, Washington Star 9/14/57

Tensions were rising throughout the nation. The people of the South were virtually unanimous in opposition to the federal court's usurpation of the heretofore unquestioned right of the states to establish, maintain and control their own schools. Ike and Faubus agreed that tensions were growing but both of us maintained our positions.

OH, WHERE IS MY WANDERING BOY? By Kennedy, Ark. Democrat, 9/15/57

Kennedy's cartoon showed that darkness had fallen with only the dim light of a waning moon. The mother "Sid" (McMath) had placed a lighted lamp in the window of the old home (Liberal Wing of the Democratic Party) and with clasped hands looked from the doorway in concern and wondered, "Oh, where is my wandering boy," the boy that was once part of the organization.

McMATH AND THE LIBERALS

I first came to statewide notice as a member of former Gov. Sid McMath's organization, — beginning as an unknown campaign worker in the primaries of 1948. After McMath's election I became a member of the Highway Commission, then administrative assistant to the governor and finally Highway Director. I went down to defeat with McMath in his third term bid in 1952, but my county (Madison) voted for him by a margin of 10 to 1.

After his loss to Senator John L. McClellan in his race for the U.S. Senate in 1954, McMath quietly supported me in the runoff with Gov. Francis Cherry, the man who had defeated him two years before.

Before the 1957 crisis developed, some differences had already developed between McMath and my administration over the race track at Hot Springs, but in the public mind we were still political allies.

When the '57 crisis developed McMath openly joined the *Gazette* editors and my other critics. He frequented the Little Rock Press Club which became headquarters for my critics and the visiting press. There with the whiskey and conversation flowing freely, he visited with the out-of-state and foreign press representatives, becoming quite a hero to them as he helped Harry Ashmore and the *Gazette* editors indoctrinate the strangers against me.

At the time McMath became governor and I became a part of his administration, Madison County had no completed hard-surfaced roads to the outside world. As a highway commissioner by McMath's appointment I secured the improvement of the remaining unimproved gap of State Highway number 68, thus giving the county its first connection by hard-surfaced road from the county seat of Huntsville to Springdale and the outside road network.

During these conversations at the press club in 1957 McMath remarked to the visiting newsmen, "The only mistake I made as governor was building that road and letting Orval out." The statement was carried nationwide in *Time* and *Life* magazines and quoted widely in other periodicals.

Another remark quoted by *Life* from the Press Club sessions was "The first time I saw Orval he came to town in a $2.00 pair of trousers with the cuffs six inches north of the socks." No source was given but I attributed the statement to Henry Woods, executive secretary to McMath while he was governor and at that time his law partner. There was no denial.

My reply to the McMath statement was, "If building the road and letting me out was a mistake, it wasn't the only one he made as governor."

So far, governors who can be charged with only one mistake during their tenure are non-existent.

RUN OF THE NEWS
by Karr Shannon
September 14, 1957

. . . Mayor Woodrow Mann said the Faubus-instituted block of integration in Little Rock's schools will set the state back 20 or 25 years. We have heard something similar from other calamity howlers. But if Arkansas had been set back half as much as these prophets of doom have been telling us the past few years, we would be in the Stone Age.

Governor Faubus wired President Eisenhower that he (Faubus) would obey both the Constitution of Arkansas and the Constitution of the United States. Impossible — if the U.S. Supreme Court is to interpret the national constitution.

CONSTITUTION WEEK

This is Constitution Week, and the grand old document is getting the acid test . . .

But the Constitution of the United States says nothing — absolutely nothing — about public schools or the regulation thereof.

September 14, 1957

South Carolina's Largest Newspaper—

THE PRESIDENT'S CHANCE

Arkansas' Governor Faubus and the President . . . have scheduled a meeting today.
It could be a momentous meeting.
It could also be a dismal failure . . .

If the President will listen to what the Governor of Arkansas should be able to tell the President, and forget some of the things the advocates of federal force have been telling him, the situation could bring some order out of chaos.

One thing has been fairly clear . . . all along. Gov. Faubus was not attempting any rebellion against the Federal government.

Gov. Faubus wants some clarification as to whether a State has any powers left to preserve the peace. He wants to know if the Supreme Court . . . meant that integration of schools should be forced in communities at the risk of the lives of the children.

President Eisenhower . . . has repeatedly indicated he thought local feelings — the imminence of danger — should be taken into account . . .

And for those who sneered there was no danger of violence in Little Rock — please let them look at Nashville, to Alabama, to Clinton, and Chicago picnics and Levittown houses. And then look at Little Rock, where there have been no bloody heads and no dynamited school houses.

Reporting has been so inflammatory . . . that the President directed his press secretary to term it "a great deal of junk."

Faubus and the President are not meeting as heads of enemy states. They are meeting to discuss the responsibilities of the President, the governors, and the lower federal courts.

Perhaps they might even discuss why Judge Davies was imported from Minnesota via North Dakota to be the "tough guy" about a question with which he is ill-suited to rule on the basis of his background. . . .

35TH DIVISION ASSOCIATION MEETS

My old war buddies of the 35th Division met in Kansas City the weekend of the Newport Conference, the first reunion I had missed since the war.

MIKE WALLACE INTERVIEW

On the night of September 15 I faced Mike Wallace, a tough adversary, in a 30-minute interview that was carried nationwide on the ABC network. The response to the encounter from the state and the nation was overwhelmingly favorable to me. I continued to receive comments for months afterward.

EXCUSE ME BOYS, I'M DUCKING INSIDE A MINUTE
By Flannery, Baltimore Sun   9/13/57

I decided to run out on my supporters under the excuse of the conference with Ike, leaving them stranded. So said the cartoonist.

Why wasn't it possible for the President and me to hold a conference honestly motivated with the hope of a solution? And without the thought of betraying any supporter or forsaking any principle?

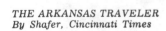

THE ARKANSAS TRAVELER
By Shafer, Cincinnati Times   9/14/57

There were many versions of The Arkansas Traveler during the Little Rock Crisis. This cartoon reflecting no malice or prejudice, showed the difficulty of making progress in the mud of "Integration." The worthwhile products in the wagon were kept from the market by the mud (controversy).

247

WITH ALL DELIBERATE SPEED
By Flannery, Baltimore Times   9/15/57

This widely used cartoon showed Charlotte, Greensboro and Winston-Salem, N.C., and Nashville, Tenn., making progress "with all deliberate speed" toward court-ordered "desegregated schools" under the watchful eye of Uncle Sam as school master. But Little Rock sat down on the steps and stopped his progress.

There was much praise by the liberal press of the other areas for achieving integration without violence. Later on, however, disorder much greater than that experienced in Little Rock, broke out in the schools of all these cities. It was erupting in Nashville at the time this cartoon appeared, and a half-million dollar school building was destroyed. No such damage occurred in Little Rock.

NO BROADCASTS TO CENTRAL ASIA
By Bristol, Source Unknown

9/15/57

While the Russian Communists were propagandizing the trouble in Little Rock, they carefully refrained from mentioning their segregated provinces in the Soviet Union.

*In June Speech Ike Said Things
To Bolster State Sovereignty Concept*

by James Free
The Birmingham News

Eisenhower Warned of Sovereignty Loss

PRESIDENT EISENHOWER *addressed a conference of state governors on June 24, 1957 at Williamsburg, Va. He issued a challenge to the states to reassert their powers and responsibilities.*

Mr. Eisenhower warned the governors that "a nation cannot be enslaved by diffused power, but only by strong centralized government." He noted a trend toward a weakening of state sovereignty, and he added that, if this trend continues, "the states are sure to degenerate into powerless satellites of the national government in Washington."

The President recalled what he told another governors' conference four years before: "That, unless we preserve the traditional power and responsibilities of state government . . . then we will not preserve the kind of America we have known, eventually, we will, instead, have another form of government and, therefore, quite another kind of an America."

Mr. Eisenhower said a lot more along this line, but these are some of the phrases that Gov. Faubus perhaps remembers best.

⌇⌇⌇⌇⌇

Shreveport Journal

September 14, 1957

ARKANSAS IN NEW LIGHT

Out of the federal-state clash . . . in Little Rock have come several developments which can only reflect credit to the great state of Arkansas . . .

Among these developments is the fact that Arkansas will receive the credit for having focused national attention upon the need for restoration of States' Rights — not just in the field of education, but in all other fields in which the federal government has usurped powers belonging to the states.

Another development is one which should go a long way toward obtaining national recognition of Arkansas as a modern, progressive state possessing many facilities and resources previously non-existent in the minds of Eastern detractors . . .

What a surprise it must have been to Northerners and Easterners, nurtured on the notion that Arkansas' educational system consists of several rows of log-cabin school houses, to learn suddenly that the City of Little Rock has beautiful million-dollar high schools for BOTH white and Negro pupils!

What a disappointment it must have been to . . . New York, Philadelphia and other points to learn . . . that Arkansas boys and girls do not . . . stammer and drawl a mountaineer jargon, but, instead, speak articulately and express themselves fluently and knowledgeably!

What an eye-opener it must have been for tenement dwellers in Chicago and Detroit to see Arkansas men and women clad — not in flour-sack aprons and overalls — but in dresses and suits from the fashion capitals of the world! . . .

What a blow it must have been to the Thomas W. Jackson joke book fans to see — not dirt streets, wagons and mules — but wide, paved thoroughfares and modern transportation facilities.

Most of all, what a jolt it must have been to the political centers of the world to learn that Arkansas' Governor Orval Faubus is not . . . a gallus-snappin', tobacco-spittin' Julius Cornpone-type vote-seeker, but a polished, courteous, tolerant statesman who . . . is more than a match for the psuedo-sophisticates of the Eastern press!

Yes, Arkansas is in a new light today as a result of the courageous action of its governor. The myth that Arkansas is a backward state has been exploded!

THEY TRYING TO SEGREGATE US?
By Williams, Detroit Free Press   9/13/57

This drawing said good results could come from the "Ike-Faubus meeting" with the extremists excluded. I am convinced that Brownell wanted no settlement of any kind in order that the ultimate use of troops would be made possible. The 101st Airborne troops at Ft. Campbell, Kentucky, as we later learned, had, even as the conference was being held, already begun special training for such a mission.

To Brownell, long before dubbed the grand political strategist of the Eisenhower administration, the use of federal troops to overcome a Southern state and effect by military might the implementation of a federal court order to integrate a Southern school, would be the ultimate political success. With one fell stroke, engineered by Brownell himself, there would be gathered up the entire bloc Negro vote, both North and South, as well as the favor of all the "liberals" throughout the nation. The losses in the legislative civil rights battle in Congress could be almost instantly regained.

THE ARKANSAS TRAVELER, *By Flannery, Baltimore Sun, 9/14/57*

Another version of the Arkansas Traveler in this distorted portrayal of the arrival at Newport. I was shown riding a donkey with blinders, with a jug of "Olde Ozark" hanging from my hip. Ike looked quizzically at my approach. "The Reverend Hays" from the clouds issued his "Reciprocal Forbearance Plea to North and South.

FACE THE NATION INTERVIEW

I was interviewed by a panel of newsmen on a nationwide television show, "Face the Nation." The broadcast was set up at the Mansion.

One of the panelists, Mr. William Hines, Jr., who had just arrived in Little Rock that day, was antagonistic and asked rough questions in an arrogant manner. Later, after Hines had been on the scene for a few days, he wrote one of the most factual and realistic reports of any of the out-of-state stories that came to my attention.

The panelists for the ABC program were: John Secondari, Chief of ABC's Washington Bureau; Bob Considine, INS Correspondent; Keith Fuller, AP Bureau Chief in Little Rock; Kenneth L. Johnson, Little Rock correspondent for the Memphis *Commercial Appeal;* and Hines, correspondent for *Telenews* and the *Washington* (D.C.) *Star.*

During the week I accepted a federal court summons from U.S. Marshal Beal Kidd to appear in Judge Davies Federal Court on September 20.

W.W. Mann, the discredited, lame-duck mayor of Little Rock, continued to act as the mouthpiece for the *Gazette* and the out-of-state press. In the capital city his influence was nil. Because of his mouthpiece role he had the open enmity and scorn of the people.

A conference between me and the President had been arranged by Congressman Brooks Hays.

Backstage At The Capitol

'VIOLENCE' IN LITTLE ROCK OCCURRED ON TYPEWRITERS

By George Douthit
Democrat Staff Writer, Sept. 15, 1957

Editorial writers and magazine editors over the nation really have had a party the last two weeks at the expense of Arkansas' Governor Faubus. They gave the words of condemnation and ridicule a heavy workout.

There was a reason for it other than the fact that they disagreed with Mr. Faubus' action in calling out the National Guard in the Central High School case. The editors got some good one-sided stories from their reporters who came rushing onto the scene looking for violence and riots.

Probably the biggest jolt the reporters received was when they came into Little Rock and discovered a quiet Southern city going about its business instead of police riding through the city brandishing riot guns.

Instead of the reporters finding white and Negro people pushing each other off the sidewalk, they saw them just as they always had lived for a hundred years — getting along together peacefully.

The reporters who had just hit Little Rock weren't getting much of a riot story to send back to their editors. So they went out to the high school where the guard was on duty.

We will admit that one lone Negro girl walked the entire block in front of the school after she had been told by the guard that the school was closed to her. We will admit that people followed her and called out things they should not have said.

But here is the pay-off. We have read descriptions of the various reporters who saw the incident. They varied from "walking with the dignity of a lady" to "she was hysterical and wept."

They had to write about her because most of them missed a few minutes later the main group of seven Negro students trying to enter the school.

There was not one word called out from the crowd, not one obscene statement made to this group. They were turned away and went quickly back from where they had come. But you should read the accounts by the foreign reporters.

Distorted Reports

They pictured these horrified Negro children being shunted away by hundreds of National Guardsmen brandishing armed carbines and rifles.

What we're trying to say is that what Little Rock lacked in "blood and thunder" the visiting press provided for the rest of the nation. They were so busy trying to be sensational about this situation here that we haven't found a single account that tried to present the situation that faces Little Rock and Arkansas.

By the end of week before last the reporters on the "battle front" had run out of material. Then Mayor Woodrow Mann took the limelight and held a few press conferences.

So, for the next few days the Little Rock story was kept alive on the front pages of the nation as the city's mayor became the hero in the face of this "dastardly" thing that the governor had pulled.

Editorials, Too

The reporters quoted and the editors editorialized that Little Rock's mayor could have handled the whole thing if the governor had stayed out of it.

In the meantime, the North Little Rock school board had decided that in view of the Little Rock situation the North Side should hold up its integration plans.

But a group of six Negroes decided to push ahead anyway, although the school board had ordered them not to try it. North Little Rock students took things in their own hands and pushed them back. No one was hurt but what a great story the foreign press had. And what pictures.

Governor Faubus was blamed for the North Little Rock action, although he had made no plans to interfere with integration in North Little Rock. It sounded better blaming it on him. So that punch was directed at him, too.

No sooner had the North Little Rock incident cooled off than over in Nashville, Tenn., citizens there resisted integration. John Kasper, the Northern troublemaker, had been walking free around Nashville for several weeks trying to stir up some action.

Faubus Blamed

One night a school was dynamited. The Nashville school superintendent called it the "backwash" of Governor Faubus' action in Little Rock. In other words, whatever happened anywhere it was blamed on Faubus. Yes, the nation's editors certainly have had a field day at his expense.

Now, after two weeks, what have we got? No one has tried to understand the problem facing the South. It has millions of law abiding people who will accept integration because the U.S. Supreme Court says we must.

Our people were given only two choices by the courts; integration without violence, or integration with violence. The majority of the people, against integration, prefer no violence.

So, now the big question is to the South: Will you accept integration without violence? We know most of the people will. But there is still a small minority of persons who, law abiding in everything else, cannot bring themselves to the point of ending the century-old tradition of segregation.

Until these few people are willing to accept this new thing quietly and peacefully, we have a problem.

And we need not expect the editors of the nation to understand. Anyway, many reporters didn't come here to seek out the real story; they came here for a sensation — riots, violence, guns, uniforms.

And in the period in which millions of words were written and hundreds of pictures taken, NOT ONE PERSON RECEIVED THE TINIEST LITTLE SCRATCH ON HIS BODY. (emphasis added)

COURT LIGHTS SHORT FUSE
By Roberts, St. Petersburg, Fla. Independent   9/14/57

This cartoonist showed the U.S. Supreme Court as the lighter of the fuse of the bomb underneath the "Public Education" school house.

OH, BOY, LOTS OF HEADLINES
By Herblock, Washington Post   9/13/57

Another extreme personal ciriticism drawing.

Up to this point the violence in Little Rock had been only on the typewriters of the visiting press and the pens of cartoonists like Block. Also, no ordinary citizen of any country in Africa or Asia enjoyed the freedom and opportunity of the ordinary citizen of the United States, regardless of creed, color or station in life.

THE SENTINEL RECORD, HOT SPRINGS, ARKANSAS

From the *Christian Science Monitor,* Boston, Mass.

September 15, 1957

The *Sentinel Record* of Hot Springs, in an editorial of its own, quoted from an editorial in the *Christian Science Monitor* of Boston, Mass., which said in part:

> *They (the majority) will have to make it very clear that racial problems must be accommodated and resolved within the national family by good will, reason, and legal processes.*
>
> *It is only fair to note that in this the South labors under extra difficulties. In that section millions of kindly, intelligent Americans are convinced that both races can progress better if a degree of separateness is maintained. Most of the South's critics would very likely find themselves taking this same position if they lived under the same conditions. Usually transplanted Northerners become more ardent segregationists.*
>
> *Non-Southerners will be able to help improve race relations better if they grasp these facts.*

THE HIGH ROAD
By Fischetti, NEA Service, Tulsa, Okla. Tribune   9/14/57

The "Eisenhower Faubus Integration Talk" was shown as the high road approach to the Little Rock problem. The low road was "precipitate action," which should be avoided. This cartoon attempted to plant a hopeful idea.

'BIRDIE'
By Knox, Nashville Banner   9/15/57

Even before I arrived at the conference with President Eisenhower, the know-it-alls in the news media were telling the world what was going to happen. One version said I had gone to

Newport to "throw in the sponge." The speculation was 100 percent erroneous and 95 percent anti-South propaganda. The President, to his credit, issued a blistering statement branding the speculation as false and saying it served no useful purpose. Thus, the cartoon showed Ike's golf ball striking the "anti-South propaganda carriers."

AND ALL THIS TIME I WAS HOPING YOU'D SPEAK UP
By Herblock, Washington Post   9/15/57

Block attempted to make President Eisenhower look bad because he counseled patience and understanding with the difficult problems created by the federal court orders on integration.

A REPORTER'S RETROSPECTION

Many Share the Blame for Little Rock's Experience

The Sunday Star, Washington, D.C., September 15, 1957

By William Hines

Peace settled like a pall last week over Little Rock, and the 200,000 residents of the Arkansas capital and its environs had an opportunity to ask themselves what had happened.

Except for the inevitable few who enjoy and thrive on strife, controversy and violence, no one in Little Rock was very proud of the spectacle in which all — to some degree — were involved. There were not a few sighs of relief over the fact that no

one had been hurt. There was gratification that the so-called "violence" at North Little Rock High School was actually no more than the kind of jostling one would experience in a New York subway.

In the aftermath of Little Rock's week of trouble, there was some effort to place the blame — and to find a scapegoat.

Casual observers found it easy to identify Gov. Orval E. Faubus as the author of Little Rock's problems. Die-hards in the extreme segregationist camp conveniently blamed the National Association for the Advancement of Colored People (NAACP). Others had other nominees — the Supreme Court, Mayor Woodrow Wilson Mann, Federal Judge Ronald N. Davies, School Superintendent Virgil T. Blossom, and many watchers from afar saw not a person but a situation to blame, the situation being a struggle between integrationists and segregationists.

Taking the last point first, there are almost no grounds for the suggestion that such a struggle exists. It is this reporter's opinion — based on conversations with dozens of Arkansans from all walks of life — that 99 percent of the white people of Little Rock oppose the idea of sending their children to school with Negroes. Among the white citizens of the Arkansas capital there is no "integrationist" movement.

The battle lines are drawn, rather, between the "compliers" and "non-compliers." The former take the attitude that integration, while undesirable, is inevitable and that the best should be made of a bad situation. The latter group holds that no education at all is better than integrated education.

Some Basic Facts

Before either side's viewpoint is dismissed with a shrug or a sneer, these two facts should be understood:

• The compliers are, by and large, the better educated, better paid, better placed people of the town. Among many of them the question of integrated education is purely a philosophical one because they either have no children, send them to a private school or otherwise do not have to face the issue frontally.

• The non-compliers, with some exceptions, are a lower economic stratum than their foes. Many of them compete directly with Negroes economically, come in contact with Negroes more frequently on a day-to-day basis, and in general cherish more dearly the old, deep-seated racial dislikes and distrusts.

Gov. Faubus appears, strangely enough, to stand in the camp of the compliers, despite the fact that he is this week the darling of the non-compliers. He pointed out on television last Sunday that he sends his son to an integrated college, and on a number of occasions in the last week he has reaffirmed both his respect for and his eventual intention to comply with court orders. But not just now, he says.

The Governor's action in calling out the National Guard at Little Rock Central High School September 2 has been the subject of much criticism both within and without Arkansas. It also has been hailed as a proper precaution. The Governor's own motives in taking this action are locked in his mind.

The point is that he has given the non-compliers a new lease on life, and for this they are grateful.

Gov. Faubus has been criticized for allowing a situation of violence to arise. As a matter of fact, IT DID NOT ARISE — either because of or in spite of his National Guard mobilization order and his public pronouncements during the week of crisis. (emphasis added)

It has been suggested that North Carolina was able to avoid an ugly situation because Gov. Luther Hodges of North Carolina had the wholehearted support of civic leaders in his State while Arkansas businessmen were not concerned about what happened in the schools.

An Implication

Is there any validity to this suggestion? No one can really know, but this may be an answer by implication:

Last May, this reporter talked in Winston-Salem, N.C., with a number of civic leaders and nabobs of the business community. One of them told of a meeting a handful of leading Winston citizens had held on the subject of the forthcoming integration.

"Among us, we represent probably 95 percent of the financial resources of Forsyth County," he said. "We quietly passed the word that trouble here would be bad for business and we weren't going to have any. We have this thing so well locked up that a cab driver couldn't get a gasoline credit card without our sayso."

"No, there isn't going to be any trouble."

A half a dozen millionaires spoke and the city obeyed. There was no trouble in Winston-Salem. [The trouble there was merely postponed. It came later — OEF.]

In Little Rock the interest of civic and financial leaders lay in another direction.

When integration became inevitable, the school district officials built a second white high school, Hall High, out on the heights west of town. That's where the well-to-do of Little Rock live.

When school opened Sept. 3, Central High was slated for integration of about a dozen Negroes [but eventually to be 50 percent or more black students, which it now is — OEF]. *No Negroes lived in the Hall High district, so the issue did not arise there. One leading Little Rock citizen told this reporter that the Hall High district is so carefully gerrymandered that it probably will be 25 years before any Negro qualifies for attendance. The integration problem will be solved — if it is ever solved — downtown.*

Inasmuch as the members of the school board participated in the decision to build Hall High, they are obliged to share — with the Governor, the business and financial leaders, the NAACP, the rednecks and the rest — blame for what happened last week at Fourteenth Street and Park Avenue.

And what of the Mayor, who criticized the Governor's action? On only one topic in Little Rock today can one find almost universal agreement. That is that Mayor Woodrow Wilson Mann is washed up and that no one would pay any attention to him under any circumstances. There are complex reasons for this, but his low estate is a matter of fact. [Yet the Mayor was hailed as the spokesman for the people of Little Rock by all the critics, and his utterances were recognized by Federal Judge Davies as the basis for his rulings in the Federal court — OEF.]

Question of Motivation

However the blame should be divided, a question that plagues everyone is: What motivates the Governor of Arkansas? Again, one cannot get into the locked recesses of another's mind. One can only put together known facts and well-grounded opinions and from these arrive at a conjecture.

Gov. Faubus is in his second term. He has been a reasonably good Governor whose administration has done much to pull Arkansas up out of the economic and social doghouse which she has shared for so long with Mississippi.

The tradition in Arkansas is against a third term for Governors. Gov. Faubus' present two-year term expires in January 1959, which means he will have to make a decision on running again in November 1958. Against him will be his own attorney general, Bruce Bennett, who will be watching like a hawk between now and next year for one false move by the Governor.

It is generally believed — without Gov. Faubus' confirmation or denial — that the Governor will go up against Sen. John L. McClellan for a six-year Senate term in the 1960 election. . . . It then follows that it is in Gov. Faubus' interest to make himself look as good as possible to the greatest number of Arkansans. It seems likely that up to now he has done just that. If an election were to be held today, many persons familiar with Arkansas politics believe Mr. Faubus would win re-election hands down. . . .

After his broadcast Sunday night, Gov. Faubus was asked by a newsman whether he thought integration would eventually come to Little Rock. "Oh, certainly," the Governor replied, "but it will take time."

Asked how much time, the Governor estimated a couple of years.

* * *

The Hines story confirmed a number of facts which were being deliberately overlooked and obscured by the great majority of the news media.

1. There was peace in Little Rock — see the first sentence of the story.

2. People were gratified that no one had been hurt.

3. The "violence" in North Little Rock was no violence at all.

4. The people were almost solidly opposed to forcible integration of the schools.

5. The rich or well-to-do class of people, who advocated compliance with the court order, had arranged, by the building of Hall High School, to avoid the integration which they urged others to accept.

6. People who understood the situation hailed my action in calling out the Guard as a proper precaution.

7. It was a situation which had developed for which no single individual or group was to blame. In my opinion, those who sought to become overnight heroes in solving an age-old, almost unsolvable problem, and pushed the integration plan for that purpose, were largely to blame.

8. Mayor Mann, the synthetic hero of my critics, was a completely discredited public figure.

9. As to the question which plagued Hines — what motivated my actions? — my immediate number one aim was to prevent violence. Subsequent events revealed that I was not motivated by a desire to replace John L. McClellan in the Senate, nor to oppose any other official on the scene at the time.

Hines is to be especially commended for stressing one point. That was the building of Hall High school by the school board for the use of the rich, leaving the poorer, working class of people, both black and white, to bear any integration problems that might arise.

'DANGEROUS'
By Rosen, Albany, N.Y. Times Union   9/15/57

Uncle Sam suffered from a black eye, "integration violence," which came from the Little Rock story. There had been no violence in Little Rock at the time this cartoon appeared.

THE NEWPORT CONFERENCE
Sept. 14, 1957

I took off from the Little Rock airport at 9:16 a.m. Friday, September 13, 1957, in a chartered Texas twin-motored plane for the conference with the president in Mr. Eisenhower's vacation retreat at the naval base at Newport, R.I. The conference was scheduled for 9 a.m. the next day.

Accompanying me were Congressman Brooks Hays and my executive secretary, Arnold Sikes.

The plane was provided by the Brown Aero Corporation of Dallas and Texarkana, through the Howard Webb Flying Service of Texarkana.

The pilots were W. C. White, Jr., Vice President and General Manager, and Ed Moore, both of Dallas.

The reporters questioned me persistently at a press conference before takeoff, but I declined to discuss the conference in advance, or to speculate on the outcome. Congressman Hays also declined comment on those subjects, but claimed full credit for arranging the conference.

In the same paper which carried news of our departure from Little Rock appeared a story by Relman Morin about the mysterious role of Hays in arranging the conference and his role of interpreter of the conflicting viewpoints of the adversaries. The story also mentioned the reports, current at the time, "that Hays may be named federal judge in eastern Arkansas — and his role as mediator . . . may lend greater probability to the report."

Somewhere about mid-journey — as I recall in eastern Tennessee — we landed for refueling and refreshment. We secured newspapers and scanned through them as we ate. All carried banner headlines and stories on the coming conference. So far as I could detect, no one in our party was recognized, and we ate without being interrupted.

We landed at Providence and were transported to the Sheraton-Biltmore Hotel. There large crowds lined the streets and watched as we got out of the cars and went inside. The people were not unfriendly but quiet and undemonstrative. (One of those watching, as he informed me years later, was a future governor of Rhode Island, and later one of my colleagues at the National Governors' Conferences.)

After a restful night we were transported the next morning by Marine helicopter to the conference site, according to news reports about 35 miles, and arrived at the appointed time.

We were met at the disembarkation point by Presidential Aide Sherman Adams and Press Secretary James C. Hagerty. We shouldered our way through a crowd of shoving, pushing, shouting reporters and photographers a few hundred feet up a gentle slope to the building used by the President as vacation headquarters.

The President greeted us in the first room inside the structure, following which he and I went almost immediately into an adjoining room where he had his desk, and the door was closed. Adams and Hays remained in the first room while Sikes remained outside in an adjoining room with Hagerty and others. I recall no sign at that time of the presence of Attorney General Herbert Brownell.

Then the President began to speak. He did not begin by saying, "Governor, what can we do about this situation?" or "Do you have any suggestions or proposals?" Nor did he ask for any information on the situation.

His speech was in the nature of a lecture and was often halting. I got the impression at times that he was attempting to recall just what he was supposed to say to me, as if he were trying to remember instructions on a subject on which he was not completely assured in his own mind.

From the President's attitude and train of thought, I got the definite impression that I had been called in for a lecture, just as a general would summon a lieutenant before him for a reprimand for an alleged transgression of military rules.

I have no doubt, now, that the President had been advised that this method was "the way to handle this fellow, Faubus." I have a strong feeling that his advisers had counseled that a firm and unyielding attitude would get results — that I would be cowed by the august position of the presidency; that I would yield, scurry back to Little Rock and carry out whatever I was told to do by either the national administration or the federal courts.

I listened most attentively and quietly until the President had finished. To say that I was unimpressed by his method would be putting it mildly, except that I was disappointed. However, I doubt if he could have detected that from my attitude.

Then I began to speak by saying, "Mr. President, there are some things I'd like to tell you about the situation."

I began by reminding him of the Supreme Court's language which said that compliance with its decision on integration would be brought about "with all deliberate speed." Then, from the viewpoint of the Justice Department and the federal courts, I told him of the progress that had been made in Arkansas.

All institutions of higher learning in Arkansas were integrated except one, and there were no applications by Negroes there. (The University of Arkansas had been previously integrated during Gov. Ben Laney's administration.) My son was attending one of these integrated colleges.

All transportation systems — trains, buses and local systems — had been integrated.

Almost all state agencies had integrated work forces. My staff meetings were integrated, and had been since I first assumed office almost three years before.

Many private businesses were integrated, and a number of hotels, motels and eating places.

At the beginning of the school year, there were more integrated public schools in Arkansas than eleven other states combined with comparable problems.

I was the first Southern governor to place Negroes on the Arkansas Democratic State Central Committee; the Republican State Central Committee also had black members.

During the course of my remarks I could detect that the President became very interested. He asked a few questions which I, of course, answered fully and completely. I became aware that the President was totally and completely uninformed on the situation in Arkansas. I had the fleeting thought that if he were still a military commander, and his staff permitted him to become involved in a conference of such magnitude while so completely ignorant of the facts, such negligence would be grounds for court martial.

I then summed up the "progress" report by referring again to the Supreme Court's term "deliberate speed," and emphasized that if any state had approached or attained the speed called for by this nebulous term, then certainly Arkansas had done so when compared to others of comparable circumstances. The people of Arkansas felt, I told the President, that they were entitled to some consideration for this "progress" in this difficult field of human relations, and I felt they were justified in that attitude.

I noted that the President's desk was bare; he apparently had no facts and figures or information of any kind on the situation. At one time, in mentioning the pressures and advice he was receiving, as well as the expressions of alarm, he pulled from a desk drawer, which appeared to be otherwise empty, a letter. It appeared to be a handwritten epistle and was several pages long.

The President said it was from a friend whom he knew personally. The person, he said, was known as a responsible individual, and to indicate to me the alarm felt by some, and the extreme advice coming to him from some sources, he read to me a part of the letter.

The writer warned of strong feeling and sectional disloyalty in the military and advised the President to remove from all positions of command all Southerners in the Armed Forces everywhere.

"Of course," commented the President as he placed the letter back in the desk drawer, "I think he's nuts."

I had the very strong thought at the time, "So this is the kind of material that is being permitted to sift through to the President while keeping him in total ignorance of the circumstances surrounding the Little Rock situation." After that, I understood more fully the role being played by those to whom many Washington reporters referred as the "Palace Guard."

After I had related to the President the progress made in Arkansas in compliance with the Supreme Court's 1954 decision and later modifying orders, I explained how Little Rock had become a focal point of conflict by contending forces.

Those who had promulgated the so-called Little Rock plan — a mere handful of the total Little Rock school district population — had become deluded with visions of grandeur. They had become imbued with the idea of becoming overnight heroes by the quick and easy solution of a problem which has defied easy solution throughout the history of mankind.

I explained how editorials and feature news stories had been written and published to the effect that the Little Rock plan would become a model for Arkansas and indeed all the South.

In fact, many reporters on the national scene had already been lured to Little Rock, not with the thought of reporting the events which did occur, but to report to the nation and the world the "great success story" which was about to unfold. Some advance stories to that effect were filed on Sunday, and also on Monday preceding the placing of the National Guard early in the evening of that day. Some of the stories were printed in various papers across the land.

These stories were of the same nature as the one filed from Africa by a reporter covering the activities of United Nations Secretary General Dag Hammerskjold. The reporter told how the Secretary General had taken off by air from one point, and of his safe arrival at his destination. The Secretary was killed in the crash of his plane, never reaching his destination, as had been reported.

These Little Rock stories filed on Sunday and Monday were too late to materially affect the immediate situation but they are proof of the aims for glory of the sponsors of the Little Rock school plan. The volatile situation was due in large part to the advance publicity brought about by these sponsors in their dreams of becoming overnight heroes.

When Citizens Council leaders and members continued to read of how the Little Rock plan was to become a model for all other areas, statewide and South-wide, they became aroused. They were joined by others who, up to that time, had manifested little interest in the Little Rock district's problems. Concern among those who opposed integration spread across the state and beyond its borders. It was manifested by the summoning of Governor Marvin Griffin of Georgia, along with other segregation leaders, to Little Rock to address meetings to which segregation leaders from other states, had been invited.

The opponents to the Little Rock integration plan were now thoroughly aroused. The determination among them grew that if the plan was to be a model for other areas of Arkansas and the South, they would bend every effort to make it a model their way. Thus, forces outside the Little Rock district became involved.

The school board and the federal courts were already out on a limb with the integration plan. The lines were drawn with the positions of the contending forces becoming more and more inflexible. Little Rock had become a focal point of contest. My action in placing the Guard around Central High School to keep order, which had the effect of preventing the implementation of the integration plan, had so far avoided a clash between these opposing forces.

"What we need," I told the President, "is a cooling off period — time for emotions to subside — for determination to wane."

I did not tell the President this would solve the problem. I told him that, in my opinion, it was the only approach that might solve the problem without demonstrations which could lead to violence and possible bloodshed.

The President was a military man. He could understand a focal point of contest and how it could develop. He was impressed. I think he was equally impressed by my earlier recital of Arkansas's progress toward compliance with the Supreme Court decision, facts of which he had been in total ignorance.

The President and I then went out into the next room to join Hays and Adams. He questioned Hays about the "progress" report I had given him and the Congressman confirmed each fact that was mentioned, sometimes adding information of his own. Hays also affirmed to the President that a cooling off period "could be very helpful."

The discussion between the four of us, with the other three doing most of the talking, lasted longer than the time the President and I had spent in private. This phase was concluded when the President had Adams summon Brownell. As I recall, this was my first knowledge of Brownell's presence at the vacation headquarters. If I had known that he was to be there, I might have taken along my personal attorney, William J. (Bill) Smith. However, I wanted to avoid legal arguments, for they can be interminable and, I thought, offered little hope of any compromise or understanding on the immediate problem.

The President said to Brownell, "The Governor tells me this about Arkansas, and Congressman Hays here confirms it." He then ticked off in rather rapid fashion a number of the things which had been done in Arkansas toward compliance with the Supreme Court decision. He concluded with:

"They've even got Negroes on the —," at this point, because of his unfamiliarity with civil government and political organizations, he couldn't recall the term "Party Central Committee" and ended with, " — aw, you know, the set-up."

Then Eisenhower mentioned the need for "a cooling off period." After some discussion of this point in which Hays was again consulted, the President said:

"Herb, can't you go down there [to Little Rock] and ask the court to postpone this thing for a few days?"

I shall never forget Brownell's attitude nor his reply. A sickly half-smile bathed his sharp, pallid features. He appeared surprised, and hesitated. Then, in the quietness, with all eyes on him as we awaited his answer, he said:

"No, we can't do that. It isn't possible." The President continued to look at Brownell as if he couldn't comprehend why it wasn't possible. Then Brownell added, "It isn't legally possible. It just can't be done." •

The President, sitting astride a chair facing Brownell, dropped his head. He appeared nonplussed, crestfallen, disappointed. Then, after a pause, with a shake of his head as if in disbelief, he arose. He did not question his Attorney General further. He had accepted the verdict rendered by Brownell. Nothing could be done.

Not once did Brownell address me or Hays while in the room.

I had remained silent during the President's discourse with Brownell. At that moment, I started to take issue with Brownell's opinion, and the words were on the tip of my tongue. But I remained conscious that I was not an attorney, and Brownell was the Attorney General of the United States giving a legal opinion to the President of the greatest nation in the world. With that thought I restrained myself and the moment passed. I had the thought, "Brooks is a lawyer and a member of the Congress that makes the laws," and looked toward Hays. His eyes were on the floor and he remained silent. Perhaps Hays recognized that if he embarrassed Brownell at that point by correcting him that it would destroy any chance he had for appointment as a federal judge. It was well known that the Attorney General was making most, if not all, the selections for the judgeships.

There were some more remarks — small talk, it appeared to me. There was to be no more serious discussion, it seemed, of the matter which had brought us together. I arose and crossed the small room and sat down on the sofa where Hays and Adams had been seated. As I took my seat, I said to the President, "I guess one solution would be to let you crucify me."

The most startled look I have ever witnessed came quickly across Eisenhower's countenance. He turned abruptly toward me, glanced momentarily at my face with amazement, then looked at the floor and turned away silently.

Just preceding that moment, as I recall, Brownell left the room, but I am not positive of this. Since it appeared that all serious discussion had ended Adams suggested, "Brooks, tell us some of your good stories."

Seldom does Hays need a second invitation and sometimes none at all, to regale hearers with his jokes and humorous anecdotes. He then told three or four amusing stories and had everyone laughing with his inimitable style and manner of relating them. But deep within me there was no mirth.

We then arose to end the conference, labeled by the press as historic. Everyone put on a good front but I felt that nothing had been accomplished. The thought recurred to me that the whole aim of the "Palace Guard," aided and abetted by their co-conspirators at Little Rock, was to accomplish what the President had appeared to attempt in the first few moments of our private conference — intimidate me into submission. Armed with facts and information which had been kept from the President, I had effectively upset that apple cart and but for the flint-faced Brownell's adamant attitude and falsehood to the President, would have won a cooling-off period that might have helped all concerned.

As Brooks, Sikes and myself accompanied by Adams walked to the helicopter for the return flight to Providence, I noticed the President on the way to the golf course swinging a club as he walked.

There was no opportunity to talk above the noise of the helicopter with crew members present on the flight back to Providence. But as soon as we were in the privacy of our hotel room I said to Hays: "Brooks, Mr. Brownell is wrong about what he told the President. The court order issued by Judge Davies inviting the Justice Department into the case for the purpose of the FBI investigation also says 'to make any suggestion or recommendation [to the Court] which it sees fit'."

After pondering a moment Hays replied, "Yes, Governor, I believe you're right."

I knew I was right and so stated and sat down dejectedly with the remark, "What can be done when we're dealing with that kind of a situation. I'll just go on back and bear the burden and the abuse." The press and liberal politicians were giving me more than my share of the latter.

"Now, don't feel like that," consoled Hays. "Maybe we can work something out. There's still hope."

So we began work on the statement for the press. Hays stayed in touch with the vacation White House by telephone and advised me what must be included to be acceptable to the advisers there. Every phrase of my statement had to be approved or dictated by those who remained at the presidential headquarters.

In mentioning the Supreme Court decision of 1954 and subsequent rulings, the statement read.

"That is not relevant. The decision is the law of the land and must be obeyed."

I knew that a court decision was not the law of the land, and so did Brooks Hays, or at least he should have known, being a member of Congress. However, upon the advice of Hays and the insistence of the vacation White House, I allowed the statement to be included in my press release. My thought was that if any compromise or cooling off period was to be obtained there had to be some give-and-take. Also I was entertaining the hope that somehow Eisenhower would learn that Brownell's advice was wrong, and something might yet be done about the suggested delay of integration in Little Rock.

It did not dawn on me at the time but I realized later that the Palace Guard was attempting to gain the advantage over me by dictating the press releases. A victory not gained in the conference was sought in the prepared statements.

Hays was very guarded about whom he was talking to in his

several calls, saying he was in touch with "all of them." Left at the vacation headquarters at the time of our departure were Adams, Hagerty and Brownell. The presence of others may have been undisclosed.

The press release finished, Hays re-read it to the White House advisers for final approval. We then went downstairs where I read it to about 75 reporters and photographers in a crowded room. Hays advised, and I agreed, to avoid answers to all other questions, even in the face of the inconclusive press release. The statement released for the President at Newport was likewise unclear as to any results of the conference.

I have the strong feeling that the President did not even see his press release, unless he read it much later. It was prepared for him by Brownell, Adams, or Hagerty, or by all three, and was released while he was still on the golf course.

The press conference concluded, we hastily packed for departure. Before leaving, Hays carefully gathered all his handwritten notes, made during his telephone conversations with White House aides as we prepared my press release, and destroyed them.

Hays stopped at New York on the return journey. My last words to him were to affirm an understanding that immediately on arrival in Little Rock I would obtain a copy of the court order and send it to him by air mail, special delivery in Washington. Upon receipt of the copy, he would get it into the hands of the President as quickly as possible.

We flew non-stop from New York to Little Rock arriving at 10:40 p.m., September 14. There, as the press reports stated, I was "swamped by newsmen at Adams Field who had waited over three hours expecting an explanation of the ambiguous statements the President and the Governor had issued early in the afternoon."

"The Governor returned to the applause of about 200 persons who had waited several hours. He stuck to his original noncommittal statement, and brushed aside all other questions with no comment," the press reports said.

I went to the executive residence, directed my aides to obtain a copy of the court order, and put it in the mail to Congressman Hays.

Did the President receive the copy of the court order? Evidently not for some time.

On October 24, some six weeks after the Newport meeting, Brownell suddenly resigned.

Informants on the Washington scene, whom I had every reason to believe, told me that President Eisenhower had finally learned how Brownell had deceived him at the Newport Conference. He was enraged, my informants said. As they described the scene, "The White House had never seen such a temper tantrum by a furious President." The Attorney General was peremptorily fired. Presidential aides announced his departure as a resignation.

I cannot vouch for the manner or reason for Brownell's termination as U.S. Attorney General. I can only reiterate that I have faith in my informants.

I do know that in my presence Brownell, either through design or ignorance, lied to the President about the court order. Whether through design or ignorance, it was inexcusable of the Attorney General of the United States in advising the President whom he served.

THE COURT ORDER

IN THE UNITED STATES DISTRICT COURT
FOR THE EASTERN DISTRICT OF ARKANSAS
WESTERN DIVISION

John Aaron et al .... Plaintiffs

vs.   Civil No. 3113

William G. Cooper et al .... Defendants

ORDER

On the date hereof, the Court having received a report from the United States Attorney for the Eastern District of Arkansas, made pursuant to the Court's request, from which it appears that negro students are not being permitted to attend Little Rock Central High School in accordance with the plan of integration of the Little Rock School Directors approved by this Court and by the Court of Appeals for the Eighth Circuit,

And the Court being of the opinion that the public interest in the administration of justice should be represented in these proceedings and that it will be of assistance to the Court to have the benefit of the views of counsel for the United States as amici curiae, and this Court being entitled at any time to call upon the law officers of the United States to serve in that capacity, now, therefore,

IT IS ORDERED that the Attorney General of the United States or his designate, and the United States Attorney for the Eastern District of Arkansas or his designate, are hereby requested and authorized to appear in these proceedings as amici curiae and to accord the Court the benefit of their views and recommendations with the right to submit to the Court pleadings, evidence, arguments and briefs, and for the further purpose, under the direction of this Court, to initiate such further proceedings as may be appropriate.

IT IS FURTHER ORDERED that the Attorney General of the United States and the United States Attorney for the Eastern District of Arkansas be and they are hereby directed to file immediately a petition against Orval E. Faubus, Governor of the State of Arkansas; Major General Sherman T. Clinger, Adjutant General, Arkansas National Guard; and Lt. Colonel Marion E. Johnson, Unit Commander, Arkansas National Guard, seeking such injunctive and other relief as may be appropriate to prevent the existing interferences with and obstructions to the carrying out of the orders heretofore entered by this Court in this case.

Dated at Little Rock, Arkansas, this 9th day of September, 1957.

RONALD N. DAVIES
United States District Judge
(Sitting by Assignment)

CHAPTER 13
INJUNCTION ISSUED; GUARD WITHDRAWN;
MAYOR MANN FAILS TO KEEP ORDER;
FEDERAL TROOPS OCCUPY LITTLE ROCK

WHITE HOUSE ACCUSATION

The White House accused a group of top Democrats of "trying to play politics" with the school controversy. The accusation was a reaction to an assertion by 15 members of the 24-member Democratic advisory council that Eisenhower "failed to use the prestige and power of his office . . . against defiance of law" at Little Rock.

MANSFIELD STATEMENT

Sen. Mike Mansfield (D-Mont.) said that the Little Rock dispute was outside the jurisdiction of Congress.

"It has no application to any law passed by Congress," Mansfield said.

So, to what "law" did these Democrats have reference?

"The president is concerned with solutions and not with political speeches," Hagerty said.

In his accusation of certain Democrats, Hagerty was 100 per cent correct. Ike may not have been interested in playing politics but he yielded to the political pressures and the mis-advice of Brownell.

Sen. Mansfield's statement was particularly significant. There was no law passed by Congress and therefore no "law of the land" in the Supreme Court ruling.

GOVERNOR'S ENGLISH DEFENDED

Editorial in Arkansas Democrat, Sept. 16, 1954

Governor Faubus is being ridiculed for saying "preservator" instead of preserver and for his "me-lish-ee" pronunciation of militia. But bear in mind that he's a native of the Ozark hill country which has richer and more colorful forms of English than urban regions speak.

Hill speech retains words and usages of every period of our language from its birth in Anglo-Saxon. Listen to the talk of ordinary hill folk who haven't lost regional usages under the impact of charmless radio, movie and television standardized speech and you will hear words that spring straight from Anglo-Saxon, Norman French, Latin, Elizabethan and 18th century English.

Mr. Faubus' way of pronouncing militia has long historical precedence. If you doubt it, just consult a Latin dictionary.

U.S. TO SUBPOENA OVER 200 WITNESSES IN PREPARATION FOR FRIDAY'S INJUNCTION HEARING

Osro Cobb revealed that upwards of 200 persons were being subpoenaed for the Sept. 20 federal court hearing in the injunctive action.

Mr. Cobb said the large number of witnesses was being called so that the government could be prepared on "every conceivable thing of material interest to the court."

The court action petitioned for an injunction against me and two National Guard officers, Gen. Clinger and Col. Johnson.

Some observers saw in the subpoena action the federal government's determination to go ahead with the case with no thought of compromise. I saw the action in the same light, but it appeared that finally a full and complete hearing would be held on the matter.

LOCAL BRINKMANSHIP
By Graham, Ark. Gazette   9/17/57

The cartoon title was a takeoff on Secretary of State John Foster Dulles' international brinksmanship. There were errors in the cartoon. The integration plan was about a year old, having been approved in federal court Aug. 28, 1956.

The National Guardsmen under my command never used bayonets or loaded weapons.

MANN ASKS REMOVAL OF GUARD: ADVANCE NOTICE OF ACTION REQUESTED IN NOTE TO FAUBUS

The opposition's mouthpiece, Mayor Mann, got into the act again.

Mann's letter to me read in part:

"As chief executive of the city and charged under the constitutional obligation of preserving peace and maintaining law and order in the City of Little Rock, I ask your cooperation in notifying me personally at least 24 hours prior to the time such withdrawal [of the Guard] is to be effective. . . ."

In a statement to the press, Mann said:

"This disgrace which has befallen the city has gone on long enough. . . . it has subjected us to state and worldwide ridicule. It's time it is brought to a halt — long past time."

—0—

Run of the News
by Karr Shannon
Arkansas Democrat, Sept. 17, 1957

Little Rock Negro Schools Have High Rating

There are over 300 high schools (almost 75% of all state schools) for white children in 68 of Arkansas' 75 counties that have a lower rating than the Negro high schools in Little Rock.

HAYS, FAUBUS CLOSETED IN NEW SESSION

Rep. Brooks Hays came to see me at the Mansion the morning of the 17th. He had nothing new to offer. He later told the press that he would continue his talks with me.

Mr. Hays said, "We enjoyed a nice talk" but that there was no news to report.

EMBARRASSING SMUDGE
By Goldberg, N.Y. Journal American   9/17/57

The cartoonist said the controversy at Little Rock was a smudge on the torch in the hand of the Statue of Liberty. However, those who opposed what they deemed to be illegal court decisions, and who agreed with my actions to prevent disorder, had an entirely opposite view.

What kind of smudge did Goldberg draw on the statue when portions of New York and Washington were later burned to the ground in racial rioting?

U.S. CALLING 200 IN FAUBUS CASE

The Toledo (Ohio) *Times,* September 18, 1957

The above was the banner headline all the way across the front page of this northern newspaper on September 18. A story datelined Little Rock, September 17, said in part:

The Federal Government, moving toward a critical test of strength with Gov. Orval E. Faubus, drew up a list of some 200 witnesses today for Friday's court hearing on his use of armed troops to block integration in a Little Rock high school.

Advice and appeals swept in on Governor Faubus as the zero hour neared.

. . . Governor Faubus has been summoned to appear Friday (Sept. 20) before Judge Davies. The Government is asking for a preliminary injunction to end Mr. Faubus' blockade of Negro students at Central High.

The mass of prospective witnesses will testify as to whether Governor Faubus was justified in calling out the guardsmen. He says he did it because he received warnings that violence would break out when the Negroes attempted to enroll.

The story of more than 200 witnesses being subpoenaed by the Justice Department was big news with blazing headlines all across the country.

The witnesses were served with subpoenas some time before the news stories appeared. But by the time this story appeared on September 18, the witnesses had received letters from the Justice Department telling them not to appear — that their testimony would not be needed.

Several of the witnesses contacted me, wondering about the motives of the Justice Department. Others contacted Department officials and offered to appear in Court, saying they wanted to testify about the matter of possible violence at Central High School. They were brusquely informed they were not wanted and directed not to appear.

The fact of the matter is, that if more than 200 knowledgeable Little Rock citizens had testified in Judge Davies' court, the evidence would have supported my action in using the National Guard to prevent disorder. The Washington attorneys for the federal government may have reached this conclusion, who then directed that all witnesses be notified not to appear. Those who offered to appear anyway met with blunt refusals.

I suspect that District Attorney Cobb, who had issued the subpoenas, was overruled by superior authority.

At the brief hearing Judge Davies for the second time in a court hearing, relied on the press statements of Mayor Mann that there was "no threat of violence" and that there "would be no violence" in the integration of Central High School.

Such was the basis of Judge Davies' ruling on September 20, when the Governor of Arkansas and the National Guard commanders were enjoined from the use of the Guard.

By denying hundreds of witnesses the opportunity to testify, and basing its whole case on such flimsy evidence — which was, in fact, no evidence at all — the federal government left many of its defenders way out on a limb. Such a case was the following editorial from the *Washington Post.*

"In any event, the surest way to convince Mr. Faubus, and to uphold the prestige of the Federal Government, is to prepare fully and without hesitation for the Federal Court hearing . . . Happily, the Department of Justice has been doing this through the subpoenas issued by the District Attorney.

Surely the Governor cannot relish the thought that the evidence gathered by the FBI — evidence reportedly showing that there was no real threat of violence until he manufactured it — may be laid before the people of Arkansas."

An interesting sidelight on Mayor Mann: While contending that there was no evidence of possible violence, city policemen had been assigned to guard his residence around the clock.

━●━o━o━●━

DAVID LAWRENCE SAYS:

Arkansas Governor Not Breaking Any State Law

Are we witnessing the beginning of the end of state government in America, and the emergence of a supreme dictatorship over the states by the federal government in Washington?

Does the silence of so many of the governors . . . mean that they have already been cowed into submissiveness as their sovereign rights are taken from them by an edict from Washington?

One governor — in Arkansas — calls out the troops to prevent bloodshed, and immediately the federal government undertakes to pass judgment upon his motives and his right to maintain order in a sovereign state.

Another governor — in Tennessee — says he must wait until an overt act occurs before he can call out the state troops. Now a school building has been blown up in Nashville. Might not vigilant action in advance have prevented such a tragedy?

If the governor of Arkansas now withdraws the troops and lives are lost, will the federal government accept the responsibility . . . ?

These are questions which have been generated by the arbitrary action of a single federal official in Little Rock who has taken it upon himself to serve as judge, prosecutor and jury to inquire into the motives and efficiency of the governor of the state of Arkansas. The Department of Justice in Washington . . . has helped to prepare an injunction which conceivably can prevent the governor of Arkansas from performing the duties of his office. This means that the representative or republican system of government in one of the sovereign states would be suspended by the order of a federal judge.

Never before in American history has the Constitution been so flagrantly defied and disregarded by the executive. Article IV says:

"The United States shall guarantee to every state in this union a republican form of government."

Only the people of Arkansas . . . can decide whether their chief executive is efficient and whether he is complying in good faith with the requirements of state law as well as federal law. They can impeach him and remove him — but the federal government does not have any such power. . . .

The issue raised in the Arkansas case is whether the governor, in calling out the state militia to prevent bloodshed, is acting in good faith. . . . where does a federal judge get the right to try a state governor in a federal court for malfeasance — for failure to do his duty?

There are people who say that, when there is a conflict between state and "federal law" the government of Washington must prevail. But there is no "federal law" involved here. No law has been passed by Congress on the subject of "integration."

JOHN TEMPLE GRAVES SAID:

What did the governor of Arkansas say to the President of the United States? . . .

Liberal Editor Harry Ashmore, fathering a wish with a thought, says his governor "capitulated."

Harry is one with the God-playing New Dealers but he can't dictate history off the cuff.

Even if Gov. Faubus withdraws the guard . . . his only visible capitulating is his acceptance of the Federal summons to court. Mr. Brownell's Tom Dewey refused to do that in 1953 as governor of New York and Former United States Supreme Court Justice James F. Byrnes refused even more vigorously as governor of South Carolina . . . Gov. Byrnes said no branch of the Federal government has a right to order a state's chief executive to be at any particular place at any particular time. . . .

WHAT A LOT OF STEW ONE OYSTER CAN MAKE
By Talbert, Washington Daily News   9/17/57

This cartoon had an ingrained inconsistency. It inferred that a bad action on my part would turn out to be beneficial to me. If I were so wrong in my actions how would such bad conduct constitute good politics for me? The people are not so dumb.

o━●━o━o━●━o

RUN OF THE NEWS
by Karr Shannon, September 19, 1957

States' Rights is the Real Issue

What has been happening . . . during the past few weeks cannot be charged totally to sentiment against integration . . . Arkansas, especially, has taken integration very much in stride, even before the 1954 Supreme Court decree . . .

The state has no school of law or medicine for the Negro. And when Negro students began enrolling in these departments of the University of Arkansas nearly 10 years ago, there were no "incidents." Also, in recent months there have been few disturbances when Negroes, without high school facilities in their respective districts, entered the white high schools.

Mainly what the South resents is forced integration as result of the Supreme Court ruling which was based on sociology and psychology, and not on precedent or constitutional edict. . . .

. . . the South sees the destruction of states' rights; it sees the federal government, not the elective school board, running the local school with a mailed fist. It is the rights of the sovereign states, the survival of our republican form of government, that is involved, not the principle of integrated schools. It is a question of whether these United States are to come under totalitarian regime with appointive federal judges, not elective officials, running the government down to and including the most remote school district.

In the last sentence Shannon was quite prophetic.

IN A WORLD WIRED FOR SOUND
By Fitzpatrick, St. Louis Post Dispatch   9/18/57

In a world "wired for sound" — encompassed by radio and television communication, the week just passed had heard the names of Faubus and Hays in the world news in connection with the Little Rock situation.

Other national and international names drummed on the air waves that week were:

GLUCK and BANDARANAIKE

Maxwell Gluck, newly appointed U.S. ambassador to Ceylon, touched off a storm of protest in that country when he admitted to a Senate committee that he was not familiar with the name of Ceylon's prime minister, Solomon W. R. D. Bandaranaike.

TITO and GOMULKA

Wladyslaw Gomulka had come again to power as the Communist ruler of Poland. With great fanfare Gomulka paid a visit to President Tito of Yugoslavia, the independent Communist ruler who had led bands of partisans against the Nazi forces in WWII.

SARIT AND SONGGRAM

In Thailand, the Army's strong man, Sarit Thanarat, seized control of the government in a military coup on September 17, ousting the premier, P. Pibul Songgram.

FAUBUS' ATTORNEYS WALK OUT ON COURT, DEFY JURISDICTION

Arkansas Democrat

by Bobbie Forster and Margaret Frick
September 20, 1957

Four attorneys representing Governor Faubus walked out on a federal court injunction hearing against the governor today after Federal Judge Ronald N. Davies had knocked down in rapid-fire succession a series of defense motions.

A statement read to the Court by Tom Harper, Chairman of the State Democratic Party, said that "the position of Governor Faubus and the military officials of the state is that the governor and the state will not concede that the U.S. in this court or anywhere else can question the authority of the governor to exercise his judgment in administering the affairs of the state."

The statement continued: "And since he does not concede this responsibility, we will not proceed any further in this action."

He asked Judge Davies "to be excused."

. . . Judge Davies said: "You are excused, gentlemen, but you understand that this is a moot question and that the hearing will proceed."

———

This was one point on which all my attorneys agreed, as well as our adviser, Sen. Richard Russell of Georgia, plus legal counsel from Virginia and other points. Many attorneys outside the South offered the same advice — do not concede the authority of any court over the discretionary and administrative powers guaranteed to the executive branch of government by the Constitution.

Motions filed by my attorneys included: the request for a three-judge federal court to pass on the matters, since a constitutional question was involved; that Judge Davies disqualify himself in the case on the grounds of prejudice; to quash the subpoenas served on the military officers, Clinger and Johnson, on the grounds that military men on duty are exempt from subpoena. All these motions were overruled by Judge Davies as fast as they were presented.

Other paragraphs in the story read:

"Numerous persons were subpoenaed to appear today: Newsmen, school board members, Supt. Blossom, Mayor Mann, Chief Potts, hardware and variety store men and others.

"The government's case was handled by U.S. Atty. Osro Cobb, and his assistant, Jim Gallman, plus assistant U.S. attorneys Ralph Sloan and Walter Riddick, who researched and investigated; Donald MacGuinness and Carl Eardley, both of Washington, top men in the U.S. Department of Justice.

"Representing Governor Faubus are Kay Matthews, Tom Harper, and Walter L. Pope, and W. J. (Bill) Smith, who did not participate in the court room proceedings."

In an interview with Democrat Reporter Robert McCord, I showed a mimeographed letter that had been mailed to prospective witnesses cancelling the subpoenas that had been served, and telling them that it was not necessary to appear in court.

Another story said Hays' talks with me had ended, which was news to me.

TO THE REAR MARCH
By Graham, Ark. Gazette   9/21/57

This was wishful thinking of the *Gazette* editors. They desperately hoped I would digress from my program and that all progress would stop, a circumstance which could be used for my political downfall. However, progress continued in every field of state service. Industrial development even accelerated in the years ahead. And I declined to join any "Dixiecrat" movement.

JUDGE DAVIES ISSUES INJUNCTION

Judge Davies signed an injunction on September 20 barring my use of the Guard at Central High School. The following headline and story appeared the next day.

GOVERNOR FAUBUS EXPLAINS 'WALKOUT' OF FEDERAL COURT, ORDER DISBANDING GUARD

September 21, 1957

The governor, in a dramatic telecast last night, announced he was bowing to the authority of a federal court injunction, . . . and that the National Guard "are now gone, or they are moving from the school grounds."

Faubus emphasized he was not giving up the fight because he had instructed his attorneys to carry it to the 8th Circuit Court of Appeals.

Little Rock was growing tense over the situation, and everywhere persons were expressing apprehension as to what would happen if integration were attempted Monday.

—0—

GOVERNOR SUPPORTED BY ALC

The Arkansas Legislative Council today unanimously endorsed Governor Faubus' effort "to prevent racial strife" in the Central High School integration controversy.

The motion defending the chief executive was made by Prairie Representative John Bethel.

—0—

RUN OF THE NEWS

—by Karr Shannon

"When the governor of Arkansas . . . orders out his troops to prevent rioting and bloodshed, he is accused of making solely a 'political gesture' — as if nobody in Washington has been making gestures to get the Negro vote without regard to the consequences to the people of the South.

—Columnist David Lawrence"

LITTLE ROCK POSES LOSS OF FREEDOM

Northern Virginia Daily, September 21, 1957

Governor Orval E. Faubus in actions and words last night dramatically answered his critics and at the same time gave renewed faith to his supporters.

By ordering the National Guard troops away from Central High School and by announcing "I will comply" to the Federal court injunction, the Arkansas governor clearly showed that he was not one who could rightly be accused of usurpation of power even by his most severe critics.

On the other hand he renewed the faith of his supporters by asserting he would exhaust all avenues of appeal to overturn the injunction . . .

. . . the Little Rock situation . . . narrows down to the question of upholding or flagrantly violating the 10th Amendment to the Constitution of the United States — guaranteeing clearly defined states' rights.

Even though Governor Faubus must have felt frustrated when . . . Judge Davies refused the motions made by his attorneys, . . . the Governor was man enough to appeal to the citizens of Little Rock for order and peace.

"Now is the time for the utmost precaution and forbearance on the part of all persons," he said. The Governor added that he hoped the NAACP . . . would "not be so reckless as to push integration . . . until a cooling off period has passed."

. . .

Governor Faubus' attorney, Tom Harper, nailed down the big issue in his final remarks before walking out . . . Mr. Harper said, "May I state our position to the court. . . . That is, that the position of Governor Faubus and his military commanders must be firmly, unequivocally, and unalterably that the Governor of the State of Arkansas cannot and will not concede that the U.S. government in this court or anywhere else can question his judgment and discretion acting as the chief executive officer of the sovereign State of Arkansas in the performance of his duties, or question his acts under the Constitution and laws of the State." This is not defiance in placing this stand to a test in the courts.

. . .

The people of America should see a solemn warning in Little Rock that if they allow the Constitution to be flouted by denying the 10th Amendment guarantee they might as well prepare themselves for other losses of freedom and future rule by court edict — and not based on law but on sociological rulings.

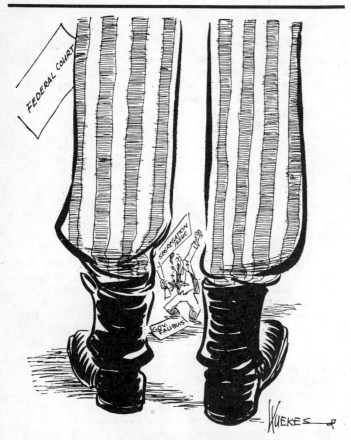

LITTLE MAN YOU'RE GONNA HAVE A BUSY DAY!
By Wuekes, Cleveland Plain Dealer   9/21/57

This cartoon was inspired by my acceptance of the summons to federal court for the injunctive proceedings. There were some much busier days with racial problems later on in other cities which included Cleveland.

UNDERSTANDING, NOT PREJUDICE

Sept. 20, 1957

(Editorial from the Dallas Morning News)

Officials of the East Texas Peace Officers Association sent a wire to Governor Faubus commending him for trying to "uphold the law" and "maintain the traditional rights of the sovereign states." It was sent in the name of its 538 members.

If there is anyone who sincerely wants peace it is the peace officer. If there is anyone who knows the peaceful way to peace it should be the peace officer. The peace officers of East Texas think that Governor Faubus is upholding the peace. Maybe the East Texans are seeing farther and more accurately than some might think.

. . .

. . . People closest to the problems have enough intelligence to comprehend it. They understand it better than the supreme court understands it. . . .

〜〜〜〜〜

Arkansas Gazette

FAUBUS APPEARS UNRUFFLED IN FACE OF MOUNTING CRISIS

September 21, 1957

by Relman Morin
Of the Associated Press

Through two fantastic weeks, Orval Eugene Faubus, governor of Arkansas, has been sleeping soundly, eating regularly, chatting by telephone with his son in college, perusing his mail and relaxing in books about his favorite character, Abraham Lincoln.

In short, they say at the Governor's Mansion, "he's going along just about as he always did before this thing came up." Mr. Faubus was pitted yesterday against the awesome might of the United States government.

He stands in the white-hot center of one of the greatest political and social struggles in the history of the Republic.

Yet he seems unruffled, completely at ease. He keeps a smile around the corners of his mouth. He listens patiently, answers carefully in quiet effortless speech.

He looks like anything but a man confronting a crisis.

This could be the crossroads of his career in politics, the long long road that led from a one-room school in the Ozark Mountains to the gracious mansion of the state's chief executive.

For when Mr. Faubus ordered the Arkansas National Guard to take stations around Little Rock Central High School, he touched emotions and split allegiances that go deep beneath the surface of day-to-day politics.

There are people at Little Rock who are against integration — and against Mr. Faubus.

Others grudgingly admire Mr. Faubus for "standing up to" the federal government — but wish it were on some other issue.

. . .

Some tell Mr. Faubus they would like to see him president.

Still others . . . are worried about the effect on the state's campaign to attract business and industry . . .

Has he gained or lost strength, politically?

His critics say Mr. Faubus alienated the Negro vote (estimated 60,000), plus the liberals, plus the people who are working to bring industry to Arkansas.

As against that, other analysts are inclined to agree with his assertions, "82 per cent of the people are against integration." They say he has won state-wide support if he runs for a third term.

10,000 Telegrams

One of his intimates says Mr. Faubus has received nearly 10,000 telegrams and even more letters since the great dispute broke out at Little Rock.

"He's read 'em all — and they're 98 per cent for him," the aide said.

Is he concerned about the fearful, nation-wide uproar that rose in the wake of his action, not to mention the repercussions overseas?

"Sure, he's concerned — but he's more concerned about violence. He can take the criticism but he just won't stand for any violence," they say at the Mansion.

Through it all two qualities have appeared, over and over again, in Mr. Faubus — monumental patience and a dogged, slogging manner.

He has always been that way, people say.

When he went into politics, he built up a reputation for fulfilling promises to his supporters and dealing swift retribution to his enemies.

Dark Horse

During his first campaign for governor, in 1954, he was one of four candidates, the darkest horse in the field.

"That's when you first saw that dogged characteristic," said a newspaperman who covered the campaign. . . . "It looked as though everything was against him. But he decided to stay in there and slug it out, and he won."

The governor is a stocky man with an ever-present smile. . . .

He dresses neatly, has well-groomed black hair. Sometimes in a photograph, he looks like the late Wendell Willkie. Sometimes, in profile, he resembles the actor, Frederic March.

The groomed appearance has neither cracked nor chipped since the night of September 2, when he sent the National Guard to Central High School, setting off both a cyclone of criticism and a roar of approval.

HUMAN EVENTS, WASHINGTON, D.C.
September 21, 1957

Arkansas Story — Uncensored: The metropolitan press in the North has so obscured the real outlines of the Faubus-Federal Government struggle that only a handful in this politically cynical Capital see through the smoke screen. A few correspondents have come back from Little Rock . . . and have privately admitted several things which they dared not send in their dispatches.

(1) Mayor Woodrow Wilson Mann, the Northern favorite in the fighting ring, has no more prestige in his town than Herman Talmadge would have in New York City.

He is an outgoing official and is thoroughly discredited; he represents virtually no important segment of Arkansas public opinion.

(2) About 98 percent of the white people of Arkansas are segregationists in sentiment — according to any "cold turkey" estimate. In legislation and referenda, Arkansans have shown overwhelmingly their opposition to desegregation. The only difference of opinion among them is between those who won't yield an inch and those reluctantly prepared to give way — well — a couple of inches.

(3) Faubus, instead of immediately (after Judge Davies' initial action) bowing to the power of the Federal Government, proceeded on his chosen course. . . .

(4) Faubus did not run to Eisenhower to win a "facesaving" exit from his situation — as Northern papers suggested. Actually, the true picture was almost the reverse of this version. . . . through intermediaries, the Palace Guard in effect invited the Arkansas Governor to visit Newport. Adams and aides hoped that a face-to-face meeting, dominated by Ike's reputed "glamor," would make Faubus surrender. Faubus apparently had other ideas — as the equivocal communiques issued after the meeting showed.

NEGROES TO ENTER CENTRAL MONDAY; POLICE ON ALERT

Arkansas Democrat, Sept. 22, 1957

*by Bob Troutt
Democrat staff writer*

. . . Negro students . . . told the DEMOCRAT last night they definitely plan to attend Central High School tomorrow.

Mayor Mann warned that troublemakers will be dealt with "firmly" by city police, who are taking over the job of preserving the peace . . .

Both friends and foes of integration issued pleas for non-violence . . .

Mayor Mann indicated . . . that city police will not actually "escort" Negro students into the school. But, he added:

"Our policy is one that will permit compliance with the law instead of obstructing it."

. . .

Text of the mayor's statement:

"The eyes of the nation and the world will be on Little Rock Monday and the period immediately following. We will be cast in a different light than during the past 18 days. Military force will be at an end. The maintenance of law and order will now be where it belongs — in the hands of local law enforcement authorities and the citizens of this community.

"Local law enforcement officers will be on hand to deal firmly with any individual or groups who might try to create trouble. . . .

THE GOVERNOR'S WEEK:

SEVERAL CONFERENCES WITH BROOKS HAYS FAILED TO PRODUCE A COMPROMISE...

no thanks!

RETURNS SUBPOENA TO APPEAR FOR HEARING ON FOUR SOVEREIGNTY LAWS.... STAY WAS GRANTED TO ARK.

FAUBUS' ATTORNEYS—

we've had enough!

—WALK OUT ON HEARING...

the order is issued........... I will comply.

JUDGE DAVIES GRANTS THE INJUNCTION...

GOVERNOR TOOK TO TV TO ANNOUNCE WITHDRAWAL OF GUARD AND TO DEFEND HIS POSITION.

HIGHLIGHTS OF THE NEWSWEEK
By Kennedy, Ark. Democrat   9/29/57

Congressman Hays had returned to Arkansas from his speaking engagements. We conferred almost daily — sometimes more than once in a day, but all proposals or suggestions ran into the adamant attitude of the Justice Department (Brownell) or the NAACP leadership.

I returned the subpoena to appear for hearing on the four states rights laws. A chief executive is not subject to indiscriminate subpoena for just any purpose.

The Faubus attorneys walked out of the injunctive hearing with the court's permission.

Judge Davies granted the injunction requested by the Justice Department attorneys.

In a TV address I explained to the people what had occurred, and announced the withdrawal of the Guard. I closed the speech with an appeal for the people to accept the situation calmly, and then departed for Atlanta, Ga., on the way to the Southern Governors' Conference.

REMOVAL OF THE GUARD; TRIP TO SEA ISLAND

On Friday, Sept. 20, at 3:30 p.m., Judge Davies issued the injunction against my use of the National Guard at Central High School. The injunction was served by Marshal Beal Kidd on my aide, Kay L. Matthews, who delivered it to me at the Mansion.

At 6:20 p.m., I issued an order disbanding and removing the Guard from the school premises. That same evening I appeared on television to announce the decision, and to explain the walkout of my attorneys from the federal court proceedings.

My attorneys and I were advised on the court withdrawal move by lawyers and statesmen throughout the country. Sen. Richard Russell of Georgia, noted nationally as an authority on the Constitution, was one of those advisers. Sen. Russell had also agreed to join my defense counsel if I were jailed or threatened with imprisonment by federal authorities.

Before leaving Arkansas, I alerted Lt. Gov. Nathan Gordon, who came to Little Rock to be in charge as governor during my absence from the state. The press related that Gordon stated that he would act only in case of an emergency.

On the 21st I arrived at Atlanta, Ga., where the Southern Governors were attending a meeting of the Southern Regional Education Board. Later we were guests of Gov. Marvin Griffin for two football games, Georgia vs. Texas and Georgia-Tech vs. Kentucky. The following day, Sept. 22, we proceeded to Sea Island, Ga., for the beginning of the Southern Governors' Conference.

At the Georgia-Texas game the evening of Sept. 21, the names of the visiting governors were announced. When my name was called, there occurred one of the greatest ovations I have ever witnessed. It equaled or excelled those for Americans by the liberated peoples of Europe during WW II.

Repeatedly, the 33,000 fans rose en masse to cheer, at one time interrupting the progress of the football game, the only time I have ever seen this happen. The ovation, as I later told the press, was not for me. It was for my stand in defense of the people's right to control their own schools. The members of the national press were visibly subdued by the occurrence. As I often noted, they were always subdued when things were breaking in my favor, as they were equally elated when events were going against me.

An article in the *Arkansas Historical Quarterly*, Summer 1979, Number 2, entitled "Governor LeRoy Collins of Florida and the Little Rock Crisis of 1957," by Thomas R. Wagy, Florida State University, the author wrote:

> Shortly after the second half kick-off, the governors were introduced. Some were amiably booed, although Collins received polite applause. In contrast to the disinterest shown in the other governors, the announcement of Faubus's name evoked an unrestrained emotional outburst from the 33,000 Southerners. Officials delayed the game several minutes as wave after wave of applause poured down upon the Arkansas governor. People jammed the aisles and leaped over seats to get nearer. The press swarmed over Faubus. Order was finally restored, but following the game crowds thronged the streets shouting "Faubus, Faubus." Dixie had a new folk hero.

FAUBUS SAYS OBEDIENCE "WAS MY ONLY CHOICE"; DOUTHIT ASKS NO VIOLENCE

by George Douthit in the Democrat
Sept. 22, 1957

> The Faubus stage of the Central High School integration has ended. It is now in the hands of the people of Little Rock and the state of Arkansas.
>
> Governor Faubus obeyed the federal court order to remove his national guardsmen from around the school . . .
>
> "It was my only choice," Mr. Faubus told this newsman . . . after a television address in which he . . . pleaded for tolerance.
>
> . . . There was speculation among reporters as to whether the troops would be removed. This

writer wrote the end of the story the day before because he, too, felt there was only one course of action for the governor.

If he had taken the other road by refusing to budge and insisting on keeping his guardsmen in place there is no way of knowing what it would lead to. . . .

As it now stands the governor has obeyed the federal government. The school is open to Negro students and the case is now in the hands of the people.

Whether we will have violence at the school when the Negroes try to enter will depend upon the people. We think there is no need for violence because nothing will be gained by it. We also would like to warn irate segregationists that federal agents are here in numbers.

The federal court has shown the lengths to which it will go to get Central High School, or any school, integrated. You may be a father of several school children, who has never harmed a thing, never stolen anything and stand as an upright citizen in your community.

Yet you may be standing in a crowd when Negroes go into the school and you yell something at them. You can be charged, convicted and tried for inciting a riot and go to the penitentiary — just for opening your mouth. You are not protected there by the law of freedom of speech.

Here is another point. Any violence that occurs will be charged up to Governor Faubus . . . So, we certainly hope that cool heads will prevail and fists will remain unclenched or there may be some broken heads.

The U.S. Supreme Court says that Negroes will go to Central High School. The federal court of Arkansas says that Negroes will go to Central High School.

If the governor and all his national guardsmen can't keep them out why should any individual or group of individuals get themselves into a lot of trouble by trying to stop them. So, for the sake of the peace of the community, we urge no violence.

Arkansas has had some bad publicity. But that publicity isn't half as bad as it will be if violence commences. The attention of the nation has been focused on Little Rock for three weeks. Now the rest of the nation is waiting to see whether the people of Arkansas are going to blow up in violence or show respect for law and order.

If there were any victory to be gained we wouldn't make this appeal to the people who are resentful of integration. But we already have an example — Clinton, Tenn. . . .

We have talked with many segregationists since this thing started. We listened to their rebellious spirit pour out against the supreme court and the federal judges. And we asked them: "Are you ready to start violence over this thing?" Everyone answered like this: "Indeed not."

Others we have talked to are certain in their minds that "things are going to bust loose, now." We asked them if they were going to commit it. Emphatically not, but someone will, they said.

"It's just in the air, you can feel it; you can cut the tension with a knife," we were told. We replied that there is nothing in the air but peace if the peo-

ple of this community and Arkansas are determined for it to be so.

From the beginning of this incident we have been one of the few writers and one of the few newspapers who gave Governor Faubus a chance to have his say. Now it is our say. No violence, please.

Douthit's column appeared in the *Arkansas Democrat* Sunday before school the next day, after I had departed from the state. I did not see the article until some days later.

Douthit had been one of the fairest and most objective reporters of the so-called Little Rock crisis.

The tension had begun building long before when the arrangement of gradual integration was born which eventually became known as the Blossom Plan. The interest gradually grew, the cross-currents developed. A part of the animosity was spawned when it became plainer and plainer that the plan called for integration for those working class people who lived in certain sections of the district, while the well-to-do professional white people and the rich nabobs of industry who lived in the silk stocking area to be served by the new high school, Hall High, would escape the consequences of the "new experiment." Already certain influential parents remaining in the attendance zone of Central were receiving transfers for their children to Hall High.

People talk about such things and so the news was out. The information became common knowledge in the district. The arrangement would spare the rich from whatever burdens and difficulties that developed and place them on those too poor or too lacking in influence to escape.

The rich and well-to-do, some of whom advocated integration, were not to participate after all — at least not for now.

The working class people were to have no choice in the matter. Their children would attend the integrated schools. The mention of transfers for them was brusquely turned aside by Blossom and the Cooper-led school board.

And so the cross-currents grew stronger, the animosities swelled, and fears, even in the hearts of the plan's designers, began to grow.

Now to this inner turmoil add the fact that Blossom, the members of the school board, the *Gazette* editor and publisher and some Negro publishers, proclaimed the plan a success even before school began. It was said the plan would become the model for all of Arkansas, and perhaps the South. These boasts by the Blossom plan advocates made the issue a matter of state-wide interest.

As the weeks progressed, state-wide interest in the integration in the capital city continued to grow. The interest spread beyond the state, and Little Rock developed into a focal point of contest.

The plan's main sponsors and advocates, including Blossom, had become imbued with the glamorous idea of becoming instant celebrities by solving overnight a problem which has never had an easy solution in the history of mankind. If they could have avoided this vainglorious ambition, and treated everyone in the district, rich or poor, the same, the beginning of the gradual integration plan might have been more peaceful.

Trouble might have come sooner or later, as it had to every area where the mixing was extensive, but the plan at least might have had a quieter beginning.

Douthit wrote a powerful plea for no violence, and his paper likewise editorialized strongly for peaceful school integration. There would have been opposition even if integration had been handled properly, but the integrationists had already done too much to aggravate the situation. The people had already heard so much double-talk and false propaganda that those who would have been reasonable were no longer in the mood to listen, even to straight, truthful talk.

LET'S KEEP IT UNTARNISHED
By Kennedy, Ark. Democrat   *9/22/57*

This cartoon was part of an intensive propaganda campaign ᴠ.aged by both Little Rock newspapers, by some church leaders, civic groups and others, to discourage disorder in opposition to the integration of Central High School. This campaign effort included peaceful acceptance statements by Brooks Hays, who hurried back to the city "to keep the president advised," and at least three statements by President Eisenhower urging "peaceful acceptance" of integration and "peaceful compliance with the orders of the court."

Coupled with these cartoons, editorials, news stories, public statements and pleas such as George Douthit's, were the threats by Mayor Mann of the use of force by the city police. There were also statements of the Justice Department threatening arrest and jail for anyone who in any way interfered with integration. Judge Davies likewise threatened objectors with contempt of court citations and imprisonment.

All of these pronouncements and threats were given the widest publicity in every manner possible.

As the cartoon aptly portrays, there had been no disorder or violence worthy of note during the three weeks I had exercised control, except, as George Douthit so truthfully wrote, "on the typewriters of the visiting press."

In the same issue the *Democrat* had an editorial affirming the fact of no violence to date, and making a strong plea for quiet acceptance of the court-ordered integration. There was also the *Gazette* editorial against any disorder.

Now, in my absence and with the Guard removed, Mayor Mann, the *Gazette* forces, and the federal judge were in charge. It was announced the Negro students would enter Central High on Monday, Sept. 23. Repeatedly, my critics had maintained there would have been no violence, and there would be no violence, with me out of the way. Their theory was now to be put to the test.

MAYOR MANN DENIES HE SOUGHT GUARD HELP; SAYS LITTLE ROCK POLICE CAN HANDLE SITUATION

Mayor Mann asked Lt. Gov. Nathan Gordon for the use of National Guardsmen in preparation for school opening, then denied having done so when Gov. Gordon made public the request. Mann then reiterated that the Little Rock police could handle the situation, although he had already requested the use of 50 state police.

If, as Mayor Mann had stated over and over, there was to be "no violence," why did he request the use of 50 state troopers?

I acceded to the request and from Sea Island instructed Police Director Herman Lindsey to make the troopers available.

Mann also asked the federal authorities for the assistance of U.S. marshals and FBI agents. The request was refused. Why? Did Brownell want violence to break out in order to open the way for the dramatic use of federal troops — and a political coup? Wouldn't it have been better to help prevent disorder by the use of FBI agents and U.S. marshals than to send in U.S. paratroopers later? However, the paratroopers were trained and ready at nearby Ft. Campbell, Ky., and Brownell evidently wanted to use them.

WELL, BOYS, WHAT'S UNDER YOUR HATS?
By Baldy, Atlanta Journal and Constitution   *9/22/57*

The governors were seated around the conference table at Sea Island, Ga., as host Governor Marvin Griffin made his inquiry. There was no abundance of press releases on the Little Rock situation. Most governors tried to avoid comment on the matter.

CONGRESSMAN HAYS ACTS AS GO-BETWEEN

Congressman Brooks Hays acted as a go-between for the White House and the integration forces in Little Rock. But efforts to save the day for Eisenhower and the *Gazette* were unsuccessful.

Hays had purposely returned to Little Rock to "keep the President advised." If everything had gone well from the federal standpoint, Brooks would have been something of a hero to Brownell and the national administration. He might have received the federal judge appointment. However, his predictions of "peaceful compliance" proved sadly in error. The judgeship went to another.

ANOTHER RESCUE SQUAD
By Fitzpatrick, St. Louis Post Dispatch   9/23/57

With this cartoon, the *Gazette* carried excerpts from editorials appearing in newspapers around the world. Most of them were unfavorable to me and Arkansas. It carried one excerpt from England.

London Daily Telegraph — "*If the federal government backs the Supreme Court in enforcing integration, race relations will certainly worsen to a deplorable degree, and there may be even uglier consequences (than the incident at Little Rock) . . . (A)ttempts to change a traditional social climate by coercive legislation are seldom productive of lasting good.*"

—0—0—0—

VIOLENCE EXPLODES AS 8 NEGROES ENROLL AT CHS, THEN ARE WITHDRAWN

—by Robert Troutt,
Democrat staff writer, Sept. 23, 1957

Eight Negro students entered Central High School this morning amid uncontrolled violence that grew so swiftly school and law enforcement officers decided to withdraw them shortly after noon. A milling, shouting mob of more than 1,000 persons ringed the school area.

Two city police cars took the Negro students to their homes shortly after noon.

Earlier they had entered by a side door while a diversionary group of Negroes appeared at the front.

Numerous fights broke out immediately and an appeal for state police brought 50 troopers racing to the scene to aid city patrolmen in battling the crowd.

Shortly after the Negro students slipped in and went to the principal's office, many white students began leaving the building.

Supt. Blossom confirmed that the Negroes had been withdrawn after Mayor Mann had radioed an announcement on the police network: "Tell the crowd the Negroes have been removed from Central High School."

The announcement came to the growing crowd, which numbered several thousand by noon.

—0—

In Washington the press reported Ike was mum on the situation.

The Pulaski County prosecuting attorney, under pressure from the integrationists, outlined in a public statement the charges that would be made against those arrested in disorders at Central High School.

A Pulaski County grand jury then in session at Little Rock, displaying a different attitude, announced that the school disorder was no problem for it to consider at the time.

0—0—0—0—0

IKE CALLS ARKANSAS GUARD INTO FEDERAL SERVICE IN CRISIS

Arkansas Democrat, Sept. 24, 1957

NEWPORT, R.I. — President Eisenhower today ordered federalization of the Arkansas National Guard and the state's Air National Guard to deal with Little Rock school integration crisis.

. . .

Eisenhower ordered Secretary of Defense Wilson to federalize the Arkansas Guard units in an executive order which said a presidential cease and desist order to Little Rock rioters had not been obeyed. . . .

Eisenhower also authorized Wilson to call out such United States troops — aside from the guard units — as Wilson may deem necessary to deal with the situation.

Eisenhower said he would use the full power of the United States — including whatever force necessary — to prevent any obstruction of the law in the Little Rock school integration crisis. . . .

Eisenhower signed his executive order shortly after a crowd of several hundred white men and women watched at Little Rock's Central High School today. There had been no violence — in contrast to yesterday — but the nine Negroes . . . were not on hand today. . . .

Eisenhower's legal right to order troops into Little Rock already has been challenged by Governor Faubus, among others. . . .

. . . In the past Eisenhower had spoken out forcibly against use of force to compel integration.

Then yesterday came his momentous decision — and change of mind. . . .

Then he put his name to a history making proclamation clearing the legal way to use of force by the federal government.

The President's actions in using troops to enforce a court order may have assumed the "color of law" by the use of documents, but it was directly contrary to the federal code, annotated in 1956, which specifically forbade such action. The use of federal troops to enforce a court order was illegal, as the national administration decided some time thereafter. The legal manner of enforcement would have been the use of U.S. marshals. But it was too late to turn back even if the national administration had been inclined to switch from illegal to legal means to enforce the order.

The 101st Airbourne Division had been training at Ft. Campbell, Ky. for more than two weeks and was ready for immediate use. It would have taken time to muster and train a force of U.S. marshals.

The President flew back to Washington to announce the occupation of Little Rock in a television address from the White House. I flew back to Little Rock the afternoon of Sept. 24.

THEY ALWAYS CALL THEM BETTER FROM THE BLEACHERS
By Alley, Memphis Commercial Appeal　　9/22/57

The "South's Far-Off Critics" seldom understood the developments in the region, but were not hesitant in offering advice and criticism.

GEN. WALKER TO ACTIVATE GUARDSMEN

Sept. 24, 1957

Lt. Gov. Gordon said he had received Army Secretary Brucker's orders to federalize the National Guard over the telephone and Maj. Gen.

Edwin A. Walker, chief of the Arkansas Military District, will activate the state troops.

Maj. Gen. Walker will be in charge and will call out whatever troops are necessary to cope with the situation. . . .

USE OF TROOPS DRAWS FIRE OF GOVERNORS

—by Jack Bell
Arkansas Democrat, Sept. 24, 1957

SEA ISLAND, Ga. — Southern and border state governors presented a solid front today against any use of the federal troops to enforce school integration in Arkansas or elsewhere in Dixie.

President Eisenhower's statement said he would use the full power of the United States — "including whatever force may be necessary — . . . to carry out the orders of the federal court," shocked this conference of southern governors into the general interpretation the president was threatening the use of federal troops to enforce desegregation in classrooms.

The immediate reaction from Republican as well as Democratic governors was against an assumption of presidential authority paralleling President Grover Cleveland's use of federal troops to break the Pullman strike in the past century. . . .

POLITICAL GOLD HUNT
By Hutton, Philadelphia Inquirer　　9/24/57

The cartoon idea was as false as fool's gold. I attended the Sea Island Conference with the intention of keeping my own counsel. After repeatedly declining to hold a press conference, Mr. Frank Bane, the Governors' Conference Secretary, came to me and said the reporters were constantly after him and that he knew they must be bothering me. He suggested I hold a conference for all of the newsmen, which might ease the situation and then perhaps he and I would get some relief. I agreed, and that was the only reason for the press meeting.

Nashville (Tenn.) *Banner*
Sept. 24, 1957

Events at Little Rock have vindicated the initial judgment of Gov. Orval Faubus . . .
. . . the chief executive of Arkansas did know more about . . . his own capital city than did smart alec commentators . . . hundreds of miles distant.

RETREAT FROM LITTLE ROCK, By Conrad, Denver Post, 9/23/57

The cartoonist portrayed me as "Faubus I" riding the decrepit steed, "States Rights" followed by the "Arkansas National Guard," retreating from Little Rock. The retreat was in response to the federal court order of Judge Davies on Sept. 20.

He DID know what he was talking about, despite furious denials by Mayor Mann and Superintendent Blossom; and despite amazing contradiction by a newly arrived federal judge presuming to dispute him both as to motive and to facts, and his right of acting to protect the public safety.

Under Governor Faubus law and order did not abdicate. He exercised the authority of his office to enforce the one in preservation of the other. That was his sworn duty and he did not default on it.

In removing the National Guard from around that school, he was complying with the order of the federal court. That was not in the belief that the crisis was past — or that the cause of it would vanish with the withdrawal of troops. He was right. . . .

* * *

. . . the outsider was a judge brought in from North Dakota, picked for the job of prescribing integration in the school system of that city.

Were there no jurists available in Arkansas to sit on that case?

STILL A PROBLEM
Artist unknown, Charleston, S.C. Gazette   9/24/57

Uncle Sam obtained all the federal court orders requested, including the one to enjoin my use of the National Guard. He now looked with amazement at the erupting violence in Little Rock which the court orders failed to prevent.

THEY HAD GUNS, BOMBS AND KNIVES!
By Conrad, Denver Post   9/22/57

The State Police confiscated dozens of knives, one rifle and other weapons during the first few days the police and National Guard were on duty.

But don't I look ridiculous as the cartoonist said the police couldn't find anything. If he had waited until after Sept. 23 he would have canceled the cartoon.

INGREDIENTS FOR AN EXPLOSION
By Werner, Indianapolis Star   9/24/57

According to this cartoonist the ingredients for the Little Rock explosion were: invasion of states rights powder, politics acid, Negro vote dynamite caps, NAACP fuse and bigotry matches. Some ingredients came from outside the South.

A GOVERNOR SCORNED —
AND THE TRAGIC EVENTS WHICH RESULTED

Ft. Smith (Ark.) Times Record
Sept. 24, 1957

(AN EDITORIAL)

It's a terrible thing when it takes an outbreak of elemental violence to prove that a man is not a fool or a liar.

Various and sundry people have come mighty close recently to accusing Governor Faubus of being one or the other of those things — either so stupid as to mistake a "bogeyman" for signs of impending violence or of making his story up out of the "whole cloth."

A federal judge had the last word on that — by a ruling which seems to us to have held that there were no signs of violence.

Today, the governor is a vindicated man — if there ever was one — but ironically and tragically, the vindication took place in the very violence of which Faubus had warned, had tried to guard against, and had been overruled in federal court.

And the question of why he was overruled is one which could stand some answering — because it has seemed to us that the signs of danger had been evident for some time.

People at Little Rock knew it — and felt it — that is, many of those who know how to read the signs did.
. . .

Anyway a lot of northern reporters have charged they "couldn't find any evidence of violence." The New York Herald-Tribune editorially has stated flatly that of course there was no danger of violence, and many others have said the same thing.

To our notion, any child of seven years could have sensed the danger — although the "sensing" would have been based on "intangibles" — not concrete facts.

Anyway, no one would listen to the governor.

So the answer was written in hate and violence yesterday at Little Rock, before even Mayor (There Is No Threat) Mann would accept it.

—o—()—()—o—

Texarkana, Ark., Gazette

September 24, 1957

WELCOME TO THE DOG HOUSE, MAYOR MANN

Events of Monday would appear to support the contention of Governor Faubus that violence would erupt if attempts were made to integrate Central High School at Little Rock. . . .

. . . The man currently occupying the front room of the Arkansas dog house is Mayor Woodrow Wilson Mann. He has played politics from the first and it all caught up with him Monday.

He jumped on Faubus for calling out the National Guard, declaring that there was no threat of violence in Little Rock. Then when Faubus called off the guard and left the responsibility for preserving order in the hands of the mayor, Mann asked

Lt. Gov. Nathan Gordon to alert about 150 National Guardsmen just in case. Gordon asked for the request in writing and Mann wouldn't give it to him because he didn't want to admit that Faubus may have been right. The result was that the Negroes entered the school, violence erupted and Mann's police force couldn't handle the situation. . . .

North Carolina newspaper
September 24, 1957

Terror In Little Rock

Was Governor Faubus right? . . .

Of one thing, some of us may be certain. He more accurately appraised the Little Rock reaction than did we.

Some of us had the feeling that, after relieving to some extent its feelings — "blowing off a little steam" — Little Rock would settle back to gradual and limited integration. We were wrong. Governor Faubus was right.
. . .

"Who can say where the ugliness lies in the blame for the ugliness of the scene?" . . .

. . . With Mayor Mann, who should have known the temper of Little Rock's people but who misjudged it?
. . .

The Little Rock outbreak was, regardless of the impulses and provocations which set it off, . . . a desperate subconscious urge of self-preservation as much as an expression of anger.

It was the basic recourse, the final weapon of those who feel abandoned and alone. . . .

INJUNCTION ISSUED; GUARD WITHDRAWN

Mayor Mann Takes Over
Riot Ensues; Paratroops Occupy Little Rock

Following my withdrawal of the National Guardsmen on the evening of September 20 Mayor Mann and his cohorts took over. There were then these developments in rapid order.

The city police, under the direction of the Mayor, began throwing up barricades on the school ground.

The next day, Saturday, September 21, this headline appeared in the *Arkansas Democrat:*

All Adults Barred from Central High

The order barring adults was issued by Blossom and the School Board.

President Eisenhower, reported to be delighted with my compliance with the injunctive court order preventing my use of the Guard, said it was a step in the right direction, and called on the people of the city to obey the Federal court order for integration, and admonished them to avoid violence. The president issued two more statements the next day, September 22, in which he called for citizens to vigorously oppose any violence by "extremists" seeking to interfere with integration at Central High.

Another headline on September 21 read: "Board Acts as Guard Removed; Violence Feared at Little Rock."

A 24-hour guard was placed on Central High School by city and school authorities.

A headline on Sunday, Sept. 22, read: "Little Rock Mayor Vows Tough Policy; Police Will Arrest Troublemakers, He Says."

Then newsmen were barred from Central by the school authorities.

There was also the column of George Douthit and strong editorials in both Little Rock papers calling for order.

On the morning of Monday, Sept. 23, this headline appeared: "City and State Police To Be There Today; Officials Confident."

On Sept. 22 I approved from Sea Island the assignment of 50 state policemen to assist in keeping order at Central the next day.

I acted on the request of Mayor Mann, School Board President Cooper and Police Chief Potts to provide a special guard when the Negro pupils went to school.

Question: If no violence was in prospect, and there was to be none, as the Mayor contended and as Cooper had sworn under oath, why was this request made for state police and why all the other preparations for trouble?

Mayor Mann also asked acting Governor Nathan Gordon for 150 National Guardsmen, a request which was denied by Mann when it was made public. But there was no doubt of the truthfulness of Governor Gordon.

Then in the afternoon of September 23, headlines appeared all across the nation like the following:

—o—o—o—o

RIOT IN LITTLE ROCK
School Removes Negroes
Police Escort Children Home

After the nine Negro students were gotten into the school by a ruse, the police forces were being overwhelmed. In spite of all the Mayor's bold but empty boasts about maintaining order, it is doubtful that his forces could have gotten the Negro students safely out of the school and to their homes without the assistance of the 50 state troopers on hand.

The next day, September 24, President Eisenhower issued an order to federalize the Arkansas National Guard and ordered 1,100 troops of the 101st Airborne Division of the U.S. Army to Little Rock.

Even as the order was being announced, members of the 101st Airborne Division, in full battle gear, were loading in transports at Ft. Campbell, Ky. In the late afternoon, citizens of Eastern Arkansas going about their peaceful pursuits, were chilled at the sight of giant military transport planes, one after another, flying low over the landscape as they approached the Little Rock Air Force Base for landing.

As the lights of Greater Little Rock gleamed through the early darkness, the motorized columns of the heavily armed paratroops, 1,100 in number, occupied the city.

At the end of the next day, Wednesday, September 25, these headlines appeared:

U.S. Army Regulars in Tight Control of
Central High Area As First Integrated Day Ends

Two Whites Clubbed, Stabbed By Soldiers

Gov. Faubus' Stock Climbs As Events Confirm Fears

Reaction In South Ranges From
Disbelief To Cold Fury

On September 26 these headlines appeared:
Troops Keep Scene Quiet;
Negroes Get Escort Again

General Shows Tough Attitude

And so began as told in these headlines, for the first time since Reconstruction days, the illegal occupation of an American city by overwhelming federal military force, and the fatal breaching of the powers and rights of the states.

And the great mistake was made by employing against them the people's own military forces — forces which they, the people, had provided either as draftees or volunteers from their midst, and for which they, the people, had helped to pay.

A dangerous precedent was set by such illegal use of the nation's armed forces, a precedent later followed by other presidents.

Thus was wrought a part of the damage spawned by the illegal lawmaking role of the U.S. Supreme Court.

And the end is not yet.

SHREVEPORT JOURNAL EDITORIAL

The day following the occupation of Little Rock by the elite 101st Airborne troops, an editorial appeared in the *Shreveport Journal,* Shreveport, La. It expressed the feelings of millions of Americans.

The editorial began:
Heil Eisenhower!
Heil der great Dictator!
Lick the heels of der Fueher!
Bow down to the modern Thaddeus Stevens!
The Storm Troopers are in Little Rock! The Gestapo is investigating ... The Second Reconstruction — a la Eisenhower — is under way!

The editorial ended:
These are dark days for the South — dark days for the United States!
Heil Eisenhower!

THE ORDER FEDERALIZING THE NATIONAL GUARD

On the night of Sept. 24, after the 101st Airborne Division had occupied Little Rock and taken over Central High School, Gen. Sherman T. Clinger, Adjutant General of the National Guard, came to see me at the Executive Mansion.

For two days the news had been nationwide and worldwide that President Eisenhower had federalized the Arkansas National Guard, but actually that act had not yet been accomplished. The telegram to me from the Defense Department was in my hands at the time. I had read it carefully. Received during the day it read that the order of federalization was transmitted "through you" to the proper officers of the Guard.

This was the traditional and legal way to federalize any state National Guard or any part of it — an order or request from the national government transmitted through the chief executive of the state. No National Guard had ever before been federalized in the long history of the nation by any other means.

I was holding the telegram, which had arrived only hours before, and had taken no action. Lt. Gov. Nathan Gordon, who was acting governor until my arrival back in the state that afternoon, had been previously informed by telephone of the federal government's intention to federalize, but had taken no action.

I TRIED, By Knox, Nashville Banner, 9/24/57

Outside could be seen the dust and flying debris from the rioting at Central High School on Sept. 23. The rope binding my hands was secured by the judicial gavel of Judge Davies with the injunction forbidding my use of the Guard.

THE BATTLE IS JOINED, By Fischetti, Palo Alto, Cal. Times, 9/24/57

No federal law gave the national government any right to interfere in state schools. There was only a Supreme Court decision, considered by millions of Americans to be illegal.

Clinger informed me that he was being pressed by Gen. Walker to issue the necessary federalization orders to all units of the Arkansas Guard.

Clinger declined and replied that before taking any action, "I must first see my boss," referring to me, the chief executive.

He was told, he related to me, that "if you don't issue the order, we'll go to the next in command. If he doesn't issue the order we'll go to the next in order of command, and we'll keep going down the chain of command until we find someone who will issue the order even if it's a corporal."

This action would be unprecedented, if not clearly illegal. However, the use of federal troops to occupy a peaceful city for the purpose of enforcing a district court order, without even notifying the chief executive or any state authorities, was unprecedented and clearly in complete violation of the Constitution and the federal code as updated the previous year. With such highhanded disregard for law and precedent already an accomplished fact, there was no reason to think that the federal authorities would hesitate to breach still further the law and precedent in the methods to federalize the Guard.

I pondered the matter and then told General Clinger:

"I am not going to transmit the order of federalization, which is the legal way as this telegram indicates. Furthermore, I am not going to instruct, advise or even assent to your transmission of the order.

"However, you know that if they pursue the course they have outlined to you, they [the federal authorities] will find someone to transmit the order. If you refuse, they will probably proceed to ruin your military career, which I know is important to you."

"Governor," interjected Clinger, "If you tell me not to do so, I won't issue the order."

"I know," I told Clinger, "but I'm not going to do that. I would take that course were it not for the jeopardy it would bring to you. But I see no reason to jeopardize your career when, in all likelihood, the order will be issued by someone."

"However," I concluded, "I'm not instructing you to issue the order; I'm not advising you to issue the order; and when it is issued it will not be with my consent. And remember, if you issue the order it will be no less unprecedented and illegal than if issued by some other in the chain of command, even, as General Walker says, a corporal."

We said no more on the matter. The understanding was unspoken between us but Clinger's course under the circumstances was clear. His only prudent decision was to issue the order.

General Clinger left the mansion near midnight. I don't know when the order was issued, nor other details. The next day the various units of the entire Arkansas National Guard were mustered at armories throughout the state and passed under federal control.

I must say this for my Adjutant General. He would, without a moment's hesitation, have sacrificed his long and distinguished military career to carry out any proper instructions from me. I had no member of my administration more loyal and efficient than Sherman T. Clinger.

Anyway, another law, and a precedent as old as the Republic, was broken by a great national leader who was generally loved and respected by the American people. He committed the act through ignorance of the civil law and history, on the advice of a cabinet member who placed politics above the law and precedent, and a dangerous new precedent was established.

To me the lesson has two morals. It is a risk to place in high office a popular and well-meaning person who is not fully qualified to deal with complex civil problems. And a high official's advisers should be persons of integrity who place the law, precedent and best interests of the country above personal or political gain.

PURPLE HEART-ACHE
By Ficklen, Dallas Morning News   9/25/57

States Rights in Little Rock was entitled to the Purple Heart medal after wounds by federal bayonets.

SPECTATOR BAYONETED, ANOTHER CLUBBED BY TOUGH PARATROOPERS

by Robert Troutt, Democrat Staff Writer
Arkansas Democrat, Sept. 25, 1957

One spectator was stabbed by a bayonet and another clubbed in the head with a rifle butt today when they hesitated before following an order to leave the area, one block from Central High School.

The stabbed man was identified as Paul Downs, Springfield, Ark. He suffered a bayonet wound in his arm, near the elbow.

The clubbed man was identified as C. E. Blake, North Little Rock, Missouri Pacific switchman. Blood streamed down his face after he was struck.

[A news photo clearly showed seven bayonets menacing Blake as he lay on the ground with the points of the knives only inches from his body.]

The remainder of the crowd was driven down the street by additional soldiers at the point of leveled bayonets. Members of the crowd sent up a loud cry of protest at the action of the troops, and several women started to scream and cry.

The incident took place with orders from the troops to "Move out."

Three unidentified white men were taken into custody and surrounded by eight soldiers a block from the school . . .

Reason for the action could not be determined, but a sergeant in charge told the soldiers: "Keep those bayonets up and straight ahead." They marched the three men to the school area . . .

At 10:35, an Army major announced to spectators: "As of now we are making collective arrests."

... They immediately took into custody a youth standing near a parked car ... and marched him to the school grounds.

Then they began arresting other spectators ... in the area.

Later, the officers warned bystanders over the public address system, "We're going to begin making arrests if more than two people are standing together."

They instructed the soldiers, "Arrest them if they give you any lip."

* * *

FEDERAL TROOPS TAKE OVER (101st Airborne); STATE GUARD FEDERALIZED AND MOBILIZED

(September 25)

Several hundred members of the tough fighting U.S. Army Unit (101st Airborne Infantry Division), bayonets fixed to their M-1 rifles, completely surrounded the school ...

... the soldiers walked into crowds of bystanders with bayonets pointed at their backs and made them move farther away from the institution.

No newsmen were allowed in the high school or on the same side of the street of the school but reports seeping out from the institution said it was "full of soldiers" in the halls.

Central was temporarily emptied by a bomb scare shortly after the federal troops took over. General Walker told students not to interfere with the military rule. Absentees at Central increased. While the troops were on the job, Ike continued to golf at Newport. A Deale, Maryland, group issued a strong condemnation of Gov. McKeldin and forced integration.

Senator Russell (D., Ga.) termed the use of federal troops illegal and accused the president of slapping totalitarian rule on the people of Arkansas.

Senator McClellan (D., Ark.) agreed with Russell that the action was "without authority of law."

The *Indianapolis Star* said the troop use was "obviously ... a deliberate effort to placate the Negro vote pending in next year's election," and the *Kansas City Star* said "beyond the principle this is a vast political battle."

U OF A TRUSTEE SCORES IKE

Jackson L. Stephens of Little Rock said today he believes the president is wrong and Gov. Orval E. Faubus is right in the Little Rock crisis. Stephens was in New York returning from a vacation on the Riviera in Southern Italy.

The Kansas City Times
September 25, 1957

Constitutional Issues
by David Lawrence

WASHINGTON — President Eisenhower's threat to use "whatever force may be necessary ... presents America with her gravest internal crisis since the reconstruction era.

It's a constitutional crisis in which the law advisers of the President have boldly sought to bypass the state of Arkansas ...

For federal court orders are not usually enforced by federal troops. They are enforced by U.S. marshals with warrants ...

. . .

The governor of Arkansas called out the National Guard to preserve order and prevent bloodshed. He was enjoined by a federal court order from continuing to do what he thought to be his duty ... Now there is disorder and the federal government is reported to be ready to ... intervene of its own accord ...

It is still up to the governor of Arkansas to preserve order. That's the constitutional way to proceed. ...

The Ft. Smith (Ark.) *Times Record*
Sept. 25, 1957

OFF THE RECORD
by C. F. Byrns

Violence in Little Rock Monday was stark tragedy. Violence always is. It solves nothing. It benefits no one. ...

What happened is what Governor Faubus has contended from the beginning might happen if Negro students were admitted to Central High School. Too few people in high places believed what the governor said. The "evidence" his critics said they couldn't find cannot now be disputed.

So long as the Arkansas National Guard was on duty, no violence occurred.

When the federal district court compelled the governor to withdraw the Guard, violence showed its ugly head.

Can anyone ask for stronger evidence to establish the validity of the governor's fears that violence would occur if integration was attempted?

* * *

. . .

The Supreme Court of the United States in 1954 rewrote the constitution, reversed all previous decisions of the same court (with different members) and the constitutions and laws of 17 states and decreed that segregation is unconstitutional.

The chain reaction began on that day in May, 1954, in the court room of the United States Supreme Court.

WHO WAS RIGHT?

Editorial, The Arkansas Gazette
September 25, 1957

As this is written the FBI report on anticipated violence in Little Rock's integration crisis has not been released and the Justice Department has left to Judge Davies the question whether it shall be made public.

It can be argued that nothing of import would be accomplished by the release of this information—which, from all reports, refutes Governor Faubus' assertion that violence was imminent in Little Rock. ...

Time magazine's "cover" article on Governor Faubus made the flat statement that 50 FBI agents had combed Little Rock and that:

> The report showed not a shred of evidence supporting Faubus' claim that Little Rock had been ripe for violence. Example: Where Faubus had said Little Rock stores were selling out of knives and pistols ("mostly to Negro youths"), the FBI agents checked 100 shops and found that weapon sales had actually been below normal.

> No one has yet denied this statement, and all reports uphold it. Certainly it couldn't be maintained now that the governor was right all along and that 50 FBI agents were wrong. The basic question still remains: Would all of this have happened if it had not been incited by the ill-advised statement and acts of the state's chief executive?

> The FBI report could shed some light on that question and we trust Judge Davies in time will release it.

––––

If the FBI report had confirmed that the contentions of "no violence" by Mayor Mann, the *Gazette* and Judge Davies were right, does anyone doubt that it would have been released? And that the *Gazette* would have published it in full?

The paragraph quoted from *Time* magazine is absolutely false. It is a lie out of whole cloth. For example it said, "agents checked 100 shops." There weren't a fourth that many in the whole area.

The State Police check on the sale of knives in Little Rock found that sales in some shops were high. Some store owners reported to me personally that they had taken knives off the shelves and voluntarily stopped the sales. No store reported sales below normal.

No greater falsehood was promulgated from any source during the whole Little Rock affair than in this editorial by the *Arkansas Gazette* and *Time* magazine.

Now, more than 20 years later, the FBI report has not yet been released.

WAY DOWN SOUTH IN THE STATE OF ARKANSAS
By Russell, Los Angeles Times   *9/25/57*

This western newspaper questioned the sanity of the use of the bayonet to enforce a court order.

In an editorial accompanying the cartoon the paper stated:

> "Gov. Faubus ... is inclined to question the constitutionality of the President's action. He relies, apparently, on Section 4 of Article IV, which says that the United States shall protect each of the States against invasion and on application of the Legislature or of the executive ... against domestic violence."

The editorial had a lot of misinformation. It said the federalized National Guard was in charge and 500 federal troops were flown in as a back-up force. It termed this "the best possible retort to Sen. Talmadge of Georgia, who likened the president's interference at Little Rock to the Russian suppression of Hungary." The paper also stated that with the use of local troops "the charge of carpet-bagging loses its edge."

All of this was untrue. The Guardsmen were not then in use. The 1,100 paratroopers of the U.S. 101st Airborne Division were used as the occupation force.

THE LONGER IT STICKS, THE HARDER IT WEARS
By Knox, Nashville Banner   *9/25/57*

Uncle Sam pinned on his hat with a bayonet — military occupation of Little Rock. He was unhappy with the situation and the longer it stuck, the more uncomfortable the arrangement.

EDITORIAL SHORT, TO POINT

Sept. 25, 1957

JACKSON — *The following appeared in today's Jackson Miss. Daily News:*
"To the president
"An editorial:
"Nuts!"

––––

At that time, only twelve years after World War II, nearly everyone could recall the Battle of the Bulge in the Ardennes, when the Germans surrounded and besieged the City of Bastogne, Belgium. A part of the forces defending the city was the 101st Airborne Division.

The German commander sent an emissary to American headquarters in the besieged town to ask for the surrender of the defenders. The 101st Division Commander, General McAuliffe, rejected the offer with the shortest reply in military history.

"Nuts!"

The Jackson newspaper declines to surrender to Eisenhower and the 101st Airborne troops with the same message.

Ironically I was a member of the 35th Infantry Division which, under Gen. Patton's command, held the right flank of the attack, the hottest point of conflict, as the 4th Armored Division led the spearhead into Bastogne to relieve the besieged 101st Division. In that attack the 35th met and defeated the crack infantry unit of the Nazi forces, the Adolph Hitler Division. Units of the 35th Division were the first infantry ground troops to make contact with the besieged garrison.

Now the 101st Airborne Division in a hostile action had occupied the capital of my native state.

"VINDICATED!" By Yardley, Baltimore Sun, 9/25/57
Some critics went far in their bigoted attempts to blame me for the short period of disorder in Little Rock.

The Gastonia (N.C.) Gazette, Sept. 25, 1957

FAUBUS VINDICATED

. . . *There is one obvious conclusion, Governor Orval Faubus is vindicated . . . in calling out the National Guard . . . It was the contention of the governor that circumstances . . . deemed this step necessary.*

Others . . . had different views. . . .

. . . federal court orders resulted in the Guard being called off the high school premises. The result need not be recounted here . . This forced the President to federalize the Arkansas guard units and return them to the places Governor Faubus assigned them originally.

"On the spot coverage," a newspaper axiom, well might be used to illustrate what happened in Little Rock . . .

When the Arkansas tempest began to boil Governor Faubus was on the spot. . . . he sensed what was likely to happen and called out the National Guard. . . . President Eisenhower was at a fashionable Newport . . . country club chasing a little white pellet around the golf course and being kissed by strange women. . . .

. . . Governor Faubus, on the spot, certainly sized up the situation in Arkansas much better than did the President.

. . . the governor stands vindicated in every sense of the word. . . .

The Little Rock race problem was pictured as a golf ball on the course as Ike played. He selected a club with which to address the ball and chose a rifle with affixed bayonet. The cartoonist questioned whether he chose correctly.

THE ARKANSAS TRAVELER
By Dobbins, Boston Traveler   9/25/57

Many people were of the view that the fierce figure came to Arkansas from the East via the North.

It could be said, using this newspaper's projection, that this same figure returned to the East and the cartoon caption could now well be "The Boston Traveler."

After its return to Boston the hate within the figure was fueled by a dictatorial federal district judge named W. Arthur Garrity, Jr.

The *Boston Traveler* of Sept. 25 appearing with the "Hate" cartoon said:

A miserable knot of humanity in Arkansas has forced President Eisenhower to renege on his high-minded stand in regard to civil rights.

The president said he could not imagine "any set of circumstances that would ever induce me to send Federal troops . . . into any area to enforce the orders of a Federal Court."

Well, now he's had to change his views. . . .

If Faubus had kept his mouth shut and stayed out of the picture, probably the revolting incidents . . . never would have happened . . .

Judge Garrity ordered the busing of 24,000 pupils to get more mixing of blacks and whites in Boston schools and in addition took the following dictatorial actions:

Removed South Boston High School from control of the Boston School Committee (school board) and placed it in charge of a federal court-appointed receiver;

Transferred the headmaster and football coach to other jobs outside the school;

Ordered the district to spend $125,000 to renovate the school and buy equipment to accommodate the black students bused into the school;

Ordered the library at another school removed to another room;

Ordered $25,000 spent to pave a turn-around for buses used in the busing program;

Ordered the purchase of a piano at another school; and

Ordered the spending of $110,000 of additional funds for repairs at South Boston High. (See *U.S. News and World Report*, Jan. 19, 1976.)

It was plain that the people and the elected school authorities were no longer running their own schools. Those duties and decisions had been arrogated to himself by a federal judge.

Commented John J. McDonough, Boston School Committee Chairman, of Judge Garrity's actions: "The next thing he'll be doing is counting the chalk."

These actions of Judge Garrity created a situation that the Founding Fathers sought to prevent in the division of powers between the national government and the states.

Northern Virginia, Strasburg
Sept. 25, 1957

Ike Followed Precedent In
Sending GIs Into Arkansas

by Arthur D. Davidson

When President Eisenhower sent Federal troops into . . . Arkansas without either invitation or consent of . . . that state, he had a number of outstanding historical precedents for his action.

He did precisely what Hitler did when he sent his German Legions into Austria, Poland and Czechoslovakia to enslave the free peoples of these countries. He emulated Mussolini, whose Italian troops rode through Ethiopia and drove its lawful government into exile.

He followed the exact course of Stalin whose . . . Russians seized Poland and the little Baltic states, then drove his dark empire southward through the Balkans . . .

The most recent precedent for the President's action was the bloody invasion of Hungary and the cruel butchery of its people by . . . Red Russia.

What could have induced the President to take such drastic action . . . Has the ADA and the lunatic element in both parties helped to upset his better judgment? . . .

In what was intended to be a very pious speech . . . the President attempted to lay the entire blame for conditions in Arkansas on Governor Faubus and the Arkansas people. This was grossly unfair.

Governor Faubus did not appoint Earl Warren to the Supreme Court. . . .

Mr. Eisenhower cannot escape responsibility for the deplorable invasion of the State of Arkansas by Federal troops . . .

AS GOOD A PLACE TO SETTLE AS ANY
By Dowling, N.Y. Herald Tribune   9/25/57

Sitting on a downed figure a determined Uncle Sam held a statement which read, "A challenge to federal authority will not be tolerated."

The caption "as good a place to settle it as any" was the thought which no doubt was urged upon President Eisenhower when he was advised to send federal troops to Little Rock. Many believe this viewpoint was advocated to Judge Davies by members of the school board, Harry Ashmore, Hugh Patterson, Sid McMath and others who favored integration in Little Rock.A strong show of force, they concluded among themselves and urged upon Judge Davies, will show these opponents of integration that the federal government means business. Then opposition will cease and we will have peaceful compliance, they hoped.

The fallacy of such a method — the use of force to place upon the people something with which they strongly disagree — is that the use of force, one begun, must usually be continued. Then dictatorship develops.

?,   By Knox, Nashville Banner & Charleston, S.C. News and Courier, 9/25/57

    This drawing was perhaps the best cartoon of all the many hundreds that were produced for placing in proper perspective the great legal question involved in the '57 Crisis. The caption is a question mark — ?. Had the gavel of an appointed federal judge replaced the elected governor of the state? Had the judicial branch of government now usurped the powers of the executive branch?

    The Courier placed under the cartoon these words: "Will An Army Officer Sit At This Desk?"

    An officer could have. Gen. Walker had as much right to use the governor's office for a military headquarters as he did the school superintendent's office at Central High School.

TROOPS TO LITTLE ROCK, By Sites, Cotton Trade Journal
(International Cotton Industry News Weekly), 9/27/57

The Statue of Liberty was alarmed to see rushing by its feet, armed federal troops on the way to Little Rock. An editorial in the same paper said: "Do the several States which compose this Union still possess the sovereignty which they retained when the Constitution of the United States was ratified? If the answer is in the affirmative, then undoubtedly the fateful 1954 decision of the U.S. Supreme Court ordering school integration was a usurpation of power, and the President's resort to use of Federal troops in Little Rock a flagrant violation of the Constitution. The Constitution does not delegate to the Federal Government the power to control educational systems within the States, nor does it delegate police power within the States."

In a news report on the legal proceedings it was said of Judge Davies, ". . . It was evident that his decision was already made before testimony was given."

CHAPTER 14
LITTLE ROCK OCCUPATION CONTINUES; CONTROVERSY BECOMES NATIONWIDE

TEAR GAS TEAM TO LITTLE ROCK; REPUBLICANS DEFECT

The U.S. government sent a tear gas team to Little Rock to be used in the school integration problem.

A prominent Republican resigned from the party and said he planned to join the States Rights Party in protest of the federal troop use at Little Rock.

IKE TO SEE GOVERNORS

The President planned to see a committee of Southern governors to discuss removal of the federal troops from Little Rock. The governors were chilled by Ike's statement that he didn't ask for talks on broad integration problems.

A Central High student was barred from a school bus by a 101st Airborne soldier and missed his transportation home.

CIVIL RIGHTS VIOLATIONS

During the initial period of occupation persons taken into custody by federal troops were jailed without charges being filed against them and held for indeterminate periods without bail. The procedure constituted flagrant violations of the civil rights of those persons arrested and held in this manner. Yet there were no protests of these irregular procedures by civil rights advocates.

Finally, Sheriff Tom Gulley protested the clearly illegal methods being employed by the occupation troops, and announced that no more prisoners of the federal troops would be jailed without formal charges first being preferred.

PRIOR TRAINING OF 101ST AIRBORNE

Attorney John Rye of Russellville called to report that (name withheld by request) a member of the 101st Airborne Division lives at Morrilton. He called his sister last Sunday, September 22, and told her that the 101st had been training for about three weeks on control of mob violence. The soldier said they were headed for Arkansas to arrive this week. This was before violence erupted at Central High School, and well before the official order sending the 101st Airborne troops to Little Rock.

Out-of-State Newspapers   9-26-57

Get Rid Of Faubus

(An Editorial)

FAUBUS, THE DEMOGOGUE

Faubus, the rabble rouser of the year, did a good job in training the other Little Rock rabble rousers to stir up Monday's mob scenes at the High School there and he and no one else is the direct cause of this disgrace to the nation.

He laid the plan so well that he was able to watch it work out comfortably from the long distance seat he sat in at the Southern Governors meeting in Sea Island, Ga.

Faubus should be impeached from office, tried and convicted of inciting to riot. We are sick and tired of the effort of many daily papers to build this man up into something great. He is a great foe of law and order. He is a great disseminator of hate. He is unfit to be in public office. He is a disgrace to his state and the nation. He is unfit, a dangerous demogogue, a Kasper in disguise, the leader of a planned rebellion.

POSITION OF FAUBUS

Critics of Governor Faubus are basing a case against his position . . . on the supposition the federal government is supreme in all matters of law. . . . The government is only supreme in law pertaining to fields in which the states have surrendered jurisdiction. But if the government were supreme in all matters of law, then we would not have a republic. We would have an autocracy. There would be no "sovereign states."

State sovereignty, however, is guaranteed by the 10th Amendment. It means the only powers the federal government has are those given to it by the states or the people. And when did the states hand over jurisdiction in the field of education? . . .

Certainly there is a question of law . . . but what law is to prevail, that of the Constitution or that created out of hand from ideological concepts by a legislating Supreme Court? This is the issue. Governor Faubus has courageously met it head on, and it's high time someone did.

The Austin (Texas) American
September 26, 1957

"Capitol A" Column

FAUBUS
by Sam Wood and Raymond Brooks

SEA ISLAND, Ga. — What kind of a fellow is this man Faubus, the governor of Arkansas?

Reporters at Sea Island, some of whom were meeting the Arkansas governor for the first time, were surprised at the manner in which Gov. Orval E. Faubus conducted his press conferences. The Arkansas governor, calmly and politely, answered all questions. He never volunteered information. That is he never took the "ball" away from the reporters to deliver a lecture. He never evaded an inquiry.

. . . the Arkansas governor was constantly trailed by 70 or more newsmen who were covering the southern governors' conference. He never hurried, never seemed to be in a rush. When a question was asked the Arkansas governor, with calm deliberation, seemed to repeat it to himself then cautiously roll out the answer.

Gov. Faubus is not the show type. He did not appear eager for publicity or for pictures but cooperated fully with the cameramen as they blazed away in his path. Whether he is right or wrong, you got the impression that the man whose action in Little Rock will be debated for years, acted as he thought best and with dead seriousness.

He did not appear elated when fighting in the Little Rock streets Monday "vindicated" his position that there would be violence, and that his calling the national guard was necessary to maintain law and order.

When the news reached him by telephone the impact was terrific. For a moment he seemed to be at a loss for words as he met reporters in a hall near the telephone booth. "I wouldn't want to say anything that would inflame an already inflammatory situation," he offered with sincere deliberation.

...Occasionally when a penetrating inquiry demanded a sharp answer it came with a grin rather than irritation.

At the governors' state dinner, the big formal occasion of the conference, Faubus sat deadpan as the biggest encore accorded any of the southerners resounded from the floor. It was the second big display of emotion in his behalf. The other came at Atlanta when the governors were introduced at the Texas-Georgia football game.

Governor Faubus took particular pains not to cast any reflection on the president of the United States although he made it plain he believed any use of federal force in Little Rock without request of the state government a severe breach of national authority.

As many other observers of the Arkansas chief executive the past few days, we are not so sure that all the applause he has received is a complete endorsement of his fight against integration, but more the public's expression of admiration for one who sticks to his convictions.

Gov. Faubus does not radiate arrogance. Neither does he radiate confidence. He is not the type of man who looks or acts like a leader. He merely leaves the impression he has a very difficult job to do and is willing to take the rap, to shoulder his own burden, and live with his success or his mistakes.

NORTHERN NEWSPAPER SCORES USE OF TROOPS
September 27, 1957

"You can't teach mutual respect and liking between black and white at the end of a bayonet," declared a front page editorial in the Manchester (N.H.) Union Leader.

Publisher William Loeb wired the Arkansas Democrat the text of his editorial, saying:

"As publisher of New Hampshire's largest daily and Sunday newspaper I am trying to awaken the North to the fact that the Arkansas fight for states' rights is a fight for the liberties of all of us. Believe sentiment beginning to change in North in revolt against Eisenhower's and New Hampshire's Sherman Adams' high-handed tactics."

Loeb's editorial was entitled "Paratroops, Bayonets — A Dictator's Answer."

THE POSSUM HUNT
By Cargill, Staunton, Va.   9/26/57

The federal dogs barked "treed" at a possum that went from one tree into another labeled "To the Higher Courts." While the legal process of appeal was followed from lower to higher federal courts, there was no relief. In fact, the erroneous decisions originated in the highest tribunal.

Appeals to the Warren-dominated court by law-abiding citizens in defense of state's rights were a hopeless expense and an exercise in futility. Decisions on appeals were foregone conclusions regardless of what the Constitution said or the merits of the cases.

Texarkana, Texas, Gazette

SOME HYPOCRISY AMONG INTEGRATIONISTS

. . . But we didn't start out to criticize the President . . . Obviously he had to do something when he picked the wrong horse — Mayor Mann over Gov. Faubus and wound up with a dangerous riot on his hands.

We are writing . . . to quote some information . . .

U.S. News and World Report . . . answers some questions we have been trying to get the government to answer in Washington.

Where do the children of the officials pushing integration go to school? . . .

"High government officials, as a rule, send their children either to private schools, or to those public schools where few, if any, Negroes are enrolled. . . .

"President Eisenhower's grandchildren of elementary school age — a boy and a girl — both at-

How far along the way is America?

...it's not too late to stop the clock!

1. The people go from CHAINS to spiritual faith

2. From SPIRITUAL FAITH to courage

3. From COURAGE to liberty

4. From LIBERTY to abundance

5. From ABUNDANCE to selfishness

6. From SELFISHNESS to complacency

7. From COMPLACENCY to apathy

8. From APATHY to dependency

9. From DEPENDENCY back again to bondage

THE CLOCK
Courtesy of Timken Roller
Detroit News   **9/26/57**

It has been written, and perhaps wisely so, that there are nine stages of man's growth and decline, from bondage to bondage.

---

tend private schools in the Virginia suburbs. . . .

"Vice President Nixon's daughters attend a public elementary school where their schoolmates are all white.

"Herbert Brownell, Jr., the attorney general . . . sends his children to private school.

"The new Secretary of Defense, Neil H. McElroy, has two daughters past school age; his 14-year-old son entered a private school in Washington. Ezra T. Benson, Secretary of Agriculture, received permission to transfer one of his children from a school attended by many Negroes to one attended by a few of them.

"The great majority of Senators and Representatives with children of school age either live in the suburbs, where mixing of races in schools is negligible, or they live in parts of Washington where racial mixing in schools is on a token basis.

"Among the nine Justices of the Supreme Court, only William J. Brennan, Jr. has a child of school age; his daughter attends a private school.

"Many prominent people outside of government also send their children to private schools, with the result that these institutions are filled to capacity and many have long waiting lists."

The idea seems to be in Washington that you can have segregation if you have enough money to pay for it.

The Dallas Morning News
Friday, September 27, 1957

BAYONETS AT THEIR THROATS

Cried a Little Rock housewife, as she saw paratrooper bayonets thrust at the throats of civilians: "How can they? How can they? Do they expect to keep soldiers here for nine months?"

It is the question which Gov. Price Daniel asks in his message to the President: "Does this mean you will occupy with troops every non-integrated school in the South?"

An unidentified Army officer on duty in Little Rock is credited with the soldier's answer: "Indefinitely. We stayed in Germany 15 years."

In Reconstruction I, United States troops stayed in Texas . . . for about nine years. . . .

How long this sort of thing would be necessary in East Texas is something The News does not care to guess.

. . . bayonets at the throats of Arkansas people is really an invasion of the homes of Arkansas by armed might.

The words of the title line of this editorial are not a flourish of editorial rhetoric. They are taken from the paratrooper sergeant's instruction to his platoon: "Keep 'em moving — bayonets to their throats."

By the law and by the mores of the Southern people, white and black, it is conceded that the father and mother have a divine right and duty to care for their children and to choose their associates as nearly as may be. . . .

. . .It has never been supposed in Texas that education by military occupation of the school premises is a good thing for white children, black children, red children, yellow or brown.

Nor is it reasonable to suppose that bayonets at the throats of anybody will promote good feeling between race and race.

Argument will go on as to whether Governor Faubus knew violence would happen. Well, it has happened. . . .

. . . If Major Gen. Edwin A. Walker and his self-called "Battling Bastards of Bastogne" are flown in here, the bitterness will flare up all over Texas.

Texans don't like bayonets at their throats.

Nashville, Tenn. Banner
Sept. 27, 1957

Faubus Documented It:

Issue Is Bayonet Rule
Over ANY State

(An Editorial)

If any further documentation was needed to awaken America at a brink of peril, Governor Faubus provided it last night. He spoke to the heart,

NEW TYPE "FEDERAL AID"
By Ficklen, Dallas Morning News   9/26/57

This cartoon, one of the most eloquent of the period, portrayed the use of "Force" — federal troops with fixed bayonets — as a new form of "federal aid."

The editorial page was filled with criticism of the Eisenhower action in Arkansas. A quote from an editorial said: *We have heard much of federal aid for schools. Little Rock now has it, muzzle end first.*

as to the mind and conscience of the nation. It was his state that has been invaded — and its authority usurped; but more than that, the ring of Federal bayonets . . . boasted readiness to subjugate in the same Storm Trooper fashion any city, school district, or section that fails instantly to bow its neck to the yoke of a Federal court order.

How else construe the amazing revelation by a military spokesman that "some time ago" selected Army units were alerted for this chore? . . .

Another Southern Governor, Frank G. Clement of Tennessee, spoke to the heart of this issue . . . It is whether the sovereign states of these UNITED STATES OF AMERICA are to be disestablished and occupied — ruled and run by martial law enforced by paratroopers and bayonets.

There is but one answer a free people can give to that question: An . . . eternal NO! . . .

MILITARY PASSES REQUIRED FOR STUDENTS

A news picture showed a girl student presenting a military pass to a 101st Airborne sentry in order to enter her own school.

Brotherhood by Bayonet!

"Start loving each other. That's a court order!"

BROTHERHOOD BY BAYONET!, Artist unknown, Manchester (N.H.) Union Leader, 9/26/57

This cartoon accurately portrayed, in the minds of millions of people, the mistake of enforced integration. It appeared on the front page of the Manchester Union Leader, the largest daily in New Hampshire. The front page headline for the news story read, "Guns Force Integration," and a headline stretching all the way across the front page for the column of Fulton Lewis, Jr., read, "The Iron Fist in 'Free' America." The newspaper said it had never been possible to force people into friendly, mutual acceptance of each other, or compel them to love each other. Those human relations must come by other means.

MISSISSIPPI TO RETAIN SEGREGATION, GOV. COLEMAN SAYS

Gov. J. P. Coleman, noting that Mississippi plans have authorized abolition of their public schools rather than have them integrated, said he doubts the president would get any satisfaction out of guarding an empty school.

—0—

CALL FOR CALM

I issued a statement calling on the people for calm and order, but voiced resentment at the occupation by federal troops. I asked the people to obey even the orders of the occupation forces, since resistance would be useless. I was under pressure to call the legislature into special session but did not deem legislative action feasible or timely.

BULLETIN

WASHINGTON, Sept. 26 — The Army said today "selected" regular units throughout the southern states have been placed on special alert to deal with any possible outbreaks in connection with school segregation.

An Army spokesman reported this to newsmen in an informal briefing.

He said that the orders went out to the five Army combat divisions in the seven states some time ago . . . Individual area and division commanders were being kept advised of developments and in turn were in contact with Washington. . . .

He explained that under the "special" or "partial" type of alert now in force, each division is to make sure that at least 50 per cent of its troops are within two hours of their home post or station at all times.

The special alert orders went out to the 3rd and 4th Army commands . . . at Atlanta, Ga. and San Antonio, Tex.

ARMY CLAMPS LID ON RIOT ORDER MIXUP

September 27, 1957

WASHINGTON — Secretary of the Army Wilbur Brucker said today [Sept. 27] a canceled order for stepped-up riot training for troops in the South "will not be revived." But Brucker still would not disclose just what the order said.

. . . Brucker personally killed it within hours after it became publicly known.

. . . the Army, embarrassed and angry, clamped a tight secrecy lid on its details lest they feed the fires of controversy over the use of troops to enforce racial integration at Little Rock.

———

The order for riot training of Army troops to be used against the country's own citizens was not canceled because Brownell and the Army thought it was wrong and a mistake. It was canceled because it "became known" and created a furor, both North and South, by alarmed citizens and public officials.

It was all right to secretly train the 101st airborne troops for use against citizens at Little Rock. But to train all Army troops for use against citizens anywhere in the U.S. was too much even for the Northern "liberals."

The order for the riot control training came no doubt from some member of the Eisenhower administration. It is inconceivable that any Army officer would originate such an order on his own.

THAT THING HURTS
By McClanahan, Dallas Morning News   9/27/57

The occupation of Little Rock with federal troops by the Republican administration locked a can to the tail of the GOP elephant which was of considerable discomfort.

WE WILL NOT SURRENDER

The Selma Times-Journal

An Editorial

The picture of President Dwight D. Eisenhower has been removed from the wall above the editorial desk of the Times-Journal.

Autographed by the President, this picture once was a prideful possession. Now it only is a symbol of futility and shame — the picture of a great general who proved in a grave domestic crisis to be a little man: A great American who has . . . little understanding of the true concept of America.

* * *

For the Times-Journal, first newspaper in the South to endorse Mr. Eisenhower for the presidency, this is a bitter dose.

. . .

We still think he is an honest man of good intent, but his capacity for leadership ended when he doffed his well-won five stars, because . . . military service has deprived him of understanding of the basic principles of a free civilian government.

No other explanation could be given for the fact that he has surrounded himself with constitutional rapists . . . to whom he listens. . . . The Times-Journal does not believe that President Eisenhower, himself, wanted to send troops into Arkansas, . . . he sent those troops because he was told by political opportunists, who place minority votes above the national welfare . . .

Nor can there be any logical explanation for his repeated references to "upholding the law of the land" when there are no such laws involved. . .

* * *

Obviously, the South cannot hope to actively resist this new occupation by carpetbag troops on the basis of gun to gun and man to man. We do not have the men or the guns.

But we will not surrender . . .

We have to stand our ground, without violence, and close every school ringed by federal troops.

Let there be no argument and no force. Just close the schools and leave them in the hands of federal troops as caretakers. . . .

LITTLE ROCK

END RESULT OF VIOLENCE
By Kennedy, Ark. Democrat   9/27/57

SOUTHERN GOVERNORS

The Southern Governors observed the giant "U.S. Enforcement of Integration" standing on the city of Little Rock. The occupation was meant to be a lesson to others who might resist the federal courts. Some writers pointed out that when the Red Russian troops drowned the Hungarian freedom fighters in blood, the action was meant as a lesson to others who might consider resistance to Communist tyranny.

MISTER FIXIT, By Dobbins, Boston Traveler, 9/27/57

My evaluation of the situation had proven to be correct. To many observers this cartoon was a prejudiced attempt to discredit a public figure who had been proven right.

IKE OCCUPIES ARKANSAS, By Dean, Shreveport, La. Journal, 9/27/57

The "rights reserved to the states" were pierced by the "Eisenhower, Brownell & Co." bayonet in the occupation of Little Rock. Federal troops controlled the schools, and jeep patrols were seen regularly on the streets throughout the city. The commanding general of some 12,000 federal troops said there was no limitation on the perimeter of his jurisdiction. He could expand federal troop control to the state's borders and into other states if he chose.

YOU HAVE JUST HEARD AN ADDRESS BY GOV. ORVAL
FAUBUS
By Grant, Oakland, Cal. Tribune   9/27/57

This is Grant's exaggerated version of my 25 minute statement broadcast over a national TV network on Sept. 26. It must
have been effective judging from the pained howls of my
critics. The press was present during my address and a news
conference followed the telecast.

I CANNOT IMAGINE
By Knox, Nashville Banner,
Marietta, Ga. Journal   9/27/57

U.S. soldiers subdued at bayonet point and gun butt those
who got in their way at CHS. Note the shoulder insignia,
"Brownell's SS Storm Troopers." The caption of the cartoon
comes from President Eisenhower's statement on July 17, 1957,
when he said:

"I can't imagine any set of circumstances that would ever
induce me to send federal troops . . . into any area to enforce
the orders of a Federal court . . . I would never believe that it
would be a wise thing to do in this country."

The quotation is taken from *The Bryan* (Texas) *Daily
Eagle,* Oct. 3, 1957, which had taken it from *The Standard
Times* of New Bedford, Mass.

ARKANSAS TRAVELER
By Talburt, N. Y. World Telegram   9/30/57

In another version of the Arkansas Traveler, I was shown as
a little man in a top hat trying to appear as a tearful giant,
clothed in demogoguery and making inflammatory speeches.
The idea was a long, long way from the truth, but if all the cartoonist's information came from the "violent" typewriters of
the visiting press, then his viewpoint could have been warped by
lack of accurate information.

ANOTHER EXAMPLE OF VIOLENCE IN
AMERICA
By Fischetti, N.W. Ark. Times
Longview, Tex. Daily News   10/2/57

In making propaganda against the
Free World the Communists were completely unscrupulous. Communist Russia
(USSR) pointed to the picture of a
baseball player facing the pitcher with the
bat at ready, as "another example of
violence in America." Yet there were
those who kept harping, "What will the
Communists think of us?"

"HOT" AIRBORNE TROOPS
By Ficklen, Dallas Morning News   9/27/57

The dispatch of Airborne troops to Little Rock by President Eisenhower was
shown as "politics" dropping from the sky
into Central High School. In my opinion
Brownell was far more interested in obtaining votes than helping black people.

PILKINGTON TO RUN FOR GOVERNOR

HOPE — Chancery Judge James H. Pilkington, Hope, has announced that he will be a candidate for the Democratic nomination for governor of Arkansas in 1958.

Pilkington filed today (Sept. 28) in the Secretary of State's office in Little Rock.

The 43-year-old chancellor announced his candidacy yesterday.

The thought occurred to many that Pilkington may have been encouraged by my critics to announce his candidacy as another means of bringing pressure on me in the state vs. federal power controversy. The announcement had no effect on my decisions at the time. Ultimately, the ill-timed announcement may have damaged Pilkington's prospects as a candidate for governor.

OFF THE RECORD
By C. F. Byrns

Ft. Smith Southwest American, Sept. 28, 1957

. . . Arkansas has become a stage on which is being enacted a drama with no presently visible ending.

. . .It will become clearer that integration is not an isolated issue but a part of a broader conflict which must one day be resolved. That is the struggle . . . to wipe out the powers of the states and center them in the federal government.

A few days ago, before the troops moved into Little Rock, the enormity of this states' rights problem was brilliantly presented by the senior justice of the supreme court of Arizona, where integration is no problem. Justice M. T. Phelps spoke in Phoenix, Ariz., to an overflow audience . . .

The speech was described in the Arizona Republic . . . as "a scathing criticism of the United States supreme court's thinking in relation to states' rights."

* * *

Justice Phelps charged the supreme court not only is resorting to the Fourteenth amendment to strike down rights reserved to the sovereign states by the constitution, but is also extending this coverage to embrace practically every business in the nation.

The justice is quoted as saying, "I say to you in all candor it is my honest conviction that it is the design and purpose of the court to usurp the policy-making powers of the nation.

"By its own unconstitutional pronouncements it would create an all-powerful, centralized government in Washington and subsequent destruction of every vestige of states' rights, expressly and clearly reserved to the states under the Tenth amendment of the constitution."

* * *

. . . Justice Phelps said this about the anti-segregation decision of 1954: "Regardless of what we as individuals may think about the justice or injustice of segregation, I here assert without hesitation or reservation that the decision was not based upon logic or law. I further charge that the processes followed in reaching the decision's conclusions violate all the procedures of due process known to American jurisprudence."

* * *

Referring to the recent decision of the high court in the Communist cases, the Arizona justice said "It constitutes an all-time low in the disregard of procedural due process."

BAYONETS FOR BALLOTS
By Knox, Nashville Banner   9/28/57

Brownell tried to gather the votes of blacks by pointing to the bayonet he ordered to the throat of the South.

The Dallas Morning News

Saturday, September 28, 1957

Did Faubus Give the Facts?

The Governor of Arkansas gave the facts of the military occupation of his city and state . . . Did he give them truly?

. . . the facts stressed by Governor Faubus are borne out in news accounts, by press photographs and by television recordings:

(1) Arkansas is more advanced in voluntary and peaceful integration in education than any other state in the Deep South.

(2) Blood has been shed by the Army of Occupation in Arkansas, and students are moved about on school grounds and in school rooms by armed guards.

(3) The outlander U.S. District Judge sent into Little Rock came with a preconceived notion of what to do and issued orders in three hearings, the combined length of which was an hour and 25 minutes.

(4) *Disorders which Governor Faubus sought to prevent have all occurred since he was superseded by the forces of the United States Government.*

(5) *The courts have ruled that the United States Government may not seize a steel plant, but that the United States Government may seize an Arkansas school plant and operate it under military law.*

. . .

The operation of television gives to the average beholder a chance to check upon radio and news reports by misinformed or prejudiced reporters. It is a severe check; but it is a wholesome one.

. . . Governor Faubus evidently welcomes that check upon his own words, his own deeds and his own personality.

Governor Faubus has been represented as a crude boor and a clown. Television shows him to be a man capable of restrained eloquence of the highest order.

The Governor has been called a trouble-maker, a rabble-rouser and a hillbilly. Television shows him to be a thoughtful man profoundly moved by the spectacle of the powers of a sovereign state being trampled under the armed feet of military occupation without warrant of statute, Constitution or common sense.

The President of the United States scorned to listen to him. But the nation listened.

IN A DIFFERENT WORLD
By Jensen, Chicago Daily News   9/28/57

A barefoot figure labeled "The Faubuses," was seated on a small world, "The Past," his back to a mountain cabin, watching a moonshine whiskey still in operation. A Confederate flag flew from the cabin roof. The figure had turned his back on the fine buildings labeled "The South's Future."

The drawing was meant to discredit all those who defended the constitutional right of the states to manage their own affairs. This was the time-honored means of conflict — smear the opposition; make them look bad; ignore the issues and the facts when they cannot successfully be debated.

At the time of this cartoon Arkansas through its 1957 General Assembly at my recommendation, had adopted a program which made the state the most progressive in the South, and one of the most progressive in the Union.

How did this cartoonist portray those who burned a large section of Chicago and looted millions of dollars worth of goods? Something which never happened in Arkansas.

Arkansas Gazette, Sept. 28, 1957

Governor Faubus' War Record Cited

By the Associated Press

The war record of Governor Faubus, mentioned by him Thursday in a nationwide address, included extensive combat service in World War II.

In his address he said his division, the 35th, helped relieve the 101st Airborne Division, some of whose units enforced integration orders this week at Little Rock Central High School.

The governor spent 4½ years in the Army after volunteering (as a private) in 1941. He was in combat 10 months and with the Army of Occupation in Germany a year.

When he landed in Normandy, Mr. Faubus was a lieutenant. He was separated from the service as a major. His assignment was combat intelligence — frequently a front-line job.

He received the Bronze Star but in conversation appears more proud of earning the Combat Infantryman Badge. He won the Bronze Star for helping wipe out a German machine gun nest. Mr. Faubus was at Normandy and went with the Division into Northern France, the Rhineland, Ardennes and Central Germany.

One of his frequent assignments was to lead patrols and to guide new units into position. He has retained an active interest in the 35th Division Association and was elected its president in 1954.

Official History

Washington, Sept. 27 — The official Army history shows that Governor Faubus was correct in saying that his Word War II division came to the rescue of the 101st Airborne, which had been surrounded by Germans at Bastogne, Belgium, in 1944.

Faubus was an Infantry captain in the 35th Division at the time of Bastogne.

According to the official Army history, the 35th was called from the German border in Alsace-Lorraine to go to the aid of the 101st, which had been surrounded at Bastogne but had refused to surrender on December 22, 1944.

The 35th moved to Arlon, Belgium, December 25-26, the history said, and "took part in the fighting to relieve Bastogne, throwing off the attacks of four German divisions" and taking two towns. The history credits the 4th (armored) Division with making the first breakthrough to the 101st on December 26.

———

In holding the right flank of the 4th Armored Division spearhead the 35th faced and defeated the Crack Division of Hitler's SS troops, the Adolph Hitler Division. Units of the 35th Division were the first foot soldiers to contact men of the besieged Bastogne garrison. The 35th then moved into Bastogne and after relieving the 101st troops, advanced eastward against fierce German resistance.

In the *Arizona Republic* on Sept. 28, David Lawrence wrote:

The action taken in Arkansas insured the defeat of the Republican Party in 1958 and 1960.

This is a tragic example of irresponsible government.

Government by bayonet has superseded government by the laws of Congress in supposedly free America.

WHAT A TOMBSTONE THAT'LL MAKE FOR YOU
By Talburt, N. Y. World Telegram,
Rocky Mountain News   9/28/57

Both the Republican elephant and the Democratic donkey pointed to the other and to Little Rock and said, "What a tombstone that will make for you" in the campaign of 1958. Since the Republicans were in power and sent the troops, they bore the blame and lost the '58 elections. (See editorial by David Lawrence in the New Orleans *Times-Picayune* of Oct. 6, 1957.)

JOIN THE ARMY AND SEE THE SCHOOLS

A sign in the window of a service station at Sullivan's Beach, S.C., read: Join the Army and SEE the High Schools. Your choice High School Duty. Bayonets free.

FAUBUS' SPECIAL SESSION CALL "JUST HOURS" OFF

This was the headline for a story by George Douthit. His information on the prospects of a special session was erroneous. Other parts of the story read:

Governor Faubus flew to the Arkansas-Tulsa football game at Fayetteville in a private plane accompanied by an aide, Claude Carpenter . . .

Mr. Faubus was taken inside the stadium in a car driven by his son Farrell, 18, and led by a State Police car. The governor took a seat in a section on the 40-yard line among the other spectators and a few of them knew he was present.

The governor chuckled at the opening statement of the game's announcer when he said "Good afternoon, ladies and gentlemen, and fellow subjects."

Mr. Faubus laughed . . . later in the game at another remark of the announcer. After each Arkansas touchdown a small cannon was fired. The announcer said: "That shooting you hear is not from federal troops. There is not a one in these hills."

I thought there were explosions in the nearby hills, probably blasting from construction work, which sounded much like artillery fire. The announcer finally said: "Don't be alarmed from those explosions, folks. There are no reports of any Federals anywhere in the hills."

The announcer was the humorous, well-liked and respected Glen Rose, well known U of A athletic official.

* * *

TEXANS TO PETITION EISENHOWER TO RESIGN

"We, the undersigned, believe that your actions against the State of Arkansas and the people of Little Rock make you unworthy of office as president of the United States and we request your immediate resignation."

* * *

SOUTHERN OFFICIALS FOR FAUBUS

Representatives of the Southern Regional Conference of Council of State Governments meeting at Baltimore adopted a resolution supporting Faubus and denouncing the use of federal troops to enforce school integration in Arkansas.

* * *

The North was appalled and the South both appalled and infuriated by the reckless use of bayonets on unarmed citizens, even girl students and innocent bystanders. The indiscriminate use of the dangerous daggers repelled even the one-sided Northern reporters.

There were no open official orders or proclamations to sheathe the knives but the word came down from the White House and Brownell's office, "Get those bayonets off those rifles and out of sight immediately."

The bayonets came off and were sheathed. We knew when the orders came down. Not for consideration of Arkansas people, however, but for the reasons whispered by Brownell in the cartoon.

COULD BE . . . ., By Knox, Nashville Banner, 9/28/57

This excellent cartoon showed what had happened in the federal government. The U.S. "Supreme Court" took over the "law making function of government" (the bat), while Congress stood by. The Court made laws, ordered their execution, then sat as interpreter and judge. The checks and balances of the national government were destroyed.

We can well imagine the confusion and unfairness that would ensue if the umpire in a baseball game demanded to bat, pitch and coach while he continued his official rulings.

LESSON FROM LITTLE ROCK
By Manning, Arizona Republic   9/27/57

With this cartoon I agreed 100%. If a school could not operate without guns and bayonets, then the whole atmosphere and attitude for proper education had disappeared. An editorial began with this paragraph:

PRESIDENT ERRS AGAIN

It is a sad development when a man once regarded affectionately by nearly all Americans and honored by them with their confidence and the highest office in the land, proves himself a weak and misguided tool in the hands of the political schemers surrounding him.

MPs IN CONTROL

Fromer Congressman Battle of Alabama personally visited the scene at Central and was forcibly escorted away by armed troops.

Military police of the 101st Division roamed widely through the area far from Central High School. Division officers said they were looking for stray soldiers from the Division.

REPUBLICANS CONDEMN USE OF TROOPS

Ted Dalton, GOP National Committeeman and Republican candidate for Governor of Virginia, told the president that the Republican platform on which he ran when elected, prohibited the use of troops to enforce court orders. Dalton urged the troops be withdrawn.

In Texas a number of prominent Republicans resigned from the party in protest of the President's use of troops. In Pulaski County (Little Rock) three GOP committeemen quit their posts for the same reason.

TIMMERMAN QUITS NAVY IN PROTEST

Arkansas Democrat, September 29, 1954

COLUMBIA, S.C. — Gov. George Bell Timmerman, Jr., has resigned his commission as a naval reserve officer obviously in protest against the sending of federal troops into Little Rock. . . .

. . .The governor said:

"Because of the recent change in official attitude on the federal level toward the personal and property rights of American citizens, I find that my commission as an officer in the U.S. Naval Reserve is no longer compatible with my duties as governor of South Carolina.

"It is with regret, therefore, that I find it necessary to tender my resignation as a commissioned officer . . ."

A lieutenant in the Naval Reserve, Timmerman in 1942 volunteered for the armed forces and served as an ensign on North Atlantic convoy duty. One of his ships was torpedoed and he spent three days in a life boat. He also commanded one of the first rocket launcher ships in the Pacific before taking part in the Okinawa operation.

RACIAL FLAREUPS IN PHILADELPHIA

Rep. L. H. Fountain of N.C. scored the President for the use of troops in Little Rock; 10 youths were arrested in racial flareups in Philadelphia, Pa.; and Billy Graham was advised to delay his planned visit to Little Rock until tensions lessened.

* * *

NO SERVICE RIBBONS FOR LITTLE ROCK

It was reported by federal authorities that no service ribbons would be issued to soldiers for duty in Little Rock.

FOUR QUIT U.S. POSTS IN PROTEST; PRAIRIE DRAFT BOARD, SAVINGS BOND CHIEF RAP TROOP USE

H. T. Patton, Vice President of Merchants and Planters Bank, and Chairman of the U.S. Savings Bond program in Ouachita County since its incep-

tion, resigned in a letter to W. W. Campbell, state chairman, and Speed Reavis, Jr., state director of the bond program.

Mr. Patton wrote, "I am not opposed to integration for those who want it, but do not force it on those who do not want it. The matter has gone far beyond integration now. Integration is merely a trend of the times under Eisenhower and gives us an insight into what lies ahead in any given field chosen by Mr. President and the Supreme Court which has been so thoroughly stacked. I regret that our president is so void of statesmanship, judgment and discretion that any American citizen should feel as I do toward his leadership."

Members of the Prairie County Selective Service Board No. 59 submitted their resignations . . . in a letter mailed to Col. Fred M. Croom, state Selective Service director. Signing the resignation were G. G. Purvis, president; W. E. Castleberry, secretary; and L. M. Waters, member.

The Draft Board letter stated: "When the federal government assigns troops in our state to handle problems that are strictly reserved for the states for handling, we feel we cannot continue to send boys to the Army to be used for any such purpose."

REPLACE THE TURF
By Alley, Memphis Commercial Appeal, N. Y. Times   9/29/57

Alley took his cue from the President's frequent enjoyment of golf. The President with a deep stroke tore the turf politically by uprooting the "sovereign state of Arkansas." Thus the caption "Replace the Turf" — restore the state's sovereign rights destroyed by the illegal use of federal troops.

Principals in Central High Integration Crisis

VIRGIL BLOSSOM: "Our plan... is the best answer to a difficult problem."

GOV. FAUBUS: "I feel like MacArthur. I've been relieved."

PRES. EISENHOWER: "Mob rule cannot be allowed..."

BROOKS HAYS: "I feel like a bird in a badminton game."

JUDGE DAVIES: "I have a constitutional duty .... from which I shall not shrink."

MAJ. GEN. WALKER: "There won't be any incidents when I get through."

DAISY BATES: "If the city can't do it, certainly it's the federal government's job."

MAYOR MANN: "If any racial trouble does develop, the blame rests on the doorstep of the Governor's Mansion."

JOII KEIIIEDY

WHO'S WHO IN THE BATTLE OF LITTLE ROCK, By Kennedy, Ark. Democrat, 9/29/57

Top row, left to right. Virgil Blossom, superintendent of Little Rock schools, "Our plan, is the best answer to a difficult problem." Gov. Faubus, "I feel like MacArthur; I've been relieved" (remark made when National Guard was federalized and federal troops occupied Little Rock). President Eisenhower, "Mob rule cannot be allowed."

Second row, Federal Judge Ronald L. Davies of North Dakota, "I have a constitutional duty . . . from which I will not shrink." Congressman Brooks Hays, Fifth (Little Rock) District, "I feel like a bird in a badminton game."

Third Row, Maj. Gen. Edwin A. Walker, in command of federal troops, "There won't be any incidents when I get through." Mrs. Daisy Bates, state NAACP leader, "If the city can't do it, certainly it's the federal government's job." Mayor Woodrow Wilson Mann, "If any racial trouble does develop, the blame rests on the doorstep of the Governor of Arkansas."

EVERYBODY IN THE SAME SCHOOL, By Somerville, Atlanta Journal & Constitution, 9/29/57

The school "Due Process of Law" was boarded up. "The End Justifies the Means School," was crowded with "raw force," as a result of occupation by federal troops. Strong editorials condemning Eisenhower's decision sending troops to Little Rock were reprinted from seven other Georgia newspapers.

TODAY, I AM A MAN
By Baldy, Atlanta Journal & Constitution 9/9/57

Ike posed as a strong man in a shirt labeled "Little Rock." Sending troops to Little Rock, he was told, suddenly changed him "from a five-year weakling" into a strong, decisive President. Note the hands holding up the false front from behind with only Ike's head shown. The remainder of the picture was fake, but the photographer took pictures of the "strong man" president for use in the campaigns of 1958 and 1960. Note the papers in photographer's hip pocket. The cartoon portrayed the motive of Ike's aides in sending troops to Little Rock.

TAKE IT EASY GENERAL
By Knox, Nashville Banner, N. Y. Times 9/27/57

NOBODY NEEDS ME AROUND HERE
By Somerville, Atlanta Journal & Constitution,
Toledo Blade 9/29/57

The bayonet thrust into Arkansas threatened the unity of the United States. Thus, the warning to the general to take it easy. Gen. Walker did an effective job in a high-handed manner. Sometime later he said that he was on the wrong side in the controversy involving the legal rights of the states.

I needed "time." That was what I asked for at the Newport Conference. The situation needed time. But the Court demanded implementation of its order forthwith. The people resisted by mob violence, and Brownell sent in the troops without delay.

CUTTING CORNERS
By Alley, Memphis Commercial Appeal
Montgomery, Ala. Advertiser   9/29/57

The U.S. Army tank cut the corner too sharply on the way to Little Rock, and damaged severely the sovereign state, the cornerstone of democracy.

On the same page Associate Editor J. Fred Thornton, began his column:

"I have been watching events in Arkansas with keen interest. I started to say the state of Arkansas, but is there a state of Arkansas anymore? Or is it the province of Arkansas, or the military district of Arkansas?"

➤➤

GRAPES OF WRATH IN FERMENT
By Seibel, Richmond Times Dispatch
N. Y. Herald Tribune   9/29/57

"Forced integration" was about to cause an outburst of "States Rights."

In reportng reaction across the country the *Tribune* quoted from a Connecticut weekly, *The Thompsonville Press*:

Our Federal Constitution does not call for integrated schools. In order to justify its decision, the Supreme Court had not only to stretch the vague wording of the Constitution, but buttress that wording with sociological theory — a strange means of interpreting the Constitution.

And on the basis of a decision so derived, an entire section of our country is now being forced to conform — conform to a judgment which it had no part in making, conform even though that judgment is contrary to its customs, its way of life, its historical sense of what is proper and right."

FOOD FOR THOUGHT
About Sept. 30, 1957

An item which appeared in the *Charlotte Observer* on Sept. 28 was called to my attention and the attention of newspaper readers, by Terry Parker Wallace. No state address was given but Wallace was possibly a North Carolina resident.

"People — all people — forget too many things too quickly.

"It happened less than three years ago.

"A newspaper printed the plight of a Negro youth doomed to death unless he could have a drastic heart operation.

"A sum of $2,000 was mentioned.

"From all parts of the state came an avalanche of $1 bills, oversubscribing the amount by a third before the newspaper could shut it off.

"Tenderly, the arms of a uniformed captain and major lifted the boy aboard a 21-passenger plane made available by the state's Air National Guard for the flight to Minneapolus and surgery.

"The operation made medical history. The boy lived.

"He and the National Guard commander who had made the plane available live today in their home town where it all took place.

"And you wonder how much of this has been forgotten — by a Negro boy and Maj. Gen. Sherman T. Clinger of Little Rock, Ark."

I recalled the incident. At my direction the black youth was flown in a National Guard plane to Minneapolis, Minn., at state expense by Gen. Sherman T. Clinger and the crew of Arkansas Air National Guardsmen. As I recall Air National Guard Commander Col. Frank Bailey was in charge of the plane and the crew.

NO ARMISTICE, By Ficklen, Dallas Morning News, 10/3/57

The war of Faubus versus the federals continued. This drawing was evoked by the failure to arrange for the withdrawal of the federal troops, which is related in the following pages.

CHAPTER 15
CONFERENCE OF IKE AND THE SOUTHERN GOVERNORS; AGREEMENT REJECTED

SOUTHERN GOVERNORS WILL OFFER SERVICES AS CRISIS MEDIATORS (Oct. 1)

WASHINGTON — Four so-called Moderate Southern governors will tell President Eisenhower this afternoon they are willing to act as mediators between the White House and Governor Faubus for the withdrawal of federal troops from Little Rock.

The four governors are Luther Hodges, North Carolina; Frank Clement, Tennessee; LeRoy Collins, Florida; and Theodore McKeldin, Maryland.

The governors are members of a five-man committee appointed by the Southern Governors Conference to discuss with Eisenhower the withdrawal of federal troops from the Arkansas capital.

A fifth member of the committee, Gov. Marvin Griffin, Georgia, announced yesterday he would not attend.

Thomas B. Stanley, Virginia, also reportedly refused to attend the conference this afternoon.

Stanley was sought to fill the vacancy created by Griffin's refusal.

* * *

SEGREGATED!
By Ficklen, Dallas Morning News   10/1/57

Since I was left out of their meeting Ficklen said I was segregated by the so-called moderate governors and the president.

FEDERALIZED GUARD ORDERED TO TAKE OVER AT CENTRAL

On October 1 the federalized National Guard troops, by order of General Walker, took over control of Central High School and escorted the nine black students to school.

After school began Gen. Walker brought Col. Julian Beakley, 153rd Infantry Regiment commander, and Lt. Col. Ernest Bowden, First Battalion commander, across the street to pose for pictures and to participate in a press interview. The press was told that the regiment took over at 7 p.m. the day before.

The 101st Airborne press officers said 200 of the 101st men were staioned behind the school.

The cost for the Guard had now reached a half million dollars and continued to mount at a daily rate of approximately $100,000.

THE SHOE'S ON THE OTHER FOOT
By Maples, Ft. Worth Star Telegram   10/1/57

School troubles far worse than any experienced in Little Rock broke out in New York. A headline in a Long Island, N.Y., newspaper on Sept. 28 read: "Race Hate Flares in LI School." There were highly publicized gang murders in the city.

Alabama Lt. Gov. Guy Hardwick suggested that the President move federal troops from Arkansas to New York City, where he said law and order had broken down.

The shoe had now begun to pinch the other foot, but the troubles in the North were not treated in the same light as those in the South by the federal authorities or the national news media.

IKE WRITES TO
EPISCOPAL BISHOP OF LITTLE ROCK

It was disclosed that President Eisenhower wrote to the Right Rev. Robert R. Brown, Episcopal Bishop of Little Rock, asking him to mobilize sentiment in an effort to end the school dispute.

Rev. Brown was formerly rector of a church in Richmond, Va., which was attended by Walter S. Robertson, Assistant Secretary of State. According to reports Brown had called Robertson, who told Atty. Gen. Brownell of the call, Brownell told the President, and Eisenhower wrote the letter.

At that time the Brownell forces were desperately grasping for popular support in the Little Rock area.

Bishop Brown made no public moves to carry out the presidential request. He would have found himself in conflict with some parishoners of his own church. There was no integration of any Episcopal congregations in the area.

STILL BLOWING HIS BAZOOKA
By Hesse, St. Louis Globe Democrat　　　10/1/57

According to the critics, my statements constituted "political opportunism" which engendered "hate" and "unrest." This cartoonist was evidently one of the critics.

THE WAYWARD FAU[BUS]
By Russell, Los Angeles Times　　　10/1/57

This was a most clever cartoon idea. The cartoonist made use of the well known school transportation vehicle labeled Central High, and, — note the caption — the name of the Governor of Arkansas. Note also the highway sign.

The four Southern Governors serenaded Ike at the White House with a possible means of removing the federal troops from Little Rock. The remark which the cartoonist had Ike make to the Governors proved to be prophetic. Many student bands throughout the South and the nation were soon forbidden to play Dixie on any occasion.

PLAY SOMETHING . . . ANYTHING BUT DIXIE
By Conrad, Denver Post　　　10/1/57

NEW ENGLAND PAPER CRITICAL OF PRESIDENT

Opposition to Ike's troop order was by no means confined to the South. *The Standard Times* of New Bedford, Mass., on Oct. 1 said in an editorial:

Public school education is constitutionally the domain of each State Government, but Central High School in Little Rock, a part of the Arkansas public school system, is under control of the Federal Government by edict of the President.

One purpose was political: To win back the Northern Negro vote for the Republican Party.

The Supreme Court decision, written by Warren, was precisely what Brownell had asked. It was a doctrinaire decision based not on law but on sociological precepts.

The President has assumed authority in a crisis of his own execution that may destroy the constitutional rights of all the States — North and South, East and West.

PAINTED INTO A CORNER
By Knox, Nashville Banner   10/1/57

Ike painted himself into a corner at Little Rock by sending the federal troops. The President sought desperately to find a way out. Note the brand of paint he used.

THE WASHINGTON CONFERENCE BETWEEN IKE, HIS ADVISERS AND THE FOUR SOUTHERN GOVERNORS

On October 1 the four Southern Governors, McKeldin, Hodges, Collins and Clement, engaged in a long conference at the White House with President Eisenhower, seeking an agreement by which federal troops would be withdrawn from Arkansas and the Arkansas National Guard would be returned to my control.

Hodges, acting as chairman of the Governors Committee, was the spokesman from Washington to me via telephone. I remained available at the Executive Mansion throughout the negotiations to receive messages and to communicate my own thoughts and suggestions.

The negotiations, I was informed in the beginning, must be based on two points: (1) that I would assume responsibility for maintaining law and order, and (2) that I would not obstruct the integration order of the court.

I agreed to these premises and the negotiations went forward. The conference continued throughout the afternoon and into the night with a number of exchanges by telephone between me and Hodges.

Finally it was agreed that an understanding had been reached. The announcement of the understanding would be made by the White House in Washington, I was told, to be followed by my statement to the press in Little Rock.

Never was I told that my statement was to be dictated from Washington and that I must use it verbatim (as was the case with the telegrams setting up the Newport conference and the statements which followed that meeting). I was advised only that my statement must agree with the two points on which the negotiations were based.

After being advised that an understanding had been reached with the President and his advisers, and following the President's announcement from the White House, I issued my statement to the press and retired to the mansion to rest. I felt weak and relaxed but not completely relieved for I knew that problems still remained. But at least we were to get rid of the federal occupation troops.

However, before I could get settled in my reclining chair, Hodges was back on the line from Washington. He sounded disappointed, disgruntled, even angry. My statement did not satisfy the President and his advisers, I was told.

I went back to my statement and rechecked it against the two-point premise of the negotiations. I was of the firm conviction that my statement fulfilled the requirements. I declined to change it.

I had alone written my own statement and now I made my decision alone. Any advisers during the day had departed when it was assumed the understanding had been reached.

Now any aides and secretaries who remained were busily answering the telephones which were ringing constantly with calls from the press which had learned of the possible rejection of my statement by the White House.

I felt my statement was more than sufficient. If the White House and the four "moderate" governors wanted more, they wanted too much.

END OF GOP IN SOUTH LAID TO IKE

Keaton Hardy, president of the Young Republican Club of Mobile County, Ala., resigned saying he was afraid President Eisenhower had killed the Republican Party in the South.

W. O. Spencer, Republican National Committeeman for Mississippi, and two other party leaders resigned in protest of federal troops at Little Rock.

* * *

RUN OF THE NEWS

By Karr Shannon, Oct. 2, 1957

Sen. Buck Fletcher of Scott is credited with the following "solution" to the current (CHS) problem.

The proposal to Governor Faubus: Secede from the Union; declare war on the U.S.; surrender; apply for foreign aid.

THE FEDERAL STATEMENT I WAS ASKED TO MAKE

The statement, which I was told was only a suggestion, which the White House and the four governors wanted me to issue was as follows:

"At a meeting of a committee representing the Southern Governors Conference this afternoon, the President was informed, at my request, that the orders of the federal courts will not be obstructed, and that I am prepared to assume full responsibility for maintaining law and order in Little Rock.

"The President has declared that upon such assurance on my part, the Arkansas National Guard will be returned to my command, and thereafter, as soon as practicable, all federal troops will be withdrawn.

"I now declare that I will assume full responsibility for the maintenance of law and order, and that the orders of the federal courts will not be obstructed."

The statement required, if I had accepted it, that the Governor of Arkansas and all resources at his command become the vassals and the servants of the federal courts, to carry out and enforce any federal court order that might be issued.

Under such a pledge the FBI could have been sent to Alaska, the U.S. marshals gone on vacation, and any and all federal forces dispersed elsewhere. The federal judge could have ordered me to send a courier to pick up his orders, of whatever nature on any subject, and then to use state forces to carry them out, even if they were in contravention of city ordinances, county procedures, state laws and the state constitution.

At that time a federal judge had enjoined James Hoffa, newly-elected president of the National Teamsters Union, from assuming office. Suppose Judge Davies had issued an order banning an official meeting of the Arkansas Teamsters Union, and barring Odell Smith, a Hoffa supporter, from continuing as its president, an office to which he had just been re-elected.

Under the pledge demanded of me, it would have been necessary to dispatch State Police or Guardsmen to constrain Smith from his duties and break up a meeting of Teamster Union members. That might have required tougher troops than those of the 101st Airborne Division.

Of course, the court orders immediately in mind were those having to do with integration of Central High School. But the pledge I was asked to give was not confined to those orders or any other particular set of orders.

No governor of any state had ever been asked to assume such a responsibility, even when all federal court orders were proper and constitutional, which in this case they were not.

The statement which I issued went far enough to satisfy any reasonable and logical man. But I was not dealing with a reasonable official in the person of Herbert Brownell, and the President was not sufficiently knowledgeable in civil law and history to recognize the extremity of the request.

I was not surprised that McKeldin, Hodges and Collins would agree to make such a request of me. They were either unable to recognize the utter unreasonableness of the demanded pledge, or were so desirous of Northern favor in hope of a Vice Presidential call or cabinet role, that they were quite willing to play the role of servile satellites to Northern "liberal" sentiment.

I was surprised that Gov. Clement did not object to such an unequivocal pledge in a matter which concerned the federal government alone.

But Frank had also been bitten by the bug of national ambition.

These were federal court orders. In all the previous history of the Republic, no president had ever asked a state or state officials or enforcement officers, to see that federal court orders were implemented or obeyed. That had always been the duty of the proper federal officials.

Note again the assertion, "the orders of the federal courts will not be obstructed," contained twice in the statement I was asked to make. Please note that it has no reservations whatsoever as to circumstances or conditions. It was demanded that I assume the entire burden for the entire federal government for any and all federal orders by any and all federal judges, even if a judge had gone insane.

Of course, I did not know what went on in the hours-long conference. I knew only what was told to me by Gov. Hodges in the telephone messages. I agreed to the two points which were mentioned as essential to an agreement, and my statement covered them completely.

The statement demanded of me was a perfidious effort to entrap me into doing the dirty and unpleasant enforcement of the federal court orders, such enforcement being the clear and unmistakable duty of the federal government, a duty which it was now attempting to avoid in the most cowardly fashion.

That night the press was calling the Mansion after learning of the possible rejection of my statement by the President. The callers were aware of the first statement from the White House and my statement shortly thereafter in Little Rock. I took the telephone and before speaking I could hear voices at the originating point. The speakers were puzzled that my statement was considered insufficient. One speaker was vehement as he conversed with another. "What do they want of this man?" I heard him say. "He's gone far enough! His concession now must be embarrassing. Do they [the White House] want complete humiliation?"

The other reporters were in agreement with the expressions. And these were representatives of the Northern press who were not aware that I overheard a part of their conversation.

The next day the four governors, I assume with the acquiescence of the White House, sent Mr. Frank Bane, the secretary of the Governors Conference, to Little Rock to see me. His coming was made known and the press encountered him at the airport. However, Mr. Bane, an intelligent, courteous Virginia gentleman of the highest order, knew how to handle his affairs.

"Gentlemen," he told the press, "as secretary of the Conference, I am merely a messenger boy in this case. You'll get nothing from me. Any statement will have to come from the parties involved."

He came to my office and from his brief case took a typewritten copy of the statement heretofore quoted. I read it to see if there was any modification or change. There was none.

"Governor," said Mr. Bane, "I was asked to bring you this statement and ask you if you could sign it."

I read the statement carefully again, placed it on my desk, looked at the kindly old gentleman, and smiled.

"Mr. Bane," I replied, "you can see what they want me to do. They (the federals) want me to take over the enforcement of the court order and relieve them of a very unpleasant duty. It's their court order; it's not mine, and it's contrary to state law. Besides, this statement calls for an even broader pledge as to a guarantee of no obstruction to federal court orders. How do I know what will be next, and possibly in some other field. I can't do it," (sign the statement) I concluded.

"Governor," said Mr. Bane, as he folded the statement and returned it to his briefcase, "I'm just the messenger boy and the servant of all you governors. You make the decisions."

He arose to depart, and as we shook hands he added, "However, just between you and me, I don't blame you for your decision. It would possibly be mine." We parted, and this is the first time I have related his "between you and me" remark.

Still further, these federal court orders were contrary to state laws, and contrary to the state consitution which I was sworn to uphold and enforce with the clearly written penalty of impeachment and removal from office if I failed in that sworn duty. All these laws and constitutional provisions were still on the statute books. The federal authorities had failed or refused to litigate them to a conclusion, in spite of my pleas to do so in order to clarify the situation.

FROM LITTLE ROCK, ARK., MONTGOMERY, ALA., NASHVILLE, TENN., THIS STORY WOULD HAVE MADE NEWS.!!

I ALMOST DIDN'T SEE THE "RACIAL" MENTION
By Knox, Nashville Banner   10/2/57

Knox showed the hypocrisy of "The Objective Liberal Press" in dealing with the racial problem in different sections of the country. This man is reading of disorders in the New York schools. The subject of race in difficulties in the North was subdued or ignored. In the South race was often distorted out of proportion to its contribution to difficulties.

The Washington Star
Oct. 2, 1957

Two Little Words

The exact nature of the assurance wanted from Governor Faubus is not clear. The first White House statement said that the President wanted "a declaration on the part of the Governor of Arkansas that he will not obstruct the orders of the Federal courts, and in connection therewith will maintain law and order in Little Rock. ...." The second statement, coming after the Governor had responded, said the President does not believe the Governor's language constitutes "the assurance that he

intends to use his full powers as Governor to prevent the obstruction of the orders of the United States District Court." There is quite a difference between the two. The second asks the Governor to enforce the orders of a Federal Court. For the use of a Governor's powers to "prevent obstruction" of such orders is another way of saying that the Governor must use those powers to force compliance. We doubt that many Southern Governors will give that pledge in the circumstances.

SEGREGATION
By Burch, Chicago Sun Times   10/2/57

A completely false viewpoint. Negroes served in my administration as state employees, in executive positions, as members of boards and commissions, and members of the Democratic State Central Committee. Negroes were always welcome and visited the governor's office at any time about any problem they wished to discuss. Black members of the administration attended the staff meetings called by me periodically throughout my 12-year tenure. Seldom was there a day when black people were not gathered in the waiting room of the Governor's office, along with all other callers, waiting their turn to see me or a member of my staff.

COMMENTS ON LITTLE ROCK

From Texas Newspapers

The Groesbeck Journal of Oct. 3, 1957, quoted from other newspapers as follows:
    Waco (Texas) News Tribune
    As for those who have been pushing against the segregation barriers, it would be extremely helpful in the National interest if they were to begin to show

a few signs of statesmanship. They have won hands down (in the Courts) on all the big tests but they have yet to prove that their tactics in the long run are beneficial to the children they profess to be serving. There is a real danger that they could succeed in destroying the public school systems in several Southern states . . .

The Naples (Texas) Monitor

The hypocrisy of Eisenhower's demands that integration in Little Rock will proceed at all costs is pointed up in a current report from Washington, D.C., WHERE THE SCHOOLS WERE TO BE A MODEL FOR OTHERS IN THE COUNTRY.

High government officials have not availed themselves of this opportunity to be a part of a model experiment.

The President's grandchildren attend private school in a Virginia suburb.

The Vice-President's children attend a public school where their schoolmates are all white.

The Attorney General (Brownell), loud in his defense of integration, sends his children to a private school.

The Secretary of Agriculture has transferred one of his children to a predominately white school from a predominately Negro school.

The only member of the Supreme Court who has a child of school age sends her to a private school

Yet those in Washington have no tolerance for those at Little Rock who also prefer to maintain segregation.

The same hypocrisy was apparent among the members of the Congress where many of those outside the South spoke out for enforcement of the U.S. Supreme Court's decision. The cry was not for the purpose of an improved school system and better education for children, but merely for the bloc Negro vote.

The same insincerity was true of the white integrationists of Little Rock. A proposal was made to set up a three-part school system, all black schools for those who wished to send their children there, an all white school for those who desired it, and a mixed school for both black and white who wished to send their children there.

Not a single white advocate of integration had the honesty or sincerity to volunteer his or her child for attendance at the mixed school.

Any believer in Jeffersonian democracy must have faith that the quiet, collective judgment of the many is more often right than the judgment of a few who arrogate to themselves the power to judge for all, or for others. Integrationists refused this view.

BUT FAUBUS DIDN'T 'CONVICT' HIMSELF
(An Editorial)

Ft. Smith (Ark.) Times-Record, Oct. 3, 1957

Judging by news stories and statements in Washington and elsewhere, President Eisenhower wants a flat pledge that "the orders of the federal courts will not be obstructed" as a condition for withdrawing federal troops.

Governor Faubus made that pledge — but tacked the words "by me" on the end of it.

And Mr. Eisenhower was said to have objected to those two words as "hedging" and also to some other things which he declined to specify.

Now we don't think there's a man alive who could honestly make a flat pledge that there would be no obstruction whatever to the integration orders.

Too many things could happen over which he had no immediate control — and they could happen before Faubus or anybody else could do anything about it.

As a matter of fact, some things which could be interpreted as "obstructions" have happened while federal troops were right there on the scene.

So it seems to us the governor simply was being careful to confine his pledges to something he positively could make good on.
. . .

But, now, Mr. Eisenhower objected to "some other things."

There weren't many "other things" in Faubus' statement.

But he (Faubus) did state that it had never been "my intention to obstruct the orders of the federal courts," and added: "I am prepared, AS I ALWAYS HAVE BEEN, to assume full responsibility," etc.

He contended he never had intended either — and made his contention plain.

And that, we suspect, is the "other things" to which Mr. Eisenhower objected.

A congressional investigation of the use of troops in Arkansas is practically certain, we think — and if that develops, it would be a feather in the cap of the executive department to have a statement from the Arkansas governor which practically admitted he had opposed the processes of the courts or deliberately failed to enforce any law.

We darned sure can see why Governor Faubus probably has no intention of getting himself into that position.

The statement in the pledge that he DID make seemed reasonable to us.

The rejection of it did not seem reasonable.

And of this, we're pretty sure:

If Mr. Eisenhower plans to keep federal troops in Little Rock until some ONE individual is willing to GUARANTEE that there will be nothing which the justice department would call an "obstruction to the orders of the federal court," then the troops probably are in for a long stay.

Because it's doubtful anyone is going to make a pledge so broad, that events could be beyond his power to make good on it.

We don't think Governor Faubus — or anyone else — is going to do it. . . .

Maybe the lads of the 101st had just as well plan to do their Christmas shopping in Little Rock.

Faubus' Statement Went As Far
As Anyone Could Honestly Go

(The Mobile Press, Oct. 3, 1957)

President Eisenhower desperately wants to get off the hook which snared him when he sent Army paratroopers to . . . Little Rock, but his palace guard won't let him get off.

. . . the President turned down a compromise under which federal troops were to be withdrawn

... after a long conference with Brownell and Adams.

After conferring with these string pullers, the President backed out of an agreement ... made earlier with a committee of four southern governors ... to the effect that Eisenhower would withdraw federal troops ... provided Gov. Orval Faubus issued a statement guaranteeing that Faubus would not obstruct federal court integration directives and would maintain order.

Not long after, ... Gov. Faubus issued the following statement which ... goes as far toward compliance with the President's terms as was possible:

"At a meeting of a committee representing the Southern Governors Conference this afternoon at the White House, the President was informed, at my request, that it has never been my intention to obstruct the orders of the federal courts, that the orders of the federal courts will not be obstructed by me, and that I am prepared, as I have always been, to assume full responsibility for maintaining law and order in Little Rock.

"This has been consistently my stand and viewpoint throughout the controversy.

"On the basis of this assurance, the President has declared that the Arkansas National Guard will be returned to my command, and thereafter, as soon as practicable, all federal troops will be withdrawn.

"I now declare that upon withdrawal of federal troops, I will again assume full responsibility, in cooperation with local authorities, for the maintenance of law and order, and that the orders of the federal courts will not be obstructed by me."

But the White House palace guard evidently convinced their front man that this was not sufficient. They came up with the objection that Faubus had added "by me" to the last sentence.

We do not see how the Arkansas governor could commit all people ... not to obstruct federal court directives. It would have been a dishonest statement had he done so.

But the palace guard ... is grabbing at all possible excuses not to pull U.S. troops out of Little Rock. Dictatorships cannot retreat. They must go forward, right or wrong. . . .

⸎⸎⸎

THE LOST PEACE
The Wall Street Journal, New York, N.Y., Oct. 6, 1957

(An Editorial)

With the approval of the President, the following statement was issued by the White House Tuesday (Oct. 1) after the meeting with the Southern Governors:

"The President stated that upon a declaration on the part of the Governor of Arkansas that he will not obstruct the orders of the Federal courts and will, in connection therewith, maintain law and order in Little Rock, the President will direct the Secretary of Defense to return the command of the Arkansas National Guard to the Governor. Thereupon, as soon as practicable, all Federal troops will be withdrawn."

The Governor of Arkansas then issued the following statement:

"I now declare that upon the withdrawal of Federal troops I will again assume full responsibility, in cooperation with local authorities, for the maintenance of law and order, and that the orders of the Federal courts will not be obstructed by me."

This done, most of the people of Arkansas and the country went to bed with a feeling of gratitude that good will, common sense and a spirit of accommodation had brought a peaceful resolution to the tragedy of Little Rock.

But late Tuesday night Attorney General Brownell huddled with the President and the outcome was a sudden announcement that Governor Faubus' statement was "unsatisfactory." And all was as before.

The White House explanation for this sudden reversal by the President was that Governor Faubus added the words "by me" to the words "not be obstructed" ... Those two words supposedly invalidated the Governor's pledge because they pledged only himself and not others.

At the very least, this is legal flyspecking. The picture of the Attorney General hunting deviously for semantic traps in an otherwise perfectly straightforward statement by the Governor of a state has the air of reducing a great public matter to the level of a squabble between scheming litigants.

In this instance, moreover, it is hard to find the grounds for the quibble. The original White House statement calls for nothing more than a statement from the Governor that "he will not obstruct" the courts and that he will maintain law as well as order.

Both of these terms, unless the English language has lost all meaning, were precisely met by the Governor in the exact language used by the original White House statement. To find that unsatisfactory now on the grounds that it did not say something else makes the President of the United States sound like the kind of litigant who changes his terms of settlement after each requirement is met.

But there is something far more disturbing in all this than the semantic quibbling.

Little Rock has been a tragic enough matter as it is, and the foolishness of many men has contributed to it. But Governor Faubus, whatever his past mistakes, has shown that he will obey court orders (he removed the Guard when directed to) and he pledges himself not to obstruct any Federal court orders. To reject that pledge out of hand is to defeat what ought to be the one desire of everyone, a way to put an end to bayonets and let that unhappy city get on about its business in peace and order.

The sudden reversal at the White House is bound to leave the impression that what the Administration seeks is not so much a resolution of the Little Rock affair — that was in everyone's grasp on Tuesday — but rather a political victory over the Governor of Arkansas that accepts nothing less than abject humiliation.

For only if that is what is demanded does it make sense to insist upon every jot and tittle in the surrender document and to accept nothing in good faith.

WHITE HOUSE CONFERENCE TABLE

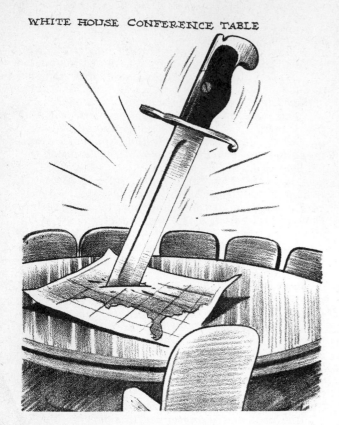

WHITE HOUSE CONFERENCE TABLE
By Knox, Nashville Banner   10/3/57

With the bayonet-wielding federal troops ruling the day in Little Rock, the bayonet dominated the conference table at the White House in Washington.

Others wrote like this:

Faubused Again
News Day, Oct. 3, 1957

Gov. Orval Faubus, Arkansas' tin-horn demagogue, has made it plain that he has no desire to maintain law and order in his state.

By blatantly double-crossing both President Eisenhower and the four Southern governors . . . Faubus proved he prefers the adulation of bigoted mobs than the respect of the decent citizens of Arkansas.

The governors . . . seriously tried to reach a solution. President Eisenhower agreed to withdraw federal troops if Faubus was prepared to assume full responsibility for maintaining law and order. The Southern governors . . . were assured he would do so. Instead Faubus issued a statement attempting to justify his actions and challenging the President.

Yesterday, Faubus made it plain . . . that his sole aim is to provoke more violence in Little Rock and thus more headline-producing notoriety for himself.

. . .

Faubus not only has disgraced his people and flouted the President, he has breached the faith with his fellow governors. As one of them, Theodore McKeldin of Maryland said yesterday: . . .

. . . *"responsible executives cannot remain silent while the spreading of the Faubus demagoguery threatens the peace, tranquility and law-abidance of other states."* . . .

STILL NO PLACE TO LAND
By Messner, Rochester, N.Y. Times   10/3/57

I hid behind a "Little Rock" ready to fire on the dove of peace. This was erroneous. Brownell and Ike were the participants who refused to put away the guns.

In downtown Rochester, the source of the cartoon, many of the buildings on which the winged creature might have landed were burned to the ground in a racial riot. All the buildings still stand undamaged in Little Rock.

➤➤

"HEEL"
By Alley, Memphis Commercial Appeal   10/3/57

My efforts to reach an understanding with the national administration had no effect on the inflexible attitude of Attorney General Brownell. This cartoon is an accurate portrayal of his position.

LITTLE ROCK!

SMOLDERING TEEN-AGE RACIAL CONFLICTS

THIS CITY OF BROTHERLY LOVE

AND IN OUR OWN BACKYARD
(Thoughtful Northerners Take a Look Around)
By Hutton, Philadelphia Inquirer,
N. Y. News & World Report   10/11/57

The "City of Brotherly Love" looking through binoculars appeared to be shocked by what it saw in the distant city of Little Rock. In the meantime the "smouldering teenage racial conflicts" of Philadelphia were getting out of hand. Without any doubt, the racial problems and animosity were more severe there than in Little Rock, and are perhaps worse now 20 years later.

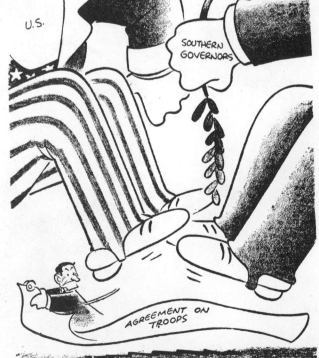

U.S.

SOUTHERN GOVERNORS

AGREEMENT ON TROOPS

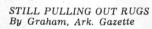

STILL PULLING OUT RUGS
By Graham, Ark. Gazette   10/3/57

The *Gazette* blamed me for the failure of Ike's conference with the four Southern governors. This cartoon and the *Gazette*'s editorial showed its inability to view events objectively and to report them fairly. It was not I who rejected the agreement. The national administration wanted to weasel out of its unpopular position and unload its enforcement responsibility on the state authorities.

NAPOLEON: 1957 MODEL
By Grenyn, Anderson, S.C. Independent   10/3/57

Ike, too, was pictured as Napoleon in the Little Rock controversy. In the background were the federal paratroopers with guns and vehicles in front of Central High School. And that was nobody's fancy or imagination. The troopers were there — vehicles, guns, bayonets and all.

A headline in a northern newspaper read:

SHOULD FAUBUS BE IMPEACHED?

Small chance there would have been for such a move in the Arkansas General Assembly at that time. Many members urged me to go even beyond the actions I had taken in my efforts to preserve control of the schools to the state and the local citizens.

Impeachment sentiment would have been strong if I had enforced the federal court order which was not a state obligation.

YOU DIDN'T SAY "CROSS MY HEART AND HOPE TO DIE"
By Somerville,
Atlanta Journal & Constitution   10/3/57

This cartoon dealt with the agreement rejected by the President and his advisers, because of the phrase "by me" in my statement. The 101st Airborne Division was kept in Little Rock, shown here sitting on me. The President's rejection of the settlement because of the two small words gave rise to Somerville's idea, "You didn't say 'cross my heart and hope to die'!"

HINNY

JOIN THE ARMY
By B. H., Source unknown   10/3/57

BH came up with a humorous appeal to be used in the U.S. Army recruiting service.

WALL STREET JOURNAL Ted Shaw

"North African campaign, Italian front, D-Day invasion, German front, Iwo Jima, South Pacific campaign, and Little Rock."

CAMPAIGN RIBBONS, 1957 STYLE
By Shaw, Wall Street Journal   10/3/57

A beribboned veteran told a new Army recruit of the various campaigns in which he had engaged. He pointed out the medals as he named them, one being for the occupation of Little Rock.

OVATION AT LIVESTOCK SHOW

I attended the State Livestock Show on Oct. 3 and appeared in the rodeo arena with Gene Autry. We received an ovation that shook the building to its rafters. Mayor Mann was seated unnoticed in the audience.

I commissioned Gail Davis, TV's Annie Oakley, an Arkansas Traveler.

SUIT FILED IN TROOP USE CASE

Mrs. Margaret Ann Jackson, Vice President of the Mothers League, filed a suit in federal court asking removal of the federal troops, declaring their presence violated the constitutional rights of her teen-age daughters, who attend the school. The defendants were Col. William A. Kuhn, commanding officer of the 101st Airborne Infantry Regiment and General Edwin A. Walker, commanding officer of the Arkansas Military District. Kenneth Coffelt was her attorney.

BUSINESS LEADERS URGE NON-VIOLENCE

25 Little Rock leaders issued a statement condemning violence and urged the citizens of the area to be peaceful. Every signer of the statement was a rich business leader in the city, and none had children who were affected by the integration of Central High School.

A TRAGIC BREW FOR AMERICA

A cartoon by Fitzpatrick in the *St. Louis Post-Dispatch*, titled "A Tragic Brew for America," said the usurpation of the people's rights by the federal judiciary concocted "a tragic brew of hate, prejudice and venom for America." The poison spread much farther than anyone could envisage at the time of the Little Rock problem.

The time came when mannerless groups shouted down speakers in public meetings. Outlaws and revolutionaries hijacked aircraft, endangering the lives of scores of innocent people while extorting huge sums of ransom for planes and passengers. Organized groups took over public buildings disrupting useful work, vandalizing and looting property to the extent of millions of dollars of senseless damage. Subversive elements invaded government offices by force and destroyed government files. Other groups took over towns and localities, occupied private property and held innocent hostages while making outrageous demands for money or other concessions.

Lawless mobs rioted in the streets, at times taking control of whole sections, defying all authority, perpetrating violence on innocent residents or passersby, burning and looting buildings and businesses for days at a time. Murder, rape and robbery became commonplace. Organized terrorism became a world-wide problem from which America was not free.

Perhaps the most tragic aspect of these episodes of hate and lawlessness was the sympathetic attitude of the federal courts and the predominantly liberal news media for the perpetrators, and the fact that little or no effort was made to apprehend and punish them according to the laws of the land. Even if apprehended and hauled into court at great effort of law enforcement agents and considerable taxpayer expense, the unruly, defiant defendants were more often freed than not by federal judges who looked diligently for any sort of technicality which could be used as a pretext for dismissal of the charges.

The federal judiciary concocted a tragic brew for America, and more and more law abiding Americans suffered therefrom day by day.

So little consideration was given the victims of this unprecedented violence and lawlessness that it seemed they had no representation in government.

DO YOU THINK WE'RE BEING AMBUSHED, By Berryman, Washington Star, 10/4/57

When I said I would stand by my original statement made following the Eisenhower conference with the four Southern governors, it gave rise to the headline, "Faubus Stands Pat." Ike showed the headline to Gen. Brucker as they discussed the federal troop order. The question of ambush was raised because the rejection of my statement left no feasible avenue for withdrawal from the unpopular federal position.

BEHIND WASHINGTON NEWS

by Bascom N. Timmons,
Chief, Democrat Washington Bureau
Oct. 3, 1954

MR. BROWNELL
SAID IT DIFFERENTLY IN FEBRUARY

On Feb. 16, 1957, under questioning from Sen. Sam J. Ervin Jr. (D., N.C.) before the Senate Judiciary Committee, Atty. Gen. Herbert Brownell Jr., made the following statement with respect to possible use of federal troops to enforce court orders in civil rights cases:

"... I think you will find the general rule is that the governor of the state must request the president."

Seven months later, September 23, Governor Faubus of Arkansas made a similar statement when President Eisenhower threatened to use federal troops to enforce desegregation . . . in Little Rock:

"It is clearly defined under the Constitution and the law that the forces of the federal government cannot be employed except on request of the governor of a sovereign state."

Less than 24 hours later, President Eisenhower ordered units of the 101st Airborne Division to Little Rock . . . without the request of Faubus.

Brownell, . . . has not shed any light on what happened in the past seven months to change his mind.

WHAT ELSE DID HE SAY?

Here are some of the things he had to say last February . . . about possible use of force to obtain compliance with federal desegregation . . .

"I am rather disturbed by you even raising these points, because, as I said so many times, public statements made by persons who intimate that there is any such thought in the minds of anyone here in Washington to use the militia in these cases does not represent the true state of the facts, and I frankly think that the only reason it can be brought into the discussion at all is to confuse the issue.

"I do not know of any responsible public official of any party of any branch of the government that has made any statement that would even lead to an inference that there is any such thought in the minds of the Congress or the courts or the executive branch of the government."

TALK OF TROOPS 'IRRESPONSIBLE'

Showing visible anger at further questioning, . . . Brownell charged that even bringing up the matter was "irresponsible" and added emphatically that *"no one has had in mind any use of the militia in this situation, and I don't think there should be any implication that they do."*

Chairman Thomas C. Hennings, Jr. (D., Mo.) . . . wanted to know if Ervin was driving at "the business that the president of the United States might send troops . . . and enforce those things at the point of a bayonet?"

Brownell's answer was flat and emphatic:

"Since there is not the slightest suggestion on the part of any responsible public official of bringing . . . the militia into the civil rights area, I think it would be misleading really to continue with an abstract discussion of a matter not pertinent . . ."

Senator Ervin, a recognized authority on constitutional law, is a hard man to stop . . .

After still further questioning, Brownell threatened to leave the hearing room if the line of questioning were pursued.

". . . I believe there is in here an implication that the president of the United States would act recklessly if not unconstitutionally, and I just cannot sit by and have the record contain any such implication of that," he said.

"I really feel this has gone far enough. It has no place in these proceedings, and I personally

cannot stay here and allow any such implication to be drawn," were his final words on the subject.

THE "IMPLICATION VS. THE ACT"

If the very "implication" that the president might use troops in the South incensed Brownell to such a point seven months ago, it is difficult to understand how the act itself has had apparently little effect on him. In fact, . . . Mr. Brownell had more than a little to do with . . . changing the "implication" into the actual fact.

WHEN THE LIGHTS WENT OUT
By Shoemaker, Toledo Blade, N.Y. Herald Tribune, Arkansas Gazette   10/6/57

It was a helpless feeling when the "Rule of Law" gave way in Little Rock. When the 101st Airborne took over, the laws ceased to have effect. Dozens of people were jailed without warrants or charges. A person could be bludgeoned, or even killed, leaving or entering his own home, if he disobeyed an order of an ordinary paratrooper. Such extreme action was not expected but it was possible, with no law or lawman for protection.

The cartoonist may have had something else in mind, but that was the way it was in Little Rock when the people's laws gave way to military force.

The Press, out-of-state newspaper

THIS MAN FAUBUS
(Oct. 4, 1947)

Even though he has been severely maligned by anti-South publications . . . Gov. Orval Faubus still looks pretty good in the fight that has developed . . . . . . this man who the detractors called an

Ozark Mountain hillbilly — and even "an uneducated farmer" — seems to be well educated and quite able in the field of politics.

In fact, he set a trap for muddling Republican political strategists into which walked President Eisenhower and his palace guard. Today, they are being chewed to pieces politically — and . . . now . . . they know it.

. . . we fail to see where the administration, coached by . . . Brownell and . . . Adams, has made the first dent in the armor of Orval Faubus as he stands firmly in defense of the rights of the sovereign state of Arkansas.

True enough, the bayonets of U.S. Army paratroopers did make a dent . . . at Central High School. But has this solved the problem? . . .

. . .

It should be humiliating to publications like TIME Magazine to observe Faubus, the man they had so cruelly belittled, standing up ably and beating Eisenhower and his political advisers at their own game.

. . . it was politics that inspired the whole chain of events . . . But the scheme has boomeranged to tear the Republican Party asunder and leave Eisenhower groping for ways out of the debacle.

And one of the chief reasons the nefarious plan boomeranged is Orval Faubus. Eisenhower, Brownell, Adams, Vice President Nixon, the U.S. Supreme Court . . . can thank or blame themselves for plummeting Orval Faubus into national political prominence.

The Kentuckian-Citizen
(Oct. 4, 1957)

USE OF BAYONETS IS AN OUTRAGE

Whether or not President Eisenhower acted within the law in sending regulars into Little Rock, . . . will doubtless be argued at great length . . . But the paratroopers' presence, which Governor Faubus called "the military occupation of Arkansas," . . . their herding school-children with naked bayonets, and with what Senator . . . Russell has called "Hitler-like conduct," supersedes theories of Constitutional law to compound an error that can not be soon erased. Yet it is only one of a series of errors that began with . . . sending a northern judge to rule on the most explosive problem of our time.

. . .

It is all very well to affirm piously that there must be law or there will be anarchy. But . . . there must be patience and understanding. . . .

It has been reported that when a paratroop officer was asked how long the regulars would stay, he replied: "Indefinitely. We stayed in Germany for years."

. . . Already the ill-advised act of Eisenhower has roused . . . feeling that was not present before his ill-starred order.

Who cares what Russia thinks of us? Will any phase of the incident look as bad as the arrival of federal troops . . . It would be far better to work for a united country here at home than to further pacify those who are plotting our downfall . . .

. . .

The president has done this nation a disservice through his use of bayonets . . .

HIS MOVE
By Williams, Detroit Free Press   10/4/57

This idea was wishful thinking. I settled down to the work of state administration and left the problems of Central High School to the federal troops and Judge Davies. They with Ike, were out on the limb in the unpopular troop occupation of an American city.

FAUBUS CHEERED AT STOCK SHOW LUNCH

Sentinel Record, Hot Springs, Arkansas
October 5, 1957

LITTLE ROCK, Oct. 4 — Gov. Orval Faubus, who has made as much news in recent weeks as any other American, got a standing ovation today from Arkansas newspapermen at an annual livestock show press luncheon.

Faubus relaxed and chatted with newsmen but made no speeches.

The only reference to the Little Rock school controversy came from the toastmaster, who quipped:

"There has been some news in Arkansas in recent weeks, Gov. Faubus began his fall television series, and the United States Army began its fall war games."

PUBLIC OPINION ON COURT RULING

A survey by the American Institute of Public Opinion showed the following sentiment in the South in September 1957:

ON THE SUPREME COURT RULING ON INTEGRATION

Disapprove the ruling -78%

Approve the ruling -16%

No opinion - 6%

SCHOOL DAZE
*By Lange, Daily Oklahoman,
Ft. Worth Star Telegram*   10/5/57

Since Army troops were now on duty in public schools, some new lessons were in order for the students. They were taught the insignia for the various ranks. Note the soldier with rifle in the doorway.

*"WHAT DID YOU HEAR ON YOUR TRIP TO
TENNESSEE, SHERM?"*
By Knox, Nashville Banner   10/4/57

Presidential Assistant Sherman Adams, after a trip to Tennessee, reported to Ike and Brownell. Sherm's burning ears attested to what he heard. He met an editorial which said the use of federal troops in Little Rock had destroyed the Republican Party in Tennessee. Papers on Ike's desk read: "Little Rock," "troops" and "force." The desk drawer was filled with golf balls and score cards.

OL' STONEWALL FAUBUS
By Grant, Oakland, Cal. Tribune   10/4/57

Federal law was not involved. The dispute was over a U.S. Supreme Court ruling. I ran into illegal federal force — not federal law. Referring to the federal troop use Sen. Mike Mansfield of Montana said on September 16, "It has no application to any law passed by Congress."

MAN BEHIND THE MAN BEHIND THE GUN
By Somerville,
   Atlanta Journal & Constitution   10/6/57

Without doubt, politics was the motivating force behind the GOP move for "over-night integration" at bayonet point in "The South." The President himself may not have been politically motivated but he yielded to his advisers and party leaders who were. The Northern Democratic bogus liberal leaders were no less imbued with selfish political motives than the Republicans.

UNCLE REMUS, 1957 VERSION
By R. D. B.,
South Deering, Ill. Bulletin   10/4/57

This drawing appeared in the *South Deering Bulletin*, a weekly publication in a Chicago, Illinois, suburb, in early October 1957, after the President and Brownell failed to get the troops out of Little Rock. "Brer Ike" got stuck with the "Tar Baby" (the Little Rock situation), and the more he struggled the tighter he was bound. His golf clubs lay where they had fallen. Brownell approached through the brambles in response to Ike's calls for help. Barred by Judge Davies' injunction of Sept. 20, I stood by as an observer.

GOVERNOR FAUBUS CAREFULLY WEIGHED OPINIONS

The New York Times
Oct. 6, 1957

By Homer Bigart
LITTLE ROCK, Oct. 5 — Orval Eugene Faubus, Governor of Arkansas, is a normally cautious politician . . .

The crisis in which he finds himself seems just as fantastic to Orval Faubus as to the rest of the world. Basically a middle-of-the-roader on racial integration, Governor Faubus cannot understand why the lightning of Federal disapproval fell on him rather than on some red-hot segregationist Governor . . .

His attitude of puzzled chagrin is understandable. Even his critics concede that Orval Faubus . . . has never made a speech that could be regarded as inciting to race hatred. He is not a typical ranter from the hill country. Even in the rough and

tumble of Arkansas politics, Faubus seems to have kept — to use his favorite word — "circumspect."

Governor Faubus . . . gave tentative approval to certain specific devices advanced in Virginia for circumventing school integration orders, notably a system of "assigning" . . . pupils on a basis other than race.

Ironically, the ARKANSAS GAZETTE, now one of the Governor's sharpest critics, thought Governor Faubus was on the right track.

FBI HOLDS GIRLS WITHOUT PERMISSION

In the Central High School controversy 15-year-old Annette Harper revealed that she was one of the girls to whom I had referred when I charged the FBI with holding two girls incommunicado for questioning. She said she was held for 4½ hours despite the FBI agents' promise to let her mother know where she was.

Sen. John McClellan
—seeks removal of troops...

Jimmy Karam
controversial figure in
Faubus camp...

ex-Gov.
Sid McMath
—emerges as spearhead of
state's liberal forces...

Atty. Gen.
Brownell—a favorite Faubus target...

...ALTHOUGH NONE IS A KEY
FIGURE, EACH PERSON PIC-
TURED HAS BEEN BUSY ON THE
PERIPHERY OF THE NATION'S
BIGGEST NEWS STORY.

Mrs. Margaret Jackson
—a leader in Mothers League
which asks closing of Central High...

Gov. Theo. McKeldin of Md.
—accuses Gov. Faubus of "double-
crossing" Southern Governors...

FRINGE FIGURES IN THE INTEGRATION CRISIS
By Kennedy, Ark. Democrat   10/6/57

The roles of McMath, Brownell and McClellan need no elaboration.

Mrs. Margaret Jackson was vice-president of the Little Rock Mother's League. The organization fought against the forced integration of the schools by lawsuits in the state courts. Through Mrs. Jackson the organization called for the closing of Central High School when it was occupied by federal troops. She filed a suit through her attorney, Kenneth Coffelt, calling for the removal of the federal troops.

Theodore McKeldin, Republican governor of Maryland, began issuing statements critical of my role at the beginning of the crisis. A well known, affable and friendly personality at the Governors' Conferences, he was known as a politician always trying to make the news. He was the only chief executive of the then 48, who had a statement ready for release on practically every subject on the agenda of the various conferences. In the Little Rock controversy McKeldin was an advocate of the Eisenhower-Brownell Combine in every sense of the word.

Jimmy Karam, at that time thought by some to be a devious character of not too good repute, was the owner and operator of a clothing store on Main Street in Little Rock. A former Little Rock Man of the Year in the *Democrat* poll, he had assisted me at critical times in the campaigns of 1954 and 1956, and during the race track controversy. I bought much of my clothing from him. He was a super salesman not easy to ignore who was often helpful and accommodating.

He had a hunger for the limelight, knew everything that was going on in Little Rock, both good and bad, was always the bearer of news of behind the scenes activities of whatever kind, and was constantly showing up at the "scene of action."

Karam's daughter was a student at Central High School at the time of the crisis which gave him a legitimate interest in occurrences there. Because he sometimes showed up with the crowds which gathered at the school, often appeared, uninvited, at my press conferences, and because his reputation at that time was not the best, the visiting press began to portray him as one of the "villians" in the crisis and one of my close associates.

One thing must be said for Karam's role in the whole continuing affair, then and later. The opposition tried by every means, devious and otherwise, to get him to join their forces and allow himself to be used against me. Although he at times seemed to waver, he never yielded to their blandishments. If Karam had chosen to join the opposition, the visiting press would have painted him as a public-spirited, law-abiding hero in the same manner as they handled Mayor Mann. Knowing Karam's yen for the limelight and his preference, the same as anyone, for good publicity, it is to his credit that he never succumbed to the opposition's persuasive offers and inducements.

Some months later Mr. Karam was converted through the efforts of Rev. W. O. Vaught, and joined the Calvary Baptist Church in Little Rock. Soon he was a noted Christian layman in great demand to give his Christian testimony in churches throughout the state. Later he appeared on Billy Graham's crusade programs, and was invited to speak in churches across the nation.

Karam's case is a good example of how the "liberal" press handles public figures in such controversies as the Little Rock Crisis. When his reputation was still questionable before his religious conversion, the *Gazette* invariably referred to Karam as "a close associate of Gov. Faubus." After he became noted as a Christian layman, the *Gazette* just as consistently referred to him as "a former associate of Gov. Faubus." Yet, there was never any change in our relationship.

NEW INDUSTRIES

A new industry announced it would open at Manila, Mississippi County, and a new building was started at Conway to house a new industry.

WINCHELL CONDEMNS

Oct. 6, 1957

Columnist Walter Winchell in a bitter, condemnatory article headed "Faubus Follies," wrote:

So, too, the problem of Faubus should be left to the people of Arkansas. After they speak at the next election, it will no longer be the National Guard barring the way to Negro children; it will be the people of Arkansas barring the Governor's mansion to Faubus.

Some forecaster! If Winchell was not better informed on other matters about which he wrote, his column wasn't very useful to readers looking for factual information.

NOT THE WAY!
By Brooks, Birmingham, Ala. News   10/6/57

Forced integration must be had in spite of the wishes of the people, in spite of adverse circumstances, in spite of danger of violence and bloodshed. Forced integration must be had if it destroyed the entire school system and education itself. For political purposes only. This cartoon said that was not the way.

The Times-Picayune
New Orleans Oct. 6, 1957
(and many other papers throughout the nation)

SAYS PRESIDENT, GENERAL TRAMPLE LAW

CITES ACT OF 1956 AND
PENALTIES PRESCRIBED

by David Lawrence

WASHINGTON — Many lawyers are writing to this correspondent from all parts of the country asking when President Eisenhower and the commanding general of the United States Army at Little Rock are going to uphold "the supreme law of

the land" and cease violating a specific statute passed by Congress which forbids the use of federal troops to enforce court orders.

The law in question — known as the "posse comitatus act" — was originally passed in 1878 but was re-stated and re-codified by Congress on Aug. 10, 1956, and now reads as follows:

"Whoever, except in CASES AND CIRCUMSTANCES EXPRESSLY AUTHORIZED by the Constitution or act of Congress, willfully uses any part of the Army or Air Force as a posse comitatus or otherwise to execute the laws shall be fined not more than $10,000 or imprisoned not more than two years, or both. This section does not apply to Alaska."

Originally this law, as passed in 1878, contained a reference only to the Army. But in 1956, when all federal laws were recodified, . . . the words "Air Force" were included.

As one lawyer, now retired from a legal branch of the armed services, writes:

"Obviously the only reason for this statute and its predecessor is to insure the people against the use of troops to enforce a court order; otherwise, the law has no meaning whatsoever."

* * *

There is, of course, no act of Congress which has "expressly authorized" the use of federal troops to enforce a court order. The three sections of federal law cited by President Eisenhower . . . have been restricted by the above-quoted "posse comitatus act."

There is moreover, no provision in the constitution by which the use of troops to enforce court orders is "expressly authorized." . . . The statutes specify the means whereby marshals . . . can enforce the laws of the United States. . . .

There are those who argue that, since the constitution itself mentions "the supreme law of the land," the President may take any means he wishes to enforce any law. The constitution says:

"This constitution, and the laws of the U.S. which shall be made in pursuance thereof; and all treaties made, or which shall be made, under the authority of the U.S., shall be the supreme law of the land."

Nothing is said to the effect that decisions of the supreme court . . . are "the supreme law of the land." As one eminent lawyer writes:

"No federal or state court of record in America has ever held that a decision of the supreme court of the U.S. or that of any other federal court is 'the law of the land.'

"Each decision is never anything more than the law of the case actually decided by the court and binding only upon the parties to that case and no others."

Since the supreme court has been reversing itself on several constitutional issues for more than 100 years now, THE USE OF TROOPS TO ENFORCE AN ORDER ON WHICH THE COURT COULD LATER BE PROVED WRONG MIGHT DO IRREPARABLE DAMAGE.

This is why the late Charles Warren, himself an assistant attorney general and regarded as the nation's most noted historian in the field of the *judiciary, says in his monumental "History of the Supreme Court of the United States," Page 748, Volume II:*

> *"HOWEVER THE COURT MAY INTERPRET THE PROVISIONS OF THE CONSTITUTION, IT IS STILL THE CONSTITUTION WHICH IS THE LAW AND NOT THE DECISION OF THE COURT."*
>
> *ONLY CONGRESS, THEREFORE, CAN PASS ANY LAW THAT BECOMES TRULY "THE LAW OF THE LAND." ONLY CONGRESS CAN AUTHORIZE THE USE OF FEDERAL TROOPS TO ENFORCE A LAW. ONLY THE PEOPLE THEMSELVES CAN AMEND THE CONSTITUTION.*

(emphasis added)

"YEAH? WAIT UNTIL YOU TRY TO SHAKE YOUR HEAD."
By Knox, Nashville Banner, Shreveport, La. Times   10/6/57

The Democratic donkey and the Republican elephant each said the other's throat had been cut by the bayonets of the troops sent to Little Rock, while thinking his own neck was still intact. Actually the cartoonist was right. Both throats were cut. The people of the South and millions more would not have voted for either of the "liberally" led Old Parties if there had been a reasonable alternative.

LATEST REPORTS, By Knox, Nashville Banner, 10/8/57

Uncle Sam, unhappily viewed through his field glasses the Kremlin in Moscow and the Russian sputnik beep-beeping around the earth. Ike, from the golf course was puzzled that the U.S. was losing the space race. Ike and Brownell were then happy to point out that they were winning the hot war against unarmed civilians and Little Rock school kids by the use of troops armed with bayonets.

CHAPTER 16
BROWNELL RESIGNS; CONTROVERSY CONTINUES
HORACE MANN HIGH SCHOOL BETTER THAN CENTRAL

RUN OF THE NEWS

By Karr Shannon in the Arkansas Democrat
October 7, 1957

While on vacation here are some of the things I read and heard.

North Dakota, home of Judge Davies, has the fewest Negroes of any state in the Union.

September 24, 1957, will go down in American history as an important date. It was the day we lost our last vestige of states' rights!

Faubus playing politics? So what! The whole thing started with Washington politics. If it's Faubus politics, it's a case of fighting fire with fire.

From Natty's Column in the Ashley County Leader, Hamburg:

Segregated suburbs (of integrated Washington, D.C.) have grown a thousand fold and it is among their schools that Brownell, Nixon, Eisenhower and other high level federal officials choose to send their school offspring — even unto the second generation.

Our Mule Barn philosopher says Faubus is still bringing in new industries. "The latest one," says he, "is the federalization of the National Guard....$95,000 a day in pay is not a bad industry." (plus the pay and maintenance of 1,100 federal paratroopers).

"HYDROFAUBIA"
By Burck, Chicago Sun Times   10/7/57

HOW'D THEY HANDLE IT IN LITTLE ROCK?
By Maples, Ft. Worth Star Telegram   10/7/57

This was a very clever play on words by the cartoonist — revision of hydrophobia, the disease which makes animals go mad. The old hound dog had gone mad with "hydrofaubia." A worse disease hit Chicago later and a large section of the city was reduced to ashes and an even greater area was sacked and looted by thousands of rioters. Nothing of that nature ever occurred in Little Rock.

Student riots against Communist rule broke out in Warsaw, Poland. The widespread disorders, attributed to "student unrest" in news reports of October 5 and 6th, were brought under control by massed police forces after several days of fighting.

Referring to the overpublicized troubles in the Arkansas capital, the Communist dictators asked, "How'd they handle it in Little Rock?"

LETTER TO "COMMANDER OF OCCUPATION TROOPS, LITTLE ROCK, ARKANSAS"

It was reported to me by parents of students attending Central High School, that the federal troops on duty inside the school had entered the girls' dressing rooms in the performance of their patrol duties. In a letter to General Walker on October 7 I called his attention to the reports. I addressed the letter "Major General Edwin A. Walker, Commander of Occupation Troops, Little Rock, Arkansas."

John W. Madden, evidently an aide of the General, signed for the letter, but Walker then returned the letter unopened as being improperly addressed.

Naturally all the responsible federal authorities denied the accuracy of the reports of the troops entering the dressing rooms. But the reports and the manner in which the letter was addressed stung the federal officials deeply. Those who supported the troop occupation were equally offended. A number of editorials sprouted across the country of which the following is an example.

A Chicago collector of famous letters requested the letter for his collection but it is still in my files.

Faubus Fails Again

Governor Faubus' fading prestige drops a few more points with his latest act in the Little Rock integration issue. In a letter which he addressed to "The Commander of Occupation Troops," he cited complaints that troops were "invading the privacy of the girls' dressing rooms" at Central High School.

Gen. Walker used good judgment and good taste when he returned the letter unopened. Because of the manner of the address Walker properly ignored the letter. Meanwhile the White House has assailed the letter as a vulgar means of trying to defame the troops at Little Rock... Troops were under orders to remain in corridors and not to enter any rooms unless summoned by a teacher. Officials said they have carried out these rules...

Note that even the biased editorial writer admitted that armed troops were stationed in the corridors and entered class rooms when requested.

AND THE PIG GOT UP AND SLOWLY WALKED AWAY, By Loring, Source Unknown, 10/18/57

This cartoon pertains to the reported entry of the federal troops into the girls dressing rooms at Central High School. When I released the information to the press my critics were agitated and angered. Cartoons such as this one were part of the reaction. The cartoonist said that by releasing the information, I got into the wallow with the hogs, and that neither the hogs or the frogs would stay with me.

Let's Have the FBI Report
On Violence in Little Rock
October 8, 1957

The first and last paragraphs of the editorial read:

To fill a hole that badly needs filling in the Little Rock story, the Justice Department some day will have to publish the secret FBI report on events that preceded the outbreak of violence at Central High School. Why not make it public now?

Continued suppression will strengthen the hands of the rabblerousers, who can claim the government is keeping the report secret because it doesn't dare to let the truth be known. Let's get the whole story on the record — now.

————

More than 20 years later the report still has not been released.

THROUGH VERMONT EYES
Burlington (Vt.) Daily News

. . . it took the President only two weeks to go back on his word and send federal troops into Arkansas.

This newspaper does not condone violence in Little Rock, but we feel that local authorities were handling the situation pretty well, despite the fact that the federal government had forced Governor Faubus to remove the Arkansas National Guard from the scene. But the people who held their heads in horror at the use of armed troops to halt integration now applaud the use of federal troops to force integration.

Eisenhower would say they aren't forcing integration but are seeing to it that a federal court order is complied with. That's splitting hairs, particularly when one considers that there was no violence at Central High School on the day the President called in federal troops.

This is the same Dwight Eisenhower who ...piously said that morals can not be legislated and that you can not force integration with bayonets.

All this has occurred, not in the streets of Budapest, not in Soviet Russia, but right here in America! Yet there are those who have insisted in the past that this newspaper is much too concerned over the encroachment of the federal government into the field of states' rights.

....Eisenhower journeyed all the way to Geneva to sit down and discuss with Communist tyrants. But he does not advocate caution, restraint or compromise in the situation at Little Rock.

Oh, no! After all, these are only American citizens and the Supreme Court already has ruled that Communists are the only people who have the right to advocate violence.

David Lawrence Says:
By What Law Are Federal Troops
Stationed In School at Little Rock?
WASHINGTON. — All over the front pages the news story was printed that Governor Orval Faubus had revealed complaints from parents claiming that federal troops were in or near the dressing rooms of the girls at Central High School.

This was indignantly denied by the Army secretary and by the White House. But nobody has denied that the federal troops actually have been patrolling the corridors.

Under what law of Congress and under what Federal Court order were the troops stationed inside a public school, and what have they been doing there?

This is a question that goes to the heart of the dispute over the illegality of the so-called "occupation." For there is no Supreme Court ruling and no law of Congress and no court order which gives federal troops the right to station themselves inside any public school at Little Rock.

Not Federal Issue

If there is disorder inside a school, it is something for the principal or the local police or the State authorities to deal with....

Editor Gives Report on Little Rock
————

NEWSPAPERS, NOT ARKANSAS
NOR FAUBUS, HURT BY PUBLICITY

Van Buren, Ark. Press Argus
by Hugh Park
Newspapers, almost to a press gave our state, our people, and Little Rock a low rating of esteem for the racial strife. Reading some of those which have been sent to our desk, you would think the world was against Arkansas, and that we had really been cast to the dung heap.

But a man close to us, who shared that same view as ours until he made a motor trip last week through 13 states to the north and east, has restored our pride. He says Arkansas is far from being hurt by the publicity that has flowed out of Little Rock like water pouring through a dynamited dam.

On the contrary, Arkansas stands higher than ever before in public esteem. Though the newspapers have missed the truth — the people have not — and Governor Orval Faubus, is as thoroughly respected in other states as he is among his own people who still stand behind him, probably three to one.

Our close friend turned in this conclusion: "I came home definitely feeling good when I discovered that everybody, but the people, is against us."

The above is a report that some of the newspaper folks may question; but this is not the first time that the American press has been mistaken — ...

* * *

What is the truth about Little Rock? Well there is no short and simple answer. But one basic fact to remember is this — you can't legislate morals....

There are deep rooted convictions against mixing of races, especially the kids in schools, and even in the North there is trouble, time and time again, more violent than that at Little Rock — but hardly so widely publicized — ...

The fact that the Texas governor pulled the same stunt last year as did Governor Faubus to prevent mob action was forgotten. The fact that the Tennessee governor had trouble last year when he waited until after the mobs formed was forgotten. Those were not deemed important then — but Little Rock was important — and should the Governor get away with what he was doing, integration was doomed; and on the other hand if the integrationists got away with their schedule, then the South was doomed.

Caught in such a web, Governor Faubus was doomed to crucifixion, regardless of how he turned. It was not the calling out of the National Guard — that brought him castigation from such newspapers as the ARKANSAS GAZETTE, whose editor is under fire from many quarters for having spiked the publicity barrage. Had Faubus put a ring of soldiers around the nine Negro children and protected them . . . he would have won the adulation of Editor Harry Ashmore, and others who have levelled their guns upon the governor.

* * *

But what about the other side — just what would have been done to the governor had he used the same tactics pursued by Ike Eisenhower? Well, he would have been scalped as clean as Ike's golf ball — you can lay to that.

* * *

So as we say, in one of these emotional upheavals there is no middle of the ground island to lodge in safety. Unless you are an extremist of one side, or the other, your lot is burdensome. Already, without doubt, you have got it figured out from our words above that this editor is a segregationist. Now if I should tell you that you are wrong, you instantly would charge me with being an integrator — or some title worse than unprintable — so you can see that the writer is caught, regardless of which way he turns, in trying to record the facts before him. How much more difficult then is it for a Governor to approach the problem of keeping the peace — without doing something to antagonize either one or both sides.

Those newspapers who have been dragging Orval Faubus down into the depths of hell may have to eat crow — and like it — before this thing is over with. The truth about Little Rock is beginning to leak out from the wreckage left by a hurricane of hate in a storm of newspaper stories . . .

~~~~~~~

NEW JOBS

The AIDC in its annual report on October 11 disclosed that 10,383 new industrial jobs were created in Arkansas in the past year. Success of the industrial program continued in its second full year of operation.

~~~~~~~

PRAYERS ON BOTH SIDES

More than 600 opponents of federal intervention in the schools joined Reverend M.L. Moser on October 11 in a prayer session at his church. Three Baptist ministers backed up by 35 other pastors conducted the service.

Reverend Robert R. Brown, Episcopal church leader of the pro-federal forces, had requested more than 200 churches to conduct prayer services for "compliance with the law". Only 85 churches conducted such services and 20 of those were Negro churches.

GUARD COST

It was calculated that it would cost the taxpayers $23 million dollars if the Guard stayed on duty a year at Central High School.

MAYBE THEY CAN BEAT THE YANKEES
By Berryman, Washington Star   10/13/57

With my hands tied with federal rope, I read a newspaper headline, "Milwaukee Braves Win the Pennant". After winning the pennant, the Braves defeated the New York Yankees to become the world champions. The implication was that I was glad someone could beat the "Yankees" since I couldn't overcome the Yankee federal government in the Little Rock struggle.

HORACE MANN AND CENTRAL HIGH SCHOOL

Cecil Allbright of the *Gazette* staff wrote of the high schools, Central and Horace Mann, on September 29, 1957:

School work has begun ... at the modern, streamlined education plant (Horace Mann) ...

Horace Mann High School for Negroes has begun its second full year of operation. The structure was opened May 9, 1956....

When it was opened, Horace Mann High was called "the acme in educational facilities" and "one of the finest Negro high schools in the South". It is so regarded today by Little Rock public school officials.

...

Virgil T. Blossom ... has this to say about Horace Mann High School.

"It is a complete facility; the very best this community could possibly offer. It has the same fine scholastic rating that Central High has — the highest obtainable from the North Central Association of colleges and secondary schools...."

"The North Central Association ... is based on the conditions of physical plant, staff, equipment, scope and other phases of educating students. Central High and Horace Mann High are judged on the same basis — not as a white school and a Negro school."

Their teachers are paid from the same salary schedule.

Each is called "a complete facility"....

Horace Mann, less than two years old, ... is modernistic to the last detail.

Horace Mann High offers a complete curriculum plus elective "extras"....

Central High School, the largest in Arkansas, will observe its 30th birthday November 17 (1957)....

Central High offers the same three general courses of education found at Horace Mann. And, as is the case throughout the system, all are co-ordinated and supervised by the same people.

The principal (at Horace Mann) is L.M. Christophe a ... Negro who holds the only doctor's degree in the Little Rock public school system other than Blossom's. Christophe has been in the system 30 years.

RUN OF THE NEWS

By KARR SHANNON, October 13, 1957

Story The Magazines Failed To Publish

Since the integration troubles started at Central High School, LIFE, TIME, and several other Northern magazines and newspapers have had a field day in publishing the seamy side of the controversy. ...they have resorted to journalistic tirades that cast aspersions upon the citizens of the entire state. Calumny, not basic facts, seems to be the stock-in-trade of some of the New York journals.

People with no other source of information ... could easily get the opinion that Little Rock provides little or no high school facilities for the Negroes. So —

Here's the factual story - devoid of bias or emotionalism - that has never been told in the slicks:

While nine Negro students attend Central High School where 1,981 white students are enrolled... 700 other Negroes go to classes at the ultra-modern Horace Mann High School... The Negro high school... is housed in a brick and metal building with the latest equipment and designs.

Schools Have Same Rating

The Negro school is less crowded . . . Last year the Negro school had one faculty member to each 19 students in average daily attendance while the white school had one teacher to each 28 . . .

The two schools have the same rating, . . . the highest any school in the nation can achieve. There are 29 faculty members for the Negro school. Fourteen have A.B. degrees and 14 have Master's degrees . . . Of the 87 faculty members at Central High, 38 have the A.B. and 48 are M.A.s . . . The same transportation facilities are available to students attending both schools, except the nine Negroes attending Central High get free transportation under military guard.

STILL BOGGED DOWN
By Kennedy, Ark. Democrat   10/13/57

The auto "Little Rock Impasse" was mired in the mudhole "Troops (federal) at Central High." A lot of people were working on the problem.

The pry pole of the four Southern Governors had already broken; Brooks Hays was still working with his pole; five Republican Southern lawmakers expressed their intention of getting into the act; the White House in Washington said "I'm hopeful;" a day of prayer was called by many churches in Little Rock, some on one side of the problem, some on the other. As indicated by my attitude, all efforts were failing.

...the Negro school cost nearly as much as the white school — $925,000. Central cost $1,500,000....

The number enrolled at the Negro school last year was 593; the number enrolled at Central High was 2,346.... The enrollment is less at Central High this year because some are attending the new Hall High School for whites in the Heights area.

Negro School Ultra-modern

The Horace Mann High School for Negroes is more modern than the 30-year-old Central High. It is a one-story affair with mezzanine-type porches and flat roofs. The classrooms surround an outlay of neat courtyards with beautiful lawns. The 37 classrooms are trimmed outside with yellow and blue pastel metals. Window space is more generous than at Central High and with the best lighting facilities today's architecture can provide.

Ample parking space is available for students and visitors. The school area ... comprises 22 acres.

Also, Dunbar School

Little Rock provides another high school for Negroes - the Paul Lawrence Dunbar. This school, dedicated in 1930, also maintains a North Central Association rating. It is a three-story red brick institution, and on the date of dedication was termed "the dream of the colored people of Little Rock come true...far beyond in beauty, and modernity, and size than the boldest had ever hoped for"...

As a practical matter and in fairness to Arkansas' capital city, all facets of Little Rock's school system should have been brought out in the avalanche of publicity that has encircled the globe. But most out-of-state newsmen, so it seems, are interested only in the shoddy side of the picture.

Gates Opened by Password: "Occupation"

CONWAY, October 14—Three Conway men in Dallas last week end had no tickets to the Oklahoma-Texas football game and forlornly stood with 10,000 other non-ticket holders trying to buy some.

Then George Curtis, a railroad agent from Conway got an idea. He improvised a sign which said: "From Occupied Arkansas; Need Three Tickets".

Almost immediately, Curtis said, a man walked up and said "you can have mine" and produced two tickets. A few minutes later a third ticket was obtained from a second man.

To top it off, Curtis sold his sign for $1.

* * *

There were many instances of this nature throughout the country.

A young man, his wife and family were driving from Arkansas to Florida. They stopped for an evening meal at a large eating establishment in a Southeastern state. Shortly after they were seated an announcement requested to know the presence of the owner of a certain automobile bearing Arkansas license plates number so-and-so.

The car belonged to the Arkansas travelers. The young man, fearing he had committed some parking transgression,

hesitantly arose and said he was the owner. Whereupon, the manager of the eating establishment came over to the table, introduced himself, and announced for all to hear that the meal, anything the family wanted, was "on the house in honor of Arkansas."

Judge Murray O. Reed, the Chancellor who issued the court order barring integration in Central High School, was traveling in the East on vacation shortly afterward. Often, as he related later, when his Arkansas car license was observed, his car was stopped as crowds gathered to ask questions and express strong support for the Arkansas attitude. When they learned the identity of Judge Reed and his role in the controversy, he was highly praised, had offers of meals and lodging and was pressed for interviews by news media.

A delegation of the Arkansas National Guard attending a national convention, upon the announcement of their presence, received a standing ovation from other Guardsmen that was unprecedented in the history of the organization's meetings.

Because of their first role in the crisis the morale of the Guardsmen was never higher. The same was true as to morale of the State Police. And never was the respect and support of the people for the members of the organizations higher than during that same period.

The reason: They were looked upon as the people's friends and protectors, rather than "enemies of the people."

STILL JUMPING
By Hesse, St. Louis Globe Democrat   10/14/57

It was ironic as I look back, to recall how the extremists of both sides of the South's racial issue viewed with suspicion my attitude toward the problem. I helped Negroes in many ways to make progress, but never encouraged at any time the interference of the federal government in strictly state and local affairs.

Yet, in spite of my record of friendship and help to Negroes in their legitimate asperations, and the progress of integration in Arkansas, this record was now overlooked, or deliberately ignored, by the extremists who favored federal intervention. Many of these Northern extremists began to portray me as a

WITH ALL DELIBERATE SPEED, Artist unknown, Chicago Daily News, 10/14/57

Ike and I were engaged in a country store checker game — "peaceful integration of Central High." Note the old fashioned stove and the sleeping hound dog. Ike was irked and impatient for my next move, but unperturbed I took my time. The caption indicated I was following the Supreme Court pace of "all deliberate speed."

southern extremist, or the tool of "Southern extremists," as in this cartoon.

The suspicion of the extreme segregationists was well known, even at the time of Governor Griffin's visit to Little Rock.

An editorial in the Monroe (La.) *Morning Sun* of October 21, quoted in part, sheds some light on the background and the situation.

Integration Cart Upset

In the race-mixing scheme mapped by Eisenhower, Nixon, Brownell and Justice Warren, Little Rock was supposed to be only a very small sideshow. Virginia was scheduled to be the scene of the real big top, "the greatest show on earth".

No violent opposition to mongrelization was expected in Arkansas for the reason that Governor Orval E. Faubus was considered by the integrationists to be no more than lukewarm at worst and it was believed he would play along with the politicians who were using integration as a means of trying to get the 10 percent of the nation's votes represented by the Negroes.

Faubus jarred the apple cart so violently that there is every reason to believe that the grand show in Virginia has been delayed to some extent.

WASHINGTON REPORT
from Arkansas Gazette, Oct. 14, 1957

FBI'S REPORT ON LITTLE ROCK TO BE MADE PUBLIC

Robert S. Allen's report on Oct. 14 said in part:

The much-discussed FBI report on Little Rock will be made public — but not for the present.

Similarly, the Justice Department is proceeding cautiously on prosecutions.

Reasons behind these backstage policies are: The explosive nature of the FBI findings which were submitted to Federal Judge Davies; and Attorney General Brownell's insistence that only "air-tight" cases be instituted against accused rioters.

The FBI is still gathering evidence . . .

This activity extends into other states. The FBI has information that certain reputed leaders in the Little Rock disturbances were not Arkansans. Also, that Governor Faubus figured in their being brought there to block the court's integration edict.

St. John Bartlett, head of the civil rights section of the Justice Department's Criminal Division, is in charge of possible prosecutions.

The 34-year-old Californian has spent some time in Little Rock . . .

* * *

This column indicates that leaders from outside Arkansas were present in Little Rock during the troubles. This tends to confirm my early contention that the city had become a focal point of contest, and therefore violence was probable.

However, the suggestion that I had anything to do with bringing anyone to Little Rock was completely without foundation. I seriously doubt that the FBI report contained any such information. Most of Allen's report is newspaper propaganda.

336

More than 22 years later no FBI report has yet been made public. No charges were filed against anyone by the Justice Department, and there were no prosecutions.

THE LESSON OF THE 101ST
By Kennedy, Ark. Democrat   10/16/57

The Democrat continued to speak against opposition to the federal court orders by the mass demonstrations. Here that route was shown to be blocked by armed federal troops, the lesson of the 101st Airborne Division. The proper way was shown to be "opposition to court orders through legal channels." However, the majority of the people felt that channel was hopelessly closed by judicial prejudice no matter what the law or evidence. A states righter or a segregationist, many people were convinced, had no chance to get justice in the federal courts.

To many that opinion was confirmed as fact when, the day following the publication of this cartoon, Judge Davies dismissed without a hearing the suit filed by Attorney Kenneth Coffelt for Mrs. Margaret Jackson challenging the legality of the federal troop use in Arkansas to enforce a court order. Davies ruled out the lawsuit on the grounds that it "raised no substantial constitutional issue."

The federal code, updated in 1956, specifically forbad the use of troops to enforce a federal court order. There could have been no clearer instance of a constitutional question. And what better example could be found of the bias and prejudice of the federal courts? Because of this prejudice, opposition to illegal control of the schools through court action was closed.

KARR SHANNON'S RUN OF THE NEWS

I still state, but not too emphatically, that Orval Faubus will not be a third-term governor. But since Brooks Hays is a whole-soul buddy to Sherman Adams, the man who runs the White House while Ike plays golf, I am withdrawing my prediction that Osro Cobb will be appointed federal judge.

Chris Finkbeiner is making a good many speeches in various parts of the state and otherwise acting like a gubernatorial candidate.

—0—

REFUGEES FROM OCCUPIED ARKANSAS

A news picture showed the bus which carried the Arkansas delegation to the National Legislative Conference in Oklahoma City with a huge sign, "Refugees From Occupied Arkansas." The bus with the sign was a major attraction all along the way and at the conference.

GALLUP POLL:
FAUBUS KNOWN TO 58 MILLION AMERICANS

The Gallup Poll revealed on October 18 that my name was known to 58 million Americans. Other prominent governors, said the poll, were known to only 3 million.

BACKSTAGE AT THE CAPITOL

GOVERNOR CAN'T CONTROL INTEGRATION RESISTANCE

by George Douthit
October 20, 1957

Arkansas' Governor Faubus has become a nationwide symbol of resistance to integration, but few people understand that he does not control either the resistance or the removal of it.

Opposition to integration is ingrained deeply in thousands of individuals — in Little Rock, in Arkansas and in the South. Nothing Mr. Faubus can do or say can change that.

So long as he moves in the direction they want him to move, he is their accepted leader and they will cheer him. Anytime he reverses himself and starts enforcing integration, they will desert him.

It should be evident that Arkansas' governor does not have the power to turn the resistance to integration on and off like a water faucet.

ARKANSAS FARM BOY
By Poinier, Detroit News   10/19/57

My critics accused me of political motivation in my actions in the Central High School crisis. Here I busily filled pail after pail with milk — "Third Term Political Capital" — from the cow, "Little Rock Integration Problem." According to many Northern writers my actions were unpopular even in Arkansas. If this were the case, how could I possibly profit politically from the situation?

...the removal of Mr. Faubus from the political scene would not remove the resistance of Arkansas people to integration.

Some of the large magazines in the North are leaving the impression to the rest of the nation that if Governor Faubus had kept still that integration would have gone off very smoothly in Arkansas. Here is one writer that knows better.

LONG TIME

Integration is going to be a political issue in Arkansas long after Mr. Faubus decides to . . . leave the political furnace to someone else to stoke.

Any person planning a political race next summer in Arkansas will have to make known his stand in the integration matter. A former politician told us last week:

"I told a county clerk in Arkansas that there isn't a thing he can do about segregation one way or another but when he seeks re-election next summer he's going to have to announce himself on the question one way or another."

What we are trying to point out is that the integration problem in Arkansas is created by the people, not by the politicians. The people are expecting the politicians to do something about it.
. . .

We do know this. When Vice President Richard Nixon accused Faubus of causing it all, the GOP No. 2 man really meant that if the governor had enforced integration at Central High School the Republican administration wouldn't be in its present pickle.

But what kind of a fix would Mr. Faubus have been in with his people in Arkansas?
. . .

GOVERNOR FOLSOM (Ala.)
EYES GUARD DISCHARGE

Governor James E. Folsom said he would discharge every member of the Alabama National Guard if any attempt were made to call the troops into federal service to enforce racial integration.

TEXANS CONDEMN IKE

A group of Texans on October 22 denounced integration by force and condemned the use of U.S. troops to enforce federal court orders.

* * *

IKE SAYS TROOPS NOT 'INTEGRATORS'; FORCE DISPATCHED TO UPHOLD COURT RULING, PRESIDENT ASSERTS

TAMPA, Fla. — Enforcement of integration was not the basis of the decision to send federal troops to Arkansas, President Eisenhower has advised Rep. A.S. Herlong of Leesburg.

Rather it was the need to sustain decision of the courts, he added in a letter.

(Of all the hair splitting ever attempted in any controversy, this case probably takes the prize.)

GAZETTE PUBLISHER HITS FAUBUS, PROVINCIALISM

Arkansas Democrat, October 22, 1957

NEW ORLEANS — Hugh B. Patterson, Jr., publisher of the Arkansas Gazette, predicted the next Congress will enact a forceful civil rights bill. And he said Governor Faubus will be the person to blame for it.

Patterson called Faubus the "mad-man who tried to deceive the president of the United States."...

Despite Faubus' recent set-backs, Patterson said, he believed the Arkansas governor would be elected if an election were held tomorrow.

He said the main fault of the Arkansas residents is that they suffer from provincialism....

AND ALL I WANTED WAS A THIRD TERM
By Stockett, The Afro-American   10/19/57

The use of federal troops in the Little Rock problem turned loose a ferocious beast which was about to devour me. The wish was father to the cartoon thought.

FLORIDA WOULD CLOSE UP SCHOOLS IF TROOPS CAME

By Earl Mazo

TALLAHASSE, Fla., Oct. 22, — Governor LeRoy Collins has signed a bill closing any public school in Florida to which Federal troops may be sent to enforce integration. The bill was passed by the special session of the Legislature, which Governor Collins had called....

Although continually touted as a "moderate" Governor Collins signed into law a school closing bill far stronger than any similar measure ever enacted in Arkansas.

By Karr Shannon,
October 22, 1957

By Karr Shannon, October 23, 1957

THE TROOPS ARE THERE TO ENFORCE WHAT LAW?

Why are troops — airborne infantrymen and National Guardsmen — in control at Little Rock's Central High School?

The official answer: "To see that the federal law is obeyed." Sometimes the answer from authoritative sources is modified thusly: "To see that federal court orders are obeyed."

But what is the "federal law" that is being forced to obedience?

The last sentence in the 14th Amendment...reads thusly:

"The Congress shall have power to enforce, by appropriate legislation, the provisions of this article."

The Congress has not enacted a single law relative to integration of races in the public schools — neither before nor since the Supreme Court's ruling on May 17, 1954.

Therefore there is no law that requires integration of Negroes with whites.

Since the troops occupied CHS, President Eisenhower has been asked to quote the law that the troops are enforcing. Attorney General Brownell has been asked to quote the law....

QUESTION FOR IKE

Some two weeks ago Governor Timmerman of South Carolina issued a statement which . . . said in part:

"I publicly call upon General Eisenhower to tell the American people what law he thinks armed terror troops were sent to Little Rock to enforce. Vague references to law and order or courts are no answer...."

NO ANSWER!

The palace guard greeted the statement with deafening silence.

Eisenhower did not quote the text of the law he had sent the troops to enforce. He did not name the law. Brownell has never opened his head. And the same goes for his partners in political club-swinging and the allies and underlings thereof.

The reason: There is no law to quote....

The Supreme Court ordered integration "with all deliberate speed." Deliberate, Websterly speaking, means "slow in action, unhurried, studied, premeditated."

"Deliberate speed" would give Congress time to enact "appropriate legislation," as required in the 14th Amendment. Congress has not enacted ANY legislation...ANY law. Hence there is no "law of the land" that requires integration. That's the reason Ike, Brownell & Company ducks when asked to give the text of the law that troops were sent to CHS to enforce.

—o—o—o—o—

Overheard: FBI agents go in pairs so they can take care of all the double-talk.

Political club-swinging

From a reader: "You stated in Sunday's column that Arkansas ratified the 14th Amendment April 6, 1868, but did not approve the State Constitution of 1868 (the one sent down from Washington) until April 23, the same year, and Congress did not reinstate Arkansas as a full-fledged state until July 28, still the same year. Then, according to Congress' own terms, Arkansas was not a state at the time she ratified the 14th Amendment but the ratification was "counted." Did I understand you right?"

You did. It was all a sordid, fraudulent mess. But the political club-swinging of Thad Stevens made it "legal" back in that day, just as the political club-swinging of Brownell, Warren, et al, makes things just as absurd "legal" today.

An experienced member of the press said Governor Faubus is hard to handle in a press conference. "He can duck under the 5th Amendment without even taking the 5th Amendment," he said.

TEXAS SOLONS SCORE IKE ON USE OF TROOPS

AUSTIN, Texas October 24 — (A resolution of the Texas House of Representatives) condemning President Eisenhower's dispatch of federal troops to Little Rock was ... passed by a vote of 112 to 24 after hours of some heated argument.

It charges President Eisenhower disregarded every precedent of law and the federal constitution in sending troops to Little Rock. It also declares Arkansas was deprived of its constitutional rights "at the point of federal bayonets."

JOE GARAGIOLA COMES TO TOWN

Joe Garagiola, former St. Louis Cardinal baseball player, then on the public speaking circuit, was the speaker for the Little Rock Rotary Club on October 24. News reports said he batted 1,000.

LITTLE ROCK 'MISTAKE' BRINGS BROWNELL'S SUDDEN DEPARTURE

By Jack Cleland, Democrat Washington Bureau.
Oct. 24, 1957

WASHINGTON — The "mistake" at Little Rock prompted the resignation of Attorney General Herbert Brownell, Washington sources indicated today. . . .

Brownell's resignation...was prompted by the international repercussions of the president's use of bayonet-wielding paratroopers to restore order in Little Rock.

It is conceded that the use of federal troops and the federalization of the Arkansas National Guard was a decision of Brownell...

Departure Gives Hope to Faubus

Governor Faubus said "I hope his resignation means a change in attitude of the attorney general's office from political motivation to impartial enforcement of the federal laws.

"Under his (Brownell's) leadership he has made the FBI a political arm of the national administration rather than the impartial law enforcement agency it once was."

William P. Rogers, Deputy of Brownell, took over as Attorney General.

"HUP - TWO - THREE - FOUR . . . !"
By Alley, Memphis Commercial Appeal   10/24/57

Herbert Brownell suddenly resigned as U.S. Attorney General. Through his maneuvering the 101st Airborne Division was sent to Little Rock. The improper use of the 101st troops pushed Brownell out of office. Thus the 101st soldier counting cadence as Brownell marches to the exit of the Attorney General's office.

Teamsters Turn Out For Fete;
Upward of 5,000 Jam Coliseum
For 20th Anniversary

I was the speaker at the Arkansas Teamsters Union anniversary banquet in the Hotel Marion ballroom, held on October 25 in honor of state president Odell Smith. Other state officials at the table of honor were Secretary of State C.G. "Crip" Hall, Labor Commissioner Clarence Thornbrough, and Roy Finch, an assistant attorney general.

—0—

TAKE BACK GUARDSMEN

On October 25 I took back 8,500 Arkansas National Guardsmen who were defederalized, and asked Congress to investigate why 1,800 were still being held on federal duty.

Assistant Adjutant General William C. Page was named acting adjutant general to command the returned Guardsmen. Adjutant General Sherman T. Clinger was retained on federal duty.

NEW INDUSTRIES

In industrial news the following new manufacturing plants were announced in the state. Monsanto Chemical Company at El Dorado; Chemical Processing Company at Magnolia, both on October 24; a plant to manufacture pre-fabricated houses at Dumas on October 25.

ANOTHER NORTHERN JUDGE

Another Northern federal judge, Richard E. Robinson, Omaha, Nebraska, arrived in Little Rock for a six-months assignment.

NAACP FILES SUITS

The NAACP filed lawsuits challenging all the 1957 legislative acts pertaining to integration and city ordinances pertaining to activities of the Arkansas NAACP.

STILL THE TOP ORDER OF BUSINESS
By Knox, Nashville Banner, Commercial Appeal   10/27/57

Protests against the illegal use of troops to enforce a court order at Central High poured in to the President's office from all across the nation. This cartoonist ranked the problem of troop removal from Little Rock above all others.

"IT'S NOTHING REALLY ... I'VE BEEN PLANNING TO RESIGN ALL ALONG."
By Kennedy, Ark. Democrat, 10/25/57

Herbert Brownell's sudden resignation brought Kennedy's version of the cause. It is my information, that the President finally learned that he had been misinformed at the Newport conference by the Attorney General, whereupon he dismissed his cabinet member. My Washington informants, one of them now a federal official with a lifetime appointment, said that when Eisenhower learned of Brownell's wrong advice there was the "greatest temper tantrum ever seen in the White House by an infuriated president."

Eisenhower peremptorily fired Brownell, but other White House advisers prevailed on the President to permit the attorney general's departure to be announced as a resignation.

LEFT---FACE! FORWARD---MARCH!

EXIT

LEFT FACE! FORWARD MARCH!
By Knox, Nashville Banner   10/24/57

Brownell, once known as the grand political strategist of the Eisenhower administration, now had to shoulder the responsibility for the giant bayoneted rifle, used in Little Rock at his instigation. "Left face" headed him toward the exit; "Forward, march" took him through the door and out of the government.

RUN OF THE NEWS

By Karr Shannon, October 26, 1957
Queen Elizabeth made headlines, but Faubus continues the most headlined man of the year.
A lot of folks are saying we can settle the integration dilemma in the courts. But . . . we can't settle anything in courts so long as the courts dismiss cases without so much as a hearing, as Davies did the one attacking the CHS troops.

MRS. LORCH SUBPOENAED BY SENATOR

By John R. Starr, Associated Press Writer,

October 27, 1957

Mrs. Lee Lorch, a white woman was subpoenaed to appear before a Senate Internal Security Subcommittee in Memphis tomorrow.

Mrs. Lorch, wife of a white mathematics professor at the Philander Smith College, promptly charged that there was "a connection between the subpoena and my helping the Echford girl."

Mrs. Lorch's 43-year old husband was cited for contempt of Congress in 1954 for refusing to answer questions about his Communist background asked by a House UnAmerican Activities Subcommittee.

Mrs. Lorch on October 27 in Memphis refused to go into executive session with the Senate Committee investigating Communist activity in the South. She likewise ignored Republican Senator William E. Jenner's warning that she might be in contempt of the committee by her refusal. She also ignored the advice of Committee Council to obtain legal advice and the offer to allow her time to do so.

On October 30 Mrs. Lorch created a disorderly scene by defying the committee. She refused to answer any questions and attempted over and over to read a prepared statement she brought to the hearing.

The Senate committee told the press it was considering whether to cite her for contempt. However, no contempt citation was issued and Mrs. Lorch successfully avoided giving any information about her alleged Communist activities.

* * *

TROOP USE ILLEGAL, EXPERT SAYS AUTHORITY ASSERTS IKE OVERSTEPPED POWERS IN CRISIS

October 28, 1957

WASHINGTON — *A former dean of the University of Washington Law School said today President Eisenhower overstepped his powers in using federal troops in the Little Rock school segregation dispute.*

Alfred J. Schweppe of Seattle, former teacher of constitutional law, contended there are no laws of the United States authorizing the president to assist the U.S. marshal in enforcing federal court decrees.

In a copyrighted article in . . . U.S. NEWS & WORLD REPORT, Schweppe said "Congress intended no such law of the United States to be in existence."

The president, he said, "does not have by virtue of constitutional office alone, the power to execute federal court decrees by force of arms. Federal court decrees are not laws of the United States but merely adjudications between particular parties and are merely the 'law of that case.' If the president has that power today, it must exist by virtue of some act of Congress."

But, Schweppe adds, Congress has made no such laws and has "left the entire enforcement of federal-court decrees to the U.S. marshal and his posse comitatus . . ."

* * *

SMITH BECOMES POLICE CHIEF

Eugene Smith of the Little Rock police, was named acting Chief of the Department on October 29 to succeed Marvin Potts who resigned.

RUN OF THE NEWS

By Karr Shannon in the Arkansas Democrat,
October 30, 1957
David Lawrence and the "14th Amendment"

A mistaken belief — that there is a valid article in the Constitution known as the "Fourteenth Amendment" — is responsible for the Supreme Court decision of 1954 and the ensuing controversy over desegregation of the public schools of America.

No such amendment was ever legally ratified by three fourths of the states of the Union as required by the Constitution itself.

The so-called "Fourteenth Amendment" was dubiously proclaimed by the Secretary of State on July 20, 1868. The president shared that doubt.

There were 37 states in the Union at the time, so ratification by at least 29 was necessary to make the amendment an integral part of the constitution. Actually, only 21 states legally ratified it. So it failed of ratification.

———

The foregoing is an excerpt from an editorial by Editor David Lawrence in a recent issue of U.S. News and World Report.

Karr Shannon then added:

Many historians have recorded details of the sordid manner in which the 14th Amendment was "adopted". Public records and history books of the Southern states, *** lend conclusive evidence that David Lawrence is absolutely right in his contention that the 14th Amendment was fraudulently adopted...

There were many discussions and arguments by many people, some of them learned scholars, based on historical facts concerning the fraudulent adoption of the 14th Amendment. However, they were of no avail. No matter how illegal the ratification of the 14th Amendment, no U.S. authority was going to do anything about it. The question was moot. The amendment would remain a part of the U.S. Constitution.

When a superior force determines to work its will by whatever means on an inferior force, all documents, no matter how wise, fair or valid, become mere scraps of paper. They are of no consequence irrespective of all arguments to the contrary. On the other hand any kind of legal-sounding jargon is used to justify illegal use of superior force. Such was the situation following the Civil War, and such was the case in the Little Rock school controversy.

APPOINTMENTS, OCTOBER 1957

C. Hugh Wyman, Little Rock, Board of Accountancy. Eagle Street, Cave City, Board of Public Welfare. Dr. George Cone, Osceola, Board of Dental Examiners. Dr. Hugh R. Edwards, Searcy, Medical Board. Dr. Hardy G. Wilcoxen, Fayetteville, Psychology Examiners Board. Board of Massage: Julian L. Aldrich, Little Rock; Salome May, Atkins; Fred Farmere, Jr., Hot Springs. W. R. Legg, Little Rock, native of Nashville, Tenn. to AIDC as Senior Communications Engineer. Robert E. Howell, West Memphis, director of Water Conservation Commission, announced by Chairman Marvin Melton. Dr. Bernard Paul, Ft. Smith, Chiropody Examining Board. T. E. "Tom" Tyler, Little Rock, legislative member of the Regional Board of Southern Governors Conference, to succeed Rep. L. H. Autry of Burdette.

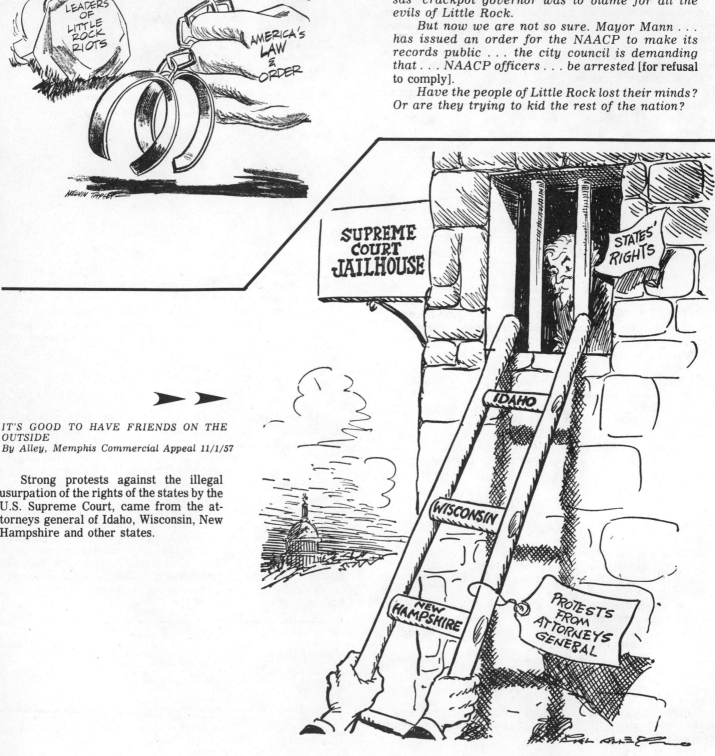

The law and order suggestion came from a strange source. There occurred more violence, injury and death from mob action in one week in New York, than transpired in Arkansas in its 148-year history of statehood.

An editorial in the same paper said:

We have just about lost all patience with Little Rock. There was a time when we felt that Arkansas' crackpot governor was to blame for all the evils of Little Rock.

But now we are not so sure. Mayor Mann . . . has issued an order for the NAACP to make its records public . . . the city council is demanding that . . . NAACP officers . . . be arrested [for refusal to comply].

Have the people of Little Rock lost their minds? Or are they trying to kid the rest of the nation?

IT'S GOOD TO HAVE FRIENDS ON THE OUTSIDE
By Alley, Memphis Commercial Appeal 11/1/57

Strong protests against the illegal usurpation of the rights of the states by the U.S. Supreme Court, came from the attorneys general of Idaho, Wisconsin, New Hampshire and other states.

CHAPTER 17
DAISY COMPANY COMES TO ROGERS; BROYLES TO UNIVERSITY.
GOP LOSES ELECTIONS; GOVERNORS MEET AT HOT SPRINGS.
FIRST 9-MONTH SCHOOL TERMS FOR ALL STUDENTS IN ARKANSAS HISTORY.

GOVERNOR'S OFFICE IS BUSY
ANSWERING LETTERS BACKLOG

The governor's large reception room was converted into a big typing center. More than 250,000 letters had already been received and more were still coming in the mail. The work of answering and filing the letters was done by volunteers or the workers were paid by voluntary contributions. The contributed funds also paid for postage and supplies. Arch Tipton of my staff assisted in this work.

LIONS INTERNATIONAL BOARD AT HOT SPRINGS

On November 1, I addressed a meeting of the Board of Directors of Lions International and received an excellent welcome and attention. Delegates from 82 Nations gathered at Hot Springs where Edward G. Barry, Little Rock, president of the international organization, presided over the sessions.

LOSS OF TEACHERS CHECKED,
FORD TELLS NLR KIWANIANS

Education Commissioner Arch Ford told a North Little Rock audience of Kiwanians that the turnover of teachers in Arkansas, both black and white, was now ten per cent, equal to the national average. The turnover was checked by the increase in teachers salaries provided in my program adopted by the 1957 General Assembly.

FUNDS FOR HELENA BRIDGE

On November 5 the Arkansas Highway Department pledged $5,250,000 for construction of a new bridge across the Mississippi River at Helena.

Progress in all fields continued.

SEGREGATION VOTE STRENGTH SURPRISES;
COUNT CHALLENGED

The talk of the town following the election for the new board of managers for the new city manager government, was the surprising strength shown by the slate of candidates endorsed by the Capital Citizens Council. Even the *Gazette* wrote the "strength had not been anticipated," and that "all six races were hair-breadth close" in which the GGC candidates were winners.

The most decisive winner was Letcher C. Langford, a Capital Citizens Council endorsed candidate, over Leland F. Leatherman of the GGC slate.

All candidates attempted to avoid an integrationist label, but Leatherman, a fine man and able attorney, was a member of the McMath law firm and McMath was openly identified with the integrationists. For Leatherman the McMath association could not be denied and it proved fatal to his candidacy.

The Citizens Council was elated with the one decisive victory and the showing made in the other races. Another fact add-

ed to their satisfaction — no candidate known as an integrationist had been elected. The main theme of the GGC was to establish stable, efficient city government and get rid of the weak and inefficient Mayor Mann who had been a lackey for the integrationists.

If the Citizens Council vote had not been split among various candidates, they would have swept the field against their better known opponents of the Good Government Committee.

Even then a strange alliance was necessary to give the GGC candidates victory. The rich, white residential section of the city, whose residents had little concern about integrated schools because of segregated Hall High, joined with the bloc vote in the Negro section in support of the GGC. Without doubt all Citizens Council endorsed candidates received a majority of white votes but the strange alliance denied victory to six of their seven candidates.

GGC winners, able, respected citizens, were Warren Baldwin, H. L. Winburn, Mrs. Edgar F. Dixon, D. W. Blankenship, Leo H. Griffin and Werner C. Knoop.

DAISY AIR RIFLE COMPANY WILL MOVE TO
ROGERS; A $10 MILLION DOLLAR OPERATION

Cass S. Hough, Executive Vice President of Daisy Manufacturing Company, said on November 8 the company would leave the town it founded in Michigan 70 years ago. "The situation in Michigan deteriorates daily," Mr. Hough said. The plant was moving to Arkansas, according to Mr. Hough, because of more favorable tax base, the state's interest in new industry, high productivity of workmen, the pay scale, a good business climate and more moderate weather.

The plant would provide 600 new industrial jobs in the Rogers area.

AEA TO FIGHT SALES TAX REPEAL

The Arkansas Education Association on November 7 announced organizational plans to fight the repeal of the 3% sales tax. The tax, enacted by the 1957 General Assembly, provided millions of dollars of additional state funds for the public schools.

In a private conference with me, AEA Executive Secretary Forrest Rozzell said, "Hell, Faubus, you've got to run again (for a third term) to save the program we all worked so hard to pass."

A survey published in the *Gazette* revealed that I was still very popular with the teachers. The Little Rock crisis did not alter their feelings after my all-out support of an adequate program for education.

NEW INDUSTRY AT HOPE

A new industry, Wire Products, from Holland, Michigan, located at Hope in Hempstead County.

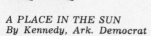

The Daisy Manufacturing Company, maker of the world famous Daisy Air Rifle, announced its forthcoming move to Rogers.

William Loeb, publisher of the *Manchester Guardian* contacted me personally about the matter. Loeb, a close personal friend of Cass Hough, the head of the Daisy Company, asked me to get in touch personally with Mr. Hough (pronounced Huff) to assure him of a warm welcome, which I did. My personal effort may have had no bearing on the eventual decision, but I mention it here out of gratitude to Loeb and satisfaction with the company's move to Arkansas.

I liked all the inducements except the lower wage scale. Arkansas workers are worth as much as the workers of other states.

Cass Hough later became a well-known Republican leader, a trusted political aide of Winthrop Rockefeller and Chairman of the AIDC.

DISILLUSIONED SNIPE HUNTER
By Seibel, Richmond Times Dispatch   11/10/57

The pale moonlight shadows revealed the barren trees of the "elections in New York City and New Jersey," and fell across a forlorn waiting Republican elephant. Taking his position at "Little Rock," he held a bag labeled "Hopes of capturing the Negro vote in the North."

Sending federal troops to Little Rock to enforce integration at bayonet point proved futile in capturing the Negro vote for the Republican Party. The Republican elephant now realized he was the victim of the age-old trick — the snipe hunt — as he sat in the lonely darkness holding the empty bag.

HOPE FADES FOR CHS CONVICTIONS; ROGERS FEARS FBI EVIDENCE NOT SUFFICIENT

By Jack Cleland,
Democrat Washington Bureau, Nov. 10, 1957

WASHINGTON — *The hopes of Brownell to obtain conviction of the persons who took part in the September 23 disorders at Little Rock Central High School appear to be no longer held in the Department of Justice.*

Neither the new attorney general, William Rogers, nor St. John Barret, head of the Civil Rights division, are satisfied that the evidence obtained by the FBI is sufficient to convict.

Rogers is reported to be under heavy pressure from the NAACP to obtain indictments.

Upward of 50 FBI agents participated in the investigation following disorders at the school.

Perhaps the main reason for no prosecutions for opposing Judge Davies' injunction of non-interference with integration at CHS, was because a trial would have revealed the double-dealing of the school authorities. Likewise much evidence of probable disorder would have been disclosed, thus giving the lie to the position taken by school officials, Mayor Mann, the *Gazette*, Judge Davies and the Justice Department.

In such trials evidence of my reasons for using the Guard would have been disclosed. Rather than risk the discredit of my critics, the Justice Department and its allies in Little Rock, chose to let the rioters of September 23 go free without prosecution.

HOAX SEEN IN GUARD 'RELEASE'

Token Discharge Denounced by Searcy Paper
November 11, 1957

SEARCY — *The SEARCY CITIZEN said today in a page-one editorial "The families and employers of 38 members of the Searcy Service Co. of the federalized National Guard were the victims this weekend of a cleverly contrived hoax which was carried out either on orders of or with approval of the United States government."*

The newspaper referred to an announcement by the Army that the company would be defederalized at midnight Saturday and said families expected the men home.

The CITIZEN said later it developed that only 17 guardsmen were released and the other 38 were sinply transferred.

"We demand," the editorial said, "that the military either release forthwith the members of the Searcy unit of the guard or give some satisfactory explanation of the hoax perpetrated in keeping them on duty."

The *Citizen* was edited by Perrin Jones with M. P. Jones publisher.

NEW INDUSTRY FOR MAGNOLIA

A new $3 million industrial plant announced on Nov. 12 its location at Magnolia. The coming of this and other new industries was proof that the Little Rock controversy was having little if any effect on the industrial program.

The lead in a long story in *Look Magazine*, Nov. 12, 1957:

THE REAL LITTLE ROCK STORY

Governor Faubus' defiance: How it really started — Who was behind it What stirred up the mob

by FLETCHER KNEBEL
Look Washington Bureau

The day Gov. Orval Eugene Faubus called out the Arkansas National Guard, he told William J. Smith, his personal attorney and close friend: "I can't win, Bill."

The governor sat in his high leather-backed chair behind a plywood-veneer desk. The place was the governor's office in the state capitol in Little Rock. The time was 3 p.m., Monday, Labor Day, September 2, 1957, less than 18 hours before Little Rock's Central High School was due to open its doors to Negro students for the first time.

"If there's trouble or violence out there tomorrow, the integration crowd will say I provoked it by bringing in troops," said Faubus.

"But if I don't call the guard and some children are killed, the other side will say the blood is on my hands. I've got to act on the side of safety. When I testified in Chancery Court last week, I said there might be violence. Now, I'm convinced of it."

Was this a sincere man voicing the dilemma of authority, or was he a man who had yielded to the pressure of racial extremists and who sought to rationalize his surrender? Only Orval Faubus knows the true answer, but his countrymen may judge him by what actually happened.

Events leading to the showdown . . . had rushed with a kind of Wagnerian fatalism in the last 13 days in the slow, orderly city of Little Rock.

The first incident occurred August 20, when Governor Faubus telephoned Gov. Marvin Griffin of Georgia, No. 1 spokesman of Dixie resistance, at Atlanta. Griffin was due in Little Rock two days later to address the Capital Citizens Council . . .

"Governor," said Faubus, "I've heard that one of your party may make inflammatory statements here. Our town is tense. If that's true, I'd rather you wouldn't come."

"Naw," said Griffin. "I'm gonna give 'em hell on the Constitution and Roy (Roy V. Harris, former Georgia state senator and Citizens Council leader) is gonna give 'em hell on the civil-rights thing. But nobody will advocate violence."

"In that case," said Faubus, "you're welcome. You and your party come stay at the mansion. I'm speaking out of town that night, but you have breakfast with me."

Harris Sets Them Straight

When the Georgians arrived at Little Rock . . . state troopers met them. Governor Griffin took the honors. Harris pulled a Capital Citizens Council delegation aside. He explained why his party had accepted the mansion invitation from Faubus, then considered by segregationists to be a "moderate" in the grip of enemy advocates of integration.

"Why," said Harris, "havin' us at the mansion's the worst thing could happen to Faubus. It'll ruin him with the integrationists and the liberals."

That night of August 22, Griffin and Harris spoke at a $10-a-plate Capital Citizens Council dinner . . . A crowd of 350 heard Griffin vow that Georgia public schools would never be integrated while he was governor. Harris went further and said the guard, state patrol and posses would be used to keep Negroes out of the schools.

"That's what put Faubus on the spot," Harris recalled later.

—0—

RUN OF THE NEWS

By Karr Shannon, Nov. 14, 1957

REPORT ON BROOKS HAYS

The Reporter magazine, ultra-liberal New York publication which has been highly critical of Governor Faubus, carries an article in the Nov. 14 edition captioned "Mr. Hays of Arkansas Meets His Responsibilities."

The magazine says that Congressman Brooks Hays "has been profoundly disturbed by the events which have followed that 'terrible Monday' when the trouble in Little Rock prompted him to call his old friend Sherman Adams and ask if there was anything he could do to help."

The article states that it is Mr. Hays' conviction "that the Supreme Court decision on integration must be upheld in Little Rock." "He (Mr. Hays) considers himself a moderate," the magazine says.

"In Little Rock," Mr. Hays is quoted as saying, "the governor is not seeking the favor of the city but of the county-courthouse politicians. In his bid for their support, he is making a coldly calculated response to a political situation."

The above excerpt from Shannon's column showed that Congressman Hays, when away from home, was not as discreet in his remarks on the Little Rock situation as he was while in Arkansas. Although he may have been sincere his remark about my attitude toward county politicians was in error.

It was not the politicians generally who were aroused. It was the people. In this Hays completely misjudged the situation.

The report certainly harmed Mr. Hays' standing with the Arkansas people as well as the county-courthouse politicians. The statement "that the Supreme Court decision on integration must be upheld in Little Rock" attributed to Hays was extremely harmful to his political standing.

The magazine article may have been unfair to Hays but if so he should have said so for his own protection. It was in error when it said Hays was prompted to call Adams by the "events which followed that terrible Monday." Hays was in touch with Adams long before that. In fact the Newport conference was arranged and held ten days before the "terrible Monday" in Little Rock.

SAME TURNING POINT

An editorial in the *Gazette* began:

In a quiet, reflective interview with Relman Morin . . . Governor Faubus has restated his position in the Little Rock school crisis without wrapping it in the bombast that has characterized his essentially political statements on the subject.

The only conclusion, however, is that the governor is right back where he started.

A cartoon showed my stand as getting nowhere, while the 'school board' was off on the road of "compliance with law and order."

But the people of Arkansas kept asking "what law?" Their Congressmen had not enacted any law giving the federal government authority to control local and state supported schools.

Many great constitutional lawyers kept making the same query.

So the question remained unsettled, and it is yet unsettled. Some authorities say that the Constitution does not give the Congress or the courts the power to regulate or control education. They contend the only legal way to grant such authority to Congress or the Courts is to amend the Constitution.

The controversy continues with greater loss each day of the people's faith in their own government.

RESOLUTION OF ARKANSAS MISSIONARY BAPTIST ASSOCIATION

These are excerpts from a resolution passed at the annual session of the Arkansas Missionary Baptist churches on November 19, 1957, and run as an ad paid with an offering by the ministers and delegates at the statewide meeting. No finer people could be found in the state, which showed that opposition to the invasion of the state and the Supreme Court ruling was not coming from the "pool-room crowd," as Brooks Hays once expressed during a conference with me, W. J. Smith and Pat Mehaffy.

A similar resolution was passed by 485 churches of the Texas Missionary Baptist Association.

ARKANSAS DEMOCRAT, November 22, 1957

Whereas, various religious bodies and church groups have publicly set forth their attitudes and beliefs concerning the proposals and plans to integrate the black and white races in our schools and society;

Whereas, both political and legal action have been taken . . . to force this change upon many of both races who do not want it, . . . without counting the ultimate cost or the end result of weakening our nation . . . ;

Whereas, being law-abiding citizens, . . . with a genuine love for all humanity and the souls of men, regardless of race or color, having proved our loyalty by giving the blood of our sons to defend the laws of our country, having never practiced violence to force the beliefs of Baptists upon others, and, consequently, being opposed to the use of physical force either to hinder or to promote the integration of free men anywhere;

Be it therefore resolved that we, . . . herewith voice our opposition to any force within or without our country, . . . which seeks to destroy our democratic and American way of life; . . . and that we hereby describe the Supreme Court rulings, . . . and the use of Federal troops to enforce those rulings, as being deplorable, unscriptural, and not in harmony with previous decisions of that body, nor with the beliefs and purposes of the Godfearing and democratic minded men who at the first drafted the Constitution of the United States of America.

(Signed) Gordon Reddin, Moderator
G. W. Fox, Clerk

CAUGHT IN THE TIDE
By Kennedy, Ark. Democrat　　　11/6/57

The GGC (Good Government Committee) candidates for directors of the new Little Rock city manager government were caught up in the tide of the federal vs. states rights controversy (race issue). They barely survived the onslaught of opponents who were, for the most part, unknown. Most of the GGC opponents were considered less qualified, yet one GGC candidate was defeated, and the other six survived by narrow margins when all were expected to enjoy overwhelming victories.

TEXAS HOUSE VOTES TO CLOSE SCHOOLS

The Texas House of Representatives by a vote of 115 to 26 approved a measure to close all schools to avoid occupation by federal troops.

FARM BUREAU PRESIDENT FOR SALES TAX

The Arkansas Farm Bureau was urged by its president, Harold F. Ohlendorf, to work to keep the 3% sales tax in effect. This was welcome support needed to save the program of progress.

TWO NEW INDUSTRIES

On November 26 an Iowa furniture firm announced it would build a branch factory in Harrison which would employ 150 workers. The next day a new industry revealed plans to locate at Atkins in Pope County.

CHANGING THE GUARD
By Knox, Nashville Banner　　　11/22/57

The daily cost of federalization of the National Guard was approximately $100,000. Total cost had reached $3,750,000 near the end of November. And, as the seated taxpayer remarked, "that doesn't count the paratroopers."

349

HOPE YOU HAVE BETTER LUCK THAN I DID, By Kennedy, Ark. Democrat, 11/22/57

Arkansas being a great duck hunting state, Kennedy used the duck hunting idea to make his point. Congressman Hays in a speech to the Louisiana Baptist Convention at Baton Rouge on Nov. 13, said we must try "friendly persuasion," and voiced a plea for a "breather period on racial problems." I had already tried that method but expressed the hope that Hays would have better luck.

SPEECH AT SHREVEPORT

I was guest speaker at the Shreveport News Club luncheon on Nov. 19. An editorial commending my remarks appearing in the *Shreveport Times* on the 21st also said "Never before has there been such a turnout for any guest speaker at a Shreveport luncheon." Many waited outside without food to hear my speech.

PARATROOPERS LEAVE

As November drew toward a close the last of the 101st paratroopers left Little Rock, departing Nov. 18. However the city was still occupied and controlled by federal troops. Federalized National Guardsmen were still on duty under the overall command of Gen. Walker who had been in charge from the beginning of the occupation.

Arkansas Gazette, Sunday, Nov. 24, 1957

AS ARKANSAS POLITICAL OBSERVERS SEE IT
Re-election Seems a Cinch for Faubus

The nation, and much of the world, now knows of Governor Faubus of Arkansas, the storm center of the Little Rock controversy. What does his own state think of him? This article assesses his chances in the light of the racial issue.

By ADREN COOPER
Of the Associated Press

Orval E. Faubus, a man who frequently thrives in a paradoxical climate, today is both a popular leader and an underdog in the minds of Arkansas voters.

. . .

. . . Mr. Faubus . . . now is in an ideal position from the standpoint of Arkansas politics.

If the Democratic . . . primary were held this week — instead of next July — a tide of . . . ballots would sweep away any opposition now in sight. That is the opinion of about 30 editors, legislators and other political observers representing every section of the state.

Some political analysts think though that the governor might lose if he should draw a strong segregationist as an opponent and if the campaign were based on taxes and other non-racial issues.

. . .

Three Other Issues
Some observers said that three strong issues could be exploited by Mr. Faubus' opponents: The Arkansas Highway Commission, taxes and the third term.

Only one man in Arkansas history has been elected to three terms and that was 50 years ago.

. . .

A third term would give him a third appointment and a majority on the five-man Highway Commission. It was to prevent a governor from getting this kind of control that the present system of appointments was set up in 1952. . . .

Mr. Faubus is credited with pushing through the 1957 Arkansas legislature a program of increased sales, income and severance taxes.

The deadline for the first collection of the income tax under the new rates is only two months before election. The sales tax increase . . . drew strong opposition and will be on the general election ballot next November.

But These May Fade
These issues may fade into the background in the minds of people . . .

Even in the northern and western areas of the state — where there are few Negroes and lukewarm feelings on the racial issue — Faubus still is considered a front-runner.

At Fayetteville, where both the University of Arkansas and junior and senior high schools are integrated, Editor Ted Wylie of the Northwest Arkansas Times said:

"I think he is stronger now — in this area — than he was the first time (1954). . . ."

There are few reservations from East Arkansas observers.

"I don't believe another segregationist, even a strong one, would be accepted by the people unless he had done something outstanding," said Perrin Jones Jr., editor of the Searcy Citizen. "Right after the federal troops arrived we ran an editorial backing Faubus' standing and criticizing Eisenhower's action and 800 people either came by the office, telephoned or wrote letters about it.

"Only one person disagreed with our view. . . . I believe they are more worked up over states rights than they are over segregation. The people resent the presence of federal troops in Arkansas and the longer they stay the better Faubus' chances."

What About Opposition?
Who would provide the opposition for Mr. Faubus?

Chris Finkbeiner, Little Rock meat packer, and Chancellor James H. Pilkinton of Hope are the only announced candidates . . .

. . .

It's possible that Mr. Faubus alienated elements at each end of the racial spectrum. He will not say that he is a segregationist but lets his actions speak for themselves.

. . .

There remains the question of whether Mr. Faubus will run. He has said repeatedly: "I don't know myself."

ARKANSAS NEAR TO REALIZING
TWO SCHOOL GOALS: 9-MONTH TERMS,
PAY EQUALIZATION VIRTUALLY ATTAINED

In spite of all the furor and trouble with the federal government as it intruded into state affairs, progress in many fields continued at accelerated rate. During the school year 1957-58, Arkansas, for the first time in all its history, had a full 9-month term of school for every child, rural or urban, black or white, in every school district, rich or poor, great or small.

The pay equalization effort — meaning the same rate of pay for black and white teachers — had nearly reached its goal. Thus black teachers were benefiting more proportionately than others from my administration's efforts to improve education. The additional benefits were justified and there was no slackening of efforts to equalize salaries because of the difficulties at Central High School.

FOREIGN AID AND FAUBUS
By Interland, News and Courier   11/30/57

Washington officials read the news of the departure of the 101st Airborne troops from Little Rock and my statement that Arkansas has been invaded and occupied by federal forces. One of the officials reported, "It's rumored that now that federal troops have left Arkansas, Gov. Faubus will apply for foreign aid!" Federal troops had not left. The 101st Airborne Division had been removed but federalized Guardsmen were still on duty.

UNHAPPY SOUTH TALKING THIRD PARTY AGAIN
By Morris, Memphis Commercial Appeal   12/1/57

Under the above heading Associated Press writer Relman Morin discussed the prospects of a Third Party movement based in the South:

"The politically unsure South is pictured . . . as a not-quite runaway boy whose thoughts are turning toward home. The South is dissatisfied with both the Democrats and Republicans but fears a third party is not the answer. Question is how much fire is behind the smoke in Dixie?"

The same page carried the pictures of three political figures. Senator Strom Thurmond of South Carolina who headed a States Rights ticket in 1948, T. Coleman Andrews of Virginia, who ran on the same ticket in 1956, and myself, who could run on such a ticket in 1960.

There is no doubt I could have led such a ticket, garnered a lot of votes and perhaps carried a number of states. I considered such an effort to be a futile gesture at the time and openly advocated remaining within the Democratic Party.

But the Southern area is no longer the Democratic "solid South." The Goldwater vote in 1964, Wallace's American Party vote in 1968, followed by Nixon's Republican sweep in 1972, show clearly that the South's solid ties with the national Democratic Party have been effectively broken, perhaps forever.

VOTERS TO DECIDE FATE OF SALES TAX

If the effort to repeal the sales tax increase was successful the student would be pulled back into the hole where education had for so long languished in Arkansas.

After the successful petition drive to refer the 3% sales tax to a vote, headed by Hope Publisher Alex Washburn, I visited with Forrest Rozzell. We both knew that it was difficult to obtain approval of a tax increase by a popular vote of the people. Besides being confusing, the measure would appear on the general election ballot along with all state and local candidates and other issues.

"Hell, Governor," Rozell reiterated to me as he had once before, "you've got to run again. If you don't we could lose everything we've gained."

We knew that a new governor would not be fully committed to the program of progress, especially the sales tax increase.

The school difficulties did not alter Rozzell's view that I should run in 1958 in order to save the progress made in education and in other fields.

I had made no decision on whether to seek a third term and gave Rozzell no commitment. I'm sure he knew I wanted to save the progressive program I had so strongly recommended and supported.

GOVERNORS MEET AT HOT SPRINGS

The members of the executive committee of the National Governors Conference met in Hot Springs on Dec. 5. Official sessions were held on Friday and Saturday, Dec. 6 and 7. The members were: Governor Thomas H. Stanley, Virginia; Faubus; Wm. G. Stratton, Illinois; Luther H. Hodges, N. Carolina; Albert D. Rosellini, Washington; John E. Davis, N. Dakota; Lane Dwinell, New Hampshire; Edmund S. Muskie, Maine; Joseph B. Johnson, Vermont; and Leroy Collins, Florida. Present also were former Governor Thomas E. Dewey of New York and Howard Pyle, former Arizona governor, then a presidential assistant.

GOP Governor Dwinell presented the proposal of the Eisenhower administration to shift funds and taxing power from the national government to the states. It was a very modest beginning involving a franchise tax placed on telephone companies and telephone users during WWII. The tax would be repealed by Congress, and the states, through their legislatures, could levy it as a state tax.

Frank Bane, executive secretary for the conferences of governors for 20 years, announced his retirement and submitted his resignation effective as of May 1, 1958.

Governor Stratton, then one of the leading Republican governors, was angry at the national administration. The Secretary of Defense with President Eisenhower's consent, had federalized some units of the Illinois Air National Guard without the governor's consent and without informing him beforehand. As a result, all the complaints from his constituents fell on Gov. Stratton.

This action by the federal government was unprecedented in the affairs of the National Guard, except in the case of Arkansas some three months before, when the entire Arkansas National Guard was federalized without my consent. This method had been considered illegal throughout the history of the nation. I have always thought that the action in Illinois — there was no emergency — was deliberately planned by Attorney General Brownell and the national administration to confirm the illegal precedent set in Arkansas.

Gov. Stratton presented a strong resolution condemning the action of the national administration to the executive committee for its approval. Before the committee convened the resolution was the main topic of conversation, and Stratton asked the governors for their support.

I told Gov. Stratton I favored his resolution because it was right, and that I would vote for it. Otherwise, I would keep quiet for two reasons: first, I was the host for the visiting governors, and second, any statement of mine might involve the so-called Little Rock affair and be detrimental in holding support from some Northern governors. No doubt every governor present favored Stratton's resolution.

But, unknown to me, the highest officials of the national administration were applying strong pressure to stop the resolution. The presence of former Gov. Dewey at the executive committee meeting was never publicly explained, but he had been sent by the national administration with the specific mission of stopping the Stratton resolution. He persuaded or pressured Gov. Stratton not to present it. The resolution just seemed to fade into oblivion and was never brought up or even mentioned at the committee's official sessions. The "disappearing act" of the resolution was amazing.

Gov. Dewey, his mission accomplished, relaxed and enjoyed himself. He remained on hand until the three-day committee meetings were concluded. It would have been a bombshell to the Eisenhower administration if the resolution had been presented by a leading Northern GOP governor and adopted by the executive committee of the National Governors Conference.

One evening Dewey and Governors Muskie, Johnson and myself fell into conversation.

Gov. Dewey grew loquacious while the rest of us listened. To me it was meeting and listening to a legend. I had read of Tom Dewey since his name first splashed across the front pages of the press in national headlines as a gang-busting district attorney in New York. He was governor of New York for three terms and the GOP presidential nominee in 1944 and 1948.

After his upset defeat by Truman in 1948, Dewey assumed the role of Republican elder statesman.

Gov. Dewey talked of many things. Of Eisenhower he said, "He has his own private pipeline to the American people." That was the best description I have ever heard of the Eisenhower popularity, and I agreed with Dewey 100 per cent. With all his ignorance of civil government and his sometimes neglect of official duties, Eisenhower could always escape the blame for anything that went wrong in national affairs. To the common people, Eisenhower always meant well and, to them, any mistakes were the fault of the Palace Guard.

As he grew more confidential in his analysis of events, evaluation of political personalities and reminiscing, Dewey would say, "Now if you quote me on this you're a liar," and then continue. We kept filling his glass and he kept talking, and every minute of his discourse on politics and political figures was filled with interest to his hearers.

Our informal discourse was discontinued and we parted at four o'clock a.m. I never saw the distinguished New Yorker again.

I recalled that two Madison County Republican leaders, former Sheriffs Dalton Dotson and Lester Keck, were personal acquaintances of Gov. Dewey and his early supporters for the presidential nomination.

Many of the personalities attending the Hot Springs meeting were transported by State Police cars to Little Rock where they made connections with commercial airlines. Gov. Dewey was one of those. On leaving Hot Springs he forgot his brief case leaving it in a conspicuous place. It was discovered by the State Police who contacted me. My office immediately contacted Gov. Dewey. I ordered the brief case rushed to Little Rock while Gov. Dewey's plane, all passengers seated ready for take off, waited for its arrival.

I would wager it contained some interesting material. For Governors Stanley and Muskie I arranged a duck hunt on the day following the conference. They were outfitted and escorted by Mack Sturgis. A friend in the Arkansas-Prairie County area made available his hunting grounds and both governors had a successful hunt.

White County Citizen, Searcy, Ark.
Dec. 19, 1957

FAUBUS AGREES TO HONOR NEGRO EDUCATOR JAN. 5

PITTSBURGH, Pa. — A Negro woman said Gov. Orval Faubus of Arkansas is willing to proclaim Jan. 5 as "George Washington Carver Day" at her request.

Dr. Alma Illery said that as founder of the National Achievement Club she has written governors of all states asking them to honor the late Negro scientist.

Thus far only 20 favorable replies have been received — including that of Gov. Faubus.

Dr. Illery said Gov. Faubus' reply said "your letter . . . only recently came to my attention. . . . I will be happy to proclaim Jan. 5 as George Washington Carver Day. . . .

Arkansas Democrat
Dec. 22, 1957

ARKANSAS DOES THE IMPOSSIBLE

. . . Right here in Arkansas, our people have been doing an impossible thing, as it seemed not so many years ago. We mean the state's advance in industry.

Governor Faubus said in a talk the other day, that Arkansas has been getting an average of nine new plants a month over the past two and one-half years. Included among these are many big-name industries.

That would have seemed an impossible feat back in the lean 1930s. When in that time we got a little canning factory, it was an occasion for the lucky community's rejoicing. Sometimes there were parades. . . .

The death of a key member of Congress elevated Second District Congressman Wilbur Mills to Chairman of the Ways and Means Committee, from which position he wielded great power for many years.

As the year ended I remained mum on campaign plans.

United Press named me Man of the Year for Arkansas.

The *Associated Press* named Mrs. Daisy Bates among the top nine women newsmakers of the year.

The launching of sputnik into outer space by the Russians was voted the biggest national and international news story of 1957. The Little Rock crisis was a close second.

THREE RING CIRCUS, By Kennedy, Ark. Democrat, 12/1/57

Razorback Head Coach Jack Mitchell, after a successful season, left Arkansas to become head coach at the University of Kansas. Athletic Director John Barnhill, surrounded by the press, old grads, high school coaches, students, "Wild Hogs" club members and fans, feverishly fished in the applications for a new coach. U. of A. President John Tyler Caldwell and the Faculty Athletic Commission, stood ready to okay Barnhill's selection before passing it to the U. of A. Board of Trustees Athletic Commission for $15,000 annual contract. I was an interested but non-participating spectator. A few days later Frank Broyles, University of Missouri head coach was selected as Razorback coach. His appointment ushered in a 19-year period of Razorback football prosperity, including two undefeated seasons and one national championship. The period became known in athletic circles as "The Broyles Era."

ARKANSAS INDUSTRIAL GROWTH

New industrial plants located in the state during calendar year 1957 provided 10,203 new jobs for Arkansas workers. Pay rolls were up by millions.

The state's industrial popularity continued to rise. On December 16 Hot Springs broke ground for a new industrial plant of substantial size. A new tubing manufacturing plant located in Conway.

The Arkansas Highway Department announced plans to spend $50 million in new highway construction in 1958.

GROUND IS BROKEN FOR $15 MILLION CEMENT PLANT AT FOREMAN

The day was very cold and my speech lasted about two minutes as we broke ground for a new, modern cement plant in Little River County on December 1. The man of the hour was W. R. "Witt" Stephens, the motivating power in the establishment of the plant. One of the happiest persons was Marion Crank, state representative. The plant was to be built in his home county and near his home town of Foreman.

BUDAPEST AND LITTLE ROCK

When the federal government sent troops to Little Rock, a number of writers compared Little Rock and Arkansas to Budapest and Hungary.

After the troops had been in charge in Little Rock for some time and the situation had grown quiet, some reporters raised the assertion this was proof that the people had accepted enforced integration. I replied that quietness prevailed in Hungary. Was this proof that the Hungarians had accepted enforced Communism?

There was no reply as the questioners slunk away.

BOYCOTT OF GAZETTE ADVERTISERS

A paid advertisement on December 13 proclaimed a boycott by segregationists against businesses which advertised in the *Arkansas Gazette*.

HARRIS HONORED — BY RAYBURN

House Speaker Sam Rayburn came to El Dorado to honor Congressman Oren Harris at a public banquet.

STATE HOSPITAL IMPROVED

One year after my fuss with State Hospital authorities, the turmoil had ended and treatment of patients was much improved, according to a *Gazette* report.

BOB BAILEY DIES

Former 3-term lieutenant governor Bob Bailey died at Russellville of a heart attack.

FEDERAL TROOPS REDUCED

The Army cut the CHS military force by 50% to 432. The greatest number of troops mobilized by me prior to the September 20 injunction was 270.

APPOINTMENTS, NOVEMBER 1957

John R. Newman, Harrison, to State Library Board. Mrs. Merlin "Bessie" Moore, Little Rock, reappointed to the State Library Board. Dr. Raymond R. Edwards, to be Director of the University of Arkansas Graduate Institute of Technology (GIT) at Little Rock. John M. Powell, Little Rock, and W. M. Carney, El Dorado, to Liquified Gas Board Advisory Committee.

APPOINTMENTS, DECEMBER 1957

J. J. Pyeatt, Fayetteville, to Real Estate Commission. A. E. Woods, Negro leader of Menifee, to Negro Boys Industrial School Board.

"I Resolve in 1958--"

—by godfrey, that's how Count Pulaski woulda wanted it!

ARCH CAMPBELL:—to paint the courthouse purple, too.

CHRIS FINKBEINER
—to get the keys to that big house at the end of Center St.

fix it—I don't wanta lose any voters!

'CRIP' HALL
—to avoid any more falling masonry.

it won't be easy

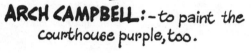

ORVILLE CHENEY
—to keep everybody current in 1958.

nothin' doin'!

ORVAL FAUBUS
—not to go up in Ike's first 'Sputnik'.

NEW YEAR'S RESOLUTIONS, By Kennedy, Ark. Democrat, 1/1/58

CHAPTER 18
THE HOYT SPEECH; THE TRUMAN DINNER; THE WASHINGTON GRIDIRON ROAST; I DEFEND IKE'S PROGRAM. I FILE FOR 3RD TERM DRAWING FINKBEINER AND WARD.

Daily Leader, Stuttgart, Ark.
Jan. 9, 1958

TWENTY-SIX WALK OUT ON CRISIS TALK

LITTLE ROCK — A Denver publisher deplored international repercussions of the Little Rock school integration crisis during an address at an Arkansas Press Assn. convention banquet, and 26 persons walked out as he spoke.

Palmer Hoyt, publisher and editor of the Denver Post made no comment on the silent protests — Not even when Keith Tudor of Arkadelphia, a vice president of the association, left the publisher's own table.

The persons who remained sat silent as Hoyt termed the Little Rock crisis one of three great dangers of the American way of life.

Hoyt said the two other major perils to U.S. civilization were contained in Russia's economic challenges and her supremacy in space age arms and sciences.

Hoyt devoted the main part of his speech to the racial controversy at Little Rock.

Gov. Orval Faubus ... introduced Hoyt and listened to the speech placidly....

The question of whether the Negro pupils should be going to classes with whites at the school is incidental, Hoyt declared.

He said the effect of the manner in which they were integrated was the important issue.

The world believes an American state tried to use its armed forces in preventing a handful of Negro children from getting an education, Hoyt said. (If the world had that false idea, the press members like Hoyt were responsible.)

"The rest of the world is not going to wait for us to make up our minds where we stand on integration." Hoyt warned.

He praised Little Rock's Gazette for its editorials...

A wave of polite applause, widespread but brief, swept the audience after Hoyt sat down.

Faubus joined in the clapping and chatted with the publisher during the rest of the banquet.

Later, the governor told newsmen he thought Hoyt's address was "the judgment of another self-styled expert from afar about a situation with which he cannot be familiar."

The bitterest reaction to Hoyt's remarks was voiced by Tom Allen of Brinkley, a state senator and newspaper publisher, who walked out during the address.

"I think the entire press association owes Gov. Orval Faubus an apology." Allen told a newsman angrily. "Mr. Hoyt's speech was in the worst taste I've ever seen, castigating the governor and the people of Arkansas."

COMMENTS ON SPEECH OF DENVER POST EDITOR

From The Arkansas Press
Jan. 16, 1958

The speech provided material for editorial comment in several Arkansas papers.

Bob Sanders of the Springdale News had this to say:

"We wish we had stayed home — or that Palmer Hoyt had stayed in Denver, ... Mr. Hoyt arose to speak after having been introduced in a very fine manner by Governor Orval Faubus. Do you know what he told us he was going to speak about — 'The Little Rock Situation.' ... Every editor present must have formed his opinion weeks and months ago. The last thing most of them wanted to hear was an outsider coming in and blowing off about the situation.

"Some of the editors didn't hear the speech. Twenty-six of them walked out right in the middle of it. Had not Governor Faubus remained at his seat, many more would have. This visitor from Denver, whose views were just as one-sided as those of Time, Life and some other publications dedicated to the task of gouging the South at every opportunity, not only was speaking on the wrong subject, at the wrong place, at the wrong time — but he wasn't even a good speaker ...

"Mr. Hoyt ... can speak anywhere he wants, but we hope it will not be our misfortune again to have to be one of his listeners."

* * *

Louis Graves of the Nashville News had this opinion:

"Palmer Hoyt, Denver editor who had a free choice of topics, tossed the Arkansas Press convention into a bit of a turmoil with his integration talk. ... Unhappily, the Convention Committee lined up Governor Faubus, publisher of the Huntsville paper, to make the introduction.

"It wasn't planned that way — it just happened.

"And despite the sensitive subject, both the governor and the Denver editor took opposing stands without embarrassing anyone by being vitriolic. I thought the governor acquired a little more stature by listening intently but without agreement, to Hoyt's words. ...

"The atmosphere wasn't charged with dynamite ...

"Most of the newspaper folks took the criticism in good stride — we didn't have to agree with the Denver editor. ...

"The governor stayed on too, and when it was over he got in the wide open informal discussions that followed the banquet. He didn't lose any sleep over the talk. Neither did he give any ground."

From John R. Newman of the Harrison Daily Times:

"The futility of speech was demonstrated. . . . The Denver Post editor said something contrary about integration. Some editors walked out and others more stupid, perhaps, stayed. * * *

* * *

Augusta Advocate
Augusta, Arkansas

It was poor taste, when Palmer Hoyt accepted an invitation to speak at the Arkansas Press Association meeting and then chose to speak on the Little Rock School integration subject. Among those in attendance was Governor Faubus, publisher of the Huntsville Record in Madison county . . . Mr. Hoyt has every right to his own opinions but it seems to us that his timing was off badly. Many publishers indicated they would have walked out on the speaker had not the governor been in the audience.

VAN BUREN PRESS ARGUS
by Hugh Park

And in his careful, concealed astonishment, if he had any, Governor Faubus came out of the explosion a bigger man than ever before. Acting the part of a gentleman, he sat through the diatribe, in which blame of course was put on the governor alone, smiled and chatted with the speaker after the dinner was over. The next day he was offered everything but an official apology of the association. He passed off the remarks of the visiting editor as "the judgment of another self-styled expert from afar about a situation with which he cannot be familiar."

* * *

BEEBE ARKANSAS NEWS
January 23, 1958

Several subscribers have asked: What about the speaker Hoyt from Denver, Colo. . . . In the first place the speaker should not have accepted the invitation to speak in occupied territory . . . and our honorable Governor Orval Faubus is to be commended for "even introducing the speaker." Governor Faubus gave the man a very nice introduction and the publisher from Denver, "took his hatred" out on the large crowd and cast reflections on our governor, but our state official withstood all of the criticism with his head held high. The speech was "bad taste"... Instead of making a spectacle by a public apology, publishers throughout the state sent personal apologies to the Governor for Hoyt's mistreatment . . . Arkansas Press Association has never in its history censored a speaker's talk. We believe in, and practice Freedom of Speech, Freedom of Press . . . Hoyt chose a subject, that he knew nothing about. He was not briefed enough with the facts, to talk intelligently. His talk is likened to an old spinster telling a mother of twelve, "How to raise children." Had Governor Faubus left the room, 98 per cent of the people would have followed. Those who sat and endured the Denver man's talk remained in respect for and to our noble Governor.

Crossett Observer, January 23, 1958
BACK TO THE BALLOT BOX

The Governor's idea of deciding the integration hassel, in which he has said each community should be allowed to vote on whether or not they want mixed classrooms, makes as much sense as anything that has been said since last September...

The Governor's idea of deciding, the integration question at the ballot box is just and fair, and should be tried...

Contending that the "founding fathers" did not want nor intend, for the Federal government to control the education of the young, Governor Faubus has rightly said that the control of the schools should rest with the local and state authorities. . . . this proposition makes sense. Who knows the local situation and how to deal with it better than local people and their own elected officials? Or, as long as the public schools are supported by state and local taxes, why then should not control of them be maintained by state and local authority?

In this day of "creeping socialism"...there are few functions left for local people to decide upon except how their schools are to be paid for and managed.

We hope the return to the ballot box plan, as advocated by the Governor . . . is carried out.

MANN TAKES CREDIT FOR CHS
TROOP CALL: PILKINGTON AIRS PLAN

A story in the Arkansas Democrat of January 30 said that Mayor Mann took credit for the calling of federal troops to Central High School during the integration crisis.

"The immediate need for federal troops is urgent," Mann said in a telegram to President Eisenhower on September 24. In conversations with the White House Mann said he recommended federalization of the Arkansas National Guard.

The 101st Airborne Division troops from Ft. Campbell arrived at the Little Rock Air Force base that same afternoon and the motorized columns occupied Little Rock as night was falling.

JOHNSON NOT TO RUN FOR GOVERNOR

Jim Johnson, in a public announcement, withdrew from the governor's race at the beginning of the year.

PILKINGTON'S PLAN

In a speech at Hot Springs January 30, Chancellor James Pilkington of Hope, who had withdrawn his candidacy for governor two weeks earlier, announced his plan for resolving the Little Rock crisis. The first of his five-point plan recommended:

"For the school board to reassign the nine students in question to the Horace Mann School for the second semester. The board has that legal right under the Arkansas Pupil Assignment Act. No federal judge in his right mind is likely to hold the school board in contempt of court for doing so under existing circumstances."

Another point recommended the resignation of the school board enmass to be followed by a special election to choose the successor members.

As I entered the second, and last year, of my second term, these were the questions and alternatives which the cartoonist had me pondering.

If I ran for re-nomination, it would be in the face of precedent. I had seen my predecessors, Governors Bailey, Adkins, Laney and McMath, fail in efforts to win a third term (Laney after being out of office for one term), or fail to win another office while still in his second term, as was the case with Adkins who lost in a bid for the U.S. Senate.

My immediate predecessor had failed to win a second term.

The only governor who had successfully sought a third term was the redoubtable Jeff Davis, a great orator, bearing an enviable political name. His victory came 54 years earlier with less than a majority of the votes.

With the runoff election law in effect a winning candidate must gather a majority.

George Douthit's column on the same page was headed, "Faubus Will Run Again, Many Factors Indicate." While making this prediction Douthit admitted that I had not indicated to him, even in private, that I would go for a third term.

On January 18 I spoke to a convention of magazine wholesalers in Little Rock attended by delegates from many states. The editorial in the *Crossett Observer* on January 23 was based on statements made in the speech.

TROUBLE IN NEW YORK SCHOOLS

Arkansas Democrat, January 31, 1958

In Washington yesterday Congressman Williams of Mississippi compared racial trouble at a Brooklyn school to the Little Rock situation.

Gov. Faubus said: "People send their children to school to be safe and under the proper influences. And in that school they are being raped and knifed and subjected to the terror of gangs.

"The people are not being told one-tenth of the trouble about racial problems going on outside the South.

"I would hate to think what the metropolitan press would have done to us if this had happened in Arkansas, or elsewhere in the South."

The Mississippi congressman told the House that school officials in New York obviously were unable to cope with violence there, and asked:

"Where are the paratroopers?"

TIME FOR DECISION, By Kennedy, Ark. Democrat, 1/19/58

"There is no comparison between Little Rock and Brooklyn," Williams said. *"No students have been raped in Little Rock, no students have been stabbed in Little Rock, no students have beaten up teachers, and there are no organized gangs roaming the streets of Little Rock."*

"Why is it that the president has not federalized the New York National Guard? Are our armed forces to be used solely in the South . . . ?"

SOIL AND WATER CONSERVATION PROGRAMS

I spoke to the members of the Poteau River Watershed Council at Heavener, Okla. on February 7. I supported strongly all soil and water conservation programs, and great progress was made in these fields during my administration. I had great favor with the leaders and members of all conservation organizations — so much that I could not accept all invitations to public functions sponsored by these groups.

TROOP COST AT CHS

By February 13 the cost of federal troops at Central High School had reached $4,285,000.

GUESS WHO?
By Kennedy, Ark. Democrat   2/24/58

In Kennedy's Valentine's Day cartoon the public was warming up to me again, having forgotten the sales tax increase. Now cupid's arrow, in the form of the income tax increase, fired (collected) by Commissioner Cheney, was about to hit the public. The cartoonist wondered if this wouldn't turn the voters against me, and jeopardize my chances for re-nomination if I decided to seek a third term.

THE DISPUTE WITH RECTOR

W. F. "Billy" Rector, Little Rock businessman, made a statement on February 13 that a contemplated ten million dollar shopping center would not be built in Little Rock because of the integration crisis.

The next day referring to Mr. Rector I said:

"In the first place this is just an excuse on their part because there is a recession on and Rector is financially interested in the project.

In the second place, Rector is an integrationist (he supported the "obey the law line" at that time). In the third place, I don't think he tells the truth. In the fourth place he lost some insurance business with the state in 1955. In the fifth place he supported the Republican candidate for governor in 1954 and is a Republican himself."

Rector's public role in the integration problem prior to this time was to file a lawsuit in Chancery Court in August challenging the validity of the four segregation laws passed by the 1957 legislature.

TWO ON THE CEILING
By Kennedy, Ark. Democrat   2/16/58

A day after my statement, Rector replied with his own blast. He started a two-page statement by describing me as a skunk. He then answered my statement point by point, denying he was an integrationist, said he was neither Republican or Democrat but an independent, admitted he had supported the Republican candidate in 1954 and stated he would continue to vote against me.

Later, a statement by the New Jersey planners of the shopping center said the primary reason for cancellation of the plans was economic.

Then, years later in 1973, who built a private school in Western Little Rock to protect his real estate investments and to avoid compulsory integration? Mr. W. F. "Billy" Rector, still a successful businessman and still going strong.

As I review and revise this in 1979, Mr. Rector is deceased (in 1975).

In the years following the time of this cartoon Billy and I became friends. Although he supported Rockefeller in the Campaign of 1964, he gave support to me, including contributions to my campaign fund, in my comeback efforts in 1970 and 1974.

I was looking forward to showing him how he figured in this writing and laughing with him over our brief controversy, until I read of his death.

JUDGE JAS. PILKINTON
OFFERS SOLUTION TO
CHS DEADLOCK...

PLAN GETS
GOVERNOR'S BLESSING

ANOTHER INCIDENT AT CHS...

WOODROW MANN
SAYS HE ASKED IKE
FOR TROOPS...

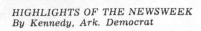
Chancellor James Pilkington of Hope, after withdrawing his candidacy for governor in the 1958 Democratic primaries, offered his plan for the solution of the Little Rock integration problem. I expressed favor for the plan. If it had been tried it would have been knocked down immediately in Judge Davies Court. George Douthit wrote that Pilkington had entered the governor's race for 1960.

Mayor Mann finally admitted he asked for the federal troops to be sent to Little Rock. Everyone knew it was not his decision. He simply did what he was told by the handful of integrationists in the city.

Incidents continued at Central High School.

► ►

VIOLENCE AND DISORDER IN BROOKLYN
SCHOOLS
By Knox, Nashville Banner   1/31/58

Cartoonist Knox had this reaction to the trouble in the Brooklyn schools in a Northern state. Rape had been committed on students in the school, gangs extorted lunch money from other students, teachers were beaten while violence and disorder went uncontrolled. Finally uniformed, armed policemen were placed on duty at the schools in an effort to keep order. Pictures of the on-duty policemen accompanied news stories of the disorder.

JUST THOUGHT I'D ANNOUNCE MY PLANS, SO YOU OTHER FOLKS'D HAVE TIME T' MAKE UP YOUR MINDS.

MOVING TO ANOTHER RINGSIDE, By Kennedy, Ark. Democrat, 2/19/58

Little Rock businessman Chris Finkbeiner, announced his candidacy for the Democratic nomination for governor on February 15. Chris had been sponsoring professional wrestling in Little Rock, a sport that had quite a following in the area. Thus the caption "moving to another ringside." Bennett correctly analyzed the 1958 situation and did not run for governor. Finkbeiner, a fine fellow but no political analyst, made a different decision.

362

THE WASHINGTON DEMOCRATIC DINNER

WARNED TO STAY AWAY,
I DECIDE TO ATTEND

ANOTHER LITTLE ROCK!
By Bristol, Cincinnati Times Star   2/21/58

A $100 a plate fund raising dinner was planned for February 22 in Washington by the Democratic Party in honor of former President Harry S. Truman. At first I gave no serious consideration to the affair. Then Harold Jenks of Piggott, a paid organizer for the party working out of Washington, a position I had helped him obtain, came to my office in Little Rock with a message from some party leaders. Jenks said that certain national Democratic leaders wanted me to stay away, that my attendance was not desired. Jenks seemed to throw his influence with them and his efforts were to dissuade me from attendance, I listened to Jenks without committing myself one way or the other.

About the same time I received word that Senator Fulbright had called Arkansas Democratic Chairman Tom Harper of Ft. Smith to say that my presence at the dinner would be embarrassing to the Party and asked him to tell me so and urge me not to attend. Harper's reply was "Bill, why don't you tell him? You've known him longer than I have."

With my attention focused on the event by these developments, I considered the matter and announced I would attend the dinner.

A private railroad car was engaged for the trip. Besides me the Arkansas group consisted of Harper, State Democratic Secretary Frank Robbins, Jr. of Conway, Rabie Rhodes of Harrison, Henry Finkbeiner and Charles Smithers of Benton, Searcy Wilcoxen of Hamburg, Olen Hendrix of Antoine, Truman Baker of Searcy, State Democratic Finance Chairmen Jack Stephens, James McHaney, George (Skeeter) Dickey, Mack Sturgis and *Democrat* reporter George Douthit, all of Little Rock.

On the day of departure I filled speaking engagements at Helena and Lepanto, then drove to Hoxie where I joined the others aboard the train.

Arkansas National Committeewoman Gressie Carnes of Camden flew to Washington for the affair. On the morning of our arrival she gave a breakfast for our party and other Arkansas people in the capital. The breakfast was more than a success. A number of national figures from other states dropped by to greet me and pay their respects to Mrs. Carnes. I noted that all the Arkansas congressional delegation was present except Senator Fulbright who was represented by Mrs. Fulbright. However the gathering was so successful that Fulbright's absence was conspicuous. I noted that Mrs. Fulbright after sizing up the situation, slipped over to a telephone and made a call. This was also noted by others, including Mr. Sturgis. Very shortly the Senator joined the breakfast party where he was a very affable, friendly participant.

At the dinner that evening the Arkansas group was the center of attention. It seemed we got three-fourths or more of the television and other news coverage, and much of the time took the spotlight from the honoree former President Truman. Our table was near the center of the room and near the head table. I was kept so busy greeting visitors to my table and signing autographs that I was unable to finish my meal.

After the program began I was induced by a member of the dinner staff to leave my table and quietly take a seat in the second banquet hall. The main speakers, including Truman, alternated between the two rooms, speaking separately to each group. Sturgis always maintained that I was purposely moved because I was getting too much attention.

The main news picture in the Washington papers the next morning was a front page photo of me and Senator McClellan paying our respects to President Truman at the head table.

Senator Fulbright did not visit with the Arkansas group. I'm not certain that he attended the dinner at all. Senator McClellan visited with us openly when the reporters and photographers were all around. I heard him remark, "There! I guess that'll show them." Many office-holders from other states came by and introduced themselves to our table.

Other Arkansawyers in attendance at the dinner were:

Mr. and Mrs. Chris Finkbeiner of Little Rock who were in Washington at the time on other business; Clifford Cole, Bill Irby and Harold Jenks of Piggott, the latter then a party worker in Washington; Les Biffle formerly of Piggott then a Washingtom resident; R.A. (Bob) Young of Ft. Smith; Dr. Shelton Rushing and Nolan Rushing of El Dorado; Paul Chambers, State Democratic National Committeeman of Helena; Miss Hank Fort of Nashville; Mr. and Mrs. John Steelman and Carroll Cone of Washington, former Arkansas residents.

Before the dinner Mrs. Carnes said that "over 3,000 tickets have been sold, and I know darn well the increased sales are because of the publicity given the attendance by Faubus."

The news said after the affair that reports that Faubus was unwanted doubled the success of the dinner when the news spread of his attendance, and he was "welcomed as a hero" by others.

One headline said: "FAUBUS WALKS OUT ON ADLAI." That came about when the staff member had me move to the second hall during the course of the program. I had no intention of walking out on anyone.

However the biased press carried many slanted and distorted reports. Some were completely false.

Arkansas was the fourth state in the nation to meet its quota of contributions for the National Party Fund, thanks to the diligence and efficiency of Jack Stephens.

LITTLE ROCK CITIZENS COMM. SUGGESTS SCHOOL BOARD ASK STAY

we've got to have relief!

I've had enough

ON THURSDAY BOARD PETITIONED U.S. COURT FOR STAY OF INTEGRATION ORDER.

ARK. FEDERAL JUDGE-SHIP DUE TO BE FILLED MONDAY. J. SMITH HENLEY IS CHOICE.

At the urging of a citizens committee among the business interests of the capital city, the school board on February 20 petitioned the federal court for a stay in the integration orders. This time the board and Blossom seemed to mean it.

Republican J. Smith Henley of Harrison was to be named a federal judge on February 24 to fill one of the Arkansas vacancies.

This column appeared in the *Piggott* (Ark.) *Banner*, Feb. 27, 1958, following the Democratic dinner in Washington.

PICKED UP HERE & THERE
by Laud Payne

We had a talk with Bill Irby and Clifford Cole, who were in Washington, D.C., to attend the Truman dinner. One of the first questions the fellows asked was "just how yellow can yellow journalism get?"

We advised them that they should have a pretty good idea after all the lies and half-truths that have been printed about the Little Rock school affair.

Bill and Coley were referring to the long stories told with the sad faces on TV and repeated by some news writers about Arkansas being slurred in the banquet as attested by the fact that our Governor Faubus was purposely seated by the committee in charge, in the basement, while the dignitaries were seated on the main floor...

Bill commented, "now we know how stinking low that some writers will stoop, and it should give us a good idea about how much truth can be placed in news accounts by certain reporters."

Both Bill and Coley joined in the statement: "Gov. Faubus was not over 20 feet from the table where President Truman was seated, he was not in the basement. Faubus and Les Biffle were together, along with members of the Arkansas delegation. We were seated in the balcony just above...and we know just how big a lie some reporters have told."

Irby went on to say, ...if you judge by reports they published of the ex-president's speech,...they

didn't even sound like the speech Mr. Truman gave. Again, I ask, just how much leeway for lying do reporters allow themselves?" Indignant about the story of Faubus being snubbed, Bill and Coley said, "Yes he was badly snubbed; so badly that people coming from all over the banquet hall to shake hands with him, jammed up the place so much passage by was impossible. Next to Mr. Truman he was the most snubbed person at the banquet."

Irby concluded his remarks with "... most of the stuff I've read about Faubus' being snubbed is pure bunk. I was there and I know they are lies."

SAM B. KIRBY

On the last day of February, 1958, Sam B. Kirby of Little Rock, Publicity and Parks Director, died in Chicago while on a trip to that city. Kirby, a devout Catholic and respected citizen of the capital city, was one of my most competent department heads and a dedicated public servant.

HUBERT MUSTEEN

During my first term Hubert Musteen of Rogers, photographer for the Publicity and Parks Agency, died on a trip to Kansas City. Musteen, one of the most skillful photographers I had ever known, was accompanying the Arkansas delegation of Jaycees to the National Convention.

The loyalty of Kirby and Musteen to the administration and their devotion to duty was beyond question. Such men were hard to replace.

-hope everybody gets the general idea!

CLUB CUT-UP

ROLLA FITCH

Rolla Fitch, director of the Alcoholic Beverage Control Agency, revoked a number of beer permits throughout the state for violations of regulations. Fitch had a difficult task but was doing it well.

lets just study the facts.

NORTH SOUTH

-all I want is to get back in CHS-

BROOKS HAYS   SAMMIE DEAN PARKER

Sammie Dean Parker, daughter of segregationist parents, was expelled from CHS. She went on television with attorney Amis Guthridge and Rev. Wesley Pruden to air grievances in the matter, and then filed suit against the school board for reinstatement. She was quickly re-admitted to CHS.

Brooks Hays filed a bill in Congress asking for a review of the facts in the segregation-integration controversy. No hope could be seen for the measure except publicity for Hays.

RIPE FOR THE PICKING
By Kennedy, Ark. Democrat   *3/9/58*

Then on March 5 I announced my plans to seek renomination for that elusive and almost unprecedented third term. I had much enthusiastic support but also some of the most bitter and determined opposition anyone ever faced.

AT THE CAPITOL
by Ernest Valachovic
Arkansas Gazette — March 16, 1958

The Buck Stops at Cornett
State Comptroller Kelly Cornett, who in length of service already has outlasted most comptrollers, may be crowding his luck.

Cornett, who has a strong feeling about right and wrong, recently asked the state Legislative Council to take some positivie action about seeing that state owned vehicles are properly identified....

The legislature...has dodged responsibility in this field, and turned over to the comptroller the task of seeing that state vehicles are properly marked.

At the same time the legislature has authroized the comptroller to make exceptions. This puts the heat on Cornett. As comptroller he serves "at the pleasure" of the governor. This means that a suggestion "from upstairs" is tantamount to an order.

Not too long ago an out-of-town state official asked Cornett to permit him to use an unmarked car...Cornett objected but was overruled and he didn't feel like making an issue...

The *Gazette* was usually trying to create discension within my administration, and raise doubts of its good intentions among the voters. This was an example.

There was never the slightest doubt in my mind about Kelly Cornett. He was one of the finest men in my administration and had my complete trust, — and support. We were old acquaintances of the White River country in South Madison County.

NOT RETURNING EMPTY HANDED
By Kennedy, Ark. Democrat   *3/21/58*

Early in 1958, in the midst of a moderate recession, President Eisenhower requested a conference with the Executive Committee of the National Governor's Conference to discuss matters he had proposed to ease the economic situation for low income groups and the unemployed. As a member of the Committee I attended the conference held in the White House.

One proposal called for the extension by executive decree, of the period in which an eligible unemployed worker could draw unemployment insurance. The president's cabinet was split on this proposal, and so were the governors present.

Governor William G. Stratton (Rep.-Ill.), chairman of the Conference, and Governor Luther Hodges (Dem.-N.C.) strongly opposed the measure and went after it hammer and tongs. Finally I came to the defense of the measure and other proposals of the president, and was joined by Governor Edmund Muskie (Dem.-Me.). It turned out we were the strongest defenders of the president's proposed moves. I noted signs of relief and gratitude from two of the cabinet members present, Labor Secretary James Mitchell and Secretary of the Treasury Anderson.

Kennedy showed me returning from the Conference with "gain in political prestige."

Other Executive Committee members present were: John E. Davis of North Dakota; Joseph B. Johnson of Vermont; Albert D. Rosellini of Washington; and Goodwin J. Knight of California.

GRIDIRON DINNER IN WASHINGTON
By Kennedy, Ark. Democrat   3/26/58

The figures of the Little Rock controversy and the decisions of the U.S. Supreme Court were main topics of the newsmen's lampooning at the gridiron dinner in Washington. The following is reprinted from the *Arkansas Democrat* with which appeared Kennedy's cartoon. Congressman Oren Harris, who attended, gave me a personal report on the affair.

WASHINGTON — Governor Faubus declined an invitation to the annual Gridiron dinner last night, pleading a previous engagement, but an impersonator sang a song which expressed Faubus' lack of repentance for anything he has done.

Before a distinguished audience, including Vice President Richard M. Nixon — President Eisenhower did not attend — members of the Supreme Court, and other officials who sided with and against the governor in the Little Rock crisis, a hillbilly garbed member of the cast, strumming a guitar, sang:

"*An unreconstructed rebel. Now, that's just what I am.*
For this fair land of freedom, I do not give a damn.
I'm glad we fought against 'em. I only wish we'd won.
And I don't want no pardon, for anything I've done.

"*I fit them pardtroopers. I showed them war is hell.*
Went flyin' down to Newport and sassed that ol' Brownell.
They snitched my Central High School. They conquered all my land.
But they didn't get my statehouse. I'm Dixie contraband.

"*I can't take down my musket and fight with them no more.*
But o' one thing I am sartin and one thing I am shore:
That I don't want no pardon for what I been and am,
But I might get re-elected·— so I don't give a damn.

The tune was an old and unidentified post-Civil War ballad. The Faubus song was part of an act parodying T-V's "Gunsmoke" in which Marshal Lyndon (Matt Dillon) Johnson of Texas, Deputy Marshal Stuart Symington of Missouri and their posse attempt to rid the Democratic party of dissension. But after hearing Faubus' defiance, Marshal Johnson, according to Symington, had: "No comment. On matters interracial, he's strictly outer-spatial."

The U.S. Supreme Court was lampooned on its civil rights decrees by a chorus of nine berobed singers, one of whom led off with a solo:

"*Mine eyes have seen the glory of a civil rights decree.*
"*We have trampled on the Democrats and also G.O.P.*
"*As for who is going to make it work, I'm glad it isn't me.*
"*Oh, boy, this job is fun.*"

"*We've opened up the files of FBI for all to see.*
"*We have emptied all the prison cells from Maine to Kankakee.*

"And any hood can take the Fifth with equanimity.
"Oh, boy, this job is fun."

"Oh, critics say we write the laws, from this I won't dissent.
"We tell the constitution's authors what they should have meant.
"Results of each election, we will never circumvent.
"Oh, boy, this job is fun."

Another news story, at variance with the *Democrat* as to the Faubus inpersonator's dress, said!

The singer portraying Faubus wore a Union Cavalry uniform with gauntlets. He was followed on stage by a guitar-bearer.
As he came onstage, Faubus said, "I'm the governor of Arkansas, Orval Faubus, now of the Union Cavalry. Just got drafted. Son, hand ol' Faubus his gee-tar."
Then Faubus strummed his guitar and sang in a hill-billy monotone the ballad.

MEASURING TIME
By Kennedy, Ark. Democrat   *3/23/58*

Taking encouragement from the anti-third term tradition a number of prospective candidates considered the race as my opponents.

Finkbeiner was already in the field and Lee Ward was almost a certain starter. Others mentioned were Mayor Jud Hout of Newport, former Governor Ben Laney, and Attorney General Bruce Bennett. Former Governor Sid McMath was still taking pot shots at me as if he might enter the hustings. In one cartoon he was portrayed as my gadfly.

The gubernatorial prospects were evaluating my strength as they considered their chances against me.

HIGHLIGHTS OF THE NEWSWEEK
By Kennedy, Ark. Democrat   *3/30/58*

Welfare Director Carl Adams went to Washington to receive instructions and allocation of funds to implement one or more of Eisenhower's programs to aid the jobless and the poor.

Candidate Finkbeiner, speaking at Fayetteville, announced he had a campaign platform that would help everyone but declined to give details until all candidates for governor were in the field.

Arkansas Democrat
March 30, 1958

BACKSTAGE AT THE CAPITOL

Faubus' Blast at Ward
May Be Tip On Campaign

By George Douthit

It would appear by Governor Faubus' frontal attack on Chancellor Lee Ward that the governor expects to see considerably more of this gentleman during the summer months. Judge Ward has said only that he might run for governor.
Candidate Sought.
It is common knowledge in political circles that a group in Little Rock which has been highly critical of Governor Faubus' actions on Central High School has been beating the bushes for a strong speaking candidate.
They want a man who can get on the stump and rip into the governor. It also is no secret that the

candidate they wanted was Sid McMath. But the former governor is just getting his financial feet on the ground in his law business...

This group isn't about to let the governor glide into a third term without a terrific fight. In fact, their search for a candidate has been going on for weeks but one after another either refused or was rejected.

Now, the big question: Have they found one in Judge Ward? Two years ago he ran a strong third for supreme court justice. He already has made speeches on integration expressing himself in the direct opposite to the governor.

He is a former state Legion commander and a good orator. Judge Ward has a record of having the courage of his convictions . . .

He may be just what the anti-Faubus faction wants to make it tough on the governor.

* * *

MARCH EVENTS

I continued to reap statewide and national publicity during March, most of it favorable and most of it due to efforts of my critics. Among the main events was the fund raising dinner in Washington where I wound up on the front page with Harry Truman with the "liberals" unnoticed. Arkansas was among the leaders in meeting its quota of funds for the national party. Another was the meeting with President Eisenhower on plans to help the under privileged and unemployed, where I was the strongest supporter of the President's proposals. I was the third governor in the nation to accept for his state the extension of benefits for the unemployed, and the first to accept and implement programs in other fields. This benefitted the poor which included the black people of Arkansas.

All this was noted by regular Democrats, unemployed workers, labor union members, under privileged people including blacks, as well as the general public. By prompt action I reaped the benefits while my enemies fumed in frustration.

A strong effort was being made by the *Gazette* powers, McMath and other critics to get more opposition to my candidacy for re-nomination. They encouraged Finkbeiner, but they didn't think he could ably, strongly and meanly attack me. So they continued to seek a candidate who would carry the battle to me personally by attacks on my policies, my administration and me.

On March 6 the *Gazette* ran an editorial which said:

If he (Faubus) manages to sweep into office for a third term it will be because he does not have opposition of the kind that can effectively remind the people that there are grave issues at stake in this election that can go far beyond the tragic events at Little Rock Central High School.

The editorial then listed the points which, it said, could be used against me.

The anti-third term tradition.

Appointment of a third member to the five-member highway commission, but failed to mention that my predecessor had appointed all five members.

The establishment of a political dynasty.

My failure to please all the segregationists.

The tax increase approved in the regular session of the Legislature early in 1957.

The perfidy of these enemy leaders, especially the *Gazette,* was most obvious in this mention of the tax increase to be used against me. The *Gazette* gave strong support to this tax increase and, in fact, had voiced disappointment that the program had not been adopted earlier at the legislative session of 1955 in my first term.

Years later Judge Lee Ward told me that Harry Ashmore had urged him to "go all out" in attacking me on the tax increase issue. Ward, in good conscience, declined the advice saying publicly that he would "pass" on the three per cent sales tax issue.

On March 6 I participated in the dedication of the Brown Shoe Company Plant in Leachville, Mississippi County.

On March 12 came another attack on me by McMath.

On March 12 the Danver's Shoe Company Inc. announced it would locate a factory in Osceola, and Imperial Bag and Paper Company announced a plant for Pine Bluff.

A newspaper story was headlined: "THIRD TERM TALLY: 7 TRY, 6 FAIL".

I met with Ike in Washington on jobless benefits March 19.

The dedication of the new, modern rehabilitation facilities, the result of administration efforts, at the TB Sanitorium near Booneville, occurred on March 21. It was a big day at Booneville and a happy day for TB patients at the sanitorium and throughout the state.

LEE WARD, Paragould

GOV. RACE

ANOTHER HAT?

it's just durn foolishness!

CHRIS FINKBEINER ATTACKS FAUBUS' TAX PROGRAM...

Finkbeiner, on March 20, hit at taxes as "durn foolishness" on my part. The press said I gave a mild reply, "Be more specific. What programs would Finkbeiner cut out? Which employees cut off?"

News on the 21st said: Lee Ward may run for governor. James P. Baker of Helena may run. Others oft-mentioned as candidates were Bennett, McMath, Ben Laney and Jack Holt, Sr. Two days later Jud Hout of Newport was mentioned as a candidate. Marvin Melton at Jonesboro took himself out of the running.

On March 30 the news said: Grand Jury to call Faubus in probe of private clubs. Rolla Fitch, ABC director, and the board members would also be called. Otho A. Cook, Little Rock, was the Pulaski County grand jury foreman. My enemies were using every artifice and method possible in their efforts to discredit me and aid the opposition.

On March 29 Senator Sam J. Ervin (D-NC) was the star speaker at a Democratic fund raising dinner in Little Rock. The news the next day carried a photo of Ervin, Jack Stephens and me. In his speech the senator said:

"The day the president sent federal troops to Little Rock" to enforce integration at Central High School was "one of the most tragic days for constitutional government in America". The problem is not solved, he said by "judicial or military coercion." Senator Ervin's appearance and speech was another plus for me, and no comfort to my critics.

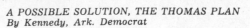

A POSSIBLE SOLUTION, THE THOMAS PLAN
By Kennedy, Ark. Democrat   4/13/58

A possible solution to tne integration-segregation controversy in the Little Rock schools continued to be of prime interest to many people.

Herbert Thomas, a Little Rock insurance executive, came up with a plan which, in my opinion, had merit. It was criticized severely by both sides and rejected outright by the blacks.

I did not take a position for or against. I thought it would have a better chance for consideration on its merits if I remained noncommital.

Evidently any compromise plan had to have some of three elements; integration, segregation and common sense. The rejection of Mr. Thomas's plan made plainer the difficulty of the Little Rock problem.

The segrcgationists in the main were willing to compromise. The integrationists and federal authorities wanted everything their way and would accept no compromise.

WEEP NO MORE FOR DIXIE
By Knox, Nashville Banner   3/13/58

Rapes, muggings and extortion among students and beatings of teachers became widespread in Chicago, Brooklyn and New York public schools. In the latter city uniformed city police were stationed in forty-one schools. In the North the bleeding hearts, mixiecrats and do-gooders, according to Knox, continued to cry about troubles in Dixie, where conditions were much better. Finally they were overwhelmed by their own problems and there was need to weep for their own plight — and not for Dixie.

Arkansas Democrat
April 13, 1958

BACKSTAGE AT THE CAPITOL
by George Douthit

They Want to Hear About
Central High School

Governor Faubus is making a lot of civic club speeches which were on schedule even before he announced for a third term. He told us the other day: "I would prefer to talk about our industrial program, educational improvements and things like that, but they want to hear something about Central High School and integration. I would like to stop talking about it, but I can't."

So, after discussing it for a few minutes he reads to his audience what he calls "the lighter side" of the situation. This side includes telegrams he has received from supporters in other states. One from Tennessee told Faubus people in that state would like for him to move over there and added: "We will trade two U.S. Senators, six congressmen and a governor and throw in Elvis Presley to boot."

"I knew they meant business," says Faubus, "when they threw in Presley."

GOOD WILL WAS KEYNOTE AS FAUBUS AND FINKBEINER FORGOT THEIR POLITICAL DIFFERENCES ON C. OF C. TRIP TO NEW ORLEANS...

FRIENDSHIP AND HARMONY
By Kennedy, Ark. Democrat   4/14/57

Chris Finkbeiner and I accompanied the Little Rock members of the C of C to New Orleans on their annual good will tour. All was friendliness and harmony.

The addition of new troopers to the State Police Force, made possible by the overall program of 1957, was credited with a remarkable 39% drop in highway deaths.

Attorney General Bruce Bennett announced for re-election, saying "I can wait" on the governor's race.

It was announced that Federal Judge Ronald Davies of North Dakota would not be sent back to Little Rock. Kennedy showed Arkansas residents as overjoyed while Davies wondered if he would be missed.

President Eisenhower vetoed the river development appropriation bill; Little Rock and North Little Rock teachers got another raise; two Republicans filed for the G.O.P. nomination for governor.

FOUL! FOUL!
By Graham, Ark. Gazette   4/22/58

Chancellor Lee Ward of Paragould officially threw his hat in the ring for governor on April 19. The cartoonist showed me holding my foot and yelling, "Foul! Foul!"

Where the cartoonist got this silly idea was hard to imagine. I never questioned the right of any citizen to seek any public office at a time of his own choosing.

HERBERT THOMAS

Herbert Thomas' plan had merit, but it ran into the brick wall attitude of the NAACP; Federal Judge Harry Lemley of Hope got the Central High School integration delay case in his court.

APRIL EVENTS

April events continued to add impetus to the political campaign.

The news on April 4 said Ward was "warmer", but Baker said no to the governor's race.

Jud Hout on April 7 hit strongly at me on the segregation issue, and said he was encouraged by support he was receiving. However, a week later he decided to "skip the race for governor."

On April 15 Attorney General Bruce Bennett filed for re-election, thus removing a prospective candidate from speculation.

MEASURE FOR MEASURE...

IF HE CAN PROVE IT, I'LL WITHDRAW. IF HE CAN'T, *HE* SHOULD WITHDRAW!

SOAP

METHINKS HE PROTEST-ETH TOO MUCH.

FAUBUS and WARD LOCK HORNS EARLY ON GOVERNOR'S CHARGE WARD MADE TRIP EAST FOR CAMPAIGN FINANCING.

MEASURE FOR MEASURE
By Kennedy, Ark. Democrat   4/27/58

Ward filed for governor on April 19. It was reported to me that just previous to filing he had made a trip to New York and Washington. I said, "Ward made a trip to the East to get campaign funds." He denied he had been to the East and fired back at me, thus giving much more publicity to my allegation.

I liked my Shakespearian reaction to Ward's upset attitude with one of my campaign jabs.

Ben Laney was still doubtful as a candidate, said press reports.

On the 24th the *Nashville News* headlined: "Ward Lashes Faubus in Declaring Candidacy, Lively Primary Forecast." An editorial favoring Ward ran in the *Warren Eagle Democrat*.

The Newport Daily Independent headlined: "Ward Hits Faubus on Three Fronts."

A headline on the 26th read: "Is He Integrationist or Segregationist? He [Faubus] Won't Say.

Herbert Thomas, author of the Thomas plan which proposed a compromise solution to the Little Rock integration problem, on the 27th severely criticized *Time* magazine for its slanted and biased reporting of the matter.

On the 28 press reports said Ward opened his campaign with a broadside attack on me, declaring I was phony on the integration issue. The next day he challenged me to a series of debates and blasted me as a pussy-footing demagogue.

On the same day both of my opponents stated their positions on the segregation issue.

Ward was quoted as saying, "I am by personal preference a segregationist."

Finkbeiner was quoted, "I do not stand for the principle of school integration. Therefore I am a segregationist". He then said he opposed the "third term power".

It was now clear that the *Gazette,* McMath and their allies had found the candidate they were seeking. Ward was articulate and daring, and carried the fight to me from the moment he announced. However, many of his charges were ineffective. For example, I had been too daring and outspoken for the pussy-footing charge to find lodging among the people. Also as Ward sought to establish his position as a segregationist, many were interested and amused at his unsuccessful efforts to make me declare myself on the issue.

BROADSIDE ATTACK BY WARD

DOGGONE EAGER BEAVER!

ORVAL

CAMPAIGN ARMOR

SUMMER WILL BE A LITTLE EARLY!
By Kennedy, Ark. Democrat   4/3/58

Ward launched his candidacy for Governor with a broadside attack on me by speeches and statements. A statewide TV address officially opened his campaign on April 28.

In the speech he called me a "fence-straddling, pussy-footing demagogue;" lashed my association with W.R. Stephens; charged that my stand on the integration issue was "as phony as snow in July;" that I used the National Guard solely as a means to a third term; that I would wreck the Highway Department, etc. etc., and challenged me to a series of debates.

I ignored the debate challenge and did not officially open my campaign until two months later.

SCHOOL'S OUT, By Hudson, Cleveland News, 5/28/58

Federal troops, on duty at the high schools in Little Rock since September 24, 1957, marched away on May 29, 1958, when the school term ended. The President's aides told the Congress the operation cost the taxpayers $5 million.

A number of civil rights leaders from throughout the nation, among them Martin Luther King, attended the graduation ceremony at Central High School. All was peace and harmony with no reports of any incidents as these civil rights leaders came and went from Little Rock.

"FREEDOM TO HIRE" AMENDMENT

BEN LANEY'S BACK IN THE NEWS...

organized labor

BEN LANEY

News reports said former Governor Ben Laney was eyed as a field general for me in the third term campaign. It was never in the cards and I never quite understood how the matter got publicized. Then Laney became chairman of a group supporting the Freedom to Hire Amendment to the State Constitution. It was speculated that the position took him out of public participation in any political race, but it didn't keep him from open opposition to my third term bid and endorsement of my opponents.

LETTER FROM DAN FELTON

On May 12 I received a letter and a campaign contribution from Dan Felton of Lee County.

A prominent businessman, planter and civic leader, Felton had inherited a strong political organization from his father which had been built over many years. While not as active as his father had been, Felton's leadership was good and he was highly respected. He had supported my opponents in the campaigns of 1954 and 1956. His support now was a welcome addition to my political strength. He wrote:

"It might be a little early, but I want you to know, Governor, that in this race I am one hundred per cent behind you...

I, personally, feel plain bad over the fact that I have not previously supported you — when there is no doubt in my mind now that your contribution to our state, the entire South and the Nation has been the greatest ever made by an individual...

Actually, Governor, there is not much I can do to help you except pledge my support, because a man with your record doesn't need to seek support — it comes to him.

I can honestly say that every person I have talked with is behind you all the way in this race — they all think that every citizen of Arkansas owes you a vote of gratitude for what you have done for us, and that for anyone to vote against you would be to tell the world that we do not believe in the right of free men to run their local governments as they so desire, but rather that they be dictated to by a centralized power.

I hope you will accept the small contribution enclosed as an expression of my gratitude for the good I think you have done for the preservation of our freedom..., and my hope that you may continue on as our good governor.

Best personal regards,
/s/ Dan
Dan Felton, Jr.

MAY EVENTS

On May 1 Little Rock Attorney Robert J. Brown filed as a candidate for governor bringing the number of my opponents to three.

The month was filled with events dramatizing the progress of Arkansas under my administration.

On May 2 I attended groundbreaking ceremonies for the states first Vo-Tech (trade) School at Pine Bluff. This facility and others to follow would provide training for workers, old and young, men and women, blacks and whites, to qualify them for the job market. The program would not only enable the trainees to earn a better livelihood, but would lend impetus to the industrial program by providing better qualified employees.

I participated in the dedication of the new $100,000 facilities at the Deaf School in Little Rock which made the Arkansas School one of the most modern in the nation. There was also a new swimming pool for the deaf and the blind students, a recreational and training facility especially useful to the latter. Many parents of the students were present from all across the state. The heads of the schools and faculty members were highly pleased with the improvements.

On May 27 we held the ground breaking ceremony for the new Children's Colony at Conway. This facility offered hope of better things for the hundreds of mentally retarded children in the state and their parents. The long frustrated efforts of many people now had promise of fulfillment.

On May 29 I visited Marked Tree to participate in the dedication of two new industries and a new state facility. The industries were Mart Manufacturing Company, and the Gotham Chalk Board & Trim Company Plant, the second headed by President Morris Miller of New York. The state facility was a new National Guard Armory at a cost of $60,000. AIDC Chairman Winthrop Rockefeller and Adjutant General Sherman T. Clinger joined in the festivities.

On May 14 I was commencement speaker for the 16 graduates of Coal Hill High School. About 1,000 people were in attendance and the press said I avoided politics in my talk.

On May 19 I appeared on the Dave Garroway nationally televised "Today Show" while attending the National Governor's Conference at Miami, Florida.

Ward was again in the headlines on May 22 with an attack on me and the statement that he opposed a hike in taxes. That was an easily taken position. I also opposed a tax hike. The tax program had been adopted in early 1957. No increase was needed now. Those who understood the situation were unimpressed by Ward's statement.

On the 24th Ward said that I conceded there would be a runoff in the governor's race. What forlorn wishful thinking. I hadn't even thought of such a concession. Johnny Sain, a popular big league baseball player of Northeast Arkansas, was announced as a Ward campaign staff worker.

Some of the high moguls of organized labor attempted to hurt my candidacy by endorsement of Finkbeiner by the political action committee (PACE) on May 25. The motion to endorse the friendly, affable Chris was voted down. Leaders then offered criticism of me but were unable to obtain any resolutions on the issue.

This action pointed up the oft-times inconsistency of some union leaders. In an effort to hurt me, perhaps because they had been directed to do so, the leaders sought to endorse one of the most anti-union business executives of the state. While a fine man in many ways Finkbeiner had for many years successfully opposed the unionization of his hundreds of employees and still maintained a non-union work force. He was a prominent member of state and local business groups who opposed practically everything that organized labor favored.

As for me, I had a good labor record while in office although I was not known as a captive of union bosses as were some political leaders. My record of performance, as contrasted with pronouncements, was better than the liberal McMath. My record was even better than my principal opponent, the *Gazette,* which once broke a strike of the *Newspaper Guild* sending its most noted columnist, Spider Rowland, into unemployment and subsequent hardship.

All these facts were not lost on the officials and members of individual unions and locals. By the dozens all across the state they endorsed my candidacy, some of them by unanimous votes.

One of the issues which my critics expected to use against me was the appointment of the third member of the five-member Highway Commission if I were re-elected. The appointments for 10-year terms for members were set up for two-year intervals. Thus it was thought no governor would ever appoint more than two members because no governor would ever serve more than two terms, and could never gain control of the agency by naming a majority of the members.

The unfortunate death of Chairman Cecil Lynch of Pine Bluff in late May changed the situation. I then had the authority to make a third appointment to fill Lynch's unexpired term. After a proper wait following Lynch's death I offered the position to former state Senator and Pine Bluff attorney Lawrence Blackwell. He accepted and was appointed.

There were good reasons for Blackwell's selection. He was a prominent attorney, an able civic minded man, a respected citizen of good judgment, restrained in his public statements and considered to be absolutely honest. Also he was a resident of the same city as his predecessor — many would have considered it unfair to place the appointment elsewhere — an area which needed highway improvements as badly as any part of the state. Also as a state senator in 1951 Blackwell was the co-author of the Mack-Blackwell Amendment to the Constitution which established the independence of the road-building agency. His appointment rendered completely futile my critics charges that I meant to destroy the independent status of the commission.

My enemies were bitterly disappointed by the development. Someone told me Henry Woods was very upset and remarked, "Well, there goes that issue".

While no doubt the Blackwell appointment worked to my advantage in the campaign, the issue of appointment of a third member of the commission would have been ineffective against me. First my predecessor had appointed all five members. Could my appointment of three members be that much worse? Second, I had faithfully kept my pledge of non-interference in highway affairs, a fact to which even the Cherry-appointed members publicly attested. In addition I had on several occasions defended the road agency from attacks by others. Third, many people wanted me to appoint other members of the commission because they felt my appointees were more responsive to their road improvement needs.

APPOINTMENTS, JANUARY 1958

Dr. H. J. Hall, Clinton, State Medical Board. Leon A. Wasson, Siloam Springs, Burial Association Board. J. L. "Bex" Shaver, Wynne, Justice Building Commission. John H. Berry, Ft. Smith, Mine Inspector. W. L. "Lloyd" Fulmer, Booneville, Parole Board. J. E. Dunlap, Jr., Harrison, Police Commission. Gene Waldon, Ozark, Arkansas Tech College Board. Dr. John H. Wilson, Magnolia, Southern State College Board. Billy G. Mabry, Conway, Stadium Commission. Mrs. Rufus Morgan, Morrilton, State Teachers College Board. J. H. Myers, Black Rock, Booneville TB Sanitorium. F. L. Archer, Hot Springs, Barber Examiners Board. F. N. Carnahan, Little Rock, Boys Industrial School Board. A. J. Baltz, Pocahontas, Forestry Commission Wallace Baker, Beebe, Training School for Girls. John Lookadoo, Arkadelphia, Henderson State Teachers College. Dr. William P. Walker, El Dorado, Chiropody Examining Board. F. A. Prewitt, Tillar, Blind & Deaf School Board. L. C. Dial, Brinkley, Publicity & Parks Commission. Carl L. Thompson, Little Rock, Veterans Service Office. Keith Tudor, Arkadelphia, Children's Colony. Board of Sanitarians: W. F. Pefferkorn, Pine Bluff; Clyde Watts, Ft. Smith; Claude L. Foster, Hamburg; Billy H. Elmore, Bentonville; C. Homer Jones, Conway. Paul Graham, Walnut Ridge, Lawrence County legislator, chosen for Advisory Board of Arkansas Association for Epileptics.

APPOINTMENTS, FEBRUARY 1958

Van Smith, Tuckerman, Arkansas State College Board. Finley Vinson, Little Rock, Merit System Council. Clifton Trigg, Dermott, A & M College Board. Dr. R. C. Dickenson, DeQueen, State Hospital Board. Mrs. Almon Faught, Jonesboro, Library Commission. C. D. Franks, Ashdown, A M & N College Board.

APPOINTMENTS, MARCH 1958

Allen Lynch, Tyronza, Board of Education. Catherine Martineau, North Little Rock, State Employees Retirement System Board. Ted Woods, Helena, Director of Publicity and Parks Agency. C. R. "Russ" Horne, Russellville, Member Publicity and Parks Commission to replace Ted Woods who became director. Sam Rorex, Little Rock, an appeals referee with Employment Security Division. Psychology Examiners Board: Dr. Jerome Schiffer, Little Rock; Dr. Hardy C. Wilcoxen, Fayetteville; Dr. Sidney J. Fields, Little Rock; Dr. H. K. Moore, Little Rock. Miss Maryella Clayton, Ft. Smith, Nurse Examiners Board.

APPOINTMENTS, APRIL 1958

S. A. Walker, Russellville, State Board of Health. Robert H. Smith Sr., Walnut Ridge, U. of A. Board of Trustees. J. C. Hawkins, Little Rock, leader of the East End Civic League of black voters, Negro Boys School Board. Howard Eichenbaum, Little Rock, Board of Architects.

APPOINTMENTS, MAY 1958

Mrs. Beatrice Cannaday, Clinton, Abstractors Licensing Board. R. L. Blair, Melbourne, Liquified Petroleum Gas Control Board. Gordon Carleton, DeQueen, prosecuting attorney. Lawrence Blackwell, Pine Bluff, Highway Commission, to fill the vacancy created by the death of Cecil Lynch of Pine Bluff from injuries suffered in a traffic accident.

FEDERAL COURT HEARING IN L.R. ATTRACTS WIDE ATTENTION... HERE ARE SOME OF THE PRINCIPALS:

"I didn't get to bed for five days after integration began!"

"The state is powerless to thwart the Constitution."

"Expert witnesses on both sides have gone astray..."

• Virgil Blossom

• Thurgood Marshall (NAACP Attorney)

"Faubus may not be governor in 1961."

• Judge Lemley

• Wayne Upton

"Lessons in good citizenship were not well learned." (at CHS)

• Dr. David Salten, N.Y.

FEDERAL COURT HEARING PRINCIPALS
By Kennedy, Ark. Democrat   6/8/58

This made Finkbeiner's proposal look ridiculous. A saving of 20% might be effected in administrative expense but not in overall expenditures.

The big money in state government lies in the millions which go to the public schools, institutions of higher learning, welfare grants, operation of the State Hospital and other similar agencies.

Some adviser to Chris goofed.

THE FORBIDDEN FRUIT
By Kennedy, Ark. Democrat   6/15/58

The hearing before Judge Lemley on the School Board's request to postpone integration for three years attracted the famous Negro NAACP lawyer, Thurgood Marshall of New York (now an associate Justice of the U.S. Supreme Court), and a so-called expert from the same state, Dr. David Salten. Salten was considered by many to be a prejudiced, biased witness who could contribute nothing worthwhile toward a solution.

Other principals were:

Supt. Blossom; School Board member Wayne Upton, who said, "Faubus may not be governor in 1961" if integration could be postponed that far; presiding Federal Judge Harry J. Lemley, who said, "Expert witnesses on both sides have gone astray."

FINKBEINER PROPOSAL

Chris Finkbeiner, as his main campaign plank, promised to reduce state expenses by 20% by practicing efficiency in state government.

We did some figuring and found that if all seven constitutional offices, including that of governor, were abolished, along with the revenue department, comptroller's department and several others, and all the expenditures for these departments and offices avoided, the entire savings would amount to only about 6% of the total cost of state government.

Sherman Adams, conservative, economical, efficient New Englander, was President Eisenhower's right hand man at the White House. Because of the president's ignorance of civil government procedures and his propensity to let staff members make decisions for him, Adams was for a time perhaps the most powerful figure in the national government.

I became fairly well acquainted with Adams beginning with the White House conference on Civil Defense and international problems in 1955, followed by the Newport Conference in 1957 and the meeting of the Governor's Executive Committee with the president in 1958.

The conduct of the presidential assistant was considered by many as above reproach. Then came the disclosures of his friendship with Bernard Goldfine and acceptance of gifts and favors from the influence peddler. The incidents were so distorted by the press and an unfriendly Democratic Congress that Adams was forced to resign.

Cartoonist Kennedy produced this clever cartoon on the subject.

Now two of the five principals of the Newport Conference were gone.

GOV. FAUBUS CAN HOLD HIS OWN

Editorial from an out-of-state newspaper

Gov. Averill Harriman of New York, the darling of many of the radical groups . . . is always quick to criticize, particularly if the person is a Southern Governor . . .

His latest blast . . . (June 13, 1958) was at Gov. Faubus of Arkansas. The New York chief executive called Mr. Faubus a "Quisling" who had failed "to uphold the public interest" in the Little Rock . . . integration troubles.

The word quisling was developed in Norway during WW II. It was the name of a Norwegian who betrayed his country during the war by supporting the German invaders. (He became the puppet ruler of Norway with the backing of the Nazi troops.)

Calling attention to this fact, Gov. Faubus took Harriman's criticism in stride and pointed up the historical fallacy in the New York governor's use of the word.

Said Gov. Faubus:

"I would like to point out that I was working against the occupation forces in Arkansas and not with them. We have some Quislings in Arkansas, but I was not one of them."

TOUCHE! our dear Mr. Harriman.

Arkansas Democrat
June 15, 1958

Backstage at the Capitol

State's View of Faubus
Only Interest to Nation
By GEORGE DOUTHIT
(Democrat Staff Writer.)

An Eastern magazine writer was in town last week, sizing up the Arkansas governor's race, and said it will get national attention — not over who is elected governor but whether the people of the state will reject or re-elect Governor Faubus. . . .

The 1957 crisis brought dozens of newspapermen into Arkansas and millions of words were written pro and con on the subject. One viewpoint which circulated over the nation was that the people of Arkansas really want integration but that Governor Faubus was blocking it.

The coming election will be the first concrete test as to what the majority of the people actually think about the Faubus actions. . . .

This magazine writer . . . said people out in the nation will accept only one answer — that the result proves Arkansas wants integration or doesn't want it.

As an example, when Chris Finkbeiner announced for governor several months ago, his picture was carried in an English-speaking newspaper in Japan. . . . The headline said: "He is opposing Faubus."

SPILT MILK IS SPILT MILK
By Kennedy, Ark. Democrat   6/19/58

AT LEAST SOMEBODY'S HAPPY
By McClanahan, Dallas Morning News   6/16/58

Many Supreme Court rulings continued to favor criminals over law abiding citizens and enforcement officers, in the view of many people.

My disagreement with Blossom at this particular time was over statements attributed to him in a magazine interview in which he was quoted as saying that he and the School Board never asked for police protection or assistance in the integration of Central High School. The statement was contrary to all the facts. I had no desire to dispute with Blossom but I had to take issue with the false statements in the magazine article.

Rep.
★ OREN HARRIS

heads house committee investigating Adams-Goldfine tie-up.

I'M ALL EARS

SUPREME COURT PROMISES TO RULE ON PATIENT-QUOTA LAW BY JULY 1.

LITTLE ROCK

CHICKEN FRY AT MT. NEBO DRAWS THREE FRIENDLY CANDIDATES FOR GOVERNOR..
RULES CALLED FOR NON-POLITICAL SPEECHES, HELD TO 10 MINUTES.

Congressman Oren Harris, chairman of the House committee investigating the Adams-Goldfine tie-up, was dubbed "Arkansan of the Week." The disclosures of his committee contributed to the resignation of Sherman Adams as White House assistant to President Eisenhower.

The State Supreme Court promised to rule on the state's patient-quota law for the Medical Center. Senator Robert Harvey of Swifton sponsored the measure in an attempt to assure fair treatment for indigent patients from all counties of the state. The great Medical Center had been built and was being operated by state funds paid by all the people, but had become almost entirely a charity facility for the Little Rock area only. Legislators considered this practice grossly unfair.

Ward, Finkbeiner and I ate chicken together at the annual Mt. Nebo chicken fry.

The cartoons were those of Jon Kennedy in the *Arkansas Democrat* Weekly Highlights, 6/22/58.

- - - - -

LITTLE ROCK EXPECTS HARROWING EXPERIENCE

Claude Sitton, in a New York Times article on the Little Rock situation had this to say:

The change in the attitude of the moderates toward the problems arising out of desegregation was demonstrated by the Arkansas Gazette. The newspaper and its executive editor, Harry Ashmore, received two Pulitzer prizes this year for the Gazette's editorial coverage of the Central High crisis.

Mr. Ashmore, in an editorial entitled "The Alternative Before the Court," noted that the newspaper has bent its efforts toward finding means by which the South could comply with the 1954 ruling in Brown v. Board of Education.

"We, and those who shared our view across the South, have failed," he wrote. "There is no way, for the time being at least, to obtain such compliance without doing irreparable harm to the system of public education upon which all our children, colored no less than white, are dependent."

Ashmore was in no wise beholden to public sentiment for job security with the Gazette, but the paper's loss of some 30,-000 in circulation and more than a million dollars may have had some bearing in cooling his ardor in advocating immediate compliance with the federal court orders. If Ashmore had reached this conclusion through observation of developments, then certainly those whose positions were determined by public sentiment must have recognized the signals even more clearly.

The Little Rock School Board refused a strong demand of a Justice Department official to issue a firm statement and ask for injunctive proceedings against opponents of the court order. Instead the Board said it would comply with state laws.

The City Manager Board of Directors issued a public statement saying it would not direct city police to attempt enforcement of the court order as Mayor Mann had done. The enforcement, said the city fathers, was entirely up to federal authorities.

In the face of these developments, and after the people voted against opening the schools on an integrated basis, the federal authorities decided later not to attempt to open the schools. They likewise refrained from any action against state officials for carrying out the provisions of the laws later enacted at the special session of the legislature.

The federal officials, wisely, I think, avoided a confrontation at the time. They did not wish to attempt the difficult task of enforcement alone without any Quislings to assist them. Their decision may have been in the best interest of everyone — granting that the ultimate outcome was to be the same with the passage of time — in avoiding disorder and violence.

———0—0—0—0———

JUNE EVENTS

Affairs continued which highlighted state progress. On June 10 came the dedication of the new Justice Building in Little Rock. Among the agencies housed were the State Supreme Court, the Attorney General's Office, the Commerce Commission, Public Service Commission and the Workmen's Compensation Commission.

On Sunday, June 29, we dedicated a new dormitory for the Boy's Training School at Pine Bluff.

On June 13 I signed the agreement with the federal authorities for the extension of jobless pay for Arkansas. The contract made available $3,255,212 for unemployed workers in the state.

The Camden local of the Carpenters Union endorsed my candidacy. The announcement came from local Secretary Jack Dorris on June 12.

On June 17, Ward got back in the headlines on the segregation-integration issue. He challenged me "Are you segregationist or integrationist?"

Ward then said, "I believe in segregation and I practice segregation, and that's more than Faubus." He went on to accuse me of being the "biggest practicing integrationist in Arkansas."

Actually there was some truth in Ward's accusation. However, the integration I practiced was by choice, not by compulsion at bayonet point.

It was strange that neither Ward nor Finkbeiner ever attacked the illegal use of federal troops in Little Rock. So long as they approved this by their silence, their stance as segregationists was ineffective in gaining support.

I ignored Ward's railings at the time and went my way declining to say whether I was a segregationist or an integrationist.

Arnold Sikes on June 18, and J. L. Bland on the 25th resigned their state positions to participate in my campaign, Sikes as manager, Bland as advertising manager.

A BUSY POLITICAL WEEK
By Kennedy, Ark. Democrat
6/29/58

On June 25 an advertisement, run nationwide from a Denver, Colo. headquarters, asked for funds to fight my re-election effort.

There was welcome news on June 22 when Judge Lemley approved a 30-month delay in integration of the Little Rock schools.

On June 26 the news said Ward intensified his attack on me. I announced I would open my campaign with a TV address. I defended my "program of progress", and said the effort to defeat me was nationwide.

Robert J. Brown, candidate for governor, withdrew from the race in time to have his name removed from the ballot. I formally opened my campaign with a statewide TV-radio address. The words attributed to me "are y' listenin', Denver?" were evoked by a fund raising effort set up in Denver to oppose me in the campaign. Ward's campaign helicopter ran out of gas forcing a landing on U.S. Highway No. 62, and Finkbeiner was campaigning in South Arkansas.

SUMMER REPLACEMENT ON T.V., *By Kennedy, Ark. Democrat, 6/26/58*

During any political year in Arkansas political telecasts, of necessity, preempt regular television programs. In the campaign of 1958 the cartoonist took a unique slant, posing the candidates as the principal characters in three popular current TV programs.

FIRST THINGS FIRST, By Kennedy, Ark. Democrat, 6/22/58

Federal Judge Harry J. Lemley on June 21, after an extensive hearing, granted the Little Rock School Board's petition for a delay in integration until the mid-semester of the 1960-61 school year. The ruling made national and international news. The cartoon sums up the wisdom and the essence of the judge's ruling — when the "right to a peaceful education" of the school children was moved ahead of "forced integration." Judge Lemley's decision won nationwide acclaim among constitutional lawyers, and had the support of all advocates of states rights. He was flooded with messages of approval from all parts of the nation.

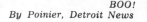

BOO!
By Poinier, Detroit News   6/22/58

Following the decision of Judge Lemley delaying integration at Little Rock, the cartoonist portrayed "Uncle Sam," the "Federal Court" and the "Little Rock Board of Education" as frightened into "integration postponement" by merely a "BOO!" from "Gov. Faubus." The aim of the cartoonist, perhaps, was to goad the federal government and the federal courts into proceeding with integration regardless of state laws and the will of the people, and regardless of the harm that might come to the children, parents, the community or education itself. Judge Lemley was a jurist of the highest integrity who was not intimidated by anyone.

THE CRITICS GRASP AT STRAWS

After the delay decision by Judge Lemley, a story written for the *Wall Street Journal*, appeared in the *Arkansas Gazette* of June 29. A lengthy article, it said the following:

"Gov. Faubus isn't needed to meet federal integration orders now. I think the race issue was a phony; now the governor will have a much harder time cashing in on it."

"The Court ruling . . . has taken a lot of wind out of Gov. Faubus' sail."

These opinions came from a Stuttgart, Ark. businessman and a worker in the camp of his political enemies.

. . . ironically, there's evidence that Gov. Faubus' task may become tougher as a result of Lemley's ruling.

"Judge Lemley's ruling has just about taken the governor's integration issue out of the picture. He's going to have to hunt for some other issues to get elected," said state Senator Roy Milum of Harrison. (Milum had been in the anti-Faubus camp since 1956 when he supported Jim Snoddy.)

My critics in the state, and especially the out-of-state journalists, seized upon all issues and occurrences, both major and trivial, and attempted to interpret them into unfavorable developments for me. The above is a good example. They were like drowning men grasping at straws.

As for the integration-segregation issue, I would have been glad for it to fade away entirely. I never liked the controversy and always regretted the fact that I could not avoid becoming embroiled. Other political leaders had much the same feeling about the matter.

As to other issues mentioned by Senator Milum, I had them, and spent 95% of my campaign speeches on these other issues after the official opening of my campaign.

Anyway, Sen. Milum's opposition to me stemmed from his demand to control all patronage and appointments in his 5-county senatorial district. I alwasy considered the senator's requests on appointments but I declined to give him the complete control he demanded. My opinion of Sen. Milum, based on long observation and experience in dealing with him, was that, although a very able legislator, he didn't care what stand a governor took on any issue just so long as the senator had carte blanche to control all patronage, projects and appointments in his district.

As to the *Arkansas Gazette*, my principal opponent, one contributor to the People's Column wrote: "We find you grabbing at straws in the wind in your effort to dig up campaign chaff for Ward and Finkbeiner." — Mrs. John D. McBurnett, North Little Rock.

Peoria, Ill., Journal Star, June 24
Reprinted in Walnut Ridge, Ark., Times-Dispatch, July 3, 1958

Maybe Faubus Was Right

U.S. District Judge Harry J. Lemley in his Little Rock decision last week said, in effect, that Governor Faubus was right.

It is bitter medicine for the anti-Faubus people . . . Anti-segregation people point out that Judge Lemley himself is an Arkansas man, implying that his decision may have been influenced by personal prejudice.

Nevertheless . . . he is a federal judge and he has ordered the postponement of racial integration in Central high school at Little Rock for exactly the same reasons that Governor Faubus gave last fall when he tried to do the same thing.

Whether Judge Lemley's ruling is right will, of course, be debated. But is a judicial opinion, arrived at by orderly processes of law after hearing evidence for and against a school board petition to postpone integration, and stated in a 35-page decision. And even if it is eventually overruled . . . it gives respectability to the position of Governor Faubus, who was thoroughly smeared last fall, from coast to coast, as a 100 per cent demagogue.

Judge Lemley said that Little Rock needed a peaceful interlude so that "the unfortunate racial strife and tension" of the city could be quieted down. Governor Faubus said the same thing.

There is now at least a question whether the Northern extremists who so furiously lambasted Governor Faubus last year were not more harmful to the cause of racial amity than Mr. Faubus was.

Arkansas Gazette, July 10, 1958

The *Gazette*, in what must have been an unguarded moment, admitted that Arkansas (during my administration) "had entered a new era of progress," and "our race relations were such that Arkansas was considered a model among the Southern states."

That was what I kept telling the national Republican administration in an effort to dissuade them from strictly political policies which did not make any contribution toward peaceful progress. I also disagreed with their cowardly failure to assume any responsibility for the enforcement of their own court orders and political decisions.

At this point the *Gazette* wanted all progress to end just so it would be more difficult for me to win an election.

State Pride

It is true that Arkansans traditionally have borne an inferiority complex inspired by statistical comparisons of per capita income that left room only to thank God for Mississippi. But until Candidate Ward's third-term opponent, Governor Orval Faubus, bucked a federal court order and made Arkansas an object of scorn over much of the na-

tion and, indeed, the world, Arkansas had entered a new era of progress and its citizens walked with a new pride.

Our industrial development program had reached such proportions that even Texas — speaking of "braggarts" — was asking how we did it. Our race relations were such that Arkansas was considered a model among the Southern states. . . .

But now Governor Faubus wants to "serve" for a third term — and to that end he is trying to convince the people that the great world is against them, not him.

BAPTIST LEADER SENDS CLIPPINGS

On July 15 a letter from Rev. Rel Gray, former Arkansas Baptist Association president for two years, was accompanied by some interesting clippings. Rev. Gray was then Pastor of Temple Baptist Church of Ruston, La.

Shreveport, La., Times
July, 13, 1958

Right Out of His Own Mouth

Elsewhere on this page, the Banner reproduces a letter written by Harry S. Ashmore, executive editor of the ARKANSAS GAZETTE, addressed to William Loeb, editor of the Manchester (N.H.) TIMES-UNION, in reply to some pointed questions.

The inquiries were not inappropriate. The answers were revealing.

In publishing this reply on page one, Mr. Loeb appended the pointed observation:

"Harry S. Ashmore . . . reveals in the above letter that although he believes integration to be fine for Central High School, it is not so fine for the GAZETTE."

Far better than one of the Ashmore speeches, or books about the "Epitaph For Dixie" or editorial columns, the Ashmore letter speaks for itself.

It is a revealing admission on pertinent points as significant to readers in New Hampshire as to those closer to home, who must have wondered what portion of Mr. Ashmore's "epitaph" he voluntarily embraced for the organ of his present attachment, how much of his "crusading" substance he was allowed to track into the house, and how large a dose of the nux vomica he prescribed for others he was willing to take himself.

Straight from Ashmore the answers have come.

It makes odd reading . . . if not wholly surprising.

Doesn't it?

The letter from Ashmore to Editor Loeb said in part:

We do not at this time have any Negro editorial employee on the Gazette. . . . We see no particular need for one now and recognize that any Negro staff member would operate under considerable restrictions due to the prevailing mores and customs of the community.

Of course we segregate Negro obituary notices as we segregate advertisements in the classified section dealing with Negro real estate. It has long been our policy and will continue to be to identify persons in all news stories by race.

Harry S. Ashmore
Executive Editor

STILL ON THE OLD 'THATAWAY' TRAIL
By Graham, Ark. Gazette   7/3/58

The cartoonist was more confused than me or the voters, as the election results later showed.

I pointed out the money raising headquarters in Denver, Colo., which mailed out letters soliciting funds to be used against me in the campaign. Certain high-up national labor leaders issued statements against me, but the union members in Arkansas paid them no heed.

The *Gazette* found two state editors to quote.

J. R. McKinley said in the *DeQueen Bee*: "Right now local people are reasonably sure there'll be a runoff with Ward tabbed as the man most likely to succeed."

David Pryor said in the *Ouachita Citizen*: "It is regretful that this entire situation has feathered the nest for some politicians throughout the state."

David didn't say whose nests were feathered, but one of those he certainly had in mind was W. R. (Witt) Stephens. Others on this list were John Cooper, Truman Baker, Olen Hendrix, Harry Parkin, W. E. (Bill) Darby, D. P. (Pete) Raney and Leon Catlett.

LETTER FROM BOYD TACKETT

Former Congressman Boyd Tackett of Texarkana joined openly in my support. Tackett helped to defeat McMath for a third term in 1952, fought me hard in 1954 and, I suspect, supported one of my opponents in 1956.

On July 14, he wrote:

Dear Orval,

You have Southwest Arkansas in the bag — no run-off in sight. I receive the same report from the other areas of the State. Therefore, while you don't need to answer the statement of your opposition that "Harry Ashmore and his Arkansas Gazette supported you in your first race for Governor," I am hopeful that you will avail yourself of the oppor-

tunity to give a true answer. That answer necessarily brings to my mind distasteful memories, but, at the same time, to the contrary notwithstanding, it can serve to your advantage to advise people of the truth, and that is: Harry Ashmore supported you because he thought you were a "pink," and he is so disappointed in finding that you are not, he is willing to fight you as a newspaper has never before openly fought any candidate for any office.

Yours sincerely,
Boyd Tackett

Boyd was 100 per cent right in his evaluation of Ashmore and his reason for supporting me, belatedly, in 1954 and then in 1956. And for his determined opposition in 1958.

QUESTION ANSWERED
By Kennedy, Ark. Democrat   7/25/58

Beginning several weeks before the 1958 Democratic Primary election, a series of small ads were run in the Little Rock newspapers hinting at some irregular connection between me and a person named Clara Lessem involving Southland Race Track in West Memphis. The ads were signed with the name Ida Thompson.

I had no idea who Clara Lessem could be, whether such a person existed, and knew nothing of the implied connection with Southland. The matter was finally cleared up in a front page story by the enterprising reporter George Douthit in the *Arkansas Democrat* of July 24.

The person was Clara Upton, sister of Charles Upton, prominent West Memphis insurance man and official of Southland Racing Corporation. Her husband, Mr. Lessem, had died and she was then using her maiden name. The family had lived in Little Rock for 55 years.

Miss Upton said she had never met me but was supporting my candidacy. Her married name of Clara Lessem had been used in the ads without her knowledge or consent. She gave a statement to the reporter in which she said: "If they (who are running the ads) damage Mr. Faubus or damage me I am going

383

to come out with a battery of lawyers and go into court and when I get through they will know who Clara Lessem is."

Following the story Kennedy produced the cartoon showing the puncture of the balloon so diligently floated by the anti-Faubus forces.

So far as I can recall I have never yet met Clara Lessem.

HANDWRITING ON THE WALL
By Graham, Ark. Gazette   6/27/58

The *Gazette* took great hope from the fact that three former governors of Arkansas came out in opposition to my candidacy.

Former Gov. Sid McMath, while attempting to avoid the label of integrationist, made a number of speeches and issued press statements opposing my candidacy. Finally he went on statewide television in a paid telecast against me.

Former Gov. Ben T. Laney joined a television panel opposing my candidacy.

Former Gov. Francis Cherry issued his statement of opposition from Washington where he was serving as a member of the National Subversive Control Board by appointment of President Eisenhower.

The only other former governor, Homer M. Adkins, issued a statement on July 27, two days before the election, saying, "I am supporting Gov. Faubus wholeheartedly as I have done in all of his previous races."

Meanwhile the *Gazette* reproduced all the newspaper comment against me it could find. The editorials included one from the Camden *Ouachita Citizen* by Editor David Pryor.

Pryor speculated that "the great silent, unheard of mass electors who are not demonstrators, who are seeking nothing but honesty and decency in return for the vote" would "commit itself on the basic issue — the great issue of a third-term governor who would be granted dictatorial powers."

Editor Pryor's implication was plain. He hoped the silent vote would reject my candidacy because of the third term.

CHRIS HOLDS 400th COFFEE PARTY...

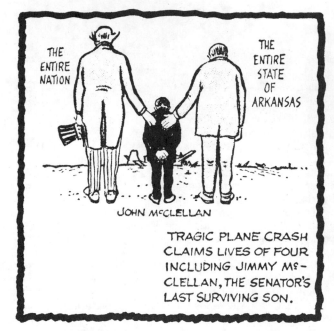

you can slow down now, chief!

FAUBUS HEADQUARTERS SAYS POLL SHOWS ORVAL TO RECEIVE 79% OF VOTES CAST.

HIGHLIGHTS OF THE NEWSWEEK
By Kennedy, Ark. Democrat   6/27/58

The first Democratic primary was two days away. Chris Finkbeiner was having coffees, and Lee Ward inferred or stated in a TV speech that someone had offered to pay him to get out of the race.

The last of Sen. John L. McClellan's three sons was tragically killed in a plane crash.

My headquarters issued a statement that I would receive 79% of the vote. I did not authorize use of the 79% figure as I knew it was a little too high.

―•―o―o―•―o―o

THE QUESTION

New York (N.Y.) *Times,* July 27, 1958

Claude Sitton, in a special report to the *New York Times* on the Arkansas election, used a question mark cartoon to help explain the situation in the campaign.

Sitton's report was grossly erroneous in one respect. He wrote: "The Governor views his opposition to forced integration as a most valuable political asset and brings it to the voters' attention at every available opportunity."

The latter part of the statement is exaggerated. In speeches that lasted from 30 minutes to an hour on the progress of Arkansas in many fields, and my hopes for still further gains, the portion of the speech devoted to the illegal use of federal force in Little Rock ranged from two to five minutes. This fact is noted in an editorial in the Fayetteville *Northwest Arkansas Times* after the election.

―•―o―•―o―•―

JULY EVENTS

On the first day of the month Roy M. Nelson, Hughes superintendent of schools for 21 years, joined the campaign staff as head of public relations division on education. Garland County Treasurer Mrs. Mary Jess Langford also joined the headquarters as a division manager.

A headline in the Hot Springs *New Era* of July 3 said: "McMath in Denunciation of Faubus."

Ward was again in the news on the integration issue. These headlines appeared on July 5:

WARD HITS FAUBUS INTEGRATION
SILENCE—*SW Times Record*

WHERE DOES FAUBUS STAND?
WARD DEMANDS — *Arkansas Gazette*

WARD THROWS INTEGRATION GAUNTLETT
AT GOVERNOR — *Newport Independent*

WARD TO BY-PASS SALES TAX—IF NOMINATED

FAUBUS SWITCHES ATTACK TO HIT
HIGH LABOR MOGULS

The news reports said I spoke to 23,000 people in a number of places on July 4. One headline read: "Roar Greets Mention of Calling Out the Guard."

On July 8 I toured the restored and preserved Civil War Capital of Washington. Judge James Pilkington and I rode in an ancient horse drawn buggy driven by Joe Booker on a tour of the area, followed by a dinner served in the building used as the Capitol during the last years of the Civil War.

I spoke that night to a political rally in Hope attended by 2,000.

On the same date I received a copy of the fund raising letter being mailed from Denver, Colo. seeking money for my opponents. It came from O. K. Leabo, a dentist, 2601 Parallel, Kansas City, Mo., who wrote:

Here's $5.00 to add to your campaign fund. I received this "junk" [the Denver letter] in the mail today. I live in Missouri, have my dental office in Kansas and am sorry I can't vote for you in Arkansas.

I used the letter and $5 check in my campaign speeches. I never cashed the check. Its value was far greater than its face value for use in the campaign. The Denver letter, Mr. Leabo's message and the check are still in my files. Similar letters came in from time to time throughout the campaign, proof that the Denver money raising effort was widespread.

The news of July 10 said I spoke to 5,000 in a night rally at Monticello. Ward had a crowd of 100 when he appeared there.

July 12 was a day the TV networks chose to cover my campaign. My first speaking engagement was at 10 a.m. at the small, picturesque county seat town of Mt. Ida in beautiful, rural Montgomery County. It was a friendly area which gave me good support in every election. I made a speech in the town in every campaign.

Two of my loyal supporters in Mt. Ida were the able, well-educated country lawyer, Jerry Witt, and his son.

My customary speaking location was the west lawn of the courthouse. The audience gathered at the low stone wall which encircled the building and grounds, at a point where trees provided some shade. My stand was in the open in the bright sun.

When I arrived I noted the microphone for my use was set beside the courthouse perhaps 100 feet from the crowd. A TV network photographer, I was told later, had set up at the stone wall to one side of the crowd, and had carefully measured the distance and adjusted his cameras.

As soon as I was introduced I picked up the mike and carried it to a point within 6 to 8 feet of the people gathered along the wall. Whenever possible I liked to be close enough to my audience to look them in the face when I spoke. I did not know of the inconvenience to the TV camera crews, but I later learned that my road crewmen were amused by the incident.

Among my hearers that day at Mt. Ida was a newcomer to the state who had never before seen or heard me. He had made a considerable investment in lakeside property at nearby Lake Ouachita, and naturally was interested in the promotion of tourism and the general progress of the state.

When I finished speaking I was engulfed by those in the crowd who wanted to shake my hand and assure me of their support. The newcomer sought out some members of my staff to say. "That's the first time I've heard that man. He is able and sincere. I'm going to support him. These newspapers had me wondering if he was a rascal."

He then asked my staff members to convey to me and my party his invitation to be his guest at his resort when the campaign was over, or whenever I chose.

I'm sorry I never had opportunity to enjoy the man's offered hospitality. The life of a governor is very busy.

McMATH IGNORED AT MURFREESBORO

Another mid-day speech was at Murfreesboro, county seat of Pike County, the site of the diamond mines. A large crowd had gathered in the bright July sun. The diamond mine owners, Mr. and Mrs. Millar were in the audience. My crew chief, "Rabbit" Burnett and other staff members had exciting news to report when I arrived. Sid McMath, accompanied by Mrs. McMath, was there. They had learned that McMath meant to "horn in," demand the use of my sound equipment and speak against me when my speech was ended. This intrusion and confrontation would be filmed by the networks and make nationwide news.

I received the information without comment, then went inside the building to use the restroom. As I crossed an empty room on the way out I noted the large TV network cable had been plugged to an outlet in the wall. Near the center of the room the cable had been neatly severed. I am reasonably certain the act was not committed by any member of my crew for I frowned on such tactics. However, it was widely felt that the TV networks had been unkind and unfair to Arkansas. Someone evidently took the opportunity to retaliate, or the network crew had cut the cable in order to claim harrassment.

I had already noted the shirtsleeved McMath lingering near the edge of the crowd. I sometimes mentioned him in my speeches but the mention was not by any means regular. I made a mental note to ignore McMath in the Murfreesboro speech. There was no necessity to open the door for the grandstanding which I had no doubt had been planned with the collaboration of the *Gazette* and the TV networks.

During the course of my speech McMath took a strategic location to my right rear where he could be photographed by the same cameras that covered me and also be near the mike and speakers stand. Farrell placed a member of my crew to the rear of the TV cameramen. Unseen by them this man directed the former governor's movements. McMath thought he was an aide of the network men, followed his directions and kept changing his position. Consequently the cameramen were kept so busy readjusting their equipment that they may have gotten few, if any, good pictures. Farrell and other young members of my road crew were elated with the success of their strategy and hilariously related the story afterward.

I later learned there was no reason to think that McMath would be heard following my address. Unknown to me my supporters in the audience and my crewmen had decided to take matters into their hands.

As the sound of my last word died away, there was a mad rush of hundreds of people to surround me and shake my hand. I noted the Millars in the forefront of the charge. A road crew member grabbed the microphone and whisked it away. All the sound equipment disappeared as if by magic. The network TV crews had all they could do to protect themselves and their equipment in the jam of people. Out of the corner of my eye I noted McMath looking on from the side with an air of puzzlement.

The crowd began to disperse as I shook hands with the last ones. Mrs. McMath lingering nearby said to me through a fixed, mirthless smile, "Orval, I thought you could do better than that," referring to my speech.

"Mrs. McMath," I replied, "I keep trying. I hope to do better."

I turned to greet more supporters and then went on my way.

A newspaper headline following the speech read:
Verbal Fight Doesn't Materialize at Murfreesboro Campaign Speech Where Faubus Ignores Sid McMath

In retrospect, I doubt that a McMath speech would have been successful if it had been attempted. Most of the crowd, after greeting me, would have disappeared just as the crowd did at Mountain Home where I was confronted by Curt Copeland two years earlier in the 1956 campaign.

10,000 AT BENTON

A July 13 headline said: "10,000 Hear Faubus at Benton."

A mile long caravan of cars filled with supporters drove to Benton from Little Rock to swell the crowd. However, the size of the audience indicated strong labor support, for Benton was a stronghold of the labor unions.

McMATH TAKES TO TV

July 14 headline: "McMath on TV; Faubus at Paragould."

McMath leveled his strongest guns on me in a statewide network TV address. With some of my youthful crew members I watched the speech from a motel room. McMath was a good speaker and I commented that it was a good speech. Farrell and the youthful workers were unimpressed and labeled it ineffective. They were right.

I spoke to the largest crowd ever to gather at the outdoor drive-in movie theatre at Paragould. A fine organization of supporters there made all the arrangements. They did other organizational work including a series of ads written and paid for locally. The ads were signed by Joe Howard, Greene County Faubus for Governor chairman.

On July 16 I was greeted by a crowd of 2,500 at Blytheville which included the city officials and the Mississippi County office holders. I was assured that the county was mine.

DAN PORTIS SUPPORT

On the same day I toured towns in Poinsett County including Lepanto. A headline read: "Faubus Gets Backing of Dan Portis." There were three definite factions in that area of the county. When I entered Lepanto, Portis, who, with his brother, J. C. Portis, was the leader of perhaps the strongest faction, was waiting with the leaders of the other two groups. Together the three leaders escorted me through the town introducing me to businessmen, employees and visitors on the streets. The unity of the factions as evidenced by their leaders meant near unanimous support in the Lepanto area and widespread favor throughout the county.

ELECTRICAL WORKERS ENDORSE ME

"Electrical Workers for Faubus," read a headline on July 20. Fifteen delegates representing 4,000 union workers statewide endorsed my candidacy. The announcement was made by Eddie Jones, the legislative representative.

On the same day a huge political rally at Pine Bluff was addressed by all three candidates. Following the event a headline read: "Faubus Cheered, Ward and Finkbeiner Hooted by Crowd."

CHERRY ASKS VOTERS TO REJECT MY BID

On the 22nd Ward was well received by a quiet, courteous crowd at my hometown of Huntsville.

On the 23rd the news said I slowed my pace with only two afternoon speeches, one at night at Clarksville.

Former Gov. Cherry, in a statement issued from Washington on July 24, strongly condemned me and asked the voters to reject my third term bid.

On the same day prominent news stories said the "silent vote" may make the experts wonder. The question raised, was it for me or against me?

News reported an overflow crowd at my open house in Little Rock. All could not gain entrance to the Marion Hotel ballroom.

NO OUTSIDE INTERFERENCE, By Kennedy, Ark. Democrat, 7/27/58

As the world watched, all eyes were on Arkansas as the July 29 Democratic primary approached. Many efforts, some from outside the state, had been made to influence the voting as the people determined "the fate of Orval Faubus." The words of the Arkansas voters to the outside world were appropriate: "You do the watching and I'll do the voting!" One of Kennedy's great cartoons.

BEN LANEY AND PANEL OPPOSE

On July 25 former Gov. Ben Laney came out openly against me. He joined a TV panel in Little Rock which included former highway commissioner Miss Willie Lawson, Little Rock business executives Everett Tucker and W. F. "Billy" Rector (one replaced the other on the panel), labor leader George H. Ellison of Ft. Smith and former Democratic national committeeman Dr. R. B. Robins of Camden.

STRANGE BEDFELLOWS

On July 27, responding to Cherry's opposition, McMath's activities and the TV panel which included Ben Laney, I said:

"I never expected to live long enough to see Harry Ashmore, Ben Laney, Sid McMath, Francis Cherry and Sherman Adams in the same political bed together.

"Can't you just see their confusion trying to make a decision for one of their candidates if he should win?"

When I made this statement in my stump speeches it was greeted with shouts of acclaim and derisive laughter.

CARPENTERS AND GOV. ADKINS ENDORSE ME

On July 27 the news said "Carpenters Endorse Faubus." Leon Bush of Local No. 690 made the announcement.

Former Gov. Homer Adkins, responding to the opposition TV panel and the three opposing former chief executives, openly endorsed my candidacy.

A *Democrat* headline read: "Nation's Eyes Turn on Arkansas as Vote for Governor Nears."

I closed my stumping tour with a speech to a giant rally at Jonesboro. Some of the best political organizers in the state made arrangements and managed my campaign there.

On the 29th, election day, the *Gazette* headlined: "World Turns Eyes to Arkansas Vote on Governor Issue."

I told the press, "It's voters turn now."

The *Democrat* reported that showers failed to check the surge to the polls, and the voting places in the twin cities were jammed. The higher vote indicated a victory for me, the newspaper said.

That night the television and radio told the amazing results, and on the 30th the headlines read: "Faubus Sweeps to Third Term; Landslide Margin Tops 2 to 1.

A *Democrat* editorial said in part:

Governor Faubus broke the half-century-old tradition against a third term for the state executive, and broke it thoroughly — flung the pieces far and wide.

There will be no run-off. Mr. Faubus is the next governor by the people's overwhelming choice.

The third term was never much of an issue. Neither, apparently, was the increase of taxes, or any other phase of the state's business. The governor himself — his record on the Little Rock High School problem — was the issue of overriding importance.

The governor handled his campaign with high political skill. A unique feature of the opposition he faced was that it included three former governors.

We congratulate Mr. Faubus on his resounding triumph. It lays a heavy responsibility on him as he steps into the long-forbidden field of no third term for the executive head of the state's business.

AVALANCHE IN JULY
Artist unknown, Richmond Times Dispatch   7/30/58

With "Third Term Nomination" in my pocket, I sat on a ballot box from which cascaded a "July Avalanche" of ballots culminating in an "Arkansas Landslide" of votes.

Five new election records were set in the primary: The highest percentage of qualified voters casting ballots, the size of the vote, success in every county, the margin of victory, and the highest number of votes ever received by a candidate for governor.

Mrs. E. Lee Tidd, Richmond, Va., who mailed the cartoon wrote on it: "Come on now, be President."

Arkansas Democrat, July 30, 1958

FAUBUS' APPEAL TO VOTERS EVEN GREATER THAN THAT OF JEFF DAVIS

by Martin Holmes
(Democrat Staff Writer)

Even his enemies were ready to concede today that Orval Faubus is the greatest vote-getter Arkansas has seen since the reign of Jeff Davis over five decades ago.

The Huntsville publisher received an overwhelming third-term endorsement to the governor's chair which hasn't been matched since the inimitable Davis did it the first time in 1904.

Times have changed since Jeff Davis stumped Arkansas by horse and buggy, but Orval Faubus saw fit to use much the same approach as his predecessor — he campaigned hard for the "common man's" vote.

The governor made some use of television in his campaign, but he also visited personally most key voting centers in Arkansas and many that are not.

NO DOUBT ABOUT IT, By Kennedy, Ark. Democrat, 7/30/58

According to Jon Kennedy, the cartoonist, I stood on a mountain of ballots, the people by my side shouting, "We Like Faubus!" Garnering 70% of the votes I carried every county in the state, as one writer penned, "sweeping all from the mountains to the delta."

Every voter had an opportunity to see him and a great many did. And history has shown it is difficult for the average person to resist a personal appeal from Faubus, who has closely identified himself with the grass-roots voters of the state and knows their instincts perhaps better than they do. . . .

VINDICATED!
By Brooks, Birmingham News   7/31/58

This drawing interpreted my primary victory as vindication of my stand in defense of the people's right to control their own schools, and in opposition to illegal federal interference in state affairs. "Faubus policies" were endorsed by an "overwhelming vote."

An editorial in the Battle Creek, Mich., *Inquirer and News* of July 31, said:

There's no accounting for tastes," said the old lady as she kissed a cow.

That's probably as good a comment as anyone can make on the Arkansas election which saw the people overwhelmingly re-elect Gov. Orval Faubus.

Faubus, the rabblerouser, had already discredited himself, the state and nation. The people of Arkansas, in endorsing his actions, have further discredited themselves.

Apparently the South, which has been the Union's great burden for a century, appears anxious to continue in the same role. As for the people of the North, they can only apologize to the world for people like Orval Faubus and the people who elect him to office.

One wonders what this same newspaper said after the Detroit riots, which paled into insignificance anything that happened in Arkansas. Or what it said after the protests in Pontiac, Michigan, over the busing orders, including the bombing of the buses, or over the court orders for Detroit which were opposed by the people.

One also wonders if this same newspaper said the people of Michigan had discredited themselves when another well known "rabblerouser," (their term, not mine) Gov. George Wallace of Alabama, got more votes than all other candidates combined for the Democratic nomination for president in the Michigan primary in 1972.

WAY DOWN SOUTH IN THE LAND OF LITTLE ROCKS
By Russell, Los Angeles Times   7/31/58

This cartoon showed the "Third Term Segregation Vote" which spelled Faubus, was fashioned of little rocks, but over them hung the "Big Rock Law of the Land." "INTEGRATION." There was no law on integration, it was just the opposite.

All across the nation headlines read like the one in the *Seattle* (Wash.) *Post Intelligencer* — "Gov. Faubus Wins By Landslide In Arkansas."

Las Vegas, Nev., *Review Journal*
July 31, 1958

IT SEEMS TO US

Faubus Victory

There is little doubt about how the people of Arkansas feel about Gov. Orval Faubus . . .

Gov. Faubus piled up more than 250,000 votes while his closest opposition was able to garner slightly more than 60,000. The combined totals of his two opponents were less than half the votes tallied by the governor.

The Arkansas governor was pilloried viciously during the Little Rock squabble, and he was pictured as a demon with horns who should be banished to the nether world. The Arkansas Gazette . . . was especially abusive to Faubus and attempted every trick in the political bag in an effort to defeat him.

However, the people of Arkansas . . . placed the stamp of overwhelming approval on his actions.

We are not about to get into an argument of whether integration is good or bad for Arkansas.

We prefer to allow the people of that state to make their own decisions, just as we want to make our own verdict on our liberal laws here in Nevada.

However, when the United States government seeks, by force of arms, to enforce an edict of the Supreme Court — which is not the law of the land but merely an interpretation of what the justices think the law should be, then we are verging on a police state which we might never be able to counter.

We have maintained . . . that states' rights are as much a part of the Constitution of the United States as the right to cast a ballot. When the federal government goes beyond those rights, then we are in trouble.

THE SILENT VOTERS FINALLY SPOKE UP, By Graham, Ark. Gazette, 7/31/58

Throughout the campaign the opposition led by the Gazette had placed great emphasis on "the silent vote." The Gazette harped repeatedly that it would go heavily for Ward and Finkbeiner. The wish was father to the thought. Graham in one of his most honest and factual cartoons, showed the silent voters blasting my two opponents and their principal backer, "The Arkansas Gazette," with the shout "ORVAL!"

WHAT A BIG BOY AM I!
By Crawford, Source unknown   7/31/58

Some just couldn't take my victory gracefully.

Taking his idea from the school book poem, "Little Jack Horner," Crawford came up with this cartoon. I have always believed I could have won a third term nomination if the Little Rock controversy had never developed. Now we'll never know.

THAT DID IT!
By Ink, Source unknown   7/31/58

An approaching boat, "Hope for Moderate Southern Views," which some people regarded as a "Federal Fifth Column," was sunk. A figure on the shore, which should have been labeled "Voters," blasted a hole in the craft with a double barrelled shotgun labeled, "Faubus Landslide."

SAVE YOUR CONFEDERATE MONEY!
Artist unknown, San Francisco Chronicle   7/31/58

A smug appearing figure held a Confederate flag and the news of the "Faubus Landslide in Arkansas Primary."

The figure said:

"Hang onto your Confederate money, folks — the South will rise again."

(If the dollar continues to be devalued and inflation continues in the nation, will the time come when U.S. money and Confederate money will be about the same value? Many Northern areas are now near bankruptcy with government employes sometimes going without pay. On the other hand bonds of Southern states are selling at a premium at lower rates of interest, all of which indicates that Southern states could issue money based on their fiscal stability, and the currency would be more valuable than Northern bonds or U.S. currency.)

THE THIRD TERM VICTORY

A *Democrat* news story on July 30 said:

Governor Faubus singled out two developments which gratified him most — the big turn out and the fact that he was endorsed by all the state, not just a particular section.

In referring to his statement of last night that the people have expressed their sentiments on states rights, he said, "Up until now it has been my word against the critics; now the people have expressed themselves on the issues."

He continued: "I remember when all the out-of-state reporters were questioning me and I would tell them that I was doing what the people wanted me to do, they would give me that look of doubt. Now they have their answer from the people."

—0—

Another story said:

In one of the enlivening paradoxes of politics, Gov. Faubus' runaway victory . . . has boosted the presidential stock of Sen. Lyndon B. Johnson.

Southern Congress members who fear a party split . . are talking . . . of Johnson as the kind of moderate . . . who might keep the [Democratic] Party united.

—0—

A 4-column picture in the *North Little Rock Times* bore this cutline and comment:

Governor Again — Almost by Acclamation

Orval E. Faubus was nominated for a third term . . . with the most thundering endorsement ever given by the voters of Arkansas. He becomes the second man in history and the first since Jeff Davis in 1904 to be nominated for a third term, and he is the first to carry every one of the 75 counties. A record number of voters went to the polls.

Across the state there were hundreds of editorials, thousands across the nation and many in foreign lands.

The Boone County Headlight
J. E. Dunlap, Jr., Harrison, Ark.
July 31, 1958

Ever since that cold night in January of 1954 when a neighboring publisher Orval Faubus came by my house to ask me for his support for governor that coming summer, I'll always remember the conversation at that time and the many incidents which have followed since.

Of all the reams of newspaper copy, magazine articles and pictures of Orval Faubus, the most vivid in my mind was him discussing his possibilities for unseating Gov. Francis Cherry.

The "Man of Destiny," as he has been labeled by newsmen, had it figured right — he won.

During ensuing years, Faubus has conducted the affairs of the office of governor apparently to the satisfaction of all classes of people. He can talk to the rich and poor alike. His background as a youth from the mountains of North Arkansas prepared him for the job which he fills with honor, dignity, common sense and with malice toward no man.

His election to an almost unprecedented third term by the biggest majority ever given a candidate for governor in any election in Arkansas should be the answer for outside critics of the way Faubus has conducted the affairs of the governor's office in Arkansas.

. . .

To say that history is being made and that Orval Faubus has been a big factor in that history would indeed be a trite statement. . . .

Editorial
Searcy (Ark.) Daily Citizen
July 30, 1958

WHEN THE MAJORITY
IS ALLOWED TO RULE . . .

Yesterday, the people of an American state struck a blow that will reverberate through the legal and legislative structure of the nation. Shattering all the records, Orval Faubus was nominated by the largest vote . . . in a primary posting the largest total vote ever cast in an Arkansas primary.

. . . it was obvious that the overriding issue of the campaign was federal intervention vs. state sovereignty. State sovereignty carried the day in Arkansas . . .

. . . If we believe in the rule of the majority as we say we do as free Americans, there can be no doubt whatsoever as to what the majority of our people want.

. . . Basically, we believe that it was a race between the rule of the majority over local affairs and the rule of federally decreed orders enforced at bayonet point.

America has long had reason to be proud of its citizens who were willing to go against tremendous odds to enforce the will of the majority. . . . yesterday's tremendous endorsement of Governor Faubus was in the same spirit as was the action in Boston's famous Tea Party.

. . . it is our opinion that the people of America will never submit to the use of federal force against the will of the majority of the people. . . . the people of Arkansas proved that in yesterday's balloting . . .

Was the editorial writer correct in the opinion expressed in the last paragraph?

MOB VICTORY
By Darcy, Source unknown   7/31/58

The person who mailed this cartoon from a Northern state wrote, "This is how biased the Northern newspapers are."

When upwards of 70% of a record number of eligible voters turn out in a primary, and renominate a candidate by a margin of 70% over two worthy, well-financed opponents, does that constitute a "mob victory?"

The Camden (Ark.) News
July 30, 1958

EDITORIAL COMMENT ACROSS U.S. FOLLOWS VICTORY OF GOV. FAUBUS

Gov. Orval Faubus' sweeping triumph in the Arkansas Democratic primary touched off a wave of comment . . .

Editorial reaction varied from a statement that the victory was "a tragedy for Arkansas and the nation" to a contention that it was "a restatement of the spirit of independence that created the United States of America."

Those views were taken, respectively, by the New York Herald Tribune and the Charleston, S.C., News & Courier.

The Shreveport Journal
July 31, 1958

GOV. LONG HAILS FAUBUS' VICTORY

BATON ROUGE — Gov. Earl Long, with a knowing grin, said today he was "delighted" at Arkansas Gov. Orval Faubus' landslide victory for a third term.

"He is one of the finest men I have ever known — liberal, tolerant," Long said. "I was delighted at the overwhelming victory.

"Faubus is one of the most intelligent public officials in the United States, with his feet on the ground at all times."

The Louisiana governor, close personal friend of the Arkansas chief executive, said Negroes have "nothing to fear . . . I know he feels kindly toward the colored people as well as towards other underprivileged people, and I know he will do the right thing by them."

Long said it is a "pity there are not more people like him at the helm of government throughout our country. He is not a showoff and really means what he says."

The Arkansas Gazette said:

"Whether the judges of the Eighth Circuit Court of Appeals, and beyond them the justices of the United States Supreme Court, can or will be influenced by the Arkansas election returns we cannot know."

"Certainly the interests of the people of Little Rock and Arkansas cry out for the relief granted in the decision by Judge Harry Lemley . . . (who) found the conditions that existed in the high school during the last session intolerable. It is a mild word for the conditions that will exist in September if the Negro children are ordered back to school by the higher court."

". . . We can only hope that if this dread eventuality does arise Mr. Faubus can find a way to bring about a peaceful settlement."

CHANGE THE NAME OF ARKANSAS?
By Alley,
Memphis Commercial Appeal   6/30/58

The "Furriners" who came into Arkansas under the flag of "Occupied Territory," now with tattered banners were in precipitate flight from the "Pro-Faubus Barrage" of votes. The caption was taken from the reports of a speech made in the halls of the legislature in the state's early history. There was a disagreement over the spelling and the pronunciation of the state's name. A proposal was made to change the name of the state. A speaker strongly opposing the change ended a stirring oration with the words:

"Change the name of Arkansas? Not no, but hell no!"

"Change the name of Arkansas? NEVER!"

Ashmore came in for a rap by the Augusta, Ga., Chronicle which said:

"Harry Ashmore won the Pulitzer Prize, but Gov. Orval Faubus won the election."

Washington Evening Star. "We do not think the intervention (by the federal government in the Little Rock dispute) was illegal. But there is not the slightest doubt that it was bitterly resented in Arkansas, and that this resentment set the stage for the Faubus triumph."

Nashville Tennessean: "One result of the Arkansas election can be taken for granted: It is not likely there will be another federal occupation of any other city over the elastic Supreme Court ruling on integration . . ."

Louisville Courier-Journal: "His appeal to the voters of Arkansas was the sure-fire stuff of the racist demagogue. He ignored issues that in normal times would have defeated his bid . . . It is a dark day for Arkansas, for the South, for America." [The statement that I ignored other issues in the campaign was completely false.]

Mobile, Ala., Register: The overwhelmingly heavy vote cast for Faubus was a particularly sharp rebuke for President Eisenhower in using troops . . . and for Little Rock Editor Harry Ashmore in his knifing of the governor in a play for a Pulitzer Prize . . ."

Hot Springs, Ark., Sentinel Record: "Gov. Faubus' nomination to a third term seemed predestined almost from the day he injected himself into the Little Rock school integration crisis. One fact stands out in Faubus' landslide victory: The people of Arkansas . . . wanted their voice heard all the way to Washington."

Columbia S.C. State. "The landslide for Faubus is not surprising . . . Arkansas did not follow the liberal thinking of some of its leaders and some of its press. . . .

New York Daily News: ". . . The Faubus victory also indicates that solution of race problems in the South is going to be a long time coming — quite possibly a longer time than if the Supreme Court had stayed out of the picture. . . . The Earl Warren court, instead of softening racial enmities in the South, has up to now only intensified them."

Baltimore Evening Sun: "If this is an index of sentiment in the South generally — and there is good reason to think that it is — there is trouble ahead."

Greenville, S.C. News: "Gov. Faubus became a symbol of popular resentment against . . . the use of armed federal troops . . . The outcome of the Arkansas election should serve as a warning to the integrationists as to how the public feels about the matter in all of its aspects."

Harrison, Ark., Times: "We've seen nothing to resemble his victory since the days of Huey Long. He won on the emotional race issue but he had the ability to win without it . . . In the integration dispute, Faubus holds that the consent of the governed is required and the will of the people should prevail. This premise holds that Eisenhower and the Supreme Court are servants of the people rather than their masters . . . The situation makes Faubus a national leader in the resistance to federal encroachment on states rights and he already has followers in all the states.

As a political scientist he violated all the accepted rules and came out with a landslide."

One commentator said the state sentiment was summed up in a telegram from J. L. "Jess" Crosser, an astute political observer of Calico Rock. It read:

"It's all over. We laughed with Chris, cried with Ward and voted for Faubus."

OZARK MOONSHINE
By Hutton, Philadelphia Inquirer   7/31/58

The old mountaineer, (That Arkansas Rebellion) drank from the jug, "Faubus Vote." However, he didn't get the words for his toast from me.

"NO, THIS IS MY LEBANON RIBBON, THE OTHER ONE IS FOR LITTLE ROCK," By Mauldin, St. Louis Post Dispatch, 8/1/58

A soldier who had engaged in only two military campaigns, shows a recruit his service ribbons. One was for Lebanon where he landed with the troops ordered there, and the other was for the occupation of Little Rock.

CHAPTER 20
UNION MEMBERS AND BLACKS SUPPORT FAUBUS; DAVIS AND FAUBUS COMPARED. LEMLEY DECISION OVERRULED; SPECIAL SESSION OF LEGISLATURE

The Daily Banner News
Magnolia, Ark., August 3, 1958

An Editorial
NEGRO VOTE HELPED

There is one factor in the landslide victory of Governor Orval Faubus over two well-meaning opponents, which has apparently been overlooked in most of the editorial comment. . . .

And this factor might help in easing some of the state's troubled waters.

The record of Negro voting, organized or not, shows more cohesion in selection than that of most minority groups. . . .

A careful study of the results of the Tuesday election would indicate that the modest vote received by Judge Lee Ward and Chris Finkbeiner is easily accounted for by their friends and well-wishers over the state. Had either of them received a considerable number of Negro votes, . . . that candidate would have forged sharply ahead of the other, even if Faubus still had won by a wide margin. . . .

From any standpoint that the tally can be analyzed, . . . the huge proportion of the Negro Vote went to Faubus.

. . .

The Negroes backing Faubus could indicate . . . that they feel the governor has stood well by their people in most situations and on most issues.

. . .

Quite a few Northern residents, particularly the not-always well-meaning ultra liberals, . . . should be made aware that the Negro vote . . . contributed to the . . . startling landslide given to Governor Orval Faubus.

This editorial is correct about the vote of the black people in the election. Before I was well into the campaign I knew that a majority would support me. Of the many indications, I cite only two.

I received a very intelligent, well-written letter from a black man in rural Cleveland County. "I am a shut-in," he wrote, "and before now I could not leave the house. I had no means to go anywhere."

"After you put your program in effect and helped me," he continued, "I can now go to town twice a month, or more often if needed, and I have the means to buy the necessities of life. I will support you and I know many more of my race will."

In Van Buren on the outskirts of urban Ft. Smith I had taken my position to speak from the platform of the railroad depot. There was a large crowd in the bright sunshine "in the heat of the day." As I took the microphone a tall, comely looking black lady of perhaps 30 years of age broke from the crowd and approached me. I paused as hundreds looked on.

With well-mannered demeanor the lady came up to me, shook my hand and said, "Governor, I'm a school teacher. I know where the greatest pay raise I ever got came from. I'm going to vote for you."

I thanked her; she merged back into the crowd and I began my speech.

Aside from these and other similar incidents, hundreds of black citizens came to hear my campaign speeches in Eastern and South Arkansas. I knew that they were favorably inclined to my candidacy, or they would not have been present.

Although my white critics and some militant black leaders strove to organize the black voters against me, they were, for the most part, unsuccessful. Even McMath couldn't sway them. Their most notable success was in some of the black wards in Little Rock.

The rank and file voters of the state, both black and white, both poor and middle class, had a feeling of mutuality with me. We had a mutual aim, a mutual desire, a mutual interest in a goal. That goal was for a better way of life — an improved way of life for everyone "struggling to make it."

That vast group included workers who for too long couldn't find jobs, or, if employed, had labored long for inadequate wages. It included insurance agents and automobile dealers who couldn't sell policies or cars to people without money. It included operators of motels, boat docks and sporting goods stores catering to the tourist trade — a trade formerly not sufficiently promoted. It included teachers and other public workers who were among the lowest paid in the nation.

The group included the poorest of the poor, the downtrodden, the left out, the left behind. It included those who could never help themselves, as the shut-in who wrote to me, and the children who would be admitted to the Children's Colony.

I was not the first to preach or advocate a program of progress for Arkansas people. But I had preached it with an understanding born of hardship, and in language that came from the grass roots of the economic life of the people.

The people believed that I was the first, in a very long time at least, who not only advocated a program of hope, but had actually implemented one that was working. I had not permitted the blandishments of office, ill-gotten gains or controversy to sway me from my chosen course of progress for all.

A good example of the progress the people of Arkansas desired was the Mohawk Tire and Rubber Company of Helena, the first plant established in the state using the governmental machinery of the AIDC. My friend, John Sheffield of Helena, accompanied me to the plant during my campaign for a second term in 1956.

In the establishment of the plant we had striven diligently and successfully to cut through the maze of legalities and bureaucratic red tape which all too often hinders and delays the implementation of any new program of this kind. Therefore, the company owners were favorably inclined toward my administration because of this help, and the management shut down the plant operations for some 20 minutes to permit me to talk to the employees.

Before beginning my remarks I looked out at the seated audience of several hundred men respectfully awaiting what I had to say. The number of black faces were comparable to the number of whites, all looking back at me expectantly. Here were workers of both races, all working together in a friendly, harmonious atmosphere, all earning a living at jobs that would not have been there without the planning and work of my administration.

That was the kind of progress the people wanted.

The progress being made helped all citizens. That was the reason both blacks and whites supported my candidacy.

If the state continued to move forward in many fields, the businessman and the farmer could "get ahead" (an oft-used expression of my father), the laborer find a job at higher wages, professional people and public workers be better paid, the downtrodden could rise, the left out be included, the left behind could catch up, and there would be help for the helpless.

That hope, that aim, that goal, is what bound me to the people, and the people to me. I understood our problems and I articulated our hopes. That was my political strength. If I had a weakness in that field it was my inability to articulate more clearly the problem and the hope.

Like Abraham Lincoln, I tried to use terms that could be understood by all the people.

It seemed to me the groups who understood more clearly were beauticians and barbers, the operators of beer parlors and grocery stores, and the Rural Electric Co-operatives. They seemed to realize more clearly that goods or services could not be sold for cash, or debts collected from people who had no or inadequate income. I had almost unanimous support from these sources.

Even Big Business in the state, including the oil companies and giant utilities, understood that more customers were better than less customers, and that paying customers were better than non-paying.

The states rights issue, standing alone, had overwhelming support. However, every candidate gave lip service to that sentiment. But, I had risked my political career to defend states rights. Bound, as the issue was at the time, to the emotional factor of race, the situation, no doubt, intensified my support in some areas and lost votes in others. But, the issue of race, or race prejudice, had never alone been sufficient to determine the outcome of a race for public office in Arkansas. That fact has been demonstrated a number of times before, during and after the so-called 1957-58 crisis.

Realizing all the above, I talked of programs and progress in my campaign speeches of 1958, devoting no more than 3 to 5 minutes of sometimes hour-long talks to the "Trouble" in Little Rock and the state-wide problem. However, a few inside critics and hundreds outside the state, falsely proclaimed that I was running on that one issue.

My critics and main opponents possibly never fully understood the situation. Even that literary genius, the "wizard of words," Harry Ashmore, never had a full comprehension of the source of my political strength. He, like other critics, spent his time attempting to attribute to me ulterior motives and chicanery as the basis of my political decisions and actions.

However, if he and others had understood the situation, I don't know any way their knowledge could have been successfully used against me.

We, the people and I, were guiding the plow. The crops in the sterile Arkansas economic fields were growing greener, and we were determined to pursue our goal — a better way of life for all of us.

"AH LIKES THE TASTE"
By Burck, Chicago Sun Times   8/1/58

A countryman, bleary-eyed from drinking "Ol' Faubus" at the "Arkansas Primary," avowed he liked the taste. The psuedo liberals who knew not constitutional law thought this was terrible, and pictured the voters as intoxicated. Actually, millions of Americans thought the U.S. Supreme Court was intoxicated with usurped power.

LOOK AWAY DOWN SOUTH IN DIXIE
By Hungerford, Pittsburgh Post Gazette   8/2/58

Uncle Sam holding the "integration law" while standing on "Arkansas," was struck between the eyes by a "Little Rock" — the "Faubus Victory." Actually the vote should have been a victory for Uncle Sam, and a blow to those who authored the illegal methods of the Republican administration.

THAT HOT POTATO AGAIN
By Kennedy, Ark. Democrat   8/1/58

Kennedy said my overwhelming victory handed some National Democratic leaders a hot potato hard to handle.

U.S. News and World Report
Aug. 8, 1958

THE PEOPLE SPEAK
by David Lawrence

Arkansas has not merely upheld its governor. It has gone beyond any question of personalities. It has upheld a great principle — the doctrine of "States Rights" which Thomas Jefferson gave us.

The people of Arkansas have said that the Constitution itself is the only "supreme law of the land."

The *Arkansas Union Labor Bulletin* of August 1, reported:

Union members rejected the recommendations of the State COPE and voted decisively for Governor Faubus.

All labor areas gave the governor a large majority vote . . . Three of the heaviest Union counties — Saline, Hot Spring and Union — voted for him in higher ratios than the State as a whole.

—0—

BIG ROCK
By Alley, Memphis Commercial Appeal   8/2/58

The "Arkansas Vote" proved to be a BIG Rock — big enough to blunt and bend the "federal bayonets" sent into Arkansas. The use of overwhelming federal power had failed to cow the citizenry of a state into meek compliance with what they considered illegal interference in state affairs.

IN CONTEMPT OF DEMOCRACY, By Knox, Nashville Banner, 8/2/58

The people of Arkansas and Little Rock voted three times in a period of 100 days with the main issue being the right of the people versus federal authority to control the local and state schools.

The results were overwhelmingly against the judicial dictatorship of the U.S. Supreme Court.

Democratic Primary, July 27, 1958

Faubus	-	264,346
Finkbeiner	-	60,173
Ward	-	59,385

School Election, Little Rock School District,
September 27, 1958
Question of closed schools or
forced integration

| For closed schools | - | 19,470 |
| For integration of schools | - | 7,561 |

(About 7,000 Negro voters in the District)

General Election, November 4, 1958

| Faubus, Democratic Nominee | - | 236,598 |
| Johnson, Republican Nominee | - | 50,287 |

Another general election result, a startling upset in a congressional race, was without doubt a reflection of anti-federal interference sentiment. In this cartoon idea Knox correctly portrayed the results of the Democratic Primary as "The Calm Deliberate Expression of the People of Arkansas" at the ballot box.

The ballot box results said no to the frantic, berobed Chief Justice of the Supreme Court and his associate justices shouting for "Judicial Dictatorship." By the expression of their will at the ballot box the people ruled the Court "In Contempt of Democracy."

However, the people had no means of enforcing their will no matter how overwhelming their democratic expression. The armed federal minions of enforcement, including the all-powerful military, were controlled by the executive branch of the federal government which backed up the "judicial dictatorship." There lay the power of force; the people had none. Even though their claims were considered legal and constitutional the law could not protect them. The people were helpless in the face of illegal use of police power.

＊＊＊

Arkansas Democrat
Aug. 3, 1958

Backstage at the Capitol
FAUBUS SAYS HE SENSED THE OUTCOME EARLY

By George Douthit
(Democrat Staff Writer)

In looking back over four weeks of campaigning, Governor Faubus said he got "that feeling" that he had won the election in about the second week. This would be around July 15. . . .

. . .

He had been out with the people about 10 days and their reactions were good. They were giving him their attention as he talked to them.
Hand Shakes
Then after he had finished they came around to shake his hand and express confidence in him and assure him of their support.

Also, in counties where his opponents were supposed to be "gaining ground," Mr. Faubus

found this wasn't true. Then and there he became convinced.

A terrifying lull crept in during the first of the final week of the campaign. The governor was tired, his workers with him were tired. . . . and the voters were weary.
Shot in Arm
Then came the shot in the arm from Washington; former Gov. Francis Cherry issued a statement that he was opposing Mr. Faubus. The opposition opened up a newspaper advertising campaign against him. Former Gov. Sid McMath already was against him. Then another "ex," Ben Laney, jumped into the fight.

At Fayetteville, some students, called "left wingers" by the governor, heckled him. The entire campaign took on new life. Mr. Faubus got his second wind and the campaign workers went out and started working again.

. . .

Arnold Sikes, the governor's executive secretary and campaign manager, said he thought the most valuable achievement was that Mr. Faubus was once more placed in the "underdog" role.

"Everybody was jumping on him and the people didn't like it," Mr. Sikes said. "He stood up and fought them by himself and was defending the people of Arkansas against those who would kick the state around. So, the voters reacted just like I knew they would do."

. . .

On the road — we were with him for four weeks — the governor never lost patience with his workers. At times he became terribly exhausted but he was always able to go a little further and a little longer at the end of the day to see people who wanted to talk to him.

In fact he almost drove himself too hard but he wanted it no other way. . . .

SECOND MAN TO WIN A THIRD TERM
By Kennedy, Ark. Democrat   8/3/58

The picture of former Gov. Jeff Davis said, "Welcome to Posterity" after my third term victory. First elected in 1900 Gov. Davis went on to his second and third victories in 1902 and 1904 (served 1901 to 1907). During his last term he was elected U.S. Senator which position he held until his death in 1913.

If I served out a full third term my tenure in office would equal that of Davis. To exceed his record it would be necessary to win and serve a fourth term. At the end of a fourth term my tenure would equal in years the time served by Gov. Elias N. Conway who served two 4-year terms, Nov. 15, 1852 to Nov. 15, 1860. To exceed Conway's length of time in office would require five 2-year terms as governor.

"NO SWEAT"
By Kennedy, Ark. Democrat   8/3/58

Congressman Jim Trimble and Brooks Hays registered victories over primary opponents.

Arkansas Democrat
August 3, 1958

RUN OF THE NEWS
by Karr Shannon

Why Faubus Won The Third Term

The landslide vote Governor Faubus received was the people's vehement rejection of federal absolutism, their wholesale denunciation of the relentless Warren court, their repudiation of the ludicrous "law of the land," their passionate resentment of the illegal directives of a president of the United States. . . .

The vote was a protest against education by bayonet, infringement upon a state's rights . . . it was a protest against federal disregard for the Constitution of the United States.

Opponents verbally chastized Governor Faubus for his moves and motives in connection with the Central High tragedy. But they never got around to finding any violation of the state's constitution or statutes, or even a violation of the federal constitution — by the governor. . . .

Opponents talked, vaguely, about settling the integration controversy in the courts. One opponent exuded lavishly about a plan for peaceful disposal of the wrangle in the Congress.

The People Remembered

But the people of Arkansas . . . remembered the succinct sessions of court presided over by . . . Judge Davies. His snap decisions. His curt language. And they remembered the adamant Brownell.

A full term of education a la troops had expired — a term hampered by confusion, nervous strain, fear, rebellion and excessive cost — before a hearing was permitted in a federal court that gave due consideration to all facets of the controversy. Judge . . . Lemley allowed the hearing to go into the third day in order to get all the facts. The leisure and dignity of the Lemley court was in sharp contrast to the Davies court of last September.

The people remembered this when they cast their votes. . . .

Congress Indifferent

The opponents' plea to settle the matter in Congress fell on deaf ears. The voters remembered . . . that Congress was in session during the . . . troop occupation . . . and that although thousands of letters of resentment were mailed to representatives of both House and Senate and reams and reams of editorials and columns were published in denunciation of the occupation, . . . Congress did` absolutely nothing!

. . . Opponents tried to establish issues pertaining to the governor's extravagance, broken promises, inconsistency, high taxes . . . They warned against the dictatorial potential and possibilities of a third term and the dire threats to the Mack-Blackwell Amendment. In these pleas they were aided and abetted by three former governors.
. . .

Maybe Faubus took his firm stand against the federals because it was politically expedient to do so. . . . Prior to the CHS "incident" he had appeared rather lukewarm and apathetic toward the integration issue. He certainly was not susceptible to the hotheads. . . .

Once he took a stand he didn't depart therefrom. The people of Arkansas were so infuriated about their treatment by the high court and Department of Justice they were grabbing at . . . any chance to express their indignation.

On Sound Footing

Governor Faubus never did say he was a "segregationist," although his opponents so tagged themselves and railed upon the governor to tell the people whether he was a "segregationist" or "integrationist." He ignored their demands.

It wasn't necessary that the governor label himself a "segregationist." . . . He was openly opposed to forced integration or any other infringement upon state's rights, the Constitution of Arkansas and the Constitution of the United States. That was sufficient.

The following was mailed to me, with an expression of his moral support, by Sen. I. N. Curtis of the New Mexico State Senate, on Aug. 4, 1958.

ELSINORE (CALIFORNIA) VALLEY SUN

. . . The United States grew in stature and became a great nation when each of the separate states operated as a sovereign state. But the Supreme Court has now decided contrary to the provisions of the Constitution of the United States,

that only Washington is capable of telling the folks in California, and in Montana and Arkansas, and in Florida and Maine, how to run their internal affairs ...

Arkansas Democrat

August 5, 1958

FAUBUS GETS ANOTHER LANDSLIDE: THOUSANDS OF LETTERS FROM NATION

It has been almost a week since Governor Faubus received his landslide endorsement . . . and the letters and telegrams of congratulations are pouring in by the thousands.

. . . the messages are coming in from every state in the Union. Every mail brings a new batch.

Girls in the governor's office have been sorting them and sending them to the mansion because the governor . . . will sit up for hours reading them.

Did So Before

He did just that when the thousands of letters and wire messages came in last September during the Central High School crisis. . . .

Picked at random, here are some one-line excerpts from the letters outside the South:

Essex Junction, Vt.: "May God bless you for your great work and the democratic principles for which you stand."

Auburn, Calif.: "We sincerely hope that other Southern leaders will immediately take steps that will bring about the same results."

Find an Adams

New York: "Even if you don't want to head a third party surely you could find yourself a Sherman Adams and one without a Goldfine in the background."

Las Cruces, N. Mex.: "May the Good Lord bless and keep you and help you with the many important tasks before you and especially integration."

Marblehead, O.: "As a nation we can still turn back to freedom, but we had better start turning."

Indianapolis, Ind.: "Your re-election shows plainly how the American people would vote if given the opportunity to express themselves . . ."

Kansas City, Mo.: "We knew you would show them and how. Wow!"

Sympathetic Republican

Chicago: "I am a Republican but I can assure you, your excellency, you have numerous supporters who have always lived in the North but are sympathetic with the South in its struggle to uphold states' rights. Millions of Americans are alarmed at the rate states' rights have been eaten away . . ."

Batesville, Ark., News-Review

August 7, 1958

CONNER'S CORNER

by Farrell Conner

AROUND THE WORLD

The people of Arkansas spoke so loudly in favor of Governor Faubus for an unprecedented third term . . . that it was heard around the world.

. . .

He is the most popular governor in modern Arkansas history. . . . In fact, if a poll of voters in the Southern States should be taken on who is the most popular governor, Faubus would win that contest too.

MRS. JOE T. ROBINSON DIES

Mrs. Joe T. (Ewilda M.) Robinson died in a Little Rock hospital at 3:30 a.m. Aug. 7, 1958. She was the widow of U.S. Senator Robinson, the Democratic vice-presidential nominee and running mate of presidential nominee, Governor Al Smith of New York in 1928. Senator Robinson went on to become a stalwart leader in the Senate during the administration of Franklin D. Roosevelt, and helped to fashion and enact many of the Roosevelt reforms.

Mrs. Robinson was hospitalized in mid-July. Some time later the venerable lady called me at the Executive Mansion to chat briefly and wish me well. Near the conclusion of the telephone conversation I expressed my hope for her quick recovery, and a personal visit with her soon.

"No, Governor Faubus," she replied, "that will not be possible."

I knew then that the call was her well wishes and goodbye to me. I felt quite saddened as I replaced the receiver after that final visit with the very prominent and respected lady.

"WITH THIS ISSUE I COULDN'T LOSE"
By Berryman, Washington Star   8/18/58

The cartoonist said the use of federal bayonets in Little Rock was the winning issue. That played its part in deciding the election, but there were other important issues, as the sales tax increase, the industrial program and progress in education.

It will always be a matter of speculation, but I shall always believe I could have won a third term if the Little Rock Crisis had never occurred.

Arkansas Gazette
August 10, 1958

THE ARKANSAS PRESS—
Third Term For Faubus
Is Still Major Subject

Politics continues to dominate the editorial columns of the state's newspapers, with Governor Faubus' third term nomination taking most of the space.

Here are samples:

Jay W. Jackson, Van Buren County Democrat, Clinton: His election to a third term was all but a foregone conclusion many days before the actual balloting took place . . . We have already noticed an interesting commentary . . . We have started hearing people already say we need a law giving a governor one four-year term only. . . .

Lincoln Ledger, Star City: Such a massive endorsement of a gubernatorial candidate has never before taken place in Arkansas. The people spoke with their votes in greater numbers than even seasoned watchers . . . had predicted. Yes, the people have spoken for their candidate and his program. Now, we can get back to work on that program of progress in Arkansas. One other word: Our congratulations go to the governor not only on his victory, but on the campaign he waged preceding it. He worked long, hard and earnestly carrying his message to the people themselves, making speech after speech, shaking hand after hand of persons in all walks of life. . . .

Esther Bindursky, Lepanto News Record: For weeks the political writers have been phrasing and re-phrasing their sentences into predictions about "the big silent vote." Never did I see a silence broken so conclusively. . . . The people voted and went about their daily pursuit of business. . . . Whatever the reason for the silence, they let their vote do the talking.

Northwest Arkansas Times, Fayetteville: We see one thing for sure — Mr. Faubus has accepted a tremendous responsibility. Winner of a third term . . . by a great majority, and a much larger total vote than ever before, he has set several precedents. . . . Not only the stand he took concerning the situation at Central High School won votes for Mr. Faubus . . . His tax program to help the schools, the leadership he exhibited in helping to iron out a badly irregular assessment system — these and other things were recognized in support of his candidacy. All through his campaign he set out in detail points of his legislative program. The record was cited, including his efforts to help both the public schools and the institutions of higher learning, through tax intake.

LeRoy Tyson, Augusta Advocate: [The] landslide victory represented a personal triumph for Governor Faubus, but more than anything else it reflects the deep resentment of the people of Arkansas against the sending of federal troops to Little Rock. . . . There were a number of important issues brought forward in the campaign, but all took back seat to the all-important matter of states rights.

E. L. Huff, Jackson County Democrat, Newport: The overwhelming vote given to Governor Faubus . . . indicates to us the strongest manifesto that could be given to the world that Arkansas definitely does not feel that the opinion[s] of the Supreme Court . . . should be accepted as the "law of the land" and that the states still have some rights left to solve their own difficulties.

El Dorado (Ark.) Daily News
August 10, 1958

Faubus, Davis; Oldtimers Ponder
How Men Were Alike, How Different

By Clayte Whitten

"What similarity do you see between Orval Faubus and Jeff Davis?"

An El Dorado resident, Hosea Ezekiel Breazeal, 91, says he's been asked that question many times this past week since the publication of a story regarding his unbroken voting record since 1888 . . .

The fact that at the time of Davis' celebrated 1904 third-term victory Breazeal was already a "seasoned" voter of 16 primaries and a judge on the Union County Election Board lends "status" to his recollections of the event.

Old-timers Speak Up

Delegated to find out just what those recollections were, this reporter felt especially fortunate at discussing the Davis-Faubus comparison with not one but three persons who say they voted for the winner in each of the elections.

William M. Ramsey, 81, one-time Union County tax assessor and retired farmer . . . and W. P. McKinnon, now 79 but then a farmer and so young he cast his "maiden vote" during Davis' first race for governor, joined Breazeal, a long-time local power in the Democratic Party set-up, in a staunch, Davis trio representative of the "common people."

Asked about any similarities between the two third-term governors, the trio insisted that the only outstanding likenesses they could recall was their overpowering popularity with the rank-and-file and their inclination to "get up and do, not just sit."

Faubus and Davis Unlike

In appearance, personality traits, and methods of campaigning they considered the two decidedly different. So were the issues at stake, they insisted, unless one . . . centered the race around "performance in office" during each man's first two terms.

But even their "things accomplished" differences were pretty hazy in the minds of these aged supporters. While they could and did rattle off the late, oft-repeated Faubus slogans on "industrial progress, teacher-salary hikes, etc." they were hardpressed to name with published statements by Karr Shannon that "Neither (Davis or Faubus) was possessed of over zealousness for truth," "each claimed credit for just about every progressive move in the state during his administration," and the implication that both spent much of their time as governor "running for office," the trio of long-time voters admitted it "might possibly have been partly true" of Davis but staunchly denied its application to Faubus. The latter, they insisted, was acquitted of any such charge last month when a . . . final jury, "Arkansas voters hundreds of thousands strong, swept him to victory with a landslide in every county in the state."

Quizzed about an editorial comment that the third-term winner owed his overwhelming victory to a "wave of emotionalism" and asked if it wasn't some such "emotional factor" that handed Jeff Davis his third term, Breazeal, Ramsey, and McKinnon said it depended upon one's definition of "emotionalism." By any ordinary definition, they ruled it out for Faubus. If one meant "feelings deliberately aroused in a listener," they allowed it certainly did fit Davis.

'Jeff: One of the Boys'

"Jeff was always 'one of the boys,' full of jokes yet quick with a tear," said Breazeal. "Most of the time the 'boys' — us common folks — were on the right side of a question, but if maybe the 'boys' were a shade off 'pure white,' Jeff was for them just the same. Now Faubus is not that way. He makes you feel he's deadly serious and fighting for something mighty important to all of us. He hasn't got time to laugh and clown around like Jeff did."

Asked if he thought Jeff Davis would have lost the election July 29, Breazeal was quick to defend the adaptability of the 54-year-ago hero.

"I wouldn't say that. Times are different now. We know what this is all about now and we want our man to be serious. Jeff was smart enough to have known that and to have obliged. Then we were a pretty 'ignorant' crew of voters — no television, no radio, and mighty few newspapers. Us fellows back in the hills and down on the farms didn't know much and long speeches full of dry facts would have put us to sleep. We didn't know enough to make 'head or tail' of say Faubus's last television speech if we'd heard it. Jeff knew all this and kept us awake and rocking with laughter."

"What I liked about Jeff was that he was as quick to tell a joke on himself as on the other fellow." This from Ramsey, who went on to recall Davis' loyalty to his friends as evidenced by an unscheduled "stumping" trip through Union County in the spring of 1904 to aid the cause of the late Emon Mahoney, who had run into unexpected opposition in his race for county judge.

Loyal to Mahoney

The event as retold by Ramsey was also sketched in a book called "What a Preacher Saw Through a Keyhole in Arkansas" by the late "Sharpe" Dunaway of Conway. It seems that Jeff Davis, bone tired from weeks of campaigning for himself and for "old Cotton Top" (U.S. Senator James P. Clark, who was being opposed by James K. Jones), refused to attend a series of political rallies being staged in the El Dorado area. Over the telephone he told Clark he'd "rather lose the governor's race and Clark's rather than get up and catch the midnight train for El Dorado."

Counting on Davis' self-sacraficing devotion to a friend in need, Sen. Clark, according to the story, then threw in the line about "Emon Mahoney having to fight a whole gang down there on account of his being for you and me."

That did it. Morning found Jeff Davis facing a hissing, booing, pro-Jones crowd on El Dorado's Court House lawn. The Dunaway book quotes him as having the crowd eating out of his hands after a tear-jerking introduction containing these words: "You may scratch the name of James P. Clark and Jeff Davis from your ballot if you will, but for God's sake save Emon Mahoney, the Irish lad who was born and reared upon the streets of El Dorado."

'Fun' Davis' Trademark

Ramsey added his own fun-provoking memory of the speech. He said that during the talk Davis complained of a sore neck from trying to sleep on the train during the night. From some source he produced a bottle of old-fashioned linament. "When Jeff loosened his tie, pulled back the shirt collar and dumped that firey stuff right down his back, the crowd howled with glee. Can you imagine Faubus pulling a stunt like that?" It was Ramsey's telling point on the difference between the two men.

"But Jeff Davis wouldn't have campaigned that way today," McKinnon hastened to add. "He was smart as well as funny. He knew exactly what would work and he used it. I'm not saying that if he had been in Mr. Faubus' shoes this summer he would have campaigned just like Mr. Faubus did, but I do think he would have made his speeches fit the times."

"My 'maiden vote' went to Jeff Davis, but I didn't know why. 'Everybody's for Davis' was the only reason I knew to give," continued McKinnon. "If my grandson and granddaughter gave their "first vote" to Faubus this summer, they had a reason. In the same way Jeff Davis would have known these young people couldn't be fooled by funny stories or crazy stunts and would have settled down to 'facts' just like Faubus did."

Likeness, Difference

Point after point the three admitted supporters of Arkansas' only successful third-term gubernatorial candidates covered the field . . .

Sometimes the three mentioned minor Faubus-Davis similarities, but more often they mentioned glaring differences. Ever they came back to their original contention: Neither Davis nor Faubus sat still. Both got in there and did something. One did it with side-splitting yarns or tear-provoking sentiment. The other resorted to logic with a solemn face. But the end results were the same — an unheard-of third term in the governor's chair and a reputation for popularity not likely to be equaled soon.

"Very little similarity between Jeff Davis and Orval Faubus.

Such is the final verdict of Breazeal, Ramsey, and McKinnon. They could be way off the beam, but these three veteran voters totaling 188 Democratic primaries have one advantage over most of us — they were there!

Arkansas Democrat
Aug. 10, 1958

By George Douthit
(Democrat Staff Writer)

When Arkansas voters overwhelmingly endorsed the stand Governor Faubus had taken on the integration issue, they did not at the same time . . . invite extremists like John Kasper.

[One of Gov. Faubus' aides] said, "You can rest assured that the governor has not changed his attitude; Kasper still is not welcome in Arkansas."
. . .

Acceptance Conditional

Now, there is another segregation group which supported Governor Faubus, and he accepted that support, but only conditionally. This was the Capital Citizens Council. Its leaders were in many conferences with Governor Faubus. Another was the Central High School Mothers League.

According to the governor's aide who sat in on many of the conferences, the governor made it plain that he wasn't becoming their leader and also emphasized his attitude on integration — that anywhere a majority of a community was willing to integrate its schools, then no minority group should interfere. . . . Apparently [Citizens Council leaders] accepted the governor's viewpoint, because they have continued to see him throughout the past months.

Arkansas has an example of "voluntary integration" in Bentonville schools in Benton County. The county population includes about 15 Negroes, with two youngsters of school age, both boys in the same family.

At first a Negro teacher was provided for the lone Negro, before his brother became of school age. Then the people of Bentonville, without any outside pressure, put the two boys into the regular classrooms.

Those people sized up their problem and met it, in a way that apparently suited that community. It would have been too costly to set up a Negro school
. . .

We asked several residents what would they have done if they had had 100 or 150 Negro students. They said: "We would set up a Negro school system. With only two boys, we have no problem."

It was in Bentonville that the NAACP sought to buy a downtown hotel and turn it into a rest home for Negroes. The townspeople held a meeting and in 20 minutes raised $24,000 and bought the hotel.

The Bentonville cases supports Governor Faubus' stand that, if the majority of the people in any community want to voluntarily integrate their schools, they should be able to do so without any outside interference.

His philosophy that each community should be allowed to work out its own problems has gained wide support. . . .

━●━○━●━○━●━○━

Van Buren (Ark.) Press Argus
by Editor Hugh Park
August 14, 1958

[Park would have agreed that I could win a third term without the Little Rock crisis. — OEF]

A REVIEW OF THE GOVERNOR'S RACE

Editor's Explanation

This Editorial was written on July 27, two days before the primary in which Orval Faubus won . . . a third term.

. . .

Last week we almost "threw the whole thing away" — and then came bursts of "disgrace" from such people as . . . Harry Truman, and . . . Eleanor Roosevelt.

Then we decided to read it over again — and this week we are printing it — knowing that we know the truth better than those who are crying "shame," . . . upon . . . Arkansas.

We well know that Little Rock was "hurt," . . . but we are sick and tired of laying the blame for it all on one man and the people of our state. . . . .

* * *

Governor Faubus won his campaign for a third term in spite of, and not because of, the Little Rock fracas . . .

It is true that the incident furnished an emotional surge of interest that could well be pointed to, especially from abroad, as the only thing at stake in the governor's campaign.

But such is not the facts in the case, and the Governor's campaign, like the Little Rock incident itself, has been "colored" more to suit the desires of hungry hunters for hot headlines than reported for the good of humankind.

Out-of-state reporters have ignorantly, or deliberately, ignored the fact that . . . Faubus has proved to be a most able governor; a governor who has had the political ingenuity to take such things as tax increases, and turn them into blessings of popularity, rather than millstones to drown him in floods of disfavor.

Orval Faubus literally boxed himself into impregnable armor against political foes' . . . campaign charges. For instance — the taxes — we're all against them, but when his worthy opponents attacked them, he could quickly say — tis true, but would you do away with the pensions for the old folks, the better wages for the teachers, the better services of government? And thus armed, the governor could never be reached by his antagonists.

Reporters ignored the better schools, the better pensions, the better roads, better salaries for public officials, especially those in the judicial system . . . and above all these the enlarged program for more industry, and higher wages, and tourist traffic — with its better fishing, hunting, and less manslaughter on the highways.

But the people had such things in their minds.

* * *

Coupled with this feeling of progress was an administration with a minimum of abuse in patronage and political favors. Though at times opponents seemed to have unearthed a termite in the Faubus house, at no time have they . . . convinced any portion of the electorate that they were digging up the dirt for anything more than plowing politics. And in that art, . . . all his critics have proved to be "second-best" when it comes to Faubus. . . .

Four years ago Orval Faubus stood alone — and through his own courage and aggressive attitude, . . . towards Francis Cherry, built a fire that . . . consumed the second term candidate. Orval Faubus became famous then — as the second man in all Arkansas history to defeat a Governor for a Second Term.

Once in office, Orval Faubus proceeded to demonstrate his political ingenuity in getting in and out of hot spots. He "handled" the legislature . . . with a finesse that few men could equal. He appointed a nationally famous Republican, Winthrop Rockefeller, to head up industrial commission in a Democratic state. . . .

* * *

But it was his handling of the tax situation that demonstrates, more than anything else, the ability of Orval Faubus. . . . Many a Governor has got beat, by the simple suggestion, of raising taxes. But Orval Faubus raised them — and his own political fortune — by steering a three cent sales tax through the legislature, of passing a law to equalize assessments on tax property, and above all, mind you, of doubling the tax to drive your car, or hunt or fish in your favorite creek.

Once there was a man named Midas, who turned into gold everything he touched. And Orval Faubus seems to turn into political fortune every move he makes in public service. Were we not a close observer of the way he talks, the way he moves toward making a decision, and the timing of his actions, we would venture to say he has been running on a "streak of luck." But it has not been luck, it has been political sagacity, a rare gift, that has brought him another triumph — the second man in Arkansas history to be elected to a Third Term as Governor.

* * *

Somehow or other, every time we think of Harry Ashmore and Orval Faubus, we think of . . Alvis Smith, . . . The story goes that back at the turn of the century, the Frisco folks sent down from St. Louis one of their brilliant executives to buy railroad ties at a bargain from the hillbillies in Arkansas. And he was doing a good job of it. But he had a most irritating habit of wearing above his ear, a long, sharp, yellow pencil. To make an impression on the natives, he would grab this pencil from its perch between the ear and skull, and flourish it with authority to those about him. Few men, . . . made anything off Alvis Smith, who in a squeaking . . . voice, spoke his mind on all matters. . . . On this particular occasion, he let go, with this warning to the Frisco tie buyer: "Young fellow, some of these days you're gonna pull that pencil off your ear one time too much, for one of these Old Country Boys is coming down here in patched pants, and he's gonna reach down in his overall pocket, and pull out a stub pencil not two inches long, and outfigure you on every tie from Fayetteville to Fort Smith."

Orval Faubus outfigured Harry Ashmore on his political ties.

—0—

HIGHLIGHTS OF THE NEWSWEEK, By Kennedy, Ark. Democrat, 8/10/58

The integration delay ruling by Judge Lemley was appealed to the 8th Circuit Court of Appeals at St. Louis. All eyes were now on that city as school time approached in Little Rock. I took a vacation in the Ozarks spending some of the time on Lake Norfork on the house boat of Fayetteville business executive L. L. Baxter. I told him the press would seek out my hiding place, which he doubted. The press did, and Baxter's picture along with mine went nationwide, even appearing in LIFE Magazine. The education groups went to work to save the 3% sales tax from repeal at the general election. With my help after my stunning victory the prospects were much brighter.

MONUMENT PREDICTED AT LITTLE ROCK

Nationally known columnist Holmes Alexander in one of his columns in August predicted that some day a monument would be erected in honor of the people at Little Rock. He wrote that "an unsung but significant victory was taken from the Communist invaders and their mercenaries."

"The collapse of the enemy thrust, as seen in Gov. Faubus' re-election . . . has been the surest sign in recent years that we have ramparts at the home front and men to mount them," Alexander wrote.

"New England and the South have combined to make this fight," he continued. "It took a newspaper in New Hampshire . . . to reduce to absurdity the posturings of a Pulitizer Prize Arkansas editor who came out for bayonet-point integration at Central High School but who kept his own office segregated."

Alexander's choice for the best reporting "on the Little Rock battle" was "the New Bedford (Mass.) *Standard-Times* and their star reporter Edward B. Simmons." Simmons wrote a five-part series of articles on the conflict dealing with (1) the fallen leaders, (2) the Communist line, (3) sociology above law, (4) the police state and (5) the continuing conspiracy.

Holmes concluded "As the years advance, we will know that an American victory has been scored for law, state sovereignty and common sense. Some day it will be worth a monument."

TWO WRONGS DON'T MAKE A RIGHT, By Robinson, Indianapolis News, 8/20/58

This cartoonist showed the difficulties on both sides of the troublesome issue. "Segregation Extremists" armed with "Mob Rule" faced "Integration Extremists" armed with "Court Orders" and "U.S. Troops." Caught in the middle of the conflict were "our schools" as the giants maneuvered against each other.

408

I returned from vacation to a desk piled high with work. Soon a special session of the Legislature was in order. Another period of intense maneuvering with the federal government approached with the Central High School situation as tense and dangerous, if not more so, than a year before.

"WHAT, AGAIN!"
By Kennedy, Ark. Democrat   8/20/58

The Eighth Circuit Court of Appeals on August 18 reversed the decision of Judge Lemley granting the Little Rock School District a delay in the court ordered, bayonet-enforced desegregation. Thus a year after the crisis began President Eisenhower again found himself with the "problem of enforcing integration" in his hands, with cries of "Southern Resentment" ringing in his ears.

HIGHLIGHTS OF THE NEWSWEEK
By Kennedy, Ark. Democrat   8/17/58

GEORGE W. JOHNSON, GOP NOMINEE

The Republicans nominated George W. Johnson of Greenwood in South Sebastian County as their candidate for governor. While working Greenwood during the primary campaign I approached an acquaintance — it may have been Means Wilkerson, one of my leaders there — standing in the street with another man whom I did not recognize. After greeting my acquaintance I turned to the other person — he may have proffered his hand first — and introduced myself. Said the affable gentleman in reply, "I'm the man who's going to beat all of you in the general election. I'm George Johnson." We had a good laugh and a nice visit. I liked my soon-to-be opponent. In retrospect, he chose a most inopportune time to bear the GOP banner in Arkansas.

—0—

A one million dollar research center would be built at the U. of A. Little Rock Medical Center.

MORE NEWS HIGHLIGHTS
By Kennedy, Ark. Democrat   8/17/58

Jim Johnson's lead over Justice Minor Milwee in the Supreme Court race was so slim that certainty of victory had to wait for official certification.

—0—

SPECIAL SESSION OF THE LEGISLATURE

The reversal of the Lemley delay made the court-ordered integration of the Little Rock schools again an imminent problem of crisis proportion. Although the case was being appealed to the Supreme Court, little hope of relief from that august body existed in the minds of anyone.

The people wanted something done and the Legislature as a whole wanted to take action. Faced with this situation there was no alternative to a special session. Work was begun on legislative measures to deal with the problem.

On Aug. 23 I issued the call for a special session to convene on August 26. The action met with wholehearted approval of the people and the legislators.

Press reports of legislative comment on my address included the following: "The best speech Faubus ever made." Some said it was the best speech they had ever heard.

Excerpts of the speech were carried by some out-of-state newspapers with favorable comment. The extremely "liberal" press failed to use any quotes and largely ignored the contents.

HIGHLIGHTS OF THE NEWSWEEK
By Kennedy, Ark. Democrat   8/24/58

The fast moving integration story completely overshadowed all other news developments in Arkansas. In the reversal of the Lemley decision, Judge Gardner wrote an eloquent dissent to the majority opinion, and granted a stay until the case could be appealed.

I met with the School Board and Supt. Blossom with inconclusive results. President Eisenhower and I were shown resuming our original positions on the CHS problem.

Chancellor Guy Williams upheld the State Sovereignty Act. The NAACP rushed to force integration and the Legislature stood ready for action.

Jim Johnson became Justice Jim by upsetting Judge Minor Milwee by 2,307 votes in a race for the Supreme Court. A known segregationist, Johnson's election was an upset and another indication of public sentiment.

SPECIAL SESSION CONVENES

The special session convened on August 26 in an air of impending crisis. I addressed the solemn faced members in a joint session in the House Chamber. There were ready sponsors for the seven bills prepared for introduction.

AND BACK TO LITTLE ROCK?
By Martin, Houston Chronicle   8/22/58

President Eisenhower ordered U.S. troops to Lebanon in a Mid-East crisis to prevent the fall of a pro-United States government. Now it appeared he would order the troops back to occupy schools in the nation because of disorders over integration problems. Notice the caption "and back to Little Rock?" is a question.

IT'S NOT AS IF WE'D CRITICIZED MARGARET
By Kennedy, Ark. Democrat   8/24/58

Former President Harry S. Truman in a speech in the North, commented on my victory of July 29. According to press reports he said, "The people of Arkansas voted in ignorance and hysteria."

I made no response to the Truman statement. I considered his remarks on the Arkansas election in the same light as his comment on the Marine Corps when he said it was merely a branch of the Navy, a statement he soon "took back," and his angry letter to the music critic who wrote unfavorably of the singing of his daughter, Margaret.

The Arkansas State Democratic Committee was not so restrained. The Committee wrote and unanimously approved a strongly worded resolution of disapproval of the former President's statement. Note Harry's picture turned to the wall, and the caption of the cartoon.

BIG ROCKS . . . . LITTLE ROCKS
By Grant, Oakland Tribune   8/25/58

Uncle Sam, pondering his problems with "big rocks" — "Nuclear Disarmament," "Summit Delay," "Inflation," "Labor Investigations," and "Middle East" got hit by a "little rock" — the "Faubus" problem.

My address to the special session of the Arkansas Legislature had indicated "no surrender" in the battle for rights guaranteed to the states by the Constitution. The address prompted the following editorial.

EDUCATION OR SOCIOLOGY?

(Dallas Morning News
Aug. 28, 1958)

Gov. Orval Faubus is growing in stature as the . . . crisis sharpens in Arkansas. His message to the legislature of his state is of a dignity and thought-fulness such as to challenge the attention of even his critics.

The Governor pitches his appeal on the clear note of liberty under law. For integration with liberty to all, he has no gesture of opposition, no word of dissent. But against schooling at the bayonet point he is determined to be the big rock in Little Rock.

Schooling at the bayonet point is not liberty for anybody. It is not schooling for anybody. It is outrage and uproar and sullen submission all jammed down into the constriction of sheer force. There is no psychology in the books that can prove that anything of the sort is a good thing. And Governor Faubus reminds the Supreme Court that it was psychology, and not law, upon which the integration decision was based.

The Supreme Court of the United States has tried to play God with Arkansas. From the Ozarks to the swamps and all over the plains in between, Arkansas people are traditionally, inherently and stubbornly averse to outside rule of their own intimate lives, their private concerns and their children.

. . .

"The Supreme Court has been usurping the rights reserved to the states by the Constitution. The Supreme Court has been making hasty, impatient decisions without proper judicial restraint. Recent decisions raise considerable doubt as to the validity of the American boast that we have a government of laws and not of men."

These words . . . are the considered and voted judgment of the conference of the Chief Justices of the State Supreme Courts of America. If the court at Washington continues on its mad course, impeachment is the only remedy. . . .

Law which can not be enforced without martial force is not law for any freedom-loving people. And a judge who can not keep his personal beliefs out of his application of law ceases to be a judge and becomes, at best, a doctrinaire and, at worst, a tyrant.

Fort Smith Times Record
August 28, 1958

AS WE SEE IT
by C. F. Byrns

The Legislature Makes It Clear

It's practically a record which the Arkansas legislature set yesterday, in approving all the bills which Governor Faubus had proposed, to help meet any possible crisis at Central high school.

. . .

And they make perfectly clear that the legislature is strictly in agreement with the governor that:

1. There shall be no "crisis" at any Arkansas school, if there's any way at all to prevent it.

2. The people of Arkansas want members of all races protected and are determined to do it — that violence is to be blocked at any price.

3. That the state and its people are willing to take drastic means to prevent any such emergencies — and to protect their rights to administer their internal public affairs. . . .

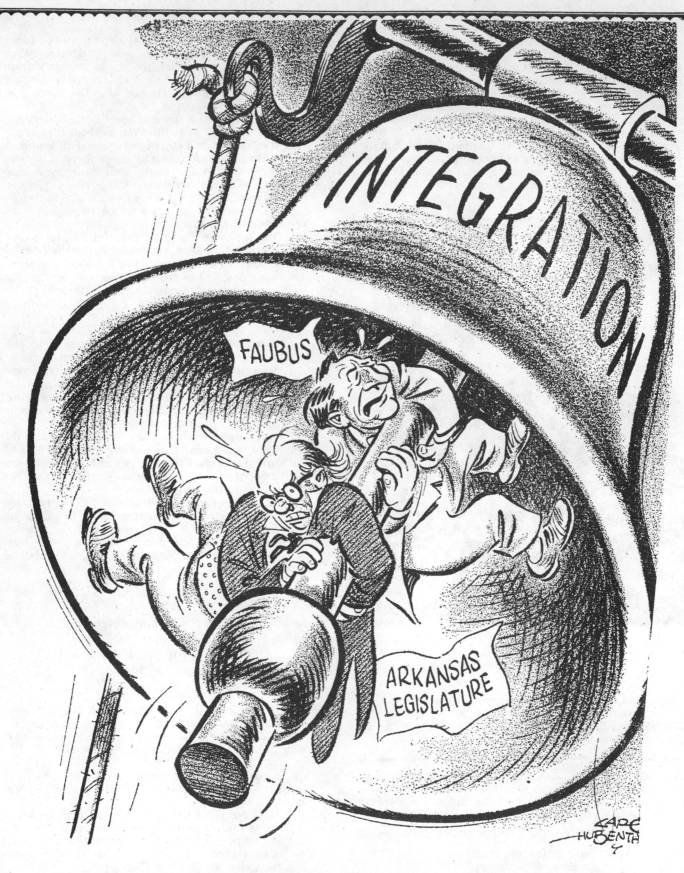

CURFEW SHALL NOT RING TONIGHT! By Hubenth, Los Angeles Examiner, 8/28/58

The cartoon was evoked by the action of the Special Session of the Legislature in passing laws to aid the people in their efforts to retain control of their schools.

GREETINGS! By Knox, Nashville Banner, Chattanooga News Free Press, 8/27/58

The U.S. Supreme Court received greetings from the State Supreme Court Chief Justices of the various states.

Meeting in national convention in California the state chief justices considered and adopted on August 27, a resolution censuring the U.S. High Tribunal for lack of judicial restraint — for going beyond its authority by making laws rather than interpreting those passed by Congress.

The vote for the resolution was 36 state chief justices for with only 8 against. It was a damning indictment of the U.S. Court for its extremism in a number of fields.

The report accused the Supreme Court of making "hasty, impatient" decisions "without proper judicial restraint" and with acting as a policy maker.

"Recent decisions raise considerable doubt as to the validity of the American boast that we have a government of laws and not of men," the strongly-worded document said.

The report stated, "The overall tendency of its decisions during the last 25 years has been to press the extension of federal power and to press it rapidly."

The resolution continued, "This Conference hereby respectfully urges that the Supreme Court of the U.S., in exercising the great powers confided to it for the determination of questions as to allocation and extent of national and state powers . . . exercise one of the greatest of all judicial powers — the power of judicial self-restraint."

TIRELESS ARSONIST
By Goldberg, N.Y. Journal American   8/26/58

Goldberg ignored the constitutional questions involved. The Supreme Court can never legally make the "Law of the Land." That is done by the Congress in harmony with the Constitution.

However, Goldberg probably cared little about the legality or illegality of the questions involved. He was a most prejudiced cartoonist. He failed to print any of the law on the book's blank pages. Because there was no law to quote.

SWIFT ACTION BY THE LEGISLATURE

All measures proposed for consideration by the Legislature were adopted in the shortest possible time for the legal passage of any bill — three days. All won unanimous approval except one. In the 100-member House a single vote was registered against the measure authorizing the closing of a school integrated by force.

There was a brief discussion of this measure between me and a joint House-Senate committee.

The committee came to my office and requested that the measure be amended to give the governor full power to close any school threatened with integration by force. I demurred, saying I did not want such power over the schools. I would accept the power to close a school as a ministerial function during the time required to hold an election, with provision for the people to vote on the measure in not more than 30 days. I argued that the people of the district should have the authority to make the decision for themselves, rather than any single official making it for them.

If the people voted to open the school on an integrated basis, it would be opened. On the other hand if the people of the district voted against school opening on an integrated basis, the school would remain closed.

In fact I told the legislators I would veto the measure if it did not contain a provision authorizing the people to vote on the matter.

In the face of this determined stand on my part, the legislators agreed not to amend the bill and passed it with the election provision.

————

Some August 28 headlines in the national press on the legislative action and the integration problem read:

Legislators Rally to Faubus; Vast School
Powers Voted — *Boston Christian Science Monitor*

Segregation Bills Go To Faubus
For Signing — *St. Louis Post-Dispatch*

Eisenhower Hints Desire for Slower
Integration; Faubus Program Voted

Slower Integration Policy Held Wish
of Entire Nation — *Columnist David Lawrence*

Supreme Court Meets, Hears Arguments,
Adjourns to Sept. 11 for More Arguments

On the same day nationally known reporter Bob Considine wrote:

"If my mail is any criterion, Gov. Faubus' stand against forced or hasty integration at Little Rock Central High School, has won hot support in all sections of the country — not just the South. If the presidential elections were held this year he could conceivably constitute the balance of power."

On August 29 the Arkansas legislators recessed the special session and returned home. The recess meant they could reconvene for further action at a time of their own choosing.

The recess also meant I could hold the enacted measures on my desk and sign them at a time of my own choosing. Since all the bills bore the emergency clause any measure would become law upon my signature.

With the advice and consent of my legislative adviser and attorney, W. J. "Bill" Smith and my other attorneys, I laid the bills aside. We waited on the decision of the U.S. Supreme Court on the Lemley delay which the Court then had under consideration and on which it heard arguments on August 28.

Some 14 measures in all had been approved by the legislators of which only six were administration measures.

The total cost of the special session was $11,996.00, a modest sum in comparison to federal spending during the Little Rock controversy.

A MEETING AT THE SUMMIT
By Hungerford, Pittsburgh Post Gazette   8/27/58

We have heard much of summit meetings in recent years. They were in vogue in 1958. Hungerford pictured me as a ridiculous figure in armor on the summit of "Little Rock" challenging the Supreme Court. Labeled the "Segregation Gladiator" my shield was the "Arkansas State Legislature."

The cartoon sought to leave an erroneous impression that I was a diehard defender of segregation. I never sought to defend or oppose segregation as such, but to defend the right of the people to make their own decisions and determine their own policies, as set out in the constitution.

MESSAGE FROM A SUPREME COURT JUSTICE?

The U.S. Supreme Court convened a special session in Washington on August 28, to hear arguments and rule on the Eighth Circuit Court of Appeals reversal of Judge Lemley's decision delaying integration in the Little Rock schools for two and one-half years.

The Court heard arguments of opposing counsel on the same day the Arkansas Legislature, also in special session, was stamping final approval on bills designed to thwart the forcible integration of the schools.

The two simultaneous special sessions, the Supreme Court in Washington and the Arkansas Legislature in Little Rock, on a matter already publicized world-wide, added still further to the national and international interest.

Then to the surprise of everyone, the Court after hearing arguments, recessed for two weeks to Sept. 11 for still further pleadings on the Lemley delay. (See cartoon On Second Thought, by Knox 8-29-58)

It was during that delay period that I received a most confidential message from a member of the Court, delivered to me orally in person by a confidential messenger. The messenger, a federal official, declined to divulge the identity of the Justice from whom the message came.

The message was to the effect that the prospects were good for "something to be worked out" in which the Court would recede from its heretofore inflexible stand on the controversy. No information was given on how this might be accomplished, but I assumed it meant at least a delay in the Little Rock problem. I fully believe there was division in the Court at that time as to the course it should take. That must have been the reason for the continuance of the case.

It would be interesting indeed if a full disclosure could be made of the discussions of the Justices. It would be interesting to know of the pressures which undoubtedly were brought to bear to obtain a unanimous verdict in the Lemley case.

The messenger was a responsible federal official of unquestioned integrity and to me well known. I have no reason whatsoever to doubt his truthfulness in this particular case.

NO SURRENDER!
By Ficklen, Dallas Morning News   8/28/58

REVIEW AND OUTLOOK

The Wall Street Journal
August 29, 1958

Its wisdom (Eisenhower's statement urging a slower pace for integration) lies first in the realization that laws are not made by lawmakers, whether they be legislators or judges. They may inscribe laws on the books but they become law only when they are recognized as just and proper by the vast majority of the people who must live under them.

For that reason the Supreme Court decision, whatever its legal standing or even whatever its probity, cannot instantly make law in the deeper and truer meaning of that word.

. . . *Even if segregation had been outlawed by a Constitutional amendment, and even if that amendment had been approved by the Southern states, the process of ending segregation would still have been long, laborious and full of trouble. It will be no less so because done by a judicial decree that says what was Constitutional yesterday is not Constitutional today.*

Of that we now have hard, and somewhat frightening evidence. The vote in Arkansas is known to all. Other states too have voted to close their schools rather than accept this new decree as a law that governs them. . . .

It will do no good to dismiss all these people in the South as fools, knaves or bigots. No one really believes that. . . .

So it seems to us that . . . here is a situation where legal logic must give way to wisdom about human affairs. What must be avoided at all costs is a head-on collision between unyielding forces. The tragedy of Little Rock must not be repeated.

ANOTHER ATTEMPT TO REACH LITTLE ROCK
By Hesse, St. Louis Globe Democrat   8/26/58

Uncle Sam with a bucket — "Court Orders," — of water — "Integration," was again attempting to reach Little Rock. The bucket had holes and he hurried to reach the city before the water was gone.

THE RABBIT GETS A RESPITE
By Kennedy, Ark. Democrat   8/24/58

The Little Rock School rabbit was chased all over the woods by the big dog of "U.S. Enforcement." The rabbit ducked into and was chased out of the logs of "new state laws," "pupil placement" and "Lemley delay." Judge Gardner of the Circuit Court granted a stay, giving the school board 30 days to take the case to the U.S. Supreme Court, and "as much longer as proceedings there may require." Thus the rabbit was safe for the moment in the "stay" log. One other log has not yet been used, "closing of schools."

*TRIED BY HIS PEERS AND FOUND
WANTING*
By Batchelor, Source unknown 8/28/58

The "Warren Court" was indicted by the "Court of Public Opinion" on charges of "Nullification of the Constitution," "Jail Delivery Simplified" and the "Right of Rape in Washington, D.C." The jury of State Chief Justices said the U.S. Supreme Court was guilty.

RACE RIOTS IN LONDON
By B H, Source unknown 8/31/58

Hinny viewed a headline in a newspaper which read "Race Riots in London." His words revealed his conclusion. Headlines on news dispatches from London on September 1, 1958, read, "Mobs Again Fight London Negroes" — "Windows Smashed, Bottles Hurled in 3rd Night of Riots." Difficulties were never that serious in Little Rock.

LATEST RUMOR IN LEBANON
By Miller, Des Moines Register 8/30/58

U. S. troops landed in Lebanon by order of the President. As usual, rumors were circulating among them as to their next destination.

417

ON SECOND THOUGHT
By Knox, Nashville Banner   8/29/58

The Warren Court in the special session of August 28 approached the "Little Rock" controversy with its judicial gavel, then turned away hesitating to strike the stone. The Court set a new session for September 11 for further arguments.

MAYBE INTEGRATION SHOULD GO AT A SLOWER PACE!

NO DELAY IN INTEGRATION!

IKE

JUSTICE DEPARTMENT

WHAT KIND OF CRITTER IS THIS ANYHOW?
By Seibel
Richmond Times Dispatch   8/29/58

This cartoon pointed up the dilemma of the people in dealing with the integration problem. When Eisenhower spoke of patience in regard to the difficult and emotional problem of compulsory integration, he indicated a slow approach might be appropriate.

His own Justice Department never spoke of understanding or patience but called for forthright compliance with the Supreme Court's ruling. The Department was motivated by narrow politics. And not closely controlled by the President.

418

PACK UP YOUR TROUBLES
By Hungerford, Pittsburgh Post Gazette   8/31/58

Two major troubles continued to bother Ike, Red China's threat to our ally, Formosa (Free China), and the opposition by me to the federal takeover of the Little Rock schools. Ike packed the troubles in his golf bag and went vacationing anyway. But his smile was a bit forced.

The troops of the 1957 Occupation of Little Rock were scarcely out of sight after their withdrawal before the controversy erupted again as schools prepared to open in September 1958.

Ike was again on the golf course, as he was when we conferred in September 1957. The world was pictured as a giant golf ball on a tee. War was about to break out in the Middle East. The Chinese Reds on the mainland were firing on Free China's (Formosa) Matsu and Quemoy garrisons in the dispute over those islands and the Pescadores.

PRESIDENTIAL VACATION
By Dowling, N.Y. Herald Tribune   8/30/58

As Ike pondered those problems, rain fell from the cloud of controversy between the States and the federal government. Since the dispute in Arkansas where I was chief executive was the most publicized, the lightning from the cloud was labeled "Gov. Faubus."

"FACE THE NATION" PROGRAM

On August 31 I appeared on the CBS Network program, "Face the Nation," from Channel 11, KTHV at Little Rock. CBS personnel flew to the capital city to produce the program.

The moderator was Daniel Schorr of CBS. The panelists were John Steele of *Time-Life*'s Washington Bureau, Jack V. Fox of UPI, and Victor Eubanks of the *Christian Science Monitor*.

On the same day Harry Ashmore appeared on NBC's Comment Program from Little Rock.

TOO FAST FOR THE REFEREE
By Hungerford, Pittsburgh Post Gazette   8/30/58

The move and countermove, lawsuit and counter suit between state and federal authority was pictured as a wrestling match between me and the U.S. Supreme Court. Ike as the referee of the fast moving event had difficulty keeping up with the struggle.

FAUBUS AT CENTRAL HIGH
Artist unknown, The Worker   *8/31/58*

The Worker, the official newspaper of the Communist Party, on August 31 in the New York edition carried this prejudiced cartoon. A figure labeled "Faubus" threatened small Negro children with a club with Central High School in the background.

The Communists were following the Party's well established line — make propaganda by distortion, exaggeration or falsification of any issue that would create distrust, fear, hate and disunity among free people.

APPOINTMENTS, August 1958

Dr. J. G. Simpson, El Dorado, Optometry Board. Fred Carter, Sr., Lake City, State Bank Commission. Ben M. Hogan, Sr., Little Rock, Game & Fish Commission. Glenn Will, Fayetteville, Pea Ridge National Park Commission. Board of Psychiatric Examiners: David J. Parma, Oliver C. Henry, Mrs. Marie Noll and Mrs. Mary Kathleen Ezell.

CHAPTER 21
SUPREME COURT OVERRULES JUDGE LEMLEY;
8TH DISTRICT COURT BREAKS ALL PRECEDENTS;
PEOPLE VOTE TO CLOSE SCHOOLS;
U.S. MARSHALS SWARM INTO LITTLE ROCK

Batesville (Ark.) Guard
Sept. 1, 1958

Paul Buchanan's
TWO CENTS WORTH

A Governor And His Power —

After out-doing some of the country's most sagacious politicians in the past year, Governor Faubus thus far has demonstrated a rare brand of resourcefulness by managing to out-maneuver just about every authority connected with the . . . tug-of-war at Central High. What's more, he seemingly has put Washington officialdom on the defensive in this sizzling, portentous controversy.

Powerful as he now is, Mr. Faubus of course had the full-fledged help of a . . . Legislature....

At any rate,... the VIP's in Washington are bothered with their ulcers and insomnia these days, all because of an unflinching governor who has befuddled them with a bold, shrewd type of aggressiveness.

━०━०━०━

Ft. Smith Southwest American

September 1, 1958

FAUBUS ASSERTS:
LAWS ARE ACTS OF CONGRESS

Governor Orval E. Faubus Sunday asserted that the "laws of the land" are acts of congress. And Congress has not acted, he said, on the school integration-segregation issue.

He quoted a 1957 circuit court decision on another matter which said a particular ruling "is the law of this case, but not the law of the land."

Faubus made the statements on a television panel interview. The question was asked the governor: "Why have you changed your mind?" after saying last year the supreme court's 1954 decision is the law of the land.

"I really haven't changed my mind," the governor said, "I was required to issue that statement as a basis for negotiations with the White House.

"Because I said it didn't make it so."

* * *

A questioner said "will you close Central High School if the supreme court orders integration." and the governor shot back: "If necessary for the peace of the community, I will."

Issued Power

The legislature last week handed Faubus the power to close any Arkansas school facing forcible integration. . . .

"Federal-state authority is at issue here," Faubus told the nationwide television audience.

"My actions up to this time have been to preserve the peace." Faubus insisted.

The panel repeatedly questioned the governor about his earlier statement he was "required" to declare the 1954 supreme court decision the law of the land.

" Did Ike insist in your making it?" a panel member asked.

The governor said Representative Brooks Hays of Arkansas and presidential assistant Sherman Adams insisted.

Asked if he believed a governor must accept a federal court decision, Faubus answered:

"Abraham Lincoln disagreed with the Dred Scott case. There are many people in the U.S. and Arkansas who firmly believe the supreme court had no authority for its 1954 decision.

"Many people — millions — think the supreme court made a law itself in that case...

-0-

The next day the following report appeared after a news conference at the Newport, R.I. Summer White House.

Hagerty Won't Answer
Faubus on 'Laws' Issue
New York Herald Tribune — September 2, 1958

Gov. Faubus said on a television program yesterday that Adams and Hays, had required him publicly to recognize the Supreme Court ruling as the law of the land as a prerequisite to further negotiation with the President on the Little Rock high school situation. . . .

The matter came up at a Hagerty news conference today. Mr. Hagerty was asked whether he had seen Gov. Faubus' remarks, and the exchange with reporters went like this:

HAGERTY: "Oh, yeah, I have seen what Gov. Faubus says,"

REPORTER: "What comment do you have?"

HAGERTY: "I think the only comment I have is no comment. You wouldn't print the comment I feel like giving."

REPORTER: "Well, let me ask you the direct question: Did the White House force Faubus to make his statement?"

HAGERTY: "That's all I'm going to say on Gov. Faubus."

The Governor conferred with the President here last September 14. The Arkansas Governor a few hours later made a statement which said in part:

"I have never expressed any personal opinion regarding the Supreme Court decision of 1954 which ordered integration. That is not relevant. That decision is the law of the land and must be obeyed...."

In Little Rock today, Gov. Faubus laughed when he heard about Mr. Hagerty's reaction.

"They hate very badly to get caught," he said.

Hagerty could easily have denied my statement. The press knew it was significant when he failed to do so, but did not directly challenge his evasion.

MORE GROUND CUT FROM UNDER....
By Knox, Nashville Banner   9/4/58

The admission of Alaska to the Union as a state cut more ground from beneath the Earl Warren Supreme Court's claim of legality for its federal school control decree.

The Alaskan statehood provisions were enacted by the 85th Congress and signed by President Eisenhower. The admission act read: the public schools and colleges "shall forever remain under the exclusive control of the state, or its governmental subdivisions".

Many people inquire that if a state has "exclusive control" over its schools, how can the federal courts legally thrust their authority into the state's school affairs in a manner now being done?

Millions of citizens believe that all court-made law is clearly contrary to the U.S. Constitution, the constitutions of the states, and contrary to the Congress-enacted, president-approved admission acts of the states to the Union.

HIGHLIGHTS OF THE NEWSWEEK
By Kennedy, Ark. Democrat   9/7/58

For those ministers who favored integration, the best leadership would have been to integrate their churches which they refused to do.

The school board postponed the school opening date waiting on the U.S. Supreme Court decision.

The U.S. Department of Justice was recruiting deputy U.S. marshals for use at Central High School. It had difficulty recruiting any highly reputable citizens for such duty.

I was interviewed on the largest radio hookup ever attempted, originating with the British Broadcasting Company of London, England. I was questioned by newsmen from Great Britain, Holland, South Africa, Brazil and France.

Senator McClellan challenged a federal court decision as the law of the land and was strongly applauded by delegates to the state Democratic Convention on September 6. Among those escorting me to the stage for my third term nomination acceptance speech were McClellan, Congressmen Oren Harris and Brooks Hays. Congressman Wilbur Mills was again permanent chairman of the convention.

Conway in the shadow of Little Rock got a new industry, a Baldwin Piano plant.

— — —

Judge Harry J. Lemley, age 75, announced on September 5, his plans to retire.

The average life of a democracy is approximately 200 years
HISTORY
JUDICIAL DICTATORSHIP
THE WILL OF THE PEOPLE
BALLOT
CONSTITUTIONAL GUARANTEES OF STATE SOVEREIGNTY
LOCAL SELF GOVT
KNOX

"HERE'S THE LAW" AND "HERE'S THE LESSON," By Knox, Nashville Banner, 9/2/58

Discarded and cast aside were "The Will of the People" as expressed at the ballot box, the "Constitutional Guarantees of State Sovereignty," and the right of "Local Self-Government." Held aloft and pointed out as the policy of the Republic was "Judicial Dictatorship."

Viewing this scene as dictatorship prevailed over local self-government was the sage, ancient figure of "History." What he saw in the American Republic recalled a lesson recorded in the pages of the book he had written — "The average life of a democracy is approximately 200 years." Now twenty-one years after the date of this cartoon our republic is past its 200th year.

Nashville, Tenn. Banner
September 4, 1958

On School Controls:
'LAW OF THE LAND' WAS WRITTEN BY CONGRESS

IF THE "LAW OF THE LAND" — as formally enacted by Congress — is clear on any point, it is that the states are invested with exclusive powers of school control. . . . at least TEN times, the only law-making body of the Federal Government has written that provision into the statutory framework of these components. And when it incorporated that clause in the Federal act admitting Alaska to statehood, it was restating a point of law recognized as legal and binding as long as the states have had public schools....

In 1889, South Dakota, North Dakota, Montana, and Washington, were admitted. The law creating them put their public school systems under their exclusive jurisdiction. In 1890 it was Idaho and Wyoming; in 1907 it was Oklahoma; in 1912 it was Arizona and New Mexico — and in every case Congress not only accepted the principle, but spelled it out. It took statutory form which never has been repealed, and still is on the books.

Its constitutionality never has been challenged...

* * *

What is the "Law of the Land" regarding schools? It is that the STATES shall exercise, not just requisite or paramount jurisdiction, but EXCLUSIVE CONTROL over their school systems.

If the U.S. Supreme Court can by a wave of the wand, a ukase, or a bland reference to "See Myrdal," wipe out the law and the Constitution on that point, there is not a point of law or Constitution safe from such treatment.

When Richard C. Butler, attorney representing the Little Rock Board, spoke of the need for time to "establish a national policy, Justice Frankfurter asked:

"Why aren't two decisions of this Court a national policy?"

The answer should have been obvious: Because no where in the Constitution or elsewhere is it provided that the judicial branch shall enact a law or MAKE national policy. Nine men named to that bench have not that AUTHORITY..

It was answered right effectively in the simple statement by Gov. Orval Faubus that the Supreme Court does not make the law. Congress does that. And on this point Congress has spoken.

Arkansas Democrat
September 7, 1958

STATE FACES FATEFUL WEEK AS COURT DECISION NEARS
by George Douthit

This is a serious week for Arkansas. The U.S. Supreme Court's decision on Central High School integration,...will decide what the weeks and months ahead will be like.

All signs point to a court rejection of the Lemley decision ... the federal enforcement agencies are ready to take over.

A decision to delay integration would be about the most sensational news that could come to Arkansas people . . .

A masterful effort was done by Sen. Fulbright in his petition two weeks ago to the Supreme Court. He described the "Southern mind" as something that should be taken into account. . . .

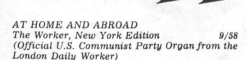

AT HOME AND ABROAD
The Worker, New York Edition   *9/58*
(Official U.S. Communist Party Organ from the London Daily Worker)

The Communist Party viewpoint in Great Britain, classified my re-election as one of two bad events. The other was sending arms to the Middle East to Israel.

Senator Fulbright's accurate description of the true feelings in Little Rock and Arkansas couldn't very well be called intimidation....

We know of no one trying to intimidate the high court, not even Governor Faubus... He can lead his people on the road to segregation, but he could never lead them on the road the other way, toward integration.

On that point we would like to repeat something we said in this column some months ago. If and when the governor ever decides to renounce his present stand and follow the dictates of the federal court, the people of Arkansas will ditch him and get a new leader.

Also, he does not control the emotions or the actions of thousands of segregationists in this state. If integration is forced once more on Central High School and there should be trouble, Governor Faubus doesn't have to instigate it. All the ingredients for violence already are present.

It doesn't take a genius to originate integration violence, but it takes a lot of sound thinking to prevent it.

AGE OLD QUESTION
By Lange, Shreveport, La. Times   9/9/58

The cartoonist raised the old unanswerable question, "What happens when an irresistible force meets an immovable object?"

IRRESISTABLE FORCE AND IMMOVABLE OBJECT
By Warren, Philadelphia Inquirer   9/15/58

Following the Supreme Court decision of September 12, I signed into law the measures passed at the special session of the legislature, and the battle intensified between the irresistible force (federal authority) and the immovable object (states rights).

SPREAD MIGHTY THIN
By Kennedy, Ark. Democrat   9/12/58

Federal Judge John E. Miller presided in the Eastern District, his own Western District and also on roving assignment.

The judge was being overworked because of the long delayed appointments to fill vacancies in Arkansas. Many people suspected the judgeships were purposely left vacant so that the Justice Department could send northern judges into the area at will.

THE WHITE HOUSE GOLFER'S VACATION, By Hungerford, Pittsburgh Post Gazette, 9/10/58

The "Maine" election, lost to the Democrats, tied a can to the "G.O.P." elephant's tail. It angrily chased "Ike's caddy," Sherman Adams, as the Democrat Donkey, "Faubus," showed up again with the Little Rock problem, to distract Ike from his golf game.

THE NEWS SAID NO SURRENDER IN LITTLE ROCK

On September 12, in the face of the U.S. Supreme Court decision of the same date ordering forced integration immediately, in the face of widespread tension, and the presence in Little Rock of hundreds of U.S. marshalls from all across the nation, I signed into law the measures enacted by the special session of the Arkansas General Assembly. Under the authority granted in the acts, I ordered the high schools not to open the following Monday, and set the election date to vote on the matter for October 7. (On September 17 I moved the election date up to September 27.)

Blazing headlines in newspapers read:

FAUBUS CLOSES CHS AFTER COURT DENIES DELAY OF INTEGRATION

FAUBUS ARREST RUMORED IN CAPITAL

LITTLE ROCK GIRDS FOR SHOWDOWN

U.S. MAPS MOVE AS FAUBUS RESTS

LITTLE ROCK MAYOR SAYS HANDS OFF

The Little Rock City Government in a special meeting decided not to enforce the federal court order. A statement signed by Mayor Werner C. Knoop said:

"If and when Central High School is integrated, the responsibility is clearly that of the federal government."

Faubus Hears School News
With Flush, Impassive Quiet

Arkansas Gazette
September 13, 1958

Governor Faubus reddened slightly when he first was told of the Supreme Court decision.

Otherwise he betrayed no emotion.

He was presiding over a state Election Commission meeting in the Reception Room adjacent to his office Sept. 12. Mr. Faubus was about 15 minutes late getting to the session. He smiled at about 50 persons on hand and sat down at the head of the conference table.

He had called the meeting of the Board, comprised of state constitutional officers and the heads of the state Democratic and Republican parties, to order when a reporter came in and whispered the news to Mr. Faubus.

The governor nodded and reddened slightly.

Other reporters fanned through the room while television and news cameras, set up for the purpose of recording the historic moment, ground away.

Mr. Faubus arose and jammed his hand into a coat pocket. Reporters surged forward to hear Mr. Faubus tell the onlookers what he heard.

The governor disappointed them. He calmly advised the persons at the meeting that they would be given a chance to speak for their choice of county election board candidates.

As he sat down, newsmen thronged around the governor asking him to comment on the court decision and what he intended to do.

"I have no comment, gentlemen," the governor said.

As the questions flew at him the governor elaborated: "I just plain will not comment."

The governor finished the Board meeting behind closed doors. He slipped back into his office without making himself available to the press.

His associates and advisors flocked to his office to vie with newsmen for seats and standing room. The governor closeted himself with Tom Harper of Fort Smith state chairman of the Democratic Party and one of the governor's lawyers.

Newsmen waited around until midafternoon to see whether or not Mr. Faubus changed his mind about a statement. The governor left the building himself to attend a meeting of the Arkansas-Industrial Development Commission.

Flanked by his ever-present plainclothes State Police guard and companion, Floyd Weaver, he returned back about 4 p.m. and attended to what his aides said was routine business.

Twenty-five minutes later the governor sent out the first of the special session bills he signed into law.

⚊⚊⚊⚊⚊

ARKANSAS GOVERNOR RESTS;
RUMORS OF U.S. ACTION FLY
Chicago News, September 13, 1958

Governor Orval E. Faubus was in seclusion today but he denied he was trying to avoid possible federal court action.

In a telephone conversation with the Arkansas Democrat he appeared unconcerned about reports circulating that the Justice Department has obtained a warrant for his arrest.

In Washington a spokesman for the Justice Department emphatically denied the reports as "complete nonsense."

"I don't think the federal authorities have any legal right to stop me" (from carrying out the laws passed by the legislature) he said.

Faubus late yesterday ordered the four senior high schools closed. (The order was for the schools not to open until the people of the district could vote on whether they should open on an integrated basis or not open at all, and a time was immediately set for the election.)

"I don't think there is any law under which they can cause my arrest for taking action I think is necessary as the head of a sovereign state," Faubus asserted.

Then he added, "I wouldn't want to hide from the federal authorities if I could. I have simply taken my action and there is nothing more to be done this weekend. I wanted to get away and rest."

He said he would be in his office Monday.

Again the governor said he was backed by the people of Arkansas.

"I received a big batch of telegrams yesterday... All of them urged me to go ahead and close the schools and call the election."

In the meantime Henry V. Rath resigned from the six-man school board in protest of the Supreme Court's decision. Other members were expected to follow.

"The U.S. Supreme Court, in denying this request, has acted in complete disregard of the social customs of the South." Rath said. "In setting aside Judge Lemley's decision, the court indicated an unwillingness to consider local officials."

QUESTIONS
By Knox, Nashville Banner,
Chattanooga News Free Press   9/11/58

Justice Felix Frankfurter of the U.S. Supreme Court during the September 11 hearing on the Little Rock case, asked "Why aren't two decisions of this Court a national policy?" Uncle Sam, speaking for the American people, replied, "Is the policy of 170 million Americans to be fixed irrevocably by nine men appointed for life? This was a capsule summation of the great controversy. And the controversy continues. The outcome will determine the fate of democracy in America.

"GOVERNMENT OF THE COURT, BY THE COURT SHALL NOT PERISH . . .!"
By Knox, Nashville Banner
9/12/58

Abraham Lincoln once said:
    ..."Government of the people, by the people, and for the people, shall not perish from the earth."
    The Earl Warren Supreme Court on September 12 affirmed, without constitutional authority, that the Court had control of the people's schools; and that the court's decisions on school matters would be enforced with the bayonet. Thus "the vote of the people of Arkansas" was nullified by the use of the court gavel and the federal bayonet.
    Lincoln's statement was changed by the Court to read:
    "Government of the Court, by the Court, for the Court, shall not perish..."

EPITAPH FOR DEMOCRACY, *By Knox, Nashville Banner, 9/13/58*

The arrogant black robed figure of the Earl Warren Supreme Court presided at an open grave funeral service. Uncle Sam was puzzled as he saw in the open grave ready to be interred, the liberty won in "1776," the right to decide issues by the "ballot," the "Bill of Rights," "Constitutional guarantees" and "government by the people." The presiding figure, Chief Justice Earl Warren, read from a statement which said "I am the law of the land; I am the Constitution of the United States." To millions of people the cartoon vividly portrayed the arrogant, dictatorial attitude of the federal judicial branch of government at the time.

Immediately following my signing of the legislative act and the proclamation setting the election, Sheriff Tom Gulley was admitted to the office to serve a state injunction on me forbidding me to close the schools. The injunction was the result of a lawsuit filed by Attorney Kenneth Coffelt for Mrs. Gertie Garrett. Press reports said both were strong segregationists and expressed puzzlement over the lawsuit. I never learned its purpose, and it was unsuccessful.

Press reports also said 150 U.S. marshalls swarmed about the office of U.S. Marshall Beal Kidd in the Federal Building. Many wore western style hats. They wouldn't talk to reporters and went to a courtroom for a secret briefing. The story said they would arrest people and take them to jail and Little Rock Police would be left with the direct duty of putting down violence.

●──●──●──●──●──○

MARSHALS, JUDGE SET FOR TROUBLE
Boston (Mass.) GLOBE, September 13, 1958
By BOB CONSIDINE

Governor Faubus has knocked the chip off the shoulder of the Supreme Court's latest edict (by signing into law the bills passed by the legislature at the special session).

But there is every indication...that the Federal Government will take no punitive action until Faubus makes his next move.

JAIL FOR DEFIANT

The troubled, jittery capital city is filled with strange faces, particularly in the area of the Federal Building. Youngish looking, muscular men with loaded shoulder holsters — U.S. marshals — have been flown in from other states.

The Justice Department has at least ten of its top attorneys on hand....

The best Justice Department legal talent is divided on whether the Government has the authority to order the schools opened or to pronounce their closing a violation of the Supreme Court order.

The Government probably will not move until Faubus makes his next move. What that will be no man can fairly foretell....

Faubus' decision to close the schools met with general agreement in this area....

Many who shrugged it (court-ordered integration) off with "Well, it's the law" last year now are part of the hard core resistance lined up behind the governor, whose personal popularity has spread from Little Rock through the South to such a degree that he is being spoken of as a possible "third party" candidate in the 1960 presidential race.

* * *

Another reason the Feds are said to plan no action against the governor, is that — as one Little Rock "moderate" said last night — "if the Government drags Orval out of his mansion and flings him in a cell he'll be a greater figure, a bigger martyr, than he is today, and the government knows it."

* * *

Meanwhile, this city sat tense and fearful as the greatest states right struggle since the Civil War swirled through it.

* * *

There were headlines throughout the nation:

ALCORN PREDICTS THIRD PARTY IN SOUTH
Fayetteville N.W. Arkansas Times

U.S. MAPS MOVES AS GOVERNOR RESTS
Little Rock Arkansas Democrat

THE SUPREME COURT REJECTS PRAYER FOR MODERATION
Charlotte, N.C. Observer

CLOSE PUBLIC SCHOOLS IN VIRGINIA
Kalamazoo, Michigan, Gazette

RACE VIOLENCE IN GREAT BRITAIN
Denver, Colorado, Post

STUNNED LITTLE ROCK FOLKS PRAYING FOR WAY OUT
Dallas, Texas, News

NO SIDESTEPPING THE ISSUE
Columbus, Ohio, State Journal

INTEGRATION STRUGGLE ENTERS A NEW PHASE
New York, N.Y., Times

AREA BAPTIST (30) CHURCHES BEHIND FAUBUS
S.W. American, Ft. Smith, Ark.

The Supreme Court upheld the decision of the 8th Circuit Court of appeals thus nullifying the delay in school integration granted by Judge Lemley. A *Gazette* editorial of September 13 said in part.

The Next Move Is Mr. Faubus'

The Little Rock School Board has now taken its plea for a delay . . . to the court of last resort. The United States Supreme Court has denied the Board's petition...

Thus the hope for any immediate legal remedy...has been exhausted. The responsibility shifts from the School Board to the principal antagonists — Governor Faubus, acting for the government of Arkansas, and representatives of the Department of Justice, acting for the government of the United States.

The next move is Mr. Faubus'. He has been armed by the legislature with full powers to act, and the School Board has indicated that it considers itself bound by the state laws...

The first question before Mr. Faubus...appears to be whether he will prevent the opening of the city's high schools on Monday while he seeks the possibility of delay through further maneuvering in the courts. If he does not, the schools presumably will open on schedule with the Negro children applying for admission — and quite possibly with a mob on hand to try to turn them back.

Late yesterday afternoon Mr. Faubus apparently met this first test in good faith when he signed a proclamation providing that the high schools of the city will not open on Monday...

It seems to us that Mr. Faubus' first obligation is to use his powers to prevent any possibility of violence and we hope he has now done so. We accept the fact that he has a mandate from the people to resist desegregation of these schools, and that he considers himself bound by it. We recognize, too, that yesterday's decision by the Supreme Court drastically limits the area of maneuver in which Mr. Faubus might re-open segregated schools without running into a direct collision with the federal laws...

Yet we believe that even Mr. Faubus' most militant supporters are still counting on him to find a way out of the impasse without the shedding of blood...

In any event the showdown...has come... The citizens of this community must resign themselves to suffering still more. The one certainty...is that there will be no easy answer, and no quick resolution of the issues...

The first and most pressing obligation of those in official position is to preserve order — and we believe those who discharge it will have the support of this community no matter how divided the people may be on the central question...

The *Gazette* and I appeared to be in agreement on one point — to preserve order was the first priority.

LET'S KEEP THE CONFLICT IN THIS ARENA
By Kennedy, Ark. Democrat   9/14/58

As Justice Department attorneys squared off against my legal staff, the cartoonist hoped the conflict could be confined to the legal field and not revert to violence in the streets. That was my hope also, and the surest way to prevent violence was to carry out the laws enacted by the legislature at the special session.

I strongly suspect that my critics and even those who favored integration, even including the federal authorities, were glad to see me sign the legislative measures into law, and continue the conflict in the courts. The *Gazette* as much as said so in its editorial of September 13. Certainly the Justice Department, which before had cowardly refused to assume its clear obligation for enforcement of the federal court order, didn't want the conflict on its hands without assistance from local authorities which had now been refused.

GOV. FAUBUS NOT WITHSTANDING
By Grant, Los Angeles Examiner   9/14/58

This would be a good cartoon in its proper perspective with a proper constitutional role of the Court. The "Birthright of future generations" should be protected and preserved. No one in Little Rock sought to deny this.

However, many questions now face the American people.

Will not the flood of crime, lawless disorder, subversion, drug abuse and pornography let loose on the nation by decisions of the Supreme Court, if not soon controlled, destroy the birthright of future generations?

Speaking further of the "birthright of future generations," the Supreme Court has now ruled, without benefit of any federal law or constitutional provision, that new lives growing in their mothers' wombs do not have the right to be born at all. These new lives can now be legally destroyed, according to the court's ruling. The Supreme Court, or anyone else, will never rock a cradle for those who are killed before they are born. Is not their birthright denied by the court ruling?

I'LL LEARN YE HOW T' DRAW, By Knox, Nashville Banner, 9/14/58

Instead of federal troops the federal government planned to use U.S. marshals and deputy marshals to enforce integration at Central. Regularly appointed marshals were sent to Little Rock from all across the nation, with the recruitment of deputy marshals from Arkansas and surrounding states. Here a two-gun U.S. marshal replaced the teacher — and says "I'll learn ye how t' draw!"

Lemley
Miller
Trimble

FEDERAL BENCH IN ARK.

sho'nuff!
SHO'NUFF!

ARK.   MISS.
HELENA BRIDGE ASSURED...

CARTOON HIGHLIGHTS of the ARKANSAS NEWSWEEK
by Jon Kennedy

HISTORIC 'DECISION WEEK' NEWS CAME IN 3 PARTS -- ARGUMENT, DENIAL, and REACTION...

...the public interest is superior to the interests of seven Negro children.

Atty. Richard C. Butler

-the judgment of the Court of Appeals must be affirmed.

chief justice

the game is now underway.

FAUBUS SIGNS THE 14 'PACKAGE' BILLS—ORDERS HIGH SCHOOLS CLOSED IN L.R.

?? ?

FEDERAL COURTROOM

KEEP OUT

MARSHALS GET SECRET BRIEFING ON SCHOOL DUTIES...

HIGHLIGHTS OF THE NEWSWEEK
By Kennedy, Ark. Democrat   9/14/58

With the retirement of Judge Lemley and Judge Trimble, only Judge John Miller remained on the federal bench in Arkansas.

The federal courtroom in Little Rock was barred to the people including the press as U.S. marshalls were secretly briefed by Justice Department personnel from Washington.

The big news was the hearing on the school controversy before the special session of the Supreme Court in Washington, the Court's decision and the reaction in Arkansas.

On the positive side the Helena bridge over the Mississippi River was assured when Arkansas and Mississippi agreed on the final plans for construction.

Also positive, the AIDC announced two new industries, the Johnson Brothers Shoe Co., Inc., at Corning, and a poultry and feed processing plant at Waldron.

In Fayetteville the new 2½ million dollar plant of Standard Register Company was dedicated before a crowd of 1,500 with hundreds more going through the plant during the day. Company president M.A. Spayd said the plant would begin operating with an annual pay roll of $400,000. William R. (Bill) Smith, AIDC member of Lake Village, represented me at the festivities, and Elmer Yancey, AIDC member of Searcy, represented the commission. State and local dignitaries attended along with other company officials.

THE WOODROW LETTER FROM ST. LOUIS

In the September 14 issue of the *Gazette* appeared a letter in "From the People" column from an attorney in St. Louis by the name Arley R. Woodrow, a former citizen of Arkansas. The letter contained statements derogatory to Arkansas and took issue with efforts of the people in opposition to what they considered illegal court orders.

Somehow the name rang a bell in my mind. I finally recalled that during my brief sojourn at Commonwealth College in the Spring of 1935, an Arley Woodrow had a law office in Mena and was attorney for the college and attorney for individuals at the college. Some of the personnel at the college, I learned, were

obtaining divorces under Arkansas' 90-day residence divorce law with Woodrow as their attorney.

Once while in Mena with a small number of college officials and students, I accompanied the group on a visit to Woodrow's office where I was introduced to him. I sat by while the college officials discussed with the attorney some legal and business matters pertaining to the institution.

There was a strong Communist group, or cell, among the students and faculty members of the college. I soon learned that Woodrow was close to this group, or at least some of the leaders. The Communists acted and spoke as if Mr. Woodrow were a trusted member of their group, — that he was one of them. I have no way of knowing now if attorney Woodrow was then a card carrying Communist, a fellow traveler or merely attorney for the group. He appeared to be more than the latter.

Woodrow's letter in the *Gazette* showed he was then a practicing attorney in St. Louis. The letter indicated he was backing the official Communist party position on the Little Rock controversy.

SCHOOL LOCK-UP

PUBLIC NEED FOR EDUCATION

SOUTH

HE MIGHT GET HUNGRY
By Hesse, St. Louis Globe Democrat   9/14/58

The great hope of the federal authorities and the integrationists was that dissatisfaction with closed schools would cause the people to favor, however reluctantly, the opening of the schools in compliance with the court orders for integration.

There were editorials, cartoons, comments and news stories by the thousands promoting this theme. Some writers seized upon the slightest pretext to promote the idea that the people were becoming disgusted and discouraged and would soon surrender. The media scene of big newspapers and TV, with some notable exceptions, constituted a propaganda campaign of the greatest magnitude.

But, as will be seen, the people were not ready to surrender but were determined to continue the struggle. They still had hope that the great national constitution would be observed thus assuring them control of their own schools.

One viewer of this cartoon commented, "Better to be hungry for a time than to be poisoned."

The people would not immediately surrender. Even with the vast resources and might of the federal government which made the outcome of the struggle inevitable, the subjugation of the people would take time.

UNWANTED

On the Ku Klux Klan, the *El Dorado Daily News* commented on September 14, 1958:

> Law-abiding citizens of Arkansas must have been gratified by Governor Faubus' expression of dislike for the Ku Klux Klan, although they probably would have preferred that he used stronger language. . . . The governor said, "I never did like the Klan. . . .

> The KKK should be looked upon with the same contempt as the people look upon the hoods who have invaded union labor. Both thrive on violence and intimidation.

FAUBUS RECEIVES ENCOURAGEMENT, PRAISE FROM THROUGHOUT NATION

Arkansas Democrat, Sept. 15, 1958

Telegrams of congratulations to Governor Faubus for his stand in closing the high schools . . . continued to pour in to his office today.

A big batch came in from all over the state of Mississippi. A big percentage came from out of the South. Here are some samples:

North Chicago — Sir, superb maneuver. Congratulations. Accept our wholehearted support.

Charlotte, N.C. — Millions of Americans now look to you as the foremost leader in the struggle to regain the freedoms which we once enjoyed under the Constitution as intended by our forefathers. Do not yield to tyranny, if we can't keep you out of jail, we will go with you.

Rialto, Calif. — Courage. One man against a nation. Josie Smith. (Fictitious name.)

Ft. Worth — Your untiring leadership and fight in upholding state rights against encroachment by a despotic court is to be commended by all true Americans. I pray that your leadership will not falter.

Atlantic City — The honest people of the United States are back of your stand...

Baton Rouge — ...backed you 100 per cent in your first rebuttal. I am more than 100 per cent backing you now. If you have the weapons to fire let me fire. I fought World War II. I worked for Mr. Eisenhower and I quit now.

Jackson, Miss. — Any services required call on us.

Utica, Mich. — We up north are backing you on each and every decision you have made. Please keep fighting for states rights and our individual rights for each and every state in the United States of America.

Birmingham, Mich. — I admire your determination but abhor your judgement. However, my son would like your personal quotable short opinion

for debate scheduled for Monday. He would appreciate anything you would like to wire him for his discussion.

West Palm Beach, Fla. — You were wonderful in your news conference. You are the South's only hope. Patrick Henry said give me liberty or give me death. He got his second choice. He's dead. Better that we die than live at bayonet point.

Snohomish, Wash. — Sacred heritage civil rights at lowest ebb since the Book of Kings First Chapter 3 Verse 9 we have lost our God and people in a political arena and offered peace offerings and made a feast to all his servants. A wise and understanding heart to walk and keep God's statutes and commandments. An ardent admirer to a great leader.

OAKLAND, Calif. — There are many with you here.

CINCINNATI, Ohio — Sir: You have many friends here in the north.

BALTIMORE — Cannot believe that any government can stop the rights of man as state's rights. You have the feelings of many people tonight. News wire states your arrest cannot be done according to the constitution of the U.S. Government. Your answer and your advice is for the nation.

WASHINGTON, D.C. — At this time of year when the leaves are beginning to display their tone of color you are having to display your stand at Central High School. Please believe me the people of Alabama are behind you. And, some of my friends from Washington, D.C.... (Former Alabamian.)

LOS ANGELES — Hold your guns.

WASHINGTON, D.C. — I am (gives name) and I go along with Mr. Day's letter to you earlier. Integration here is abominable. I have lived here all my life and please may I say too do not relinquish your stand.

Gary, Ind. — Stick to your guns. Federal government is based on state government, but federal government cannot usurp state government. Good luck.

MILWAUKEE, Wis. — Suggest high school integration be only on non co-educational basis.

RICHMOND, Va. — Millions are giving you moral support unexpressed.

DREXEL HILL, Penn. — Thank God there is somebody for states rights. Continue the good work. Don't give up.

JACKSONVILLE, Fla. — Thank you for having more guts than our governor's got.

DULUTH — Minn. — If the rights and laws of any state in this democracy of the United States is jeopardized or denied by any person, even the president of the USA or his representatives, then we are not a group of states as individuals but 48 states governed as one by dictator and or for his representatives. A country can be democratic only as long as it is governed by representatives which are chosen by a vote of the people. If the voting and the choosing of the laws by any state as an individual state is not recognized by a president then any law becomes meaningless . . . If the government of the USA wishes to overthrow the people and their representatives then the people have no other choice than to overthrow the non-democratic government.

WASHINGTON, D.C. — Congratulations. You have delivered the first decisive blow to Communism in these United States. Keep going. The informed populace is with you.

LONG BEACH, Calif. — Congratulations on school closing. Gratifying to see someone with power of their convictions and courage enough to assert them.

NEW YORK — Millions of us Northern Yankees are pulling for you in this crisis brought about by a handful of old men. . . . This is more dangerous to the unity and security of America than the rumblings of old Khrushchev so please take courage and may the vast majority win to continue a democracy of the people.

(These are but a few of the thousands of wires and letters the governor is getting. He is reading practically all of them and those with addresses — and most of them have them — will be answered.)

―=0―0―●―0―0

Editorial
BUFFALO, N.Y. COURIER EXPRESS
September 16, 1958

Enforce What 'Law of the Land'?

The integration-segregation debate is so fraught with emotionalism on both sides that it is difficult to get the issue defined in cool, hard, objective terms. It ought to be possible, however, to clear the air of at least one of the misleading catch phrases that becloud the issue and confuse the public.

This catch phrase ... is that integration must be enforced as "the law of the land." Let us ask a practical question:

Who must do the enforcing of what law of the land?

To the first part of the question the more zealous advocates of immediate integration are likely to reply that it is up to President Eisenhower,...to compel Faubus to enforce the aforesaid "law of the land."

This gives rise to another query: Just how does a President go about the task of compelling the Governor to enforce a "law of the land" which never has been written into the federal statutes and which conflicts with state laws that the Governor is sworn to enforce?

Advocates of drastic action will retort that the United States Supreme Court decision of May, 1954, made integration the law of the land and no further legislation, federal or state, is necessary.

Well, if that is the right answer, Congress and the various state Legislatures have wasted a lot of time, in the last century and a half, passing laws when all they had to do was to stand aside and let the Supreme Court hand down decisions...

If you are getting confused...don't blame me... The Supreme Court decision of May, 1954, set aside as unconstitutional the education laws of certain Southern states requiring separate schools for white and Negro pupils.

...There was no federal statute involved. Indeed, since the beginning of the Republic, public education has been regarded as a field reserved to state and local governments...

GOVERNMENT MAY LET FAUBUS 'STEW IN OWN JUICE'

So read a headline in the Minneapolis, Minnesota, Tribune, September 16 over a story by Carl T. Rowan in which he wrote:

"The assumption here is that parental and student unhappiness over the closing of the schools will mount swiftly and that Faubus will be forced to act soon."

The wish was father to the thought.

It was not I who wanted to continue the fight. In fact, as Democrat reporter George Douthit wrote a year before, I never wanted the fight in the first place.

Soon after this , on September 27, I let the people decide at the ballot box about continuing the fight. The decision was made in an election conducted by election commissioners and election officials over which I exercised no control whatsoever.

As to the "Government letting me stew in my own juice," that was a pretext and a dodge by federal officials to cover up their unwillingness or inability to do anything about the situation. In fact, the federal authorities wanted as much as any one to avoid a confrontation at the time and their sympathizers in the press were willing to cover for them.

PRIVATE SCHOOL CORPORATION ORGANIZED

A private school corporation was organized in Little Rock, with Attorney Leon Catlett drawing up the necessary papers. The incorporators were Dr. T.J. Raney, Herschel Goodman, Dr. Malcolm G. Taylor, J.C. Mitchell, Mrs. Gordon P. (Willie) Oates and Ben C. Isgreg. Raney was elected president of the corporation.

The charter was officially granted in Pulaski Circuit Court on September 17, Judge J. Mitchell Cockrell presiding.

SUPPORT CONTINUES NATIONWIDE

Support for the effort in defense of states rights continued to be manifested by thousands of letters and telegrams from across the nation. On September 18 a wire from Nacogdoches, Texas, bore the names of 460 signers. Earlier a telegram from Louisiana contained 2,300 signatures.

The support came not from individuals alone but from labor union locals, church groups, conventions of various groups of all kinds, associations representing professional groups, family gatherings, neighborhood house parties or truckers gathered at a truck stop.

FEDERAL MARSHALS

Finally, the Eisenhower Administration had wised up to the legal way to enforce a federal court order — the use of U.S. marshals.

To rely on local and state authorities to enforce a federal court order which was clearly in conflict with state law, was a mistake from the very beginning. Even worse, it was a scheming, dishonest attempt by federal authority to evade a responsibility solely its own, and a cowardly effort to avoid the dirty work involved.

The main reliance of the Justice Department, it appeared, was placed on the recruitment of deputy marshals. They came not from the ranks of proud, law abiding citizens ready to help in law enforcement. Evidently the federal authorities were unsuccessful in recruiting such persons. Many of the deputy marshals, we soon learned, were less than reputable citizens who were lured by the urge to pack a gun and the monetary

"WHICH WAY TO LITTLE ROCK, SONNY?"
By Mauldin, St. Louis Post Dispatch, 9/18/58

This excellent cartoon by Bill Mauldin, the great World War II cartoonist, showed the great and famous U.S. marshals making their way to Little Rock. How many regular marshals were ordered to the city, we never knew. It remained a closely guarded secret of the Eisenhower Administration. Great lawmen like Matt Dillon, Chester, Wyatt Earp and Bat Masterson, the sight of whom caused the little farm boy to drop his hoe as his hat flew off, were notable for their scarcity at Little Rock. In this respect Mauldin's cartoon was in error.

reward. Some had court records of their own. Others were considered undesirable characters in their own communities where they couldn't have been elected constable even without an opponent.

During the service of these marshals in Little Rock the State Police picked up several on various minor charges. At my direction they were quietly released without any publicity. One of these deputized U.S. marshals was apprehended by the State Police security force one night in a drunken condition, trying to break into the Executive Mansion. I was informed by the troopers on duty and personally interviewed the inebriated deputy marshal in the West Guest House. Following his apprehension he professed friendliness, and after giving us considerable information was released. The deputy marshal's apprehension and committment to jail for the attempted entry by force to the governor's residence would have made a story of considerable embarrassment to the federal officials. But, contrary to the thoughts of many of my critics, I was not playing to the grandstand. I was trying to avoid violence, property damage and bloodshed.

●—○—●—○—●—○

LITTLE ROCK'S PRIVATE SCHOOLS GROUP MEETS, FACES LEGAL FIGHT

LITTLE ROCK PEOPLE PUT FAITH IN FAUBUS

Governor Has Public's Support
In Move for Private Schools
September 18, 1958
By T. GRADY GALLANT

LITTLE ROCK — Though sorrowful at having to close their high schools, the people of this city seem to have an abiding faith that Governor Orval Faubus will lead them from the wilderness of discontent. It was this feeling that led to the overwhelming return of the governor to a third term in office . . .

By their ballots . . . the forces of resistance for Arkansas were drawn for battle, the legal breastworks were carefully erected and shelters provided for an incessant rain of political pressures, words and deeds that fell upon them from Washington, New York and other areas.

Now the great lines of battle are clear. The strategy is strikingly similar to that of another day, when the sword was drawn and the brave fell under an onslaught of an economy too great, and a measure of time they could not endure.

ENDS WITH CLOSING

As one of the government attorneys said here the other day, Washington does not care whether Arkansas has a school system or not. If the state closes up its school system, that ends the conflict here. . . .

Neither is the government concerned with discrimination of individual against individual, as that is a private matter, at least for now....

Thus, the great problem of Governor Faubus and his school system — and it is his school system, for the people have placed its life in his hands — is to offer it up for adoption... That will be the ultimate solution here.

This solution is no secret. It has been announced. But it is not easy.

As the future days dawn, some of the greatest legal minds of the nation will give almost undivided attention to the school "adoption papers," Are they legal? That will be the burning question.

It is in this light that the events in Little Rock must be considered. The Supreme Court has ordered integration here. The schools must be integrated, if the government and the locality that created them keep them.

If they are destroyed, closed forever, sold, or given away, the government will no longer have them to integrate. They will be gone.

The formation of a private school corporation here yesterday is a first step that may lead to a system of private schools throughout the state of Arkansas.

There are two significant statements in the above story.

The first and most significant is that of the government attorney that "Washington does not care whether Arkansas has a school system or not."

This is most remarkable, and a bit terrifying. The first aim of any government, what ever the degree of freedom, should be the maintenance of an atmosphere in which schools could be established and supported for the education of all children. All public officials, even government attorneys, and all good citizens of a republic such as ours, should be deeply concerned that school systems be maintained. The concern should be for proper school systems with an atmosphere conducive to quality education. The aim should be to produce good citizens properly educated, not well trained outlaws.

That irresistible federal power was exerted in Little Rock, not with the prime motive of maintaining a good school system, but to destroy it if necessary if it could not be bent to the federal will, is an alarming commentary on the attitude of the federal government and the federal courts. From this statement of a federal official that Washington did not care whether Arkansas had a school system or not, a statement borne out by the attitude and actions of the federal authorities, one must reach the inescapable conclusion that the sole motivation of the national administration was political.

The reason for the federal government's judicial rulings — without benefit of law or constitutional justification — its executive decisions, and the use of naked, military force, was to gain raw political power — brutal, corrupt political power if it had to be but political power nevertheless.

Under such circumstances it becomes easy to understand why it was so useless to quote the Constitution and legal precedents or the law in opposition to illegal federal actions, or to cite the absence of any law for actions taken. The recitation of proper actions taken by the state, local authorities or the people themselves in relation to schools and the racial problem, were likewise futile in gaining any consideration for the difficulties that must be met. Reason and logic were likewise ignored.

A particular political position had been adopted with the aim of acquiring votes and political power. Supported by vocal, militant, well organized groups, that viewpoint, supported by police power, proved predominant, — and successful.

But what of the school systems, society itself, and the very fabric of the Republic?

That is another question.

The other statement: "Neither is the government concerned with discrimination of individual against individual, as that is a private matter," is likewise amazing.

This indicates a callous disregard for the welfare of those for whom the federal authorities professed to be concerned.

Any good citizen should be concerned with improper discrimination of one individual toward another, or the attitude of government toward individuals or groups. Any good citizen will attempt to correct his own conduct in this regard, or use his influence to help remedy such situations. There are many ways to take action without the use of law or rules. In fact the law is useless in the face of contrary human attitudes, unless police state methods are used in which case everyone ultimately suffers the loss of freedom and dignity.

It was deplorable that so many of the advocates of integration refused to accept personally their own professed theory. In fact many of them set deplorably bad examples by practicing the opposite of what they preached.

It seems that never before have so many leaders in so many fields, including government and the ministry, been saying one thing and doing another. And this attitude is tragically typified by the statements of the government attorney, in Little Rock at the time as a representative of an allpowerful federal government, which cared not whether Arkansas had any school system at all, and was indifferent to improper individual discrimination.

Never before has there been such widespread lack of faith in our institutions, once the pillars of our society-government,

the courts, political parties, business, the schools, the church.

To the general public there are too few heroes, if any at all, and too many leaders in too many fields are portrayed as rascals, and sometimes proven to be. Mistrust is so prevalent that even those who point out and bring down the "rascals" are themselves viewed with doubt and misgiving.

Is it any wonder then that disillusionment exists in racial and ethnic groups, among the poor, the old, the handicapped, war veterans, labor unions, women, the professions, and even the great, silent majority. Even the youths, — in ordinary times the idealistic dreamers, — seeking now the lost anchors of integrity, struggling on a minimum wage inadequate to support them in an age of inflation, price gouging and rip offs, — are cynical.

In such a time a true disciple speaking in sincerity of those verities without which no society can endure, is apt to be met with the sarcastic query, "Yeah, What's your angle?"

AND NOW A WORD FROM OUR SPONSOR
By Jenkins, N.Y. Journal American   9/22/58

Classes by television on the Little Rock stations beginning September 22, authorized by the school board, gave rise to this cartoon. I had nothing whatsoever to do with the television classes although I personally approved of the activity. I never appeared on any program.

PLAYING 'EM CLOSE TO THE VEST
By Kennedy, Ark. Democrat   8/17/58

The election results were a mandate to me from the people. I could do no less than my best, regardless of the criticism and condemnation from some sources. The chips of the Justice Department were labeled "U.S. Authority" while my chips were "Arkansas Laws."

The "Supreme Court" and "Governor Faubus" battle it out Western, two-gun style, as the "Little Rock Schools" were caught in the line of fire.

THE NEW ORDER
By Dale, San Antonio Express   9/21/58

This was another make-the-opposition-look-bad cartoon which ignored the issues and the facts.

On September 16 I reset from October 7 to September 27 the date for the election on which the people of the Little Rock district would vote on the forced integration question.

Reports on the press conference said, "that if voters in the school district decide they want Little Rock's four high schools opened on an integrated basis, he (Faubus) will let them open integrated."

"If voters decide for segregation, he said, he has a plan for reopening them, but declined to say what it was."

On the same date a small group of Presbyterian ministers meeting in Little Rock adopted a resolution urging:

"Faubus to consider countermanding the proclamation with which he closed the schools Monday."

"Faubus to refrain from closing schools in any other section of the state."

"All citizens to think . . . and to obey all laws and duly constituted authorities."

The crux of the matter was contained in the phrase "obey all laws and duly constituted authorities." I had been elected by the people of Arkansas to enforce state laws, carry out state policies and obey the constitution of the State of Arkansas and the United States.

The people overwhelmingly and sincerely believed that the federal court orders were NOT "duly constituted authority."

A Little Rock minister who had a part in formulating the resolution adopted by the Presbyterian group was the Rev. Dunbar Ogden. A militant integrationist, Ogden had played an active role from the very beginning and even prior to the start of the controversy in September 1957. He had worked closely with the two known Communists, Lee and Grace Lorch, who were deeply involved. But Rev. Ogden had **not** integrated his church.

When questioned by the press about the resolution, I commented:

"I am aware that a number of ministers in the Presbyterian Church have been very effectively brainwashed . . . by the left wingers and the Communists."

Thus the cartoon of me throwing mud "Arkansas Pastors 'Brainwashed' by Commies charge."

This comment brought angry charges from this particular group of ministers that I had "insulted the entire Presbyterian Church" and demands for an apology. The matter was played up by part of the press with such headlines as "Faubus Rakes Clergy."

This, of course, was a great exaggeration. I had commented that **some** of the Presbyterian ministers had been brainwashed. On the other hand, one of the most powerful writers and speakers in my defense was a prominent Presbyterian minister in Tennessee.

Letters poured in from all across the country, many from Presbyterians, backing up the comment I had made.

It was interesting to note that all churches represented by these ministers were segregated.

It was likewise interesting to note that the Communist Party of the U.S.A., in a statement in their official organ of September 14, 1958, took the following stand:

The National Executive Committee of the Communist Party last week issued an urgent "call to action." Appearing over the signature of James E. Jackson, party secretary for Negro affairs, the Communist Party urged: "Stop segregationists' outrages against Negroes. Uphold Constitutional rights."

The statement went on to condemn the entire South in general, endorsed the Supreme Court's decisions and called for implementation of the court orders by the use of force.

NEW HOPE BAPTIST RESOLUTION

On the other hand there was this reaction from patriotic Americans:

On the same date (*Ft. Smith Southwest American,* September 14) ministers representing the churches of the New Hope Baptist Association, in their annual meeting at Mulberry, Arkansas, unanimously adopted a resolution commending me for signing the bills passed by the special session of the legislature. The ministers urged me to continue to act to "preserve our God-given rights."

STUDENT PROTEST FAILS

In Little Rock a determined effort was made by integrationists to drum up a student protest to the school closing. A wire service on September 27 reported the results thusly:

"A so-called 'student protest' against the action of Faubus drew only 10 boys to Hall High yesterday, and the knot quickly dissolved."

ATTORNEYS' STATEMENT ON SCHOOL LEASING

On or about Sept. 21 61 Little Rock attorneys signed a statement saying that the contemplated leasing of the public school buildings to a private school corporation for use in operating private schools was illegal. An Arkansas law on the statute books for many years clearly indicated that the leasing of school facilities was lawful. Furthermore the practice had been customary throughout the nation since the establishment of public schools in Colonial days.

One of the signers of the attorneys' statement was Steele Hays, son of Congressman Brooks Hays.

The statement brought strong reaction from a number of sources. A spokesman for the States Rights Council said of the lawyers who signed the statement, "The people of Arkansas will long remember their names and in the future shun them like poison. It is recalled that the actions of prejudiced men are to be no more respected than the sweat from the blankets of jackasses."

"I SAID, DRINK NOW!"
By Brooks, Birmingham, Ala. News   9/21/58

This cartoon used the old saying, "You can lead a mule to water, but you can't make him drink" — something everyone understood except the U.S. Supreme Court and the fuzzy-minded "Liberals."

WOMEN'S EMERGENCY COMMITTEE FORMED

The Women's Emergency Committee was formed to fight for the opening of the schools on an integrated basis. The officials chosen were Mrs. Joe R. Brewer, president, a federal employee of North Little Rock who had no children in school; Miss Ada May Smith, treasurer; Mrs. Woodbridge E. Morris, secretary; and Mrs. David D. Terry, listed as one of the organizers, and like Mrs. Brewer with no children in school.

A steering committee was named to direct the campaign effort for the opening of integrated schools with Mrs. Samuel E. Cottrell as chairman. Steering committee members were Mrs. Robert Schultz, Mrs. Charles Stevens, Mrs. Nathan Graham, Mrs. L. Prentice Booe, Mrs. Graham Wilson and Mrs. Edward Lester. The husbands of Mrs. Schultz and Mrs. Lester were signers of the attorneys' statement.

The committee members and their allies put on a strong, well-financed campaign to promote their viewpoint with the voters of the school district. They obtained much free publicity in the newspapers of the city especially from the *Gazette,* and ran advertisements in the papers and by radio and television.

"ORVAL, HERE COME THEM REVENOORS BACK AGIN!"
By Conrad, Denver Post,
N.Y. Herald Tribune   9/21/58

I was pictured as a moonshiner brewing up a concoction in a contraption labeled "Ol' Segregation." A friend or partner warned that the "Revenoors" (federals) were coming back again and I loaded up a double barrelled shotgun.

Shreveport, La., Times
September 22, 1958

FAUBUS DISPLAYS FINEST TRAITS OF LEADERSHIP

Gov. Orval Faubus of Arkansas is developing, under the pressure of events, into one of the most astute, bold and imaginative political figures of our time. Some of his actions are more than clever. They display genuine tactical brilliance.

One such action is the calling of the Sept. 27 special election on reopening the schools. All along, integrationists have been able to maintain . . . that Faubus represented a clique of extremists while most of the people of Little Rock . . . would not resist the edict of the Supreme Court.

By calling a special election and giving the citizens of Little Rock a chance to express themselves, Faubus will lay that question to rest once and for all. . . .

Gov. Faubus has always declared himself to be at the disposal of the MAJORITY of the people. If they want integration, he has said repeatedly, they can have it. If they want segregation, he will fight for that. Whatever his personal feelings, he will subordinate them to the will of the majority. . . .

These things are, however, mere side skirmishes in the battle Faubus is waging. The governor's really great achievement, . . . has been to make the entire nation aware of the fact . . . that every citizen and every state has a stake in this attempted invasion of states' rights. Faubus has raised for everyone the spectre of arbitrary federal invasion of the lives and rights of individuals. . . .

To be sure, Faubus has not done all of this alone. But he more than any other man has done it, and he more than any other man has borne the brunt of the attack.

Louisville, Ky., Courier Journal
September 23, 1958

NEGRO GIVEN POST BY FAUBUS PRAISES HIM

Arkansas Governor, Center of 3-Ring Show, Is Target For Number of Quips, Too

by Kyle Vance

LEXINGTON, Ky. — *Arkansas Governor Orval E. Faubus received warm praise from a Negro educator during Monday's business session of the Southern Governors Conference.*

He also was the favorite target of integration quips thrown by the chief executives in some of their less serious moments.

A reporter's notebook on random topics of the 3-ring Conference Show was filled full of Faubus. He was the main performer in the social and integration-controversy rings and shared top billing in the business ring.

During a discussion of the South's school problems at a session of the Southern Regional Education Board, Faubus left his seat at the governors table to greet Dr. Lawrence A. Davis, president of the all-Negro Arkansas A.M.&N. College.

Moments later, Davis was recognized for some remarks and said:

"This seems to be a moment to recognize the contributions of our governors. I would like to commend the work of our Governor in a great need of our times. That is, a co-operative attack on the problems of Negro colleges."

Faubus told newsmen after the meeting that Davis "is my appointment" to the SREB. [I was the only governor in the conference to appoint a black to the Board. Each state was represented by three appointed members.]

Faubus joined other governors during the afternoon in posing with the celebrated show horse, Wing Commander, at Castleton Farm, one of the story-book establishments of the horse-loving Bluegrass.

"Look at the Commander's pretty brown coat and white feet," North Carolina's Luther H. Hodges ribbed Faubus. "He's a desegregated horse."

"I don't know about that," Faubus responded, "but it's good to see a horse getting some attention for a change."

Texas Governor Price Daniel was introduced as head of the Union's "second largest state," a tongue-in-cheek reference to the pending admission of Alaska.

Daniel smilingly pleaded to "let us enjoy these last few days we remain the largest state."

———

Richard Harwood of the same newspaper wrote:

Gov. A. B. "Happy" Chandler of Kentucky . . . cast aside his burdens last night to burst into song, . . . before a throng that gathered to eat fried chicken at his mansion in Frankfort. With support from the Tate Blakely Negro Chorus, he warbled through verse and chorus of "Steal Away" and "Old Black Joe." Magazine photographers greedily recorded the performance.

Maryland's Gov. Theodore McKeldin dropped for a moment his high seriousness on the issue of integration to make a joke at the expense of Faubus. The television cameras recorded the scene.

He's The Man of The Hour

Faubus doesn't have to tell jokes to get attention. He is being pursued by reporters, male and female, wherever he goes.

There is no end to the questions and, apparently, no end to his willingness to answer them. He'll talk any time and any place and he doesn't look around for his public relations man to backstop his answers.

He is a most accommodating and mild-mannered man to have caused such an international stir.

A Break for Newsmen

It is the Faubuses, the Chandlers, the McKeldins who lift these conferences from the doldroms into which they would otherwise sink. . .

———

In another news story it was reported that upwards of 120 people saw my press conference, including about 75 newsmen, the greatest attendance at any press conference.

Gov. Cecil Underwood of West Virginia told his press conference, "We don't have a [integration] problem in West Virginia and I don't intend to create one by sitting here and talking about it." His press conference ended after that statement.

AND LET THE PEOPLE SPEAK!
By Graham, Ark. Gazette   9/22/58

Although they made determined efforts to turn the tide, the advocates of federal authority sensed they were going to lose the school election on the question of forced integration. This outrageously false cartoon was an attempt to make it appear that the election was rigged.

RECORD TURN OUT IN SCHOOL ELECTION

The largest turn out in the history of the Little Rock School District was recorded in the September 27 election on the controversy of court-ordered integration for the Little Rock Schools.

Although a strong campaign was waged by those favoring the opening of the schools on an integrated basis, they lost on the issue by a lop-sided margin.

The vote to keep the schools closed rather than submit to the federal court order to integrate was 19,470. Those favoring opened high schools on an integrated basis polled 7,561.

With some 6,000 to 7,000 black voters in the district, they evidently did not vote overwhelmingly for integrated schools, or there was a low turn out of black voters. The women's Emergency Committee failed in persuading other white voters to the viewpoint it espoused.

The election result was decisive. Everyone now recognized the schools would not open on an integrated basis as directed by the federal courts.

On the day the election was held I was in Fayetteville watching the Razorback-Tulsa football game.

DE WITT (ARK.) ERA ENTERPRISE
Sept. 28, 1958

Brought Big Applause In Chicago

The banner pictured here was carried by Robert Lane, Chief de Gare of Voiture Local 854 in the 40 et 8 parade down Chicago's famous State Street during the 99th annual convention of the American Legion held in Chicago the first week in September.

This Promenade Nationale was viewed by some 300,000 people who lined each side of State Street. The Arkansas delegation and banner received cheer after cheer all along the line of march. There were also repeated calls for Governor Faubus.

Lane said, "If anyone had any doubt as to the popularity of Faubus and his stand for states rights before going to Chicago, that doubt was certainly erased by the cheers as the banner passed and calls were made for Governor Faubus and they were calls of approval and not cat-calls".

Brought Big Applause In Chicago

Pictured holding the banner are, from left to right, W.R. Smith, Bill Norsworthy, Robert Lane and H.N. Siems.

Other voyagers marching in the parade in addition to those with the banner were Past Grand Chief, Joel Bunch, Thompson Hargraves, Jr., Doug Wells, Bill Burns, Doyle Daniels, Pete Slater and the present Grand Chief Wilber Barker.

COMPLETION OF HIGHWAY 68

On Sunday September 28 I attended a celebration of the completion of hardsurfacing of the last unimproved gap in state highway 68. The affair was held at Dry Fork in South Carroll County near Congressman Jim Trimble's boyhood home. Previously at Dry Fork and Osage cars were often stuck in the unbridged streams. In times of high water the roads were closed to all traffic.

It was a glad day for me. I had begun efforts for improvement of the road when I went on the Highway Commission by Governor McMath's appointment in 1949. Completion that year of the unimproved gap in the highway between Huntsville and Springdale had given Huntsville its first connection to the outside world by improved highway, and led to McMath's now famous remark to the outside press about building that road and "letting Orval out" of Madison County.

The highway was now hardsurfaced, with new concrete bridges over a number of streams, from Siloam Springs on the Oklahoma border eastward to Springdale, Huntsville, Alpena and thence by Highway 62 to Harrison and across the state to the Mississippi River, affording the first direct crossing of North Arkansas by improved highway. It was a great day for the people of that section and for many far beyond the area.

Joining me in the speaking duties were Congressman Trimble who had returned from Washington for the occasion, and Highway Director Herbert Eldridge of Little Rock. It was a significant occasion for both of them. Not only did the highway traverse Congressman Trimble's district but his boyhood playgrounds. It removed a problem he had faced throughout his congressional career for he had been beseiged from the very first with requests for assistance in securing the needed improvements. Director Eldridge was privileged to participate in a ceremony marking the completion of the first direct east-west improved highway in the northern half of the state.

Participating with me and Eldridge in the ribbon cutting ceremony were some Carroll County residents who were indeed happy. County Judge Arthur Carter of Berryville who acquired the right-of-way for the project, Clint Suggs, master of ceremonies for the occasion and Raymond McKinney, president of the Highway 68 Association. Suggs and McKinney were both Dry Fork residents.

NEWSPAPER COMMENTS
September, 1958

IS FAUBUS A POTENTIAL LEADER?

The left-wing press, aware that Gov. Faubus may become a national symbol of resistance to illegal Federal tyranny, have tried to pin the label of "segregationist" on him. This tactic proved woefully unsuccessful insofar as one of Faubus' own children attends an integrated school!

During the past few weeks Gov. Faubus has succeeded in basing his cause on the principle of States Rights versus Federal Tyranny - and the illegal and unconstitutional decisions of the Warren Court. These issues affect every citizen of this country.

The WALL STREET JOURNAL quoted Gov. Faubus as saying: "There is no clear-cut Federal Statute regarding the integration of schools. If there were, it would be unconstitutional, for the authority to control public education has never been delegated by the States to the Federal Government."

And THE TOLEDO (Ohio) TIMES stated editorially after a recent televised broadcast by Gov. Faubus: "Arkansas' Orval Faubus defended himself very well when he faced a nation-wide television show with some Washington reporters who gave him quite a grilling. His resource of forensics was as good as ever, but this time he was armed with some infrangible facts ... What he said, in making his two major points, is true, wholly supportable by Constitution and law ... Those points are: (1) A Supreme Court decision is not the law of the land and (2) Only the Acts of Congress are the law of the Union and Congress has passed no law making segregation in the schools illegal."

And THE INDIANAPOLIS STAR states: "But the issue is no longer integration or education. Faubus rightly termed it a battle for States rights and Constitutional Government." Then THE STAR adds: "Orval Faubus is a politician and a successful one (Ed. note: overwhelmingly re-elected as Governor this Summer)...with all the faults, failings and virtues which may be found in the various connotations of the term. He has the solid support of the majority of citizens in Arkansas, and he has the firm backing of most of the members of his Legislature. If this is not an adequate expression of the democratic process, it is hard to understand what would be..But like him or not, Orval Faubus has in the past days spoken some truths which need to be pondered carefully, and prayerfully by all of the country."

FORTY-EIGHT SOVEREIGN STATES AWAIT ....
By Knox, Nashville Banner   9/28/58

"And if I were Ike, I'd say, look here Faubus, when the supreme court makes a ruling it's the law of the land, get it? Then I'd give him a whack with the putter."

THE CYNICS CORNER
Artist unknown, St. Petersburg, Fla. Register   9/26/58

Discussion of the problem had its humorous aspects, as shown by the comment with this drawing.

The people had voted in Little Rock. Would they be permitted to carry out their will freely expressed at the ballot box? The people of other states watched and waited for the answer.

LOWER COURT CARRIES OUT SUPREME COURT EDICT

The U.S. Supreme Court issued its clarifying ruling on the Little Rock school case on September 29.

On that same day a two-judge court in Omaha, Nebraska composed of federal judges Joseph W. Wood and Harvey J. Johnson, issued orders in the Little Rock case. With the two-judge court ruling coming on the same day, orders or instructions had to be transmitted by telephone or telegraph, or by fast special planes from Washington.

The orders of Judges Wood and Johnson were dictated by telephone to Federal District Attorney Osro Cobb at Little Rock, where they were mimeographed for distribution. Marshall Beal Kidd's force of U.S. marshalls then began serving hundreds of mimeographed orders on school board members, school teachers, state officials and others.

The action was an unprecedented display of haste, as well as an unprecedented method of transmitting federal court orders by federal authorities.

Still further actions by the Justice Department were likewise unprecedented. The order by the two-judge court was made retroactive to the previous Thursday, September 25. It blanketed in the period to the following Monday October 6, at which time the judge said a hearing on the Little Rock school matter would be held.

The unseemly haste and unprecedented action by the courts and the Justice Department was due to the possible lease of the school buildings to the private school corporation. If the lease had been consummated and the schools opened, the federal authorities would have had to close them as not in compliance with court orders. Faced with the prospect of ousting teachers and students from their own schools by the use of U.S. marshalls, a state of near panic prevailed among federal authorities and Little Rock integrationists.

U.S. SUPREME COURT RULING

The U.S. Supreme Court ruling of September 29 spelling out its decision of September 12, caused thousands of headlines of news stories, editorials and columns to blossom throughout the nation. In Little Rock and Arkansas the people appeared to be more angry and determined to resist than in 1957 when the city was occupied by federal troops. The court went even beyond the Little Rock case in its ruling.

Here are some of the headlines across the country:

INTEGRATION RULE SETS SHOWDOWN
—Boston, Mass., *Christian Science Monitor*

SUPREME COURT RULES OUT EVASION
—Johnstown, Pa., *Tribune-Democrat*

ALL RESISTANCE SEEMS RULED OUT BY OPINION
—Columbia, S.C., *State*

OUT OF BOUNDS, By Jenkins, N.Y. Journal American, 9/29/58

The cartoonist said "Fearless Faubus" ran out of bounds in avoiding the "Supreme Court" team. The out of bounds steps were labeled "Private School Evasion." This drawing inferred that private schools were illegal, a patent falsehood. Thousands of private schools operated throughout the nation. Millions of people, including many constitutional lawyers, believed the Supreme Court judges lined up completely off the legal field when they ruled that federal authorities could control local and state public schools.

AND HE HAD SUCH A PROMISING FUTURE
By Parrish, Chicago Daily Tribune, 9/23/58

This front page cartoon in color said that "Arkansas," with "blue prints for progress" in "industrial expansion," "business opportunities" and "national prestige," had gotten drunk on a brew labeled "Old Faubus." It failed to note that I was the author of the program that was bringing much of the progress to the state. Some months later, a large section of Chicago was burned and looted in racial riots. The resulting damage and deaths in the one riot, exceeded the damage and deaths that occurred in the entire South in half a century. What concoction made Chicago so drunk? While Arkansas is debt free and its local bonds sell at a premium, Chicago (in January 1980) cannot pay its teachers.

ANGRY ARKANSAS 'PLAYING IT BY EAR'
—Ft. Lauderdale, Fla., *News*

THE COURT PRESSES HARDER
—Norfolk, Va., *Ledger-Dispatch*

HUNDREDS ARE SERVED WITH INTEGRATION ORDER
—New York, N.Y., *Herald Tribune*

WILL SCHOOLS OPEN? JURISTS BLOCK PRIVATE PLAN
—Miami, Fla., *Herald*

PRIVATE SCHOOLS DROPPED;
LITTLE ROCK GROUP BOWS TO COURT RULING
—New York, N.Y., *World Telegram and Sun*

U.S. COURT ORDER STOPS
LITTLE ROCK PRIVATE SCHOOLS
—San Francisco, Calif., *Chronicle*

'OBITUARY' OF SCHOOL PLAN READ IN RAIN
—Seattle, Wash., *Times*

LITTLE ROCK HEEDS EDICT,
SCHOOLS REMAIN CLOSED
—New York, N.Y., *World Telegram and Sun*

ORDER BLOCKS LEASE PLAN
—*Mirror*, New York City

ORDER BANS PRIVATE SCHOOLS
EVASIVE SCHEMES SCORED:
STILL PLAN REOPENING TODAY
—Los Angeles, Calif., *Examiner*

LITTLE ROCK CORPORATION GETS LEASE BUT
APPEAL BENCH ORDERED CHECK ON
ACTION BY BOARD
—Washington D.C., *Post Times Herald*

THE DIXIE SLUGGER DISPUTED A DECISION
By Hungerford,
Pittsburgh Post Gazette   9/30/58

The cartoon was prompted by the Supreme Court ruling of September 29 barring the use of the school buildings by the Private School Corporaton on the grounds that it was an evasive scheme to avoid the court's ruling that integration must proceed forthwith. However, the Corporation was not out of the game. It went ahead with private schools in other facilities.

GIVING UNTO THE PEOPLE A NEW COMMANDMENT . . .
By Knox, Nashville Banner   9/30/58

The U.S.A. viewed with concern the handing down by Chief Justice Earl Warren of a new commandment for the American people.

"Thou shalt not challenge the Laws of Warren, either through an elected executive, or an elected legislative body."

Knox, an eloquent defender of the Constitution through the cartoon medium, could have added "or an election on any issue."

HIGHROAD, U.S.A.
By Knox, Nashville Banner   9/29/58

The "Will of the People" proceeding down the road "Democratic processes," ran into the roadblock "Judicial dictatorship" set up by the Earl Warren U.S. Supreme Court. The dictatorship showed its power in its all-encompassing decision of September 29, thwarting the will of the people as expressed by the legislature and at the ballot box.

THE COURT STANDS FIRM
—New York, N.Y., *Post*

THE COURT SPELLS IT OUT
—Minneapolis, Minn., *Tribune*

ARROGANT DECREE
—Augusta, Ga., *Chronicle*

HISTORIC PRECEDENTS SEEN BROKEN
BY SUPREME COURT
—New York, N.Y., *Herald Tribune*

LITTLE ROCK HIGH SCHOOLS REMAIN
CLOSED: U.S. COURT RULINGS ADD TO
CONFUSION; PRIVATE GROUP ASSAILS ORDER
AS BLOCKING ALL EFFORTS TO OPEN
—St. Louis, Mo., *Post Dispatch*

U.S. COURT FORBIDS FAUBUS SCHOOL PLAN
—Houston, Texas, *POST*

SOUTH PUSHING PRIVATE CLASSES
—Denver, Colo., *Post*

REMOVING ALL DOUBTS
—Cleveland, Ohio, *Press*

LITTLE ROCK SCHOOLS TO STAY SHUT
—New York, N.Y., *Journal American*

DICTATORSHIP SPEAKS (U.S. SUPREME COURT)
—Chattanooga, Tenn., *News-Free Press*

THE COURT CLOSES THE DOOR
—Memphis, Tenn., *Press-Scimitar*

A SUBTERFUGE STRUCK DOWN
—Des Moines, Iowa, *Register*

CHILDREN VICTIMS OF LITTLE ROCK VOTE
—Syracuse, N.Y. *Post Standard*

STALEMATE AT LITTLE ROCK
—Lincoln, Nebraska, *Evening Journal*

THE SUPREME COURT BRINGS DIXIE
TO BRINK OF REALITY
—Harrisburg, Pa., *News*

DR. RANEY SAYS PRIVATE BOARD
FAR FROM FINISHED IN FIGHT
—Little Rock, *Arkansas Democrat*

A LOCAL VOTE COUNTERMANDED
(VOTE OF SEPTEMBER 27 IN LITTLE ROCK)
—Phoenix, Ariz., *Gazette*

And the Private School corporation was not finished. Private schools were established and opened as U.S. marshals and U.S. Justice Department lawyers swarmed into Little Rock, and thousands of headlines and editorials continued to appear from coast to coast.

APPOINTMENTS, SEPTEMBER 1958

Dan W. McBrice, Rector, Embalmers and Funeral Directors Board. Sam Rorex, Little Rock, Chairman, Board of Review. Commission to Study Educational Television for Arkansas: Selected by Senate, Sen. Guy Jones, Conway; Sen. Tom Allen, Brinkley. Selected by House, Tom E. Tyler, Little Rock; O. P. Hammons, Forrest City; H. H. Howard, Blytheville. Appointed by Governor, Hal Robbins, Conway; Mrs. J. R. Sink, Newport; Cooper M. Burley, Little Rock; Ed I. McKinley, Little Rock.

THAT'S THE DYNAMITE, By Knox, Nashville Banner, 10/1/58

CHAPTER 22
THE LUBELL ANALYSIS. PRIVATE SCHOOL GETS UNDER WAY. IRS CHECKS MY INCOME TAX. ALFORD FILES AS WRITE-IN CANDIDATE AGAINST HAYS.

Much has been written concerning blame for resistance, some of it violent, to the decrees of the U.S. Supreme Court. Lawabiding, tax-paying citizens who wanted quality education for their children and who tried to raise them in a proper moral atmosphere, were charged with prejudice, bigotry and lawlessness, simply because they resisted radical, court-made law, which they regarded as inimical to their interests, and in which they had no voice.

On the facing page, Knox points out the lighter of the fuse to the dynamite in the explosions of resistance.

To blame the people, North or South, for resistance to "law by decree" which was considered unconstitutional and illegal, and clearly without the consent of the people or their representatives in Congress or legislature, was the same as blaming the Colonists for resistance to King George's decrees at the time of the American Revolution.

To blame those leaders of the nation of whatever section who spoke out for their people in resistance to illegal, court-made law, was the same as blaming Patrick Henry, James Otis, Samuel Adams, Benjamin Franklin, Thomas Jefferson and George Washington for speaking out against the repressive acts of the mother country in Colonial times.

To say that the people without being consulted should quietly accept unconstitutional law by decree on pronography, subversion, reapportionment, abortion and integration, was to say that the Colonists should have accepted without protest the Stamp Act, the tax on tea, the Writs of Assistance and the quartering of troops in their midst without their consent.

If the Colonists had not successfully resisted the repressive measures placed on them without their consent, our democratic form of government would not have been born.

Millions of Americans now believe that if the people do not now successfully resist the repressive, unconstitutionally court-made laws placed on them without their consent, our democratic form of government will die.

Those who agree with certain changes brought about by the usurpation of power through unconstitutional court decrees, should remember there are proper ways to remedy ills and bring about change. The liberty of all the people will be more secure if proper, legal means are used.

It would be well for all to bear in mind George Washington's admonition:

Let there be no usurpation, for though in one instance it may be the instrument of good, it is the customary weapon by which free governments are destroyed.

THE GOVERNMENT IS US . . .

A cartoon by S. B. Warren in *The Independent* on October 2 entitled "The Government Is Us: We Are the Government, You and I", explains to the three branches of government in Washington that in our form of democracy the people are sovereign; that rule by Washington officials is by consent of the governed; that the officials are not supreme with the people as servants; but that the officials are the servants of the people by the people's consent.

Edicts are not to be handed down from Washington against the people's will, but the people's will determined by the expression of the majority is to be carried out within the framework of the Constitution.

An editorial in the same paper said:

CAN THE PEOPLE BE WRONG?

"Up in Washington the nine little Caesars must be feeling pretty smart and smug. By a rape of the powers of the people, the berobed usurpers have turned Communists out of jail and American children out of school. The Kremlin must be doubly jubilant. . . .

This is for sure a helluva democracy when the people are wrong and nine little men are right. Some say there will be a revolution in this country. We say there has already been one. The people have been overthrown, the Constitution has been stretched to cover a deliberate abrogation of the instrument itself.

. . . Where will it end?"

WHAT! NO STUNTS
By Justus, Minneapolis Star   10/1/58

To lease public school buildings for use in the operation of "subscription schools" had always been legal. As a youth, I had attended such a school. The parents paid tuition to a qualified teacher who established the rules and procedures and accepted those students who paid tuition on a monthly basis. The school board allowed the use of the public school facilities, ofttimes without charge. This had been a general practice for many years, and was no different legally than the plan that was devised at Little Rock.

"YOU'RE TOO LATE, COMRADE!" *By Alley, Memphis Commercial Appeal 10/1/58*

The Soviet dictator, Nikita Khrushchev, once said of the Western democracies including the United States, "We will bury you!" Khrushchev came with his shovel to bury the democratic form of government in America. In the view of the cartoonist, he was too late. Freedom as we had known it — government of the people, by the people and for the people — was already buried by the usurpation of power by the U.S. Supreme Court, mainly under the leadership of Chief Justice Earl Warren.

CAUGHT IN THE GALE
By Hungerford, Pittsburgh Post Gazette   10/1/58

No one ever claimed the public schools were private property, and they certainly were not federal property, nor were they legally subject to federal control.

FAUBUS PREPARED TO GO TO JAIL; COURT ATTEMPTS TO BLOCK PRIVATE SCHOOL

October 2, 1958
by Robert L. McCord
Special to The Christian Science Monitor

Little Rock — Gov. Faubus, . . . his intimates indicate, is prepared to go to jail if necessary — to support the mandates given to him in two elections by the people of Arkansas and of Little Rock.
. . .

Request Granted

. . . the Governor ordered the schools not to open after the . . . Supreme Court declared that the integration plan . . . must proceed. A private school corporation was formed, and it leased the four high-school buildings from the Little Rock School Board Sept. 29.

A few hours later the Eighth Circuit Court of Appeals . . . issued a temporary restraining order forbidding the school board to release the schools. . . .

Cited in the restraining order were not only the school board and its superintendent, but school employees, agents of the school district and "all persons in active concert or participation with

them," which, of course, included the Governor and the private school group. It is estimated that more than 175 copies of the order were served by U.S. marshals.

Teachers Warned

Attorneys advised the school board not to turn over the buildings or any funds to the private school corporation. Teachers were warned not to enter into any negotiations with the private school group, and . . . the school board cancelled its system of television classes.

The first new development came Oct. 1 . . . Dr. T. J. Raney, president of the private school corporation, . . . read a statement that said in part:

"Federal government officials, from the President on down, . . . must somehow be made to understand that the course they have chosen is leading our nation to destruction. We have no alternative but to stand fast until there is an awakening by the people of our nation.
. . .

. . . We have chosen our course, and as long as the people of Little Rock and our public officials give us their support there will be no turning back. . . ."
. . .

. . . His final sentence was: "Any contributions should be directed to the Little Rock Private School Corporation in care of the trust department of the First National Bank of Little Rock."

Schools Stay Closed
. . .

Meanwhile, the four Little Rock high schools remain closed, . . .

In front of each of the closed schools a sign was erected (by some one). . . . The signs read: "This school closed by order of the federal government." . . .

DEAD END
By Lange, Daily Oklahoman   10/2/58

As the fight continued to preserve the people's rights to manage their own local and state affairs, the setting was erroneously portrayed as "Segregation Alley." Political leaders who sought to assist the people in the defense of their rights were depicted butting their heads against the stone wall.

—o—o—o—

Appleton, Wisc., Post-Cresent, Oct. 2, 1958

LITTLE ROCK WANTS PEACE, SEES INTEGRATION AS COMING

*Some Families Suggest Starting
Over on Lower Grade Levels*

by SAMUEL LUBELL

The mood of most of the citizens of Little Rock is not really that of the irreconcilable defiance of the supreme court that is suggested by nearly three-to-one vote for desegregated schools.

Of more than two score families interviewed, an overwhelming majority voiced strong support of Gov. Orval Faubus. Yet most of these Faubus supporters also felt that "eventually we're going to have to take" some form of integration.

In their groping for a peaceful way out at least a dozen families volunteered "maybe we ought to start all over again in the lower grades."

. . .

Another typical reaction was voiced by a laundry route driver to whom I talked as he sat . . . on the porch of his home, about a block from a Negro residential district. Strong for Faubus, he said, "The reds are behind this. They're trying to pull America down from inside as they have with every other country they've taken over."

Forced to Give Up

Still he conceded, "I guess we're going to have to take it." . . .

After a pause he added, "There must be some way of moving into this peacefully."

Actually, public opinion in Little Rock can be divided into three parts. A small minority of the white population is openly for integration. . . . It feels, as one insurance agent put it, "If Faubus hadn't called out the national guard there wouldn't have been any trouble."

At the other end is a much larger minority that could be termed irreconcilable, last-ditch foes of integration. Profane in their denunciation of "those communists in the supreme court," they tend to be violent in their language. . . . A man swore, "I'd rather see the schools burned down."

Somewhere in between these two extremes will be found the majority of the Little Rock citizenry. The bulk of them voted to back Faubus in his re-election bid because "he stood up for the south" or "to show the north we can handle our own affairs." But when they discuss the segregation problem their voices are more troubled than defiant.

"I wouldn't want my daughter going to school with Negroes," one mother told me, "But I suppose it must come." . . .

Afraid of Violence

Others feel "it is all right to close the schools for a short time but not for long." Still others are less afraid of racial difficulties than violence. "I'm a pacifist in this struggle," said another mother.

"I'd like my child to learn to live with others but I wouldn't want her in a school someone may blow up."

Some families say, "Maybe if we fight this hard enough the supreme court will change its decision." Others echo one young housewife's remark, "I'll say 'no' as long as I can even though I don't think integration will hurt my child."

A few mothers confessed they hoped for a long enough delay "so my son will be out of high school." But more than a few others said, "My child is in grammar school now. It would be terrible if this isn't settled before she gets to high school."

In sum, most of the Little Rock citizenry, even while backing Gov. Faubus, still yearn . . . for a peaceful solution to the whole school crisis.

Two thoughts crossed my mind. One was how eager people are to have me think well of the people of Little Rock. This defensiveness characterized nearly everyone I talked with in the city. I heard many complaints of "how those northern newspapers write us up" and demands of "why don't they run a picture of that new Negro high school we have built?"

Good People Here

One man, to reinforce his argument that "the people down here are good people," waved down the street and exclaimed, "Everyone on this block owns his home! That's more than you can say of people up north."

The second thought that crossed my mind was how hungry the people of Little Rock must be for what was described as "some kind of compromise that will bring peace to this community." . . .

REAPING THE WHIRLWIND
By Thiele, Chicago Sun Times   10/2/58

Subsequent events proved the cartoonists's projection sadly in error, as the Arkansas general election of November and the Gallup Poll of December 1958 showed.

LUBELL'S ANALYSIS

In reference to Lubell's last statement, the segregationists offered a compromise — a school for blacks, a school for whites, and an integrated school. Labeled a freedom of choice plan it was a major concession on the part of the leading segregationists. It was rejected outright by the integrationists. The federal courts likewise rejected any thought of compromise. With this adamant, unyielding attitude on the part of the integrationists and the politically motivated federal authorities, the struggle continued much longer than it otherwise would have.

This partly accurate analysis of the situation in Little Rock applied, I believe, to the South as a whole, and perhaps to other areas of the nation. The people were tiring of the struggle, as I knew they would, but they were not yet ready to give up. They wanted leaders to fight for them even though they feared they could not win when they felt by every right they should win. If those in positions of leadership failed to stand up and fight for their rights, they would reject them and find other leaders who would. This was dramatically demonstrated in the general election in the Fifth Congressional District one month after Lubell's article was written, as it had been earlier in the rejection of the Southern congressmen who failed to sign the Southern Manifesto.

This seems a good place to point out the difficulties of my position in the controversy and the reasons for the difficulties involved in my objectives. My immediate main aim was to prevent violence leading to property destruction, injury to persons and loss of life, coupled with the effort to provide proper leadership to the great majority of people in their fight to preserve their constitutional rights. The feeling over forcible integration and the federal usurpation of the prople's rights was so strong that firmness, strong measures and often dramatic action were required to prevent disorder so long as there was hope of success in blocking forcible integration by violent means. While few people were willing to resort to physical violence in opposing integration in the schools, many were willing to accept success by this means so long as they did not participate.

I distinctly recall attending a dinner in my honor by the civic leaders of Warren, county seat of Bradley County in South Central Arkansas. The area had long been a hot bed of segregation sentiment. The invitation was conveyed to me by Representative Carroll Hollensworth, one of the most able legislators in the history of the General Assembly, who was Speaker of the House in 1953 and was then seeking re-election to his House seat. Hollensworth was openly advocating that I should seek a third term and said to me frankly, "Governor, this is the first time in my long career that I have ever openly come out for a candidate for governor. I am doing it for my own good. It would be unpopular to take any other stand."

That evening at the banquet I was seated beside a minister at the head table. During the course of the meal he said to me, "Governor, when there's any demonstration in opposition to court-ordered integration, I will not be there. I will not be there because it is not my nature to participate in any activity that may turn into violence. But at home or wherever I am I will be praying that others will be there, and that they will be successful in blocking the integration."

The words burned into my memory. I never forgot them.

The words and the sincerity of the speaker pointed up clearly the difficulty of preventing completely any acts of violence in opposition to integration by force. While few were willing to resort to these physical means of resistance, those few who would had the moral support and encouragement of much greater numbers of people. And they would be protected by large numbers of their fellow citizens.

Therefore, in order to avoid confrontation that would lead to violence the conflict between proponents and opponents of court-ordered integration must be kept in the legal and political fields. If the opponents, who were in the great majority, were to heed my pleas and the pleas of others to remain non-violent in their activity, they must be convinced that the battle was being fought by their leaders with determination and sincerity.

If fought to a conclusion in this manner the results would be accepted. But not until the great question was litigated to a final conclusion in the courts, not until they were convinced that opposition by any method was hopeless and futile, not until they were convinced the federal authorities would enforce by any means the court orders — only then would the matter be settled. Then and only then would the moral support and encouragement of large numbers of opponents be withdrawn from that smaller number who would oppose forcible integration by violence. Then even though the great majority might still consider the U.S. Supreme Court decision illegal, the change being wrought not according to majority will, and not for the best, then adamant, open opposition would cease. In other words, the great majority of people must come to the conclusion and realization that continued opposition to the federal courts was futile. Then, like the freedom fighters of Hungary, they would become quiet in subdued acceptance of the change. They would be conquered but their attitude would be unchanged. To the great majority this would be tyranny, but they would have the satisfaction of knowing they had resisted the imposition of this tyranny by a superior force, and that it was imposed in spite of legal guarantees and over their determined opposition.

My two-fold task was to lead the people in their fight in the legal and political fields while keeping the lid on violence, until we had won some concessions in the courts or with the federal authorities, or until the people could see that the struggle was hopeless.

According to Mr. Lubell's analysis, which I think is fairly accurate, the fight had progressed almost to that point. Many people were approaching that hopeless state of mind which is preliminary to surrender. But woe to any leader who surrendered before they were ready.

As I set my course and maneuvered against the politically motivated officials of the national administration, I had a third objective. If integration had to be brought about by force, I was determined that the cowardly, hypocritical federal authorities would assume the responsibility for the enforcement of their own orders.

I say cowardly because these officials feared the danger in the confrontations, and the political consequences of the enforcement; I say hypocritical because these same officials were unwilling to practice what they sought to force upon others.

The adamant Herbert Brownell, the proponent of integration by any means and at any costs, even to destruction of the public schools, who sought to recover from his political losses in the civil rights debate by sending the federal troops to Little Rock, sent his child to a private segregated school. He could have set a more honest example by sending the student to a public integrated school. Other high federal officials were guilty of the same practice.

In Little Rock the small band of ardent integrationists was guilty of the same offense. The *Gazette* editors advocated integration for others in the schools while writing to Editor Loeb in New Hampshire that they couldn't integrate the paper's work force "because of the mores" of the community. The Rev. Ogden accompanied the black students to Central High School while refusing blacks the privilege of worshipping at the altar of his segregated white church. Mrs. Brewer heading the Women's Emergency Committee to work for the integration of the schools while she had no children to attend school, and who worked outside the district.

Former Gov. McMath by whose side I walked when his administration was crumbling and indictments were threatened after his defeat for a third term in 1952, he, accompanied by his alter ego, Henry Woods, went down to the Little Rock press club where all the outside reporters gathered. There they joined Ashmore, Patterson and others in propagandizing the incoming reporters against me. In the dim hazy light of the smoke-filled room and the bourbon inflamed minds, they may have appeared as great heroes — to the outside reporters. But if the masses of Arkansas people could have seen them there they would have had a different viewpoint.

As the people's freely elected governor I managed state affairs and directed their struggle as best I could. In the so-called Little Rock crisis I succeeded in preventing violence. No one was killed; no one, black or white, was injured sufficiently to require hospitalization. (The worst injuries occurred while the 101st Airborne troops were in control and were inflicted by the soldiers.) No building was looted, burned or otherwise damaged or destroyed. No businessman or laborer lost his means of livelihood.

In the second objective, we lost the struggle to retain for the people the right to manage their own schools. We were overcome by the judicial dictatorship backed up by federal force, but we fought the battle all the way to a conclusion.

In the third part of the controversy, the federal authorities were compelled to take some action to enforce their own court orders. And to the national administration and the federal authorities this was the most unpleasant development of the whole situation, especially when they found it resulted in political loss rather than gain.

EDUCATION BE HANGED!
By Knox, Nashville Banner　　　　　　　　*10/3/58*

The Earl Warren Supreme Court rewrote the phrase of the original 1954 decision, "with all deliberate speed," to read "with all breakneck speed." The Court's written decision of September 29, 1958, confirmed its oral decision of September 12, which reversed Judge Lemley's decision to delay integration in the Little Rock high schools. The district court at St. Louis implemented the decision with unprecedented speed and unprecedented methods.

The caption expressed the Court's regard for education.

PRIVATE SCHOOL
By Sloggatt, N.Y. Mirror　　　　　　　　*10/3/58*

The Private School Corporation moved to establish private schools after the people ballotted to close the senior high schools rather than accept forced integration. This cartoon inferred that I would be the only student — humorous and sarcastic but not factual.

Arkansas Democrat, Oct. 5, 1958

DELIBERATE SPEED NOW SHIFTED INTO HIGH GEAR

by BOBBIE FORSTER
(Democrat Staff Writer)

. . . The federal emphasis on speed in handling integration matters has been more apparent since various polls have indicated that a rather surprising percentage of people in other parts of the country are not unsympathetic toward the South these days.

. . .

Record in Making

Some type of speed record seems to be in the making in the alacrity with which the Justice Department attended to integration matters in the Little Rock case this past week. And the current emphasis on speed, apparently, works in several directions: Reaching backwards, clipping along in the present, and stretching into the future.

For one thing, a restraining order was elasticized back to a date five days preceding that on which the application for the order was filed.

For another thing, the telephone and the mimeograph machine replaced the usual certified orders from a district clerk's office.

And for still another point, the justices in Washington branded as "evasive schemes" so-called private schools before any case actually involving them had been brought to Washington.

. . .

Consider the time table on the so-called "private school lease":

When the Little Rock School Board asked Federal Judge John E. Miller if it could lease the four empty buildings to a private corporation, . . . it did so in a petition that virtually cried out for a three-judge court to rule on the constitutionality of an 1875 state law and several 1958 laws.

. . .

There is also the matter of the NAACP by-pass of the clerk of the appeals court. To the clerk's office went a copy of the school board's petition for instruction, but only as an exhibit for a pleading that "would be filed." The pleading itself was sent to a circuit justice. And it was the justice, rather than the U.S. mails or a lawyer, who filed it with the clerk a few hours before two other justices were hearing the pleadings.

The U.S. marshal's office made the service of a resulting restraining order after it was telephoned down, rather than waiting for the official certified copy to be filed with the local district clerk.

And one final point. Special helpers from the Justice Department in Washington reached Little Rock the very next day after the restraining orders were served. They arrived just as fast as airplane wings and engines could deliver them.

———o—o—o———

Arkansas Democrat, October 5, 1958

Dred Scott and Little Rock

HISTORY REPEATS SELF IN INTEGRATION RULING

by CHARLES O. GRIDLEY
Democrat Washington Bureau)

History has now repeated itself in the Supreme Court's interpretation of its own initial stand on school integration.

Its decision has brought about a spirit of defiance to the high court's authority among millions of Americans which parallels that which resulted from the Dred Scott decision of 1857, in which the judicial tribunal ruled that Dred Scott, a Negro, did not become free when taken to a free state and did not have rights as a citizen.

. . .

Shocking Opinions

Over a span of 101 years, the court has twice given opinions which shocked a great number of citizens. It is true that those opinions went from one extreme to the other, but what is essentially important is that the court in both instances seemed to exceed the authority which common consent has given it under the Constitution.

. . . In the Little Rock case, the court has made clear that it assumes the right to make the Constitution conform to some of its own conclusions, rather than vice versa.

Lincoln's Court

The authority of the Supreme Court was never challenged more vigorously by a prominent political figure than it was by Abraham Lincoln in his 1858 debates with Stephen A. Douglas. . . . There again the point he made was that the court had exceeded any authority granted it by the Constitution, and that it had read into the Constitution language and interpretations which could not be justified.

. . .

ON SAME DAY SCHOOL LEASE PAPERS SIGNED, FEDERAL COURT ISSUED RESTRAINING ORDER.... U.S. SUPREME COURT OUTLAWED "EVASIVE SCHEMES."

PRIVATE SCHOOL BOARD THEN BEGAN ON PLAN TO HAVE THEIR SCHOOLS FINANCED BY PUBLIC CONTRIBUTIONS...

NOT SO FAST!
By Kennedy, Ark. Democrat   10/5/58

The integrationist forces of both Washington and Little Rock were thrown into a state of panic by the prospect of private schools in the public school facilities under lease to the private school corporation. They moved in great haste into federal court to block the lease, and the courts acted in unseeming haste for the same reason. For example two judges formulated a court in St. Louis and ruled on the matter before the case had been filed, made the decision retroactive to a date prior to the school lease, and made it applicable to a time period to follow. The case was then filed by one of the judges rather than an attorney. The orders of the hastily assembled two-judge court were then telegraphed to U.S. marshalls in Little Rock whereas the customary method was to transmit certified orders by mail.

If the private school corporation had gotten the schools opened in the leased buildings, it would have been necessary to issue federal court orders and send U.S. marshalls or troops to arrest the teachers and force the children out of the school buildings. The federal authorities and integrationists were struck with consternation at the thought of being caught in such a role. Then if students and teachers had adopted Communist methods by refusing to move and going limp, what a job it would have been for the marshalls to carry more than 2,000 of them from the building.

The panic-stricken attitude of the national administration naturally became apparent to me and the members of the private school corporation. As the federal restraining order was being served on hundreds of people, some one had the thought of posting a sign on the school grounds which read:

"This school closed by order of the federal government."

WHODUNIT?
By Kennedy, Ark. Democrat   10/5/58

In the haste of printing the sign, government was misspelled.

However, the erection of the sign made the point. The mistake in spelling brought about wider publicity than would otherwise have been obtained.

The private school corporation then moved ahead to secure finances and other facilities in which to operate private schools.

Arkansas Democrat, Oct. 5, 1958

RUN OF THE NEWS
by KARR SHANNON

There Are Nine Members On Little Rock School Board

The Little Rock School Board no longer consists of five or six men, locally elected. The board is made up of nine men, none of whom lives in Little Rock or anywhere else in Arkansas.

Not one of these Little Rock school board members ever lived in the district, ever voted in the district, ever paid a penny of tax in the district. Not one owns a dime's worth of property here.

They were not elected by the people.

Yet, they are in major control of the Little Rock school system. They tell us who can go to school and where. They tell us how we can spend our own tax money. They apparently are custodians of the buildings.

Right now, they dictate enrollment in the senior high schools. And there's a plan that gives them the same control over the lower schools as the years go by.

Calling the Roll

The names of the Little Rock School Board members are as follows:

Earl Warren who, as chief justice of the U.S. Supreme Court, has voted for Communism 36 out of 39 cases before the court. . . . Hugo L. Black, voting for Communism 71 out of 71 cases. . . . Felix Frankfurter, voting for Communism 56 out of 72 cases. . . . William O. Douglas, voting for Communism 66 out of 69 cases. . . . Harold H. Burton, voting for Communism 32 out of 69 cases. . . . John Marshall Harlan, voting for Communism 20 out of 36 cases. . . . William J. Brennan, voting for Communism 20 out of 34 cases. . . . Charles E. Whittaker, voting for Communism four out of 11 cases. . . . Tom Clark, voting for Communism 18 out of 51 cases. . . . (Data take from Congressional Record, Page 12120, July 10, 1958.)

They Made the Law

That's the kind of school board in charge of Little Rock schools.

There is no law on the Arkansas statutes that permits this group to run our schools.

There is nothing in the State Constitution that gives them such position or power.

There is nothing in the U.S. Constitution or enactments of the Congress that gives this group such authority over our schools.

The only law that bestows upon the nine the right to dictate policy for the Little Rock School District is a law that the nine men made of their own free will — without consulting a single, solitary resident of the district.

The Great Declaration

Is that the kind of democracy Thomas Jefferson had in mind when he wrote the Declaration of Independence? . . .

Is that the kind of democracy the 55 signers of the Declaration of Independence declared for?

Is that the kind of democracy our forbears fought, bled and died for in the American Revolution?

Is it the kind of democracy the framers of our Constitution planned?

Preamble Made a Sham

Is the policy of this nine-man school board that sits in Washington in harmony with provisions of the Preamble to the Constitution? . . .

Is it the kind of democracy that Woodrow Wilson wanted to make the world safe for? Is it the cause that thousands of Americans who now sleep in Flanders Field gave their lives for?

What Liberty!

When Patrick Henry, back in the days of greatness, got upon his subsequent legs and said "Give me liberty, or give me death," was he asking for the kind of liberty the Warren-Myrdal court is giving us today?

The South suffered agony for years during the "Reconstruction" that followed the close of the Civil War. Federal regulations were little short of terrifying. Carpetbaggers rode herd.

But even in those trying times the people were allowed to operate their own schools.

DEMOCRACY!
By Knox, Nashville Banner   *10/5/58*

Knox raises the question — was it any longer democracy when the will of the overwhelming majority was throttled by a court decree — a decree not based on law or the constitution but on the sociological thinking of the court as obtained from a book by a Marxist author.

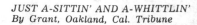

JUST A-SITTIN' AND A-WHITTLIN'
By Grant, Oakland, Cal. Tribune   *10/4/58*

No act of Congress or amendment to the constitution made federal school control the law of the land to be exercised through a court gavel. Despite challenge after challenge **no one** came forward to quote any federal "law of the land" on state schools.

459

DARK DAYS AHEAD
By Alley, Memphis Commercial Appeal   10/5/58

The gavel, "Law by Court Decree" was substituted for the torch of freedom in the uplifted hand of the Statue of Liberty. In the other hand of the statue was a plaque which read "Reaffirmed 1958." The caption of this drawing, "Dark Days Ahead," by one of the nation's best cartoonists, was prophetic.

THE ARKANSAS TRAVELER
By Hungerford, Pittsburgh Post Gazette   10/7/58

Uncle Sam, driving the "Integration School Bus," represented as a modern vehicle, was help up by a chin-whiskered "Little Rock" in an old fashioned wagon drawn by a "Segregation" mule.

REV. BROWN SEES "OUTSIDE" FORCES IN LITTLE ROCK

On October 6 the Rt. Rev. Robert R. Brown, Episcopal Bishop of Little Rock, in a press release charged that there is evidence to indicate that "outside" forces organized, inspired and financed the buildup of opposition to integration at Central High School last year.

Rev. Brown may have had correct information but three points can be made about his statement. First he was one year behind on his information. Second, plenty of opposition to forcible integration was on hand in the school district — the outside forces didn't vote in the September 27 school election. Third, there were also "outside" forces which "helped to organize, inspire and finance" the integration movement in Little Rock.

Little Rock, as I had informed President Eisenhower, became a focal point of contest.

JUSTICE FRANKFURTER ATTACKS ARKANSAS

Justice Felix Frankfurter in a public statement attacked the officials of Arkansas. Many people thought the Justice's denunciation was unbecoming of one who was supposed to sit in unbiased judgment on matters in dispute. The officials of Arkansas were elected and served with the consent of the people. That was not the case with Frankfurter.

IF A BEAR VISITS, IGNORE HIM!
By Kennedy, Ark. Democrat   10/24/58

The Arkansas Game and Fish Commission had imported bears from Northern states and Canada and released them in the mountain sections of the state in a restocking program.

The Commission insisted that the bears not be harmed or killed. At a loss how to deal with these visitors, concerned citizens and officials inquired of the Game and Fish Agency how to handle the invaders. The Commissioners replied, "Ignore them."

AMERICA'S OFF-SHORE ISLAND, By Grant, Oakland, Cal. Tribune, 10/7/58

In 1957-58 the United States as an ally of Free China (Formosa) experienced a serious confrontation with Red China over the offshore islands of Quemoy and Matsu, which threatened to erupt in a major conflict. The islands were beseiged by Red guns on the mainland with guns of the Free China forces replying. The duel continued for months. Here Little Rock was pictured as an off-shore island with me in command, firing "Defiance of the Courts" blasts at the mainland and federal courts. Like the Free China troops, my forces were outnumbered but still fighting. (We lost in our defense of the people's constitutional rights, and now, 1979, Formosa has lost also. U.S. recognition of Formosa has been withdrawn to please the Chinese Communist regime.)

461

EENY, MEENY, MINEY, ORVAL! JUST LIKE THAT! By Knox, Nashville Banner, 10/8/58

In 1958 the Internal Revenue Service was making a check of my income tax return. An agent of the Little Rock office sent me a bill for a large amount due, in which I was charged as income the appropriation for salaries of the employees and for maintenance and upkeep of the Governor's mansion.

Charged to me as personal income also was the fair rental value of the executive residence, and the gift of a car in 1954. With those items charged to the governor as personal income, his entire annual salary of $10,000 would have been insufficient to pay the taxes.

Instead of being cowed by the bill, I released copies to the press including a large number of out-of-state reporters. Then on the advice of my attorney, W.J. (Bill) Smith, I sent telegrams to the governors of other states inquiring if they were required to pay taxes on the salaries appropriated for their employees, and if the fair rental value of their executive mansions was charged to them as income. I made the same inquiry of the President in relation to the White House.

None of the items have ever been chargeable as income to any public official. The mansion was owned by the state which was responsible for its upkeep. The checks to the employees did not even pass through my hands.

After my release of the IRS letter it was hastily withdrawn. The examination of my tax returns was soon completed, although I had to produce documents and figures dating back as far as 20 years. The IRS ruled that no additional tax was due.

The cartoon idea of "Eeny, Meeny, Miney" selection of my report, expressed serious doubt of the Internal Revenue Service statement that it was just a routine check.

I still carry in my mind a vivid recollection of the press conference. That was the manner in which a great number of the out-of-state reporters slunk away, quiet, cowed and subdued after receiving copies of the IRS statement. "Their side" had suffered a damaging blow.

An objective, unbiased national press? The thought is enough to provoke sarcastic laughter.

The goof of the Internal Revenue Service in checking my income tax return and my reply to the letter of charges placed the Service in the dunce cap. There was the inescapable thought that the check was to bring pressure on me in the state vs. federal power controversy.

HIGHLIGHTS OF THE NEWSWEEK
By Kennedy, Ark. Democrat   10/12/58

LATEST DOPE ON LITTLE ROCK INTEGRATION
By Alley, Memphis Commercial Appeal   10/12/58

Kennedy said the IRS goofed when they charged me with taxes not due.

W. D. Brashears, a Little Rock professor, was engaged as superintendent of the private school, and letters were mailed by the corporation asking for contributions.

Frank Lambright, Little Rock businessman, was named a Little Rock School board member to fill a vacancy created by the resignation of Henry Rath.

EDITORIAL

The Philadelphia (Pa.) Afro-American
October 11, 1958

"For four long and bitter years, politicians and officials of the Confederate states have not only been running —

They have been lying, ducking, evading, fooling, cheating, misrepresenting, defying and rebelling.

But Chief Justice Warren's new opinion says in language that even a Faubus can understand: Come on boys. The game is over.

There's no reason for an Eastland, a Talmadge, a Thurmond or Byrd to plead that he didn't understand."

TIME TO PUT FAUBUS IN JAIL

"Presuming Uncle Sam means business in sending 170 U.S. marshalls to Little Rock and alerting hundreds of others from as far away as Maryland—
The time has come to put Faubus in jail.
He has defied the government long enough.
. . . The federal government is known to maintain a very nice boarding house and retreat at Alcatraz. No one has been known to escape from there and live to tell about it.
And there is a nice new lockup for Federal Offenders in Alaska.
Prisoners do not escape there either, because they would freeze to death before they could get two miles away.
With the weather, an Arctic prison is the safest place to stay alive."

Louisville, Ky., Times
Oct. 11, 1958

INTERNAL REVENUE SERVICE BLUNDER IS A BREAK FOR FAUBUS

Somebody certainly goofed when the Internal Revenue Service notified Governor Faubus that he owed income taxes on $105,499.14. . . . The I.R.S. was counting as income the rent and operating expenses of the state's executive mansion, campaign expenses, and a gift automobile.
. . . If governors had to pay income tax on the amount of money they save by living in rent-free accommodations provided by the state, few men could afford to be governor. And, as Faubus was quick to point out:
If "demands for payment of personal income tax can be made upon me for this gift (automobile) then it is reasonable to assume that demands will be made upon the President of the United States for personal income taxes on all the gifts he has been
receiving at his Gettysburg farm, including tractors, purebred hogs, cattle, etc."
The blunder enables Faubus to wear the cloak of a man who is being discriminated against by the federal government. . . .
. . . The I.R.S. did Faubus a favor and gave itself a black eye when it counted the executive mansion as income.

FAUBUS HAS OVERWHELMING SUPPORT

The Chicago Tribune, Chicago, Illinois
Oct. 9, 1958

The CHICAGO TRIBUNE sent a staff writer to Little Rock to study Gov. Orval E. Faubus' mail — a deluge of 30,000 letters from all parts of the country on that regrettable school crisis.
Communications favor Faubus' battle against federally ordered school integration by 50 to 1. From Chicago, which now has its own race problem, letters favored Faubus by the same ratio.
Here's the encouraging theme in most of the letters: They do not condemn Negroes. They do not stress the color angle. They do condemn the Federal Government for attempting to wield power in what letter writers feel is strictly a local and state issue.
That is the theme the country has not grasped. More important in the integration decision than the emotion of color mixing is this dangerously unwarranted power of Washington.
If an all-powerful government can tell an Arkansas city who must sit next to whom in schools, it can tell what books they must study; what courses they must take; what authors they must learn.
Hitler's first move, after burning the Reichstag, was to take over Germany's school system. The Nazis were ready to march.

Memphis, Tenn., Commercial Appeal
October 12, 1958

PRIVATE SCHOOL DONATIONS COME FROM FAR AND NEAR

by KENNETH JOHNSON

LITTLE ROCK, Oct. 11 — They're coming from just about everywhere.
They come in the form of muchly-worn one-dollar bills and in $25, $50 — sometimes even $500 and $1,000 checks.
And usually they bear with them expressions of ire against the Federal Government; pledges of continued help to Arkansas and Gov. Orval Faubus.
That's the way those sorting out the mail describe the flood of donations pouring in here in support of the move for privately-financed segregated schools.
Most From South
A reporter observed some of the mail as it came into Gov. Orval Faubus' office Friday. Most of the letters received that day were from Southern states. But there showed up messages and checks, or bills, from other sections of the country.
A surprising number of the donations come from California. There are also some from New York.

One of the Governor's aides . . . said there are "perhaps less than a half a dozen states that haven't contributed." Another said contributions have come even from Canada and points overseas.

One man from Louisiana sent a $50 donation, in the form of two $25 checks, and to Governor Faubus for use of private schools. He wanted the two canceled checks, bearing the Governor's signature, as souvenirs for his two grandchildren.

Wants None Back

A man from New York sent a five-dollar bill and with it a letter. He signed his name, but no address —didn't want any of it back, he said. And it was to be the "first of monthly five-dollar donations for white schools or for any purpose decided by Governor Faubus," he added.

A man from Utah sent $25 with the notation, that's what he "would have sent to the Republican Party" if the integration controversy had been handled differently by the national Administration.

The Governor . . . says he plans to personally sign most of the letters of acknowledgment. . . .

. . . Also getting mail and donations daily is the office of the Little Rock Private Schools Corporation, as well as First National Bank, which the corporation has designated as its official trust-fund bank.

. . . The Governor said his office was receiving from $3,000 to $4,000 a day.

GOING NOWHERE FAST
Artist unknown, Ft. Dodge, Ia. Messenger   10/14/58

As the anti-integrationists and Gov. Faubus were being crushed, the cartoonist raised the question, "What's your next move, Orval?" The caption said "Going Nowhere Fast". The federal government didn't accomplish anything at the time except to cause the closing of four senior high schools. The private schools were successfully established, so we were going where we intended at the time.

BROTHER FAUBUS WILL NOW PASS THE HAT
By Dowling, N.Y. Herald Tribune   10/10/58

A ruffian — "Disobedience to Law" — stood with a club — "Evasion of Court Orders" — and announced that "Brother Faubus" will now pass the hat. I held a sign which read "National Contributions" and a huge hat bearing a $ sign. The announcement that contributions would be accepted for the private schools in Little Rock evoked the cartoon. The critics were shocked by the ready response from every section of the nation.

On Oct. 9 a federal court ruled against a system of private schools in Virginia.

Orlando (Fla.) Sentinel, Oct. 25, 1958

WHEN LAWS ARE NOT LAWS

Mr. Dozier A. DeVane, a retired U.S. district judge, has put his finger squarely on the Supreme Court's weakness which has caused all Americans so much concern:

"The Court has asserted its right not to be bound by its own prior decisions whenever it desires to construe the Constitution or an act of Congress otherwise," Judge DeVane said.

"If this is the law of the land, then the Constitution means nothing."

Judge DeVane was discussing specifically the earlier decisions of the Supreme Court which established the doctrine of equal but separate facilities for children in public schools.

. . .

Without some consistency, some constraint, it is not inconceivable that the Supreme Court could interpret the same law differently every time it went into session.

. . .

He urges attorneys "to rise in unison and be leaders in the effort to save this Republic of ours."

The alternative is deepening and destructive chaos centered around a judicial oligarchy.

THAT SUPREME COURT'S NOT GONNA MAKE MONKEYS OUT OF US . . .
By Conrad, Denver Post   10/14/58

If in truth I had been responsible for collecting all the funds for the private school, then for a monkey I did pretty well. Contributions came to my office from every state in the Union and from eight foreign countries.

This was another make-them-look-bad cartoon, never mind the issues.

NOMINATIONS, DEDICATIONS AND PRIVATE SCHOOL OPENINGS

On October 16 I was nominated for the George Washington Honor Medal awarded by the Freedoms Foundation of Valley Forge. I reasoned that the chances for approval of my nomination were not the best when I learned that President Eisenhower was a member of the board.

Progress continued in Arkansas in spite of controversy. On October 17 Oklahoma Governor Raymond Gary joined me in the dedication of a new section of Highways 270 and 59 connecting our states. The well-attended mid-day ceremony was at Page, Okla. near the state line, north of Mena where Gary and I clipped the ribbon officially opening the new road.

In Little Rock there was quick response to the announcement of the private school opening plans. Hundreds of students were ready to enroll.

BOUQUET AMONG BRICKBATS
By Kennedy, Ark. Democrat   10/16/58

Because of the school difficulties, Little Rock was criticized by almost every leftwing speaker, preacher, politician, columnist and commentator, as well as Communists, all across the land.

During that time the Federal Housing Administrator announced the city was a leader in the nation in slum clearance and urban renewal. Little Rock had an excellent urban renewal program and deserved the bouquet. Much of the new housing was in the sections inhabited by blacks.

HIGHLIGHTS OF THE NEWSWEEK
By Kennedy, Ark. Democrat   10/26/58

Late starting seniors at the T. J. Rainey High School worked to catch up on their studies. The Baptist churches registered about 500 students in their private schools. Some students transferred to other public schools. About 40 were accepted at Hazen and traveled daily by bus from Little Rock.

Help came from the Legislature. It approved a measure authorizing the transfer by the State Board of Education to the school, private or public, attended by each student, an amount equal to the per capita spending of state funds for the education of each student in the public schools.

———

In other highlights, Arkansas Democrats, angered at public criticism by National Democratic Chairman Paul Butler, refused to contribute to the National Democratic Campaign Fund.

———

Plans were announced for construction of an 18-story office building in Little Rock — an indication business was good.

———

The Razorbacks met the Ole Miss Rebels at Little Rock War Memorial Stadium. Mississippi Governor J. P. Coleman and Mrs. Coleman, in the city to attend the game, were our guests at the executive mansion.

➤➤

UNDER SCRUTINY
By Kennedy, Ark. Democrat   10/22/58

The private school in Little Rock was named the T. J. Raney High School in honor of the chairman of the board. The federal Justice Department watched for any opportunity to impede its operation. The school proceeded without difficulty.

➤➤

A PERPLEXING REQUEST TO THE JUSTICES
Artist and source unknown   10/7/58

The U.S. Supreme Court was in session. Subjects for the session as shown on the papers were: "Commies We Should Turn Loose Today," "Commands from NAACP," "Subversive Program," "Other Ways We Can Mess Up Everything," etc. One of the Justices brought startling news, "You fellow honors, we have a most distressing situation — the people are asking us to integrate." The children and grandchildren of the justices and other high Washington officials attended public or private segregated schools.

STOP! By Pletcher, Sioux City, Ia. Journal, 10/27/58

The law forbids any vehicle to pass a school bus while it is halted. As the driver of the bus "Private School System" I held up the "integration schedules" caught in the rear and driven by Uncle Sam — actually the Federal Courts. The cartoon was an admission that the private school plan was working at the time.

TRYING TIMES FOR FAUBUS PREP, By Green, Providence, R.I. Journal, 10/23/58

An effort was made to throw doubt on the status and quality of the private school set up by the Private School Corporation. The wish was father to the thought. Its status was never in doubt. A cartoonist as far away as Rhode Island was not informed on the situation.

ALFORD SURPRISE CANDIDATE FOR CONGRESS

On Monday October 27 Little Rock school board member Dale Alford announced his candidacy as a write-in candidate for Congress against the Democratic nominee Brooks Hays.

Early that morning Alford with two or three advisers came to the Mansion to discuss the matter with me before I went to the office. I soon was aware they were serious about Alford's candidacy.

As is the case in such conferences much was said of perhaps little importance, and which cannot be recalled because no record was made of the conversation.

Finally I summed up the situation by enumerating the difficulties faced by a write-in candidate. I told my visitors:

(1) Almost all county office holders and nominees for office will feel constrained to vote for Hays as the Democratic nominee because they are likewise Democratic nominees bound by a pledge to support the party nominees. This would deprive Alford of a number of votes but more important would deprive him of any active leadership among them which he might otherwise obtain.

(2) Alford's name was not on the ballot which meant that any supporter must take the trouble of writing in his name. This was a difficulty which always cost votes to a write-in candidate.

(3) The shortness of time remaining for an active campaign would make difficult the organizational work necessary for a successful effort.

Then those present analyzed Congressman Hays' situation. His political standing had been severely impaired by his son's signature on the statement by the Little Rock attorneys challenging the legality of leasing the public school facilities to the private school corporation. The congressman's standing was still further damaged by his own remarks, especially the speech to a North Little Rock audience in which he publicly classified himself as a moderate. Furthermore, they said, many people now knew he was close to the *Gazette* editors and constantly advised with them.

Then, Alford's friends concluded, many people also knew that both Hays and his son, Steele, were on the losing side in the recent school election of September 27. Many people, they said, were angry at Hays and anxious to vote against him, and more important, would work hard for Alford's candidacy.

I was asked the question, as I recall, by Alford, "Do I have a chance to win?"

My honest answer based on my evaluation had to be, "Yes, you have a chance, but it is a slim chance, a bare chance based on the difficulties I have enumerated."

I was asked for advice on making the race.

"I am not going to advise you," I told Alford. "I have told you of the difficulties. You must make your own decision."

I had to leave for appointments at the office as Alford and his advisers continued to discuss the matter. I had no idea what Alford's conclusion would be. It was apparent he wanted to run for the office but I felt his decision would be negative.

Caught up in a hectic office schedule the matter was dismissed from my thoughts. Later in the day my receptionist, Mrs. Patsy Ellis, conveyed to me the news that Alford had announced his candidacy. That was the first I knew of his affirmative decision.

I do not recall having any contact with Alford during the campaign. Neither was there any contact with Hays. I was out of the city and out of the state most of the time during the eight days remaining before the election.

For the next link in the story I must go back to a previous occurrence.

Some time following the July 29 Democratic primary in which I won a third term nomination, and Brooks Hays was renominated to Congress, I received a call on my private line in my office from Forrest Rozzell. A group wanted to confer with me, he said. Could it be arranged that day following my office hours. I checked and told him that it could and he asked me to come to his office in the nearby AEA building. I agreed.

When I arrived at Rozzell's office some time after five p.m., the group Forrest mentioned proved to be only him and Brooks Hays.

Hays, backstopped by Rozzell, wanted to discuss the Little Rock integration situation. The gist of a rambling discourse by Hays was to persuade me to change my position and support the forcible integration of Central High School.

After fully hearing them out I finally said, "I hope you fellows don't think I've lost my mind," meaning sufficiently to follow Hays' suggestion.

"Aw, now, Governor," remonstrated Brooks, "I've checked this city. I know my people. This will be perfectly safe to do."

"Brooks," I replied, "I know your crowd and I know their thinking. Even they are divided. I also know the other groups in this city and I know their thinking. They are not divided.

"Furthermore," I told him, "you're already in trouble and you're going to be in worse trouble if you're not careful."

Then turning to Rozzell I said, "And Forrest, you're going to get into trouble also. You can't push this thing (the integration problem) on the people. They're angry and frustrated and looking for someone to take it out on. Only time and events will change the public sentiment. No individuals or groups can change it now. You're both wrong in your evaluation. You're treading on dangerous ground and I'm not going to be foolish enough to join you. You're gathering sentiment from only one group, and that group is out of touch with reality and the conditions around them."

Both men heard me out as I spoke strongly. In fact all opinions were strongly expressed. Forrest, in particular, was not noted for mildness in discussions or arguments. I don't know whether they agreed with my evaluation of the situation, but they subsided in their argument.

Events proved the accuracy of my evaluation of the Congressman's situation.

Forrest also, true to my prediction, got into serious trouble. If there had been a vote of the AEA membership he would have been thrown out of his position as executive secretary. However

his position was subject only to the AEA executive committee and Forrest always managed to have the favor of a majority of the committee. A number of times the teachers elected new members who were anti-Rozzell. However, by the time other anti-Rozzell members could be chosen at the annual elections, Forrest, by his diligence and zeal in behalf of teachers and education generally, and "diplomacy" with the committee, would have converted one or more of the previously elected anti-Rozzell members. He continued this successfully until he was ready to retire in the late 70s.

When the conference ended we parted amicably on good terms. It was a frank discussion among friends all engaged in the hazardous field of public service. There was no animosity or bitterness on my part, and I hope none on theirs. They had requested the conference, and I had given them my honest viewpoint on an issue as volatile and emotional as any that had arisen in the lifetime of each of us. I feel sure the two of them, like myself, wished deeply that the issue had never arisen.

"DRAT THAT BOY"
By Kennedy, Ark. Democrat   *10/31/58*

Many people, including the cartoonist, were not aware of it at the time but write-in candidate Dale Alford in his 8-day write-in campaign was doing more than putting Halloween marks on the campaign office window of Democratic nominee Brooks Hays.

———

It appears I was in disagreement with both Rozzell and Hays on the great constitutional question that was involved. I regretted to see the national government interfere in a purely state matter. It is a historical fact that once big government gets a foot in the door, it continues to intrude with the consequent loss of liberty to the people.

I related the incident to no one except possibly a few of my closest associates. If I had wanted to hurt Congressman Hays a public statement on his position in our discussion would have done him great injury at that time. However, I considered the matter confidential, as I still feel it should have been. If such

LINE FORMS TO THE RIGHT, By Kennedy, Ark. Democrat, 10/26/58

All the bogus "Liberals" and many Northern politicians who were either trying to attract some attention to themselves, or gather up some minority group votes, took verbal punches at "mean ole Orval." Tallulah Bankhead, movie star noted for her drinking ability (note the champagne glass) and Democratic Chairman Paul Butler have finished their punching session. Vice-President Richard Nixon worked off steam while Republican Chairman Meade Alcorn, Sen. Pastore of Rhode Island and others waited in line.

matters are not so treated under particular circumstances, it would become impossible for sincere people to exchange views on matters on which they disagreed.

Anyway, shortly after Alford's announcement was on the radio news my private telephone rang. The caller was Rozzell.

"Governor," he inquired with concern in his voice, "has this announcement for Congress got anything to do with the conference we had some time ago?"

I assured him that it did not. "In fact," I told Rozzell, "the announcement on the news was the first I knew of Alford's decision to run. I've talked to him about the matter but I did not put him in the race. It's his own decision."

"Also," I added, "I've told no one about our conference. Since I've told no one, nothing could have come out of our meeting from me that could have contributed to Alford's decision."

As I recall Rozzell responded, "That's what I wanted to know." He thanked me and hung up.

On Oct. 29 Claude D. Carpenter, Jr., considered a close associate in my administration, resigned as attorney for the Public Service Commission to manage Alford's campaign. Carpenter took the action with my knowledge and consent. Those who wanted him in the Alford campaign were nearly all my strong supporters.

That same night Alford made a campaign speech by television which was well received.

On October 31 Conway County Sheriff Marlin Hawkins, one of my chief lieutenants in his area, announced his support for Hays and urged all loyal Democrats to support all Democratic nominees. The Sheriff was sounded out by Alford people seeking his help. He declined and gave all out support to Hays.

Sheriff Hawkins also made public his support for the 3% sales tax.

A news story on October 31 said:

"In Little Rock a Faubus administration friend pointed out that the governor had left the state in the week before the election.

"Mr. Faubus has not commented on the Hays-Alford race, pointing out that he does not vote in the Fifth District.

"In Pulaski County, many of the persons who supported Mr. Faubus in his successful third term bid for the nomination are speaking out in favor of Mr. Alford. They feel, as does Alford, that Hays has been too moderate on the matter of integration."

APPOINTMENTS, OCTOBER 1958

Bob Evans, Helena, Publicity and Parks Commission, to fill the vacancy created by the death of my good friend, Helena Mayor John C. Sheffield. Dr. Hugh Moseley Jr., Warren, Dental Examiners Board. James M. East, Little Rock, Real Estate Commission. Howard F. Pratt, Little Rock, Board of Accountancy. Dr. Marvin F. Cohen, Little Rock, Chiropody Examiners Board. State Athletic Commission: Rocky Dunn, Conway; Marshall Blackard, Blytheville; Dr. Garland Murphy, El Dorado. W. L. "Doc" Hinton, Little Rock, resigned as director of the Assessment Coordination Department to join a professional appraisal firm. Freeda W. Canaday of England named director to succeed Hinton.

HOPE YOU MAKE IT, SONNY!
By Kennedy, Ark. Democrat

10/29/58

The increase of the state sales tax from two to three per cent had been referred to a vote of the people at the November 4 general election. The "integration controversy", "property assessment grumbling", and other problems clouded its successful passage at the polls. Kennedy gave the tax increase a friendly gesture in the caption, which may have indicated a change of attitude by the *Democrat* from its original opposition. There is no doubt that my stand on the states rights issue and my renomination greatly helped the sales tax cause.

CHAPTER 23
ALFORD UPSETS HAYS. FAUBUS INCLUDED IN PRESIDENTIAL POLLS AND GALLUP'S TEN MOST ADMIRED MEN. ARROGANT FEDERAL COURT RULING FORCES SCHOOL BOARD RESIGNATION.

POTENTIAL PRESIDENTIAL CANDIDATES

Ike and Harry, senior leaders of their parties, looked over the prospects for presidential nominees in 1960. On the Republican side were Nixon, Knight and Knowland of California and Nelson Rockefeller of New York. The Democratic hopefuls were more numerous: Pat Brown of California, Symington of Missouri, Harriman of New York, Muskie of Maine, John F. Kennedy of Massachusetts, Stevenson of Illinois, Williams of Michigan and Meyner of New Jersey.

Over in the lefthand corner was Faubus of Arkansas with a paper under his arm which read "Dixiecrat," a cartoonist miscalculation. I soon had more support percentagewise for the Democratic nomination than most of the other Democrats shown.

At that time millionaires Harriman and Rockefeller were battling for the governorship of New York. Rockefeller won in the Nov. 4 general election.

FAUBUS DAY AT TIPTONVILLE, TENN.

On the first day of November I was a guest of the people of Tiptonville, Tenn., where a street was named in my honor. Press reports said "Faubus was given a hero's welcome."

On November 2 a third party group at Milton, Florida, called for me to be a candidate for president on a Third Party ticket.

STICKERS LEGAL IN ELECTIONS

In Little Rock an attorney general's opinion requested by Wylie Cavin, Sr., member of the Pulaski County Election Commission, ruled that it was legal to use stickers of a candidate's name on the ballot. Instead of writing the name an elector could cast a vote for a candidate by placing a sticker bearing his name on the ballot. The ruling was considered a favorable development for Alford in his race against Hays.

WHO WILL BE RUNNING FOR PRESIDENT WHEN TIME ROLLS AROUND TO PICK IN 1960, by Wilcox, Boston Globe, 11/2/58

—now is the time for all good men—

Brooks Hays

LITTLE ROCK EYE DOCTOR LAUNCHES LATE WRITE-IN CAMPAIGN TO UNSEAT VETERAN CONGRESSMAN BROOKS HAYS...ALFORD BELIEVED TO HAVE FAUBUS BACKING...

—I see a chance to win...

Dr. Dale Alford

HIGHLIGHTS OF THE NEWSWEEK
By Kennedy, Ark. Democrat   11/2/58

Dale Alford became a write-in candidate for Congress against the Democratic nominee, incumbent Brooks Hays, launching his campaign only eight days before the election.

U.S. Senator John McClellan vowed to try again to curb the run-away U.S. Supreme Court.

The Arkansas Legislative Council (ALC) found it difficult to formulate realistic state budgets until the fate of the 3% sales tax was known.

The people of Bastrop, La. by public solicitation raised $11,-100 for use of the private school and sent a delegation to present the funds to me at the governor's office.

THAT'S REAL NEIGHBORLY OF YOU.

Bastrop, La.

$11,100.00

PRIVATE SCHOOL FUND

—if at first you don't succeed—

SEN. McCLELLAN PROMISES NEW TRY TO CURB COURT.

—we don't know exactly where we are—yet.

ALC TAKES UP STATE BUDGETS WITH FATE OF 3% SALES TAX UNDECIDED.

GOV. COLEMAN ENDORSES HAYS

Gov. J. P. Coleman of Mississippi in a taped telephone interview from Chicago, endorsed the re-election candidacy of Brooks Hays. Based on his public statements Coleman was one of the strongest segregationists in the South. The endorsement was an effort to offset the prevailing view of Hays as an integrationist.

FLORIDA VOTERS FOR FAUBUS

A news dispatch from Crestview, Fla., where I was scheduled to speak on November 8, said:

Many Crestview people are boosting Faubus for President . . . as a Democratic candidate and not a third party candidate. Mayor-elect Harry Booth said the old folks wanted Faubus for speaker at the Old-Folks Crestview picnic. Faubus for President signs were already in evidence, Booth said.

CLEAN SWEEP AT MT. OLIVE

On election day, Nov. 4, a news headline read: "Faubus makes clean sweep of Mt. Olive, 13 to 0."

ALFORD IN UPSET VICTORY

On Nov. 5 a news headline read: "Alford in Stunning Win; Hays Concedes." I wondered if Hays recalled the conference between me, him and Forrest Rozzell, and the warning I had given.

Of the five principals in the Newport Conference on Sept. 14, 1957, three had now been toppled from their positions of prominence — Brownell, Adams and Hays. Only Ike and I remained.

OTHER HEADLINES

Other news headlines on Nov. 5 read:
Faubus Leads GOP Nominee
George W. Johnson, 5½ to 1

Both Faubus, Sales Tax Act Are Victorious

Faubus Strength Blasts Sales Tax
To Victory

One news dispatch said, "Voters agreed in overwhelming numbers to retain the 3% sales tax, thus handing another mighty political triumph to Governor Faubus."

MANY DEFENDERS

My stand for constitutional government as opposed to government by court decree won many defenders across the nation. There were personal calls from prominent figures in the screen and entertainment world from Hollywood, from successful men in the field of business, from experts on the Constitution, from lawyers, professors, editors and columnists. The calls, telegrams and letters came from all across the nation.

One of those prominent defenders, then a resident of Houston, Texas, was a native of Arkansas who had won worldwide reknown from Hollywood in the entertainment field, first with a radio program, then as a public speaker and as an actor on the screen. The following news item tells the story.

SUPREME COURT ATTACKED BY FAMED MAN OF MIRTH

Jackson, Miss., Clarion-Ledger
Nov. 4, 1958

A man reknowned for bringing smiles to faces struck a sober knell . . . here as he sidetracked humor and warned of "the losing battle we're fighting in Washington."

Chester Lauck, whose portrayal of Lum in the famed "Lum and Abner" radio series helped dispel gloom for listeners (before and) during WWII, warned a Ladies Night crowd at a meeting of the Jackson Touchdown Club that American citizens are giving up their personal liberty by sitting back . . .

In defense of states rights and constitutional government, the famed humorist . . . attacked the Supreme Court as a judicial group turned legislative and called for support of Arkansas Gov. Orval E. Faubus.

Referring to Faubus, Lauck said: "He's kind of fighting a lone battle over there; he needs and deserves the support of the South." This remark brought a rash of applause from the audience.

Lauck said the Little Rock situation is not merely a question of integration. He said the true issue is the right of states to govern their own affairs. Lauck called Faubus' stand "the last stand of states rights."

"We're fighting a losing battle in Washington that's more important than football victories," Lauck grimly warned the gridiron enthusiasts.

The man of mirth charged the nation as a people of "dissipating its inheritance." He deplored a national debt of $288 billion [$600 billion in 1979]. . . . He accused both Democrats and Republicans of placing their organizations above their country . . . He called for political leaders who will restore constitutional government, be they Democrats or Republicans.

The humorist served Touchdown Clubbers their dessert (of humor) first before hitting them with his main course.

PENCIL PUSHERS LAUNCH ALFORD
By Kennedy, Ark. Democrat   11/9/58

475

The results of the Congressional election for Fifth District were, in the words of a *Democrat* editorial, "One of the most spectacular upsets in the national election picture."

Karr Shannon, the noted *Democrat* columnist, interpreted the outcome as a rejection of the "party loyalty" tradition which once insured any Democratic nominee a victory in the general election. "Mr. Hays played it (party loyalty) for all it was worth — and lost," wrote Mr. Shannon.

The *Gazette* and other extremist liberal elements sought to blame me for Hays' defeat. This was untrue. Congressman Hays, with an able assist from his son, Steele Hays of Little Rock, brought about his own loss, as letter after letter and other sources said to me during the aftermath of the upset Alford victory. This does not in any sense, question the honesty or integrity of Brooks and his son. It merely recognizes the reality of the situation.

The "moderation" stand in the cartoon was not generally accepted. Many who voted against Hays felt he had joined the extremists when he spoke favorably of forced integration and appeared willing to surrender to the federal usurpation of state authority.

━━◦━◦━●━◦━◦━

ARKANSAS STRIFE'S ECONOMIC RESULTS WORRIES CITIZENS

Miami, Fla., Herald, Nov. 8, 1958

by Relman Morin

[The story did not bear out the headline, as the following quotes indicate.]

How has the battle of Little Rock affected business conditions in Arkansas and the state's drive to attract new industry?

Statistically, the answer seems to be, "Not at all."

Many economic barometers — employment and unemployment, payrolls, department store sales, bank debits — indicate a very healthy condition.

The record for the state as a whole, in the year since the riots at Central High School, is good. As for Little Rock itself, an economist says:

"Little Rock never had it so good."

. . .

The Arkansas businessman, and the group working to bring new industry into the state, confront the question:

"If this deadlock (between state and federal authority) is not resolved, what will it do to business and development in another year?"

Some figures . . . are generally encouraging. For example —

The AIDC reporting for the year ending last July, announced 63 new industries and 28 expanded plants in Arkansas. Jobs created, it said, totaled 8,-527.

Manufacturing employment in Little Rock itself reached an all-time high, the Chamber of Commerce reported last June 30. "It is one of 12 cities in the nation to show an increase over 1957 in a report released by the U.S. Department of Labor," the Chamber said. [Little Rock was fourth in percentage of increase among the 12 cities.]

In bank debits Little Rock was the only one of the "six largest centers" in the Eighth Federal Reserve District to show an increase in July, this year, compared with July 1957. . . .

In department store sales . . . Little Rock showed the same level for Sept. 27 as for Jan. 1, 1958. Other major cities as St. Louis, Louisville and Memphis showed an appreciable decline.

[After much more of a speculative nature, Morin wrote:]

This reporter queried some firms around the country which, according to Arkansas sources, had been considering locating plants in the State. Only one indicated that the race problem in Arkansas may have influenced the decision against going there.

VOTERS ACCENTUATE THE POSITIVE...

HIGHLIGHTS OF THE NEWSWEEK
By Kennedy, Ark. Democrat   11/9/58

According to the cartoonist:

Arkansas voters disapproved moderates as they gave Alford victory in his write-in campaign against Hays.

Were in a positive mood as they okayed the 3% sales tax; industrialization bonds for new industry (another of my programs); kept the state out of the property tax field; approved raises for state legislators; and kept the railroad full crew law.

Before departing for speaking engagements at Crestview, Fla. on Nov. 8 and New Orleans, La. on Nov. 11, I announced that I would remain in the Democratic Party and had no intention of promoting a Third Party movement.

According to press reports Hays charged, or inferred, that I engineered his defeat.

Arkansas Democrat
Nov. 9, 1958

BACKSTAGE AT THE CAPITOL

Traditions in the South
Outpull Loyalty to Party

by George Douthit
(Democrat Staff Writer)

There is a good lesson for politicians in the defeat of . . . Hays by . . . Alford, The feelings of the majority of the people in the South for their traditions . . . are a lot deeper than their party loyalty.

One Democratic voter told us after election: *"The people were mad at Brooks Hays for his integration stand. And when the people get mad at a politician he is heading for defeat."*
. . .

Mr. Hays arranged the conference between Governor Faubus and President Eisenhower at Newport, R.I.

Details of Meet Leaked

While Mr. Hays' part in these conferences and those subsequent to it were kept secret, the word gradually leaked out that the 5th District congressman was taking the stand of "gradual integration."

. . . Rumor also has it, he was meeting with some other people who were outspoken against the stand taken by Governor Faubus. Further rumors had it that Mr. Hays, if he could get Governor Faubus to back down, could get a federal judgeship. . . .

. . . [In the Democratic Primary] Amis Guthridge, attorney for the Capitol Citizens Council, filed and polled 18,000 votes to Mr. Hays' 28,000. . . . the feelings against Mr. Hays had not crystalized to the point they had reached last week.

Victory Was Doubtful

. . . With his Democratic nomination in hand, Mr. Hays, instead of swinging toward the segregationist views, swung the other way. His speech in North Little Rock that he was a moderate was politically damaging.

Dr. Alford didn't really appear on the political scene until after the primaries. As the lone segregationist member of the Little Rock School Board, he took to television in behalf of the vote to keep the Little Rock schools segregated.

His personality and ability to present his cause, even without one iota of experience, got a lot of folks to talking. . . .

Dr. Alford got the bug. More and more people were expressing dissatisfaction with Congressman Hays' stand and more and more were urging Dr. Alford to oppose him. Dr. Alford discussed it with veteran politicians. He went in with his eyes wide open. He knew what he faced. . . . A majority of the voters have spoken again. . . .

I'm no eye-doctor, but I can see some things clearly —

HAYS CHARGES FAUBUS ENGINEERED HIS DEFEAT.

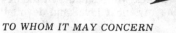

TO WHOM IT MAY CONCERN
By Kennedy, Ark. Democrat   11/9/58

MODERATION

BROOKS HAYS

WARNING UNSAFE STAND

NEW RULING BY
8TH CIRCUIT COURT OF APPEALS

On Nov. 10, 27 days after final arguments were heard on its hasty oral decisions of Sept. 27 and the unprecedented actions in carrying them out, the 8th Circuit Court of Appeals of St. Louis, Mo., handed down new rulings. Press reports read:

The federal appeals court directed the Little Rock School Board to take positive steps to accomplish integration of the Little Rock School District. The court did not spell out how this should be done.

The Court assailed Faubus and the Legislature for their efforts to use public school buildings for segregated schools through the Little Rock private school corporation.

The Court directed Judge Miller to enjoin the School Board "from taking any further steps or action without the approval of the District Court." (The schools would now, in effect, be run by the Court from St. Louis.)

The Court also directed Miller to enjoin the Board "from engaging in any other acts whether independently or in participation with anyone else, which are capable of serving to impede, thwart, or frustrate the execution of the integration plan mandated against them."

Truly it was a sweeping and arrogant order.

A federal court had assailed a state legislative body for exercising its constitutional right to enact laws in accordance with the wishes of its constituents, and assailed a state's chief executive for carrying out a legislative mandate, his constitutional duty.

The Court had told an independent school board elected by the people, that it had no power to act, that it could do nothing without first clearing its actions with the Court.

The officials of the private school corporation announced the private school would stay open, and I stated that I could see no conflict with the ruling of the Court in the operation of private schools.

The Little Rock School Board was in a far different situation. Faced with the order to take "positive steps" to integrate the schools without any directions as to how it should be accomplished, and at the same time enjoined from any action without first clearing it with the District Court in St. Louis, the Board found itself in a near impossible situation.

The board members viewed the difficult and intolerable conditions, and resigned the night of November 12 effective November 14. Before resigning, the Board terminated Supt. Virgil Blossom and bought up his contract for $19,900.

Board member Wayne Upton stated, "All members of this school board are segregationists in feeling," and blamed me for the resignation of the five members.

Dale Alford, the Congressman-elect, still a member of the Board, did not join in the resignations. However, he had to resign later to take his seat in Congress.

DEDICATE LAKE ERLING

I participated in the dedication of the 7,000 acre Lake Erling in South Arkansas near Spring Hill, La., on Nov. 11, flying from New Orleans where I addressed a large Veterans Day crowd in front of City Hall. Lake Erling was a project of the International Paper Company which would be open to public use.

DEPUTY MARSHALS TERMINATED

News reports said the special deputy U.S. marshal project in Little Rock was ended by the Justice Department.

I SAID I WOULDN'T STAND IN YOUR WAY
By Herblock, Washington Post   11/11/58

This prejudiced cartoon came from the defeat of Hays in the general election by write-in candidate Dale Alford.

The cartoonist did not infer, he stated, in substance, that while Hays was engaged in "efforts to settle the Little Rock Crisis," I stabbed him in the back. The idea was as false as the cartoon was vicious.

The role of Hays as a go-between in the conference with the President, was not a major factor, if a factor at all, in Hays' defeat. The opposition to Hays and his loss of the election was due almost wholly to two things — the pro-integration stand of his son, Steele Hays, and the Congressman's speeches and statements favoring court-ordered integration following his renomination in the Democratic Primary. Also his close association with the *Gazette* integrationists had become known.

The federal power advocates sought some way, other than the truth, to explain the Hays defeat. This does not infer that Hays was guilty of the same offense.

G. B. PHILLIPS DIES

I cancelled a speaking engagement before the Neosho-Cottonwood Flood Control Association at Chanute, Kansas, on Nov. 18, to return to Little Rock from North Arkansas, to attend the funeral of Green Berry Phillips, a mansion employee. Mr. Phillips, age 75, died of a heart attack while on duty at the executive mansion. He was among my most loyal and devoted friends.

AFL-CIO CONVENTION

I addressed the Arkansas AFL-CIO Convention in the capital city on Nov. 19.

"WHEN SHERMAN SAID WAR WAS HELL, HE WASN'T JUST
A-WHISTLIN' DIXIE!"
By Mauldin, St. Louis Post Dispatch   11/12/58

SCRAMBLE
By Kennedy, Ark. Democrat   11/16/58

Mauldin used a theme with which I was most familiar. With an ally, I was in a fox-hole almost filled with water (the kind we saw so often in the WWII Alsace-Lorraine Campaign), trying to hold off a superior force attacking with superior arms. The huge cannon ball from heavy artillery was the "Latest Court Order on Schools," from St. Louis Nov. 10. The caption was a realistic reaction of the fox-hole occupants.

IRS REPRIMANDS SUPERVISOR

It was announced the Internal Revenue Service would reprimand a supervisor of the clerk who sent me the letter charging me with income tax on the rental value of the mansion.

SONG: WE LIKE FAUBUS

On Nov. 21 a song "We Like Faubus" went on sale in Little Rock. Written by Kansas City composer Nick Morris the song was recorded by a Little Rock quartet, the Warners, produced by the Morrisey Music Company of Little Rock and distributed by Siebert's News Agency. For months afterward I heard the record on juke boxes throughout the state.

DEDICATION AT McRAE SANATORIUM

On Nov. 23 we dedicated the new Rehabilitation Building at McRae Memorial TB Sanatorium, an administration project in a facility for black people. Dr. Hugh A. Browne, superintendent since 1931, was in charge of the program. The Rehabilitation Center was the first new structure at the facility in many years. Dr. Browne, a most able administrator, ran a very smooth operation with practically no trouble for my administration.

This excellent cartoon portrayed the struggle of the county governments and equalization boards to equalize property assessments at the required 18% of true market value set by state law.

The equalization program was one of the most difficult undertakings of my administration, and one fraught with the greatest political jeopardy. In spite of the difficulty and political danger, I gave solid support to the program from the time of its enactment in the 1955 session of the General Assembly. We furnished every assistance to the local units of government and kept up constant but friendly pressure for them to meet all requirements of the law.

Two very capable and qualified men, W. H. "Doc" Hinton of Little Rock, succeeded by Jack Cato of Walnut Ridge, headed the program during my tenure. They are due much credit for the program's success.

Soon our success in this difficult field of government became known beyond the state's boundaries. Other states, including some of the most progressive, were sending representatives to Arkansas to study our program and its methods.

In 1958 a check by the state reassessment agency found a number of counties below the minimum level of 18% required by law.

They were diligently working to attain the required level to avoid losing a portion of their state turnback funds. Other counties which had already attained the required level were waiting at the top.

"Re-assessment Mountain" was difficult to climb for the counties but they succeeded with the able assistance of the state agency.

Arkansas's property assessment and taxation system equalled or excelled any other in the nation for fairness and equity.

479

APPEALS COURT ORDERS
SCHOOL BOARD TO TAKE
'AFFIRMATIVE STEPS', BUT
DIDN'T SAY HOW OR WHEN...

WILBUR MILLS TO BACK ALFORD FOR DEMOCRATIC SEAT.

HIGHLIGHTS OF THE NEWSWEEK
By Kennedy, Ark. Democrat   11/16/58

The federal Appeals Court ordered the Little Rock school district to "accomplish integration" but didn't say how or when. In the face of the sweeping and extreme order Federal Judge John Miller said he was going on vacation.

The Little Rock school board resigned before the petitions seeking their recall were filed. A lawsuit was filed seeking to prevent the buying up of Supt. Virgil Blossom's contract.

Some "liberal" members of Congress talked of barring Dale Alford from taking his seat in the House. The powerful Arkansas Congressman Wilbur Mills announced he would back Alford to be seated as a Democrat.

The Little Rock private school planned a 178-day school term under Supt. Brashears.

Publisher John Wells of Little Rock, a rank conservative, asked for a recount of ballots in an effort to help Brooks Hays who was classified as a liberal. The Wells-Hays alliance was difficult to understand.

Attorney Bob Laster assumed an extreme attitude on the school controversy by stating he would open the schools on a segregated basis regardless of anyone or the consequences. His statement was a prelude to more political activity on his part.

I announced I would stay with the Democratic Party and fight my battles in its ranks.

Wayne Glenn, personable and able labor leader of Little Rock, was elected president of the merged AFL-CIO of Arkansas.

Congressman Brooks Hays received an ovation at the state Baptist Convention, it was reported, and wondered where all the Baptist brethren were on election day when he lost to Alford. Some of them were at the polls voting for his opponent.

Defeated candidate Chris Finkbeiner said in a speech at Miami, Fla. that the situation would get worse in the Little Rock school controversy.

THE "OTHER" LEGISLATIVE BODY'S IN SESSION, WE HEAR . . .
By Knox, Nashville Banner   11/25/58

The U. S. Congress is the constitutionally created legislative body, but another had been illegally established by the usurpation of power. Frustrated by their failures in Little Rock, the power-bloated Supreme Court, "that other legislative body," was conversing with the Justice Department which handled the difficulties. The Court said: "We've got to make a law to make the law we made, make the people . . .''

HIGHLIGHTS OF THE NEWSWEEK, By Kennedy, Ark. Democrat, 11/23/58

Citizen-News
Nov. 27, 1958

ASIA VIEWS U.S. NEGROES

Japanese Critic Finds
Little Rock 'Beautiful'

TOKYO — A caustic Japanese critic of the United States has expressed sympathy for America's efforts to solve its Negro problem.

Ashihei Hino, Japanese novelist just returned from a two-month trip to the United States, said he saw improvement in the status of Negroes in many places, including Little Rock.

In an article in the newspaper Tokyo Shimbun, Kino said the Negro "if he demands outright equality, without improving his own record of crime, ignorance and uncleanliness, is bound to fail."

. . .

"I visited Little Rock, Ark., with a preconception mixed with dread," he writes. "I had thought it was a fearsome place of bigotry where poor Negroes were ruthlessly persecuted by whites.

"I found out quickly my preconception was completely wrong. It was a quiet, beautiful city . . . Whites and colored people were living together in harmony.

"Facilities for the Negroes were as good as those in New York, Boston and Chicago I had seen earlier.

"Now I know it is wrong to consider the Little Rock school incident as a peak of the Negro problem. It is indeed far more complex and deep rooted."

MORE NEWS HIGHLIGHTS
By Kennedy, Ark. Democrat   11/30/58

Arkla gas rates increased by use of the escalator clause in the contracts, and the customer wonders why the rates never "escalate" downward.

HIGHLIGHTS OF THE NEWSWEEK
By Kennedy, Ark. Democrat   11/30/58

On a hunting trip to Wyoming I bagged a nine-point buck. It is likely that my hunting companion's shot felled the large deer. My boast (the cartoonist's idea) pertained to State Trooper Floyd Weaver, my personal driver and bodyguard most of the time during the '57 Crisis and for some years afterward. Later John Hicks and Richard "Dick" Rail, two loyal and dedicated state policemen, served me in the same capacity.

THE FINAL SCREENER
By Kennedy, Ark. Democrat   12/5/58

Soon I would make my third appointment to a full 10-year term on the Highway Commission. The *Democrat* still editorialized vigorously for the non-political status of the road agency. The cartoon indicated the general public would be interested in evaluating my selection. I knew that as well, or better than anyone.

FAUBUS

WILLIAMS

SYMINGTON

JOHNSON

KEFAUVER

KENNEDY

STEVENSON

Jerry Shaw

DEMOCRATIC PRESIDENTIAL CHOICES

GALLUP PRESIDENTIAL POLL

Miami (Fla.) Herald, Nov. 30, 1958

STEVENSON LED AS DEMOCRATIC CHOICE IN 1958; KENNEDY CLOSE BEHIND

In the Gallup Poll of Nov. 30, 1958, Adlai E. Stevenson led the field as the 1960 choice for president among rank and file Democratic voters . . . Sen. John F. Kennedy . . . was a close second.

. . .

The third most popular choice was Sen. Estes Kefauver of Tennessee, followed by Sen. Lyndon Johnson of Texas.

. . .

Following is the vote among Democrats, as compared with a similar survey in June:

	Today Pct.	June Pct.
Stevenson	29	23
Kennedy	23	19
Kefauver	11	16
Johnson	6	12
Symington	5	4
Williams	5	2
Faubus	4	
Other	3	9
None of these, no opinion	14	15

"*Other candidates receiving 2 per cent or less among Democratic Party members were Sen. Hubert Humphrey of Minnesota and New Jersey's Gov. Robert B. Meyner.*

. . .

. . . Independent voters lined up on Democratic candidate possibilities as follows:

	Today Pct.	June Pct.
Kennedy	30	27
Stevenson	20	16
Kefauver	10	13
Johnson	6	3
Symington	4	5
Faubus	4	
Meyner	4	5
None of these, no opinion	19	17

NEW SCHOOL BOARD ELECTED

A new school board of six members was elected at the school election of Dec. 6. The two opposing sides each won 3 posts, making it an evenly divided group. All candidates ran as avowed segregationists but everyone knew that three winners, Everett Tucker, Ted Lamb and Russell Matson, would favor compliance with the federal court order. In the eyes of the people this made them integrationists.

Winners on the other slate were businessman Ed I. McKinley, attorney Ben Rowland and Little Rock Traffic Judge Bob Laster. All the candidates on this slate would have won had not their backers been torn by discension and personal jealousy. The segregationists never had effective leadership and never remained united for long.

The divided board portended discension in Little Rock school affairs. Also failure to win complete victory in the election signaled the beginning of the decline in the political strength of the extreme segregationists.

During the school election campaign I joined in labeling Lamb's slate of candidates as integrationists. Lamb squeaked to a victory over a weak opponent and leveled a blast at me.

LAMB TURNS LOOSE BLAST AT FAUBUS; INTERPRETS ELECTION AS BEGINNING OF END FOR GOVERNOR

Ted Lamb . . . saw the outcome of the balloting as a defeat for governor Faubus. Lamb later said Everett Tucker concurred in his statement. . . .

He and other members of the "businessmen's slate" campaigned as segregationists.

. . . The Little Rock advertising executive said:

"Our victory is the beginning of the end for Orval Faubus, a 20th Century Michiavelli. This is the first crack in the Faubus edifice and I predict that his entire political empire, founded as it is upon misrepresentation and bigotry, will soon be crumbling at his feet.

"The attempt of this unscrupulous demagogue to wreck the Little Rock School Board has now been thwarted." . . .

SPEECH IN HOUSTON, TEXAS

I accepted an invitation to speak at a "Bill of Rights Day" observance in Houston, Texas, on December 12. The affair was sponsored by a dozen or more patriotic organizations including veterans groups.

A bomb threat kept early arrivals standing in the cold for about an hour. A check of the premises was made by Houston police officers after which the meeting was permitted to proceed.

I spoke to a capacity crowd of more than 3,000 in the Music Hall and was enthusiastically received.

Leaders of the sponsoring groups were seated on stage. One invitee, a Houston judge, was missing. When I got back to the hotel accompanied by my hosts, he called.

"I was there," he told my hosts, "seated in the audience. That man made a fine speech," he continued. "It was in good taste and well received. I'm sorry I allowed some adverse criticism to keep me from appearing on stage with him," he concluded.

I was introduced at the meeting by Wright Morrow of Houston, former Democratic national committeeman for Texas.

THE DAISY CHAIN
Political ad, Ark. Democrat   *12/4/58*

The campaign was under way to choose six new school board members to replace those who had resigned. Alford had now submitted his resignation in preparation to assume his seat in Congress.

Five candidates shown in this cartoon ran as a team, and were alleged to have the backing of the NAACP. Dewey Coffman who supported six other candidates ran this cartoon against the five named.

"GIDDAP, I SAY!"
By Graham, Ark. Gazette

12/5/58

Claude Carpenter, Jr., Alford's campaign manager in his victory over Hays, was chosen by the Democrats to head the fund raising drive for the national party. State Democrats refused to contribute to the national Democratic fund.

Carpenter announced the money would remain in the state to be used only to defray state party expenses, and the quota was met. Later I raised the funds for the national party from selected sources.

Carpenter was designated by National Committeewoman Gressie Carnes to represent her at a meeting of the Democratic National Committee. The *Gazette* said the national party was puzzled by the choice.

MOVE TO BLOCK
ALFORD FROM SEAT IN CONGRESS

The news of Dec. 18 revealed a move by Northern Congressmen to block Congressman-elect Alford from taking his seat in the National House of Representatives. The move was aided by Little Rock publisher John F. Wells and was understood to have the tacit approval of Congressman Hays.

—0—

SOVEREIGNTY COMMISSION
DECLINES INVESTIGATION

The State Sovereignty Commission, of which I was chairman, declined to conduct investigations of alleged subversive activities by Communists in the state.

Atty. Gen. Bruce Bennett under authorization granted by the Legislature, presided over a 3-day public hearing of Communist activities in Arkansas in connection with the integration problem. The hearings were conducted by the Special Education Committee of the Arkansas Legislative Council.

On Dec. 19 in a press statement I questioned the value of further generalized hearings into alleged subversion in the racial unrest in Arkansas.

No doubt the Communists were as active in the unrest as they could possibly be, but in the emotional atmosphere which prevailed I felt there was danger of such inquiries going too far afield. Injustice could be done to innocent people in generalized hearings. Also, there would be the constant effort of the leftists, aided by some liberals, to discredit any such hearings no matter how fairly conducted.

No further investigations on the subject of subversion were made by any official state agency or group.

ARMY-NAVY HOSPITAL

In the face of probable closing of the Army-Navy Hospital at Hot Springs by federal authorities we began the formulation of plans to convert the hospital to a state facility. Later through plans worked out by my administration, it was converted to a state-owned and operated rehabilitation center for the handicapped. The facility became one of the largest and finest centers of its kind in the nation, and continues in operation.

IRS CONTINUES

On Dec. 25 the Internal Revenue Service was engaged in an examination of the Executive Mansion expenditure records. The agents were seeking, no doubt, to discover any evidence of conversion of state funds in the mansion account to private use. To the contrary they discovered that the account was insufficient to cover all Mansion expenses and that on some occasions my own personal money and funds contributed by personal friends were used to help pay state activity costs.

THE GALLUP POLL OF ADMIRED MEN

Arkansas Democrat, December 28, 1958

The Sunday issue of the *Arkansas Democrat* carried Gallup's annual list of "The Ten Men in the World Most Admired by Americans."

To the complete surprise of many people, both friend and foe, my name was included in the top ten. The list was as follows:

1. President Dwight D. Eisenhower
2. Sir Winston Churchill
3. Dr. Albert Schweitzer
4. Rev. Billy Graham
5. Former President Harry S. Truman
6. Gen. Douglas MacArthur
7. Vice-President Richard M. Nixon
8. Dr. Jonas Salk
9. Bernard Baruch
10. Orval E. Faubus

No other governor had ever made the list and no U.S. Senator or member of Congress up to that time.

The three new names in the top ten were Nixon, Baruch and Faubus. Among those replaced was Adlai E. Stevenson, on the list the previous year.

Names most prominently mentioned after the top ten included:

Public Affairs: Adlai Stevenson, Herbert Hoover, John Foster Dulles, Sen. John Kennedy, Gov.-elect Nelson A. Rockefeller, Dr. Ralph Bunche, Gov. Herman Talmadge, J. Edgar Hoover, Sen. Richard Russell, Gov. Luther Hodges, Sen. Lyndon Johnson, Sen. Estes Kefauver, John Nance Garner, Supreme Court Chief Justice Earl Warren.

And Sen. William F. Knowland, Gov. A. B. Chandler, Gov. Theodore R. McKeldin, Sen. Albert Gore, Sen. Harry Byrd, Gov. Frank Clement, Sen. Frank J. Lausche, Speaker Sam Rayburn, Gov.-elect David Lawrence, Rep. Melvin Price, and many others.

Now there could be listed four things, among others, which vindicated my stand against federal usurpation of the rights of the states. They also justified my diligence and tenacity in long and difficult struggle, and were some compensation for the severe criticism which I had so long endured, of which many of these cartoons are good examples.

1. My overwhelming re-election for a third time by a record vote exceeding all previous margins of victory.

2. The endorsement of the overall program of progress I had recommended to the General Assembly at its 1957 regular session, by the vote to retain the three percent sales tax.

3. The almost unanimous support of the General Assembly in the special sessions dealing with the Little Rock Crisis.

4. Inclusion in this list of admired men.

APPOINTMENTS, NOVEMBER 1958

Leon B. Catlett, Little Rock, appointed a special justice for State Supreme Court. Fred Carter, Lake City, reappointed to State Bank Commission. W. J. "Bill" Smith, Little Rock, Associate Justice of State Supreme Court to fill vacancy created by retirement of Justice Minor Milwee. J. W. Durden, Ft. Smith, Prosecuting Attorney, 12th Judicial District.

APPOINTMENTS, DECEMBER 1958

N. D. Early, Brinkley, Fargo Training School for Girls. Arnold B. Sikes, Little Rock, Commerce Commission. John Fogleman, West Memphis, Justice Building Commission. Rolla Fitch, Hindsville, Executive Secretary to Governor on 12/15/58. Sherman V. Zinn, Little Rock, Workmen's Compensation Commission. Forrest Rogers, Lincoln, State Plant Board. J. L. Erwin, McGehee, Desha County Judge and noted historian, to Civil War Centennial Commission. Dr. Sam J. Kuykendall, Little Rock, McRae Memorial Sanatorium.

CHAPTER 24
COMMENT ON GALLUP'S LIST. THIRD INAUGURATION. INDUSTRIAL PROGRESS. THE PRESS CONFERENCE AT HOT SPRINGS. CONCLUSION

GALLUP'S LIST OF "TEN MOST ADMIRED MEN IN THE WORLD"

The (Crossett, Ark.) News Observer
January 1, 1959

EDITORIALS
Arkansas' Famous Governor

Depending on how they feel personally about the man, Arkansans . . . were either shocked or thrilled by the news . . . that their Governor, Orval Faubus, had been named as one of the top ten men in the world most admired by Americans.

The selection of Mr. Faubus also came as a surprise to many of his followers, . . . because even though the Faubus name has become a household word in Arkansas, many folks did not realize the fame of the backwoods boy from the hills of Madison County had spread the world around. But famous he is, as the Gallup poll shows. Mr. Faubus was the only Governor so selected and his nationwide popularity places him beside President Eisenhower and a few other men of international fame, as being held in the highest regard by their fellow citizens.

Mr. Faubus has received this fame . . . because he has become a symbol to the whole world of the theory of states rights versus central government. He is the personal hero . . . to those . . . who see the dire danger which lurks in an all powerful rule from Washington. Mr. Faubus is the David who has stood up to the Goliath and regardless of their personal feelings pro or con about his motives, . . . many people have cheered him for his individual courage.

. . .

Regardless of his future, Mr. Faubus is without peer the most famous Arkansan . . .

Shreveport, La., Times
January 2, 1959

HIGH TRIBUTE IS PAID FAUBUS IN NATIONAL POLL

. . . It is, indeed, amazing that Governor Faubus should be included in this particular Top Ten and that statement is not meant to imply . . . that he does not deserve the honor. "Amazement" comes because no man in this particular era of American history has been subjected to organized attack embracing ridicule, belittling and general condemnation in the manner or in the volume in which such attack has been directed at the Arkansas Governor.

. . .

Various left-leaning political or comparable organizations around the country have carried on an organized campaign to make this Chief Executive of a sovereign state appear to be some kind of a nitwitted bumpkin or a horrible ogre against whom the shutters of homes should be barred at night.

Yet, in a national poll . . . conducted in all 48 states, Governor Faubus is selected as one of the ten most admired not only in the United States but in the entire world; most admired by Americans, that is. And, an overwhelming majority of those polled must have been residents of areas outside the South. This is, indeed an amazing tribute to the Arkansas Governor when all the factors involved are considered.

* * *

Dallas, Tex., News

No. 10 is interesting. The Governor . . . has been lampooned by every commentator and newspaper outside the South because of his resistance to the U.S. Supreme School Board.

But maybe that's why he's admired, even outside Arkansas.

. . . seems to be a man of conviction . . . dedicated to [a] principle.

. . . The world admires a man who stands up for what he believes and is willing to fight the mob for his convictions.

* * *

Arkansas Democrat

. . . With him the State shares the international spotlight of public opinion.

Never before have Arkansas people had so strong feelings about a governor. . . . no native or adopted son . . . heretofore has been so widely known.

. . . people . . . praise his courage in carrying out the will of the majority of the citizens who elected him. Among those admirers are persons who favor integration, but who believe that the federal government has no right to change a social system against the will of the people and no right to interfere in state and local operation of schools.

Gov. Faubus's administration has brought much progress to Arkansas.

In having become a world figure, Gov. Faubus owes considerable to his enemies. They have tried to paint him as an uncouth, heartless demagogue, and despite the rancor and rudeness of some "foreign" interviewers he remained calm and courteous.

The effort to "demonize" him has been so extreme that his name has spanned the planet.

* * *

Gary, Ind., Post-Tribune

The addition of Faubus [to the list of 10] is not pleasant to contemplate. . . . It is discouraging when a man so obviously a demagogue is included, even in 10th place, on a list of men most admired by the American public.

Fond Hopes for 1959

by Jon Kennedy

Buffalo, N.Y., Courier Express
Jan. 5, 1959

HALOES, HORNS AND HOOFS
AND GOV. FAUBUS

Americans . . . have a tendency to depict public figures either with haloes or with horns and hoofs. Consistently depicted throughout the North as having horns and hoofs is Gov. Faubus of Arkansas. In view of this, the following AP dispatch from Little Rock has some interest.

"A convicted Negro slayer will get a review of his death sentence even if Gov. Faubus has to pay the costs himself.

"The Governor . . . has reprieved Lawrence Smith, 19, who had been scheduled to die in the electric chair for the robbery slaying of a white farmer.

"Faubus said everyone sentenced to death ought to be able to exhaust all avenues of appeal, Smith apparently could not raise the money to take his case to the high court.

"It looks like I will have to pay it out of my own pocket or get it from some of my friends," the Governor said.

Gov. Faubus' critics undoubtedly will accuse him of a grandstand play. His friends undoubtedly will cite his action as disproving that his opposition to school integration is based on hatred of Negroes. [My worst critics never accused me of hatred — of anyone.]

. . .An objective observer might point out that he (Faubus) has taken . . . an action based on an attitude assailed by certain Northern extremists as "paternalistic."

. . . Such a "paternalistic" attitude is not confined to Southern Governors or to cases involving Negro prisoners. Some years ago, when Alfred E. Smith was Governor of New York State, he learned of a convicted murderer who had filed no appeal because he had no funds, no friends and apparently no one interested in taking the necessary legal action. So Gov. Smith reprieved the prisoner and filed such an appeal on his own initiative.

This brings us back to public men and haloes and horns and hoofs — and the quirks of public opinion which result from thinking in such terms.

DAN STEPHENS JOINS MY STAFF

The media on January 7 carried the news that Dan Stephens of Clinton would shortly join my staff as administrative assistant in the governor's office. Stephens had just concluded two terms as prosecuting attorney of his district. He had served as head of the Bureau of Vital Statistics in the State Health Department during the McMath Administration while attending law school at night, and it was during that time we first became acquainted.

Stephens went on to fill a number of positions in state government during my administration. He performed his duties well with credit to himself, the agency he served and the administration.

R. W. (BOB) MEDLOCK

Another who joined my staff in later months as administrative assistant and became prominently known in my administration was R. E. (Bob) Medlock of Independence County. At a very early age he served as county clerk in Batesville, but he did not stop with claiming that beautiful county seat as his home town. He always went further to the small settlement of Bethesda near the banks of White River as the place of his origin.

Once with Truman Baker and other officials of the Highway Department I accompanied Bob on a trip to Bethesda where we held a dedication ceremony for a new, improved highway, the first constructed into the area. He introduced me that day in the public ceremony to his home town people, and claimed the occasion as a highlight of his political career.

Of all the people who served in my administration, none were more loyal and diligent in my service than Bob Medlock. Also he never ceased to be grateful for help or favors, a warm and endearing attribute all too lacking in many others. "Bob's middle name is Loyalty," his friends said of him. Could they say much more?

I joined Bob in Bethesda another time. It was general election day, Nov. 5, 1974, after we had lost in the Democratic Primary earlier in the year. It was a day that had always been important to Bob, for any election day was important to him. Perhaps it was the first election in which he had failed to vote, unless he missed one during his war time service as a member of the armed forces.

Bob had died of cancer and had come home for the last time. The bugle blew the lonely call of taps over his casket; I presented the folded flag to his widow, and saluted the remains of a friend I shall always remember.

Hot Springs Sentinel Record
Jan. 13, 1959

FAUBUS INAUGURATED
IN COLORFUL CEREMONY

LITTLE ROCK — Gov. Orval E. Faubus did something today that only one other man in the history of Arkansas had done before him.

He became governor of the state for the third time.

On Jan. 11, 1905, Gov. Jeff Davis set the precedent that Faubus followed.

The ceremony today was a colorful one.

Lieut. Gov. Nathan Gordon presided, and presented the Rev. Wayne Smith, pastor of the First Baptist Church in Little Rock, for the invocation.

House Speaker Gene C. Fleeman of Mississippi County, declared the results of the general election for the constitutional officers, excluding the governor, and Chief Justice Carleton Harris of the state Supreme Court gave them the oath of office.

Fleeman then declared results of the general election for the governor, and appointed a committee of senators and representatives to escort Faubus into the joint session.

The committee returned to the jampacked house chamber. Faubus was in the lead, followed by Mrs. Faubus and their son.

Faubus was solemn-faced, Mrs. Faubus smiling.

Both stepped to the speakers stand as a junior high school band in the balcony burst into strains of "Dixie." . . .

Fleeman officially declared Faubus elected, and Harris administered the oath . . .

More applause, and Faubus' face broke into a wide grin.

Gordon then presented the governor with a certificate of election, and then introduced Faubus for his inaugural address.

. . .

He made little departure from the prepared text, changing words only to make sentences read more smoothly.

Faubus was wearing his characteristic blue suit, white carnation in the lapel, and a red tie.

As he read, he clinched his hands and waved his arms for emphasis.

There was little early reaction from the legislators who listened attentively. . . .

Later in his speech, the governor touched on the Little Rock conflict of September, 1957.

Speaking of decisions, the governor said he made them "prayerfully and fearfully at times, but the decisions were mine."

Heavy applause.

"There has not yet been brought to bear any fact, information, reason, logic or law which led me to think for one minute that I was wrong."

More heavy applause.

The governor went on:

"The fence-straddler is sooner or later toppled from his perch to join one force or the other, or to crawl away and disappear into the brush."

Heavy applause again.

✧✧✧✧

Arkansas Democrat
Jan. 13, 1959

FAUBUS MAKES 3RD TRIP
UP MARBLE STAIRS
TO TAKE OATH AS GOVERNOR

by Bobbie Forster
(Democrat Staff Writer)

For the third time in less than five years Orval Eugene Faubus, Huntsville, today walked up the 41 marble steps from the executive offices on the 2nd floor of the capitol to the House of Representatives on the 3rd floor.

Twice before the weekly newspaper owner has climbed those marble steps to take the oath of office as governor of Arkansas, the second man in the state's history to make that ascent more than twice. Today, he used his family Bible for the ceremony.

On all three occasions, a special legislative committee has escorted the man who already knew the way . . .

In 1955 he faced a legislature restive after one-term Governor Cherry had recommended in a farewell address no new taxes to a body not wanting new taxes. It was a body divided in sentiment toward a retiring governor and toward a newcomer.

Establishes Leadership

. . . A month later the new governor made another speech at a joint session to establish his leadership firmly after having astutely waited for a legislative move to develop a program, a legislative move that never came.

On Jan. 11, 1955, first-term Governor Faubus questioned the need of the schools for an additional $12 million, asked for the scrapping of the bulky Cherry Fiscal Code and the establishment of a comptroller's office, recommended the elimination of the poll tax . . . recommended encouraging industry.

. . .

He agreed to a property reassessment program and an industrial development program.

On Jan. 15, 1957, he climbed the 41 steps to ask for $22 million in new taxes. And he marshalled through this session a 3 percent sales tax, lowering income tax exemptions, an increase in severance taxes and higher driver's license. . . . He has said he would not ask for any new taxes of the 1959 session.

. . .

The legislature today apparently is willing to go along with most of whatever legislation he recommended, strongly drawn to that view by the overwhelming vote he piled up for a 3rd term.

The following were new members of the Sixty-Second General Assembly of 1959:

SENATE

Jack Yates, Ozark, Third District
Rudolph Bates, Mt. Ida, Fifth
Olen Hendrix, Antoine, Seventh
Jimmy Slack, Malvern, Eleventh
Bob Dodson, Camden, Twelfth
Dr. Herbert H. Price, Pocahontas, Seventeenth.
(Dr. Price died and Thomas Penn, Black Rock, was elected to fill the vacancy at a special election on Jan. 26, 1959.)
John D. Eldridge, Augusta, Nineteenth
Doug Bradley, Jonesboro, Twenty-fourth
Joe Lee Anderson, Helena, Twenty-sixth

HOUSE OF REPRESENTATIVES

E. C. "Gene" Fleeman, Speaker, Leachville, Mississippi County

Hal Moody, Chief Clerk, Searcy, White County

Grover C. Carnes, Stuttgart, Arkansas County
N. B. "Nap" Murphy, Crossett, Ashley
Sam Powell, Mountain Home, Baxter
Roy H. Galyean, Rogers, Benton
J. Hugh Lookadoo, Arkadelphia, Clark
Clifford F. Cole, Piggott, Clay
Gean P. Houston, Heber Springs, Cleburne
John States, Jonesboro, Craighead
Edwin E. Hopson, Jr., McGehee, Desha
Lowell Whittington, Ozark, Franklin
Eugene "Bud" Canada, Hot Springs, Garland
Tony F. McDonald, Paragould, Greene
Donnie Bryant, Batesville, Independence
John E. Miller, Melbourne, Izard
Virgil C. Kolb, Clarksville, Johnson
Mattie Garner Hackett, Stamps, LaFayette
Roy S. Dunn, Booneville, Logan
Clyde O. Wahlquist, Prescott, Nevada
W. D. Baker, Jasper, Newton

Gus L. Ladd, Jr., Helena, Phillips
Alvis W. Stokes, Umpire, Pike
Ben Allen; Mrs. Gordon P. "Willie" Oates, Little Rock, Pulaski
Roland Morris, Pocahontas, Randolph
O. P. Hammons; Clarke Kinney, Forrest City, St. Francis
Ezra Horton, Marshall, Searcy
Milt Earnhart; Johnny Boatright, Ft. Smith, Sebastian
George W. Davis, DeQueen, Sevier
Cecil L. Gibson, Evening Shade, Sharp
David J. Burleson, Fayetteville, Washington
Ralph Underhill, Searcy, White
Boss Mitchell, Danville, Yell

HIGHLIGHTS OF THE NEWSWEEK
By Kennedy, Ark. Democrat   1/18/59

I was inaugurated for a third term. Among the legislative proposals I recommended was a student aid plan to assist youths of all races and creeds to secure college training. The plan was approved by the Legislature.

The NAACP filed suit to nullify Acts 4 and 5 enacted at the special legislative session in August, 1958.

I stood off an attack by legislators and businessmen on the re-assessment program.

State Senator Robert Harvey of Swifton wanted to revise the state income tax laws.

The Legislative Council laid the integration troubles at Central High School to actions of the Communist Party — and there was more than a grain of truth to the charges.

R. B. "Dick" Winfrey, a former Highway Department employee who went to Oklahoma and later returned to Arkan-

sas, was named acting highway director to replace Eldridge who resigned.

Dale Alford was seated in Congress as a Democrat.

The first Sports Hall of Fame banquet for Arkansas was a great success in Little Rock with the eloquent and humorous Joe Garagiola of St. Louis as emcee. Joe filled that role at the installation banquets for a number of years, with his ability contributing much to the success of the events. I became one of the favorite objects for his jokes.

CHENEY AND LANEY
LEGISLATIVE ADVISERS

My legislative advisers for the regular session of the General Assembly for my third term beginning January 13, 1959, were J. Orville Cheney with Bill Laney as assistant. They left their positions as Revenue Commissioner and Assistant Labor Commissioner respectively to serve during the term of the legislative session. Cheney with former service in the Senate was respected by his former colleagues and was familiar with legislative procedures. Laney as a member of organized labor was very helpful in the field of legislation affecting labor laws and working people.

HOLLENSWORTH SUFFERS HEART ATTACK

Representative Carroll Hollensworth of Warren, Bradley County, suffered a heart attack and was hospitalized at St. Vincent's without visitors on January 20. His great ability and skill as a legislator was lost to the General Assembly.

Hollensworth recovered sufficiently to return to the legislative halls before the session ended but could not be active as before. After returning home he succumbed to the heart ailment some months later. His death left a void in legislative leadership which was difficult to fill.

DEDICATION OF
$15,000,000 CEMENT PLANT AT FOREMAN

We traveled by train from Little Rock to the dedication of the $15 million cement plant at Foreman, built as a subsidiary of Arkla Gas Company. Several cars were filled with businessmen and legislators invited by W. R. "Witt" Stephens, the power behind the construction of the facility, and Representative Marion Crank of Foreman. It was a bitterly cold day with speeches and the ceremony held to a minimum of time. Following is a newspaper report of the event on Jan. 20, 1959:

In a 5-minute address from an ice-covered platform, Gov. Faubus cited the Foreman Cement Plant as a "true indication of the type of spirit and cooperation" which will mean continued progress for the state.

W. R. Stephens, president of Arkla which owns Arkansas Cement Corporation, also spoke.

Faubus told the audience that he had "boundless faith in Arkansas, and Witt Stephens has boundless money. With my faith and his money, we will build Arkansas."

There were 1,200 in attendance including about 100 members of the Legislature.

Because of the temperature (27 degrees with wind) Faubus and others kept remarks brief and on the light side.

Stephens recalled a colder day and said:

"I was one of the people who told Orval Faubus he couldn't be elected governor [in 1954]. And then I tried to help carry out that program [defeat me]. The day I had to go to the governor's office and ask him for something was colder than today.

"But Gov. Faubus turned on the charm and made me feel warm, so I offered my services as his

491

political adviser. He said that if he had taken my advice he wouldn't be governor, and he told me to go back to my chosen profession of making money, which I did."

The plant, perhaps the most modern in the world, was already in production at the time of the dedication ceremony.

COMPTROLLER KELLY CORNETT DIES

In January 1959 I lost one of the finest, most loyal and trustworthy members of my administration. Comptroller Kelly Cornett, native of St. Paul, later a resident of Huntsville and for a brief period in 1939, my deputy circuit clerk, died of a heart ailment on Jan. 20. A press report of Jan. 21, said:

Gov. Faubus called Mr. Cornett "an exceptional man."

"I am not saying this because he is dead — he was an exceptional man. In attempting to run an administration, sometimes you have concern or a second thought about someone in your administration. But I never had any concern or a second thought about him," Mr. Faubus said.

PRESS INTERVIEW AT HOT SPRINGS

The Arkansas Press Association and the National Editorial Association held a joint meeting at Hot Springs on January 8, 9 and 10. I made the welcoming address the first day and then held a press conference in which all those in attendance participated. After my speech I faced and fielded the questions of some 300 publishers, editors and reporters for more than two hours. Following is some of the newspaper comment afterward in newspapers across the state and nation.

The Manila, Ark., Sentinel
Jan. 22, 1959

This will undoubtedly be only one of many editorial articles written this week that will be concerned with . . . a press interview with our Governor, Orval E. Faubus.

. . . the best way to get the true measure of a man's sincerity and knowledge is . . . a press conference with a group of experienced newsmen. If they can't upset his equilibrium it can't be done . . . and I am convinced . . . with Orval Faubus it can't be done.

He is an experienced and capable politician . . . He is also a sincere and dedicated man, and this is far more important. He is sincerely and diligently working for the people . . . of Arkansas to the best of his ability. He is doing what he believes to be the things that those people want him to do (and the voting last year proves that he knows what they want him to do).

He is conscientious and capable . . . well informed on all phases of government . . . He answered every question that was asked, personal or public, . . . did not dodge or attempt to avoid any specific question or subject. There were many of both. His answers were honest and complete, without bitterness or temper. . . .

. . . questions . . . covered a variety of subjects — integration, racial misunderstandings in many parts of the country, states rights, political problems, and even personal subjects . . . In each instance the Governor was straightforward and never evasive.

. . . Governor Faubus gained respect and admiration, not only for himself, but for . . . Arkansas as well. There will be many editorials written . . . throughout the country . . . most of them will be complimentary. The Governor made many new friends.

————

WE VISIT GOVERNOR FAUBUS

The Mitchell, Ind., Tribune
(Republished in the Beebe, Ark., News)

One of the highlights of the Convention was a press conference with Gov. Faubus. We had the governor pictured as a demon with horns or a gestapo type individual. We found our opinions entirely unfounded. The governor had a pleasing personality and impressed us as being very intelligent and capable of handling any situation. . . . [He] was confronted with hitherto unknown questions from about 300 editors from all over the United States. . . . Most of the questions concerned the Little Rock problem.

. . . Never before . . . have the rights of states and local governments to control their own affairs been so threatened by the federal government, he said.

It was also brought out . . . that the Negroes in Little Rock have adequate school facilities, having a high school building . . . rated in a national builders magazine as one of the five best in the nation . . . more modern than Central High School.

The governor probably has received more publicity and unjust criticism than any other man in the nation. But he impressed us as a man capable and most sincere in trying to solve local problems. . . . We certainly are sympathetic with his problem.

•—o—o—o—•

Publisher and Editor Laud Payne of the Piggott Banner wrote on January 16:

The Arkansas Press was represented by 500 people. The NEA Ass'n. was represented by about 300 editors and their wives from practically all the 48 states.

. . . a large percentage of the visitors considered one of the highlights of the program the opportunity of seeing and hearing Gov. Faubus. The Governor gave the group a two-hour press conference at which he answered all the questions sent his way.

We found some of the people (before the conference) openly antagonistic toward the Governor, some non-comittal; many had been "brainwashed" 100% by some large dailies, some radio and TV reporters, who had them thinking that the Governor had already been sent his horns and forked tail.

. . . about 90% of the editors were in Arkansas for the first time . . .

Naturally, as the press conference got under way, the questions were almost 100% on the line of integration.

A few of the visiting editors . . . asked questions that we classify as "loaded," designed to put the Governor "on the spot." However, he "took very good care of himself."

One visiting high school girl, daughter of a Northern editor, was a bit sarcastic sounding as she asked "If we as students don't object, why should you?"

The Governor asked her to what extent her home school was integrated, and she said 390 white and 18 Negro students. He then told her that 11 schools in Arkansas were integrated, some on about the same basis. He also told her the state-supported colleges were integrated. She seemed dumbfounded and virtually said she didn't believe him. Finally convinced, she admitted that she had never been told there was any integration whatsoever in Arkansas, and that the Little Rock incident was the first effort to integrate. She said the papers up that way never gave those facts.

A lady editor of a Kansas weekly asked the Governor to explain the charge that he (Faubus) was Communistic, as recently charged by Confidential Magazine. The Governor told the story of his brief stay at Commonwealth College and (then related briefly) the communists' role in the Little Rock school trouble. At the conclusion (of the conference) the lady rushed to the Governor, shook his hand . . . said: "Governor, many papers, including mine, have been very cruel to you with the distorted lies we have published about you. Thank God for you, Gov. Faubus. My readers are going to learn the truth about you and about the Arkansas case when I get back home."

A New York State editor took the floor and praised the Governor for . . . standing up to the Communists and . . . to call names.

ᴓᴦᴓᴦᴓᴦ

The Republican
Paoli, Indiana

Reprinted in
Bald Knob (Ark.) Banner
Jan. 29, 1959

CLOSE-UP OF GOVERNOR FAUBUS

We have attended only a very few press conferences in our years in newspaper work. Certainly we never before attended one of the significance of one held . . . in Hot Springs, Ark., at which delegates . . . interviewed Gov. Orval Faubus.

This interview was spontaneous. Anyone was privileged to ask any question he chose, and the governor dodged none of them. More than 300 small town editors were present. 32 states were represented . . . a few of the questions from northerners were quite sharply edged, . . .

The conference lasted two hours and covered far more ground than we have space to report. The very first question and its reply were typical. It was asked by Mrs. Margaret Wyatt, editor of the Brown County Democrat at Nashville, Ind. She asked if the governor foresaw any time when the schools of Little Rock would be integrated.

He replied that no one man had the answer to that. His position from the first has been that integration is a local problem. Only people who live in a given community are familiar enough with prevailing conditions to decide. If at any time the people of Little Rock want integrated schools, he thinks they should have them.

. . . Although his difficulties with integrationists have been more highly publicized, he has also had trouble with segregationists who oppose integrated schools under any condition. . . . He pointed out that Arkansas has more integrated schools than nine other southern states combined.

We came to Arkansas wondering whether Faubus was merely a rabble-rouser who was capitalizing on an unfortunate situation for his own personal political future. After listening to him for two hours we are convinced that he is an honest man who was caught in an impossible situation; that he sincerely believes in states' rights and local self government. We found him to be highly intelligent with a sharp wit that brought good natured humor to many of his answers.

As to facts about the Little Rock situation, one of great significance . . . has been little publicized in the North. This was that Horace Mann High School, the Negro school there, has better facilities than 30-year-old Central High, scene of the disturbance. In fact, . . . Horace Mann was chosen by an architectural magazine as fifth among all the schools in the nation in having modern school facilities.

ᴓᴦᴓᴦᴓᴦ

Here are excerpts from a critic's observations.
Arkansas Democrat, Jan. 23, 1959

They go . . . to see a virtuoso performance of standard material. . . . disappointments are . . . rare at the governor's meetings with the press.

More evidence of this was offered at a joint meeting . . . of the NEA and APA. . . . local reporters (went) to see Gov. Faubus face the out-of-state newsmen, who presumably would pose some pointed questions . . .

The Hot Springs gathering . . . promised to be a sort of grass roots affair with questioners from 32 states.

A luncheon preceded the interview; . . . the visitors were openly hostile to Gov. Faubus, or expectant and wondering, . . . or just neutral. None of this is desirable in an audience, and the governor set about changing this with his welcome to Arkansas.

He was, he said, just a small-town (Huntsville) newspaper publisher and editor who stumbled into the governor's office." . . . (then) a sizeable list of good jokes, . . . a cataloguing of the wonders of Arkansas: bauxite, diamond mines, thermal baths and growing industrialization.

All hands retired to the press conference.

Faubus bearing . . . ranges from smiling humility to triumphant confidence, just as listeners . . . pass from skepticism to applauding good humor.

. . . (a) Kansas (questioner) wondered if Faubus' inclusion on Gallup's "Ten Most Admired" list was a slap at Adlai Stevenson, who had been excluded this year. That, said the governor, brought to mind the dying man who was told to renounce the devil and replied: "I'm in no position to renounce anyone."

"That's the way I feel," the governor insisted.

. . . later . . . he displayed a newspaper clipping headed, "Faubusites Fail in Seventh Attempt to Burn Bates Home." [The ridiculous perfidy of the story made the point.] *Lusty laughter . . . indicated they had followed the governor . . . and were having a high time . . .*

. . . Many Southern politicians fret and fume under fire, feeling . . . that the rest of the world is conspiring to cause the South discomfort. Faubus cuts a singular figure. If others look like frightened high school ballplayers, . . . he is the icy professional quarterback, calmly passing from behind his own goal line. This is his general manner, rather than the extreme high and low-pressure examples listed.

. . .

. . . the interview . . . ended with a standing ovation for Faubus — a spectacle to cheer his supporters and chill his opponents.

Arkansas Democrat
Jan. 24, 1959

PUBLISHER HITS FAUBUS' VIEW

BOSTON — *Little Rock publisher Hugh Patterson Jr., said last night Arkansas has a citizenry "aroused and led by a man more intent on personal political ambition than the general welfare."*

Patterson, publisher of the ARKANSAS GAZETTE, said Governor Faubus "has learned the technique of using an issue of emotion and prejudice to overturn a long-time tradition in Arkansas against a third term."

. . .

Patterson said "Little Rock, Arkansas and Faubus are bad words today throughout much of this country and the world." . . .

"Public education," Patterson said, "is suffering severely in two states today and is likely to suffer more, and for a time become non-existent in others. . . .

Arkansas Democrat, Jan. 25, 1959

BACKSTAGE AT THE CAPITOL

Visiting Press Not As Welcome; Digest to Blame

by George Douthit
(Democrat Staff Writer)

Visiting reporters from the North and East have found Governor Faubus an easy target for interviews with virtually no red tape. . . .

All of the magazines . . . have had their reporters spend many hours gathering information from him and then slanting it as much against him as they dared.

Governor Faubus' philosophy about all of this has been that, while they were doing their slanting, they were unsuspectedly presenting some very valuable information to the American public . . .

New Angle

But Charles Morrow Wilson, in his free-lance article for READER'S DIGEST, attacked the governor from a new angle. He has depicted Mr. Faubus as a backwoods character with hardly any knowledge of grammar.

. . . a Houston newspaper only a few weeks ago . . . said the Arkansas governor had the appearance of a Wall Street banker and spoke in perfect English.

Mr. Faubus has had millions of words written about him in the last 18 months, most of them devoted to unkindnesses, but even in the most vengeful attacks no writer described him as backwoodsie.

Wilson's Language

. . . Mr. Wilson himself uses backwoods English in his own language. The editors have carefully used correct spelling of Mr. Wilson's own words, but the tenor of the language is the same.

For instance, this paragraph:

"At the age of seven, Li'l Orval was already 'Axin alongside' Pappy Sam, helping to take out hickory splits for sale to the local ax-handle factory and ash blocks for the barrel-stave plant."

Those are the words of the writer, Mr. Wilson, not Governor Faubus. Here is how he has the governor talking:

" 'The burn man must have a natural feelin' for fire,' Faubus explains. 'If he's a fraidy cat or too cautious, he don't get the burnin' done. And if he ain't real smart, he's sure to start a forest fire.' "

. . . We have been close to the governor for over four years and have never heard him make such grammatical mistakes, even before he became the polished speaker he is now.

We remember the day Mr. Wilson stood in the middle of the governor's reception room waiting to get in to see him. Mrs. Patsy Ellis, the governor's secretary, recalls it, too.

She said: "I didn't want him to go in. He was so poorly dressed that I just didn't believe he represented the READER'S DIGEST. He didn't say he was a free-lance writer. He said he was with the magazine."

He Looked Part

In fact, to us, Mr. Wilson had all the appearances of the character he has tried to paint Mr. Faubus to be.

. . .

. . . A woman editor of the READER'S DIGEST talked to Gov. Faubus over the telephone for an hour about the article. . . . She did not ask, however, whether Mr. Faubus used the type language that was used in the article.

. . . the description that he is without knowledge of good English, when all who have heard him know better.

Of Wilson's story Karr Shannon wrote in the *Democrat* on Jan. 25:

. . . Wilson has been a reporter for the ARKANSAS GAZETTE, the ST. LOUIS POST-DISPATCH and the NEW YORK TIMES.

It is a rambling piece of third-rate reporting, far beneath the dignity of the magazine that carries it. Although aimed at aspersion and calumny, it runs . . . some six pages of insipid, dull, boresome composition . . .

Stamps (Ark.) Democrat
January 29, 1959

PEOPLE OF ARKANSAS LIKE GOV. FAUBUS

When Governor Faubus entered the Marion Hotel Banquet room Tuesday night to attend the dinner given by Arkansas Power and Light Company for Senators and Representatives and State Officials, the people attending the dinner stood and applauded him till he had reached his seat at the speakers table.

The people of this great state honor Faubus for what he is and what he has done rather than for who he is or who his ancestors were.

In his opening remarks, the governor . . . referred to an article the DIGEST had published criticizing the governor and poking fun at the people of Arkansas for stooping so low as to elect such a man as governor of the state.

The majority of the people of Arkansas are proud of Governor Faubus . . . and it is easy to see that he is head and shoulders above all those who are trying to tell the world that he is a boob. These hecklers remind me of a dog running alongside a car and barking their heads off, they know they have no way in the world of attracting attention other than yapping at something bigger than they are and they could no more take the place of Faubus than the dog could drive the car.

. . . So the rest of the country hears only the voices of those who do not possess the facts about conditions in the South. Anyway, we are proud of our governor, and the only thing accomplished by such articles as READER'S DIGEST published is that it binds us closer to the man who has stood up against all opposition and has returned answers of logic to questions asked in scorn.

Baxter Bulletin, Mountain Home, Ark.

January 29, 1959

THE OZARK OUTLOOK
by Tom Dearmore

Reader's Digest Article
Gives Distorted Picture

When the ARKANSAS GAZETTE flies to the defense of Orval E. Faubus it is plain that something of a drastic nature has happened.

This was the case last week when the READER'S DIGEST appeared on newsstands . . .

The piece . . . is easily the worst job of reporting we've ever seen. It seems incredible that the READER'S DIGEST would have bought it without checking into the facts more thoroughly.

It will undoubtedly help Faubus a thousandfold more than it will harm him in the state.

Wilson . . . made him appear as a Li'l Abner-type ignoramus, lacing the article with hillbilly colloquialisms.

We've never, in all our years of being a hillbilly, heard most of the "sayings" which babble throughout this literary effort, and, in years of knowing the subject of the article, have never heard him use any of them.

The ARKANSAS GAZETTE gave an accurate editorial review, stating in part:

"It seems remarkable that the author . . . could have compounded so many factual errors in so brief a sketch . . . Its great fault is that it succeeds in conveying a wholly false image of the man Faubus by confusing and often altering the details of his early personal and political career, and by heavily larding the whole business with a hillbilly vernacular that seems to be largely the personal creation of Mr. Wilson."

Whatever else may be said about Faubus, he has developed to a high degree his speech, conversation and appearance.

. . .

. . . He is a man of keen instinct and quick mental reflex — . . . and fast on his feet in any company or on any platform. . . .

The DIGEST article will help enlarge the untrue mental image which many non-Arkansans have conjured up about the personality who has figured largely in stirring up the greatest defiance of federal authority since the Cvil War. . . .

THIS ONE'S ON ME

by Esther Bindursky
in Lepanto, Ark., News

A current article in the February issue of READER'S DIGEST on Gov. Faubus entitled "How He Got That Way" was written by Charles Morrow Wilson . . .

To quote a Little Rock newspaper, regarding one segment of the article, "This quotation shows the Governor talking with worse grammar and less precision than local reporters have ever heard him use. Wilson in other ways gives the impression that Mr. Faubus is an uneducated hillbilly."

Which reminds me of what a newspaper woman from Lawrence, Kans. said after the Governor's news conference during the NEA and APA (meeting) in Hot Springs.

. . . The newspaper woman grabbed the microphone away from the Governor and expressed her appreciation for the hospitality extended by Arkansas and said she had changed her mind about a lot of things since coming to Arkansas . . . especially Gov. Faubus.

. . . The COMMERCIAL APPEAL (Memphis) quoted the Governor as saying in regard to the (Wilson) article he had learned it was best "to keep my temper" about critical articles appearing in print.

Wilson's title . . . of his article . . . will resound with furore as it reverberates the question "How did Wilson get that Way?"

"I'M CONTENT JUST BEING THE CONSTITUTION"
By Daniel, Knoxville Journal   Early 1959

As Chief Justice of the U.S. Supreme Court, with the acquiescence of the associate justices and complete disregard for the provisions of the Constitution, he could interpret the document to be whatever he personally wanted it to be.

This cartoonist explained why Earl Warren had no desire to be president.

Thus, Warren was more powerful than any president, more powerful than the Congress. And he could overrule the will of the people whenever he was personally inclined, no matter how strongly that will was expressed by ballots or legislation. The caption, "I'm content just being the Constitution," aptly and truly described the situation.

The fault lay in a pliant chief executive and a dilatory, fearful Congress, each of which declined or refused to sufficiently challenge the usurpation of power by a runaway Court headed by a chief justice with delusions of great power.

Why should Chief Justice Earl Warren want to be president? He would have been giving up two-thirds of his power.

In his position, with no formidable opposition, he exercised more power than either the President or the Congress. In fact, he exercised the power of all three branches of the government. Not only did the Court make laws. It directed their enforcement by the executive branch, or the states. And then the Court ruled on litigation involving the laws.

In this role Warren made new laws, forbade the Congress to interfere and ordered the executive branch to carry them out.

Through the executive branch he created new armies by federalizing the entire National Guard of various states. He then ordered the new armies to enforce upon their own people his newly-created laws.

He overruled at will a cowed Congress composed of the people's representatives. Thus, his new laws, created without constitutional authority, went unchallenged.

By direct action of the Supreme Court or indirectly through the lower courts, he overruled the authority of the elected governors of the states. Whenever they challenged the Court's illegal edicts he threatened them with jail and imposed fines of enormous amounts until they were subdued.

State legislators were threatened with imprisonment for daring to perform their constitutional duty of legislating the will of their people. In fact, they were forbidden to perform their constitutional duty to legislate — the only reason for their existence — unless the legislation conformed to Earl Warren's personal ideas of what the legislation should be.

Time after time in state after state, the results of elections and the enactment of legislation, all through legal, democratic processes, were overruled and nullified by the Warren Court without the blink of an eye.

And what are the results of this now deeply entrenched judicial dictatorship on the country?

More crime, more lawless disorder, juvenile delinquency, pornography, drug abuse and subversion, and less fidelity, patriotism and faith in government than at any time in the history of the Republic.

NEWS ITEM: U. S. PLANS TO SHOOT MAN INTO SPACE
Artist and source unknown   Early 1959

Keeping the caption in mind note that Uncle Sam, with space rocket and launching tower in the background, looked at a figure with a question on his mind. The figure — Faubus — burned a book, "The Law," with a closed and locked school in the background. Another gross distortion of facts.

Some time during the controversy the inimitable Bob Hope cracked a joke:

"Ike wanted to send a man to the moon, . . . but Gov. Faubus refused to go."

Much later, Hope was guest speaker at the State Dinner of the National Governors Conference at Hershey, Pa., July 1-5, 1962. One of his wise cracks there in reference to a Supreme Court decision was:

"They used to teach us to pray in school. Now it's a federal rap."

WRONG GUY HIT WITH THE BOOK
By McClanahan
Dallas Morning News   1/59

Many cartoonists continued to portray the federal courts, with some state courts following suit, as biased in favor of law violators.

◀◀
ACHILLES' HEEL
By Ficklen, Dallas Morning News   2/59

The Republican Party's strength nationally in 1958 sank to its lowest point since the days of Herbert Hoover in the midst of the Great Depression. In the South the fortunes of the Party were ruined by the national Republican Administration's actions at Little Rock. That the party regained strength in the region in the years which followed was not so much due to Republican efforts as to the unpopular policies of the national Democrats.

ORVAL FAUBUS
GROWING IN POPULARITY

(From a California newspaper,
March 1959)

An exchange that comes to my desk says, "Governor Orval Faubus is growing in popularity every day, not only in Arkansas but throughout the South." Really, this is true throughout the nation. The politicians and federal "big brass" hate Faubus. His name has become a challenge. What he has done in Arkansas means much more than segregation or even States Rights. It means the lone stand of a single man for genuine Americanism. Slowly and surely the sane people of the United States are coming to see in the stubborn stand of Faubus something akin to the stand of Horatius, defending the bridge over the Tiber, and of the valiant fighters on "Flanders Field" who cried, "They shall not pass." The stand of Faubus no longer savors of sectionalism. It is a stand for the fundamental constitutional rights of the sovereign states. It is a battle to preserve the meaning of the contract, entered into and signed by the thirteen original colonies. When the fog and smog have rifted, the name of Orval Faubus will be written high on the list of the nation's defenders.

━0━0━0━

Rogers, Ark. Daily News
May 1, 1959

ROGERS WRITER SAYS GOV. FAUBUS DOESN'T MIND SKATING ON THIN ICE; IS RESPECTED BY NEGROES

(Editor's Note: The following profile of Governor Faubus entitled "The Most Unpredictable Man," appears in the current issue of the national magazine, The Chiropractic Home. It was written by David Baxter a former California newspaperman who has lived near Rogers since 1956.)

By David Baxter

No one knows what niche Orval E. Faubus will occupy in history . . . Some southerners think he's a twentieth century Robert E. Lee while others chew their tobacco disdainfully at the mention of his name. The average northerner takes it for granted he's a rabid segregationist.

If there was ever a study in contrasts, Orval is. Take a session of the Arkansas legislature, for example. Faubus, a former school teacher, demanded an increase in state taxes to get more money for schools.

The legislature went along and the increase went into effect. Came the Little Rock imbroglio and the governor closed the schools, . . . promoting private schools to replace them.

This seems paradoxical but he said he had a reason — to carry out the will of the vast majority of the people of the state and preserve order.

That sounds as though he favored segregation but no, he has repeatedly declared he is not opposed to integration of public schools but to the methods used to accomplish it, in violation of states rights.

While segregationists regard him as a hero he has pointedly told them he is not against integration. Nevertheless, he opposes it. Why?

Behind this, too, lies his reasoning. He thinks, like Jefferson, that it is the duty of any representative to find out what the majority want, then carry out their will, even though he personally may disagree with his own constituents.

So, while Faubus himself had no scruples against school integration, the people did as they proved by the landslide vote they gave him at the past election and as even his arch enemy, Harry Ashmore of the Arkansas Gazette, tacitly admitted.

So Orval kept his own ideas on integration to himself and represented the sentiment of the people.
. . .

In carrying out the will of his home staters Faubus has alienated many in other states, particularly in the north.

Some politicians think this dooms any ambition he may have had for high national office but others point out that if he swallowed his own opinions on integration in order to represent his constituents, he might equally well carry out the will of the people on a national scale, regardless of his personal opinions.

The Arkansas voter is no more predictable than the governor. Before the Little Rock affair Faubus seemed to have gotten out of step in an unpopular proposal to reappraise all property for assessment purposes. The legislature went along on that, too.

It fell to county judges to take the necessary steps to carry out the reappraisal in their areas.

Yet at the last election Faubus, who had originated the program, was re-elected to an unprecedented third term due to indignation over the integration issue while the same voters angrily threw out of office many county judges and state legislators who had carried out the legislation. . . .

Whether the redoubtable Orval is liberal, conservative or in between is conjectural. When he first sought the office his opponent, Governor Francis Cherry, and the right wingers blasted him as a near-communist, pointing to the fact that he had attended Commonwealth College at Mena, a notorious hotbed of extreme leftists that was closed due to public clamor. Up to the Little Rock business his critics called him either a bolshevik or arch New Dealer. Today many one-time liberal friends such as former Governor Sid McMath denounce him as a reactionary after his resistance to integration.

Ex-critics now warmly welcome him to their bosoms as an upholder of the traditions of the old south. The bulk of the Negroes showed in . . . the vote they gave him (about 85 percent) hold him in high regard and that he has given them better, more impartial treatment than any other administration.

The governor's associates indicate no particular trend of thought, either. One of his close friends is Jimmie Karam, a Little Rock haberdasher. . . . If Karam has a liberal leaning no one has ever detected it. On the other hand, Faubus is quite at home with millionaire Republican Winthrop Rockefeller, . . . who . . . is more than mildly liberal and who openly criticized the governor during the state-federal dispute. Many suspect the governor of keeping people guessing but he himself simply says, "I carry out the people's will."

Faubus seems to have progressive industrial views. The average Arkansawyer hates even a hint of taxation yet the governor, in asking for a three cent sales tax, remarked, "If Arkansas is going to grow industrially it might as well be now." The people voted overwhelmingly for the tax and the state is looking up industrially, many old established northern and western plants having moved there. Faubus proudly points to dozens of photos of big factories where there had been none before.

The Governor seems unafraid to skate on thin ice sometimes but many people like his personal touch. For instance, recently an old couple posted their farm as bail for their son, charged with burglary. The son skipped and the judge ordered the bail forfeited. The son was promptly captured in Kansas but the bail forfeiture stood and the old folks were to lose their farm. Faubus heard about it and dug up an old authority whereby he could overrule the judge, since he did not want the parents to lose all they had. A county grand jury challenged his authority to cancel the bail forfeiture order but he stood his ground and no more has been heard of it.

Another case was that of an Arkansas grandmother to whom the courts had awarded custody of her grandson, the father and mother being separated. Grandma took the child to Texas to visit his mother who utilized the occasion to run off with him. Grandma, like a vexed bloodhound, trailed them to Kansas where the daughter-in-law had placed the child in an orphanage. Grandma stalked into the institution, said she was the boy's legal guardian and demanded him. When the state institution refused she came up with a six-shooter, held them up and took her grandson out.

She was back in Arkansas before Kansas authorities could apprehend her. They requested Faubus to extradite her.

"Don't you think for a minute Orval's going to send me back up there," she told reporters.

He didn't.

A few weeks ago a colored man who was scheduled to die in the electric chair wanted special permission from the state Supreme Court to review his case. He lacked money, so the Governor, who always avoids capital punishment if he can and takes a personal interest in seeing his people get a square deal, dug down into his own pocket to put up the money for the Negro's appeal.

That could probably only happen in Arkansas.

◖━◗◖━◗◖━◗

Dallas, Texas, Morning News
May 1, 1959

LITTLE ROCK BUSY

It is the vogue among commentators of a sort to deplore, depreciate and denounce Little Rock. Little Rock troubles, it is said, have blighted the capital city of Arkansas.

Is it true? Nonfarm jobs are up in Little Rock 2 per cent — down 1.8 per cent for the nation as a whole. Weekly factory pay in Little Rock is up 6.4 per cent — up 4.4 per cent for the country at large.

Department store sales are 3 per cent above what they were a year ago. The corresponding figure for the United States is only 1 per cent above a year ago. Little Rock building permits are up in value 16.5 per cent over 1958 at the same time. For the nation the increase is only 8.9 per cent. Little Rock banking activity shows a gain of 6.6 per cent as against 3.5 per cent gain for the nation.

A little more of this kind of "ruin" for Little Rock and there will be a business stampede to get there and set up shop.

On Dec. 6, 1959, a headline in the *Democrat* read "State Shucks Recession As Income Soars." The story related that during 1959, the last year of major controversy over the segregation-integration issue, personal income for the state had increased more than $100,000,000. The information was according to the University of Arkansas *Business Bulletin*.

◖━◗◖━◗◖━◗

RUN OF THE NEWS
by Karr Shannon
Arkansas Democrat, Sept. 25, 1970

Karr Shannon wrote the following years after I left office:
Faubus Obeyed Law

During the summer's race for Democratic gubernatorial nominee, some of the liberal newspapers lambasted Orval Faubus — again — for his official acts as governor during the Central High School crisis in September, 1957, and for months following. The liberals never forget. And they'll bring up the matter again and again at the slightest chance. Yet —

Faubus never at any time violated any law of the federal government or state. He was perverse, contumacious . . . but never in contempt of the Constitution of the United States or of the state of Arkansas. He had a legal right — legal from the laws of both state and nation — to call out the State Guard.

What Governor Faubus did back there — all legal — and what happened, as a consequence, was as tame as a Wednesday night prayer meeting compared to the violence, property destruction, murder . . . that has since rocked the nation — all as a consequence of the high court's 1954 decree. And dissension and violence continue to worsen.

LITTLE ROCK INTEGRATION PLAN VOIDED BY COURT

On May 13, 1970, the 8th U.S. Circuit Court of Appeals struck down the Little Rock School District's original desegregation plan, which was based on the neighborhood-school concept. The news report said:

The Court ordered the school board, under supervision of the federal District Court at Little Rock, to implement . . . a plan under which no pupil would be excluded from any school because of race or color.

The Court ruled the plan for faculty integration was unacceptable.

Judge Pat Mehaffy of Little Rock, then a member of the Court, excused himself from the case and the Court split 5-2 in its decision.

The neighborhood school concept, the basis of the original school integration suit in Little Rock, was now scrapped. Although the federal government had ordered thousands of heavily armed, bayonet-weilding troops into the city to enforce the court order based on the original lawsuit, and would have slaughtered opposing American citizens if necessary to bring about compliance, that order, enforced by such extreme means, was now nullified by a new directive by the same federal courts.

From the time in September 1959 when school authorities began compliance with the original order without federal military enforcement, only slightly more than ten years had passed. Now the plans, painstakingly evolved, implementing the order were declared null and void and of no effect.

Now new plans, using busing as a tool to bring about certain nebulous racial ratios in all schools, must be evolved to comply with the new court ruling. And in all the legal verbiage of the courts and the bureaucratic instructions of the Department of Health, Education and Welfare, no mention was ever made of quality education, or even a proper education of the students, black or white, who were affected by the new federal orders.

There was opposition to the new ruling by both black and white parents. Black patrons of the College Station area lodged strong protests against the busing of their children from their neighborhood school to more distant school facilities, even gaining an audience with Senator McClellan to voice their discontent. Protests likewise came from white patrons in various areas of the district. All protests were in vain. School authorities and lawmakers at all levels were powerless to change the situation. The federal judicial dictatorship held firm and remained in full control.

On June 10, 1975, patrons in the College Station area, filed a lawsuit in U.S. District Court in the names of 45 black students seeking to halt busing from the area for racial balance. The suit was against the board of Pulaski County Special School District and Supt. J. K. Williams.

The College Station Elementary School and the Cook Elementary School were being phased out and turned into kindergarten facilities over the objections of the plaintiffs. Students in the College Station area would be bused to schools 10 to 20 miles distant, the complaint said.

The plaintiffs attorney, Robert Morehead, asked a temporary restraining order and a permanent injunction to prevent the plan from being implemented.

The lawsuit was unsuccessful, the schools were phased out and busing continued.

One result of the busing program was the acceleration in the growth in numbers and size of private schools. By October 1973 approximately 7,000 students were enrolled in private schools in the Greater Little Rock area. Private and parochial schools established in Pulaski County drained 1,554 students from the public schools in the period 1968 to 1973, according to an article in the *Arkansas Gazette* (page 17A, Oct. 14, 1973).

The private schools continue to grow. The enrollment of their children in private school facilities places a heavy burden on those parents who must pay tuition there and also taxes to support the public schools which they do not choose to use.

In this matter the federal courts have also assumed control, considered by many to be illegal, and forbidden the states to allow tax credits to parents sending their children to private or parochial schools.

And so the confusion with its attendant discontent continues. Often when school officials and patrons have adjusted to one set of court rulings governing school affairs, they find themselves faced with new federal court rulings and new regulations by Washington bureaucrats. Thus public education suffers to the detriment of all students, and private schools continue to proliferate.

The question is, would all this have happened if the federal courts had not injected their power into the field of education in contravention of the U.S. Constitution and state laws?

In the opinion of many people problems would not have been so great, and public education would not have suffered so severely if the courts had not intervened. The changes sought could have been made legally and constitutionally, thus avoiding the widespread resentment and disrespect for authority which were created by the illegal means which were employed.

It is a certainty that compulsory segregation could have been abolished by legal means — a constitutional amendment is one method — and equally certain that, sooner or later, given the tenor of the times, the change would have been effected.

The use of illegal judicial means to effect the change set a precedent which, carried into other fields, may well destroy the Republic.

APPOINTMENTS, Early 1959

Bert Dickey, Sr., Earle; John Tyson, Springdale; State Racing Commission. Lewis M. Robinson, Little Rock, Public Service Commission. Armel Taylor, Clarksville, Highway Commission. Dr. Joe Shuffield, Little Rock, State Hospital Board. Benny Ryburn, Monticello; W. A. Stone, Pine Bluff; A & M College Board. J. C. Mitchell, Little Rock; Cleddie Harper, Carlisle; State Teachers College Board. J. C. Mitchell, Little Rock, Merit System Council. Fred Martin, Hot Springs; Ralph Van Meter, Judsonia, Negro Boys Industrial School. L. M. Greene, Siloam Springs, Prison and Parole Board. Carl Burger, Bentonville, State Police Commission. John Chambers, Danville, Ark. Tech College Board. Ted Larimer, Green Forest; George Reynolds, Petit Jean Mountain, Publicity and Parks Commission. Gordon Carleton, DeQueen, Southern State College Board. Sister Mary Humbeline, Hot Springs; Miss Elva Holland, Little Rock, Nurse Examiners Board. Mrs. Ruth Rankin, Little Rock, Practical Nurse Division Board. Dr. John P. Wood, Mena, Booneville TB Sanitorium. R. A. Young, Jr., Ft. Smith, U of A Board of Trustees. Dr. O. D. Campbell, Warren; Dr. John Smith, Stuttgart; Veterinary Examiners Board. Walter L. Pope, Little Rock, Workmen's Compensation Commission replacing Bayard Taylor who resigned. Max Coger, Danville; Dan Felton, Marianna; Welfare Board. Austin Franks, Pine Bluff, Alcoholic Beverage Control Board. Dr. N. T. Hollis, Little Rock; Dr. M. Edward Wheat, Springdale, Commission on Alcoholism. J. P. Wahl, Helena, A M & N College Board. Julian B. Davidson, Little Rock, Board of Architects. William H. Wyatt, Blytheville, Ark. State College Board. Lawson T. Garner, Crawfordsville, Bank Commission. Robert Mays, Fordyce, Blind and Deaf School. Byron D. Brown, Sheridan, Boys Industrial School. Walter Priest, Beebe; John A. Healey, Little Rock; Harold Todd, England; Burial Association Board. Dr. W. R. Brooksher, Ft. Smith, Cancer Commission. Robert D. Nabholtz, Conway, Children's Colony Board. Dr. Roy Eugene Mathis, Texarkana; Dr. Tina S. Murphy, Little Rock; Chiropractic Examiners Board. Arthur Shirey, Texarkana, Commerce Commission. Mrs. Elah Miles Lovelace, Hot Springs, Cosmetology Board. M. P. Jones, Searcy, State Board of Education. Thomas Gaughan, Camden, Forestry Commission. Raymond J. Hartlieb, Hazen, Training School for Girls. M. H. Russell, Crossett, Henderson State Teachers College Board. C. F. Fitch, Hindsville, Livestock Sanitary Board. Dr. Earl D. McKelvy, Paragould, State Medical Board. Dr. Charles M. Bowers, Paragould, Optometry Board. V. B. McCloy, Monticello, Board of Review. J. Lester Booker, Little Rock, Commerce Commission. Physical Therapy Board: Leland Wicke, Ft. Smith; Mike Kumpuris, Little Rock; Miss Ruth Burnett, Jacksonville. Healing Arts Board: Dr. Jack W. Sears, Searcy; Dr. James L. Stevenson, Little Rock; Dr. Warren W. Nedrow, Jonesboro; Dr. Joe Robbins, Conway; Dr. Ralph Sloan, Jonesboro; Dr. W. O. Langston, Little Rock. Water Conservation Commission: J. F. Reeves, West Memphis; Jeff Davis, El Dorado; John Luce, Ft. Smith; Morris Bowman, Newport; Ed I. McKinley, Little Rock; Wayne Hampton, Stuttgart; Harold Snyder, Dardanelle. Tommy Russell, North Little Rock, resigned as administrative assistant to the Governor. Advisory Council for Employment Security Division — Representing the Public: Henry C. Armstrong, Ft. Smith; Rev. H. O. Bolin, Little Rock; Horace H. Fisher, Malvern; Dr. Orville J. Hall, U of A, Fayetteville; Mrs. Johnnie Mae Mackey, Hot Springs. Representing Employees: Judge Rogers, Camden; Howard Pierce, Little Rock; Floyd Taylor, North Little Rock; Cory Ball, Bauxite; Schuyler Smith, Jonesboro. Members representing Employers: Ray Kimball, DeQueen; Rex L. Morgan, Corning; H. T. "Red" Crawford, Benton; J. G. Smith, Pine Bluff.

CONCLUSION

As I entered into and progressed through my third and succeeding terms as Governor, tens of thousands of words continued to be written about me, many in criticism, some in praise, others in attempts at subjective analysis.

A man returning from a tour of Europe reported that the names of three American governors were well known there. They were Rockefeller (Nelson), Faubus and Nixon. (The latter didn't make it; he lost to Pat Brown.)

W. O. Vaught, the well known, long time pastor of Immanuel Baptist Church in Little Rock, made a visit to the Soviet Union. After returning home he related to his church that he had attended a notable function in the Communist capital where he encountered a nationally known American religious leader. When the leader learned where the Little Rock pastor was from, he promptly paraphrased a well known Scriptural quotation, "If God be Faubus, who can be against us."

The investigation of my income tax reports was completed and no additional tax was levied. Some regarded the finding as victory and vindication for me over a vengeful national administration. I like to think it was because the Internal Revenue Service learned the facts and wanted to be fair.

The industrial program continued to flourish and accelerate in spite of the efforts of some to create a contrary impression. New records were set in the establishment and expansion of Arkansas factories and the creation of new jobs for Arkansas workmen.

In 1959 the Borge-Warner Company constructed at Ft. Smith the largest industrial plant built in the United States that year. For several years thereafter its size was not exceeded by any other newly constructed industrial facility in the nation.

The Pickens-Bond Construction Company of Little Rock grew larger and richer as, under the live wire leadership of Jack Pickens, its president and prime mover, it constructed plant after plant all across the state. As I attended a lengthening string of ground breakings and dedication ceremonies for new factories in town after town, I could almost always see the affable Pickens either on the platform among the dignitaries or in the crowd of happy spectators, be the affair at Batesville, Little Rock, Osceola or Ft. Smith.

The members of the AIDC became well known figures across the state, especially that of its chairman, Winthrop Rockefeller.

The sight of the new industrial plants was proof to the people of the success of the program. Any words to the contrary fell on deaf ears among the Arkansas people. But there was other evidence. Some time before my administration ended the population shifted from basically rural to urban. For the first time in the long history of Arkansas the residents of towns and cities of 2,500 population or more exceeded the number of those who lived in the smaller towns and the countryside. Industrial growth continues and the imbalance between rural and city residents steadily widens. That this development was inevitable will be little disputed. That the development with the consequent enrichment of the state came much sooner because of my work and leadership in the field of industrial growth is, I think, equally well established. It is also my opinion, that the Arkansas example, and Arkansas methods which were often copied by others, had considerable impact on the entire South in economic growth.

Authorities in Washington recognized the state's programs in industrial development and tourism and recreation as among the finest in the nation. Delegations in the United States from foreign countries to study such matters were directed to Arkansas by Washington officials of both Republican and Democratic administrations.

One such delegation from a newly independent nation of the Carribean area was placed under the guidance of Mrs. Daisy Bates of Little Rock, who called my office to set up an appointment. While other officials were flustered with concern, I granted the interview without hesitation.

Following the conference in my office the reporters came in and photographs were made. The black official from the foreign country seemed both pleased and surprised at the attention. Incidentally, he was one of the best informed men on politics, history and government with whom I ever conversed. And come to think of it, where else could he have received so much notice, as well as the information which he sought.

A photograph showing Mrs. Bates and me shaking hands with the official standing between us, was published statewide, nationwide and around the world. News copies were mailed to me from South America, Africa, Europe and Hong Kong.

Later I was told that a state politician with ambition to be governor, grabbed a Little Rock paper in which the picture appeared, rushed back to his office and with his staff began an early celebration of his anticipated victory over me in the next election. Alas, for counting chickens before they are hatched.

In Washington the national administration and the Congress authorized the establishment of Job Corps camps for underprivileged youths. They were patterned after the Conservation Corps Camps (CCC) of the Roosevelt era. By the very nature of things many black youths were among those to be helped. While many states, some in the North, and some with so-called "liberal" leadership, were rejecting the camps, a right granted by the act of authorization, as unwanted nuisances which would be detrimental, I was informed by Washington authorities that two sites had been selected in Arkansas for the creation of two such facilities. After clearing the matter with civic and business leaders of the affected areas, I readily accepted the plans for the establishment of the camps.

Agriculture Secretary Orville Freeman, former governor of Minnesota for six years during my tenure and a personal friend, came to Arkansas to participate in the dedication of the first camp in the nation at a point west of Hot Springs. (On that occasion I became acquainted with Mike O'Callaghan, then a minor official under Freeman who later became governor of Nevada.) The second camp in the nation was at the small community of Cass, 15 miles north of Ozark and just 15 miles south of my birthplace of Combs.

While in Arkansas Freeman, accompanied by me, went to Little River County in Southwest Arkansas to inspect a Rural Economic Development area, another pioneer project for the nation. There under the leadership of State Representative Marion Crank one of the most successful projects of its kind had been initiated and developed. Freeman was highly pleased with what he saw, and the national press corps which accompanied him, at first highly skeptical of what they might find in Arkansas, were amazed with the success of the program and the leadership ability of Crank.

Arkansas by act of the Legislature was the second state in the Union to authorize condominiums, a new form of housing development and ownership. The new method is now used nationwide.

Arkansas was the sixth state to sign a contract with the proper federal authority to assume regulation of nuclear materials used in medicine and industry. With the contract regulation and control passed from federal officials to state authority under the Health Department.

As state service improved in all fields and factories dotted the state, many forms of enterprise grew.

Rural co-operatives established rural telephone systems. The private companies extended their lines to new customers and modernized the service. In Madison County the independent telephone company under the leadership of the owner and manager, Curtis Shrum, established a highly modern system. There were no unsightly poles and wires that could be broken by falling trees or ice storms. The entire system is underground. Now, where no service was formerly available, a countryman can pick up a receiver and dial a number in any part of the nation.

The Rural Electric Co-Operatives, the bedrock of progress in the countryside, continued to extend their lines into remote areas and to modernize their service. Their service and growth was often matched by the private utilities. Together these co-ops and private companies have done such a good job that now more than 98% of all homes and businesses in Arkansas are electrified.

The Ark La Gas Company, once it was firmly established under the leadership and genius of W. R. "Witt" Stephens, began a program of modernization and expansion. It was not long before approximately 100 new towns and settlements, and the areas in between, were enjoying the convenience of natural gas. Perhaps three-fourths or more of the towns were on the Ark La system.

When President Lyndon Johnson initiated his "poverty programs" as a part of his Great Society, we accepted most, if not all of them in Arkansas, and made them work more successfully than in any other state. Much credit for their successful implementation must go to J. L. Bland, director of the Employment Security Division, and Director Carl Adams and Assistant Director A. J. "Red" Moss of the Welfare Department.

In implementing a number of these programs we had able assistance from a man who was not on the state pay roll. Lewis "Red" Johnson of Little Rock, head of the Arkansas Farmers Union, sponsored the Green Thumb program for the employ-

ment of older workers and made it a model for the nation. In the Youth Employment program, also under Johnson's leadership, there were more young people gainfully employed in useful projects than any time before or since in Arkansas. The records revealed that approximately 87 per cent of these young workers, both black and white, both male and female, used their earnings to pay for their continued education in high school and college. The cost of administering these projects under Johnson's direction was less than one per cent of the amount spent, while in other states the administrative costs ranged from 12½ to 27 percent.

Much of this progress had not yet been accomplished as I entered my third term, and was yet to be achieved. So, that is another story.

J. Orville Cheney continued to collect more and more revenue, which was used for continued improvement of state service. Many officials in my administration set all-time records for tenure in their positions. But, that is part of the continuing story.

Contrary to opinion in some circles, Mrs. Daisy Bates and I did not become personal enemies. Although sometimes cast in opposing roles, we continued to work together on many matters of mutual interest to the benefit of the people of the state. Later she was succeeded by her husband, L. C. Bates, as head of the Arkansas NAACP. He became one of my frequent advisers on a number of matters and I found him to be calm, logical and objective. Finally, near the end of my tenure I was requested by a delegation of three leaders of statewide black organizations to seek re-election. I declined, but I appreciated the gesture of confidence as manifested by their pledge of support. That is also another story.

Progress continued. Campaigns continued. Controversy continued.

In one campaign I was attacked from both flanks by former allies who had become opponents. Assisted by three other opposing candidates one attacked from the "left," the other from the "right." Middle ground is sometimes hard to defend, so that is an interesting story.

Finally, an administration man with service in a popular agency, resigned to oppose me for governor. That was a hard battle with some unusual angles.

The editorials and the cartoons continued. There were more drawings by Kennedy and Graham, other cartoons from coast to coast, and another Arkansas artist, a confirmed critic, made his fortune largely from my face and at the same time made the farkleberry bush well known in Arkansas.

All this, and much more, is enough for another book.

INDEX

Cartoons and quotes are taken from many newspapers throughout the state. the nation and some from overseas. None are indexed.

Down from the hills